A RASA READER

Historical Sourcebooks in Classical Indian Thought

HISTORICAL SOURCEBOOKS IN CLASSICAL INDIAN THOUGHT

Sheldon Pollock, Series Editor

The Historical Sourcebooks in Classical Indian Thought series provides text-based introductions to the most important forms of classical Indian thought, from epistemology, rhetoric, and hermeneutics to astral science, yoga, and medicine. Each volume offers fresh translations of key works, headnotes that orient the reader to the selections, a comprehensive introduction analyzing the major lines of development of the discipline, and exegetical and text-critical endnotes as well as an extensive bibliography. A unique feature, the reconstruction of the principal intellectual debates in the given discipline, clarifies the arguments and captures the dynamism that marked classical thought. Designed to be fully accessible to comparativists and interested general readers, the Historical Sourcebooks also offer authoritative commentary for advanced students and scholars.

A Rasa Reader

CLASSICAL INDIAN AESTHETICS

Translated and edited by
SHELDON POLLOCK

COLUMBIA UNIVERSITY PRESS
NEW YORK

Columbia University Press
Publishers Since 1893
New York Chichester, West Sussex
cup.columbia.edu

Paperback edition, 2018

Library of Congress Cataloging-in-Publication Data

Names: Pollock, Sheldon I., translator, editor.
Title: A rasa reader : classical Indian aesthetics / translated and edited by Sheldon Pollock.
Description: New York : Columbia University Press, 2016. | Series: Historical sourcebooks in classical indian thought | Includes bibliographical references and index. | Includes translations from Sanskrit.
Identifiers: LCCN 2015020974 | ISBN 9780231173902 (cloth) | ISBN 9780231173919 (pbk.) | ISBN 9780231540698 (e-book)
Subjects: LCSH: Rasas—Early works to 1800. | Aesthetics, Indic—Translations into English. | Sanskrit literature—Translations into English.
Classification: LCC BH221.I52 R43 2016 | DDC 111/.850954—dc23
LC record available at http://lccn.loc.gov/2015020974

COVER DESIGN: Jennifer Heuer

FOR ALLISON

यदेव रोचते मह्यं तदेव कुरुते प्रिया |
इति वेत्ति न जानाति तत्प्रियं यत्करोति सा || (भोजराजस्य)

Contents

PREFACE XI
ACKNOWLEDGMENTS XIX
ENGLISH TRANSLATIONS OF SANSKRIT TITLES XXI
LIST OF ABBREVIATIONS XXIII

Introduction: An Intellectual History of Rasa 1

CHAPTER ONE
The Foundational Text, c. 300, and Early Theorists, 650–1025 47

1. The Basis of Rasa Theory in Drama 47
   Treatise on Drama of Bharata (c. 300) 47

2. Rasa as a Figure of Speech in Narrative Poetry: The Early Views 55
   Ornament of Poetry of Bhamaha (c. 650) 55
   Looking Glass of Poetry of Dandin (c. 700) with the Commentaries *Ratna's Glory* of Ratnashrijnana (c. 950) and *Guarding the Tradition* of Vadijanghala (c. 950) 58

3. Rasa as a Figure of Speech: The Late View 65
   Essential Compendium of the Ornament of Poetry of Udbhata (c. 800) with the *Brief Elucidation* of Pratiharenduraja (c. 900) and the *Exegesis* of Tilaka (c. 1100) 65

4. Rasa as the Character's Emotion, and How We Know It 74
   **Commentary on the* Treatise on Drama, of Bhatta Lollata (c. 825) 74
   **Commentary on the* Treatise on Drama, of Shri Shankuka (c. 850) 77

5. There Are No Rules for the Number of Rasas 84
Ornament of Poetry of Rudrata (c. 850) with *Notes* of Namisadhu (1068) 84

6. Rasa Cannot Be Expressed or Implied, Only "Manifested" 87
Light on Implicature of Anandavardhana (c. 875) 87

7. Rasa Cannot Be a Figure of Speech; It Is What Figures of Speech Ornament 98
The Vital Force of Literary Language of Kuntaka (c. 975) 98

8. There Can Be No "Manifestation" of Rasa 106
Analysis of "Manifestation" of Mahima Bhatta (c. 1025) 106

CHAPTER TWO
The Great Synthesis of Bhoja, 1025–1055 110

1. One Rasa Underlies All Multiplicity 110
Necklace for the Goddess of Language of Bhoja (c. 1025) with the *Commentary* of Bhatta Narasimha (undated) 110

2. One Rasa Underlies All Multiplicity: The Late Statement 119
Light on Passion of Bhoja (c. 1050) 119

CHAPTER THREE
An Aesthetics Revolution, 900–1000 144

1. From Rasa in the Text to Rasa in the Reader: Core Ideas 144
**Commentary on the* Treatise on Drama, and *Mirror of the Heart* of Bhatta Nayaka (c. 900) 144

2. From Rasa in the Text to Rasa in the Reader: Elaboration 154
The Ten Dramatic Forms of Dhanamjaya (c. 975) and the *Observations* of Dhanika (c. 975), with *The Lamp* (on the *Ten Forms*) of Bahurupa Mishra (undated) and the *Brief Annotation* (on the *Observations*) of Bhatta Nrisimha (undated) 154

CHAPTER FOUR
Abhinavagupta and His School, 1000–1200 181

1. Rasa and the Critique of Imitation 181
Literary Investigations of Bhatta Tota (c. 975) 181

2. The Theory of Rasa Purified 187
The New Dramatic Art, of Abhinavagupta (c. 1000) 187

3. Potential Flaws of Rasa 224
Light on Poetry of Mammata (c. 1050) with the Commentaries of Shridhara (c. 1225), Chandidasa (c. 1300), Vishvanatha (c. 1350), and Paramananda Chakravartin (c. 1500) 224

4. The Purified Theory in Abstract 235
Short Explanation of Light on Poetry, and *Commentary on* Analysis of "Manifestation" of Ruyyaka (1150) 235

CHAPTER FIVE
Continuing the Controversies Beyond Kashmir, 1200–1400 239

1. Where Is Rasa? Is Rasa Always Pleasurable? 239
Mirror of Drama of Ramachandra and Gunachandra (c. 1200) 239
The Single Strand of Vidyadhara (c. 1300) with the *Central Gem* of Mallinatha (c. 1400) 247
Ornament of the Fame of King Prataparudra of Vidyanatha (c. 1320) with *The Jewel Store* of Kumarasvamin (c. 1430) 255

2. A Philosophical Précis of the Rasa Problematic 261
Mirror of Literary Art of Vishvanatha (c. 1350) with *The Eye* of Anantadasa (c. 1400) 261

3. Rethinking "Semblance of Rasa" 269
The Moon on the Rasa Ocean of Singabhupala (c. 1385) 269

CHAPTER SIX
Rasa in the Early Modern World, 1200–1650 276

1. A Reader Reading for Rasa 276
Elixir for the Rasika, of Arjunavarmadeva (c. 1215) 276

2. A Poet Writing of Rasa 280
The River of Rasa of Bhanudatta (c. 1500) 280

3. Devotees Experiencing Rasa 285
Pearls of the Bhāgavata, of Vopadeva (c. 1300) with the *Lamp for Transcendence* of Hemadri (c. 1300) 285

Divine Jewel of Ornamentation of Kavikarnapura (c. 1550) with the *Commentary* of Lokanatha Chakravartin (c. 1690) 290

Ambrosial River of the Rasa of Devotion of Rupa Gosvamin (1541) with the *Passage Through the Impassable* of Jiva Gosvamin (1541), and *Treatise on Divine Love* of Jiva Gosvamin (c. 1550) 300

4. Vedanticizing Rasa 310

The Nectar Ocean of Literary Art of Vishvanathadeva (1592) 310

The Bearer of the Ganges of Rasa of Jagannatha (c. 1650) 314

ENGLISH-SANSKRIT GLOSSARY 327

NOTES 333

BIBLIOGRAPHY 421

INDEX 431

Preface

The world of classical Indian literary theory is vast and complex, and it had long seemed to me that any attempt to produce a historical reconstruction of even a part of it, such as the discourse on aesthetic experience, was foolhardy. Given that this theory is among India's most luminous contributions to humanistic knowledge, however, and that there is so little of it, in translation or in exposition, that one can confidently recommend to students and general readers, the attempt seemed worth making. I first tried assembling a small team to produce a *Rasa Reader*, distributing the different chapters to different specialist scholars. My colleagues were perfectly willing—but their schedules were not. When months of delay had turned into years, I decided to take on the task alone. After half a decade of work on it, I can affirm that my initial cautions were fully justified.

The *Rasa Reader* is the first in a new series of historical sourcebooks that aims to make available to a contemporary reading public—students, comparativists, and interested generalists no less than specialists—translated and annotated texts from the major scholarly disciplines of classical India, arranged in such a way that the principal arguments and disputes can be observed in their historical development. That no such works exist, whether dealing with Indian aesthetics or rhetoric, hermeneutics, logic, or anything else, is a result, as series contributors are learning, of the serious difficulties involved on every front.

In the case of classical Indian aesthetics, the original works have often been very poorly transmitted (a trait that distinguishes this field from the others), and even when the integrity of the texts is assured, some of them can be obscure to the point of impenetrability. The arguments are often complex in themselves and presuppose knowledge of many different disciplines—hermeneutics, logic, philosophy of language, psychology—and deep familiarity with literary texts, some of which have vanished. The thought world the Western reader is entering here is remarkably sophisticated and subtle, and even those inside the tradition were sometimes confused or simply uncomprehending; this *Reader*'s jungle of endnotes is testimony to both the text-critical and the interpretive challenges the materials present. Making sense of the conceptual shape of this world, moreover, requires confronting very real intellectual-historical and theoretical problems. And this is to say nothing of the challenges of translation. The unhappy history of English versions of Sanskrit technical writings demonstrates how enormously difficult it is to achieve clarity, consistency, and accessibility, to say nothing of readability. Even after engagement with core questions of Indian aesthetics for almost twenty years and continual work on this book for five, I am sometimes uncertain whether I have come much closer to resolving some basic problems than when I first encountered them, or to giving them an English form that does the original justice.

Let me address some of these matters in a little greater detail, starting with the texts I have included in the *Reader* and how I have structured it.

Although it is painful to think of the many extraordinary works of classical Indian aesthetics that have been lost, fragments are sometimes quoted by later authors, and a large number of complete works have indeed been preserved. As for the fragments, I have assembled all available for a given author and ordered them as coherently as possible; the arrangement and some attributions remain speculative. From the major works, I have tried my best not to omit any significant argument from fifteen centuries of discourse (save in the rare case where an outstanding translation has recently appeared).[1] I have not suppressed material that is sure to seem perplexing (here Bhoja is exemplary), in order to illustrate the very real conceptual challenges that confront us, or even material I am unsure I understand myself (Abhinavagupta presents numerous instances), in the hope that others may learn from my shortcomings and do a better job. Some texts were excluded, either because of space constraints or because I view them as redundant.[2] The word "classical" in the subtitle of this book refers to a tradition of theorists who grappled with the problem of rasa in Sanskrit. The reception of this theory within other South Asian traditions—its acceptance as the basis for Brajbhasha poetics, its complex interaction with Sufi mysticism in Avadhi poetry, its relation to the very different conceptual orientation of classical Tamil poets—is outside the scope of this book (and the competence of its author).

However varied the historiographical conceptions among the thinkers themselves represented here, I present their texts for the most part in strict chronological order. There are some problems with this approach. The *Treatise on Drama* was undoubtedly revised, possibly in Kashmir in the eighth century,[3] but the work as a whole is as much as five centuries older. It therefore must come first, despite the likelihood that its earliest commentators knew nothing of some ideas it advances in the form we now have it. The commitment to chronological presentation has been broken in only a few cases. The *Mirror of the Heart* of Bhatta Nayaka and its rich elaboration in Dhanamjaya and Dhanika's *Ten Dramatic Forms* and *Observations* antedate Bhoja (Bhatta Nayaka by as much as a century, the latter pair by a generation or two), but Bhoja is, puzzlingly, ignorant of their innovations. Instead he offers, for all the apparent idiosyncrasy of his overall system, what I regard as a *summa* of the classical tradition, and hence I place him earlier in the *Reader.* Vopadeva's early fourteenth-century *Pearls of the* Bhāgavata is placed after Bhanudatta's early sixteenth-century *River of Rasa* to illuminate its links to the development of the devotional rasa. But Kavikarnapura's *Divine Jewel of Ornamentation*, though slightly later than Rupa and Jiva Gosvamin, precedes them in the *Reader* because it represents, to my mind, an older viewpoint that those works critique.

An additional complication to chronological order and intellectual-historical coherence is entailed by the presence of commentaries. On the one hand, these are works intimately related to their primary texts—which can sometimes be almost incomprehensible without them—and it is reasonable to present them together. On the other, commentaries often exhibit much later thinking, and to present them along with the texts risks violating a core historical principle of this collection. Some (or parts of some) approximate stand-alone works, and I have placed them on their own (preeminently Abhinavagupta's *The New* Dramatic Art). Others, however, are so intimately related to their main texts that such sequestration was not an option, despite their conceptual distance. We need to keep this in mind when reading Bhatta Narasimha, of perhaps the sixteenth century, who raises issues that would never have entered the mind of Bhoja, the eleventh-century author of the *Necklace for the Goddess of Language*; similarly, the twelfth-century Tilaka sometimes approaches the early ninth-century Udbhata with entirely anachronistic presuppositions. Vigilance is clearly required when commentators contradict their authors on the basis of concepts unavailable to them: Ruyyaka, for example, applies Abhinava's ideas in evaluating the *Analysis of "Manifestation"* of Mahima Bhatta (who knew but was uninterested in them), and Lokanatha Chakravartin puts forward those of Jiva Gosvamin when critiquing Kavikarnapura's *Divine Jewel.*

For reasons of space no less than coherence, anything in the commentaries not pertaining to rasa has been excluded. The same holds for the illustrative verses adduced as examples, even though these were often chosen as the best that Sanskrit poetry has to offer. This is an even more unfortunate loss in the case of the poetry composed by the poet-scholars themselves to illustrate their propositions (Vidyanatha and Bhanudatta are among the most significant), for which the reader may have no other translations available. But to have included these poems would have swollen the size of this work beyond all manageable proportions. I only give them when the main argument would otherwise become unintelligible, as in the selections from Mammata's *Light on Poetry*.

It will quickly become clear from the style of argument that Indian aesthetics was a discipline intimately tied up with other aspects of philosophical thought; the standard format of most later treatises, "memorial verse" followed by prose "exegesis," offers a formal sign of this kinship. And clearly, if we are to gain a granular understanding of rasa theory and do justice to the often profound ideas at work in its historical transformation, we need to have a better grasp of the complex and sometimes strikingly discordant ontologies and epistemologies that marked Indian thought over these fifteen centuries—Vedic, Samkhya, Buddhist, Jain, Shaiva, Vaishnava, and so on. It has not been possible to include that background here to any high degree, but I console myself with the knowledge that the series this book inaugurates is intended to provide the foundations for precisely this sort of historical-philosophical analysis.

The translation of technical terminology has offered special difficulties. Any reader of contemporary Western scholarship will be familiar with the vexations caused by specialist vocabularies, and classical Indian theory has them too, only more so. For one thing, the Sanskrit intellectual tradition throughout its history displays a preoccupation, often maligned as obsession, with both taxonomic comprehensiveness and descriptive precision, and the two tendencies worked together to expand the terminological domain relentlessly in every discipline. For another, classical aesthetics in particular felt called upon to invent an entirely new lexicon precisely to make sense of the entirely new sort of experience that the aesthetic represents—something our authors never tire, century after century, of explaining. The woman who is a cause of desire in a man in everyday life is not in the same way a cause of desire in the character on the stage, the actor playing the character on the stage, or the spectator in the audience watching the actor play the character. New terms were needed to capture the difference in these two processes and the panoply of their associated components.

The problem the translator confronts, besides grasping these distinctions in the first place (and in some cases this is exceedingly hard), is to render them in intelligible English. "Foundational factor" for the aesthetic counterpart of that mundane "cause" may not be a phrase that rolls off the tongue, but it is close to the original and immediately makes clear (or clearer than the usual translation, "determinant") exactly what is meant. Indian thinkers usually refer to these components—foundational (*ālambana-*) and stimulant (*uddīpana-*) factors (*vibhāva*), transitory emotions (*vyabhicāri-bhāva*), psychophysical responses (*sāttvika-bhāva*), and physical reactions (*anu-bhāva*)—as a single category (*vibhāvādi*), which I translate as "aesthetic elements" (similarly, "desire, etc.," *ratyādi*, is often used for the category "stable emotion," *sthāyi-bhāva*, and is so translated).

Inventing new terminology to make sense of newly perceived phenomena was an ongoing process in the history of Indian aesthetics. Bhatta Nayaka's hermeneutical revolution in the tenth century required the coinage of a range of new terms, such as "commonization" (*sādhāraṇīkaraṇa*) and "experientialization" (*bhogīkṛttva, bhogīkaraṇa*), and the repurposing of older ones. Thus *bhāvanā*, or "actualization," used in scriptural hermeneutics to explain the verbal force of Vedic commandments, was reconceived as the mechanism for experiencing literary emotions.[4] Abhinavagupta a few generations later would speak, for the first time, of the phenomena of "factoring," "reactionizing," and "colorizing" (*vibhāvana, anubhāvana, samuparañjakatva*), and borrow from Shaiva theology a term at once earthy and numinous to describe the "rapture" of aesthetic experience (*camatkāra*).[5] Old words were also being used in new senses, such as Anandavardhana's *dhvani*, originally just "sound," and accordingly need marking as such; hence the term "implicature," rather than the quotidian "implication," borrowed from the philosopher H. P. Grice (not an exact fit, since Grice's word could also translate the contending term "sentence purport," *tātparya*, borrowed from Vedic hermeneutics). Any clumsiness should usually be chalked up to my failure, though sometimes it does reflect the original. Readers of Heidegger will understand.

It is banal but true to say that successful translation finds the sweet spot between domestication and estrangement. Take the Samkhya theory, vastly disseminated across the Sanskrit knowledge systems including aesthetics, with its three elements of psychophysical reality, *sattva*, *rajaḥ*, and *tamaḥ*. To leave such terms untranslated would simply deepen the darkness for the lay reader. Rendering them as "sensitivity," "volatility," and "stolidity," while not necessarily providing perfect translations in all circumstances, preserves something of the unfamiliarity of the original while conveying a digestible notion of the basic arguments in which they are invoked in aesthetics: one's mind must be *receptive* to the aesthetic object,[6] while one's natural *inability to focus* and preternatural *indifference* to whatever is outside one's self have to be overcome for this to happen. For the same reason and in the hope of recovering a sense more faithful to the tradition, I have sometimes rejected a widely used translation—"love in separation," for example, in favor of "the erotic thwarted," which reflects the aesthetic system's own understanding of *vipralambha-śṛṅgāra*.[7] Of course, "traditional" understandings themselves have histories, and while I have considered it essential to maintain consistency in translating technical terms to enable the reader to follow the discourse over time, when change occurs, I have tried to signal it in translation.[8]

A problem of a more complex sort is presented by the word *bhāva*, translated here as "emotion," since its semantic field extends to notions sometimes dramatically at variance with what the English word would suggest. "Emotion" itself is a nebulous category in English. "Devotion," "boredom," "interest," and "surprise" have been included in it (and think of the history of its predecessors "passion" and "sentiment"), but the Sanskrit term can be even more elastic. Although Abhinavagupta at the end of the tenth century defines it in a way entirely familiar to us ("an experience pertaining to oneself and consisting of an awareness of pleasure or pain"),[9] for many early writers *bhāva* can comprise physical as well as affective states. The thirty-three listed by Bharata include torpor, numbness, sleepiness, and the like; Abhinava claims the list is really an open one and encompasses such states as hunger and thirst. Not all thinkers felt comfortable with this latitude or perhaps even with the physicality of *bhāva* itself (whereas Bhanudatta in the early sixteenth century defends the traditional category vigorously, Bhoja in the early eleventh replaces "possession" and "dying" with "jealousy" and "attachment"). However variously "emotion" itself may have been understood in the West, clearly no single English word is capable of communicating *bhāva*'s very wide domain of reference. Add to this the fact that *bhāva* comprises not only the subjective sense of emotion but also its objective cause; sometimes it even stands for the *vibhāva* itself, the foundational factor (the same can be true of their underlying nouns: *bhaya* in Sanskrit can mean both fear and whatever induces fear, i.e., danger; *kautuhala*, both wonder and whatever excites wonder), and can therefore require the translation "factors and emotions." Then too, Sanskrit aestheticians were sometimes as unclear about some of the affective states as we are; *dhṛti,* one of the transitory emotions, is sometimes understood as "satisfaction," sometimes as "constancy."[10]

Analogous in the degree of its cultural unfamiliarity and relative fluidity is the broader sphere of Sanskrit terms for the cognitive faculties. Lacking as we do an adequate historical psychology for India, it is hard to gauge how accurate are the English translations "intellect," "mind," "heart," and "mental state" for terms such as *buddhi*, *manas*, *antaḥkaraṇa*, and *cittavṛtti*. Part of the issue is the superabundance of subdivisions in the categories of classical psychology, far more than English vocabulary can differentiate. But again this is compounded by contending definitions across the philosophical systems and occasional uncertainties. The logician Bhasarvajna of Kashmir, a generation prior to Abhinava, says about the *manas*: "It is through the *manas* that we become aware of pleasure and pain." Such an account would seem to equip us well for grasping Abhinava's observation that the spectator's apprehension of a stable emotion en route to becoming rasa has the character of "direct awareness" and occurs in the *manas*. Perhaps Abhinava means to contrast *manas* here to the *buddhi*, intellect (which has a component of volition), or *antaḥkaraṇa*, "inner organ" (often seen as a combination of *buddhi*, *manas*, and ego, *ahaṃkāra*; perhaps "heart"), where linguistically mediated understanding occurs. But uncertainty grows when, in trying to make sense of the old category "actions of mind (*manas*), speech, intellect (*buddhi*), or body" (which preceded, or at least complemented, that of the four types of acting that later became standard), we bump up against the remark of the earlier logician Vatsyayana that "By *buddhi* is actually meant *manas*."[11]

Otherwise, the psychological vocabulary in English usually aligns reasonably well with the Indian categories once we figure them out.[12] What makes the translation of Indian emotion terms harder than it has to be is the impoverishment of contemporary English idiom for talking about feelings. We no longer have acceptable words for describing sexual love, for example. "Erotic" is all that is left, and I have adopted it perforce for *śṛṅgāra*, since that rasa is concerned above all with physical desire, and not primarily with "love" (later writers such as Kavikarnapura make this distinction crystal clear). Worse, and oddly so, is the situation with the comic rasa. There is no simple word to describe the feeling that something is funny; "amusement" is our one resort, however rare that may have now become in the emotional sense.

The one exception to these general rules guiding the translation concerns the term that I have chosen not to translate at all: *rasa* itself. It is not simply that rasa is the very unit of analysis and the object of study; rather, much of the discourse of Indian aesthetics is directed toward answering the question of what exactly it is. Translating the term would unhelpfully predetermine the answer, and so the range of possibilities has been allowed to emerge from the discussions—which turn out to offer in their own way an account of what the best translation(s) would be. I have treated in the same manner the derivative *rasika*, literally "he who, or that which, has or tastes or experiences rasa"; and like the class categories discussed earlier, *rasādi*, "rasa, etc.," though it technically includes all the rasas, emotions, semblances of emotions, and other subcategories, is generally rendered simply as "rasa."

A few less problematic choices require only brief comment. The word *kāvya* is at once a superordinate term, "literature," which includes poetry, poetic prose, drama (thus, "belles lettres"), and a subordinate term, used to distinguish literature meant to be recited before an audience from literature meant to be performed in a theater. When that distinction is clearly drawn—and it is an important one in this context, given the history of the extension of rasa theory from the latter domain to the former—I translate *kāvya* as "poetry" in contrast to "drama," though sometimes also as "literature heard" in contrast to "literature seen" when the Sanskrit terms (*śravya* and *dṛśya*) are used and seem specifically to require it. By contrast, I render it as "literature" when both genres are meant or no decision as to their differentiation can be made. Indian theorists, incidentally, never unambiguously refer to readers, only to listeners. But I feel certain that many Indian authors meant "listener" to include "reader" (just as classical Greek critics used *akroātēs* to refer to both). I thus consistently refer to "the viewer/reader" (and not "viewer/listener") as the audience of *kāvya* in its combined sense, and also use "viewer" and "reader" when drama and poetry, respectively, are specifically under discussion. All technical terms are organized in an English-Sanskrit glossary that lists the choices I have made.

The aim of producing as readable a sourcebook as possible has encouraged me to really try to translate the thought as well as the words of our authors. I therefore put into the translation what is implied in the text and consistently eschew the tangle of brackets that chokes so many translations of technical Sanskrit with pedantry. Anyone who knows Sanskrit will not need brackets to understand how I translate as I do, and those who do not will not care (the same holds for diacritics in proper names, which I have eliminated). Brackets are used only for numbers or letters to help the reader follow an argument, and for the page numbers of the original within a selection. Parentheses enclose material that is itself parenthetical in the original, as well as page numbers at the start of a selection.

I have tried wherever possible to consult manuscripts in the case of textual uncertainties. The most important are those of the *Abhinavabhāratī*, but copies of materials held in Trivandrum were able to be acquired very late in my work, and could be used only sparingly. Where multiple editions of a Sanskrit text are listed in the bibliography, the translation is based on the one listed first. In citing prose texts, where chapter and verse number are not available, I supply both page and line number (e.g., 282.1; when there is more than one volume, 1.282.1).[13] An asterisk indicates conjectured names of works no longer extant (e.g., **Commentary on the* Treatise on Drama, of Bhatta Lollata). In the annotations, references to the original verse number or pages of texts (identified by their abbreviations) include "above" or "below" when the passage is excerpted in the *Reader*; actual page numbers in the *Reader* have been added only when deemed essential.

Acknowledgments

I first began thinking seriously about rasa when I had the privilege of reading Bhoja's *Śṛṅgāraprakāśa* with the late K. Krishnamoorthy in Mysore in 1995, and while that text often mystified us both equally, I learned much from him about Indian aesthetics and have remained gripped ever since by the deep problems it raises. Rewaprasad Dwivedi, a leading modern-day *ālaṅkārika*, has been a stimulating conversation partner over the years since our first meeting in Varanasi in 1984. Radhavallabh Tripathi shared his learning at a seminar on rasa I offered at Columbia University in autumn 2011. Indian hermeneutics plays a small but critical role in this book, and I must acknowledge the two great, now-departed scholars who taught me what I know of this discipline, P. N. Pattabhirama Sastrigal (Varanasi) and K. Balasubrahmanya Sastrigal (Mylapore/Mantralayam).

I am deeply indebted to Lawrence McCrea and Andrew Ollett, who read carefully through the entire manuscript and offered numerous insights and corrections. Yigal Bronner did the same for parts of chapter 1, and Guy Leavitt for parts of chapter 4. Two true *rasika*s and old friends, Robert Goldman and Lyne Bansat-Boudon, made a number of valuable suggestions. My thanks are also due to the students, too many to name, with whom I read rasa texts in Sanskrit seminars over the years.

Thanks for help in acquiring copies of manuscripts are owed to Shrikant Bahulkar, Bhandarkar Oriental Research Institute; Ramesh Gaur, formerly of the Indira Gandhi National Centre for the Arts, New Delhi; and Sitanshu Yashaschandra, Baroda. Dragomir Dimitrov of Marburg University made available to me unpublished manuscript materials of the *Kāvyādarśa* and Ratnashrijnana's commentary. Ramesh Mittal of DK Agencies supplied me with books at a time when they were critical to my work and libraries were nowhere in sight.

At Columbia University Press I am grateful to Wendy Lochner for support and guidance from the start of the Historical Sourcebooks project, and to Leslie Kriesel for expert help both as developmental editor and as editor for this volume. The Andrew W. Mellon Foundation of New York honored me with a Distinguished Achievement Award that funded the research for this work and provided major support for the series in which it is appearing.

I began this book in India in September 2008 and completed it in India in March 2014. On both occasions, and in all the time in between, I had the joy of endlessly enriching conversation with Allison Busch. This is the least of the reasons for dedicating the book to her.

English Translations of Sanskrit Titles, with Approximate Dates

WORKS ON RASA

Ambrosial River of the Rasa of Devotion	*Bhaktirasāmṛtasindhu* (1540)
Analysis of Literature	*Kāvyanirṇaya* (975)
Analysis of "Manifestation"	*Vyaktiviveka* (1025)
Bearer of the Ganges of Rasa	*Rasagaṅgādhara* (1650)
Brief Annotation	*Laghuṭīkā* (of Bhatta Nrisimha) (undated)
Brief Elucidation	*Laghuvṛtti* (of Pratiharenduraja) (900)
Bud of Rasa	*Rasakalikā* (1200)
Commentary	*Vyākhyā*
**Commentary on the* Treatise on Drama	**Nāṭyaśāstravyākhyā* (of Bhatta Lollata, 825; of Shri Shankuka, 859; of Bhatta Nayaka, 900)
Compendium of Tropes	*Alaṅkārasarvasva* (c. 1150)
Divine Jewel of Ornamentation	*Alaṅkārakaustubha* (1550)
Elixir for the Rasika	*Rasikasaṃjīvinī* (1215)
Essential Compendium of the Ornament of Poetry	*Kāvyālaṅkārasārasaṃgraha* (800)
Exegesis	*Vivṛti* (of Tilaka) (1100)
Guarding the Tradition	*Śrutānupālinī* (950)
Jewel Mine of Symphony	*Saṃgītaratnākara* (1225)
Lamp for Transcendence	*Kaivalyadīpikā* (1300)
Light on Emotion	*Bhāvaprakāśana* (1200)
Light on Implicature	*Dhvanyāloka* (875)
Light on Passion	*Śṛṅgāraprakāśa* (1050)
Light on Poetry	*Kāvyaprakāśa* (1050)

Literary Investigations	*Kāvyakautuka* (975)
Looking Glass of Poetry	*Kāvyādarśa* (700)
Manual of Poetry	*Kāvyānuśāsana* (1150)
Mirror of Drama	*Nāṭyadarpaṇa* (1200)
Mirror of Literary Art	*Sāhityadarpaṇa* (1350)
Mirror of Poetry	*Kāvyadarpaṇa* (1650)
Mirror of the Heart	*Hṛdayadarpaṇa* (900)
Necklace for the Goddess of Language	*Sarasvatīkaṇṭhābharaṇa* (1025)
Notes	*Ṭippaṇī* (of Namisadhu) (1068)
Observations	*Avaloka* (975)
Ornament of Poetry	*Kāvyālaṅkāra* (of Bhamaha, 650; of Rudrata, 850)
Ornament of the Fame of King Prataparudra	*Pratāparudrayaśobhūṣaṇa* (1320)
Passage Through the Impassable	*Durgamasaṃgamanī* (1541)
Pearls of the Bhāgavata	*Bhāgavatamuktāphala* (1300)
Ratna's Glory	*Ratnaśrī* (950)
The Central Gem	*Taralā* (1400)
The Eye for Light on Implicature	*Dhvanyālokalocana* (990)
The Jewel Store	*Ratnāpaṇa* (1430)
The Lamp	*Dīpikā* (of Bahurupa Mishra)
The Moon on the Rasa Ocean	*Rasārṇavasudhākara* (1385)
The Nectar Ocean of Literary Art	*Sāhityasudhāsindhu* (1592)
The New Dramatic Art	*Abhinavabhāratī* (1000)
The River of Rasa	*Rasataraṅgiṇī* (1500)
The Short Explanation of Light on Poetry	*Kāvyaprakāśasaṃketa* (1150)
The Single Strand	*Ekāvalī* (1300)
The Ten Dramatic Forms	*Daśarūpaka* (975)
The Vital Force of Literary Language	*Vakroktijīvita* (975)
Treatise on Divine Love	*Prītisandarbha* (1550)
Treatise on Drama	*Nāṭyaśāstra* (early centuries C.E.)

OTHER WORKS

Great Commentary on Grammar	*Mahābhāṣya*
The Ascetic King of Vatsa	*Tāpasavatsarāja*
The River of Kings	*Rājataraṅgiṇī*
Tying Up the Braid	*Veṇīsaṃhāra*

Abbreviations

ABh *Abhinavabhāratī*
AK *Alaṅkārakaustubha*
AmŚ *Amaruśataka*
AS *Alaṅkārasarvasva*
AŚ *Abhijñānaśakuntalā*
AVM *Abhidhāvṛttimātṛkā*
BhM *Bhāgavatamuktāphala*
BhP *Bhāvaprakāśana*
BhPu *Bhāgavatapurāṇa*
BhR *Bhaktirasāyana*
BhRAS *Bhaktirasāmṛtasindhu*
BKA *Bhāmahakāvyalaṅkāra*
CC *Camatkāracandrikā*
DhĀ *Dhvanyāloka*
DhĀL *Dhvanyālokalocana*
DR *Daśarūpaka*
IPVV *Īśvarapratyabhijñāvivṛtivimarśinī*
KA *Kāvyānuśāsana*
KĀ *Kāvyādarśa*
KAS *Kāvyālaṅkārasūtra*
KASS *Kāvyālaṅkārasārasaṃgraha*
KD *Kāvyadarpaṇa*
KLV *Kalpalatāviveka*
KM *Kāvyamīmāṃsā*
KP *Kāvyaprakāśa*
KS *Kumārasambhava*
MBh *Mahābhārata*
MM *Mālatimādhava*
MVC *Mahāvīracarita*
ND *Nāṭyadarpaṇa*
NŚ *Nāṭyaśāstra*
P *Pāṇini*
PMS *Pūrvamīmāṃsāsūtra*
PR *Pratāparudrayaśobhūṣaṇa*
PS *Prītisandarbha*
RAS *Rasārṇavasudhākara*
RK *Rasakalikā*
RKA *Rudraṭa Kāvyālaṅkāra*
RT *Rasataraṅgiṇī*
RV *Raghuvaṃśa*
SD *Sāhityadarpaṇa*
SKĀ *Sarasvatīkaṇṭhābharaṇa*
SRĀ *Saṃgītaratnākara*
SSS *Sāhityasudhāsindhu*

ŚP	*Śṛṅgāraprakāśa*
TV	*Tantravārttika*
URC	*Uttararāmacarita*
VJ	*Vakroktijīvita*
VP	*Vākyapadīya*
VS	*Veṇīsaṃhāra*
VU	*Vikramorvaśīya*
VV	*Vyaktiviveka*
v.	verse
v.l.	varia lectio

A RASA READER

Introduction

An Intellectual History of Rasa

kān pṛcchāmaḥ surāḥ svarge nivasāmo vayaṃ bhuvi/
kiṃ vā kāvyarasaḥ svādhuḥ kiṃ vā svādhīyasī sudhā//

The gods live in heaven and we on earth, so whom can we ask
which is sweeter, the rasa of poetry or the nectar of immortality?

—ANONYMOUS

1. WHAT WAS "AESTHETICS" IN CLASSICAL INDIA?

What exactly we are experiencing when we see a play or read a novel is one of the core questions of the humanities, because that experience is one of the core aspects of what it means to be human. Entering into another world, by some measure an unreal one, and losing ourselves in it completely is an almost everyday occurrence, but one that only gains in mystery because it is quotidian. To watch ourselves watching something unreal, and willingly embracing that real unreality, no matter how sad or terrifying, is to enter into a fascinating hall of mirrors. Making sense of the reflections in this hall is what "aesthetics" in part is concerned to do. Although storytelling in drama or poetry is a universal human practice, few people have meditated as deeply and systematically on the questions it raises as thinkers in India, who over a period of 1,500 years, between the third and the eighteenth centuries, carried on an intense conversation about the emotional world of the story and its complex relationships to the world of the audience.

In gauging the contributions of what, for reasons I will specify momentarily, we may call Indian aesthetics, it would seem prudent to put the empirical horse before the theoretical cart and ask first what the thought world of classical India actually looked like, and only then to see how, if at all, it might align with present-day conceptual categories. The series in which this book appears, however, is intended not only for specialists but also for generalists and comparativists, who not unreasonably would want to know at the outset something about how their own thought world maps against what they are about to encounter.

To this end, it makes sense to begin by clarifying what we mean by "aesthetics" and asking how it has come to be what it is today. To address the first question, it is less helpful to know what people now abstractly take "aesthetics" to mean than to see what they pragmatically do with it. We can gauge something of this pragmatic understanding by looking at a contemporary overview of the subject, like a recent Oxford anthology.[1] This consists of six sections of readings; the titles of four are: "Why identify anything as art?"; "What do artists do?"; "Can we ever understand an artwork?"; and "How can we evaluate art?" These are all questions no Indian thinkers before modernity, at least none who wrote in Sanskrit, ever systematically raised, not because of their incompetence but because of their different cultural presuppositions and conceptual needs. For one thing, there was no unified sphere with a particular designation we could translate by the English term "art." There were separate cultural domains of poetry (*kāvya*), drama (*nāṭya*), music (*saṃgīta*, consisting of vocal and instrumental music and dance), and less carefully thematized practices, with terminology also less settled, including painting (*citra*), sculpture (often *pusta*), architecture (for which there was no common term at all), and the crafts (*kalā*), which could include many of the preceding when that was deemed necessary. In these separate domains there was never any dispute, at least overtly, about what was and was not to be included, though sometimes works passed into and out of a given category, according to historically changing reading or viewing practices. Furthermore, almost everything outside the literary realm, let alone the cultural realm, remained outside classical Indian aesthetic analysis (including nature: though Shiva was a dancer, God in India was generally not an artist). There are exhaustive normative descriptions of painting and music technique, but these comprise no systematic aesthetic reflection. Painting is referred to only once in all our texts, in a celebrated analogy on imitation framed by Shri Shankuka around 850 and repeated down the centuries.[2] Music is mentioned only a handful of times in passing, and although a celebrated musicological treatise does frame rasa as its central aesthetic problem, what it offers is standard literary rasa;[3] the question whether music can be narrative or programmatic, or why and how we respond emotionally to it at all—questions that intrigue contemporary aesthetics—was never asked. Indian aesthetic theory was founded upon representation of human emotion in the literary artwork and our capacity not just to find the representation "beautiful" but to *get inside* it.

As for questions of creativity and genius (*pratibhā*), Indian thinkers certainly were interested in them,[4] but they never thought it necessary to develop a robust theory to account for their nature or impact on the work. Interpretation was never thematized as a discrete problem of knowledge in literary texts. Hermeneutical theory was expanded from scriptural to literary studies beginning in the mid-ninth century, but literary interpretation as such was something to be pragmatically addressed in the course of exegesis. And although larger theses were offered about how meaning is produced, a work's overall meaning was rarely posed as an explicit, let alone as a theoretical, question.[5] Critical judgments were certainly rendered, strengths and weaknesses were recorded, and forms of practical canonization were widespread (in anthologies, praise poems, imitation), but literary evaluation itself was not framed as a philosophical problem. Last, while careful attention was directed to beauty (*saundarya*), especially in literature (which does have a role to play in aesthetic reflection), beauty was typically disaggregated into its constituents—figuration, naturalistic description, verbal texture, modes of meaning production (such as implicature), and emotional register—and never became an object of abstract consideration in and of itself.

In two other sections of the Oxford anthology, however, the Indian and the contemporary Western disciplines overlap: "Why describe anything as aesthetic?" and "Why respond emotionally to art?" Although the second would never have been framed as an option in India, these two questions bring us to the core of the Indian concern with aesthetics, a term we may therefore unhesitatingly adopt despite the fact that no single word in Sanskrit is available to translate it.[6] (Remember that even in English "aesthetics" is not found in the intended sense before the eighteenth century.) What Indian thinkers wanted to figure out above all was what exactly distinguishes an aesthetic from a nonaesthetic object or event, and how that distinction plays out in audience response. But this was something they were able to do only once they had analyzed how emotion was *formally* created—and the analysis they developed provides something as yet unavailable in Western aesthetics: a systematic account of how emotions are represented, a "general inquiry into the character of the emotional structure specific to what we call literature."[7]

As for the particular history of aesthetics as a discourse in the West, we need only delineate what that means for our understanding of the Indian case and provide a few benchmark questions to bear in mind as we proceed. There is now widespread agreement that the origins of what we recognize as Western aesthetics have something centrally to do with the coming of Western modernity. In the eyes of Max Weber, the leading exegete of that historical rupture, art in premodernity everywhere was completely subordinated to the religious sphere. Only with the growth of the "rationalization" of life that defines modernity, and the associated shrinking, in Weber's assessment, of religion's capacity to provide salvation did the aesthetic sphere for the first time become autonomous, initially as a surrogate for and then as a competitor of religion, with its own value system of taste contending with that of religious morals (a view for which Matthew Arnold was a key representative in England). A more politically textured reading would understand the aesthetic sphere as an ideological form constructed at once in connection with the rise of class society and as a challenge to it, but also deeply shaped by the European experience of colonialism. Hegel's aesthetic theory, for example, emerged not only from the new bourgeoisie's contemplation of its own world but also from its confrontation (represented in Hegel's comparative method) with what was not of its own world.[8]

Aesthetics was famously invented as a European academic discipline by Alexander Baumgarten in 1735, though philosophical aesthetics has its origins a decade earlier in Francis Hutcheson's *An Inquiry Concerning Beauty* (1725). By far the most influential contribution to the field has been Immanuel Kant's *Critique of Judgment* (1790). For Kant, "taste is the faculty for judging," and judgments of "taste" determine whether or not something is beautiful and are based on feelings of pleasure. His principal concern is with the subjectivity of such judgments; they have nothing to do with what in his view constitutes real knowledge. The most important modern account of the modern aesthetic revolution, at once intellectual-historical and philosophical, is that of Hans-Georg Gadamer. The rise of what he calls "aesthetic consciousness" in Kant and especially Schleiermacher refers to the devaluation of aesthetic knowledge. True knowledge became exclusively scientific; the hermeneutical "knowledge" rendered by art experience was shunted off to the purely subjective realm and relegated to a place between the skeptic's quotation marks.

Core to the dominant views on the rise of Western aesthetics, then, is a set of shared assumptions: that the creation of a domain of art entirely separate from religion is a phenomenon associated with, even partly defining, modernity; that the rise of the discourse that takes this domain as its object was conditioned in part by modernity's work of "purification," to use Bruno Latour's idiom, and in part by the cultural problems posed by its evil twin, colonialism; that the rise of scientific rationalism was accompanied by a devaluation of what was not science, and that therefore the knowledge, moral and emotional and otherwise, that art offers and aesthetics aims to explain was rendered nonknowledge. This is the horizon of interpretation that modern students by default bring to the study of classical Indian aesthetics and that shapes their understanding. How far Indian thought corroborates these assumptions, or instead explodes them, will emerge from our reconstruction. This raises intellectual-historical problems of its own, as do the many parallels between the Indian and Western traditions—not least, the use of the category "taste" itself, the most literal translation of the word *rasa*.

One of these parallels lies in the overall conceptual configuration of the problem of emotion in literature. Theorization in the West, at least in the modern period, often juxtaposes concerns with the author's emotion in the creation of the literary artwork (as in "expression theory") with the emotion embedded in the text by virtue of its formal properties (as in American New Criticism) and with the reader's emotional engagement with the text (as in some versions of reception theory).[9] A strikingly analogous set of concerns can be found in India, but here the ideas take on the contours of a sharp historical development.

The earliest evidence we have of rasa, or at least a component of the rasa complex, lies in the story of the "first poet" and the creation of poetry; this was followed by a long period of intense analysis of the formal structure of the aesthetic object, beginning with the foundational text of the discourse, the *Treatise on Drama*. The aesthetic revolution in the tenth century brought to the fore the aesthetic subject—the audience and its response—though older conceptions would persist, if sometimes in strikingly new formulations.[10]

2. RASA IN THE POET

In the *Rāmāyaṇa* of Valmiki (last centuries B.C.E.), the first work of what would come to be called *kāvya*, or classical Sanskrit literature, the poet recounts how a sage passed on to him a tale about the deeds of the great Prince Rama (who, along with his wife, Sita, would supply the paradigmatic examples of hero and heroine throughout the history of Sanskrit aesthetics). When Valmiki later sees a hunter kill a bird in the act of mating, he experiences a transformative moment of *śoka*, grief, and he spontaneously utters a curse in a form of language utterly unfamiliar to him, namely *śloka*, versified poetry. In this story we find the first acknowledgment not only that the specific power of literature lies in the expression of emotion—the phonemic correspondence *śoka/śloka* maps an ontological one—but also that the expression of the poet's own emotion constitutes this power.

That "the poetry is in the pity" of the poet was a conception still alive almost a millennium after Valmiki, though now couched in a more theoretically sophisticated idiom. The mid-ninth-century thinker Anandavardhana, when arguing that it is rasa that makes literature literature, explains that it was to demonstrate this fact that "the grief of the first poet . . . was shown to be transformed into verse. For grief is the stable emotion of the tragic rasa."[11] The idea that the literary artwork is an expression of the author's own emotion is summarized in an oft-quoted verse of Ananda's: "If the poet is filled with passion, the whole world of his poem will consist of rasa; if not, it will be completely devoid of it."[12]

This Indian version of the expression theory of literary creation informs some of the earliest systematic thinking about rasa. We find it in the *Treatise on Drama*, in one definition of the all-important term "emotion": "'Emotion' (*bhāva*) is also so called because it serves to 'bring into being' (*bhāvayan*) the poet's inner emotion (*bhāva*), by means of the four registers of acting: verbal, physical, psychophysical, and scenic."[13] And it reappears in one of the earliest discussions of rasa in the rhetorical tradition. Around the beginning of the eighth century Dandin declares that "Rasa is found in both the language and the subject matter, and insightful people become intoxicated by it like bees by honey"; his tenth-century commentator Ratnashrijnana explains that "by 'insightful people' is meant poets who understand rasa. . . . It is they who become intoxicated by a poem filled with rasa"—that is, no doubt, by their own poem.[14]

Yet over time, Indian thinkers would move far away from this view and never really return, for they came to understand that rasa cannot be a response to the real world, the world outside the theater, for there, grief is truly grief. It was precisely the difference between the two experiences that became their preoccupation. The poet would continue to be included, if with ever diminishing frequency, in discussions of who really experiences rasa. In fact, it is surprising to see Bhatta Tota, the teacher of the celebrated Abhinavagupta (c. 1000), still asserting on the threshold of the aesthetic revolution (and in a way irreconcilable with his student's later views) that "the protagonist, the poet, and the audience . . . all have the same experience," and even the author of that revolution, Bhatta Nayaka himself, maintaining the position.[15] At the end, however, these references are more commendatory than substantial. The poet's emotion becomes a vestigial question, found only in a type of literature containing not rasa but only emotion, given that the feelings involved ("desire" for God, for example) are excluded by the canonical definition of rasa and hence can never develop into it. The "predominant element" in such work remains the speaker's, that is the poet's, emotion. Elsewhere, what the poet himself felt would become irrelevant to Sanskrit poetry and its theory.

3. RASA SEEN, IN THE PLAY

The organized presentation of aesthetics, beyond the desultory remarks of early poets, forms a subordinate component of two closely related bodies of *śāstra*, that is, a body of systematic thought, or theory. One of these, which was both earlier and more consequential for the history of classical aesthetics, is *nāṭyaśāstra*, the theory of drama. Its origins are unknown, but as a structured form of thought it is unlikely to predate the early centuries C.E. The other is *alaṅkāraśāstra*, poetics or literary theory generally, which arose around the sixth century but gradually appropriated the discourse on aesthetics, especially with the demise of dramaturgical theory after about the thirteenth century (most of the texts here are in fact from works on poetics). A key problem in aesthetic theory was finding ways to connect these two disciplines, which meant extending a system originating in "visual literature," or drama, to "aural literature," or narrative poetry.

The oldest extant text on dramaturgy in India is itself titled *Nāṭyaśāstra*, the *Treatise on Drama*, and is ascribed to the sage Bharata. The original composition (early centuries C.E.) was revised at some point, most probably in ninth-century Kashmir, where we observe a new and intense commentarial interest in the work. The *Treatise* is a comprehensive account of everything from the ritual preliminaries of a theatrical performance to the various types of acting (language, gestures, facial expressions, costume and makeup) to music, dance, and stage design, clearly addressed in the first instance to those who create and perform drama. Chapter 6 is the closest thing we have to a foundational text of the discipline of aesthetics, where the celebrated "aphorism on rasa" is found: "Rasa arises from the conjunction of factors, reactions, and transitory emotions." Explaining this compact statement remained for a full millennium and a half what it meant to explain aesthetic experience.[16]

It is in keeping with its purpose and readership that the *Treatise* should be concerned with rasa as something generated by the formal features of the drama. The analytical dissection of objects in the world that present themselves to us ready-made is at the very heart of the Sanskrit intellectual tradition, most prominently on display in the work of the Sanskrit grammarians. One of the aims of the *Treatise* is accordingly to break down the phenomenological unity of the drama into its constituent parts. These include the "leading male character" and "leading female character," the bases of the emotional structure of the play: depending on which aspect of this structure is emphasized in the story, the man can be represented as the "foundational factor" of sexual desire, say, for the woman, or (more frequently) she the foundational factor for him. Other beings (or things) function as the foundation for other emotions, but the *set* of emotions available for representation is finite; there are eight and eight only, the dominant or basic emotions. The characters move through different scenic contexts that stimulate their desire (moonlit nights, for example, or pleasure gardens), and can therefore be identified as "stimulant factors." No one experiences a basic emotion pure and unmixed, but rather conjoined with other feelings of a more ephemeral nature—the "transitory emotions," longing, disquiet, or despair, for example, in the case of sexual desire. These, which number exactly thirty-three, are more complex than the translation "emotion" might suggest, since they include physical events such as torpor, sickness, possession, and dying, and traits such as sagacity that we commonly understand as inhering in a person in a stable way. Such emotions are interior phenomena, unknowable to others except through the physical "reactions" with which they are invariably connected: seductive glances, for example, in the case of desire (physical reactions constitute an open category, and therefore are not numbered and listed). Finer distinctions can be introduced in these physical reactions by identifying those where the psychological dimension (*sattva*) is more prominent: the perspiring, horripilation, and pallor that occur in connection with desire are different from those that have purely material causes (heat, cold, illness), and may therefore be classed as "psychophysical responses" (*sāttvikabhāvas*), eight of which are identified.[17]

From such an analytical perspective the play looks like a jumble of disconnected components, but the very performative—and almost alchemical—process that characterizes drama and that forms the subject matter of the *Treatise* subordinates and homogenizes them. They are ultimately combined into a whole, where each component is at once preserved and subsumed, that constitutes the unified emotional core of a given scene and of the play as a whole. This core is its rasa, or "taste," which may be likened to the flavor of a drink of multiple ingredients, complex but unified.

Many readers new to the analysis of rasa—and some in the tradition itself—react unfavorably not only to its apparent numerological obsession, its mania for counting and listing, but also to the very supposition that emotional phenomena can be listed and counted. Yet making sense of emotion in literature is partly about making sense of emotion as such, and thus defining and delimiting it. This is all the more the case for authors and actors, who are concerned with *making emotion*, not just making sense of it. Every tradition of inquiry into the emotions, ancient Greek or imperial Chinese or early or late-modern European, has sought to define and list them, especially those held to be basic.[18] If we think carefully about the list of eight in the *Treatise*—desire, amusement, grief, anger, determination, fear, revulsion, and amazement—we will recognize that it comprises only those that can actually be communicated in performance. For "literature meant to be seen," one descriptor coined early on and perhaps in the *Treatise* itself for distinguishing drama from other types of belles lettres, emotion that can be seen was naturally counted as basic.[19] Some scholars who have studied the question of emotion and physical expression, like the philosopher William James, have found a very close, even defining, connection between them: "A woman is sad," he wrote somewhat counterintuitively, "*because* she weeps."[20] But others have held, more persuasively and more in harmony with the Indian view, that there are invisible emotions, such as motherly love. As Darwin described it, "No emotion is stronger than maternal love, but a mother may feel deepest love for her helpless infant, and yet not show it by any outward sign."[21] Such emotions could never be rasa—until such time as the boundaries of "literature that can be seen" would no longer define what rasa could in fact be.

One of the most important and fertile yet intractable questions for the entire subsequent aesthetic tradition is what Bharata thought rasa is—or in the terms that would later be used, where it resides and who experiences it. Given that the fundamental concern of the *Treatise* is performance, and that, as a result, its analytical concern is the formal features of drama, it is understandable that Bharata should consistently discuss rasa as something located in the performative event, in the actors and the characters they represent (as also, as we have seen, in the heart of the playwright). In the *Treatise*, as one scholar has observed, the words rasa and *bhāva* (emotion) "invariably" refer to the activity of the artist and not the spectator, "the aesthetic situation, the art object outside," not any subjective state of reception.[22] Both the *Treatise* taken as a whole and its earliest interpretations corroborate this judgment. The text's overriding concern and its typical descriptions show that for Bharata, rasa was an emotional state in the character that "arises" when the various formal components of the drama enumerated are successfully "conjoined" in performance. And this assessment is exactly what is presupposed by the contentious course—whose contentions would otherwise make no sense—taken by the entire later history of aesthetics.

There is more to the organizing metaphor of "taste" than the combination of diverse ingredients into a unity. A thing can certainly be said have a taste in itself, but the very idea of taste also of course presupposes a taster. The text itself unpacks the metaphor in a prose passage (most of the work is in verse): "Just as discerning people relish tastes . . . discerning viewers relish the stable emotions . . . and they feel joy."[23] We do not know whether the passage is original to the unreconstructed, pre-Kashmirian *Treatise* (aspects of its phraseology suggest it is not), but even so, it does not cloud the primary focus of the work, the "art object" of the drama itself rather than the "subjective state" of the viewer. It would be some six centuries before the formal analysis of rasa would give way to the phenomenology of its reception.

4. RASA HEARD, IN THE POEM

What happens when a theory developed for drama, for "literature that is seen," is appropriated for poetry, "literature that is heard"—read out before an audience but certainly also read privately? The fact that such an appropriation took place in classical India is transparent in the historical record, but Indian thinkers themselves were also fully aware of it. "Generally speaking," wrote one poetician at a time when the extension was already well under way, "the nature of rasa has been discussed by

Bharata and others in reference to drama. I shall examine it here, according to my own lights, in reference to poetry."[24] The consequences of this far-reaching expansion of rasa theory can be charted principally in three domains: the discursive, where a dramaturgical concept was assimilated to a new knowledge structure, the theory of rhetoric, to which it was alien; the conceptual, where the specific nature of the art form—narrative, not performative—required a new linguistic analysis of rasa; and the categorical, for the defining condition of rasa as something actually visible on the stage no longer constrained the understanding of what emotions could count as a rasa. In all three domains, however, the discourse on rasa remained formal, and attention was still squarely focused on the text.

4.1 As Figure

The theoretical analysis of poetry, which, as noted, came into being much later than dramaturgy, centers on its figurative nature. For the early theorists, poetry was above all language usage marked by "indirection," that is, by figures of sense such as metaphor or metonymy. Literary theory, hence, was predominantly a theory of "ornaments," rhetoric, or figures (*alaṅkāraśāstra*; the term itself is late); other early concerns, with language "qualities" (such as phonemic texture), for example, or regional styles, would eventually fade. The question itself, why it was felt necessary to assimilate a dramatic theory of aesthetic emotion into such a poetics, was never raised. Perhaps we need look for an explanation no further than the growing intellectual dominance of the idea itself, as embodied above all in the maturation of Sanskrit drama (the works of Kalidasa, late fourth century, are exemplary). At all events, by the ninth century thinkers like Rudrata were insisting that writers "take all possible care to endow a literary text," that is, a poem, "with rasas," for people recoil from literature without rasa—the "juicy" parts of the text, after all—as they recoil from a dry moral treatise.[25] The only way to effect this assimilation, given rhetoric's discursive constraints, was to think of aesthetic emotion as one more type of figure, and this was the course followed for the first several centuries.

In the simplest terms, the new "emotion tropes," as we might name them, all represent expressions of heightened feeling: where a given emotion clearly manifests itself; where a warmly felt compliment is conveyed; where a character's arrogance or vehemence is expressed.[26] While not embodying the indirection that defines other figures, these remain specialized uses of language and hence may be conceived of as "ornaments" and thus objects suited to a theory of ornamentation. For the early authors (of whom only the works of Bhamaha, mid-seventh century, and Dandin, early eighth century, survive), rasa was clearly subordinate to and therefore easily subsumed under the larger discourse on figures; it did not yet constitute the heart of literariness.

The last formulation of the rhetorical analysis of aesthetic emotion, and now a somewhat dissonant one, is marked by the work of Udbhata (c. 800). On the one hand, as we might expect from the first known commentator on the *Treatise on Drama*, Udbhata radically redefines the emotion tropes to approximate the full rasa typology. What for earlier writers was the "expression of heightened emotion" becomes in Udbhata the "full realization" of rasa with the complete panoply of aesthetic elements; the "emotional compliment" now becomes the "intimation" of an emotion; the "prideful expression" becomes the "semblance of rasa," defined as feeling marked by social impropriety. And along with these redefinitions, a fourth figure is added, the quiescence of an existing rasa.[27] At the same time Udbhata lists the components conducive to the full creation of rasa: a stable emotion, transitory emotions, foundational and stimulant factors, reactions, and, controversially, use of the rasa's "proper term."[28] In all these cases the conception of rasa remains precisely what it was in the past: a phenomenon immanent in the text, a formal feature related to the characters in the narrative.

However, the internal strain in the system has become apparent: despite his effort to approximate the dramaturgical model, Udbhata continues to categorize all these as figures of speech, and, like Bhamaha and Dandin, to group them with such tropes as "disingenuous expression" and the "description of providential help." By the end of the ninth century, Udbhata's commentator Pratiharenduraja was confessing how markedly the conceptual terrain had shifted from the time of his author: "Whether the rasas and the emotions, given that they are the source of the highest literary beauty, are 'ornaments' of literature or its very life force will not be a subject for consideration here lest it unduly lengthen the book."[29] The commentator's question would be answered almost immediately.

4.2 As Implicature

The primacy of rasa in literature and the difficulty of containing it within the conceptual framework of figures was first recognized by Rudrata sometime in the early ninth century. But it was Anandavardhana a generation or two later who made rasa the central organizing concept of literary analysis in his *Light on Implicature*. Adopting an idea from Mimamsa, scriptural hermeneutics or the "science of sentence meaning," foundational to the great transformation of rasa in the following generation, Ananda reasoned that, just like sentences, literary texts were "teleological," defined by having a single end or meaning, which in the case of the literary text he identified as its rasa, or emotional core.[30] The idea that rasa, thus transformed into the ultimate goal of literature, could be subsumed under the logic of tropology and function as a figure—something that ornaments something else of greater significance in the economy of the poem, the way a metaphor ornaments the message—ceased to make sense for Ananda. Or more precisely, it made sense only according to the relationship just mentioned for metaphor. Thus, where the dominant element in the poem can be clearly seen to lie in its narrative content, such as the grandeur of God or flattery of a king, any emotional expression such as the tragic or erotic would have to be ranked as subordinate. Some thinkers, like Kuntaka in the century after Ananda, would insist that even in such poems as prayers to gods or encomia to kings the rasa remained dominant, "the thing to be ornamented"—"There is no separate thing to be apprehended beyond the mental state itself that constitutes the narrative content," he argues passionately—and hence could never itself constitute an ornament.[31] For still others, by a tendency toward preservation widespread in Indian intellectual history, the notion that rasas are indeed figures of speech would survive into the thirteenth century and beyond.[32]

Anandavardhana's liberation of the rasa of poetry from the prison house of rhetoric, however, is not what earned him his important place in the intellectual history of aesthetics. His most historically consequential idea concerned the communicative medium of rasa in a world purely textual and no longer performative. How, he asked—or at least this is the question buried below the surface of his answer—can rasa be made known when there is nothing to see, when it is the rasa of "literature that is heard"?

Here again the central concern remains a formal, textual, and more specifically a linguistic process. Surprisingly, Ananda never defines rasa, just as he never discusses its reception (the Sanskrit word for "audience," *sāmājika*, key to so much later discussion, is absent from his treatise). He is concerned exclusively with poetic expression. Just as in much poetry (especially the early Prakrit tradition that first suggested the idea to Ananda), the narrative element that has overriding importance is the one that is *meant* without being directly *expressed*,[33] so rasa, Ananda argues, can never be a matter of direct denotation. Explaining how something intended but unspoken could be communicated, whether it is an emotional or narrative or even rhetorical element, and especially the first of those in a nonperformative literary environment, required hypothesizing a new linguistic modality. This Ananda named *dhvani*, "implicature," and through this, rasa (and the rest of the unsaid) is "manifested" the way an object in a dark room is manifested by a lamp.[34] The vast taxonomic elaboration of implicature that Ananda developed can be divided into two main types: "where the literal meaning is not intended at all, and where it is intended but subordinated to some other meaning." The implicature of rasa occupies a special conceptual niche: it is the only type in the second category where the succession of meanings, from literal to intended—that is, from the disaggregated aesthetic elements to the unified emotional "meaning" produced by them and viewed as a totality—is not registered by the reader but instead arises with apparent (but only apparent) immediacy.[35]

The claim that normal linguistic processes failed to explain the formal production of rasa and a new one had to be postulated would be hotly contested in the century after Ananda, most notably by Bhatta Nayaka (c. 900), who sought to completely overturn the notion of "manifestation" by rethinking the nature of rasa itself—a venture unimaginable, it would seem, to Ananda. Others, like Dhanika (c. 975) in his only fragmentarily preserved *Analysis of Literature,* insisted that the older doctrine of sentence intentionality (*tātparya*) was adequate, or, like Mahima Bhatta (c. 1000), reduced implicature to logical inference.[36] The prehistory of Ananda's theory is equally important. Udbhata had claimed that the "proper term" for a rasa—"the actual lexeme, 'desire,' for example" (as his commentator explains)—is as essential a factor in its creation as the stable emotion and other "aesthetic elements." This "gives us to understand the presence of the emotion because it refers to it."[37] The point seems natural enough, indeed inevitable: is it possible to express passion without using the word "passion"? In a poem, unlike a drama, emotions cannot be shown but have to be told—but how can you tell without naming? And in fact early writers, such as Bhavabhuti (c. 800), seem to bend over backward to meet the requirement enunciated by (though not necessarily originating with) Udbhata.[38] But some before Ananda contested the idea, and others after him saw it as a literary flaw: if rasa can *only* be implied, then directly naming it was automatically a defect. As a late writer put it, "The allure of things that should be covered, like a woman's breasts, is diminished when they are openly shown; so too are transitory emotions expressed by their own words when they should be indicated by physical reactions and the like."[39] Shri Shankuka's critique a few generations before Ananda was based on a powerful and convincing distinction he was the first to draw, between mere referential language and the expressive language required for rasa, while Kuntaka's response—long after the transition of rasa from dramatic to poetic theory was made, and its original problems were no longer thinkable—was simply ridicule.[40]

If Ananda turned this problem into a cornerstone of his theory,[41] his commentator Abhinavagupta reflected more insightfully on the matter, and, surprisingly, reasserted something of the validity of Udbhata's view. "It is essential," he says (not in his commentary on Ananda, understandably, but in *The New* Dramatic Art) for words such as those for the transitory emotions to be "expressive of rasa," because if it were not possible to use the actual words for transitory emotions, reactions, and the like, they could never be communicated; it would be "virtually impossible to comprehend them," and the words themselves would have no signification at all.[42] However interesting, even profound in its own way, this dispute may be and however complicated its history, the key point has again to do with the extension of the rasa template from play to poem. Udbhata's position becomes less controversial when viewed within the problematic of the *textual* constitution of aesthetic emotion, and in the historical context of trying to solve the problem of producing rasa not in performance, where it (or rather, its signs) can actually be seen, but in narrative, where it can only be imagined when "heard."

4.3 New Categories

Indian thinkers would puzzle over the relationship between drama and poetry for centuries. Around 950, Abhinavagupta's teacher Bhatta Tota argued that "Rasa exists only in drama, and in poetry only to the degree that it mimics drama"; it "comes into being," as Abhinava paraphrased, "only when a state of awareness simulating perception comes into being." A little later Bhoja asserted, contrarily, the primacy of poets over actors and poetry over drama, on the grounds that

> A subject does not expand the heart / so powerfully when we see it portrayed
> as when it flashes forth from the words / of great poets declaimed with art.[43]

Or, as an early thirteenth-century scholar put it, the superiority of poetic language to dramatic acting lies in "the range of its narrative power."[44] Yet, if poetry is comparable to drama in the deep visuality it can produce through that power, it offers in the end a radically different aesthetic experience.

As a consequence, the extension of the theory of aesthetic emotion from drama to poetry entailed confronting the major challenges in the discursive and conceptual domains we have reviewed: the tropological assessment of rasa in early rhetoric texts (since there was no other way to assimilate it to the discourse), and the semantic rethinking felt to be necessary by Anandavardhana (since there was no other way to make sense of its purely verbal mode of representation). It remains to explore the third domain of impact: the categorization of rasa. Once visibility had ceased to limit the understanding of what emotions could count as a rasa, a Pandora's box was opened. It was no longer a question of being able to tell simply by showing; now one could show by telling (or "implying"), and the palette of rasas could be increased theoretically to the very limits of expressive language and psychological complexity. Eventually, as the extension of rasa theory to poetics had become naturalized and its origins in dramaturgy ceased to provide justification for any limits, Indian thinkers began to react as unfavorably as their modern counterparts to the closed list of emotions (dramaturgical theorists, however, such as Dhanamjaya and Dhanika, still resisted).[45] "The conventional wisdom that the term rasa refers only to the heroic, the fantastic, and the remaining six," says Bhoja at the start of his *Light on Passion*, is mere "superstition": "our intention in this work is to put it to rest."[46] He accordingly adds a wide range of new rasas, including the vainglorious, the noble, and motherly love—this last being the most telling, since it explains all the others given its inherent lack (as Darwin argued) of visual expressibility. No longer limited by physical performability, the category of rasa was now open, and would be expanded over the centuries, sometimes—as in the case of the "devotional" rasa—in the face of intense scholarly opposition.[47] The dispute over the peaceful rasa, the emotion of emotionlessness, speaks not only to the difficult extension from performance, where it could not be represented, to narrative, where it could, but also to the movement from formalism, where it could not be embodied, to reception, where it could be felt.[48] And such rethinking was not just about classification. The expansion of rasas in narrative poetry and fiction reflects an expansion of the emotional imagination of writers as they explored new areas of human feeling.[49]

In all this intellectual ferment sparked by moving from stage to page, rasa remained what it was from the start, a phenomenon of the text, a formal feature pertaining to the characters, just as earlier it had been analyzed as a phenomenon of the performance, whether pertaining to the actor or to the character with which the actor identifies. That rasa was conceived of as a textual object, the stable emotion of the character when "strengthened" or "enhanced" by the aesthetic elements, was explicitly acknowledged by Abhinavagupta as "the view of the most ancient authorities" such as Dandin three centuries earlier: it is "the stable emotion alone"—the stable emotion of the character—"that, once intensified by the causes, reactions, and the rest, becomes rasa."[50] And this is precisely the view of our oldest preserved commentator on the *Treatise on Drama*, Bhatta Lollata, according to whom "rasa in the primary sense of the term exists in the character."[51]

Early scholars wanted to understand how rasa "arises" (Bharata's word) in the character, in other words, how the elements of the artwork formally combine to create what the American New Critics would call a "formula of emotion."[52] When they raised epistemological questions—do we "infer" rasa, for example; is it something "manifested" to us?—the object of analytical primacy always remained the emotion of the character, how it is "strengthened " (Bhatta Lollata) or attains "enhancement"

(Anandavardhana).[53] This was also the concern of the poets themselves: when Bana (c. 650) exclaims how hard it is to produce a beautiful poem and make "its rasa clear," he is referring to emotions in the text, not its impact on the reader.[54]

This view would be maintained in some quarters up to the time of Bhoja, who in this regard appears as its last great exponent. As the selections here make clear (and his commentator corroborates), Bhoja, like all the earlier thinkers, thought of rasa first and foremost as something in the character.[55] The later steps in the aesthetic process—where poetic language communicates rasa to the reader, who can be said to experience it—are only implicit, never actually discussed. Bhatta Nayaka of Kashmir was the first to turn his attention principally to those later steps, which prompted him to rethink both the ontology and the epistemology of rasa—the question of how and where rasa exists always being related to how and where rasa is made known—and thereby to spark a true Copernican revolution in Indian aesthetics.

5. RASA IN THE READER

Bhatta Nayaka's transformation of rasa theory seems to owe something to his special combination of intellectual gifts. He was celebrated as both a scholar of scriptural hermeneutics and a littérateur, a man "at once learned in the four Vedas and himself a veritable temple for poets," according to a medieval chronicle that places him around 900, a generation after Anandavardhana, whose theory of "manifestation" it was part of his goal to refute. The claims of hermeneutics as a broad heuristic were being ever more widely asserted during this period; literary studies, as Ananda shows, and jurisprudence in particular were much influenced. But Bhatta Nayaka's hermeneutic approach to aesthetics lay not just in general analogies, like Ananda's teleological comparison of sentences and literary works. It lay in full-scale homologies: between the literary text and the scriptural text, the reader and the worshiper, and aesthetic pleasure and spiritual beatitude. Aesthetics itself became a form of hermeneutics, not only in the traditional Indian sense of the term, insofar as the same interpretive method could be applied to it, but in our contemporary philosophical sense, insofar as the subjectivity of the reader became the central concern.

The most grievous loss to Indian aesthetics is Bhatta Nayaka's masterpiece, the *Mirror of the Heart*. From the extant fragments and the detailed exposition provided by the late tenth-century scholars Dhanamjaya and Dhanika, however, we can get a reasonably good sense of his thought. The aim of his critique of traditional aesthetics was to redirect attention away from the formal process by which emotion is engendered in and made accessible through the literary work, toward the reader's own experience of this emotion: away, that is, from the response to form and toward the form of response. And to make better sense of what actually occurs in the experience of response, Mimamsa theory proved especially revelatory.

Bhatta Nayaka's reconstruction was predicated upon a critique of all earlier assessments of rasa, on two scores: its ontology (how it exists, whether in the character, the actor, or the poet) and its epistemology (how it comes to be known, whether through perception, inference, or "manifestation"). Rasa now refers to an actual experience and hence cannot belong to a character like Rama, who is dead and gone; if it were something truly present in the character who appears before the audience members, they would in effect be observing someone's private life, and hence feel such entirely nonaesthetic emotions as embarrassment; in any case, the whole purpose of literature is enjoyment of rasa, and so it can only belong to the viewing or reading subject.

If Bhatta Nayaka's critique sounds more stipulative than analytical, that is no doubt a consequence of our sources. Three points come through clearly, however: the positions on rasa he was refuting were real (you do not contest ideas no one holds); they were the sole positions on offer; and his refutation of them was profound. For the reconstructive part of his project it was obviously crucial to understand how a text can actually produce a response in a reader. The preeminent method available for this was Mimamsa, and Bhatta Nayaka's genius lay in understanding how precisely to explain literary textuality by the procedures Mimamsa had perfected for scripture, and above all, the incitement to action that textuality—rather mysteriously, if we pause to think about it—can summon forth.

To put his complicated argument in simple terms, we can imagine Bhatta Nayaka starting with the basic questions his two disciplines would have forced upon him. The Veda is concerned, axiomatically for Mimamsa, exclusively with commanding religious action (which in this thought world meant sacrificial offerings), but how does the Veda actually prompt a person to act? At the same time the Veda is replete with narrative passages that seem to have nothing to do with commandments as such but merely describe meritorious ritual acts of other people at other times and places: "Now, Indrota Daivapa Shaunaka once performed this sacrifice for Janamejaya Parikshita," runs a typical instance, "and by performing it he extinguished all evildoing."[56] How do such narrative texts relate to the principal deontic thrust of Vedic commandments, such as "One who desires heaven should sacrifice"? And what can any of this tell us about literary texts in general—which qua texts should be amenable to Mimamsa's hermeneutic—and specifically about how and why readers here and now are able to experience a literary narrative that always concerns other people at other times and places? Is there some force in the literary text prompting the reader to respond that can be compared to, or elucidated by, the force in scriptural commandment and narrative?

The two cases, Bhatta Nayaka concluded, are precisely homologous, since the linguistic force that Mimamsa named the "actualization" or production of action works in both. In the operations of this force in literature, literary language plays a crucial role. Its formal properties, above all its figurative dimension, render it completely different from everyday referential language. When a word like "Sita" is used in a poem, it no longer refers to the particular historical personage who was Rama's wife—if it continued to do so, she could never become a licit "foundational factor" for the viewer or reader's desire, and hence rasa could never arise; in poetry "Sita" instead signifies woman as such. This is part of what Bhatta Nayaka named the process of "commonization," which enables the reader to make the character's emotional experience his own in such a way that he "actualizes," or reproduces, it.[57] The reader of poetry comes to feel what Rama once felt, just as the reader of scripture is prompted to do what Janamejaya once did. If Bhatta Nayaka had spoken the language of European hermeneutics, he would have said that the text can really be experienced only when one feels addressed by it, when one "applies" it to oneself.[58] This second moment, actualization, made possible by the first moment, figurative, or literary, language, is followed by what Bhatta Nayaka, with another neologism, terms the "experientialization" of the literary work, which engenders in the reader not sacrificial action, like a scriptural commandment, but aesthetic pleasure, an end in itself.[59] Although the notion of actualization is one of linguistic mediation, the focal point for both scripture and poetry is action, not understanding.

However complex Bhatta Nayaka's ideas about rasa may appear in the shape we have them now, it is easy to appreciate their brilliance. They are clearly of an order of magnitude more profound than anything earlier, and they were to utterly transform aesthetics. Henceforth nearly every thinker would return to the question "Who has rasa?" and would conclude that it belongs to the viewer/reader, that in fact *his* "stable emotion" is what is actually at issue in rasa theory, not the character's, and is what the aesthetic elements "enhance." The physical reactions that are effects of emotion in the character, for example, are causes for rasa in the viewer/reader;[60] later thinkers even argue that his own reactions become diagnostic of his own rasa (and not just the character's reactions for his). Rasa thus became entirely a matter of response, and the only remaining question was what precisely that response consists of. Even here Bhatta Nayaka set the agenda, when he described it as a state of total "absorption,"[61] where the subject experiences the pleasure of a consciousness untouched by the things of this world, superior even to the religious experience analogized to it: "Nothing can compare with aesthetic rasa," says Bhatta Nayaka, "not even the rasa spiritual adepts bring forth."[62]

Once Indian thinkers realized that the key thing about rasa is the reader's or viewer's experience, it no longer mattered whether rasa is engendered, inferred, or manifested in the character—indeed, talk of engenderment, inference, and manifestation no longer made much sense. They began to ask how literary language transforms discourse about people one does not know (Rama, Sita) into something one as a reader is somehow able to enter into and find applicable to one's own self, and how that produces a unique kind of experience and knowledge. The paradigm had truly been shifted.

6. RASA AFTER THE REVOLUTION

Nowhere did Bhatta Nayaka's new ideas exert greater influence than on the scholar who most vehemently criticized him, Abhinavagupta. Readers will see at the very beginning of Abhinava's "purification" of rasa theory in his *New* Dramatic Art that he is entirely dependent on his predecessor's hermeneutical theory.[63] In fact, Abhinava's brilliant elaboration of that theory is what enables us, in the absence of the *Mirror of the Heart* itself, to understand its full implications. But the new hermeneutical aesthetics had another equally dramatic impact that needs explaining, through the transubstantiation that Abhinava effected in the understanding of Anandavardhana's work.

From his formalist perspective Ananda was concerned to make sense of the text-internal mechanisms by which the sense of an emotion was created. To explain how rasa can be communicated at all if it cannot be an object of denotation or even connotation, he hypothesized as we saw a new linguistic modality (*śabdavṛtti*) he called "implicature" or "manifestation" (the two terms here being synonymous). In the wake of Bhatta Nayaka's ideas of rasa as reception, however, Ananda's formalist account no longer had much traction, and if the theory was to be saved in the face of the new paradigm, the concept of "manifestation" would have to be reinterpreted. For his commentator Abhinava—a century after Bhatta Nayaka and even more after Ananda—what was now "manifested" was a newly activated psychological modality, the "mental state" (*cittavṛtti*) of the viewer/reader.[64] This he equates without hesitation with Bhatta Nayaka's "experientialization"—"The so-called 'process of experientialization' is nothing but the poem's implicature of rasa"[65]—even though the refutation of implicature, in the form of the linguistic phenomenon it originally referred to, had been one of Bhatta Nayaka's principal objectives. A linguistic phenomenon is admittedly at the same time a cognitive phenomenon, but the two can be analytically separated, and when Ananda and Nayaka spoke of "manifestation" it was in the former sense. And as Dhanika would make clear (and logic suggests), there is a very close linkage of the epistemology of rasa with its ontology. Rasa can only be said to be "manifested" if it is in fact located in the character, because it already exists in him (having gotten its existence from elsewhere, like a pot from clay) and is only being brought to light (like a pot by a lamp). If rasa is located in the viewer or reader, however, it must be "actualized" in them by the literary artwork.[66]

Abhinava fuses the two ideas—manifestation of the latent meaning of a text and manifestation of the latent predispositions in the viewer—in order to preserve the now enlarged concept when moving from Anandavardhana's text-centered view of the concept of rasa to his own new reader-centered view. There is no question that Abhinava "has taken over most of the new ideas" of Bhatta Nayaka, but there is also no question that these cannot fit into the "general view" of Ananda.[67] On the contrary, Abhinava transformed the general view, but in accordance with a much broader current of thought.

The dividing line between rasa in the character and rasa in the audience would remain blurry for some time. Dhanika, writing around 975, appears to have been the first person to draw a distinction between what he calls "real-world" or mundane rasa and the "rasa of drama" and the "rasa of poetry." The distinction leads to serious conceptual difficulties if we take the terms literally.[68] For aesthetic emotion does not in fact exist in the real world, nor even in the world of the actual historical person on whom the literary character is based. The affective life of the historical person, just like our own, consists not of rasa but of emotion, the response to real pleasure and pain. For such a response, as our authors never tire of reminding us, we have the "causes" of the real world; and precisely because we do not have such responses in art, the new vocabulary of "foundational factor" and the like had to be invented. What Dhanika means by the term "real world" is the world *inside* the drama or poem—the storyworld, or, more technically, the diegetic level of the narrative (for which Sanskrit lacks any other term of art save for the confusing one Dhanika introduced). In that world people can experience rasa only and precisely because they have ceased to be historical persons and have become "characters." The contrastive notion of "real-world," i.e., storyworld, rasa can have arisen only given its new counterpositive, the "rasa of drama," produced in the dramatic performance and experienced by the audience. Scholars in later periods were to make further modifications in these concepts. Abhinavagupta, for example, appears to have found Dhanika's type of binary misleading. For him, there is no "real-world" rasa, certainly not in the real real world, but not even in the storyworld. Rasa is a phenomenon of the aesthetic *event* alone; for this "savoring" of rasa, or "rapture," as he calls it, Abhinava reserves the qualification "supermundane."[69] But even this assessment, and much of the understanding of literature that accompanied it, was to be overturned in the coming centuries.

7. RASA IN THE CHARACTER, AGAIN

The rise of a new style of religious devotionalism in the early modern era (from around 1500) opened a remarkable final chapter in the history of the idea of rasa. Indian aesthetics had always shown a certain awkwardness in dealing with religious "literature," the scare quotes signaling that sacred writings were expressly excluded from what our thinkers classified as *kāvya*. The fact that *kāvya* itself had its origin, or one of its origins, in Buddhist religious literature had long been forgotten; as for Vedic or even puranic works, Sanskrit poeticians never cite them when discussing rasa or rhetoric or any of the other features of *kāvya*. Bhatta Tota, Abhinavagupta's teacher, made it very clear that the figure of "poet" (*kavi*) mentioned in India's oldest extant religious literature was to be strictly differentiated from the poets with whom classical poetics was concerned. The latter have not only the insight of the seer but also a gift for "description," that is, for the noninjunctive, expressive language use that constitutes literature.[70] Unsurprisingly, secular poetry is the *exclusive* concern of Abhinavagupta in his aesthetic works. Bhatta Nayaka had earlier developed a three-part classification of textual forms that put religious texts and literary texts in structurally discrete categories: in scripture wording has primacy; in historical narrative, factual meaning; "when both the wording and the meaning are subordinated and the aesthetic process itself has primacy, we call it literature."[71] For the classical period the religious and the literary were separate conceptual worlds.

Poets, however, had long striven to make poetry out of prayer, from the time they began writing *stotra*, or prayer-poetry, in the early centuries C.E. From the middle of the first millennium on, and from Tamil Nadu to Kashmir, religious poets began producing works that ever more clearly sought aesthetic ends by whatever metric of "aesthetic" one might care to apply (and even began occasionally to use, or appear to use, rasa talk to describe their aims).[72] Eventually aesthetic theory would no longer be able to ignore such material.

The incorporation of the "peaceful" into the taxonomy of rasa (probably not much before the eighth century)[73] would accommodate some of this literature. For this rasa, according to Mammata (c. 1050), the stable emotion is dispassion (others would suggest impassivity), and this can be developed fully into a rasa. The example he provides is a *stotra* ascribed to the tenth-century Shaiva scholar-poet (and teacher's teacher of Abhinavagupta) Utpaladeva.[74] It quickly became clear, however, that the rasa analytic could not comfortably accommodate such literature, as an early commentator's strained effort to parse Utpaladeva's poem suggests.[75]

Aside from difficulties about the peaceful rasa, which much exercised our thinkers, above all Abhinavagupta,[76] a vast amount of religious poetry is not about dispassion at all but about passion, desire for God. Yet this too disrupted the standard typology and required a new category: "When desire is directed toward a deity," says Mammata immediately after discussing the peaceful, "we have 'emotion' rather than rasa."[77] The idea that in certain portions of a narrative a rasa will only be "intimated" and not fully "enhanced" had appeared already in Udbhata.[78] The new notion envisioned a different situation. Because desire for God, as Mammata at least conceives of it, is fundamentally at odds with sexual desire, it cannot fulfill the definition of erotic rasa as standardized in the *Treatise on Drama* (where it pertains exclusively to a young, highborn, heterosexual couple) so as to develop into rasa. Hence, the affective impact of such religious poetry must be different. But here too, disagreement among later commentators, including one in the sixteenth century who boldly rejects Mammata's position, shows the growing inadequacy of such an appraisal.[79]

With the composition of the *Bhāgavatapurāṇa*, a masterpiece of Vaishnava devotionalism, in south India sometime in the tenth century and its rapid dissemination across the subcontinent, the aesthetic aspirations of religious literature were dramatically and unequivocally asserted, and aesthetic reflection began to emerge specifically to take account of them. This began with the *Bhāgavatapurāṇa* itself, where "*rasikas*," those who can experience rasa, and "*bhāvukas*," those who "actualize" in themselves the emotion of the narrative—two keywords of later rasa discourse, the latter used first by Dhanika (*bhāvaka*) and almost certainly derived from Bhatta Nayaka—are called upon to "drink the *Bhāgavata* fruit that is rasa." The *Bhāgavata* elsewhere offers important hints that some version of a theological rasa concept was already known to it. The religious text was now both claiming an aesthetic position and being accorded one.[80]

The theologization of rasa commences, quite self-consciously, in the *Pearls of the* Bhāgavata, Vopadeva's commentary on select verses from the *purāṇa* composed in western India in the late thirteenth century. The work develops a new rasa of "devotion"—explicitly rejecting Abhinavagupta and Hemachandra[81]—to explain the overall aesthetic emotion of the poem, and the traditional rasas are subsumed as its subvarieties. But it was the appearance in eastern India of the charismatic religious figure Chaitanya (1486–1534) and the sacral practices he introduced—including a new definition, one might say, of what "desire" for God could mean—that would prove to be a historic watershed in aesthetic theory.

The aesthetic theology announced in the works of the Vaishnavas of Bengal constitutes one of the few major innovations in rasa theory in the early modern era, and marks the moment when all the strands of that theory are tangled into their most complicated knot. The most important is the age-old question of who feels rasa: is it located in the characters—that is, the devotees—in the tales told of Krishna, or in the devotees of the everyday world listening to or reading those tales? The great innovation of the devotion theorists lay in fundamentally redefining these long-standing alternatives.

Moving beyond Vopadeva's tentative and narrow assessment, the Bengali Vaishnavas offered new interpretations in the face of new religious realities. Kavikarnapura (c. 1600) sought to maintain something of the old tradition of rhetoric (for which he was attacked by his own commentator) and, by a set of new categories almost Ptolemaic in their intricacy, to preserve "secular" rasa while at the same time applying Vaishnava theological categories to religious literature. Far more radical are the views of Rupa Gosvamin and his nephew Jiva Gosvamin, but their radicalism, by an interesting historical irony, lies in part in their archaism. Their notion of rasa is close to the classic account of Bhoja, and thus to the oldest one we have, that of Bhatta Lollata, for whom rasa is in the character, since it is the enhancement of his stable emotion. Their dramatic innovation was to reevaluate who the "character" actually is: not only those who appear in the *Bhāgavatapurāṇa* as devotees of Krishna but also the real-world devotees, theologically reenvisioned as "characters" (and at the same time actors) in the drama that is God's pageant on earth, who have the same attitude toward Krishna as those primeval characters and can even can take on their identity (Rupa and Jiva were viewed by their disciples as incarnations of female attendants of Krishna's beloved Radha). Why, after all, use the language of aesthetics to describe the devotee's relationship to God if that relationship were not *aesthetic*, to be conceived of as a drama in and of itself?[82]

Rasa theory is thus brought full circle, though the circle is now a much bigger one. In the process, the Bengali Vaishnavas transformed what for Abhinava had been the supermundane rasa experience of secular poetry into the mundane—when not denying altogether that it could even be rasa. For Jiva, "supermundane" was a status to be awarded only to the rasa of those experiencing God, whether in literature (which means effectively the *Bhāgavatapurāṇa* or other Vaishnava poetry such as Rupa's own) or in life[83]—for "supermundane" rasa now became, however ironically, a phenomenon of the mundane world, if one transfigured by religious passion. With all this, the discourse of rasa was not just being transferred from poetry to theology, it was being restricted to theology. Religious consciousness, previously exiled from the world of rasa, eventually succeeded in exiling secular literature itself, which now became a matter of "worms, feces, and ash," according to one later thinker, and no longer deemed capable of producing rasa.[84] (In the real world of art, however, things were rather more complicated still, since actual poems and paintings were often meant to be understood as courtly and religious at one and the same time.)

In comparison with such elaborations and innovations in the Vaishnava tradition of Bengal, one other domain of convergence of religion and aesthetics in the early modern period may seem minor, but it is still intellectually significant. By the sixteenth century, for reasons that await scholarly analysis, Vedanta in general and monistic (Advaita) Vedanta in particular had come to exert a powerful influence across the traditional Indian knowledge systems, colonizing various earlier independent forms of thought such as hermeneutics. It seems inevitable that its impact would eventually be felt in aesthetics. To be sure, Vedantic aesthetics had a prehistory.[85] *The Ten Dramatic Forms* (c. 975), retheorizing rasa experience as something that pertains to the viewer, had already used an Upanishadic idiom when describing it as "a state of pure blissful consciousness," "the bliss that is the self," where "the self-other distinction vanishes," a hallmark concept of monistic metaphysics. This too came from Bhatta Nayaka, who was the first to draw the analogy between aesthetic experience and spiritual, in particular Upanishadic, experience, when famously asserting that the spectator's consciousness "shares something of the character of savoring supreme being [*brahma*]."[86] These few, undeveloped notions aside—their undevelopment partly a result of the fragmentary nature of our sources—the presence of a Vedantic viewpoint in the early thinkers can hardly be felt. Within a generation Abhinavagupta began to use the language of monistic Shaivism to describe the nature of rasa, though in the selections from *The New* Dramatic Art offered here, that philosophical framework is rather etiolated. Like his predecessors, he may describe the experience of rasa as a state of "uniformly blissful" consciousness, but he does not offer a theological-aesthetic program.[87]

Something quite different presents itself in the works of early seventeenth-century thinkers, among whom Vishvanathadeva and Jagannatha are especially notable. Both men hailed from Andhra and lived in Varanasi, and the latter, though far more famous, almost certainly borrowed from the former. From Vishvanathadeva's sources, which include a key text of early modern Vedanta, and from his technical language, we can see that he brings a strong Vedantic perspective to the problem of rasa.[88] Clearly the disciplinary (or sectarian) affiliation was definitive for him. But there is more to his Vedanticization, and Jagannatha's, than simply intellectual politics.

At the center of Vishvanathadeva's and Jagannatha's conception is the older notion of rasa, as the experience of consciousness itself, when consciousness is thoroughly evacuated of the dross of everyday life so as to become, as it were, self-transcendent. Vishvanathadeva authorizes this view by citing the *Taittirīya Upaniṣad*'s ancient doctrine that the self is composed of five sheaths, the last of which is the "bliss component." This component is naturally obscured by the processes of phenomenal life, but in aesthetic experience, given the peculiar nature of its revelation, everything that conceals the bliss that is consciousness is removed: the "veil of unknowing is lifted."[89] The aesthetic experience is thus a kind of perfect, objectless state of awareness.

In line with this more explicit affiliation, Vishvanathadeva is the first to draw the analogy—original and in its own way profound—between the aesthetic process and the textual basis of scriptural revelation that is central to the Vedanta vision. Both literature and scripture are in the last analysis forms of linguistic communication, providing "direct awareness derived from words and their meanings," as Vishvanathadeva puts it. But both are unlike any other such phenomena in their capacity to produce a supermundane effect through language itself. Early modern Vedanta devotes unprecedented attention to the linguistic analysis of the "great sentences" of the Upanishads ("That art Thou" and the like) to show how this linguistic model of liberation can work. It offers a very suggestive analogy to the powers of literature, though Vishvanathadeva and Jagannatha only draw it and provide no full-scale exposition.[90]

Let me try now to summarize the main plot of the complicated story I have just told, emphasizing the movement of analytical focal points. In his three-part analysis of literary modalities of beauty, Bhoja distinguishes the expression of rasa from two other aspects that can make a literary work beautiful: sonic features of the text and figures of sense.[91] The expression of rasa differs from those aspects in that it works at the level of the text's content and thus pertains to its existence as an affective phenomenon. But what exactly does it mean to speak of the literary text as an "affective phenomenon," and what does the work of rasa consist of? In these two closely related problematics lies much of the complex historical development of the idea of rasa.

As an affective phenomenon, the literary text can be analyzed either internally or externally: as representations of people, and as representations for people. In the first case it is the characters who are taken to experience the basic emotions ("stable emotions") in response to certain objects ("foundational factors") and under certain external conditions ("stimulant factors"). These emotions are nuanced in any given case by more ephemeral feelings ("transitory emotions") and made legible by physical signs ("reactions" and "psychophysical responses"). But, to move to the second case, the literary work is always representation for people, viewers and readers. It is they who, on the phenomenological level, experience the artwork, and only in their experiencing it can the artwork have meaning and come to life. The text can accordingly be analyzed from the inside—how the various necessary components are organized to provide a rich representation of human emotion—or from the outside—how viewers and readers respond to such representations. And depending on the analytical stance taken, our understanding of how this phenomenon is actually operationalized by the work will differ. Considered as an internal process, the "expression of rasa" may be seen as a formal capacity of the artwork for manifesting the emotional state of the character who is experiencing it; considered as an external process, it may be seen as a hermeneutical capacity of the artwork enabling viewers and readers to "actualize" such an emotional state.

Theoretically, therefore, rasa can be regarded as a property of a text-object, a capacity of a reader-subject, and also a transaction between the two. The whole process, in fact, exists as a totality even while its several moments can be analytically disaggregated. In this, rasa precisely resembles the "taste" it metaphorically references, which may be regarded as existing at once in the food, the taster, and the act of tasting. Something of this totality has been captured by the phenomenologist of aesthetics Mikel Dufrenne, who writes of the "primordial reality of affective quality, wherein that part belonging to the subject and that belonging to the object are still indistinguishable":

> It is for this reason that we have been led to say that the affective is in the work itself, as well as in the spectator with whom the work resonates. Feeling is as deeply embedded in the object as it is in the subject, and the spectator experiences feeling because affective quality belongs to the object.[92]

The history of aesthetic discourse in India is a history of the gradual elaboration of the components of this comprehensive view. The comprehensive view itself, however, was one Indian thinkers themselves never developed. What this means for an intellectual history of rasa will be considered below.

8. NORMAL RASA, CONFLICTED RASA, SEMBLANCE OF RASA

The *Treatise on Drama* sets out the standard components for the genesis of rasa, and these were accepted without demurral over the long history of the discipline. Thus, in the erotic rasa, the "foundational factors" must be a young, highborn, heterosexual couple; the "stimulant factors" gardens, breezes, sandalwood cream, and so on; the "transitory emotions" anxiety, fatigue, disquiet, and the like; the physical "reactions" and "psychophysical responses" sidelong glances, fainting, horripilation, and the rest that betoken the presence of the emotions. This may all sound very artificial, but Indian thinkers started from real plays and poems in their quest to understand how emotion was produced, and the analytical terminology they developed was a method for anatomizing what they found present. Aside from the dialectic typical in the history of intellectual practices, whereby description tends to morph into prescription, it was standard procedure in Indian science to reduce the phenomenal world to its constituent parts, which then come to look like building blocks. Analogous are the rules for generating correct grammatical forms that derive from an anatomy of real nouns and verbs, or the steps in producing a correct syllogism that derive from actual inference.[93]

Other aspects of the standard model seem less familiar and suggest something like a vernacular sociology of the aesthetic. The *Treatise* itself institutes this social aesthetics, rigorously relating rasa and status; although rarely discussed in later theory, it is presupposed everywhere.[94] Thus, the erotic and the heroic pertain only to characters of high status; the comic, by contrast, only to those of low or middling status. If the fearful is found in men of high status it will always be a matter of simulation: they do not, indeed cannot, fear their guru's anger, for instance, but they must simulate fear to be a dutiful devotee.[95] More complex than these correlations and more revealing of the history of rasa is the tragic, where kinship rather than status is the social element at issue.

Although the English word "tragic" has a complex history of its own deriving from Aristotelian poetics, it suitably captures the sense of the Sanskrit term *karuṇa*, which is usually but misleadingly translated "compassion" or "pity." In *karuṇa* rasa, not only must someone be lost forever,[96] they must also be beloved to the subject; the rasa accordingly refers primarily to the sense of one's own loss. By contrast, "The tragic rasa that arises when someone grieves for a person with whom one does not have a kinship bond," explains Abhinavagupta, "is a *semblance* of the tragic and hence is itself comic" (for Abhinava, *all* semblance of rasa is comic).[97] Compassion, by contrast, is a generalized "pity for the sufferings or misfortunes of others," according to its dictionary definition. This feeling, however, enters the history of Indian emotions only with Buddhism (especially Mahayana), which transvalued the dominant, quasi-aristocratic view, here as well as in other areas of Sanskrit thought. One might even say Buddhism redefined the very concept of "loved one" so as to comprise the whole world, thereby turning *karuṇa* into the active, blind (and to modern eyes almost irrational) compassion so exuberantly illustrated in the *jātaka* tales.[98] It was the Buddhists who invented compassion—and that is not the *karuṇa* of aesthetic discourse.

Abhinavagupta's mention of "semblance" raises another important issue in classical aesthetics. From the late ninth century on, lists of the standard topics of aesthetics begin to include, along with rasas and emotions, the "semblance" of rasa and of emotion.[99] The technical term, *ābhāsa*, is also used of the image of, say, a horse in a painting (*turagābhāsa*), or of a misleading reason in a syllogism (*hetvābhāsa*): something comparable to but not itself the authentic entity, and sometimes even fraudulent. In the case of "semblance of a rasa," modern scholarship is uncertain about the matter, and it is unclear how far back in the tradition this uncertainty extends. The phrase "semblance of rasa" was first used (and probably invented) by Udbhata (c. 800) to characterize narrative that was "contrary to social propriety" and thereby violated a core feature of rasa, its ethical normativity. In the erotic, for example, the mutuality of desire would obviously be violated in the case of sexual assault. Udbhata offers as illustration a poem (of his own) where the great god Shiva is so overcome with desire for the goddess Parvati that he is on the point of taking her by force.[100] However "contrary" such an act is in itself, there may nevertheless be good narrative reasons for relating it. Without Ravana's violent abduction of Sita there would be no *Rāmāyaṇa*. What Udbhata's and Valmiki's poems describe is a semblance of legitimate sexual desire; what they offer, however, is decidedly not, as some contemporary scholars have described it, only a semblance of aesthetic experience.

This point is forcefully made by Singabhupala (late fourteenth century) in the subtle interpretation offered of a great poem from the *Hundred of Amaru* (Singabhupala typically adduces as illustrations verses from the finest works of Sanskrit literature), a wife's lament for the fading of desire in her marriage. The rasa, the emotional experience in and derived from the poem, cannot be the erotic, since the conditions for the erotic are lacking; even the "erotic thwarted" is not possible, for this is always predicated upon the possible renewal of the "erotic enjoyed." Nor can it be the tragic: her relationship may be dead, but her husband is not. When Singabhupala tells us that the poem "fails to attain beauty," he is not saying the poem itself is not beautiful; the poem "fails to attain" the tenderness of the erotic, but it undoubtedly possesses some other, powerful, emotional-aesthetic force, which he calls the "semblance" of the erotic. To identify something as semblance of rasa, accordingly, is to make a judgment, not on the quality of the poem, but rather on the nature of the aesthetic experience it produces, where something is, if not always "contrary to social propriety," as Udbhata has it, at least "out of keeping." Far from marking failure to become a "genuine aesthetic experience," semblance of rasa offers an experience of another order, at once morally problematic, psychologically subtle, and aesthetically complex and one that great literature cannot forgo.[101] If rasa is the ultimate literary value, the question of how to assess the value of a literary work where rasa *as such* is absent—indeed, must be absent—requires real discernment, and this is what Indian thinkers brought to bear.

The modern interpretation of semblance as "failure" may not entirely contradict tradition, however. In the seventeenth century Jagannatha approached the problem with what seems to me a cultural consciousness rather different from what came before, and where "semblance" appears to have become a mark of censure. He offers a long list of themes—and he is the first to do so—that all "produce the semblance of rasa": desire directed toward an inappropriate object (the wife of one's teacher, a goddess, a queen) or that is not reciprocated; desire on the part of a woman for more than one lover; "a father's grief for a son who is querulous and wicked, or grief on the part of an ascetic who has given up all attachments; spiritual disenchantment with life on the part of an untouchable"; "martial determination on the part of a low-born man," "laughter directed at one's father." Although a few of these themes are part and parcel of the greatest Sanskrit literature (how could we have a *Mahābhārata* without Dhritarashtra's lamenting over his wicked son Duryodhana, or without Draupadi and her five husbands?), the remainder would never be written. No doubt earlier critics too were concerned about literary impropriety, felt that certain kinds of morally as well as physically implausible narratives could only be used if they had the stamp of tradition, and advised revising episodes even in such narratives if they violated standards of social propriety.[102] But if I am right to see it as a new prescriptive turn in the history of rasa—perhaps a sort of conservative traditionalization on the threshold of modernity—Jagannatha's very cataloguing of the transgressive subjects, the sort that elsewhere in the world would help to make modern literature modern, would mean proscribing them. And this may be a source, if we seek one in the tradition, of the understanding of semblance not as diagnostic of moral-aesthetic complexity, but as marking literary failure.[103]

The standard list of rasa topics also includes analysis of the actual narrative stages or conjunctures when a rasa comes into being or ceases, when it gives way to another rasa or coexists with another in a kind of mélange. These are rarely discussed in detail.[104] One other, however, the potential conflict of rasas, holds great theoretical interest for traditional scholars and great scope for their interpretive virtuosity.

"Flaws" were a subject of literary criticism from an early date in India, and although those relating to rasa are most fully systematized in Mammata's *Light on Poetry* (in the same section he also examines the stages in the succession of rasa just mentioned), earlier scholars had thought long and hard about which rasas can and cannot be combined with other rasas—that is, about what makes for a coherent emotional experience in art, or indeed, coherent art. Anandavardhana offers the first account in the third chapter of his *Light on Implicature* (the source of much of Mammata), while Dhanika approaches the question from a different angle, examining the definition of "stable emotion" and elaborately investigating the problems that arise when more than one of them is present in a poem.[105]

It requires no professional competence to perceive that certain combinations of rasas are inherently complementary, others inherently contradictory. The violent complements the heroic as obviously in classical India as elsewhere, while the fearful, just as obviously, contradicts it. But two qualifications must be introduced here. First, some combinations produce problems peculiar to Indian cultural sensibilities, which modern readers need to understand in order to appreciate. Second, and more consequentially, the theory of conflictual rasas encouraged especially fruitful interpretive practices.

For the first point, consider the following poem (Mammata's example of the flaw of "the use of an antithetical aesthetic factor"):

> My love, be gracious, show your favor / and put your anger away . . .
> My simple girl, time is a fleet deer / that, once fled, never returns.[106]

In a love poem to one's coy mistress of this sort, the allusion to the brevity of time (a "stimulant factor," according to Mammata) is a component of the peaceful rasa irreconcilable, for Indian readers, with the erotic rasa of the verse, and hence the poem must be judged an aesthetic failure. Alas, poor Herrick, for your admonition to virgins to make much of time.

Other poems raise far more complex questions. In some cases the apparent contradiction between rasas—say, the erotic and the macabre—is resolved by the interposition of a mediating rasa. Here is an example offered by Dhanika:

> Lucky those women who get to wear / fragrance of the finest scent.
> My husband only transfers to me / the foul smell of his battle wounds.

Here the interposed heroic rasa ("battle wounds") neutralizes the impact of the macabre ("foul smell"). Sometimes a contradiction is neutralized by the attenuated character of one of the rasas, as when a wife cries out at the sight of her husband's dismembered corpse on the battlefield (Mammata's example, borrowed from Ananda):

> This used to loosen my belt and untie / the knot holding up my skirt, and fondle
> my heavy breasts and touch my navel / and thighs and mound—this very hand.

Here, while the erotic would appear to conflict with the tragic, it is actually present only in memory; the erotic, rather than diminishing the tragic, enhances it. The hierarchy of rasas can become dizzyingly complex, as in the following celebrated poem:

> Like a husband whose betrayal is still moist
> it was driven away when trying to clutch their hand,
> it was mercilessly struck when grasping their hem,
> shaken off when stroking their hair, and spurned
> in a panic when falling at their feet,
> and when attempting an embrace forcefully rebuffed
> by the women of the Triple City, tears brimming in their eyes:
> may this fire of Shiva's arrows burn away your sins.

According to Arjunavarmadeva (c. 1215), one among many who quote the poem, the erotic (the image of the errant lover) is subordinate to the tragic (the fire's destruction of the king of the antigods inhabiting the Triple City), and the tragic to the heroic (Shiva's grandeur), or perhaps (critics disagree) to the emotion of the devotee in the face of his god's power.[107] Rasa, as these examples show, not only explained theoretically how emotion is created in literature, it also invited readers to develop ever more complex practices of interpretation.

9. RASA AND INSTRUCTION

De gustibus non est disputandum—"in matters of taste there can be no disputes," runs the old saw.[108] On the face of it, taste would seem to be an affair of the heart, not the head, and rasa as "taste" would hardly be expected to pertain to the domain of reason, preeminently moral, social, or other kind of judgment. Thinkers in classical India directly engaged this question, like their counterparts in the early modern West, though the discussion proceeded differently in the two cases, with equally divergent outcomes.

As with so much in the history of Indian aesthetics, the conversation begins with Bhatta Nayaka. Since the time of Bhamaha (c. 650) the view had been dominant that the cultivation of literature produces pleasure but also "instruction"—in this context, always instruction in the four "ends of man," love, wealth, morality, and spiritual liberation—with the two outcomes equally balanced.[109] This old view came to be embodied in the very definition of rasa at a relatively early stage. For Pratiharenduraja (c. 900), the "enhancement" of the stable emotion that leads to rasa meant its development, in all its complexity and along with all its requisite contextual elements, precisely as a source of instruction.[110] It cannot have been much later that Bhatta

Nayaka for the first time contested such didacticism. His challenge is implied in the famous differentiation of genres that is almost certainly his own: if scripture commands us like a master and history counsels us like a friend, literature seduces us like a beloved. But it is directly expressed in one of his few surviving fragments: reading literature is about experiencing rasa, not gaining knowledge of some moral precept, something his follower Dhanamjaya was thinking of when at the beginning of his *Ten Dramatic Forms* he sarcastically proclaims, "I salute the fool who turns his face from pleasure and thinks the point of literature is mere instruction, no different from historical narrative."[111] This too is the position Abhinavagupta defends early in his commentary on *Light on Implicature*: in literature, "pleasure is the predominant element"; it is "bliss that constitutes the final goal of literature, taking priority over even instruction."[112] Yet it is a position he would qualify and eventually abandon.

In his turn away from Bhatta Nayaka, Abhinava was taking a cue from his teacher Bhatta Tota (c. 975). Again, we have only a fragment that explains the latter's position, but it seems clear enough: "Pleasure is constitutive of rasa, and rasa is simply drama, and drama simply knowledge." Pleasure may still be held to be an essential component of literary art, but not an end in itself; its true purpose is "knowledge" of the four ends of man. This fragment is cited by Abhinava late in his commentary on the *Light* itself in a closely reasoned passage that seeks, or so it seems, to manage a tension with his earlier statement. Rasa, he explains,

> is made possible by virtue of the "conjunction of aesthetic elements" that are themselves inseparable from instruction in the four ends of man. In composing the elements appropriate to a given rasa, the poet's total "self-surrender to the savoring of rasa" that Anandavardhana stipulates is actually what is instrumental in making such instruction fit and apposite. Hence, literary pleasure as such is instrumental to education, as my teacher argued.

To soften the seeming contradiction with his earlier argument, he adds that pleasure and instruction are not two separate things since they converge in a single object, the propriety (*aucitya*) of the aesthetic elements: the experience of rasa is preconfigured (in terms of which elements are "appropriate" to the production of each rasa) to align with social norms (in terms of which responses are the "appropriate" ones to engender in the first place). "The source of literary pleasure as such lies, as I have repeatedly said, in the social propriety of the aesthetic elements, whereas 'instruction' is nothing other than the correct understanding of those elements, as being 'appropriate' each in its own way to the given rasa." Instruction through literature, he concludes, should concern itself with practices that conduce to the success of the protagonist or to the defeat of the antagonist.[113]

In his later commentary on the *Treatise on Drama*, a far more insistent theory of rasa as social and moral pedagogy is developed. The whole focus of aesthetic experience is shifted to the emotions that pertain to the ends of man: "The end result of the savoring is instruction in morality and the other ends of man"; the viewer of drama "comes to possess a certain form of consciousness of the sort conveyed by the deontic language of scripture—that those who do such and such a thing receive such and such a reward."[114] By a virtuosic if no doubt anachronistic reading, he links Bharata's idea of the four primary rasas, the erotic, the violent, the heroic, and the peaceful (replacing Bharata's macabre), with the four ends of man, love, wealth, morality, and liberation. And in his account of the sixth hindrance to aesthetic consciousness (concentrating on nonessential parts of the artwork), Abhinava explains that the "most essential aesthetic components are those several forms of consciousness that pertain to the ends of man," and again correlates with them the stable emotions, desire, anger, determination, and impassivity.[115] Literature's capacity to refine our moral imagination is thus continually reasserted as a central tenet of Abhinava's mature aesthetic theory.

It deserves noting, given Kant's influential "differentiation" of aesthetic judgment from social and moral judgment, that the domains of these types of judgments overlapped closely in classical India. Equally notable, however, is the actual nature of such "judgment." The pedagogy enabled by rasa experience is not learning to feel the way another has felt, to see the world through the eyes of another, to develop solidarity with another in his suffering—what the philosopher Richard Rorty, for example, understood to be the moral work of literature.[116] This may appear to be implicit in the discourse on rasa: how else, one might suppose, could what Bhatta Nayaka called "commonization" or the "heart's concurrence" achieve their effect without an ethical education that made it possible to experience the experience of another as one's own? But Indian thinkers never quite make this explicit; such an interpretation even seems to misconstrue their argument. Commonization is concerned less with positing a broadly human, and humane, way of understanding narrative—like Rorty's (widely shared) view that "by identification with Mr. Causaubon in *Middlemarch* . . . we may come to notice what we ourselves have been doing," our blindness to the pain of others, for example—than with applying the narrative to one's own life by assimilating its notions of propriety. Taking pleasure in that narrative was instrumental to the creation and confirmation of the judgment of a work's moral order, and about that order there was no dispute, since there was no dispute about the social norms with which it was to be correlated. A narrative has an essence, to which there is a "proper" way to respond.[117] The pedagogy of rasa was, thus, not a matter of working through the moral ambiguity of literature (was it just that Dushyanta should reject the pregnant Shakuntala?); traditional readers never highlight such ambiguity, however much poets may have invited them to do so. On the contrary, literature was understood to present not questions but answers, which were easier to learn through literature than through other communicative forms. One could well say, then, that for Indian aesthetics, there really is no disputing in matters of taste, not because each reader has his own in accordance with the relativist-skeptical stance of modernity, but because all readers have, ideally, the same.

Nothing said so far, however, explains how viewers and readers are able to taste rasa in the first place and to grasp its social-moral logic. Is any special knowledge required? What exactly is the role, if any, of aesthetic theory itself in the education of taste? How, in short, does a *rasika*, a person able to taste rasa, come to be a *rasika*? Rasa theory would seem to be an account of everyday aesthetic experience, of how viewers and readers react. And after all, what special training is required for getting lost in a book or film? Perhaps more than we know, since although it may seem to be a natural human capacity, Indian thinkers saw "nature" quite otherwise. A *rasika* may largely be born, not made, but who is born a *rasika*?

Not many thinkers addressed this question directly. For Vishvanatha (c. 1350), only "certain special people" have the capacity for relishing rasa, those who have a "superabundance of sensitivity" and "possess merit acquired in a former existence," or as he puts it elsewhere, the requisite "predispositions." Those lacking such capacities—here Vishvanatha cites from the lost work of Dharmadatta—"are like the walls and wooden posts and stone floor inside the theater." Predispositions are acquired in one's present existence as well as in former ones, and these are what make the savoring of rasa possible. If we did not hypothesize a causal force of predispositions cultivated in a present life, we would expect even dry-as-dust theologians to savor rasa; if we gave no causal force to those acquired in a past life, we could not explain why some who are keen to savor rasa are incapable of doing so.[118] There is no doubt a good answer to the obvious question why the endless cycle of transmigration would not eventually endow all people with all predispositions, but our thinkers do not provide it.

There is more to aesthetic sensitivity than simply one's predestination for it, to be sure. Abhinavagupta argues that receptivity comes, at least in part, from a previous study of literature. But that too requires the presence of good karma from past lives, a "heart by nature like a spotless mirror," a mind "no longer subject to the anger, confusion, craving, and so on typical of this phenomenal world." Only those traits enable rasa to manifest itself "with absolute clarity."[119] In the end, rasa theory is meant to explain the world of aesthetic response, and not—except incidentally, as knowledge that prestructures interpretation—to teach us to cultivate it.

10. THE INTELLECTUAL HISTORY OF RASA DISCOURSE

The foregoing account is one attempt to reconstruct the historical transformations of rasa thought as plausibly as evidence permits. It must be inaccurate in some particulars, given the limits of my knowledge, but it also must be untrue, in several senses of "untrue." I cannot have told the whole story of rasa, and not only because no one can know historical stories in their entirety. First, there is the question of sources. We are painfully aware of texts that have disappeared—in fact, no discipline of classical India has suffered greater losses than aesthetics.[120] In addition, some texts have been preserved in only a very few manuscripts, or only in part, or in such a state that for stretches on end they are close to unreadable, or, conversely, in so many manuscripts that the very idea of a producing coherent, let alone critical, edition seems absurd.[121] And this is to say nothing of the difficulties that confront the reader trying to make sense of texts that the tradition itself shied away from commenting on.[122]

My account can be said to be untrue in a second sense, as diverging from what the agents themselves believed about what I have come to think of as the recoding of the meaning of "manifestation," for example, or, more consequentially, about the extension of aesthetic theory from drama to poetry or the shift from formalism to reception. Disagreement with tradition raises knotty if familiar questions about what makes an interpretation valid and for whom, and about history itself—or rather, about history (the scholar's) against itself (the participants').

In one last, related sense my account cannot quite be true, given that in some cases, we have access to texts that few in the tradition did, texts that scarcely entered into circulation in their primary sphere and hence had minimal historical effects. This is surprisingly the case with two masterpieces, Abhinavagupta's *New* Dramatic Art and Bhoja's *Light on Passion*. The contemporary scholar is thereby put in the strange position, the reverse of the first predicament, of knowing more of the intellectual history of this discourse than some of its participants had access to.

It may be useful to try more precisely to characterize the foregoing history of rasa from two different directions: from the inside out, so to speak, and from the outside in. From the first perspective we can perceive ideas, presuppositions, or objectives that the actors themselves were aware of, even though we may know little about them now; from the second, we can identify conditions that structured their knowledge that the actors themselves may not have been aware of. Each perspective comprises its own kind of historical effectiveness.

One constraint on the discourse of rasa, so far little mentioned but far-reaching and largely acknowledged by the participants, pertains to their philosophical or religious affiliations. Many of our literary theorists also wrote on philosophy or theology[123] and thus, as in the Western tradition from Aristotle to Kant to Dewey, a formative if not constitutive relationship held between aesthetics and philosophical worldviews. But disentangling this relationship is no easy task in itself, and it is made harder by the unfortunate thinness in the record just where we need it to be thick: on the value commitments of most of our thinkers. If we knew that Shri Shankuka was in fact a Buddhist, we could better understand his arguments both about the place of inference in the aesthetic process (inference and perception being the only two means of valid knowledge that Buddhists accept) and, somewhat more speculatively, about the sources of his view of "imitation" (which perhaps lay in Yogachara "illusionism").[124] That Bhatta Nayaka's allegiance to Mimamsa (far deeper than Anandavardhana's) marked his entire system is crystal clear, but if we understood precisely which brand of Mimamsa this was, Kumarila's, Prabhakara's, or another, we might be able to develop a richer sense of how he thought "actualization" worked, and more particularly, how the "eventful narrative" (*arthavāda*) embedded in scripture "rouses" the ritual agent to re-create the ritual act—and, homologously, the reader the literary narrative. Bhoja is more direct about his Samkhya inheritance[125] (less so about his Shaivism), but it is a laborious task to reconstruct just how far this inflected his aesthetic theory, beyond the obvious role of the theory of the three psychophysical elements in his understanding of the "sense-of-self" that constitutes "passion." The situation does become more perspicuous as the meta-aesthetic discourse shifts from philosophy toward religion, where Abhinavagupta's theory of aesthetic consciousness shares many traits with, though is not necessarily conceptually dependent on, his theory of liberated consciousness; the reverse might be posited of the later Advaita aestheticians Vishvanathadeva and Jagannatha, about whose religious views the information in the second case is sparse, in the first case entirely absent.[126] Rupa and Jiva Gosvamin, by contrast, are known primarily as religious thinkers, and their views help us understand how religion and aesthetics were not just related but fused into a new aesthetic theology—at the same time hinting at what we are missing more generally about the religio-philosophical context of earlier aesthetic thinking.

A second dimension of intellectual history from the inside out concerns the status and practice of intellectual history in the tradition itself—how the thinkers themselves sought to grasp the development of their discipline—and the sources they had at their disposal. Abhinavagupta is the first to have brought a chronological sensibility to rasa discourse: the prologue to his own "purified" theory in *The New Dramatic Art* is clearly meant to represent ideas that succeed one another in time and in value. He was able to reconstruct this order—going back some three centuries (to the time of Dandin, c. 700)—because the actual texts were still available to him. The number and diversity of citations in his own commentary from the early writers on the *Treatise on Drama* attest to this availability; the same holds, naturally, for his familiarity with the works of his own teachers, Bhatta Tota and Bhatta Induraja.[127]

By the mid-twelfth century, however, scholars were already departing from a strict chronological approach. In his treatment of the history of rhetoric more generally, Ruyyaka places his discussion of Kuntaka and Bhatta Nayaka *before* that of Anandavardhana, a temporal displacement one of his commentators explains by noting that although both thinkers came later, they are presented as earlier "since they were following the doctrines of the ancients"; by contrast, Mahima Bhatta is said to have "put forward something of his own invention entirely" and so is treated after Ananda.[128] Here chronology is inflected by a kind of axiology (the validity of which we will assess momentarily) that comes to the fore in later discussions of rasa.

While many of those discussions adopt some version of Abhinava's account, they are subject to two important limitations. First, almost without exception, no later scholar had access to any of the original texts Abhinava cites, or even to *The New* Dramatic Art, where many are discussed; they all derive their overview from the exposition in his *Eye for* Light on Implicature (which admittedly sometimes provides more detail), or, far more frequently, from Mammata's précis of this exposition in his *Light on Poetry*. Second, and no doubt as a consequence of this documentary deficiency, the very content of the chronology and hence its structure begins to change after the eleventh century. Jagannatha (c. 1650) discusses eleven different interpretations of rasa in an order that is entirely evaluative: it starts with the doctrine he accepts (Abhinava's) and ends with those he almost certainly invented to demonstrate the slow descent into ever greater inadmissibility. (In the same spirit of anachronism, unless it is parody, he makes Bhatta Nayaka speak in the rebarbative style of the "New Logicians" that came to prominence only four centuries after his death).[129] The natural conclusion to this development of the discourse—what we might call its pure logicization—is found at its endpoint, in the work of Rajacudamani Dikshita (c. 1650, not excerpted here). His "history" of rasa dispenses entirely with historical sources, becoming an account not of what the positions actually were, but of what conceptually they should have been.

It is a rather fine line that divides this practice (and tacit theory) of intellectual history from what we can perceive when we look from the outside in. This perspective offers a view of issues that those who made the history could not or did not—so far as we can tell—perceive themselves. A few examples both minor and major, which, given his prominence, are best provided by the works and practices of Abhinavagupta, suffice to give a sense of the problematic as a whole.

The New Dramatic Art, written in Kashmir around 1000 C.E., seems to have vanished from there almost as soon as the ink was dry. The only scholars in the premodern era who evince direct knowledge of the work all lived in Gujarat during the twelfth century.[130] What others knew of Abhinava's aesthetic philosophy comes from his earlier commentary on Anandavardhana, *The Eye for* Light on Implicature, or from Mammata's précis (Mammata himself shows no evidence of having read *The New* Dramatic Art either, though the question awaits systematic study). What does this lacuna mean for intellectual history?

For one thing, since the views on rasa in the two works are not identical, Abhinava's mature theory was essentially unknown to subsequent scholars. Consider his understanding of the state of consciousness that the aesthetic experience represents. At various high points of his exposition, such as his definition of drama, Abhinava announces his name for this state: *anuvyavasāya*, secondary or reflexive knowledge of a knowledge, but he goes on to carefully gloss this in order to signal its newly charged meaning (it is "on the order of a direct awareness," "consists of the light of the bliss that is one's own pure consciousness," and so on).[131] The term—Abhinava's version of Bhatta Nayaka's "experience" through "actualization"—is used in Abhinava's aesthetic sense in no other text on rasa discourse, because no other text knew that sense or the work in which it was contained.[132]

What later texts do represent as part of Abhinava's aesthetic theory concerns the "manifestation" doctrine of rasa that he developed in his commentary on Anandavardhana. As we saw, Abhinava, confronted with the potential obsolescence of Ananda's treatment of rasa in the wake of Bhatta Nayaka's revolution, transformed an object-oriented linguistic notion into a subject-oriented psychological one—what is now "manifested" is the stable emotion in the heart of the sensitive reader rather than rasa in the text. The core terminology for this modality, "manifestation" (*vyañjanā* and its various cognates), is virtually absent from *The New* Dramatic Art. The concept clearly had no further role to play for Abhinava, since his new theory is hermeneutical. For all subsequent thinkers, however, "manifestation" became the watchword of Abhinava aesthetics, something possible only if *The New* Dramatic Art was unknown to them.

The history of the reception of Abhinava's conceptual leap in *The Eye* is even more revealing than this bibliographical lacuna. No later scholar ever comments explicitly on the transvaluation of Anandavardhana's idea of "manifestation" developed by Abhinava when he moved it out of the old thought world of formalism into the new one of reception.[133] The fact that he appropriated Bhatta Nayaka's concept of "experience" when reworking "manifestation" likewise went entirely unrecognized by subsequent thinkers.[134]

All that said, the scholarly practices in evidence here have a long history. When Abhinava ascribes to Bharata himself aspects of Bhatta Nayaka's theory, as well as the entirety of his own radically "purified" aesthetic theory ("It is simply what the sage himself has said and nothing new at all"), he is in quest of an old warrant for a new idea, a conventional move in classical thought and found elsewhere in aesthetics per se.[135] To assess Abhinava's rewriting of Ananda as a commentator's misinterpretation of his base text, however, would be to misinterpret the commentarial function in classical India. Commentary could legitimately encompass not just exegesis of the old but also promulgation of the new, no matter how much at variance the two might seem to a present-day scholar.

Beyond the transformations of rasa thought, how variously they appear when seen from the inside out and the outside in, and what the practice of intellectual history means in the two cases, there are conundrums having to do with the overall historical shape of the discourse. The three most obvious are why rasa theory came into being when it did, why it exploded into prominence when it did, and why it came to an end when it did.

Theory is related, however obscurely, to practice, and the history of rasa theory roughly maps against the history of the practice of Sanskrit literature—understanding "literature" in the sense accorded to the category in Sanskrit culture itself. In that sense, Sanskrit literature was an invention of the beginning of the Common Era, and the theory of dramatic composition arose relatively soon thereafter. The slow (and fitful) process of incorporating poetry into that theory started not much later than the true efflorescence of poetry (in non-Buddhist circles) around the fourth century.[136]

What is striking is how quickly rasa became so central to learned discourse in royal courts from Kashmir to southern India. Bhoja, for example, produced two works that engaged the theory of rasa head-on while ruling from a highly visible, even storied, court at Dhara in central India. Why the ruling elite's interest in aesthetics arose when it did (though earlier thinkers like Dandin and Udbhata were also associated with courts) is no easier to answer than the parallel question of why aesthetics in Europe should have emerged first in the early eighteenth century. One can easily coordinate the interests of the court with the cultivation of courtly norms that the aesthetic imagination was meant to reproduce—indeed, perhaps too easily, for coordination all too quickly becomes reduction. It may be true, as I once put it, that good readers—of the sort Bhoja intended his work to form—make good subjects, and, as Terry Eagleton has it, that the aesthetic lies "at the very root of social relations" as the "source of all human bonding."[137] But these are bare theoretical bones, and we need more resources, of the sort this sourcebook seeks to provide, if we are to put flesh on them.

Far more complicated than the beginnings of rasa discourse or its consolidation as an important cultural-political form is the question of its ending. Space permitting, I would have concluded the *Reader* with Rajacudamani's *Mirror of Poetry* because that work shows not only a marked discursive transformation—one entirely de-historized, as we saw, where early thinkers have become ideal types entirely disconnected from their actual works (most of which had disappeared as much as a millennium earlier)—but also a marked exhaustion. Rajacudamani reproduces the same set of topics in play from the time of Abhinava and adds nothing from his own time and place, the remarkable world of south Indian culture at the height of Nayaka power.[138] Later works advance in not one particular our understanding of either the substance of rasa theory or its history.[139] Many works purportedly dealing with rasa are actually anthologies of poetry illustrating the rasas, in imitation of Bhanudatta's *River of Rasa* (c. 1500), but containing nothing of his analytical concerns.[140] Clearly, if somewhat perplexingly, the analysis of literary emotion had ceded place to the creation of literary emotion. The remarkable flowering of a new rasa theory among Bengali Vaishnavas was accompanied by a remarkable flowering of new poetry, but while the production of poetry continued, no further theoretical contributions were made after the seventeenth century. The last work I examined from before the colonial caesura, Acyutaray Modak's *Essence of Literary Art* (*Sāhityasāra*, c. 1820), is fully representative of the endpoint of the discourse. His interests are altogether other (mostly rhetorical), and when he turns to rasa in the final chapter of his treatise, he does no more than offer a few verses illustrating the erotic.

The picture does not change even if we widen our lens beyond the sphere of Sanskrit intellectuals. Across the early modern vernacular world, poets were clearly fascinated by rasa; the pen names even Muslim poets adopted, "Raslin," "Raskhan," and the like, attest to this. Yet Sufi masters who wrote in Avadhi, aside from incorporating rasa categories into their romances, had no interest in advancing the theoretical project of classical aesthetics. Hindu intellectuals produced large numbers of studies, but again these were either restatements and anthologies on the model of Bhanudatta's specialized treatise on the typology of leading female characters (*nāyikābheda*) in his *Bouquet of Rasa* (*Rasamañjarī*), or vernacularizations of older classics (like Kulapati Mishra's 1670 *Secret of Rasa*, *Rasrahasya*, a version of Mammata's *Light on Poetry*), which embody nothing of the conceptual ferment that had marked the discourse over the previous millennium.[141] Although many works await editing, nothing, published or not, suggests that early modern intellectuals of whatever linguistic orientation or religious persuasion had anything to add to the rasa conversation.[142] That the end came on the eve of colonialism is entirely coincidental, and cannot by any means be construed as a consequence.

From one angle, rasa discourse in the period 1650–1800 presents a picture of intellectual stasis. At times it was hard to move the conversation forward, since innovation in Sanskrit thought was always threatened with Ockham's Razor. Bhanudatta in 1500 had to defend his invention of the "fantasy" rasa from the charge that it had "no traditional standing," just as centuries earlier Anandavardhana had to defend "implicature."[143] The impediment of "scholarly convention"[144] did not of course stop either scholar, or Bhoja, who directly attacked it. But Jagannatha in the mid-seventeenth century evinces a newly heightened sense of traditionalism when he refuses to entertain the possibility of any modification of the received aesthetic system—by the addition of the devotional rasa, for example—lest disciplinary chaos ensue.[145] All the other questions, of the sort that modern aesthetics learned to ask—about the criteria for identifying something as art, or interpreting it, or evaluating it beyond the traditional system of genre compliance, rhetorical exegesis, and the specification of disqualifying "flaws"—were even further removed from the agenda.

Whatever the force of such explanations for the discipline's denouement, another seems considerably less cogent, namely, that rasa theory was simply too inflexible to account for new kinds of poetry that appeared in the early modern period, since there are two unwarranted assumptions in the argument. One is that the new literature was radically incommensurate with the old, but this has yet to be convincingly demonstrated. The other is that rasa theory as such was somehow narrowly tied to that old literature, but this is based on an impoverished understanding of the theory's aim, which, as the materials offered in this *Reader* show, is to account for the emotional core of literature and why we respond to it the way we do, and which accordingly cannot be tied to any historical moment.[146] A related notion, that rasa theory was exclusive to drama and Sanskrit drama declined in the early modern era, is wrong on both counts.[147]

Viewed from another angle, and with greater hermeneutical charity, the fact that rasa discourse did come to an end might be taken as marking the attainment of a state of conceptual plenitude. After a millennium and a half of the most searching analysis the world had ever seen—on the basis of a carefully elaborated lexicon, stable categories, and fully shared assumptions of core questions—of the emotional structure of literary artworks, thinkers were perhaps justified in believing that they had carefully weighed every possible alternative and fully understood the nature of aesthetic response—and that there was nothing left to say.

11. "TASTE" COMPARISON AND THE PORTABILITY OF RASA THEORY

Why should "taste" have become the pre-eminent metaphor for understanding aesthetic response in classical India? Curiously, this is something our authorities never care to argue out on philosophical grounds. They unpack the idea only for its metaphorical implication, and then only with respect to the capacity of the aesthetic object to combine disparate elements into a whole, the way a mixed drink combines its ingredients to produce a single gustatory experience (the asymmetry between the six sensory tastes—sweet, sour, bitter, etc.—and the eight aesthetic tastes holds little interest for them). There may have been the incidental implication that rasa theory imparts "the ability to detect all the ingredients in a composition," as Hume famously defined taste, but this was never directly stated, and the very relationship between knowing rasa theory and improving reading practices went largely unexamined.[148] Occasionally the image is extended to the "chewing over" required to get the full sense of a poem, the way sugarcane must be slowly chewed to extract its juice.[149] But generally speaking, the metaphor did no further work. In particular, Indian thinkers seemed unconcerned to explain the relationship, obscure on the face of it, between nonrational "taste" and the highly rational social and moral judgments in which the rasa experience of literature is meant to school the reader. Perhaps it was too obvious to them, and only modern Western readers feel the need for such an explanation, living as they do in a world where knowledge has become the preserve of reason alone, with the relationship between taste and moral judgment severed and the "aesthetic concept of morality" lost for good.[150]

Even more curious than the presence of the metaphor is the fact that a second great tradition of aesthetic analysis, at the start of the modern era, should have independently settled on the same way of expressing the response to art. True enough, for both traditions it would have been obvious that this response occurs initially at the experiential, even physical level, and only subsequently at an intellectual one. "Aisthēsis" in the radical Greek sense of the word, as a general term for this object of study—the "feeling" part of art—makes very good sense. But "taste"? Does it really offer a "natural" metaphor for the aesthetic sensibility, and if so, in what sense?[151] It may be only their vagueness that makes other metaphorical locutions for aesthetic experience, such as being "touched" or "moved," any less curious. But on the face of it, to say, however figuratively, that taste is the medium of our interaction with art is no less strange than saying it is smell.

Unlike smell, taste admits of degrees; as a bodily sense it also has a more direct relationship with the object as well as with the object's pleasure than the "distance" senses such as sight (we *like* tastes in a more intimate way than we like sights).[152] Though natural, it can in principle be improved with training, the sort of training that, in the case of artworks, aesthetics would hypothetically be able to provide (as we have seen, there is uncertainty about this in India). It can also be "acquired." But additionally, taste seems to capture that special phenomenological truth formulated by Dufrenne. Feeling is embedded in the object no less than in the subject, and the viewer experiences feeling because affective quality belongs to the artwork; in the same way, we have the taste of a thing only because the thing itself has taste, as it does not have sight. The long debate over rasa's location can be seen as a search for an understanding already gained by the metaphor itself—this is just what Abhinavagupta argued[153]—one not attained in the West until the rise of phenomenological aesthetics.

The use of the metaphor in European intellectual history seems to have begun with the Jesuit thinker Balthasar Gracian in the early seventeenth century, for whom taste functioned more as a moral category than an aesthetic one: it is possible to refine the taste as well as the mind; in taste begins the drawing of distinctions and hence social cultivation.[154] Taste became central to aesthetics, however, only when aesthetics was first invented as a discipline in the mid-eighteenth century, in a world where the hereditary prerogatives of aristocracy were weakening and judgment itself was becoming the foundation of a new society. Hume's concern, like that of many other eighteenth-century thinkers, was to establish a standard of taste in the face of subjective aesthetic sentiment, which he does by tracing the diversity of taste to a diversity in capacities to register what are, for him, objective qualities of beauty. His emphasis on judgment may set him apart from our Indian theorists; however subjective "taste" may seem to us, there was never any doubt for Indians that a single standard could apply.[155] Yet like them Hume holds that the cultivation of art is essentially the cultivation of moral awareness, though the process is very different in the two worlds. For Hume, passion is linked with taste; it is something to be disciplined by taste, which is the true source of happiness; art refines our feelings.[156] For Indian thinkers, the relationship of emotion to reason was in general a question of little philosophical interest, but neither was emotion something to be subordinated to or dominated by knowledge, as it was for Plato and most of his successors. And in any case, aesthetic pedagogy unfolds for Indians in a far more explicit manner: the viewer of a play becomes suffused "by the desire to attain the good and to avoid the bad," as Abhinava puts it, and "he actually comes to do the one and to shun the other, given that he has now gained an understanding to this end."[157]

What is most fundamentally constitutive of the Indian discourse on rasa, namely, the relationship between taste and social propriety ("The one thing that can impair rasa is impropriety," says Anandavardhana. "Composing with customary propriety—that is rasa's deep secret"), is also most occluded, for the sources of social propriety lay far below the level of analysis. Propriety was simply a given.[158] This "miscognition" of the social determinants of judgment was largely the case in the West as well, until critique became a component of criticism and taste was identified as a marker of social status. The distinctions social subjects make—between the beautiful and the ugly, or whatever—serve to distinguish themselves ("Taste classifies, and it classifies the classifier").[159] "Good taste," "bad taste," "tasteless": these are things for which we can easily provide Sanskrit translations (*sarasa, virasa, nīrasa*, etc.), but the latter carry, or are permitted to carry, no hint of the social origins that would impugn their naturalness. Whereas the English term "taste" is always applied to the capacity of the social subject, the Sanskrit term is typically tied to the aesthetic object.

As for the Weberian account with which we started, not much is left. There was indubitably an autonomous domain of art in India before the coming of European modernity, one fully distinguished from the religious sphere. No Indian Arnold may have ever suggested that poetry could replace religion as a source of salvation, though Bhatta Nayaka came close. But it was only in the sixteenth century that thinkers claimed, or came close to claiming, religion could replace poetry. Before this, literature for Sanskrit thinkers was an affair of this world, and aesthetic theory was a way of making sense of how the world produced rasa, and rasa helped reproduce the world.

12. RASA PAST AND FUTURE

There is a proclivity in a certain strain of postcolonial thought to assert claims to conceptual priority: the precolony is always supposed to have preempted colonialism in its theoretical understanding of the world. This is demonstrated for classical Indian aesthetics by awarding it a kind of superior insight and universal applicability ("Rasa in Shakespeare" is the genre of study I have in mind). To understand rasa as a historical form of thought, however, as I try to enable the reader of this *Reader* to do, is to confront a theory clearly contingent on a nonmodern worldview and understanding of literary art. Its full conceptualization is intimately tied to a number of primary, uncontested, and largely nontransferable Indian presuppositions—about the threefold psychophysiology of Samkhya, for example, or the storage of memories of past lives, or even transmigration. That said, rasa theory does offer an account of widely shared mental processes and an analytic procedure that enable us here and now to think through more clearly and talk more precisely about features of our own aesthetic experience for which we have no ready-to-hand concepts or language. Even more fundamentally, it allows us to admit that we have such experiences in the first place.

For in fact, reading with emotion in the modern West was until recently viewed as a fallacy—indeed, it was called the "Affective Fallacy." Even before W. K. Wimsatt and Monroe Beardsley coined the phrase in their well-known essay, René Wellek sought to proscribe the "emotive" criticism of literature, reducing it to "the labeling of works of art by emotional terms like 'joyful,' 'gay,' 'melancholy,' and so forth," and denying that "even if we define these emotions as closely as we can, we are still quite removed from the specific object which induced them." Emotion "has nothing to do with the actual object" of literary study; in addition, its analyses are unverifiable and cannot contribute to a "cooperative advance in our knowledge."[160] For Wimsatt and Beardsley, attempting to understand what a poem is from what the poem does, far from being a route to overcome the obstacles to objective criticism, actually leads "away from criticism and from poetry" toward impressionism and relativism. What counts is referential meaning, not emotion: "It may well be that the contemplation of this object, or pattern of emotive knowledge, which is the poem, is the ground for some ultimate emotional state which may be termed the aesthetic. . . . But it is no concern of criticism, no part of criteria."[161]

In the last decade there has been a growing unease with these grand dismissals.[162] Emotion, in literary criticism, philosophical aesthetics, and even social theory, is staging something of an insurgency, with the rise of an "affective turn" prompting new histories of the emotions, new studies of the emotions in history, and new cognitive theories of the emotions.[163] And here rasa theory and its history may have some role to play. The theory offers an acute dissection of the elements that produce—as they undeniably produce—emotion in the literary artwork, and a perceptive analysis of the psychological process of viewer or reader response, while the very disputes that marked the theory's historical development contain a whole universe of enduring, contending assessments. In the best of cases it may even help us unlearn old modes of reading while gaining new ones, to better understand what it means to experience art and hence to be a full human being.

CHAPTER ONE

The Foundational Text, c. 300, and Early Theorists, 650–1025

1.1 THE BASIS OF RASA THEORY IN DRAMA

Treatise on Drama of Bharata (c. 300)

As with virtually all foundational texts of the Sanskrit knowledge systems, we have no secure information about the author of the *Treatise on Drama*. The early grammarian Panini (fourth century B.C.E.) refers to a text called *The Actor's Sutras*, and the late fourth-century (C.E.) playwright Kalidasa knew of a "theory of drama," if not the *Treatise*.[1] Some organized body of knowledge of the sort presented here had therefore long been in existence, but there is no way of knowing how much the *Treatise* overlaps with or draws from this older tradition. The text appropriates the authority of the sage Bharata, but he lived in time out of mind, and there is even uncertainty about the "text" itself. The extant manuscripts disagree about everything from the number of chapters to the readings of individual verses, and nothing approaching a critical edition has ever been attempted. While on formal grounds the compilation (and this is what it seems to be) can be vaguely assigned to the early centuries (perhaps third century) C.E., the material was clearly re-edited, and partly rewritten, at a later point in its history, most probably in Kashmir around the eighth or ninth century. From this time we have the first secure evidence of commentarial attention to the work, from the Kashmirian scholar Udbhata (c. 800), who is followed by a long and distinguished list of thinkers for the next two centuries.

The *Treatise* is a vast and comprehensive account, in some six thousand verses (*The Six Thousand* is its traditional name) and thirty-six (or thirty-seven, or thirty-three) chapters, of the entire domain of dramaturgy, from the construction of the theater to the languages used in plays (their grammar, figures, intonation, and so on) and the singing, musical instruments, dancing, makeup, costuming, and physical movements of the actors. But in accordance with the declaration of the *Treatise* itself that "No part of the enterprise will succeed without attention to rasa," the discussion of rasa in the sixth chapter has attracted the most sustained attention of scholars, both ancient and modern.

This discussion places in bold relief not only the signal importance of the *Treatise* for the history of Indian aesthetics but also the impediments to understanding that history entailed by the text's problematic transmission. Its celebrated *Sutra on Rasa* is the founding statement on aesthetics, and would be interpreted and reinterpreted for almost two millennia: the mid-seventeenth-century thinker Jagannatha discusses eight different readings of the aphorism that he viewed as constituting the whole history of aesthetic theory.[2] In addition, all the basic components of the theory that later thinkers would have to deal with are listed, defined, and illustrated in the *Treatise*. But the reader will also confront at the very beginning of the selection the obscurity of many of the technical terms, and the inconsistencies, even contradictions (or what sometimes seem to us today to be inconsistencies and contradictions) left by the editing process. These are such that some scholars have come to view the rasa section in its current state as incoherent beyond repair.[3]

Although the *Treatise* is undoubtedly difficult, that extreme view is readily refuted by the very substantial sense we are able to extract from the text in the state we have inherited it. Moreover, as we develop a deeper understanding of the intellectual history of rasa subsequent to Bharata, we may, by an admittedly circular process, employ interpretation to identify some of the traces of later revision and the confusion it has left in its wake. A simple but striking instance concerns the number of rasas. There is no question that a ninth, the peaceful, is a later (perhaps much later) addition to Bharata's original eight,[4] and although only a few manuscripts of the text include this addition, the eleventh-century commentator Abhinavagupta defended it, and consequently it appears in the printed editions that seek to reconstitute "Abhinavagupta's text." Abhinava protests too much, however, when he asserts that the manuscripts containing the peaceful rasa are "ancient," and he is forced to explain why, for example, other listings of eight rasas and their appurtenances—deities, colors, etc.—do not include the peaceful.[5]

If the uncertain history of the text makes it hard to understand what Bharata's view of rasa was, so too does the history of its interpretation, insofar as scholars have anachronistically read the ideas of later theorists back into the *Treatise*. This pertains particularly to the focal point of Bharata's rasa analytic. A half-century ago a leading scholar of Indian aesthetics was correct to note—and has been alone in noting—that in the *Treatise* "the words rasa and *bhāva* [emotion] are used in connection with the actor and the artist and not in connection with the spectator," and that any "historical approach" to these concepts must admit that they "describe the aesthetic situation, the art object outside, more than the subjective state of the critic."[6] Although the scholar never worked out this historical approach, his intuition was correct, and the judgment about rasa fits with the overall objective of the *Treatise*: to provide guidance above all to actors. This objective is manifest in the work's repeated references to how the components of drama, and the rasas in particular, are "to be acted out," and it was clear to the work's contemporary readers. "The theory of drama," as Kalidasa put it, "is focused on performance."

Given that subjective response is encoded in the very metaphor of "taste," rasa discourse must always have been concerned, at least implicitly, with "the subjective state," or the viewer's response. Nonetheless, the primary expository focus in the *Treatise* is the actor and, indissociably, the character the actor is representing. Although an explicit discussion is absent, no doubt because the matter was self-evident to all participants in the discourse, Bharata's language often clearly suggests that his analytic focus is on rasa in the character. The comic, for example, "is seen to exist for the most part in women and characters of low status," not in the response of the viewer.[7] Moreover, Bharata's conception of the causal process—*bhāvas*, or emotions, are the factors that "manifest" the rasa—implies, or at least later is taken to imply, the preexistence of rasa in the character and hence the character's analytic primacy.[8] And this is all in keeping with the perspective of the earliest commentator on the *Treatise*, Bhatta Lollata.

One well-known passage in prose (most of the work is in verse) seems to speak against the assumption that Bharata himself shared the perspective of his first commentator: "Discerning viewers relish the stable emotions manifested by the acting out of various transitory emotions and reactions . . . they feel joy and the like in doing so."[9] Yet even this passage, although it represents a concern with viewer response that is hardly evident elsewhere in the sixth chapter, is consistent with the general model according to which rasa is located in, and belongs to, the character. Later authors certainly took this to be Bharata's view. As for the gustatory metaphor, it determines little in and of itself. "Taste" may be said to exist as such only when tasted (a kind of secondary quality), but it nonetheless can be considered a property of the object (a kind of primary quality).[10]

The commentarial tradition on the *Treatise* cannot have begun much before the early ninth century, with a now-lost work by Udbhata.[11] All other commentaries, likewise produced in Kashmir, have also vanished; we know of them only from fragments preserved in the lone survivor, *The New* Dramatic Art, of Abhinavagupta (c. 1000, some of which are found also in his earlier *Eye for* Light on Implicature). This work often makes clear that the tradition of interpretation of the *Treatise* had long been broken, and for problematic passages Abhinava is trying to make the best of a bad situation. But although his ideas are sometimes palpably at odds with the natural reading of the text, he is a critically important guide through the work, something that becomes painfully apparent in the few selections offered here from the seventh chapter, where much of his commentary is missing. I therefore provide in the notes a number of his comments, while reserving for chapter 4 a translation of passages that showcase his own—for the most part, radically divergent—theories.

FROM *TREATISE ON DRAMA* OF BHARATA

(6.1–7) After the procedures for the stage preliminaries had been recounted to them, the great sages all addressed Bharata once again: "Answer five questions for us. Authorities on drama list various dramatic rasas. Can you tell us what it is that makes them rasas, 'tastes'? Why are the emotions (*bhāva*) so called, and can you tell us what they bring into being (*bhāvayanti*)? What exactly is meant by 'catalogue,' 'epitome,' and 'definition'?" When Bharata the sage heard the sages' words, he made the following reply regarding the analysis of rasas and emotions. "I shall explain it to you in full, holy men, as well as catalogue, epitome, and definition. It is altogether impossible to plumb the depths of drama. Why? Because the theoretical knowledges are numerous and the practical skills incalculable. The depths of even one ocean of knowledge cannot be plumbed accurately, let alone all the others.

(6.8) That said, I will present a catalogue of the topics of drama, beginning with the rasas and emotions, which briefly offers the sense of the aphorisms and their commentary,[12] yet allows for larger inferences.[13]

. . . .

(6.15–23) The erotic, comic, tragic, violent, heroic, fearful, macabre, and fantastic are the eight dramatic rasas. These are the eight that were enunciated by the great Druhin.[14] Now I shall tell you about the emotions: the stable, the transitory, and the emotions generated by one's 'sensitivity.' The stable emotions are desire, amusement, grief, anger, determination, fear, revulsion, and amazement. The transitory emotions are despair, fatigue, disquiet, resentment, intoxication, exhaustion, torpor, despondency, anxiety, confusion, remembrance, satisfaction, shame, recklessness, joy, agitation, numbness, pride, depression, longing, sleepiness, possession, dreaming, waking, vindictiveness, dissimulation, ferocity, sagacity, sickness, madness, dying, fright, perplexity. The eight sensitivities are paralysis, perspiration, horripilation, a broken voice, trembling, pallor, weeping, and fainting. The four registers of acting that pertain to drama are the physical, verbal, psychophysical, and costuming.[15]

. . . .

(6.31) Such is the compendium of drama in brief aphorisms. From this point on, I provide an analysis based on the aphorisms and commentary.

(p. 1.266) We will explain the rasas first, for no part of the enterprise[16] will succeed without attention to rasa.

Rasa arises from the conjunction of factors, reactions, and transitory emotions.[17] [281] What would be an analogy? Just as taste arises from the conjunction of various condiments, spices, and substances, so rasa arises from the presentation of various factors and emotions. That is to say, just as physical tastes, that of lassi, for instance, or other such drink, are produced by substances such as brown sugar, plus condiments and spices, so [282] the stable emotion, in the presence of the various factors and emotions, turns into rasa.

Here one might ask: What does 'rasa' actually mean? Our answer is that rasa is so called because it is something savored. And how can rasa be said to be 'savored'? Just as discerning people relish tastes when eating food prepared with various condiments[18] and in doing so find pleasure, so discerning viewers relish the stable emotions when they are manifested[19] by the acting out of various transitory emotions and reactions [283] and accompanied by the other acting registers (the verbal, physical, and psychophysical), and they find pleasure in doing so. This explains why we call them 'dramatic rasas,' or tastes. On this matter there are two traditional verses:

> (6.32–33) Just as connoisseurs eat and savor their fare when prepared with many condiments and substances, so the learned fully savor in their heart the stable emotions when conjoined with the factors, transitory emotions, and reactions.[20] That is why they are called dramatic rasas, or "tastes."

[286] On this point the question has been raised whether [1] rasas are produced by the emotions and other aesthetic elements,[21] or [2] emotions by rasas. And some have held [3] that rasas and emotions are mutually constitutive. The last two positions are false; we can readily observe that rasas are produced by the emotions and other elements and not the reverse. On these three positions there are several verses:[22]

> (6.34–38) [1] "Emotions" (*bhāvas*) are so called by the creators of drama because when conjoined[23] with the various registers of acting they bring into being (*bhāvayanti*) the rasas. Just as various substances bring a new flavor[24] into existence, so the emotions with the aid of the registers of acting bring the rasas into being. [3] There is no rasa without the emotions and other aesthetic elements, and no emotions without rasa. Their production is mutually effected in the course of acting. Just as the conjunction of condiments and spices makes food savory,[25] so the emotions and rasas bring each other into being. [2] Just as a tree grows from a seed, and flower and fruit from a tree, so rasas are a root, and the emotions and other elements are all determined from them.

[288.3] Accordingly, we shall now explain the rasas: their coming into being, their specific colors, superintending deities, and finer points. [289] Among the rasas, four are generative causes: the erotic, the violent, the heroic, and the macabre. To clarify:

(6.39–45) From the erotic arises the comic, from the violent the tragic, from the heroic the fantastic, and from the macabre the fearful.[26] The comic may be described as an imitation of the erotic, and the tragic rasa may be understood as an effect of the violent. The fantastic is declared to be an effect of the heroic, and the fearful should be understood to come about at the sight of the macabre.[27]

Their colors: the erotic is blue-black, the comic is white, the tragic is gray, and the violent red; the heroic is golden, the fearful black, the macabre blue, and the fantastic yellow.

Their superintending deities: Vishnu is presiding deity for the erotic, Shiva's goblins for the comic, Rudra for the violent, Yama for the tragic, Mahakala for the macabre, Kala for the fearful, Indra for the heroic, and Brahma for the fantastic.

[293.12] We shall now explain the definitions and give the finer points of the various rasas when conjoined with reactions, factors, and transitory emotions, and we shall show how a stable emotion becomes rasa. [294] To begin with, the erotic has its origin in the stable emotion of desire, and has the nature of radiant attire.[28] [295] In real life anything that is pure, immaculate, radiant, or beautiful is compared to love; a person dressed in radiant clothing is thus said to be "lovely." Just as men's names derive from their paternal lineage, maternal family, or professional function, and come to be established through the usage of competent speakers of the language, so the rasas and emotions and other elements of the drama derive their names from their function and are established through competent usage. Thus, the erotic rasa is established by virtue of its function and is so named because it has the nature of "lovely," radiant attire. Its cause is a woman and a man; its characters are a young couple of high status. [297] It has two states, the erotic enjoyed and the erotic thwarted. The erotic enjoyed, for its part, comes about from stimulant factors such as the enjoyment of the appropriate season, flower garlands, scented creams, jewelry, a boon companion or beloved object, a beautiful home; the experience of strolling in a garden, or hearing about or observing it; sporting in the water; mimicry of the beloved. [299] The erotic is to be acted out by such reactions[29] as the skillful play of the eyes, movements of the eyebrows and sidelong glances, and gentle and pleasing bodily motions and verbal utterances. [300] All transitory emotions can be used except for torpor, ferocity, and revulsion. The erotic thwarted, however, is to be acted out by despair, fatigue, disquiet, resentment, exhaustion, anxiety, longing, sleeping, dreaming, waking, sickness, madness, possession, numbness, death, and other reactions.[30]

[302] Here one might ask: If the erotic has its origin in the stable emotion of desire, how is it subject to transitory emotions typically pertaining to the tragic? Here is our answer: We earlier stated that the erotic is actualized in two ways, as enjoyed and

thwarted, [303] and the authors of treatises on erotics state that it has ten stages,[31] which we shall describe in the chapter on acting in general.[32] That said, the tragic rasa, arising as it does from such foundational factors as a curse or misfortune befalling a loved one, the loss of one's wealth, death, or imprisonment, is a state of hopelessness; the erotic thwarted, by contrast, is a state of hopefulness, arising as it does from longing and anxiety.[33] [304] Thus, the tragic and the erotic thwarted are entirely different; at the same time, the erotic is indeed subject to all the transitory emotions.[34] With respect to this:

(6.46) When a man is joined with a woman, feeling mostly pleasant things, and availing himself of the appropriate season, flower garlands, and so on, it is designated the erotic rasa.[35]

[305] Here are two verses in *āryā* meter that embody the meaning of the aphorism on the erotic:

> (6.47–48) The erotic rasa arises from the appropriate season, flower garlands, jewelry, a boon companion, music, engagement with poetry, pastimes like strolling in a garden. It is to be acted out by clarity of eye and face, smiles, sweet language, satisfaction and joy,[36] and gentle movements of the limbs.[37]

. . . .

(6.77–82) The erotic rasa has three different forms, depending on whether it is in essence a matter of language, action, or costume, and the same holds for the comic and the violent.[38] The tragic is likewise held to be threefold, depending on whether it is produced by a violation of morality, occasioned by the loss of one's wealth, or brought about by grief.[39] Brahma has proclaimed that the heroic is similarly threefold: the heroic in munificence, in morality, and in war. The fearful likewise has three forms: it can be simulated, or stem from a criminal act, or be anything a timid person finds frightening.[40] The macabre can be pure or impure: the former is disturbing, and is brought about by the sight of blood and the like; the latter is disgusting, and is brought about by the sight of excrement, maggots, and so on. The fantastic is twofold as well, being either heavenly, that is to say, produced by the sight of something divine; or blissful, that is, produced by joy.[41]

. . . .

(6.83) These are what are known as the eight rasas, defined according to their appropriate definitions. I shall now present the definition of emotions.

(p. 1.336) We shall now explain emotions. The author asks: Why are emotions (*bhāva*) so called? Is it because they come into being (*bhavanti*), or because they bring something else into being (*bhāvayanti*)? The answer is that they are so called because they bring into being the meaning of the literary work[42] when these are given verbal, physical, and affective form. . . . Here are verses to this effect:[43]

> (7.1–3) An emotion is something brought about by the foundational and stimulant factors, and apprehended by means of the reactions in concert with the verbal, physical, and psychophysical registers of acting. "Emotion" (*bhāva*) is also so called because it serves to "bring into being" (*bhāvayan*)[44] the poet's inner emotion (*bhāva*), by means of the four registers of acting: verbal, physical, psychophysical, and makeup. "Emotions" (*bhāvas*) are so called by the creators of drama.[45]

[342.8] These emotions include the eight stable emotions, thirty-three transitory emotions, and eight psychophysical responses. These forty-nine emotions should be understood to be the causes of the manifestation[46] of literary rasa. The rasas arise from them in combination with their common properties.[47] Here is a pertinent verse:

(7.7) The use[48] of subject matter with which the heart concurs is the source of rasa, and it can engulf the body entirely, the way fire engulfs dry wood.

[343] Here one might ask: If the rasas arise from the forty-nine emotions connected with the subject matter of a literary work, when these emotions are manifested by the factors and the physical reactions in combination with their common properties, why is it only the stable emotions that are said to become rasas? Our answer is as follows: Just as human beings, despite the fact that they have common physical traits, similar hands and feet and torsos and frames, and common major and minor limbs, will become, some of them, kings by reason of their family, character, wisdom, actions, skills, or cleverness, whereas others of lesser intelligence will become their servants, so the factors, physical reactions, and transitory emotions are subservient to the stable emotions. And the stable emotions, since the many other elements serve them, become the master; the other emotions, being subordinates like the men in the analogy, serve them in a subordinate manner; the transitory emotions are their retinue. Take as an example a king: although he has an entourage of many men, he alone acquires the title and no one else, however great. In the same way, the stable emotion alone, though surrounded by the factors, reactions, and transitory emotions, is awarded the name of rasa. Here is a traditional verse on the matter:

(7.8) Just like a king among men or a teacher among students, the stable emotion is preeminent among all emotions.

[344.3] We have in fact already given the definition of the emotions when identified as rasa. We shall now give their general definitions as emotions,[49] starting with the stable emotions.[50]

. . . .

[349.11] We shall now explain the transitory emotions. These are called *vyabhicāris*, from the preverbs *vi* and *abhi* and the verbal root *car* in the sense of "come": they "come (*caranti*) variously (*vi*[*vidham*]) into proximity (*ābhi*[*mukhyena*])." When endowed in performance with the verbal, physical, and psychophysical registers of acting, they "lead" the rasas. In what sense [350] can they be said to lead? This is a just a conventional expression, the same way we say the sun "leads" the day or an asterism, without doing so by using arms or shoulders. . . . The transitory emotions lead the rasas just as the sun does the day or an asterism.[51]

. . . .

(7.93cd) I shall now discuss the psychophysical responses in due order.

[373.3] Here one might ask whether the acting out of the other emotions is supposed to happen without psychic sensitivity, such that only these responses should be called *psycho*physical. My answer is as follows. Psychic sensitivity as defined here is something that arises from the mind; it is said to be the mind in a state of heightened awareness, since the psychic sensitivity arises when the mind is thus aware. The particular nature of each of its different emotions, such as horripilation, weeping, pallor, and the like, cannot be brought about when the actor's mind is elsewhere. Given that the drama imitates the nature of the world, the role of psychic sensitivity is essential. An example: the dramatic emotions that are effects of pleasure or pain should be so purified by psychic sensitivity that they are identical.[52] In the case of pain, for example, which consists of weeping and the like, how can it be acted out by someone not feeling pain; or pleasure, which consists of joy and the like, by someone not feeling pleasure? It is precisely thanks to the actor's psychic sensitivity that he is able, even when not feeling pleasure or pain,[53] to display horripilation or weeping, and it is for this reason that these emotions have been explained as being psychophysical."[54]

1.2 RASA AS A FIGURE OF SPEECH IN NARRATIVE POETRY: THE EARLY VIEWS

Ornament of Poetry of Bhamaha (c. 650)

From the time of the *Treatise on Drama*—assuming the existence around the third century of a work on dramaturgy that bears some relationship to the text of *The Six Thousand* we now have—some four centuries elapsed until rasa was addressed in Sanskrit literary theory. And when this occurred, in Bhamaha's *Ornament of Poetry*, rasa took a form radically different from what Bharata's account would have led us to expect.

The *Ornament of Poetry* is our first extant work on poetics in Sanskrit. Scholarly controversy long clouded Bhamaha's date and relationship with the poetician and poet Dandin (see the next section), with whose *Looking Glass of Poetry* the *Ornament* bears a complex relationship. But the question of priority at least has finally been sorted out. Bhamaha is to be dated no later than the middle of the seventh century, and must be viewed as the predecessor of Dandin (c. 700).[55] Bhamaha does cite several forerunners in the field of poetics, but all their works have vanished, and we have no idea what, if anything, they may have thought about rasa. We also have no exegeses of his work (save for some fragments of a commentary by Udbhata, c. 800), and his compressed style can make his intention difficult to grasp. In fact, it is often Dandin's fuller exposition or reworking that offers compelling (if not always decisive) illumination.

I describe the *Ornament* as a treatise on "poetics" in order to distinguish Bhamaha's work fundamentally from the domain of dramaturgy. Bhamaha is concerned exclusively with the nature of literary language in *kāvya*, poetry, which was (usually) clearly differentiated from *nāṭya*, drama.[56] Whereas Indian thinkers did use the term *kāvya* also to refer to a higher-order category of language use—what we would call belles lettres or literature as such—their subdivision of *kāvya* into literature meant to be heard (or read) and literature meant to be seen marked out two very different domains of expressive language use. And rasa as first theorized for literature in performance was emotion the spectator could *see*.

Precisely when and how the concept of rasa was extended from drama to narrative poetry, from the seen to the heard (and read), and with what consequences for aesthetic theory, is something we need to puzzle out from our textual sources. With the sole exception of Rudra Bhatta,[57] no thinker ever announced he was extrapolating from the one domain to the other, or described the reasons for doing so, or addressed head on the difficulties in adapting a performative scheme to a narrative form. In Bhamaha's work, in fact, the transition appears to be just beginning.

Not only does the *Ornament* not address rasa as a separate topic, it does not yet even recognize rasa as a separate analytical category. Instead, given Bhamaha's overall concern with figures of speech and how they "ornament" language and render it literary rather than documentary, he conceives of rasa, or more precisely, verbal expressions of emotions, as tropes, that is, particularized types of expressive language use. Three that he defines would long be discussed in relation to rasa: the "rasa-laden statement"; the "affectionate utterance"; the "haughty declaration." A fourth figure, which he characterizes as the expression of happy coincidence, will later be redefined as an "emotion trope" too; so also, to a degree, the "noble," which for some authorities has a component of emotion, though for others, a purely material dimension (I supply translations of these in brackets).[58] It is symptomatic of the inchoate stage of the understanding of emotion in literature—where the analytical focus remains entirely on literary form, not reader response—that Bhamaha should present these emotion tropes in a list of twenty-three other very heterogeneous figures of sense. Some may be statements where affect is in some sense present, if less obviously so (the "disingenuous remark," for example), but all the rest are familiar figures of speech such as intentional contradiction, false praise, or subtypes of simile. Besides his rather obscure listing, and in accordance with his spare style, Bhamaha only briefly defines the figures and exemplifies them with very abbreviated quotations from works (in most cases, lost works) of Sanskrit literature.

These diverse materials are not easy to understand at first glance. The categories themselves will be redefined over the coming centuries, so much so that by the eleventh, Bhamaha's views were considered almost incoherent.[59] Even the particulars can be hard to grasp, though here Dandin's fuller account goes some way in clarifying Bhamaha's intention. For the "rasa-laden statement," for example, Dandin's illustrative verse offers a perfect exemplification of Bhamaha's definition: it marks the moment in a lost work about the romantic king Udayana when his queen Vasavadatta's disguise as a mendicant is removed and she is revealed to be alive, returned as it were to life. At this moment the erotic rasa, as Bhamaha has it, is indeed "clearly shown."[60] Notwithstanding Bhamaha's abbreviated characterization, the figure has nothing to do with disguise as such, but rather with a *transition* in the narrative where the rasa can actually achieve full development. This is also manifestly the case with Dandin's next example, the violent rasa, which again shows the moment of climax.[61]

A "rasa-laden statement" was thus thought of as prompting the reader to focus on that specific moment in the development of a rasa when it finally and actually achieves "full development," as Dandin's exposition shows. Similarly, Bhamaha's two other related figures, while not directly linked with rasa, do flag moments of emotional climax—of joy (in the affectionate utterance and arrogance in the haughty declaration—whatever else may be going on in the overall development of the rasa. While devoid of the expressive "indirection" that characterizes metaphor, metonymy, and the other figures of sense, these emotion tropes nonetheless remain charged uses of language and hence are capable of being seen as *alaṅkāra*, literally "enhancements" of speech.

FROM *ORNAMENT OF POETRY* OF BHAMAHA

(3.1) Scholars declare the following also to be figures: affectionate utterances; rasa-laden statements; haughty declarations; expressions of disingenousness, of happy coincidence, or of nobility.[62]

. . . .

(3.5) An example of an affectionate utterance is what Vidura says to Krishna when he comes to his house:

> "The joy I experience today by your coming to my house, Govinda,
> I will have in the future only if you return."[63]

(3.6) A rasa-laden statement is one where a rasa such as the erotic is clearly shown, for example: "The queen appeared, no longer disguised as a religious mendicant."[64]

(3.7) An example of haughty declaration is when Karna rebuked the snake-arrow meant for Arjuna on its return: "Dear Shalya, does Karna shoot an arrow twice?"[65]

[(3.8–9)[66] The disingenuous is where what is said is not exactly what is meant, as when Krishna addresses Shishupala in the "Theft of the Jewel": "We do not eat, at home or abroad, food not first eaten by learned Brahmans." This is said, in fact, in order to avoid Shishupala's poisoning him.[67]

(3.10) An example of happy coincidence is when in the "King's Friend," Narada appears to the Kshatriya women as they are going to appease Parashurama.[68]

(3.11) An example of nobility is when Rama, powerful though he was, in accordance with his father's word humbly abandoned the kingship and betook himself to the forest.

(3. 12) Others interpret the figure differently, namely, when something is presented as richly appointed.

(3.13) An example: Chanakya going at night to the pleasure house of Nanda recognized that it was covered with moonstones only by the drops of water that adhered.[69]]

LOOKING GLASS OF POETRY OF DANDIN (C. 700) WITH THE COMMENTARIES *RATNA'S GLORY* OF RATNASHRIJNANA (C. 950) AND *GUARDING THE TRADITION* OF VADIJANGHALA (C. 950)

In contrast to Bhamaha, we have a reasonably clear sense of the time and place of the critic and poet Dandin, for he states in one of his works that he was attached to the Pallava court in south India at the end of the seventh century, and that his great-great-grandfather had originally come there from farther to the northwest, in today's Karnataka (which might explain Dandin's predilection for the literary style of Vidarbha, the northern Deccan). In addition to his literary-theoretical treatise, he wrote a celebrated (though now only fragmentarily preserved) prose poem, *The Story of the Beautiful Woman of Avanti* (*Avantisundarīkathā*), a portion of which, the *Adventures of the Ten Princes* (*Daśakumāracarita*), circulated independently, and also a now-lost poem where "two tales are joined"—probably the two epics—in simultaneous narration through extended double entendre (*dvisandhānakāvya*).

The *Looking Glass of Poetry* is one of the most influential works in the global history of poetics, probably second only to Aristotle's treatise in breadth of impact. It was translated into a number of South Asian languages and exerted influence on literatures as distant as Recent Style Chinese poetry of the late Tang dynasty and seventeenth-century Tibetan poetry. Like Bhamaha, though far more expansively, Dandin deals mainly with figures of speech in poetry. Unlike Bhamaha, Dandin attracted several commentaries that have been preserved; among the most important are two composed in the mid-tenth century, one by a Buddhist monk from Shri Lanka, Ratnashrijnana (also responsible for translating the *Looking Glass* into Sinhala), the other by an scholar at the court of Krishna III of the Rashtrakutas, whose actual name has been displaced by his sobriquet, "Gazelle Among Disputants."[70]

The first thing that strikes the reader of the *Looking Glass* is the profusion of literary features to which the term "rasa" is applied. Dandin uses it in three largely unrelated senses: first, as a general term for the "tasteful," or sweet, poetic style; second, as a term referring to any "sophisticated" turn of phrase, both usages being part of a broader literary theory of poetic language; third, as a technical term for the various affective dimensions of literary expression we have seen in Bhamaha. Dandin introduces the first two senses in connection with his discussion of what in Sanskrit are called *guṇas*, or "language qualities," which generally refer to linguistic aspects of words (phonological, syntactical, or lexical, such as, respectively, soft or harsh phonemes, the degree of compounding, etymologically simple or complex lexemes) or their content. "Sound rasa," as the commentator Ratnashrijnana calls the first quality, comprises a sort of phonemic echoing across words (similar to, but not fully patterned like, alliteration or assonance); "content rasa," on the other hand, refers to sophistication in expression.[71] Both these senses of rasa will be discarded in later tradition.[72]

Rasa as the affective content of literary discourse for Dandin is embodied in the same three figures of speech as for Bhamaha: "affectionate utterance," "rasa-laden statement," and "haughty declaration." While only the second is specifically connected with rasa, all three self-evidently comprise expressions of emotion, and this is clearly indicated by the definitions Dandin offers for them, which emphasize heightened feeling.[73] (Again, I include a fourth in brackets, the "noble," which, as in Bhamaha and later in Udbhata, has, on one interpretation, a component of affect.) Dandin's treatment of the "rasa-laden statement" in particular demonstrates his understanding that rasa in the sense of aesthetic emotion refers principally (perhaps even exclusively) to the intensified emotion of the character. All his illustrations exemplify this: they are the character's direct discourse, and never external description. Rasa as "the stable emotion alone . . . once intensified by the causes, reactions, and the rest" is precisely what Abhinavagupta some three centuries later will later identify, in discussing the views of Bhatta Lollata, as "the position of the most ancient" authorities, on which he cites Dandin's own words.[74] It is also manifestly the view of Dandin's commentator Ratnashrijnana: an emotion's "achieving the highest stage" of intensification means that it is made manifest by means of verbal reactions, since emotions are internal states and otherwise unknowable to others (a clear and simple explanation of "enhancement" of the sort we do not find elsewhere).[75] Accordingly, like other aspects of meaning, rasa and its related emotion tropes were thought of by Dandin as a purely internal, even formal, feature of the work, and as yet had nothing to do with reader response (even for Ratna, the only response that might count is that of the poets themselves, 1.51; 1.52).

Like Bhamaha before him and other poeticians to follow, Dandin had no category other than figuration under which to theorize the phenomenon of rasa in poetry. And in fact, explaining how affectionate utterance and the rest could or could not be thought of as figures of speech (even if the Sanskrit term *alaṅkāra* were taken, with Bhoja, to mean something like "factor of beauty" rather than trope),[76] would exercise the best literary minds of the following two centuries. Dandin himself seems untroubled by any conceptual tensions. He may be sensitive to the awkward multivalence of the term "rasa," taking pains to clarify that the second figure, the rasa-laden, relates to the eight dramatic rasas, and thus can be connected only vaguely with the quality of phonemic or semantic "sweetness" (2.290), but he otherwise makes no note of any category difficulties. For Dandin as for Bhamaha, rasa was native to another (i.e., dramaturgical) discourse, where it was more fully explained; in poetry, by contrast, the only category available for its analysis was the figure of speech. It would take several more centuries for it to be conceived of as the dominant feature of the literary work, in fact, the singular feature that distinguished literature from all other forms of language use.

FROM *LOOKING GLASS OF POETRY* OF DANDIN (D), WITH *RATNA'S GLORY* OF RATNASHRIJNANA (R) AND *GUARDING THE TRADITION* OF VADIJANGHALA (V)

(R) The author now addresses the language quality called "sweetness."

(D) (1.51) A poem is defined as "sweet" when it has rasa. Rasa is found in both the language and the subject matter, and insightful people become intoxicated by it like bees by honey.

(R) By "insightful people" is meant poets who understand rasa. . . . It is they who become intoxicated by a poem filled with rasa.[77]

(V) By specifying that this is rasa in the *words* of a poem, the author is distinguishing the language quality from what will later be defined as the ornament called the "rasa-laden" statement (2.278). For the latter is concerned with the erotic and other rasas, whereas what is meant here is the sweetness of the very words themselves.

(D) (1.52) When one word is experienced as similar to another by reason of this or that sound, we have what is called "proximity of words," i.e., such as are comparable in form and the like. This conveys rasa, and can be combined with alliteration.

(R) Words that have similar sounds and that are not placed far apart from each other produce rasa in poetry, because that is sweet. This is "word rasa," known as "proximity of similar words" or "sound similarity," and is much prized by southerners. Alliteration is word rasa too and is likewise prized by southerners. . . . Thus word rasa is shown to be of two sorts . . . proximity and alliteration, which can be used together but need not be. A poem lacking both, however, will lack rasa, and poets will not savor it.

(V) "This or that sound" refers to such things as phonemic quality, accent, or syllabic weight.

. . . .

(R) The author now proceeds to explain "content rasa":

(D) (1.62–64) Although any ornament can endow a meaning with rasa, the most important factor is sophistication. "I want you, girl, why don't you want me?" This sort of locution is vulgar, and produces poetry devoid of rasa. "The god of love, that wretch, shows me no pity, but happily he bears you no grudge, my sloe-eyed girl": a locution like this, on the other hand, which is sophisticated, conveys rasa.

. . . .

(R) The author now defines three ornaments: affectionate utterance, rasa-laden statement, and haughty declaration:

(D) (2.273) An affectionate utterance is an expression of heightened affection;[78] a rasa-laden statement is one beautified by rasa; in a haughty declaration the speaker's ego is prominent. All three, when they reach their intensified state,[79] become ornaments.

(R) An expression of "heightened," or intensified, affection . . . is an "affectionate utterance." A statement that is "beautified" by reason of the erotic or other rasa to be communicated is called "rasa-laden." A declaration in which "ego," or haughtiness, is conspicuous is "haughty." In this group of three ornaments, "intensification" is said to be present to the highest degree—that is, the expression of emotion is maximal, that of rasa unalloyed, that of haughtiness powerful. This sense is already expressed by the comparative suffix (used in the first case) and the possessive suffixes (used in the latter two), which can denote "to a high degree."[80] The added term "in their intensified state" is, hence, intentionally redundant, but it is used to make the point absolutely clear.

The author offers an example of an affectionate utterance:

(D) (2.274–275)

"The joy I experience today. . . ."[81] This is how Vidura spoke, and properly so, since such contentment can be gotten from no other source. And Krishna, who can be won over by nothing more than devotion, was overjoyed.[82]

(2.276–277)

"The moon, the sun, the wind, the earth, the sky, the sacrificer, fire, and water— who are we to bypass all your forms, Lord, and see you in your very person?"[83]

This expression of joy, felt by King Ratavarman[84] when the deity appeared right before his eyes, is to be understood as the affectionate utterance ornament.[85]

(R) The author now illustrates and explains the rasa-laden ornament:[86]

(D) (2.278)

"The woman I thought was dead and hoped to rejoin by taking my own life— here she stands, my Avanti! How could I, while still alive, have gotten this woman back?"[87]

(R) This would seem to exemplify joy, which has already been given. To clarify this the author now explains the distinction between the affectionate utterance and the rasa-laden statement.

(D) (2.279) What was shown earlier was joy, whereas in the poem just given we have sexual desire that has become the erotic rasa thanks to the full development of its form. This type of statement is called rasa-laden.

(R) In the affectionate utterance ornament previously described, the joy or contentment was shown to be directed toward a male.[88] The subsequent illustration is an example of desire or passion for a female, a particular emotion that is the source of the erotic rasa and is produced by the requisite foundational and stimulant factors and made known by the requisite reactions— as the author says, "that has become the erotic rasa," i.e., that has been transmuted into the form of that particular rasa. How exactly? "Thanks to the full development of its form." Here "form" means its nature, its own particular type of mental formation, whereas "full development" refers to a state of being stimulated or highly strengthened.[89] . . . What the author means is this: desire that remains unintensified, existing through the inner principle[90] and having the nature of a particular mental formation, will be unmanifest. In this state it is called an emotion, and that is why "emotion" is described as a purely mental transformation (and hence unmanifest). This same emotion when stimulated becomes manifest through some "reaction," understood as the verbal[91] or other register of acting. At that point it turns into what is called rasa. This is why it has been said that it is the emotions, once made manifest, that receive the name rasa. Further detail may be had from the treatises devoted to the topic.

The same reasoning can be understood to apply to the other rasas the author is about to discuss, the violent and so on, which have the form of particular transformations of the emotions anger and so on.

(D) (2.280)
"The one who dragged Draupadi by the hair before my very eyes—here he is, the vile Duhshasana! And now that I have caught him, he will not live a moment longer."[92]

(R) The author points out the rasa here:

(D) (2.281) In this poem, the anger of Bhima as he watches his enemy achieves the highest stage and becomes the violent rasa. This ornament is called a rasa-laden statement.

(R) Here "achieving the highest stage," or the high point of intensification, means reaching the state of manifestation through the reactions.

(D) (2.282)
"Without having conquered land and sea, offered many sacrifices,
and given wealth to suppliants, how could I call myself a king?"

(R) He now explains which of the several rasas this is:

(D) (2.283) In this poem, the emotion of determination is intensified and thereby comes to exist as the heroic rasa, with the power of making the words a rasa-laden statement.

(R) It is "intensified," that is, it reaches the highest stage, insofar as it is made manifest.

(D) (2.284)
"The queen, whose tender body was pained by a bed of flowers—
how can she lay herself down on a blazing funeral pyre?"

(R) The author now clarifies which of the many rasas this is:

(D) (2.285) In this poem, it is the tragic rasa that, once it has attained prominence, comes to be considered an ornament. The same holds for the remaining rasas, the macabre, the comic, the fantastic, and the fearful.

(R) Here, in the manner already discussed, the "tragic"—that is to say, the particular type of emotion called grief that provides the basis for a particular type of narrative dealing with tragic matters[93]—when it reaches "prominence," i.e., comes to manifestation,[94] transforms into the tragic rasa, and is held by knowledgeable people to be an "ornament" or adornment to the literary text.

(D) (2.286)
"Drinking the blood of your enemies time and again from cupped hands,
the ghouls garlanded with entrails go dancing with headless corpses."

(R) Here the emotion called disgust is generated by the requisite foundational factor and made manifest by a physical reaction of the corresponding form. As it takes on the nature of a rasa, the macabre, which has the form of something loathsome, is considered an ornament.

(D) (2. 287)
"My friend, you'd better move your blouse to cover this fresh line of scratches on your breast—aren't you supposed to be angry with him still?"[95]

(R) The sight of the immodest marks is the foundational factor, which brings about the emotion called amusement, and this in its intensified form becomes the comic rasa.

(D) (2.288)
"On the trees in the garden of the gods, the sprouts are silken cloths,
the flowers necklaces and other jewelry, the branches mansions—how marvelous!"

(R) Here the emotion called amazement, rendered preeminently clear, becomes the rasa of the fantastic.

(D) (2.289)
"This is the thunderbolt of Indra that bears fire on its blades,
and just thinking of it makes the demons' wives miscarry."

(R) Here the emotion called fear, which mutates into the form of the fearful rasa, is said to function as an ornament.

Since the rasa-laden statement would seem to have already been addressed under the heading of the language quality sweetness, it might be unclear why it is being discussed again. To this point the author now speaks:

(D) (2.290) Earlier it was pointed out that in the case of sweetness, rasa is the source of sophistication in discourse. Here, by contrast, we are discussing the nature of the rasa-laden ornament of language that is connected with the eight rasas.

(R) By "discourse" is meant the content conveyed by the poem . . . and by "rasa" is meant what has been called the rasa of sense. This was indicated earlier, on the occasion of distinguishing between the sound and sense aspects that are both common to sweetness, when the author stated, "Although any ornament can endow a meaning with rasa, the most important factor is sophistication."[96]

He now exemplifies and explains haughty declaration:

(D) (2.291–292)
"Do not fear I will take vengeance for your crimes:
my sword would never fall upon an enemy in retreat."
Here an enemy seized in battle has been freed by a prideful man. This and other similar kinds of expression are known as "haughty declaration."

(R) Another example:[97]

"I would sacrifice my life in the fire of battle should some powerful enemy appear before me.
But were I ever to be so cowardly—I, Ravana!—as to give back Sita, I would cease to draw breath."[98]

[(D) (2.298) According to experts the "elevated" ornament is when supreme grandeur of either sentiment or material wealth is shown.

(2.299) "Raghava was incapable to disobeying his father's command, a man who had no qualms about the heavy task of decapitating Ravana."[99]

(2.300) "Only with difficulty could Hanuman recognize the lord of Lanka since a hundred images of him were reflected on the jeweled palace walls."]

1.3 RASA AS A FIGURE OF SPEECH: THE LATE VIEW

Essential Compendium of the Ornament of Poetry of Udbhata (c. 800) with the *Brief Elucidation* of Pratiharenduraja (c. 900) and the *Exegesis* of Tilaka (c. 1100)

On the testimony of the *River of Kings*, the mid-twelfth-century history of Kashmir, Udbhata was the chief court scholar of King Jayapida of Kashmir (c. 800). Later evidence, preserved in a commentary on a text on logic, suggests that Udbhata (or *an* Udbhata) was a very independent-minded grammarian, even a contrarian, as well as a materialist (*carvāka*), and a renegade (*dhūrta*) materialist at that.[100] The extant works—*The Essential Compendium*, fragments of his commentary on the poetics of Bhamaha, vague references to followers of his commentary (Audbhatas) on the *Treatise on Drama*, along with a few quotations from an unnamed work attributed to Udbhata by Pratiharenduraja in his commentary on the present work—are inconclusive on the question of identity. Would a materialist have written a court epic on the marriage of the god Shiva and Parvati, as our Udbhata did, borrowing large selections of the work for use as examples in *The Essential Compendium*? Would a Shaiva sectarian have composed one of the great expressions in Sanskrit of the universal solidarity of humankind?[101] Why not, after all? In the absence of counterevidence, the contrarian grammarian, renegade materialist, and radical poetician can be taken to be one and the same person.

As for the commentators on his extant work, the older, Pratiharenduraja, tells us that he came from the Konkan on the west coast and was a student of Mukula Bhatta, an important language philosopher in Kashmir, which would date him to 900. Tilaka, who knew and followed Induraja closely, was the father of the poetician Ruyyaka (c. 1150), and thus lived around 1100.[102] We have no other works from either scholar.

Udbhata's treatment of aesthetic emotion marks the final—and by now contradiction-riddled—stage where the conceptual framework of the older rhetorical analysis that had contained it, so far as narrative poetry is concerned, was stressed to the breaking point. And Udbhata nearly broke it.[103] He radically redefines the earlier notions of Bhamaha and Dandin, formulated when dramaturgical rasa theory had yet to be fully adapted to poetry, and masterfully assimilates them to what was to become—or instead, here for the first time has become—the classical typology, something not unexpected from the first known commentator on the *Treatise on Drama*. Thus, the ornament known as the "rasa-laden" statement, earlier viewed as heightened or climactic emotion, now explicitly[104] becomes the "full realization" of rasa, with the complete panoply of aesthetic elements (the foundational and stimulant factors, and the rest). "Affectionate utterance" is more clearly defined as the "intimation" of an emotion, where a rasa is not fully developed.[105] "Haughty declaration" is transformed into an utterance marked by social impropriety, and hence reconceived as the "semblance of rasa"—the very idea, and the technical term, appearing here for the first time (4.7). Finally, an ornament that Bhamaha and Dandin had not even thought of as pertaining to the realm of affect, "happy coincidence" (*samāhita*), is redefined by Udbhata as "quiescence," where an existing rasa is resolved and no other takes its place, a category complemented by three others (the emergence of a rasa, the conjuncture of two rasas, the oscillation between rasas) in the works of later writers.[106]

Yet despite this close approximation to the dramaturgical model, Udbhata continues, like Bhamaha and Dandin before him, to categorize all these forms of expression as figures of speech like the tropes based on semantic indirection, such as double entendre (*śliṣṭa*), and contentual figures, such as the "elevated" (*udātta*), where "some richly appointed object" ornaments a poem, "or the deed of a great being when intended as a subordinate feature and not as the main narrative itself" (4.8).[107] By the early tenth century Induraja was registering concern over the tensions here—and at the same time marking how far the conceptual terrain had shifted over the course of the preceding century—when he wrote, "Whether the rasas and the emotions, given that they are the source of the highest literary beauty, can really be 'ornaments' of literature or are rather its very 'life force' will not be a subject for consideration here lest it unduly lengthen the book."[108]

In one of his most notable, and most controversial, innovations, Udbhata includes among the features required to indicate a rasa's presence in a poem the use of the "proper term" for an emotion (and judging from some extant literature, contemporary poets and playwrights may have felt the same way).[109] "A proper term," Induraja explains, "is the actual lexeme, 'desire,' for example. This gives us to understand the presence of the emotion because it refers to it." Udbhata's analysis would be critiqued within a generation or two by Shri Shankuka, and what for Udbhata was a component in the creation of rasa became for later scholars a literary flaw. It does not require much reflection to see that announcing "This is erotic" does not per se make a scene erotic (and can in fact be counterproductive). Then again, if an emotion's "proper term" is more broadly conceived, the issue becomes more complicated and avoidance more difficult. Saying "I love you" hardly negates the aesthetic effect of a love scene, whereas for some transitory emotions there is no way to indicate their presence *except* by naming them (as Induraja points out). The real complexities here will become apparent in Abhinavagupta's later rethinking of the question.[110]

In intellectual-historical terms, the commentary of Pratiharenduraja is especially valuable in giving us a sense of the wider understanding of rasa at the start of the tenth century. In fact, it provides the first systematic account we have since Bharata of the components of rasa theory. And little in his account deviates from Bharata, though uncertainties mark his exposition at times (transitory emotions, for example, are rather redundantly said to intimate transitory emotions, and according to his definition of "reactions," they would seem to comprise what the tradition has usually called the registers of "acting," see KASS 4.2, below). His thought, as in that of his near contemporary at the other side of India, Ratnashrijnana, continues to be dominated by the idea that rasa is nothing other than an intensified state of the stable emotion, and that the emotion in question is located in the character: when the quiescence of rasa is discussed, for example, it is Shiva who is said to have reactions to his erotic rasa (on 4.7). Induraja, accordingly, like Udbhata and his predecessors, concentrates his analysis of rasa on its features that are immanent in the text rather than on the phenomenon of reader response, though he does cite one verse (on 4.3–4) that clearly derives from the new reception theory.[111] The history of the discourse was reaching a stage where the line between seeing rasa as constructed in the text and seeing it as cognized by the reader was becoming ever more blurry.

There are some additional innovations in Induraja's thought. We encounter here for the first time the idea that the stable emotions are not understood "in their unique individuality, but rather in a general form" (*sāmānyarūpa*), which, while not the theory of "commonization" (*sādhāraṇīkaraṇa*) that Bhatta Nayaka would introduce around the same time (and of which Tilaka was fully aware), has no antecedent in Udbhata's work itself, and Induraja's use of the term may reflect something of the new thinking about rasa taking place in his time. Rasa is now also intimately linked with a didactic component, since it is a "means of attaining the four ends of man" (4.3–4), something that would be more expansively described by both Abhinavagupta and Bhoja.

One last point of interest pertains to Udbhata's redefinition of the affectionate trope, which only "intimates" emotion rather than displays it clearly, as in the rasa-laden figure. Induraja designates this "emotion poetry," a new term that will later become standard, if rare in actual usage. This refers to a poem or portion of a literary text where emotion is thought of as present but not developed—or, more properly, unable to be developed—to the point of becoming a rasa. For all later authorities, this arrested condition results from the fact that the *object* of the emotion is not of the sort required for the rasa to develop. Desire, for example, the emotion that leads to the full development of the erotic rasa, must by definition be sexual desire between a young man and young woman of high status. Yet one can feel desire for a child, a parent, or a god, and literature that addresses such feeling, where the rasa cannot be fully developed because the desire is not of the sort that can be normally consummated, will remain "emotion poetry" (so Tilaka). For Induraja, the rasa has not achieved "full enhancement" because of the treatment of the aesthetic elements, not because of the nature of the object of emotion (in this case, an animal adopted as Parvati's child). The dispute would be adjudicated in the coming decades.

FROM *ESSENTIAL COMPENDIUM OF THE ORNAMENT OF POETRY* OF UDBHATA (U) WITH THE *BRIEF ELUCIDATION* OF PRATIHARENDURAJA (P) AND THE *EXEGESIS* OF TILAKA (T)

(U) (4.1) Some scholars say that the following are also ornaments: the affectionate; the rasa-laden; the impulsive; the disingenuous statement; the quiescent; the elevated, which is twofold; and double entendre.[112]

(P) First of all, the affectionate:

(U) (4.2) When a poem is composed so as to *intimate* the emotions such as desire and so on by means of the reactions and the rest, scholars define it as the "affectionate" ornament.

(T) The desire here is the sort directed toward a deity, a guru, a king, and so on.[113] When the desire directed toward the beloved is indicated, the author will call the ornament the "rasa-laden."

(P) There are three types of emotion: stable emotions, transitory emotions, and psychophysical responses. . . .[114] All told these number fifty, and there are four things that "intimate" them:[115] the reactions, the factors, the transitory emotions, and their own proper terms. With respect to these four, the reactions are themselves of four sorts:[116] physical, verbal, psychophysical, and costuming. Physical refers to hand gestures and other such forms of acting;

verbal to the use of intonation and so on; psychophysical to paralysis and the rest; costuming to headgear, dress, and so on. This fourfold set of reactions functions as effects that give us to understand the presence of the emotions that are their causes.

[48] Factors are of two sorts, foundational and stimulant. A foundational factor is the substratum[117] that enables a stable emotion to arise: Sita, for example, is a foundational factor in the case of Rama. A stimulant factor is that by virtue of which the stable emotions become intensified: the appropriate season, for example; flower garlands; scented creams and the like in the case of the erotic rasa. These two sorts of factors function as causes of desire and the other stable emotions, and as such they give us to understand the presence of the emotions, which are their effects, just as the arrival of dense dark clouds gives us to understand the coming of rain. In the same way that a given effect, once clearly comprehended, is invariably related to its cause, so a given cause, once clearly comprehended, is invariably related to its effect, as is generally demonstrated in everyday experience. Accordingly, the factors, insofar as they are causes, give us to understand the existence of the stable emotions.

(T) (p. 33) An emotion does not become the life force of literature merely insofar as it is inferred, but rather when it is understood as being general[118] and thereby comes within the domain of the act of tasting. This applies to rasa as well. That is why experts have said that rasa, emotion, the semblances of rasas and emotions, and cessation are all "implied." What Udbhata has said so far implicitly concurs on this point. If we examine the real nature of things, rasas, emotions, and so on are not actually inferred at all, since factors, reactions, and transitory emotions are not primary causes, effects, and auxiliary causes. If they were, the *Sutra on Rasa* would have said that rasa arises from the conjunction of primary *causes, effects,* and auxiliary *causes.* To examine how this is the case, however, would expand the size of my book, so I will not dilate upon it here.[119]

(P) (p. 48) "Transitory emotion," for its part, is a particular state of a stable emotion, and comprises despair and the rest. And because it is a concomitant, the transitory emotion leads us to assume the presence of the stable emotion, the way one wheel of a cart leads us to assume the existence of the others. Finally, "proper term" means the actual lexeme, "desire," for example, which gives us to understand the presence of the emotion because it refers to it. Although of course we do not observe that such words as "desire" and so on are a *sufficient* condition for really understanding an emotion like desire—since that is something whose nature is a unique particular[120] and thus accessible only through immediate experience[121]—we nonetheless do find that they in part, like the physical reactions, can become a condition for understanding the emotions. After all, just as the reactions and so on do not give us to understand the presence of the stable emotions in their unique individuality, but rather in a general form,[122] so do their proper terms. Enough said.

These four—the reactions, factors, transitory emotions, and proper terms[123]—are thus the causes for understanding the emotions. To quote Bhatta Udbhata: "The emotions have four different elements."[124] Now, when a literary work is composed by means of things "intimating" the fifty emotions, desire and all the rest—that is, things that lead us to assume their presence not in their sheer individuality but in their general state—by means of the reactions and the other three elements, either aggregated or disaggregated[125] as appropriate, we have the "affectionate" ornament. The word for "affectionate," *preyaḥ*, a comparative of the adjective "beloved," *priya*, expresses the foundational factor of desire, whereby desire itself is indirectly connoted; and since all fifty emotions are invariably listed along with desire,[126] those in addition to desire can hereby be understood to be implied.[127] Thus, the affectionate is metonymy for emotion poetry in general. Given that the poem is the thing to be ornamented, the emotions here function as ornaments. An example of the affectionate:

(U) Feeling a yearning no different from affection for a son,
Parvati drew him into her embrace and began to comfort him.[128]

(P) Drawing to the breast is the physical [49] register of acting; comforting or consoling the verbal register; the baby animal (the antecedent of "him") is the foundational factor. The longing awakened by her affection is the transitory emotion, since her "yearning," or desire, insofar as it is said not to differ from affection for a son, must have some connection with a species of longing. "Yearning" itself is a proper term. Thus, by these four features, the physical reactions[129] and so on, we are enabled to infer[130] the presence of the emotion of desire in the form of parental affection. Other verses could similarly be adduced for the other emotions as well.

The rasa-laden:

(U) (4.3–4) The rasa-laden is where the coming into being of a rasa, the erotic and the rest, is *clearly* shown, with its basis in five features: its proper term, stable emotions, transitory emotions, factors, and registers of acting.

The erotic, comic, tragic, violent, heroic, fearful, macabre, fantastic, and peaceful are the nine rasas that have been handed down for drama.[131]

(P) The rasas, which are nine in number, consist in the full enhancement of the nine stable emotions, desire and the rest, in such a way that each becomes, as appropriate,[132] the means of attaining the four ends of man, or the grounds for avoiding their opposite. Insofar as they are savored in this enhanced form[133] they are referred to by the technical term "rasa," or taste, connected as it is with a specific kind of savoring. By contrast, since there is no such savoring of the transitory emotions, despair and the rest, we do not apply to them the technical term "rasa," connected as the word is with that specific condition of reference. If one intends merely to express savoring pure and simple, there is no contradiction in using the term in reference to the transitory emotions, any more than in reference to the physical tastes, sweet, sour, and the rest. To quote the remark Rudrata makes after listing the rasas, the erotic and so on: "They are called 'rasas' because they are tasted [*rasana*]."[134] To quote again:[135] "The special sort of 'savorable' consciousness by which the four ends of man and their opposites are understood as things to be attained and avoided,[136] respectively, is held to be rasa."[137] Here the word "sort" indicates that the use of the technical term "rasa" in the case of the erotic and so on is dependent on a special kind of savoring.

(T) (p. 33) These rasas are such insofar as they enable us to achieve the four ends of man, and avoid their opposite.

(P) These nine rasas, the erotic and so on, come to be understood through five different components. To quote Udbhata again, "The rasas have five different elements."[138] One of these elements is the proper terms that are expressive of the rasas—for example, in the case of the erotic, the word "erotic" itself.

(T) (p. 34) These proper terms have the capacity to express the rasas only generally, not in their individual manifestation. Otherwise the very verse cited above, "The erotic, comic, tragic," would provide us as complete a comprehension of rasa as drama itself does.

(P) Next, the nine stable emotions, which can be called the material cause of the rasas. [50] Then the transitory emotions, despair and so on, which are particular states of the rasas. Then the two types of factors, which are the instrumental cause of the rasas (in one case, a woman, for example; in the other, the right season, garlands, scented creams, and so on). Last, the four registers of acting, the physical and the rest, which are the effects of rasa.

(T) The term "acting" in the verse signifies the reactions.

(P) These five features, the proper term and the rest, whether aggregated or disaggregated, function as the basis of the rasas; the poem that, as a consequence,[139] has the capacity to exhibit the rasas in "clear" form is the ornament "rasa-laden." Rasas, after all, are ornaments to the poem.[140]

(T) The factors must be directly expressed in the poem, whereas the transitory emotions can be implied. The stable emotion, however, can only be understood by implication, for rasa is nothing but the stable emotion so understood.[141] If it could be directly expressed, the physical and other registers of acting meant to function as inferential signs for it would have no function—and a poem would as a result be rather silly.[142]

(P) Here is an example:

(U) As Shiva contemplated the full extent of Parvati's virtues
his passion, laden with fantasies, became overpowering.
His body grew slick with sweat and the hair so stiffened
it looked like the filaments massed in the calyx of a *kadamba* bud,
while his face was ornamented with a look now pregnant with longing,
now immobilized by anxiety, now languid with delight.

(P) What is being presented here is the erotic thwarted, of the craving sort,[143] with reference to the lord. Its proper term is "passion . . . became overpowering," with the stable emotion being revealed by the word "passion" in the same verse, for the erotic rasa is in essence the enhancement of desire, and "desire" in this discourse is the passion of two young people for each other. Thus, since it expresses a particular type of desire, the word "passion" here may be taken to function as the proper term for the stable emotion. The transitory emotions are longing, anxiety, and joy (representing "delight"), and they are revealed by their proper terms. Perspiration and horripilation, two psychophysical responses, are expressed by their proper terms; they are at the same time transitory emotions, since, like despair and the rest, they are particular states of the stable emotions, and hence transitory. The foundational factor is referred to in the phrase "As Shiva contemplated," since the goddess becomes a factor insofar as contemplated[144] as a being endowed with various virtues. As for the forms of acting, that which concerns glancing is referred to by the word "look." Thus, in these verses the erotic rasa (of the craving type) is manifested[145] by the five elements, proper terms, and so on. Other examples could be cited for the other rasas. Now, whether the rasas and the emotions, given that they are the source of the highest literary beauty, are really "ornaments" of literature or its very life force will not be a subject for consideration here lest it unduly lengthen the book. Similarly, I will not analyze the nature of rasa and emotion because it would require a great deal of comment and in any case is not directly germane.

(p. 51) Now the impulsive:[146]

(U) (4.5) When rasas or emotions are presented as contrary to propriety because they are caused by craving or anger or the like, we have what is called the impulsive.

(P) Sometimes rasas and emotions are presented in accordance with our moral sensibilities, sometimes in conflict with them. In the former case, the ornaments are referred to as the emotional and the rasa-laden. Where, however, a work presents rasas and emotions that contain a conflict with those sensibilities and with the acceptable behavior rooted in them, the poetry is designated as "impulsive." Rasas and emotions are contrary to propriety when they are presented as being caused by passion, hatred, or delusion. The ornament is therefore called "impulsive," because of the presence of impulsiveness or force as prompted by the agent's own misjudgments. An example:

(U) Shiva's craving increased to such a degree that he was ready to quit
the path of the good and take Himalaya's daughter by force.

(P) Here the text describes the taking by force of an unmarried maiden on the part of the lord—though he immeasurably excels all worldly beings—something that is caused by his powerful passion and is contrary to our established moral principles. Hence the impetuosity. His "craving increased" is the "proper term" for the erotic, since the erotic rasa, given that it is an enhancement of desire, essentially consists in the increase of craving. Furthermore, the word "craving" comprised in the phrase is the proper term for the desire that is the stable emotion of the erotic. "Himalaya's daughter" is the foundational factor; "by force" expresses the transitory emotion agitation; "ready to quit the path of the good" the transitory emotion confusion; "ready to . . . take" the bodily reaction. Thus by means of the five elements, the proper term and the rest, the erotic of the impulsive variety is indicated. The impulsive can be similarly exemplified for the other rasas and emotions.[147]

. . . .

(P) (p. 52) Next, the quiescent:

(U) (4.7) The quiescent is when the existence[148] of a rasa, emotion, or the semblances of rasas and emotions, is presented as quiescent, with a complete absence of the reactions of any other rasa or emotion.

(P) So far it has been stated that there are two sorts of rasas and emotions, depending on whether or not they are in conflict with moral standards. When the words "rasa" and "emotion" are used all by themselves, the intention is to refer to the second type; the word "semblance" is added when there is a conflict. When the "existence"—that is, the connection with their human substratum—of a rasa or emotion, or the semblance of rasa or emotion, is presented as quiescent, we have the ornament known as quiescent (*samāhita*), for we then have a resolution (*samādhāna*) or reconciliation (*samādhi*) or avoidance of rasas. One might ask whether the cessation of an antecedent rasa (since the existence of some rasa is being avoided in the poem) would not of necessity lead to the presentation of some subsequent rasa, so that one of these ornaments, the rasa-laden and so on, would wind up intruding. It is to address this concern that the author adds "with a complete absence of the reactions of any other rasa or emotion."

. . . [53] Where the force of the predisposition[149] occasioned by an earlier rasa is such that, even if the rasa has ceased, another form of rasa fails to display itself, or if it should, it disappears by virtue of some intervening matter, we have the quiescent ornament. An example:

(U) His loving eyes, the movements of his glances, the play of his brows,
his clear complexion, the horripilation[150] in his body slick with sweat—
all this the lord calmed, as well as his limbs aflame with the fever of love,
and he approached the Mountain's daughter with a salutation.

(P) "Calmed" means restored to their natural state. . . . The lord's reactions to the erotic rasa—the longing in his eyes and so on—are made to disappear by the transitory emotion termed "dissimulation," that is, covering his face. The phrase "with a salutation" indicates this concealing of the face.[151]

(U) (4.8) The elevated is either some richly appointed object or the deed of a great being when intended as a subordinate feature and not as the main narrative itself.[152]

(P) "Riches" are treasure such as gold or other wealth. A richly appointed object adorns the poem's subject matter.

(P) An example of the first.

And Shiva said, "On Himalaya pearls are produced by boar, bamboo, and elephants,[153]
and even Shabara women can use them at will to adorn themselves.
One of its peaks, Gandhamadana, scrapes the sky with its summits
made of precious stones:[154] sapphire, beryl, and rubies.
Its tablelands are made of solid gold,
and vast Emerald Mountain forms one of its foothills.
And when at the end of a cosmic age Earth falls into the underworld,
it does not fall along with her—no, it is then that its full extent is finally revealed."

(P) (p. 54) Here, masses of precious objects have been presented in the narrative, and this is what makes it elevated. It ornaments the poem by suggesting these objects' supernatural effects. The presentation of a "richly appointed object" forms only one type of elevated figure; the other is an act of a noble-minded being seeking to achieve what is good and avoid what is bad. It would be imprudent to assert that when such a narrative is being presented we have a case of the rasa-laden figure simply because it gives us a sense of the erotic or other rasa, for the noble-minded act here is a subsidiary sentence meaning, insofar as it is subordinate to some other thing. For obviously here the behavior of some great person, since it is subordinate to some other meaning, cannot be the main purport of the sentence. We have the rasa-laden figure, by contrast, only where the rasas are understood as the *main* purport: in such a case they are being savored in the form of an enhanced stable emotion (itself the means for attaining one of the four ends of man, or avoiding their opposite), since that is the point upon which the sentence comes to rest. How then could we have here even a hint of that figure?

(T) (p. 37) With the words "subordinate feature" the author shows that the elevated is not in essence the rasa-laden figure. For here the act of the great being has a secondary, not a primary, role.[155]

(P) Here follows an example of the second:

> (U) "The great Himalaya—so stable it stood unshaken even when the stout shoulder of the Primal Boar struck it repeatedly—has a daughter, and this blessed lady is she."

(P) Here the principal sentence meaning is Himalaya's stability. The act of Lord Vishnu in the Boar incarnation when engaged in saving the universe, which does give us a sense of the heroic rasa, is a subsidiary sentence, and hence intended as subordinate.

1.4 RASA AS THE CHARACTER'S EMOTION, AND HOW WE KNOW IT

**Commentary on the* Treatise on Drama, of Bhatta Lollata (c. 825)

Lamentably meager though the remaining fragments of his work may be, with Bhatta Lollata we can perceive the true commencement of the extraordinarily intense investigation into literary emotion that would make the next three centuries in India the most fertile in the history of aesthetics anywhere before European modernity. This commencement was no doubt the result of a rediscovery of, or at least reengagement with, Bharata's *Treatise on Drama* in Kashmir in the early ninth century, a work that raised, in a productive way, as many questions about rasa as it answered.

Although Bhatta Lollata is cited before Udbhata in what would appear to be a chronological listing in a verse in a fourteenth-century musicology treatise ("The commentators on the treatise of Bharata were Lollata, Udbhata, Shankuka, Abhinavagupta, and Kirtidhara"),[156] the selection below from Abhinavagupta's *New* Dramatic Art makes clear that Bhatta Lollata opposed some positions of "Udbhata's followers," so he is likely to be later than 800; and since he himself is the direct object of critique by Shri Shankuka, whom we can reasonably place around 850 (see next selection), putting Bhatta Lollata early in the first half of the ninth century would make sense of all our data.

Although a dozen short citations on technical questions of dramaturgy are preserved from his commentary on the *Treatise*, what we know about Bhatta Lollata's view of rasa is largely restricted to the brief passages presented below. But two verses from what appears to be another work of his on literary criticism, entitled the *Exegesis of Rasa* (*Rasavivaraṇa*), are cited by the late twelfth-century scholar Hemachandra when discussing complex figures of sound:

> Such figures as this have no purpose other than displaying the poet's skill, and I will not bother with defining their subtypes. They are really an excrescence on the literary work since they do not serve the purpose of teaching any of the ends of man.

> Good poets, after all, compose poetry to turn tender minds toward those ends, and a poem where the rasa is completely impeded by sound figures requiring special effort to make sense of is hardly a happy means to such a goal. And in actual fact, descriptions of rivers, mountains, oceans, and so on really just destroy the rasa; how much more so an altogether impenetrable poem. Thus Lolata [*sic*]: "Exertions in describing rivers, mountains, oceans, cities, horses, towns, and the like that have no purpose other than displaying a poet's skills are not approved by serious scholars for inclusion in literary works. All the variety of sound figures, 'twinned' forms (*yamaka*) and the rest . . . completely impede the rasa, and if not simply a poet's egotistical ostentation, are a result of his blindly following convention."[157]

Even from this brief citation, Bhatta Lollata can be seen as a forerunner of Anandavardhana in holding that rasa must constitute the core of the literary experience, so much so that anything not contributing to rasa, let alone detracting from it, must be eliminated. A twelfth-century commentator preserves a historical memory of the importance of Bhatta Lollata's views by declaring that if "Lollata, mountainlike himself, could not plumb the depths of the ocean of rasa," then who else could?[158]

Bhatta Lollata's interpretation of Bharata's *Sutra on Rasa* marks the starting point ofwhat would evolve into the standard historical narrative of the development of rasa theory, one that would endure basically unchanged to the end of the seventeenth century. Bhatta Lollata argues first that there is one crucial thing left unstated in the *Sutra on Rasa*, namely, the place in the whole process of the stable emotion itself. It is when the aesthetic elements are "conjoined" *with the stable emotion*, he asserts, that rasa arises, because rasa is in fact nothing but the stable emotion in a state of being "strengthened" or "enhanced" by these elements. Moreover, the stable emotion in question is that of the character and the character alone; it is decidedly not that of the spectator, about whom Bhatta Lollata, to judge from our fragments, is silent and apparently indifferent. The same holds for the reactions: these are responses in the main character to his own stable emotion, not those produced by his rasa in another character, let alone the reactions of the viewer/reader, as later thinkers would maintain.[159] For Bhatta Lollata, "reactions" are the sorts of physical responses discussed in the *Treatise* itself, as in the case of the erotic rasa: "The erotic is to be acted out by reactions such as the skillful play of the eyes, movements of the eyebrows, and sidelong glances."[160] Hence, it is in the character that rasa exists "in the literal sense," and in the actor only figuratively—but in no sense in the spectator, an interpretation whose reality later commentators would confirm even as they sought to refute it.[161] In fact, Bhatta Lollata's understanding of the ontology of rasa accords fully with the position of Bharata himself, for whom rasa is the intensified stable emotion and simply and naturally "arises" from the conjuncture of the aesthetic elements.[162] This view would remain dominant for many subsequent writers, including Kuntaka at the end of the tenth century, and even Bhanudatta as late as the early fifteenth.

FROM *COMMENTARY ON THE* TREATISE ON DRAMA, OF BHATTA LOLLATA

Restatements of Bhatta Lollata's doctrine

(#1a, Abhinavagupta)[163]

Bhatta Lollata and others, first of all, have interpreted the *Sutra on Rasa* of the *Treatise on Drama* ("Rasa arises from the conjunction of factors, reactions, and transitory emotions") to mean: rasa arises when there is a "conjunction of factors, etc.," i.e., a conjunction between these aesthetic elements *and the stable emotion*. With respect to the elements, the factors[164] are the cause that generates a mental state, namely, the particular stable emotion itself. The reactions meant in this analysis are not those *produced by rasa*, since they could not then be counted as *causes of rasa* as they are here;[165] they are rather reactions to the stable emotion.[166] As for the transitory emotions, although they are themselves mental states and therefore should not be able to coexist with a stable emotion,[167] nonetheless what is meant here by "stable emotion" is simply the dominant predisposition.[168] It is just as in Bharata's analogy of the mixed drink: among the various condiments,[169] spices, and substances a certain one acts as the dominant "perfuming" element,[170] and hence is like the stable emotion, whereas other ingredients appear intermittently, and hence are like transitory emotions. Therefore, it is the stable emotion alone, once strengthened by the aesthetic elements, that constitutes rasa; in the unstrengthened state it remains a stable emotion.[171] Rasa in the primary sense of the term[172] exists in the character, Rama for instance; it exists in the actor only by force of his complete identification with the part.[173]

(#2a, Abhinavagupta)[174]

Bhatta Lollata argued that, although rasas were potentially infinite in number, it was the opinion of experts that only those listed by Bharata were capable of portrayal on the stage.[175]

(#3a, Abhinavagupta)[176]

According to the followers of Udbhata . . . were the actor really to undergo the experience of rasa and emotion he would be overcome by them during a death scene, say, and utterly fail to keep the rhythm of the dance. . . . Bhatta Lollata rejects this view of Udbhata's followers. For one thing, it is perfectly possible for the actor to experience rasas and emotions as well, by way of the stimulation of his own predispositions. For another, he would be able to keep the rhythm by virtue of his complete identification[177] with the part.

(#4a, Ruyyaka)[178]

In Bhatta Lollata's view, the "conjunction" referred to in the *Sutra on Rasa* is a threefold relationship: object and means of *production*; object and means of *knowledge*; object and means of *enhancement*. These correspond, respectively, to the factors (both foundational and stimulant), the reactions, and the transitory emotions. And on this view, accordingly, the word "arises" in the *Sutra* is explained in three different ways as well. Thus, rasa in the primary sense of the term is the stable emotion coming into being in the character and present in him in an enhanced form. In an unenhanced state it remains the stable emotion.[179] In the actor rasa exists only in a figurative sense.

Commentary on the Treatise on Drama, of Shri Shankuka (c. 850)

Like the work of Bhatta Lollata—who inaugurates an era of not only reengagement with the *Treatise on Drama* but also regrettable textual loss—all the writings of Shri Shankuka have disappeared save for a few fragments of commentary and poems. This marks what is probably the most grievous loss in the history of rasa discourse after Bhatta Nayaka.

There is no reason to doubt that the literary theorist we are concerned with was the same as the poet mentioned by the twelfth-century chronicler Kalhana as the author of the court poem *Triumph of the World* (*Bhuvanābhyudaya*). According to the *River of Kings*, in 850/1 during the reign of King Ajitapida, a terrible battle took place between two royal factions, and "the poet Shankuka, a veritable moon to swell the ocean of learned minds, composed a poem about this battle called *Triumph of the World*."[180] A dozen or so verses of Shankuka are preserved in an important fifteenth-century anthology, though these tell us nothing specific about the poet; one verse cited in another (dated 1363) is ascribed to "Shankuka, son of Mayura," though whether this is the Mayura who composed the *Hundred Poems to the Sun* (*Sūryaśataka*), we have no way of determining.[181] A late twelfth- or early thirteenth-century dramaturgical work refers to Shri Shankuka as a minister who was also a dramatist and remembers at least one of his plays, a romantic comedy called *The Earring of the Many-Colored Lotus* (*Citrotpalāvalambitaka*); it also refers to a dramaturgical argument of his not known from elsewhere.[182] That the text of his commentary on the *Treatise on Drama* was still available then seems impossible to believe; neither Mammata (c. 1050) nor Hemachandra (d. 1172), to judge from their interpretations, knew anything more about it than what they had read in Abhinavagupta.[183] At all events, with a likely date of about 850, we can be sure that Shri Shankuka preceded Anandavardhana (patronized by the subsequent king, Avantivarman, whose rule commenced in 855/6), of whom he appears from the surviving materials to know nothing.

An older argument that Shri Shankuka may have been a Buddhist is worth renewed consideration.[184] While each individual piece of evidence may not be all that strong, aggregated they carry some force. Shri Shankuka quotes a verse from the work of Dharmakirti, the great Buddhist philosopher of the seventh century, though other later scholars (such as Mahima Bhatta) who were not Buddhists quote him too. The honorific "Shri" might (though does not necessarily) suggest Buddhist affiliation, but he would have had to be a recent convert if he was indeed the son of the poet Mayura. The later critic Bhatta Tota is able to challenge one of Shri Shankuka's interpretations on the (implicit) grounds that it would force him to accept the category of the universal (*sāmānya* or *jāti*) and hence to fall victim to the fallacy of defending a position at variance with his core beliefs (*apasiddhānta*)—and it was only the Buddhists who rejected universals. He accords a central place in his theory to logic in general and inference in particular—one of the only two means of valid knowledge accepted by Buddhists—so much so that when he brings the buzzsaw of inferential reasoning down on Bhatta Lollata, very little is left. But then again, other, non-Buddhist thinkers were logicians in ninth- and tenth-century Kashmir, among them two of the greatest (Bhasarvajna and Bhatta Jayanta). Last, Abhinava appears to attribute to Shri Shankuka a new understanding of the tragic rasa, as general compassion rather than grief for the loss of a loved one, which fits with developments in Mahayana Buddhism.[185]

As in the case of Bhatta Lollata, Shri Shankuka's commentary on the *Treatise on Drama* has vanished except for the quotations preserved by Abhinavagupta, who, when he is not simply referencing his interpretations on technical questions of the theater or variant readings of the text,[186] opposes him at every point. But Shri Shankuka's ideas are not easily dismissed. His important distinction between referential and expressive language, whereby he critiques Udbhata's new doctrine of the place of the "proper terms" in the creation of rasa, would be picked up by Anandavardhana in his own way and restated by Abhinava even as he dismisses it.[187] His key argument in aesthetics, while apparently primarily an epistemological one (how rasa is apprehended), is actually ontological (what rasa is): because we cannot directly perceive emotion, we must infer it, and the content of such inferring, as in all inference, obviously cannot be the real thing itself. For precisely this reason Shri Shankuka understands rasa as an imitation (*anukaraṇa*, *anukṛti*, literally an "after-making") in the actor of the stable emotion in the main character. And all the aesthetic elements—the factors, reactions, and so on—can therefore be configured as components of an inferential process whereby this emotion in the character comes to be known.

Yet the kind of knowledge involved in such aesthetic inference is unlike any other. In cognizing an entity we typically reach one of four possible conclusions: that we have cognized the real entity; that the entity we have cognized is proven to be false after we first thought it to be real; that the cognition is uncertain—it may or may not be the entity we think; or that we have only cognized something similar to what we thought we had cognized. None of these possibilities pertains to aesthetic inference. Instead, as Shri Shankuka says, introducing an analogy that would be repeated down the ages and that tells us as much about the aesthetic objectives of Indian art as about Shri Shankuka's theory, our experience of the character in a play is like our experience of a painted figure, a horse for example, in a painting: we do not say the painting is *like* a horse, or posit any other of the three cognitive relationships; we simply acknowledge, "This is a horse." Rasa for Shri Shankuka would seem then to be a theory of perfect mimesis, where the viewer is not equating an image with a thing but simply seeing the thing itself so long as the play lasts or the painting is visible (although imperfect mimesis—absence of perspective, say—could arguably produce a reality effect as well). As the literary critic Kuntaka was to put it a century and a half after Shri Shankuka: "This is in the first place to postulate a comparability: between a poem and a painting, a poem's techniques and a painting's, and a poet and painter, because in both cases the principal objective is to reference the actual nature of a thing."[188]

Of course literature may be said to create what it only imitates (or is thought to imitate), and imitation, as Indian art shows, is no selfsame thing. Yet this was not the grounds on which the theory would be attacked. It was rather the notion of imitation itself, which was viewed as more a phenomenological than an aesthetic problem—whether and what precisely the actor is imitating, not whether the poet is imitating the world—and the critique of imitation on the part of Bhatta Tota in the following century would ensure for Shri Shankuka what Shri Shankuka himself had ensured for Bhatta Lollata: that his work would be consigned (almost) to oblivion.

FROM **COMMENTARY ON THE* TREATISE ON DRAMA, OF SHRI SHANKUKA

Restatements of Shri Shankuka's doctrine

(#1a, Abhinavagupta)[189]

Shri Shankuka rejects the view of Bhatta Lollata[190] for seven reasons: [1] Logically, we cannot have any awareness of a stable emotion *prior to* its connection with the aesthetic elements, since those elements are the inferential signs required for such an awareness. [We cannot, after all, have an awareness of fire on a mountain without first perceiving smoke, KA.]

[2] It would turn out that the stable emotions would have to have been mentioned prior to the rasa. [If in the definition of rasa as understood by Bhatta Lollata (where it is the stable emotion enhanced by the aesthetic elements that is rasa) the stable emotion were in fact the subject and rasa the predicate, the former should have been mentioned first by Bharata, KLV.][191] [That is to say, if Bharata had thought it was the

stable emotion itself that turned into rasa as a result of a conjunction—having first been brought into being by the factors, indicated by the reactions, and enhanced by the transitory emotions—then it would have been appropriate to list and define the stable emotions first, which he has not done. The rasas are in fact listed and defined first, KA; and the stable emotions only later, KLV.]

[3] If rasa were simply the stable emotion enhanced, no purpose would be served in providing as Bharata does another explanation when the stable emotion is supposedly augmented so as to become a rasa. [Why, that is, does the sage first describe the factors and reactions of the rasas, and once again describe precisely the same factors and reactions of the stable emotions? KA; if rasa were simply the stable emotion enhanced, there would be no point in setting out the factors and reactions again, KLV.][192] [For when defining the rasas one after the other, Bharata will say something like the following: "Next, the heroic rasa. It is embodied in a character of high status, and consists of determination. It arises from such factors as lack of confusion, intentness, leadership, discipline, strength, valor, power, fortitude, and might." And when later on he refers again to the stable emotion he says, "The stable emotion called determination is embodied in a character of high status. It arises from such factors as power, courage, and the absence of despondency."[193] These statements are identical in meaning, but when rasa is *defined* the factors and so on are discussed at length, and only sparsely when the stable emotions are reiterated. Moreover, it would be useless to explain the cause of a thing's arising and to repeat it when the thing is enhanced, KA.]

[4] [If it is claimed that the stable emotion is the unenhanced state and rasa the enhanced state, KA], there would turn out to be an infinite number of stable emotions given the infinite degrees of enhancement to which each of them is subject, from dull to duller to dullest, and so on,[194] [as well as innumerable rasas from intense, to more intense, to most intense, KA, KLV].

[Were "rasa" the name reserved for the single point when the stable emotion reaches the state of full strengthening, we would have several problems, KA.] [5] It would be impossible for there to be the six types of comic rasa that Bharata identified.[195] [6] [Furthermore, Bharata states that desire has ten stages,[196] with each later one relatively more intense than the previous. Here too, given the possibility that each has its own relatively greater degree of intensity, KA] it would turn out that we would have innumerable erotic rasas and stable emotions of desire in each of the ten stages. [7] [It would also turn out that rasas and emotions would always progressively intensify, KLP.] [While Bhatta Lollata has argued that the stable emotion of the initial stage[197] gradually turns into rasa when it is strengthened, KA], what we find actually occurring is the opposite. Grief, for example, is powerful at first but gradually lessens rather than strengthens. This is also the case with anger, determination, and desire:

[once these stable emotions arise, each from its own cause, KA] we find them diminishing over time with the loss of indignation, resolve, and satisfaction, respectively.[198]

Therefore, [the *Sutra on Rasa* has to be interpreted differently, and as follows. The "conjunction" referred to there is an *inferential* relationship among the aesthetic elements, KA]. On the strength of inferential signs—the causes known as the factors; the effects consisting of the reactions; the auxiliary causes,[199] namely, the transitory emotions—which, though factitious, since they are acquired by human effort,[200] are not recognized as such, we apprehend as existing in the actor a stable emotion that is an *imitation* of the stable emotion in the main character, Rama, say, and precisely because it is an imitation it is designated by the special term "rasa."[201]

A distinct comprehension[202] of the foundational and stimulant factors is gained[203] on the strength of the literary narrative itself; the reactions are something the actor is trained to produce; the transitory emotions [267] are gotten by inference from their own associated factitious reactions. But we have no way of apprehending the stable emotions, not even from the literary narrative. The proper terms for them, "desire," "grief," and so on, simply render these things referents, insofar as they denote them; they do not make us *understand* them as if they were "verbal acting," or expression.[204] For *referential* language as such is not at the same time *expressive*; it is the medium whereby expression is achieved, just as the limbs of the body are not in and of themselves expressive but the medium whereby expression in acting is achieved. Accordingly, in verses such as the following,[205]

> Although my *grief* is distended, profound, endless, and vast,
> it is siphoned off by my anger, like the ocean's water by the submarine fire.[206]

or

> He was so paralyzed by *grief* that his counselors raised a hue and cry,
> and fearing that his heart might burst, they begged him to try to weep.[207]

grief is not being "acted out" or "expressed," but simply denoted. In the following poem, however,

> As she drew my portrait a stream of teardrops came falling
> that made my body appear to perspire at the touch of her hand.[208]

the sentence not only denotes its proper sense, it "acts out," or expresses, King Udayana's stable emotion (here, pleasurable desire) and does not just speak of it. For the "verbal register of acting," or verbal expression, is the power enabling us to understand something, and is above and beyond the mere saying of the thing. For precisely this reason [the fact that a stable emotion cannot be understood directly from the literary narrative, KLV] the sage does not mention "stable emotion" in the *Sutra on Rasa* itself, not even in a separate case form.[209] [It is only when conjoined with the aesthetic elements, and by no means prior to that point, that the stable emotion can be apprehended, and only as an imitation, KLV.] Accordingly, rasa must be an imitation of a stable emotion,[210] and hence it makes sense for the sage to say later that it "arises from" the stable emotion, or "consists of" it.[211] We certainly have evidence[212] that real effects (such as rasa) can arise from knowledge of something unreal (like the content of an inference based on an imitation). To quote: "Two men run toward two sparkling lights, one a gem and one a lamp, both thinking the lights a gem. Although there is no difference regarding their false knowledge, there is a difference regarding their real effects."[213]

In this inferential process none of the following notions arises in us: that [1] the actor is actually the happy Rama;[214] or that [2] the actor is not in fact Rama and not really happy when we had first thought him to be the happy Rama;[215] or that [3] he may or may not be Rama; or that [4] he is similar to Rama. Instead, the aesthetic apprehension we have is different from all four, [1] a true apprehension,[216] [2] a false one, [3] a doubt, and [4] a similitude. It is, instead, an apprehension that can be analogized to that of a painted picture of a horse, and has the form: "Here is the happy Rama."[217] To quote:[218] "There is no appearance of doubt, or indeed of truth or falsehood—we have the thought, 'This is him,' and not 'This is *actually* him.' We encounter no antithetical ideas,[219] and so nothing makes us aware of the conflation.[220] It is an experience we actually undergo, and what logical argument can confute such empirical evidence?"

(#2a, Abhinavagupta)[221]

Shri Shankuka held that, in the course of a dramatic performance, while relishing the rasa in the actor, a viewer apprehends the stable emotion in the character, whereas in the actual world depicted in the drama[222] a dramatis persona[223] causes the rasa to come into being.[224] The second position, that emotion and the other aesthetic elements precede rasa, accords with the training intended by the teachers of drama. This is why there is in fact a third option.[225]

[(#2b, Hemachandra)[226]

Therefore, emotion does not precede rasa, but just the reverse. When the sage states, "Whether rasa precedes emotion or emotion rasa is a function of the nature of the case: in the course of a dramatic performance, while relishing the rasa in the actor, viewers apprehend the stable emotion in the character," he is affirming the first option. In the actual world depicted in the drama, however, it is as a result of the character's first seeing "emotion"[227] that its essential form, namely rasa, arises.]

(#3a, Mammata)[228]

Shri Shankuka's position is as follows. The stable emotion is inferred to exist in the actor,[229] whom we grasp by a mode of comprehension different from all four normal forms of apprehension. . . . This inference arises from a "conjunction"—that is, an inferential relationship—of three elements: (1) a cause, which is designated by the term "foundational and stimulant factor"; (2) an effect, which is designated by the term "reaction"; (3) an auxiliary cause, which is designated by the term "transitory emotion." The first is distinctly comprehended from the literary narration itself, such as in the following verse, where we have a foundational factor for the erotic rasa enjoyed:

> Here she comes into view, a stream of ambrosia upon my limbs,
> a salve applied to my eyes, my heart's desire incarnate, my life breath's mistress.

Or in the next verse, where we have a stimulant factor in the erotic rasa thwarted:

> By a cruel fate I have been parted from her, that woman with large darting eyes—
> and at the same time the season has come of dense, racing clouds.[230]

The other two elements are manifested by the actor himself by revealing the effects of each, something he is able to accomplish thanks to training and practice.[231] Although these aesthetic elements are factitious, they are not recognized as such; and although the stable emotion is grasped by inference, it is different from any other thing we infer insofar as it is something tasted, thanks to the beauty of the aesthetic event [—it is like our mouth puckering on seeing someone relishing a lemon, KA]. It enters our imagination[232] as the stable emotion[233] of the character, and although it is completely nonexistent in the actor himself, it is something that can be relished by the audience members by way of their own predispositions. The inferred stable emotion thus relished is rasa.[234]

On the Tragic Rasa

(#4a, Abhinavagupta)[235]

The term *karuṇā* (with -*ā*) refers in everyday life to the sense of compassion.[236] It receives the technical designation of *karuṇa* (with -*a*), or the tragic rasa, when the spectators apprehend the presence of grief in the actor by means of inferential signs.[237]

On the Psychophysical Element

(#5a, Abhinavagupta)[238]
The following verses of Bharata,

> Special effort must be taken in the case of psychophysical acting, since drama is founded upon it. . . . The psychophysical, which is connected with a particular emotion, is unmanifest, but it can be made known by its various properties—horripilation, tears, etc.—and so endowed with the rasa appropriate to the locus.[239]

have been interpreted by Shri Shankuka and others as follows: Why does the psychophysical require such serious "effort"? Here is the answer: The psychophysical in a particular character, Rama for example, is "connected with an emotion," that is, engendered by an intense state of concentration, and is productive of such psychophysical responses as horripilation. This inner psychophysical element in the drama is "unmanifest," or invisible, and can be "known" only by way of those things that are properties of it, such as horripilation, since they prompt us to infer it as their cause (there would be no causality[240] only if those properties were ever to come into existence in the *absence* of pleasure, pain, and so on). Moreover, it is then "endowed" with the rasa that happens to be the principal one in relation to the emotion under discussion, and can be known, as pleasure or pain, only with substantial effort by means of the rasa in the character. The horripilation and so on are the effects of this element, and in the absence of this or that outcome, how could a performance pertaining to the psychophysical element from which those effects derive ever succeed without a substantial effort? Such is the gist of the matter.[241]

1.5 THERE ARE NO RULES FOR THE NUMBER OF RASAS

Ornament of Poetry of Rudrata (c. 850) with *Notes* of Namisadhu (1068)

With respect to the development of the discourse on poetics, Rudrata must certainly be placed later than Udbhata (c. 800); at the same time, he knows nothing of Anandavardhana (c. 875) and is cited, as we have seen, by Pratiharenduraja around 900. A date of around 850 thus seems reasonable. For some scholars his name (and that of his father, Vamuka) has suggested an origin in Kashmir. Namisadhu, his one surviving commentator (we know earlier ones existed) was a Jain monk who composed his commentary in 1068.[242]

Although the *Ornament of Poetry* deals mainly with figures of speech, rasa occupies a more prominent position in it than in any previous work on poetics. In addition to defining rasa, Rudrata illustrates all the varieties (with poems of his own composition) and their subdivisions, with a focus on the erotic, along with details on the characteristics of the leading man and woman that would eventually form a genre of literary criticism in its own right (the "types of hero/heroine" treatise). If there is little discussion about what rasa is or how it works, we do find some noteworthy innovations, as well as continuities.

Rudrata is the first scholar of poetics for whom rasa is no longer counted among the figures of sense. Instead, the topic is treated in a separate section of the book, which suggests to the admittedly post-Anandavardhana commentator Namisadhu that rasa has a more essential role to play in the literary work: unlike ornaments that enhance the exterior, the body of the poem, rasa is an "innate" quality. And for the first time (unless the verses ascribed to Bhatta Lollata, above, by Hemachandra are authentic), a clear linkage is found to exist between literature and the ends of man—a theory of didactic aesthetics, which would be restated by Pratiharenduraja in the generation after Rudrata and fully elaborated by Abhinavagupta and Bhoja. As for the rasas themselves, Rudrata's list includes the peaceful as well as the "affectionate," replacing the general "affectionate utterance" trope found in Bhamaha and Dandin with the specific feeling of parental, especially maternal, love (already hinted at by Udbhata). Perhaps Rudrata's most important contribution is the independence he shows in challenging Bharata's traditional list: since any emotion can be "tasted," the number of rasas is, he says, in principle limitless. This is precisely the argument Bhoja will make with far greater force a century and a half later. Last, if Namisadhu is correct in representing rasa in this account as an "enhancement" of the stable emotion, there is little to suggest that Rudrata is not still following Bhatta Lollata, for whom rasa is the stable emotion in the character under conditions of full development, and for whom, accordingly, the formal constitution of aesthetic emotion, rather than its reception by the reader, continues to constitute the focal point of the analysis.

FROM *ORNAMENT OF POETRY* OF RUDRATA (R) WITH *NOTES* OF NAMISADHU (N)

(N) The author has already described the benefit to a poet from composing a poem. But what of the benefit to the listener? To this he now speaks:

(R) (12.1–2) To be sure, literature produces, quickly and sweetly, an understanding of the four ends of man for sensitive people,[243] who shy away from learned treatises, dry as dust as they are.[244] Therefore, one must take all possible care to endow a literary text[245] with rasas. Otherwise such people will recoil from it as from the treatises.

(N) If this were the case, one might object that literature would then only be for the sensitive,[246] not for those who lack sensitivity, and would therefore not be available to all people. But this objection does not hold. We are only describing a way to ensure the attention of sensitive people, not to prohibit the attention of the insensitive; they may certainly attend to literature as well. One might also ask why the rasas were not discussed among the ornaments. We would answer: Words and meanings make up the body of a poem. Figures such as "crooked expression" and "direct description"[247] are factitious ornaments, like bracelets and earrings. The rasas, however, are innate qualities, like beauty, and accordingly require that a separate chapter be started for them.

What are these rasas? He now sets them forth:

(R) (12.3) The erotic, heroic, tragic, macabre, fearful, fantastic, comic, violent, peaceful, and affectionate—such are all the rasas.

(N) The straightforward meaning here is not all there is to it.[248] Note that the erotic is placed first in order to indicate its primacy. Moreover, the word "such" means "of this sort," and accordingly other emotions of this sort—sagacity,[249] despair, paralysis[250]—are all to be understood to be rasas.

But how is it that despair and the like become rasas? He now speaks to this:

(R) (12.4) Insofar as the teachers have identified certain emotions as "rasas" because they can be tasted (*rasanād*), the way sweetness, sourness, and the like can be tasted, other emotions such as despair can be rasas as well, since they too can by all means be tasted.

(N) The "teachers" are Bharata and others, who said that the stable emotions are rasas because they are tasted, that is, savored, just like something sweet or sour, which becomes a rasa only by virtue of being savored. To quote, "Just as connoisseurs eat and savor their fare. . . ."[251] In response to the likely objection that taste may be possible only in the case of the stable emotions, the author responds that "other emotions such as despair," i.e., the *transitory* emotions, and for this reason they too have to be understood to be rasas. Someone who believes that these cannot achieve enhancement will hold that they remain simply emotions. But the author's idea is that there is no mental state that cannot achieve enhancement and become rasa. That Bharata used the technical name only in reference to eight or nine rasas[252] was owing to the fact that they are, for the most part, the ones that attract sensitive viewers.[253]

Now the definition of the erotic:

(R) (12.5–6) The behavior, consisting of desire, of a man and woman who are mutually attracted is the erotic rasa. It is of two sorts, the erotic enjoyed and the erotic thwarted. The former is when the couple are together, the latter when they are parted. The erotic is again twofold in being either hidden or open. . . .[254]

1.6 RASA CANNOT BE EXPRESSED OR IMPLIED, ONLY "MANIFESTED"

Light on Implicature of Anandavardhana (c. 875)

With the literary theory of Anandavardhana we enter a new world of critical sophistication. In his *Light on Implicature*, rasa becomes the central phenomenon of literariness for poetic as well as dramatic forms. Theoretically, rasa now defines literature; pragmatically, it is now the element to which all other features of the literary text are subordinated.

Once again the chronicler Kalhana helps us locate our thinker historically, identifying him as one of the scholars who won fame during the reign of King Avantivarman of Kashmir (855/6–883).[255] Aside from the *Light on Implicature*, only one other work of his is extant, the devotional *Hundred Poems to the Goddess* (*Devīśataka*), which ironically embodies little of the literary theory for which he became famous. He refers in the *Light* to other compositions, but none has survived.

In one sense it is impossible to make a selection of passages on rasa from Ananda's work, since as a whole it is about rasa. Although according to his theory, not all literature is concerned with the communication of rasa, when rasa is present it becomes the central organizing component of the work, and all other aspects must be brought into harmony with it: "The first domain of action, for a good poet, is rasa." From the school of scriptural hermeneutics Ananda appropriated the notion that discourse has a "unity of purpose," and it is rasa, rather than figure of speech or language quality or anything else, that constitutes literature's unifying purpose.[256] Rasa here, finally and explicitly, has a fully developed character: it applies equally to poetry and to drama; the entire panoply of its components—the "semblance" of rasa, for example, and the notion of its "cessation"—is known, if hardly developed;[257] works as a whole are shown for the first time to have a single rasa; Ananda argues in the case of the *Mahābhārata*, for example, that the dominant rasa is the peaceful.

All that being said, however, rasa itself has an undertheorized presence in Ananda's treatise, astonishingly so given its conceptual primacy. He never tells us what rasa actually is or why it should be central to the literary work; he never comments on, or even cites, the celebrated *Sutra on Rasa*. More important, he never addresses the question of how the reader knows or experiences it. We are justified in inferring from this loud silence that for Ananda, none of these questions mattered, and that the phenomenon of rasa was basically unproblematic. He conceived of it as his predecessors had; the great insights that would transform aesthetic theory were a generation away. For all his remarkable insight into how literary meaning is engendered, Ananda plainly had no interest in how it was experienced, and in this he conformed to the formalistic analysis that he inherited.

What was important for this analysis was not so much where rasa is or who knows or experiences it—these questions were to be made central only later—but how it comes to be where it is. Though he never names Bhatta Lollata or Shri Shankuka, Ananda was aware of the disputes associated with them, in particular the processes by which rasa is produced in the literary text, for these are the disputes he sought to resolve: how "language qualities" or figures of sound or sense (DhĀ chapter 2) and "texture," or degree of compounding (chapter 3.5) relate to rasa; by what processes rasa is produced at the level of the literary work as a whole (3.10–14); what obstructs or contradicts rasa (3.18–20; here he offers an innovative discussion, which would be fleshed out and more thoroughly systematized by Mammata). What Ananda wants to understand are thus the *textual* processes by which rasa is made manifest. Rasa holds no interest as a theoretical problem, or as subjective phenomenon—the question of aesthetic reception—however much it is the viewer/reader who makes the judgments about the successful or unsuccessful manifestation of rasa, and to whom in the final analysis rasa is "manifested" or "implied" or "suggested."[258]

To all appearances, rasa for Ananda is something that exists in the text and indeed, in the main character (or in the author, insofar as he becomes a character when the narrative voice of a lyrical poem is his own). It is something to be "revealed" by the text and so presumably is located in it; the writer "composes" it and the narrative elements "possess" it. When discussing the relationship of linguistic "texture" to the suggestion of rasa, Ananda observes that the rasa must be "appropriate to the speaker and to what he is saying." "The 'speaker,'" he adds, "can be either the authorial voice or someone presented by the poet, and the latter can be either endowed with rasa and stable emotions or devoid of them." The one time Ananda actually mentions the locus of rasa, he identifies it as the character, either the protagonist or the antagonist;[259] it is "the hero's erotic rasa," for example, that "has reached the highest pitch of enhancement." Clearly, as Ananda's most recent translators point out, he is using rasa "in its old sense of a particularly vivid emotion" rather than in its emergent sense of "aesthetic delight."[260] All he is concerned to explain is the mechanism by which the text produces rasa, and here the idea of "implicature" takes on critical importance.

For Ananda, literature as such is constituted by "implicature," or meaning without saying.[261] He got the idea of this new language function from a particular genre of lyric poetry (in Prakrit) where the main point of the narrative is only implied, not openly stated. This insight led to another, that implicature could apply to figures of sense as well, since these are sometimes directly expressed but sometimes only suggested; and to rasa itself, which thus forms a third domain of implicature to complement those of narrative and figure. There is no standard language function, primary or secondary, that can actually *produce* the sense of emotion in literature. It cannot be expressed literally; Ananda firmly sets aside Udbhata's old idea about the use of the "proper terms" for the rasas. It cannot be expressed figuratively, through metaphor, metonymy, or another trope. A new function has therefore to be postulated: emotion in literature can only be communicated by implicature—or, to use Ananda's other technical term, can only be "manifested"—via the combined activity of the aesthetic elements as each generates its own meaning. Implicature is the "soul" of poetry, and rasa is the "soul" of implicature.[262]

Again it is the textual processes behind the production of implicature, not its subjective reception, that matters. Ananda had no intention of proposing a new understanding of rasa as such, only a new model of its mode of textual realization coupled with a more thoroughgoing argument about the organizing force it exerts on the literary work. His conceptual universe is that of his immediate predecessors; rather than rejecting Bhatta Lollata's ontological view that rasa actually comes into being in the character, Ananda makes it entirely a function of language, and he does the same with Shri Shankuka's epistemological view that rasa is something inferred on the basis of an imitation in the actor of the character's stable emotion. His silence about his predecessors notwithstanding, it seems likely that his new explanation may have been influenced by Shri Shankuka's distinction—to the degree we can understand it from the meager fragments available—between referential and expressive language.[263]

The new theory of implicature is complicated by multiple varieties and subvarieties, which we can pass over here. What is critical to register for the intellectual history of rasa discourse is that Ananda is positing a new linguistic modality (*śabdavṛtti*) for generating rasa in the text. And the most startling development in the coming centuries will see this turned into a psychological modality (*cittavṛtti*) for producing rasa in the viewer/reader, something that, given the actual arguments of the *Light on Implicature*, would likely have left the author mystified. If the idea of implicature transforms the entire future history of rasa discourse, the future history will, in turn, transform the idea itself.

One last small but telling innovation of Ananda's concerns the old notion of the three (or four) "emotion tropes," the rasa-laden and the like. For anyone who had absorbed the understanding of rasa made available by the new commentarial work on the *Treatise on Drama* produced in the course of the ninth century, the very idea of rasa as just another among the host of figures familiar from the rhetorical tradition can no longer have made much sense (we have seen the strains in Udbhata's model). In Ananda's account, the "rasa-laden" refers to the case where a rasa, the tragic, for instance, is present but *subordinate* to the main thrust of the poem, the poet's flattery of a king, for instance.[264] In the example given in the selection below, the tragic rasa only serves to enhance—to "ornament"—the eulogy of the king, and therefore it has a secondary, not primary status, which belongs to the eulogy (it is "rasa-laden," not rasa). Although Ananda clearly captures something real in the cases he cites, Kuntaka in the next century will attack his views, claiming that the expression of emotion remains dominant in the poems adduced, and that in general rasa can never be subordinate.

FROM *LIGHT ON IMPLICATURE* OF ANANDAVARDHANA

(p. 78) The third type of implicature concerns rasa. Here rasa is *suggested* by the expressed meaning. [80] This is something completely different from expressed meaning because rasa cannot be the object of the primary function of the words. For it to be "expressed" would mean one of two things: being directly made known by the proper terms for rasa ("the erotic" and so on), or being indirectly made known, by way of communicating the aesthetic elements.[265] With respect to the first option,[266] we would wind up with the absurdity that we could not apprehend a rasa unless its proper term were made known. [81] But rasas are not always made known by their proper terms, and where they are, we in fact apprehend them only indirectly, by their aesthetic elements being communicated; and there the proper term would only serve to restate the rasa, not produce it. That is why we do not find ourselves apprehending rasa in other sorts of contexts: [83] thus, in "poetry"[267] that merely employs the word "erotic" without communicating the aesthetic elements, we do not have the least apprehension of rasa. Because of these positive and negative concomitances—that we apprehend rasa from the particular aesthetic elements all by themselves, without use of their proper terms, whereas we do not apprehend it from the mere use of their proper terms—rasas can only be said to be *suggested* by the expressed meaning. . . .

(1.5) (p. 84) Precisely this signification is the soul of literature. And this is why long ago the first poet's grief at the separation of the pair of cranes was shown to become verse.[268]

[87] A literary text may be beautified by a whole range of words and significations, but it is this suggested meaning that constitutes its essence. [88] This is why the grief (*śoka*) of the first poet Valmiki that arose at the cry of the crane—when its beloved was slain and it was overcome by despair at being forever separated—was shown to be transformed into verse (*śloka*). [89] For grief is the stable emotion of the tragic rasa; [90] although other kinds of implied meaning are found to exist, they are all meant to be included in the implicature of rasa and emotion, since that is the most important of all. . . .

(2.1–2). Basic implicature is of two kinds: the literal meaning is not intended at all; the literal meaning is intended but is subordinated to some other meaning. The second kind itself has two varieties, depending on whether or not the temporal succession between the literal and implied meanings is registered by the reader.

[175] With respect to the two varieties of the second kind of implicature,

(2.3) Rasa (along with emotion, semblance of rasa or emotion, cessation of either, and so on) comes to light without the temporal succession being registered; and when it does so as the predominant element of the literary text,[269] it is distinguished as the very soul of implicature.

[180] Rasa comes to light at seemingly the same moment as the literal meaning. And when it does so as the predominant element, it becomes the very soul of implicature. The author goes on to show that the domain of implicature of the sort where the succession is not registered is to be differentiated from the figure of speech known as the "rasa-laden":

(2.4) The domain of implicature is where the signifier, the signified, and the various elements that lend them beauty are all directed toward rasa.

[190] We apply the designation "implicature" to a literary text in which the words, their meanings, figures, and language qualities, are all used *in subordination to* the main meaning—rasa, emotion, semblance of rasa or emotion, cessation of rasa or emotion—and are all themselves mutually differentiated from implicature.

(2.5) [191] But in a literary text where some other[270] subject matter is predominant and rasa subordinate, rasa will function as a figure of speech. Such is my view.

Although earlier scholars have argued for a domain of operation of a figure of speech called the "rasa-laden," my position is that the domain in which rasa is thought to act as a figure is simply where the rasa is *subordinate* in the text, with some other subject matter showing itself as predominant.[271] Take, for example, a verse of royal flattery: here the affectionate utterance[272] itself [193] constitutes the subject matter, whereas the rasas are seen to be subordinate.

When rasa thus does function as a figure of speech, it can be either pure or mixed with other rasas or figures. Here is an example of the former:[273]

"Don't laugh,[274] I'll never let you go again! It's been so long since I've seen you.
Why do you leave so often, cruel man, what's driving us apart?"
This is how your enemies' wives speak in their sleep, embracing their husbands tight,
until they awake—and burst into bitter tears at their empty arms.

In this poem, the tragic rasa, which is here unmixed with anything else, is subordinate,[275] and it is this that clearly makes it a figure "laden with rasa."[276] . . . [197] Where rasa itself constitutes the subject matter, however, in what way could it possibly be a figure of speech? For it goes without saying that a figure is by definition a source of beauty *for something else*, and cannot in and of itself beautify itself. Here is a précis of the matter:

> What makes a figure of speech a figure of speech is the fact that it functions in a context where the main point is a rasa.

[198] Accordingly, where rasa constitutes the main subject matter it can never be assigned to the domain of figuration, but must instead be a species of implicature, where simile and all the rest function as figures *for it*. Rasa functions as a figure only where something other than rasa constitutes the principal subject matter and rasa contributes to the beauty. Thus, implicature, on the one hand, and simile and the like as well as the "rasa-laden" figure, on the other, have entirely distinct spheres of operation.

Now, one might object that where rasa functions as a figure of speech, the subject must be a sentient being.[277] [200] But that would mean that all other figures, simile and the rest, would have no scope, or virtually no scope, to operate, since wherever the actions of insentient things are the subject, we can always find some way to construe them with actions of sentient beings.[278] One might rejoin that, regardless of such a construal, a text with insentient things as subject is beyond the scope of operation of the "rasa-laden" figure. But if that were true, vast numbers of works of literature, storehouses of rasa though they are presumed to be, would be condemned to lacking rasa [203] entirely. Take for example the following verse:

> These waves her frowns, these startled birds her belt,
> trailing foam like a wrap fallen loose in agitation,
> meandering along a broken course while brooding on my lapses . . .
> surely this unforgiving woman has been transformed into a raging river.[279]

Although here an insentient entity, the river, may be the main subject, we most certainly construe it with the action of a sentient entity. If, however, one were to admit that where we do have such a construal, we can have rasa functioning as a figure of speech, then we would have virtually no scope for the other figures, simile and the rest, to operate, since there is no action of an insentient entity that cannot be construed with that of a sentient one, at least as a stimulant factor. [204] In short, rasa can be a figure of speech only where it is subordinate; where it is dominant, it must by all means be what the figures ornament, not a figure itself—and that is the very soul of implicature.

. . . .

(p. 328) Now, while everyone knows that implicature where the temporal succession from the literal to the implied meanings is not registered—that is, the implicature of rasa—also appears at the level of the work as a whole, as in the case of the *Mahābhārata* or the *Rāmāyaṇa*, precisely how this comes about needs to be explained. . . .[280]

The literary work as a whole can manifest rasa (and emotion, and so on), and the first factor in its capacity to do so is presenting the narrative in a way beautified by "propriety" in all the aesthetic elements—in other words, when the foundational factor and the rest are appropriate to the rasa meant to be conveyed. [330] The foundational and stimulant factors are familiar to all. As for propriety with respect to the stable emotions, this derives from the proper type of character. Characters can be differentiated as human or divine and so on,[281] and among the former, as having high, middling, or low status. When the stable emotion is presented as unmixed with any other and suitably harmonizing with character, the emotion can be said to have propriety. If, on the other hand, an emotion (determination, say, or whatever it might be) that should belong exclusively to a human were presented as being located in a divine being, or the reverse, it would be inappropriate. In the same way, if in describing a king, who is a mere human, actions such as leaping over the seven seas were ascribed to him, they would of necessity lack rasa, however cleverly presented, because of their impropriety.

Now, it might be objected that legend tells of kings like Satavahana who visited the realm of the Naga serpents,[282] and other things of that sort, so what impropriety could there be in describing extraordinary feats on the part of kings capable of sustaining the entire world? But that would be incorrect. We are not saying that it is improper to describe such feats in the case of kings, only that when a *fictional* story is composed with reference to a being that is merely human, nothing appropriate to a divinity should be ascribed to him. In the case of a story concerning god-men, there is of course nothing whatever amiss in ascribing behavior as is appropriate to both, as for example in the story of the Pandavas. With respect to the exploits of Satavahana and the like that we hear of in legends, their description appears suitable to the degree that the exploits are restricted to those related in the legends; presenting anything about them in excess of this would be improper. Here is the essence of the matter:

> The one thing that can impair rasa is impropriety.
> Composing with customary propriety—that is rasa's deep secret.

[331] This is why in Bharata's *Treatise on Drama* a strict rule is given that drama should use well-known plots and a well-known noble hero, for the poet will never be confused about what is and is not appropriate for him. The poet who creates a play with a fictional plot, by contrast, risks erring when describing a hero's nature that precisely because of its unfamiliarity might seem to be inappropriate.[283]. . .

Hence, in the case of desire no less than determination, propriety with respect to the character must be observed—and this applies to all the other the stable emotions, amazement and the rest. The fact that in this context, great poets may have proceeded in their works without regard for such propriety is simply to be judged a fault, even if, as already observed, it may not always be registered because of their artistry.[284] As for propriety of the reactions, this is something already made known in Bharata's *Treatise* and elsewhere.

[334] In short, a poet must not only follow the norms enunciated in the *Treatise* and examine the works of great poets but also focus his mind and make the greatest effort to avoid any lapse in the propriety of the aesthetic elements. When we say that a factual or fictional narrative becomes capable of manifesting rasa when it embodies propriety, we mean that a poet should accept only such narratives—and no others among all the various tales of history and the like, however rasa-laden they may be—that are proper in all their aesthetic elements; and that he must take far more care with a newly invented fictional narrative than with a factual one. For if he stumbles from inattention there, he will expose himself to a serious charge of ignorance. Here is a verse that summarizes the matter:

A fictional narrative must be handled in such a way
that it appears replete with rasa throughout.

And we have already shown that the means to this end is conformity with propriety in the use of the aesthetic elements. Moreover,

In the case of narratives like the *Rāmāyaṇa* that are famous for a given rasa,
any subjective change that might introduce a conflict of rasas should be avoided.

In a word, one should avoid subjective changes in such narratives. To quote: "One must never overstep the limits of the story, however minimally."[285] That said, if one must make such a change, it must not introduce a conflict of rasas.

A second factor in the capacity of the work as a whole for manifesting rasa lies in eliminating a plot component not in harmony with the rasa in one way or another and replacing it with a narrative element, even a fictive one, more appropriate to the desired rasa; examples may be found in the works of Kalidasa, Sarvasena's *Vishnu's Victory* (*Harivijaya*), or my own *Arjuna's Deeds* (*Arjunacarita*). As we have said, in composing a poem, a poet must devote himself heart and soul to rasa, and hence, if he notices some component in the plot not in harmony with the rasa, he should go so far as to expunge it and feel free to introduce another story element in harmony with the rasa. For no purpose is served when a poet simply reproduces the storyline, something already accomplished by the historical account itself. . . .

[341] Another ingredient in the capacity of the work as a whole for manifesting rasa is, first, when the rasa is stimulated and moderated as occasion demands [342] (as for example in the drama *Ratnavali*), and, second, when the dominant rasa is called to mind again whenever it threatens to disappear (as in the drama *The Ascetic King of Vatsa*). The final ingredient for the manifestation of rasa in the work as a whole, be it a drama or whatever, is the measured use of figures of speech, however great may be the poet's talent for them. For a talented poet can sometimes become so involved in composing figures that he produces his composition without any regard to the position of rasa. I offer this advice because we actually do find poets so filled with the rasa[286] of creating figures that they completely disregard the basic rasa of their compositions.

. . . .

(p. 360) The author, having explained how rasas are essentially "manifested," now asks how rasas can come into conflict with one another:

> (3.17) In composing the rasas, whether of a whole composition or a single poem, the thoughtful poet will take care to avoid any conflict between them.

Otherwise he will not succeed in filling a single verse with rasa. With respect to the rasas whose conflict with one another a poet must take care to avoid, the author has the following to say:

> (3.18–19) [1] The use of aesthetic elements connected with a conflicting rasa; [2] discoursing at length on something unrelated to the rasa, even if that can somehow be made to construe with the rasa; [3] suddenly discontinuing or suddenly revealing the rasa; [4] continuously stimulating a rasa even after it has attained full enhancement; [5] inappropriate behavior: all this can contradict a rasa.

[1] One source of conflict lies in making use of aesthetic elements connected with one rasa that conflicts with another rasa already in play. For the use of [1a] the foundational factor of a conflicting rasa, an example would be when acknowledged factors of the peaceful rasa are first described and directly thereafter is the description of a factor of the erotic. For the use of [1b] the transitory emotion of a

conflicting rasa, an example would be a lover's talking about the transience of life and other sources of dispassion when trying to assuage his beloved's anger at his unfaithfulness. For the use of [1c] the reaction of a conflicting rasa, an example would be a poet's describing reactions associated with the violent rasa for a lover who is beside himself with anger when his beloved fails to relent in her jealous anger toward him.

[362] [2] Another thing that will disturb the rasa is when a poet discourses at length on something unrelated, even if that can somehow be made to construe with the rasa; as, for example, when he goes on endlessly describing mountains or whatever or gets lost in composing "twinned" figures and the like when he is in the midst of describing a hero in a state of the erotic thwarted.[287] [3] Another cause of disturbance is when the rasa is suddenly [363] discontinued or suddenly revealed. An example of an inopportune cessation would be when the hero's erotic rasa[288] has reached the highest pitch of enhancement thanks to a heroine with whom he yearns to be united—and it is clear that they are mutually attracted—and then the poet shows complete indifference to the activity that would unite them and arbitrarily begins to describe some wholly unrelated activity. Inopportunely revealing a rasa occurs when, for example, in the midst of an apocalyptic battle where heroes are dying[289] the poet starts describing, for no good reason, the erotic rasa of some godlike hero who has not earlier been shown to be in the least subject to it.

In the latter case it would not do to argue that the hero of the story may have been driven mad by fate, since after all the creation of rasa is rightly the poet's principal *raison d'être*;[290] plot description is simply a means to that end, as we said earlier.[291] And hence, were a poet to be preoccupied with merely describing the plot, he would wind up with a composition where the rasa and emotions have no clear hierarchical ordering, and he would thereby be liable to misstep in the ways noted. It is for this reason I have taken the trouble I have here, because it seemed right to give poets the gist of how rasa is manifested, [364] and not from an obsession with communicating every single dimension of implicature.

[4] Rasa will also be disturbed if it is continuously stimulated even after it has attained full enhancement. For once a rasa has been fully enhanced through the complement of its aesthetic elements and then come to be experienced, it will seem like a faded flower if the poet recurs to it again and again. [5] The last disturbance is inappropriate behavior, as for example if the heroine were to speak to the hero, without any obliqueness whatever, of her desire for sexual intercourse. . . .[292]

Good poets must accordingly strive to avoid such rasa conflicts as these and others along the same lines that they can come up with on their own. Here is a verse that gives the essence of the matter:

Rasa should be a good poet's chief object of concern, and he must avoid all error in creating it. A composition lacking rasa brings infamy on a poet—indeed, he ceases to be a poet at all, and his name will be lost to posterity.

(3.29) (p. 397) A good poet must be particularly attentive in the case of the erotic rasa. For if he commits an error here, it will be immediately noticed.

The erotic rasa is far more delicate than any other, and therefore a poet must be particularly attentive or careful about it. If he makes an error, he becomes an object of scorn to receptive readers. This is because the erotic is necessarily an object of every living being's experience,[293] and insofar as it is accordingly more pleasing than any other rasa, it is preeminent among them. . . .

[404] No one thinks that the rasas are nothing more than the factors, the reactions, and the transient emotions. Accordingly, the apprehension of the aesthetic elements and the apprehension of the rasa that depends upon those elements are classified as cause and effect respectively. A temporal succession must of course exist between these two, but it is not discernible because of its brevity. And so we have said that the rasas are in the category of things "manifested" with no succession being *registered*. . . .

[497][294] For mature writers it is unseemly even to try to compose literature if they do not give precedence to rasa; whereas if they do, there is nothing that does not profit by being included as a component of the intended rasa. Nothing, not even an insentient thing, cannot be a component of the rasa, whether by strictly functioning as a foundational or stimulant factor appropriate to the rasa or by being shown to behave like an sentient being. Here [498] are three apposite verses:

In the boundless world of literature the author is sole creator god: the whole
universe takes on whatever form he wills.
If the poet is filled with passion, the whole world of his poem will consist of rasa;
if not, it will be completely devoid of it.[295]
A good poet can treat insentient things as sentient, and the reverse, just as he
pleases, since he has complete autonomy in his literary work.

Therefore, anything can become a component of the intended rasa at the will of the poet who gives precedence to rasa heart and soul, and can enhance the beauty of the composition in which it is included.

1.7 RASA CANNOT BE A FIGURE OF SPEECH; IT IS WHAT FIGURES OF SPEECH ORNAMENT

The Vital Force of Literary Language of Kuntaka (c. 975)

Perhaps the only work in the Sanskrit tradition that can be likened to what today we would regard as literary criticism—sustained interpretation of the literary text, often from the vantage point of the work as a whole—Kuntaka's *Vital Force of Literary Language* was composed in Kashmir near the end of the tenth century. As often, we can determine the author's date only on the basis of relative chronology: whom he quotes (e.g., Rajasekhara, c. 920) and who quotes (or rather, seems to allude to) him (Abhinavagupta, c. 1000).

Almost from the start—and almost to the end—participants in the tradition of discourse on the literary sought to identify some singular feature around which to organize their understanding of literariness.[296] For Bhamaha and Dandin, this core feature was figuration; for the early ninth-century poetician Vamana it was "style"; for Anandavardhana, "implicature"; for Kshemendra in the early eleventh century, "propriety." For Kuntaka it was what he called *vakrokti*, literally "crooked utterance," where the term *vakra* refers not, as earlier, to indirect expression as exhibited especially in figurative language, but rather to everything from phonemic quality to the meaning of the work as a whole that renders expression notable; something like "striking usage" would be a fair translation.

Accordingly, in contrast to Ananda, rasa has a reduced role to play in Kuntaka's work, and in his understanding of that phenomenon he harkens back (without naming him directly) to the founding formulation of Bhatta Lollata. For Kuntaka, rasa is in the first instance the "enhancement" of the stable emotion of the leading character through the combined force of the aesthetic elements. The examples he provides in the selections offered here show the process whereby, in the first case, the erotic thwarted and in the second case, the tragic come to be enhanced in the male character by a range of stimulant factors.

Kuntaka's acceptance of the old formalist theorem, moreover, led him to embed his discussion of rasa in an analysis of "the subject matter" (*varṇanīya*). This he divides into sentient and insentient entities, the former further subdivided into two groups, "primarily sentient" beings—deities, demigods, and humans—and "not primarily sentient" beings—animals. Self-evidently, rasa can be placed within such an analytical framework only because Kuntaka conceives of it as a phenomenon contingent on the nature of the receptacle: rasa pertains only to higher beings ("the activity of the primarily sentient beings . . . consists essentially in their rasa"); in lower beings there can be only a "semblance of rasa," precisely because they were not thought to possess the cognitive-emotional apparatus to feel it. The complex relationship of rasa and consciousness, whether human, divine, or animal, will occupy thinkers in the following centuries (especially Vidyanatha and

Singabhupala); the very verse Kuntaka uses to contrast the "impulses" of animals to the stable emotions of higher-order beings, namely the opening verse of Kalidasa's *Shakuntala*, will be the first adduced by Abhinavagupta in his presentation of his own theory of rasa, a distinction explained by the latter's focus on aesthetic reception.[297]

All these points about rasa are largely received opinion; where Kuntaka directs new critical attention is toward the old notion of the "emotion tropes." We have seen that much of the complicated history of rasa theory's conceptual transference from drama to poetry is concentrated here. First categorized as just three figures of speech among countless others (rasa-laden expression, affectionate utterance, and haughty declaration), they were eventually rethought by Udbhata as components of a more fully realized, even dramaturgical, theory of poetry (the full realization of rasa, the intimation of an emotion, and the semblance of rasa, respectively, with the quiescence of rasa added as a fourth). But for all that, they remained figures for Udbhata, no different from simile or metaphor; even Anandavardhana made conceptual space for rasa functioning as a figure. Kuntaka is the first to deny that rasa can ever be a figural "ornament" to a literary text, directly and forcefully critiquing both Udbhata and Ananda. And he does so at a level of detail and with a degree of tenacity impossible to convey in a brief selection.

Despite the overall analytic framework that keeps Kuntaka's attention focused on the form of the literary work, he does here and there make reference to audience response. Although he nowhere mentions Bhatta Nayaka (see chapter 3.1), the notion that rasa above all concerns the aesthetic response of the viewer/reader had been fully naturalized by Kuntaka's date. Hence elements of a reception theory of rasa ("rasas produce the rapture of aesthetic relishing in any sentient creature"; "the reader . . . whose heart . . . overflows with rasa") coexist with Kuntaka's more formalistic focus, suggesting the discursive durability of the older paradigm.

Kuntaka's work has come down to us in somewhat fragmentary form, and without commentary. His often florid style adds to the challenge of following his argument. But if it is a struggle to understand this careful and deeply insightful reader of literature, it is decidedly a worthwhile one.

FROM *THE VITAL FORCE OF LITERARY LANGUAGE* OF KUNTAKA

(3.7) (p. 138) The "primary" category is made beautiful by the enhancement of their unaffected desire and the like; the other becomes adorned when reference is made to the impulses appropriate to their particular species.

The nature of the "primary," that is, principally sentient,[298] category of beings—gods, antigods, and the like—becomes fit subject matter for poets, or in other words, enters the field of their proper literary creativity, when they are "made beautiful by the enhancement of their unaffected desire and the like." Desire and so on are the stable emotions, which are "unaffected" when they are free from any constraint, that is, beautiful thanks to their naturalness.[299] They are said to be "enhanced" when they come to exist as the erotic and the other rasas, according to the axiom that rasa is nothing but the stable emotion. This makes the category of beings "beautiful," that is, enchanting. An example in the case of the erotic thwarted is the lament of the mad Pururavas in the fourth act of the *Urvasi Won by Force*:

> She might be angry and hiding herself by magic—but she would not stay angry
> so long.
> She might have flown up to heaven—but her heart would still be soft on me.
> Even the foes of the gods could not abduct her from my presence—and yet
> she is completely lost to view. How can fate ever have arranged this?[300]

[139] Here the king is almost beside himself with misery from having lost his beloved, and is confounded by his repeated failure to recover her. He tries to imagine some reason for being unable to catch sight of her, carefully making reference to each option from moment to moment, in the very first instance calling to mind her natural gentleness, and then dismissing each argument[301] by reflecting on what she would be expected to do. Given the impossibility of any sequence of events[302] that might lead to her recovery, he becomes utterly distraught with the certainty of hopelessness. This brings the rasa to the point of full enhancement. And this is further stimulated by later statements, such as the following:

> Had that shapely woman touched the earth with her feet
> where the sandy ground of the forest is wet from rain,
> I would surely see a trail of footprints, with traces of lac,
> with a deeper depression at the heel from the weight of her limbs.[303]

Here his hopefulness ("Perhaps she once touched the ground with her feet")[304] leads him to imagine he might recover her. But given that a trail of footprints would have been visible, beautified by red lac and with her figure imprinted deeply at the heel from the weight of her hips (since the sandy ground of the forest had been softened by the rain), his certitude of hopelessness grows all the stronger, and occasions the mad lamentation that marks the following sentences.

An example of the tragic rasa is the lamentation of the king of Vatsa in the second act of *The Ascetic King of Vatsa*:[305]

You only glanced at the riverside house and wandered with forlorn look from the pleasure house,
heaving with sighs and casting quick glances at the walkway of *kesara* vines.
Why now come to my side, little son, and ply me with your fawning? It was your cruel mother
who left you—and left me, too—and departed for the most distant land.[306]

Here the entire complement of foundational and stimulant factors that are the cause of the rasa's enhancement [140] has been fully developed by the poet. And the statement of the court fool that introduces this verse, "What a sad mistake for the fawn, the queen's adopted child, to be following you," has been employed for the same purpose, enabling the riverside house, the baby deer, and the rest to become stimulant factors of the tragic rasa all the more effectively. The poet has precisely the same intention when he presents the statement of the king (after the minister Rumanvat, hearing the parrot crying for the queen, says, "This is rubbing salt in a wound!"), which is addressed to the dead queen:

Your boon companion, who once touched that cheek of yours with his claw
as he tried to peck the ruby earring from your ear, thinking it a pomegranate seed . . .
this poor parrot is now crying out in utter agony.
And how, my queen, can you refuse to respond to him at all?[307]

Here the poet presents the parrot as the spoiled favorite of the queen with the intention of communicating her affection for him. The use of the word "that" referring to the cheek is meant to point toward its extreme delicacy, which the king himself had had the experience of enjoying. In this way, the tragic rasa, given that its very existence depends on such stimulant factors, is brought to the highest pitch of beauty.

It is because these two rasas, the erotic thwarted and the tragic, are extremely delicate that we have drawn our examples from them. One can easily come up with illustrations of the other rasas.

By contrast, the nature of the second, or secondary, category—those sentient beings that are animals, such as lions and so on—becomes fit subject matter for poets only when reference is made to the urges appropriate to their particular species.[308]

. . . .

[143.18] Thus, the "body" of the narrative, which can consist of either an entity's being endowed with rasa or its innate beauty[309]—the former depending on whether its rasa is predominant, as in the primary category of beings; the latter, on whether its particular nature is predominant, as in the secondary category—must be "that which is ornamented," and cannot itself be an ornament. It has already been explained why the *nature* of a thing cannot be an ornament. The author now refutes the view of other poeticians who hold that when the subject of the narrative is the activity of the primarily sentient beings, which consists essentially in their rasa, the subject can indeed function as an ornament.

> (3.11) [144] The "rasa-laden" cannot be an ornament, first, because it constitutes the very thing we are apprehending in a poem, and there is nothing above and beyond it; and second, because no coherent relationship exists between the literal meaning of the word itself ("rasa-laden") and the putative meaning ("the rasa-laden ornament").[310]

If it is the rasa itself, the erotic and so on, that constitutes the subject matter and hence the "thing to be ornamented," then something else must constitute the ornament. Conversely, if rasa is said to be an ornament itself on the grounds that it gives pleasure to connoisseurs, then something above and beyond it must be proposed as the thing to be ornamented. The ancient poeticians did not give the least thought to this simple distinction when they defined and illustrated the "rasa-laden" ornament. . . .[311] [145.23] Nor can the example they offer—given that an example's only salvation lies in the definition it is meant to exemplify—be considered an option all on its own. [146] For in the poem adduced, "The woman I thought was dead and hoped / to rejoin by taking my own life,"[312] there is no separate thing to be apprehended beyond the mental state itself that constitutes the narrative content, which is nothing other than the enhancement of the stable emotion of desire. Hence, we can only conclude it is that which is to be ornamented.

Now, one thinker has introduced into the definition the qualification that the "proper term" provides one of the five basic components of rasa.[313] The idea that rasa should be based on its proper term, however, is to our way of thinking completely bizarre. We might ask this learned scholar, who ponders so deeply the essence of rasa and pretends to know its ultimate truth: What is it actually that you are claiming is "based on its proper term," the rasa itself or the "rasa-laden" ornament? On the first alternative, the word "rasa," if we think of it being based in its proper term, means literally "to be tasted," and thus, when referring to the erotic and so on, rasa would necessarily *be tasted* by anyone who knew the word's meaning—which would amount to saying that the different rasas produce the rapture of aesthetic relishing in any sentient creature as soon as they are denoted by their proper terms and come within earshot. By the same reasoning, any object, when denoted by its proper term—like "candy"—would provide the full experience of savoring the thing, and so anyone who craved any pleasure would, without any effort, just by the word's merest denotation, be proffered by this noble sir[314] pleasures equal to a king's ransom. Thank you very much indeed!

It cannot be the second alternative, either, where it is supposed to be the "rasa-laden" ornament that is based on its own term, since that word in fact expresses rasa and, as we just saw, it cannot have that as its basis, let alone something entirely unconnected. So at the very outset the idea that the rasa-laden can be an ornament is refuted. . . .

[149.19] Then again, it has been asserted that the rasa-laden figure may be understood as something providing a special beauty and brilliance to the poem.[315] Thus one especially learned scholar has declared:

> But in a literary text where some other subject matter is predominant and rasa subordinate, rasa functions as a figure of speech. Such is my view.[316]

That is, in the case where some other subject matter may, on the grounds of its prominence in the poem, be distinguished as the thing to be ornamented, the erotic or other rasa will become an ornament, since it is being presented as something subordinate to that subject matter. In this sort of context, it is claimed,[317] a subsidiary element is adorning a principal one in such a way that the poet's own sentiment is what is made manifest, and for that reason, the differentiation of rasa as ornament becomes patently manifest. . . . [151.2][318] For example, our learned scholar cites the verse, "Don't laugh, I'll never let you go again!"[319] and argues that the main subject matter lies in its core meaning, the poet's flattery: "Here, Your Majesty, you see the kind of suffering, reaching the highest pitch of tragedy, that your enemies' wives undergo when, with their husbands slain by your hand, they are overwhelmed with sorrow and defenseless." The tragic rasa, for its part, is presented as something subordinate to that meaning, whereas the erotic (the variety known as the erotic thwarted through the lover's absence) has no reality whatever.[320] Being communicated by a sentence—an array of syntactically coherent elements—and appearing clearly as auxiliary to something else, the rasa, he concludes, here must be called ornamentation.

Now, it is certainly not the case that the definition of rasa cannot apply here: that would be so only if the full complement of its causal elements, including rasa's foundational factor, were absent. But the foundational object[321] is clearly present. Even less is there any literary fault in the introduction of two conflicting rasas, the erotic and the tragic: although the two rasas do exist in the poem in actual fact, there is no conflict between them in our cognitive experience because they are not both simultaneously vying for primacy.[322] Thus, the erotic too has the wonderful capacity here to delight sensitive readers, since there is no proof that only the tragic is at issue in the poem. The erotic thwarted, [152] elicited by its foundational factor (contained in the wives' words) that is its causal element, is found during their dreaming state; the same thing logically applies to the tragic rasa during the waking state. Hence both rasas are possible, and thus it seems hardly reasonable to argue that it is the tragic that should dominate from the very first instant. It hardly defies logic that the king's enemies and their wives should have become separated,[323] having fled hither and yon, terrified by the fierce power of the great man who is the object of the poet's flattery.

Even if it were clear that this is instead a case of the tragic rasa, we could understand the meaning as follows: the wives of your enemies, their minds overwhelmed by the calamity that has befallen them, finally attain reunion with their husbands in their dreams; they begin to converse as usual with their husbands about their experiences together; when they chance to wake up, they reflect on the difference between things before and after waking, their hearts are lacerated by the contrast in things brought on by those reflections, and they begin to weep. Hence, the erotic would be said either to enhance the tragic or to take on the traits of the transitory emotions appropriate to the tragic.[324] How then could one argue that there is no trace of the independent functioning of the erotic rasa here?

It is also problematic to argue that the affectionate utterance made to the king is predominant in the poem, whereas the tragic rasa, as something subordinate to it, must be ornamentation. First, in this example as well as the earlier one,[325] what is clearly presented as the primary subject matter is the complex transformations of the tragic rasa. Second, it is not reasonable[326] that the tragic should be *directly expressed*—on the analogy with other ornaments such as circumlocution or allegory where, though these are not separate from the expressed sense, something else is indirectly expressed[327]—precisely because, being a rasa, it is always supposed to be "manifested." Nor [153] could it be classed in the domain of what is called "subordinate implication," because the rasa, as something manifested—here in the form of the tragic—must always appear as predominant. And last, the affectionate utterance and the rasa cannot both be "manifested," because then the relationship of principal and subsidiary supposed to subsist between them would be logically untenable.

We have only sought to show to the degree possible the various unacceptable options with respect to the "rasa-laden" ornament; at all events, the analogy with normal figures of speech simply does not hold.

. . . .

[156.10] Having refuted the notion that the "emotional" utterance can be an ornament, on the grounds that it constitutes part of the narrative content, the author goes on to offer the same refutation for the remaining figures, since they too constitute narrative content. . . .

[156.18] The ancients tried to offer definitions and examples to show that these are ornaments, but being based on false reasoning, their argument is inadmissible. Let us examine both the definition and the example of the "impulsive" declaration: [157] "When rasas or emotions are presented as contrary to propriety. . . ."[328] [157.12] What sort of impropriety can permit the presentation of rasas based on it to become an ornament? Not only will a rasa apprehended as a violation of propriety fail to become fully "enhanced," but indeed, ugliness will gain entry. To quote: "The one thing that can impair rasa is impropriety."[329] Now, perhaps what is intended in the definition is not any real impropriety but, on the contrary, something in perfect harmony with the subject matter with reference to the rasa—which itself is being manifested by aesthetic elements that are indeed proper, not inapposite to the subject matter, and not objectionable. The logic behind such an argument is offered elsewhere in the definition: "because [those rasas or emotions] are caused by craving or anger or the like." But this would not be a very compelling justification either. A rasa or emotion may be presented [158] as touched by impropriety only when the rasa has been fully enhanced by propriety, and then only in reference to a lesser being, as a result of his lust or the like, and certainly not in the context cited.[330] Only when its natural charm is imparted by the beauty coruscating with the innate artistry of the poet and enlivened by the full complement of aesthetic elements can even a fully proper rasa convey its deepest beauty to the reader, who is transported by the play of the fantastic and whose heart then overflows with rasa the way a moonstone is liquefied by moonbeams. How then can a rasa that is wilting under impropriety, its very existence compromised by the suspicion that craving or the like is involved, ever attain the high status of ornament? Thus, in the aforementioned context, great poets have found a way to invest the poem with rasa, on a par with other subject matter, and have done so with utter brilliance, for example:

> Shiva himself passed those days only with difficulty,
> longing for reunion with the Mountain's daughter.
> How could such emotions not disturb a human, who is far less self-controlled,
> when they touch the lord of all?[331]

We have examined this in detail since it has come up in the course of our exposition. But it might be objected that we are disputing over matters of concern to the learned experts in the principles of Bharata's *Treatise on Drama*, namely whether or not the blessed lord, who has been cited in the example poem, should be brought into the narrative as an object of a "semblance of rasa"; deciding about propriety or impropriety, by contrast, is entirely beside the matter. Well, we are happy to concede the point to the good sirs. That said, however, what is narratively central in the poem is that particular mental state of the lord, and hence it cannot escape being the "thing to be ornamented," and not an ornament itself.[332]

1.8 THERE CAN BE NO "MANIFESTATION" OF RASA

Analysis of "Manifestation" of Mahima Bhatta (c. 1025)

Mahima Bhatta's *Analysis of "Manifestation"*—its title in Sanskrit, *Vyaktiviveka,* refers to Anandavardhana's theory of "manifestation" (*vyakti*)—must have been composed sometime in the first quarter of the eleventh century, since it cites *The Eye for* Light on Implicature (c. 1000) and was itself cited by Mammata (c. 1050). But again, like Kuntaka, Mahima seems generally to be carrying on an older conversation. He is by no means ignorant of Bhatta Nayaka—he quotes a verse that should probably be attributed to him, though he openly admits he never had the chance to read the *Mirror of the Heart*[333]—but he has nothing to say about the components of the hermeneutical revolution Nayaka inaugurated. He is similarly unconcerned with most of Abhinavagupta's key questions, though he clearly knew at least *The Eye for* Light on Implicature. What centrally interests Mahima Bhatta is what interested Shri Shankuka and Ananda, the mechanism by which rasa gets produced, and the cogency of the arguments in support of *vyakti*, or "manifestation."

There is no hint in the *Analysis* that by *vyakti* Mahima Bhatta understood anything but Ananda's linguistic modality (*śabdavṛtti*) of implicature (*dhvani*), that is, the "manifestation" of literary meaning in general and literary emotion in particular. The term is certainly never used in the treatise in the sense of a psychological modality (*cittavṛtti*), the revelation of a subjective response to the aesthetic object, as would become common in the wake of Abhinava's reinterpretation. In fact, like Ananda himself, Mahima Bhatta takes no notice of the reception theory of rasa—he says explicitly, "We hold rasa to be an imitation of a stable emotion"—and, like his fellow logician from whom he borrowed this view, Shri Shankuka, he was concerned with the cognitive process by which the presence of rasa in the literary text is made known. Of course, writing when he does, Mahima agrees that in the final analysis rasa is an "experience of rapture on the part of the responsive viewer/reader," but the only possible application of the term "manifestation" to that process, he argues, is a figurative one. What actually happens is that we *infer* rasa from the aesthetic elements; hence, though these elements do not "manifest" rasa, the use of "manifestation" in a figurative sense may be allowed as pointing toward the uniqueness of the final experience. It is toward establishing the limits of this figurative usage of "manifestation," in addition to denying its literal use in favor of inference, that Mahima Bhatta's efforts here are directed.

FROM *ANALYSIS OF "MANIFESTATION"* OF MAHIMA BHATTA

(p. 59) In the case of a sentence, where we have a cause-effect relationship between the words and the meaning, we easily mark the temporal sequentiality between the apprehension of the cause and the apprehension of the effect. We must understand the same process to be at work in the case of a narrative element and a trope, which are accordingly objects of inference.[334] It is only with respect to rasa, which is actually likewise something inferred, that we have a cognitive cause-effect relationship where the succession is *unregistered*, but this is merely a product of the illusion of their simultaneity. Our opponents consequently accept this relationship as one of "manifester and manifested,"[335] upon which their use of the word "implicature" is dependent. But in the case of rasa this can only be a metaphorical usage of "manifestation,"[336] not a literal one, since the literal sense is inapplicable given the reasoning we shall present.[337] The purpose of using a metaphorical expression is to suggest the experience of sublimity, as we might call it, on the part of the responsive viewer/reader. This is something we can observe with respect to the primary sense of the word "manifestation" in the case of a painting or sculpture.[338] . . .

[70] One might raise the following objection to our metaphor thesis: Emotions like desire and the rest are particular states of pleasure and pain. How can they offer "an experience of sublimity on the part of the responsive viewer/reader," which is a purely pleasurable process of savoring, in such a way as to justify using the metaphorical language of "manifestation" in the case of the rasas, when they are actually inferred? For in everyday life, when grief and other emotions are inferred from various signs, the person doing the inferring is not observed to experience the least bit of pleasure. On the contrary, a good man, or even a neutral one, will be found to feel fear, grief, sadness, or other pain. And nothing special distinguishes literature from everyday life so that the pleasurable savoring should be found only in the former and not in the latter. The very same everyday foundational factors and the rest, in the form of causes, effects, and ancillary causes, prompt the inference; the very same emotions, desire and the rest, in their particular states, are the things inferred. So what is special about literature that rasa is savored only there and not in everyday life? There is in fact nothing special, and hence, there being no purpose to be served, it makes no sense to use "manifestation" in a figurative sense with respect to the stable emotions.

The answer to this objection is as follows.[339] The savoring of rasa, which the sensitive reader alone can have, comes about only when an awareness of emotion arises by means of the aesthetic elements. That is the nature of things, and no serious scholar disputes it. Thus the *Sutra on Rasa* of Bharata; and to quote further:

> The purpose of literature is rasa, which is an experience consisting of savoring; it may be said to be "manifested" only by way of a manifestation called awareness revealed by the conjuncture of aesthetic elements.[340]

[71] These aesthetic elements do not exist in everyday life. What exists are real causes and effects. Nor can one imagine that the aesthetic elements and the real causes are one and the same thing; they are entirely different, with different definitions. To explain: in the real world the emotions, desire and so on, that exist in Rama, say, as particular stable states are in literature called emotions (*bhāvas*), because, when imputed to characters by poets to enhance their descriptions, they "bring into being" (*bhāvayanti*) the various rasas, as Bharata says.[341] The causal factors of these emotions—Sita in the case of Rama, for example—when conveyed by literature come to be called factors (*vibhāvas*), because they "factor" (*vibhāvaya-*) the emotions. [72] And the same with the reactions and the transitory emotions. . . .[342]

[74] Since aesthetic elements are factitious, whereas cause, effect, and ancillary causes are real, the ones pertaining to literature and the others to the world, the former differ from the latter in both their natures and their objects. Given this difference, when the aesthetic elements produce an apprehension of the stable emotions, which do not really exist, it is entirely appropriate to refer to the stable emotions as "implied" or inferred, in the primary sense of the terms, given that they are nothing but that apprehension. This comprehensive cognition of the apprehension of a stable emotion is itself the savoring of rasa, and it, by contrast, is a real, not factitious, phenomenon.

[75] Or let us say that the stable emotions are permanently imperceptible. A perceptible thing cognized directly does not provide thoughtful people with the rapturous experience of something presented by a great poet in language. To quote:

> Emotions conveyed by a poet's power conjoined with the force of identification
> flash forth from a poem in a way unequaled even by seeing with one's own two
> eyes.[343]

And even that is not as deeply savored by them as it is when the aesthetic elements enable the emotion to be inferred. This is a fact of nature and not subject to dispute. To quote again:

> An emotion inferred from real causes is not savored the way it is when inferred from the aesthetic elements, just as the express meaning does not give as much pleasure as the implied.[344]

. . . .

[78] In everyday life, causes, effects and so on, which are nonfactitious, give us to understand real emotions; they are purely inferential, and have not a hint of implicature. How then could there be even a drop of the savoring of pleasure? And precisely herein lies what is "special" about literature over against everyday life, which makes it perfectly reasonable to use, with reference to the stable emotions—which are actually inferred—the *figurative* language of "manifestation," its purpose being to suggest this savoring of pleasure. . . .

[83] As far as rasa is concerned, it would be impossible for an implied meaning to be made manifest simultaneously with the manifestation of the aesthetic elements. For these are causes and factitious, and in fact are given the name "aesthetic elements" when they are used by poets for bringing to the awareness of the cognizing subject emotions such as desire and the like. In the process the latter, which are more or less reflections,[345] acquire the name "stable emotions," and when they reach the state where they can be relished thanks to the heart's concurrence of the viewer/reader, they are called "rasas." Obviously it is not possible for effects that are more or less reflections to become manifest *simultaneously* with their causes, for the very determination of a causal relationship between them would thereby vanish.[346]

. . . .

(98–101) It cannot be, as Anandavardhana claims, that "implicature" refers to a "particular variety of poetry,"[347] because implicature is supposed to define poetry as such, and implicature consists, as he himself avers, essentially of rasa.[348] [100] Nor can the rasa implicature offers be a "particularly good" variety,[349] because rasa is defined as a savoring of pleasure that does not admit of any higher degree.[350] To quote: "When rasa attains plenitude through poetry recitation or *dhruvā* singing,[351] the viewer/reader becomes focused on its intense savor, and turns inward for a moment. Then all other sensory objects vanish, one dwells within oneself, and one's own streaming joy, the sort that spiritual adepts delight in, becomes manifest."[352] Absent this rasa, a poem cannot *be poetry* at all, let alone a "particular" variety of poetry, and no rational person would bother with it, since it would be completely useless. [101] For "poetry" is defined as the activity of a poet that consists of the "conjoining of the aesthetic elements"—which itself is invariably connected with the "manifestation" of rasa.

CHAPTER TWO

The Great Synthesis of Bhoja, 1025–1055

2.1 ONE RASA UNDERLIES ALL MULTIPLICITY

Necklace for the Goddess of Language of Bhoja (c.1025) with the *Commentary* of Bhatta Narasimha (undated); *Light on Passion* of Bhoja (c. 1050)

King Bhoja of the Paramara dynasty ruled in the city of Dhara (in today's Madhya Pradesh) for nearly half a century (d. 1055). His court would later become the stuff of legend on account of the many literati who flocked there in search of patronage from the greatest literary connoisseur of the age—and perhaps the most creative, given the number of poems and treatises ascribed to him. Kings often took credit for the compositions of their courtiers, but there is reason to think that at least a few of the works that now bear Bhoja's name are genuinely his, or rather—since authorship in this world could be complex—that he participated in some central way in their creation. The *Light on Passion* certainly bears the voice of a single author, and it is hard not to think of this voice as Bhoja's when we read, for example, in his exposition of the first verse of the work, that "it is not just anyone" who has enunciated it, but "a great king appointed by his elders to protect all that has been inherited, and who in this verse beseeches God that there should be no transgressions against the established order or against caste or life-stage practices while he is engaged in the composition of this book."[1] This is less assuredly the case with the *Necklace for the Goddess of Language*, but its author shares the same conception of literature in general and of rasa in particular as that found in the *Light*.

Two factors make Bhoja's literary works extremely difficult to interpret. One is simply the novelty and complexity of his thought. Bhoja offers an intricate, even counterintuitive, theory of rasa, set within an intricate, though comprehensive, literary system. The second factor is the absence of any detailed tradition of exegesis, which magnifies the problems produced by Bhoja's conceptual novelty and intricacy. Although both his literary treatises were read widely, at least in southern India—we can see their influence in a number of later works[2]—the *Light* was never commented on at all, and the only commentaries on the fifth (or rasa) chapter of the *Necklace*, those of Bhatta Narasimha and of an anonymous author, are each available in one poorly preserved manuscript.[3] As a result, even the most learned of Bhoja's modern students have been confounded by his work.[4] And if readers cannot fail to be astonished by Bhoja's virtuoso interpretations of Sanskrit poems, where the analytical and interpretational force of rasa theory is deployed to remarkable effect, they also stand bewildered before his ubiquitous and seemingly arbitrary lists: the "twenty-four powers ensuring the presence of rasa," the twenty-four types of figures of sense, and of figures of sound; the twelve types of word, and of meaning, and of "unity."[5] But the component that has proven most difficult to understand is also the most fundamental, his theory of rasa.

Bhoja's views on rasa are typically regarded as the most unusual and provocative that the tradition has to offer.[6] For one thing, he takes issue, often with disputatious irreverence, with Bharata's foundational text. Something so new appears to be going on here that even later traditional scholars, such as the celebrated early fifteenth-century exegete Mallinatha, viewed it with disdain ("Insofar as Bhoja's work is fatally impaired by its contradictions with the foundational works of Bharata and so on, simply ignoring it . . . is the best critique").[7] Bhoja himself is clear about his iconoclasm: "The conventional wisdom that the term 'rasa' refers only to the heroic, the fantastic, and the remaining six [traditional rasas] has . . . only been accepted because of the intellectual conformity typical of the world, and our intention in this work is to put it to rest." At the same time, he clearly inhabits a thought world radically different from what was to come—or rather, had already come (his relationship to Dhanamjaya and Dhanika will be discussed in chapter 3). How exactly we are to place him in the intellectual history of Indian aesthetics has therefore been an open question.

As the title of the greater of his two works announces, the focus of *Light on Passion*, *Śṛṅgāraprakāśa*, is *śṛṅgāra*, and in much of the text this term is understood in the sense common to earlier literary theory: "In this treatise the erotic rasa will be discussed. It is of two sorts, the erotic enjoyed and the erotic thwarted."[8] But what Bhoja perceived, as no one earlier did and few later have,[9] and what prompts a reorganization of the entire logic of his analysis, is that the psychological force at work in *śṛṅgāra* in that narrow sense, "the erotic rasa," actually can be found across the entire spectrum of emotions; there clearly exists some more basic principle that all the rasas share. "Rasa in this treatise is defined as love," he argues. "For all forms of emotion, desire and everything else, once they reach their full development, ultimately turn out to be nothing but this. Thus people are said to '*love* sex,' to '*love* quarreling,' or anger, or joking."[10] To this more fundamental principle he gives—confusingly for us—the same names, *śṛṅgāra* and rasa (to distinguish the particular phenomena, *śṛṅgāra*$_2$ or rasa$_2$, from the general *śṛṅgāra*$_1$ or rasa$_1$ from which they arise, I translate the latter as "passion"). But he also calls it, with greater analytical import, "sense of self" or "ego," notions we need to pause over given their centrality to Bhoja's thinking.

The terms are taken from Samkhya philosophy, which was foundational to Bhoja's thought, and the explanation for them offered by Vachaspatimishra, a great Samkhya exegete two generations before Bhoja, repays attention. His comment on the *Sāṃkhyakārikā* verse "'Ego' is one's 'sense of self' " runs as follows:

> Sense of self is the awareness that one is empowered to act with respect to one's experiences or thoughts; that one is capable of doing so; that phenomenal objects are meant for oneself, that no one but oneself is empowered to act upon them; accordingly, that one exists. Sense of self is equated with ego because it is unique to oneself. It is in dependence on one's sense of self that the intellect comes to determinations, that is, reaches decisions such as the thought "I must do this."[11]

As Bhoja describes it in the *Light on Fundamental Principles*, his handbook on Shaiva-Samkhya philosophy, "Ego has three forms: existential, agentive, and emotive. It is the connection with ego, so long as it exists, that enables one to engage with phenomenal existence."[12] It also has three aspects depending on the nature of the person—sensitive, volatile, and stolid (the three constituents of all physical and mental reality, according to Samkhya)—which are generally intermingled. In its purest state, ego, or "passion," is unevenly distributed: it is something that "awakens in the heart of those in whom sensitivity predominates"; "a transformation born of a special kind of untainted property." Not everyone has that sort of passion, and hence not everyone has rasa.

In short, passion, ego, or sense of self is a general psychological orientation enabling one to act in the world, something like Rousseau's *amour de soi*, and with none of the ethical disparagement carried by his *amour propre*, let alone by the English term "egotism" (for which Sanskrit would generally use the term *asmitā*). And this is why Bhoja can view it as something fundamental. Emotions for Bhoja are, radically, "things produced" (*bhāva*) through a process of "production" (*bhāvanā*) and hence are secondary; what underlies them and hence exists beyond the "plane of production" is the true (and singular) rasa, the core nature of personality.[13] This more basic principle represents, accordingly, the psychic energy at the core of all feelings, a capacity for affective intensity as such, something enabling one to experience the world richly, which is singular and can rightly be taken as the origin of all other emotional states, or rasas plural. Because the desire that underlies passion is "the paradigmatic emotion," it may stand, metonymically, for them all.[14] Hence light on "passion" sheds light on rasa as such.

At first glance, and especially in view of the transformative developments in theory around his time (chapter 3), it has appeared to most scholars that Bhoja is concerned in the first instance with understanding the passion of *readers*, and what makes it possible to respond to literature. But given both the overall framework of Bhoja's analysis and the specifics of his argument, that is a serious misinterpretation. The *Light*, like the earlier *Necklace*, is, according to its prologue, a work about "unity" (*sāhitya*), or the various processes by which sound and sense unite to produce the peculiar kind of verbal communication called literature. Bhoja very carefully differentiates among the terms he uses for what he sees as *sāhitya*'s four main principles: literature must be "without flaws," that is, flaws, being copresent with language and thus a congenital threat, must be eliminated; "qualities must be used," that is, the verbal (phonemic, syntactical, and lexical) character of the literary utterance must be carefully constituted with due attention paid to style and rasa, otherwise it will be flawed; "figures of sound and sense" may or may not be joined to the work; finally, the work must show a "presence of rasa." It is precisely because rasa is an instance of this *formal* unity, in fact its essential condition, that it is of concern to Bhoja.

The effect of this overriding purpose of rasa analysis, consistent with Bhoja's account of the other features, is to constantly redirect attention back toward the text, toward the literary process itself and the production of literary communication. Whatever else Bhoja might have thought about rasa as a readerly experience—he never directly refers to that experience anywhere in his treatises—the aspect of the rasa problematic he invested with analytical primacy was *inside* the text, the experience of the character, as the primary and "real" (not metaphorical) participant in the rasa experience. At every step Bhoja is concerned with the emotion of the character and not the reader. It is the character (Rama) who is said to "have rasa," and it is for this reason that the words he speaks can be said to be "rasa-laden." It is the character who is said to experience the latent predispositions when these are activated by the foundational and stimulant factors. It is his stable emotions that are said to arise. A "developed rasa" is accordingly "that which the protagonist, who occupies the chief role in the narrative, comes to have in reference to a commensurate object."

Bhoja wants above all to understand how literary characters can be shown to experience and express the emotions they do, what that tells us about their special psychosocial qualities, and by what means specific to it the literary artwork produces the sense of a feeling. Ultimately, as with Anandavardhana, this entire account implicitly subserves readerly pleasure, which no doubt interested Bhoja for reasons that would be as clear to him as to any other reader. But his principal focus is resolutely on the text: this is a point that Bhatta Narasimha, commenting on Bhoja's rasa theory in the *Necklace*, is keen to make when he reconstructs the larger terms of the argument (retrospectively, of course; Bhoja was not arguing against views he could not have known). Neither the rasa chapter nor anything else in his two treatises directly and unambiguously addresses the aesthetics of reception, a development in the theory of rasa of which Bhoja seems ignorant (or, at the very least, in which he was uninterested).

Thus, while Bhoja wishes at times to contest or even overturn Bharata's classifications and their restrictions—about, for example, the limit on the number of stable emotions, or the notion that rasa is the stable emotion when strengthened, or the generative relationship between emotions and rasas[15]—one could argue that he is simply introducing the flexibility necessary to account for the criticisms already made by others such as Rudrata.[16] The same attitude informs his approach to Dandin's *Looking Glass*. Much of Bhoja's treatment of rasa may seem like a simple appropriation of that work, but that is far from the case, as his use of Dandin's "emotion tropes" fully demonstrates. But whether Bhoja uses the past contentiously or creatively, it is a past with which he is conceptually akin. In this sense his continuity with his predecessors can be said to remain largely unbroken; both his analytical focus and his radical difference from the innovators who were to come—or, in Bhatta Nayaka's case but unbeknownst to Bhoja, had already come—together invite us to think of his account as a true classical synthesis. The core commitment to the formal analysis of rasa, which had lasted nearly a millennium and was about to be displaced for all the major thinkers in the field, is something Bhoja evinces throughout his two great books.

Keeping this commitment in mind will help us understand other aspects of Bhoja's very peculiar rasa analysis. One is the larger framework within which it is situated, that of a discussion of ornaments. Rasa, no less than language qualities and figures of speech, can be called "ornaments" insofar as these can be understood as factors of beauty in literature, rather than just figures of speech.[17] They accordingly represent components that may be isolated in an analysis of the process of "combination" of features that constitutes the "presence of rasa." For precisely this reason Bhoja is so preoccupied with the "emotion tropes" inherited from Dandin (the affectionate, the rasa-laden, and the haughty expression). It matters little that Bhoja's new hierarchical ordering of their intensity (with the affectionate at the top, whereas for earlier thinkers it represented a stage below the developed rasa) is driven by his own new theory of rasa as love (that is, *prema*, which is cognate with *preyaḥ*, the "affectionate"), and has no basis in Dandin's own discussion. His preoccupation again demonstrates that, with Bhoja as with all his predecessors, we remain squarely in the domain of a formalist account of the aesthetic object.

Bhoja places enormous demands on the reader, past no less than present. But he has a profound analysis to offer, if we only take the trouble to understand it.

FROM *NECKLACE FOR THE GODDESS OF LANGUAGE* OF BHOJA (BH) WITH THE *COMMENTARY* OF BHATTA NARASIMHA (BN)

(Bh) (5.1) The phenomenon called rasa is defined as sense of self, or ego, or passion, and it is the presence of rasa that makes literature beautiful.

(BN)[18] Rasa is located in the character who is the subject of the work, Rama for example, and when rasa is "present" in or conjoined with a poem about Rama through an appropriate literary composition, it delights the hearts of the audience.[19] One might, however, raise the following objection:[20] Rasa cannot be located in the character, since the character is dead and gone; it must be in the audience members, who are alive and present. Moreover, the main point of a literary work is not the character. Writers do not write literature so that characters long dead and gone can "have rasa," but so that the audience can enjoy rasa.[21] Therefore, the rasa must be in the audience, not in the character. We would answer: Not in the least. If the rasa were in the audience, the literary work would have had either to produce it in them or to make them aware of it when it already exists in them.[22] Which is it? The objector might respond: The literary work does both: the work of a good writer seems to transfer to the audience, right before their eyes as it were, the full complement of rasa elements, the foundational factor and so on, which as an aggregate brings about rasa in their hearts. "Rasa arises from the conjunction of factors, reactions, and transitory emotions."[23] Because it communicates this full complement, the literary work can be said to produce rasa. At the same time, it makes the audience aware of rasa by revealing the causal factors that underlie it. To this we would answer: That is incorrect. How can the aesthetic elements communicated by the literary work be the cause of a rasa located in the audience? Causes must necessarily preexist their effects, and when one is listening to a literary work, those factors do not actually exist at all, let alone exist as necessarily prior.[24] And as for their making the audience aware of rasa, what difference does that make? Rasa does not come about as a result of being aware of these factors; rather, it essentially is those factors themselves, as has been stated in the *Sutra on Rasa* ("Rasa arises from the conjunction . . ."). . . .[25] "Rasa" in the primary sense of the term is what is located in the character; the prevailing sense of the word (that is, with respect to the audience) is only a secondary meaning.

Moreover, a single verbal function cannot both produce something and make us aware of it. That which makes one aware of something must exist after that thing has been produced, and words, having once ceased after putatively producing rasa, no longer have the capacity to function in order to inform us of it. Therefore, rasa exists only in the character; it is communicated by the literary text and experienced by the audience. One might object that if it is the characters alone, such as Rama, that are properly to be called *rasikas*, or those who experience rasa, how can that term be applied, as it in fact is, to the audience? How, that is, does a literary work go about engendering rasa? We would answer that although rasa exists only in the character, a writer is able, by the use of words appropriate to that rasa, almost in actuality to transfer it to the mind of the audience. They experience the rasa thereby transferred . . . and so acquire the designation *rasika*. And the whole point of literature is to produce that experience.

Here one might further ask: But what about literary texts with totally fictitious plots?[26] No real character exists that can function as the locus of rasa, only someone invented by the writer's craft. We would answer: There is no law that a writer must talk only about things that really exist; that is not to the point. He can talk about nonexistent as well as existent things. All that really matters is that the character presented as the locus of rasa should delight the hearts of a receptive audience. It is similar to the problem of the language quality called "clarity of meaning." If clarity exists, that is, if the essence of a thing is clearly communicated, it is of no concern to the writer if that thing itself exists in actuality; the only matter of concern is whether, in communicating the thing, whether real or not, he is giving the audience pleasure. What is identical in the two cases is that reality attaches to something that is generically similar to what is being communicated. Thus, the effective communication of the rasa that exists in the character and there alone, with the purpose of bringing the audience pleasure, is what it means for there to be the "presence of rasa"[27] in a literary work.

(Bh) (5.2) Rasa is born of a special transcendent power within the selves of beings, and shows itself to be the sole cause for activating the self's proper qualities.

(BN) [Summary comment p. 414.1]: Thus "rasa"[28] stands above and beyond all these other particularized forms of rasa. It is singular, and in essence the act of savoring. It is that which activates the qualities in the self, and by these reactions that are its effects, it manifests itself to others. Proved to exist by the person's own experience of it, being located in the character, it is experienced by the audience when communicated through an appropriate literary composition.

(Bh) (5.3) If the poet is filled with passion, the whole world of his poem will consist of rasa; if not, it will be completely devoid of it.[29]

(BN) One might object: If the literary work only communicates the rasa that is in the character, how can one say that some *works* are "full of rasa" and some have none? We would answer: While the rasa does exist in the character, its presence or absence in a literary work depends on whether the writer producing the work has or does not have rasa. The reality or unreality of the rasa in the character is immaterial for this.[30]

(Bh) (5.4–8) In the sentence, "The woman looks," no rasa whatever appears; in "The beloved casts a glance," it can be clearly perceived.[31] In "I want you, girl, why don't you want me?" we have a vulgar sense producing an utter lack of rasa; in "The god of love, that wretch, shows me no pity, but happily he bears you no grudge, my sloe-eyed girl," the sense is sophisticated and furnishes rasa. What is required to convey rasa are the following: a new idea; sophisticated, well-turned phrasing; pleasing composition; clear articulation;[32] and propriety of meanings[33] beyond the purely mundane. From among the forms of discourse that make up literature,[34] namely, indirect expression, natural expression,[35] and the expression of rasa, I propose to show that it is the expression of rasa that finds favor among everyone.

(5.9–12). There are twenty-four powers ensuring the presence of rasa: [1] emotion; [2] generation; [3] continuity; [4] arising; [5] enhancement; [6] mixture; [7] diminution; [8] semblance; [9] cessation; [10] remnant; [11] particularity; [12] supplement. . . .[36]

[23] the ways of combining various ornaments and rasa; [24] the expressions of rasa. Whoever knows their essential nature will be able to produce poetry.

(5.13–23) [1] A rasa, when it awakens in the form of desire, for example, through its specific foundational factor, is defined as stable emotion.[37] Included in the category are the eight stable emotions (desire and the rest); the eight psychophysical responses (weeping and so on); and the thirty-three transitory emotions.[38] "Stable" emotions are those that "stay" permanently in the consciousness, come to be conjoined with their adjuncts,[39] and when amplified, become the particular rasas.[40] The mind untouched by volatility and stolidity is here called "sensitivity"; the emotions that, thanks to their connection with sensitivity, have the capacity to contribute to the production of rasa are themselves called the psychophysical responses, or "sensitivities." The "transitory" emotions are so called because they cause a stable emotion to constantly "transit" around in the body,[41] and thereby become the causes of the physical reactions. Or perhaps they are so called[42] because once present, they do not remain; transitory emotions like remembrance come into existence and go out of existence in love and its various rasas.[43] However, we ourselves insist not only that *all* the stable emotions can become transitory in the case of desire[44] but also that the transitory emotions pride, attachment, satisfaction, and sagacity can become stable emotions in the case of four additional rasas respectively: vainglory, affection, peacefulness, and nobility.[45]

(5.24–34) [2] A rasa is "generated" when, as a result of the nature of the emotion's substratum,[46] or the preeminence of its object, or the high susceptibility of the subject's innate dispositions, it has generated in its substratum a reaction, a transitory emotion, or a psychophysical response.[47] [3] A rasa's "continuity" refers to the continuation of a reaction and the like when the force of memory has become highly susceptible by virtue of the stimulant factors. [4] The "arising" of a rasa refers to the mere fact of its arising given the conjunction of the factors, physical reactions and psychophysical responses, and transitory emotions. [5] The "enhancement" of a rasa is an intensification brought about by the quality of the object of the emotion, the nature of its substratum, the high susceptibility of the innate dispositions, or the high degree of magnification[48] brought about by the stimulant factors. [6] The "mixture" of rasa is a combination when some other emotion arises whose originating cause, moment in time, and strength are equal to the first rasa.[49] [7] "Diminution" is a decrease in the strength of a rasa from its being overshadowed by another one or lending its coloring to another.[50] [8] We understand "semblance" to be the presence of rasa in characters of low status, animals, antagonists, or entities referenced in a merely metaphorical manner. [9] The "cessation" of a rasa is its complete elimination in the face of some powerful adverse cause. [10] When the rasa is not completely eliminated thereby, by virtue of the nature of the substratum[51] or the force of the innate dispositions, it has what is termed a "remnant." [11] We refer to the eight standard rasas, the erotic and so on; the four additional ones, the peaceful, vainglorious, affectionate, and noble; as well as the various stable emotions, desire and the rest, as "particularities" of rasa. [12] The "supplements" of rasa are the factors, the reactions, the transitory emotions, the substratum, and the ten forms of coquetry of lovers (mimicry and the rest). . . .[52]

. . . .

We now proceed to definitions and examples.

(5.138) Desire is a feeling of pleasure with respect to things attractive to the mind; in the case of a nonintimate relationship it is called affection.

An example of a rasa's "stable emotion" [1], here in the form of desire:

> Hara lost his calmness for a moment like the ocean when the moon begins to rise,
> and feasted all his eyes[53] on Uma's face with those ruby-red lips.[54]

Here Parvati's face is made attractive by her full lips and so on, and Lord Shiva feasts his eyes upon them. This act enables us to infer the specific nature of his craving, and this in turn, given the absence of mention of any psychophysical responses, enables us to infer only that a pleasant experience has come about.[55]

[571] An example of the "generation" of rasa [2], again in the form of desire, when we have the emergence of a psychophysical response:

> The groom's forearm had goosebumps and the maiden's fingers began to perspire
> when their hands met, as if the love god's very existence were split between them.[56]

Here we understand, from the emergence of the psychophysical responses of horripilation and perspiration, that rasa in the form of desire is coming to manifestation.

An example of the generation of rasa when we have the emergence of a transitory emotion:

> They cast their glances sidelong and turned them away when brought into
> contact,
> their eyes tactfully restrained by shame, hungry though they were to look.[57]

Here, as the transitory emotion of shame comes into being, it gives us to understand the coming into being of rasa. An example of the same thing with the emergence of a physical reaction:

When Sunanda finished speaking the princess put aside her shame
and with a glance purified by grace, like the ritual garland, chose the prince.[58]

Here a physical reaction, which in this case consists of the bodily action of glancing,[59] marks, by its coming into being, the manifestation of rasa.

2.2 ONE RASA UNDERLIES ALL MULTIPLICITY: THE LATE STATEMENT

From *Light on Passion* of Bhoja[60]

INTRODUCTION

1. May the body of Shiva, enemy of the Triple City, provide protection—a body that seems to know at once love enjoyed and thwarted: though fused with his beloved, it cannot loosen her belt or gain an embrace or obtain a kiss or see her glowing face.[61]
2. May Ganesha, blessed lord of hosts, remove all obstacles, the dust of whose lotus feet so burnishes the mind that it becomes clear as a metal mirror to reflect all the more luminously the full wealth of word and meaning.
3. "Passion" is defined as a special capacity of a person's ego; it is the very essence of love. Insofar as a person has the capacity to "taste" it, it is called rasa, or "taste." One who is endowed with the capacity to taste rasa is said to be a *rasika*, "one who can taste rasa."[62]
4. It is an indescribable transformation of primal matter consisting of one's sense of self that awakens in the heart of those in whom sensitivity predominates; a transformation born of a special untainted property, arising by way of predispositions formed by experiences in past lives, and functioning as the single source of the appearance and intensification of the entire range of the self's attributes.[63]
5. What is above all "savored" in ordinary language is the purport; in a literary work, implicature; among all a lover's qualities his firm devotion; in a woman's body her charm. And what is above all savored in the heart of man with a sense of self[64] is passion and passion alone.
6. Authorities traditionally reckon ten rasas, namely, the erotic, heroic, tragic, fantastic, violent, comic, macabre, affectionate,[65] fearful, and peaceful. We, however, admit only one rasa, passion, insofar as it alone is what is really tasted.
7. The conventional wisdom that the term "rasa" refers only to the heroic, the fantastic, and the remaining six has come out of nowhere and is hardly more than a superstition, like the belief that banyan trees are haunted by goblins. It has

only been accepted because of the world's usual intellectual conformity, and our intention in this work is to put it to rest.

8. The sense of self that produces the experience of the consciousness of pleasure and the rest of the emotions as all agreeable to the mind[66] is what we should understand to be rasa, for that is what is "tasted" through the power of the self. To apply the term to emotions such as desire when fully developed is erroneous.
9. The forty-nine emotions, desire and the rest, that arise from the various causal factors, encompass the element of passion and augment it so as to make it manifest, as a mass of flames augments the elemental form of fire to make it manifest.[67]
10. That which is produced (*bhāvyate*) by a process of production (*bhāvanā*) in the mind of a person fully absorbed while the process is occurring, is called a "thing produced" (*bhāva*), or emotion. Rasa, however, transcends the plane of production and, in transfigured form,[68] is what is really savored in a heart with developed ego.
11. If desire and the other stable emotions are to be counted as rasas when they achieve full development, then what crime are joy and the other transitory emotions guilty of that they should not get the name rasa, since as emotions they are no different from desire and the rest? If it is because they are supposed to be ephemeral, then, pray tell, how long do fear, grief, anger, amusement, and the other "stable" emotions really last?
12. If an emotion's stability is thought to derive from the preeminence of its object or the nature of its substratum, then what about "transitory" emotions such as anxiety and the like? As for the substratum, that is, the hero's temperament, it remains the same in the case of both "stable" and "transitory" emotions with respect to his self; as for the object, the capacity to excite predispositions is something common to both "stable" and "transitory" emotions.[69]

It is established, then, that desire and the rest of the forty-nine emotions themselves derive from passion; the doctrine that the heroic and so on are rasas is at bottom false. Passion is the sole rasa, and the only means of fulfilling the four ends of man. Specifying what precisely this rasa is, however, is difficult, since it is knowable only experientially and is not universally accessible. When displayed by skilled actors in correctly performed dramatic acting, it can be ascertained by the audience; when properly[70] declaimed by great poets in their compositions, it can become accessible to the minds of the learned. However, [3] things are not so sweetly savored when they are actually perceived as when they are cognized through the language of masters of language. To quote: "A subject does not expand the heart so powerfully when we see it portrayed as when it flashes forth from the words of great poets declaimed with art."[71] Therefore we prize poets far more than actors, and poetry more than dramatic acting.

Literature has traditionally been defined as the "unity" of word and meaning; to quote: "Words and meanings unified constitute literature."[72] As for the signification of "word," it is that through which, when pronounced, meaning is understood, and is of twelve sorts, beginning with base and affix and ending with sentence, section, and work. "Meaning" is what a word gives us to understand, and it is of twelve sorts, beginning with action and tense and ending with word meaning and sentence meaning. Finally, "unity" signifies a relationship of word and meaning, and it too is of twelve sorts, beginning with denotation and intention and ending with absence of flaws, use of language qualities, connection with "ornaments,"[73] and the presence of rasa.

. . . .

(p. 373.26)[74] We have already argued that purport is a kind of sentence meaning that pertains to ordinary language, whereas implicature is restricted to literature. What is the actual difference between these two? Earlier we asserted that

> [374] Ordinary language is the direct language of scholarship and everyday life; the indirect language found in "declarative statements"[75] and the like has the designation "literature." Purport is a feature of meaning, when the essential intention of a speaker is understood from his utterance; implicature, by contrast, is a feature of words. Purport is an internal quality of the goddess of speech, like a woman's sexual attraction; implicature is the goddess's external quality, like a woman's radiant physical beauty.[76] Because the difference between them is slight, both are sometimes called by both names, just as the two months Surabhi and Vaisakha may be referred to by either of the names for spring, Madhu and Madhava.[77]

True, one might object, this has been asserted, but it has yet to be expounded with appropriate examples. I will do so then; hear me out.[78]

The entire preceding passage[79] should be understood as relating to implicature in literature. "Purport" in ordinary language is of two sorts, depending on whether it is the language of scholarly discourse or of everyday life.[80] An example of the former is found in memorial verse 3 of the introduction. The first sentence there ("'Passion' is defined . . .") is based on *received knowledge* of the type known as an "authoritative testimony." The second sentence ("Insofar as a person . . .") is based on personally verifiable *perception*, in a way that conforms with the technical term ("perception") itself. The third sentence ("One who is endowed . . .") is an *inference* of the sort known as "necessary assumption." That is to say, the perfectly just, everyday description of a few exceptional persons as "ones who can taste rasa," in the sense that they have a connection with rasa when this has nothing to do with their ability to taste flavorful foods, could never be made unless we *assume* that a relationship with an existent thing called rasa obtained that could be personally validated. The communication of this intended sense by means of the three sources of valid knowledge constitutes the *explicit* sentence meaning.[81]

There are three kinds of people with whom one may communicate: one who has no understanding of a given matter at all; one who has a contrary view; one who is uncertain. Now, just as one prepares a meal on the assumption that, between a sick and a healthy man, it is the healthy man who is going to accept food, so here it is out of consideration for the man who has no understanding that received knowledge is introduced even before the other two. The doubter and the contrarian will of course not accept received knowledge, and for them a proof stronger than all the others, namely perception, is accordingly adduced. But the last, the man of opposing views, will not accept even perception because of his contrariety, so to instruct him the ultimate weapon, universally applicable reasoning, is adduced. This intention of the author's, which leads him to adduce as he does the three means of knowledge, constitutes the *implicit* sentence meaning.[82] Lastly, from the Samkhya viewpoint adopted here—shown by, among other signs, the adducing of the only three means of knowledge it accepts[83]—derives the *purport* of the communication:[84] that passion is something that must preexist and merely becomes manifest, not something previously nonexistent that then comes into being, and that it has three means of valid knowledge.[85] [375] For Samkhya thinkers argue that only something already existent can "come into being"; primal matter alone is active, spirit is passive, and matter approaches spirit, passive though the latter is, to furnish experience.

It may be objected that the Samkhyas typically adduce their proofs in the order perception, inference, and authoritative testimony, and that we should therefore explain our "purport" in adducing received knowledge first. We have of course already stated that we do so out of consideration for the man lacking all knowledge of the matter. But we might add that adducing it first is meant to suggest our belief that things grasped by perception do not please so much as they do when grasped through the words of masters of language.[86] And by abandoning the traditional order of proofs, we also want to indicate that we are not 100 percent Samkhyas, for literary art is thoroughly nonsectarian.[87]

In memorial verse 4 we indicate the causes that help manifest passion as well as the effects of passion, another term for which is sense of self. Passion is the "very essence of love" (compare memorial verse 3), the third of the ends of man and the reward of the other two, namely wealth and morality. It is, moreover, a "special capacity of a person's ego" (memorial verse 3) subsisting in the self by way of reflection. Thus: it arises in consequence of undiluted good karma from past lives, and once arisen it is the cause of the "appearance" of the "entire range of the self's attributes"[88] (memorial verse 4) that will be defined below. Passion is something strengthened by the innate dispositions produced by the experiences of countless past lives, and when thus strengthened it becomes the cause of the "intensification" of the entire range of the self's attributes. Passion is the "single" thing of this kind, it is a "transformation" of primal matter consisting of a developed "sense of self"; and in exceptional individuals it awakens, in the form of reflection, as if from sleep at places where darkness, or stolidity, is breached.[89] Such is the explicit meaning of the sentence.

With the phrase "single source" we indicate that there exists no other source of the entire range of the self's attributes, and thereby mean to say that passion alone is the means of fulfilling the four ends of man.[90] By using the figure of waking after sleep in the verb "it awakens," we mean to suggest that passion subsists in suspended animation even when as yet unmanifested, and thereby we want to deny that it then ceases to exist. Our indicating its miraculous character by the word "indescribable" in the memorial verse intends to suggest how difficult it would be to describe passion's exceptional quality even if one had a thousand lifetimes to try. "Consisting of one's sense of self" indicates that the foundation of passion, which is in essence awareness, is awareness itself, and thereby excludes any other ground for it. Such is the implied sentence meaning. The purport of the sentence is to encourage readers who seek to fulfill the four ends of man to apply themselves to this,[91] since the fact that passion is the means to achieve those ends is the sort of thing we have striven to communicate. In the same way one can analyze the explicit meaning, the implicit meaning, and the purport of nonscholarly, everyday utterances. The foregoing explains those rare instances where literature and ordinary language, and thus "implicature" and "purport," are actually mixed together in a single text, as for example in memorial verse 1.

Chapter 11: Discourse on the Presence of Rasa

[613] The body of the poem, like that of a beloved, must, in accordance with what has been said up to this point, be without flaw, endowed with qualities[92] and with ornaments. But the presence of rasa[93] is the principal source of its real beauty. That is,

> All a woman's adornment—her lovely form, good family,
> youth, beauty, firm devotion, affability, character,

sophistication, modesty, breeding—all counts for nothing
if she does not have deep love for her lover.[94]

And,

"My lady may be adorned with good birth, character, and jewelry,
but I don't find her attractive unless in a crowd of women
she holds her head high with the pride derived
from being honored as a hero's wife."[95]

Now, rasa in this treatise is defined as love. For all forms of emotion, desire and everything else, once they reach their full development,[96] ultimately turn out to be nothing but this. Thus people are said to "*love* sex," to "*love* quarreling" or anger or joking.[97]

There is no way to counteract a predilection that has no cause.
There is some thread of affection that knits living things together deep within.[98]

Thus,

"A man who loves a woman thinks she does everything to please him,
unaware that he finds pleasing whatever it is she does."[99]

Moreover,

"The person need do nothing at all, the mere joy of being together
dispels sorrow. What a gift it is, to have someone who loves you."[100]

Or:

"A person one loves gives pleasure even when causing pain.
Breasts thrill with delight even while throbbing from a lover's scratches."[101]

[614] This is something we have already argued (memorial verse 8). Now, one might object: You just said that, given such expressions as "to love sex" or "to love quarreling," all emotions when fully developed ultimately turn out to be love, and that therefore in this context rasa itself is defined as this love. How can you then say in the memorial verse: "To apply the term to emotions such as desire when fully developed is erroneous"?[102]

My answer is that rasa is not "emotions such as desire when fully developed," but instead, precisely the passion that underlies them. What we mean by "passion" is a particular aspect of the ego; the seed of any heightened state of "the entire range of the self's attributes" [memorial verse 4] that make manifest the particular preferences, views, and acts of the self; in other words, the "cause of . . . intensification" [v. 4] of intellect, pleasure, pain, predilection, aversion, volition, innate dispositions, and the rest. When this passion is "tasted" by a responsive person it is called rasa. When it exists, the person is said to be a *rasika*, "one who can taste rasa"; when it does not, he is said to "lack rasa."[103] The "emotions," which make passion manifest, are in fact *derived* from it. They are forty-nine in number. . . .[104]

[615] On this point some have argued that the erotic rasa originates from desire; in our view, the erotic—that is, passion—is itself the origin of desire and all the other stable emotions. After all, these arise only in the man of passion, not in the man lacking it; it is only the man of passion who experiences desire, amusement, determination, or attachment.[105] Desire and the rest are emotions and not rasas precisely because they are things that are brought into being; indeed, it is because they are, to the degree possible, produced (*bhāvyamāna*) that they are called "things produced" (*bhāva*), or emotions. Rasa, however, goes beyond the plane of production and hence is one's very "sense of self," that is, the experience of pleasure even in the presence of pain and the like, which thereby become agreeable to the mind.[106] Since the stable emotions, when fully developed, are therefore a source of pleasure only indirectly, the name rasa is applied to them *in a secondary sense*. They are, accordingly, not themselves rasa but rather precisely emotions, because they are the object of the process of bringing-into-being.[107]

The assertion that rasa comes about when only a stable emotion like desire is brought to its full development also has no substance.[108] For that can apply to any of the thirty-three transitory emotions too, such as fatigue, which can be "brought to full development" through overexertion and the like. And these transitory emotions are as "stable" as the others, since they too activate[109] powerful innate dispositions. Now, such innate dispositions can be activated in consequence of either the preeminence of the object of affect or the temperament of the character.[110] A character's temperament is one of the three kinds, sensitive, volatile, or stolid, and thereby a corresponding experience will be brought into being. Accordingly, these transitory emotions too may be referred to as "stable."[111]

There is actually no warrant for a division into eight stable emotions, eight psychophysical responses, and thirty-three transitory emotions, since the function of any one of these factors can be executed by any of the others. A given emotion can be now stable, now transitory; in fact, depending on the circumstances, all can be stable or transitory emotions or even "sensitivities," that is, psychophysical responses, because they all derive from the mind, and sensitivity is nothing but an unobscured mind.[112]

It is also foolish to assert that it is only a stable emotion that becomes rasa through its conjunction with factors, physical responses, and transitory emotions [616], since you can find the same conjunction in any of the transitory emotions, such as joy and so on. Therefore, desire and the rest of the "stable" entities are nothing more than emotions, whereas passion and passion alone is the sole rasa. And this rasa, when coming to light thanks to these emotions in combination with their full complement of factors and reactions, can be savored especially intensely.

With respect to this point, some[113] have argued that the rasa called the erotic is not something brought to manifestation by desire and the other emotions; they claim instead that desire (and this would hold true for the other stable emotions), having first arisen through the foundational factor and reached intensification through the physical setting and other auxiliary causes, *itself turns into* rasa and so acquires the name "the erotic." But those who hold this view may be asked the following: Do these stable emotions, each of them arising by reason of its specific foundational factor, arise the same for everyone, or only for some? If for everyone, then the whole world[114] would be *rasikas*—able to experience rasa—which is patently not the case, since we can see for ourselves that some individuals are able to experience rasa and some are not. And no postulate that is contradicted by perception is admissible. So desire and the other stable emotions do not come into play for everyone, but only for some, and for this variance we must identify some cause. It will have to be either something empirically verifiable or something transcendent. It cannot be the former since there is nothing to be observed there; as for a transcendent cause, it must be either common or unique, and if it is common, we are back with the first problem, namely, that the whole world would be able to experience rasa. If, however, this causal condition is a unique transcendent thing, it would have to be the effect of some property[115] to which the individual's beginningless predispositions are related. And it is precisely this that we call the "special capacity of a person's ego" (memorial verse 3), which we simultaneously refer to as passion, sense of self, and rasa. It is in consequence of this that the stable emotions, desire and the rest, come into play. And it is only those persons endowed with passion who can savor this rasa when it comes to be manifested by the fully developed stable emotions; it is the same as with the element of fire, which is only manifested by a mass of flames.[116]

Rasa, which arises through such conditioning factors, is of three sorts: "developed," "in the form of an emotion," and "semblance of rasa." A developed rasa is what the leading character, the protagonist who dominates the narrative, experiences in reference to a commensurate object of affect. Rasa that remains in the form of an emotion is what a supporting character experiences and is not fully developed. Semblance of rasa is what the antagonist experiences, or what is ascribed to an animal.

The aforementioned "presence of rasa" is of two sorts: at the level of the individual passage or of the whole composition. [617] So far we have discussed—whether in strict accordance with the rules of discourse or randomly as an outgrowth of other discussions—the presence of rasa at the level of the passage by way of [1] the avoidance of flaws (reference to what is indecent, inauspicious, disgusting, vulgar, and so on); [2] the use of language qualities (luminosity, "wherein the rasa appears with great brilliance,"[117] and the like); and [3] the conjunction with "ornaments"[118] (the "graceful" and other dramatic modes, and the "southern" and other verbal styles). But the presence of rasa in a passage actually reaches its full development only when these various ornaments exist in combination, since rasa is produced by a special constellation of language qualities and ornaments. Generally speaking, we never find language qualities, or figures (whether of sound or of sense or of both sound and sense, which comprise, respectively, alliteration, etc.; naturalistic description, etc.; and metaphor, etc.)[119] existing singly in the body of a poem, any more than we find only single pieces of jewelry—whether bangles, armlets, or earrings—on a woman's body. It is only in combination that they are considered to be fully developed ornamentation. As in the case of prepared food, where we have the combination of sweet, sour, salty, and the "six-spice" substance; in the case of dress, the combination of garments, creams, garlands, jewelry; in the case of incense, the combination of sandalwood, aloe, camphor, and sal-tree resin; in the case of musical performance, the combination of dance, instrumental music, singing,[120] and recitation; in the case of love, the combination of anger, repentance, forgiveness, and the pleasure of reunion; in the case of family life, the combination of acts fulfilling the four ends of man, morality, wealth, love, and liberation—so in the body of the poem it is the combination alone of the three types of figures (metaphor and the rest) along with the set of language qualities[121] that, being the thing savored most, is the cause of the presence of rasa.

. . . .[122]

(p. 624) This "combination" was earlier defined as a mixture "of various 'ornaments.'"[123] One might have called it simply a "mixture of 'ornaments,'" and the fact that we use the qualification "various" is meant to indicate that language qualities, rasas, and so on are also "ornaments" insofar as these also make a poem beautiful. This is in accordance with Dandin's pronouncements.[124] . . .

Now, while it is reasonable to say that language qualities themselves are "ornaments," it may be thought unreasonable to claim that rasas and the rest (emotions, semblances of emotions, etc.) can be ornaments, because unlike the qualities, these are not explicitly referred to as such by Dandin. But in fact it makes perfectly good sense, since [1] "the haughty," [2] the "rasa-laden," and [3] the "emotional" are actually classified among the ornaments when they are in their intensified state. . . .[125]

Let us examine these in order. [1] When Dandin defines "a haughty declaration" as one where "the speaker's ego is prominent," he is describing the first stage of rasa (otherwise known as "ego," "sense of self," or "passion") as it awakens in the form of a transformation of primal matter consisting of a developed sense of self in the hearts of sensitive persons. With his definition he encapsulates the following: rasa is a special dimension of the ego that is the source of the appearance and intensification of the entire range of the self's attributes; something found in certain special individuals and produced through an exceptional, transcendent cause;[126] its durability ("prominence") is owing to innate dispositions derived from the experiences of countless past lives.[127] Examples of a haughty declaration:

> [625] "O joy! All homage to me! She looked at me,
> that girl with eyes that flutter like a frightened doe's."[128]

Or:

> "As the lovely-eyed girl stood at twilight in the courtyard, crowded as it was,
> I could hardly control myself and began to swing my arms.
> She sighed, her head lowered in modesty, but innocently and shyly in between
> she sent looks of love toward me that shone more brilliantly than the moon."

[2] When Dandin defines the "rasa-laden statement" as "beautified by rasa," he is establishing the second stage of passion, which, in accordance with the *Sutra on Rasa* ("Rasa arises . . ."), comes to manifestation by means of all the different causal factors and becomes amplified so as to reach its full development.[129] An example:

> "At this point, the lotus-eyed girl showed rare mastery of Love's lessons:
> an allure beyond the power of language to describe,
> every possible emotion, every physical reaction,
> while casting her reserve to the winds."[130]

Or:

"By chance I came upon my love like a digit of the moon
entering the maw of Rahu, and I snatched her from the arc of that bastard's sword.
I nearly lost my mind—broken from shock, melted with pity,
agitated with amazement, aflame with anger, and blossoming with joy."[131]

[3] When Dandin defines "affectionate utterance" as "an expression of heightened affection," he is indicating the highest stage of the ego. For by the use of the term "affection(ate)" he is referring indirectly to desire, which is the paradigmatic emotion, and is indicating further that it transforms into love when it reaches full development and transcends the nature of an emotion ("transcending the plane of production").[132] He thereby gives us to understand that all the other emotions as well, upon reaching full development, are transformed into love.[133] An example:

"A man who loves a woman. . . ."[134]

[626] Or:

"Identity in joy and sorrow, consonance in every condition,
where the heart can find respite, whose rasa old age cannot spoil,
what alone abides as time removes all veils and pure love ripens—
that singular blessing is only bestowed on a good man, and only then with
luck."[135]

Last, by the words "All three, when they reach their intensified state, become ornaments," Dandin gives us to understand that when they are *not* "intensified," all three function as language qualities, not ornaments, for all three are found listed as such among these qualities.[136]

. . . .[137]

(p. 626.24) An objection might be raised: Does the suffix *-vat* ("laden") in the word *rasavat* ("rasa-laden") have a possessive or a comparative sense?[138] The former is impossible, since none of its meanings can apply. Rasas are states of pleasure or pain pertaining to conscious embodied beings. But literature consists of words and meanings and is therefore not itself conscious; accordingly, none of the meanings of the possessive suffix (abundance, censure, etc.) is possible.[139] [627] As for the comparative suffix, it too is impossible since its meanings (as an adverb, or in reference to a possessive or locative, signifying "similar")[140] are likewise inapplicable. One cannot say, for example, that a literary work is *rasavat* because it "functions like" rasa, nor is there anything in it or of it "similarly as in" rasa or "similarly as of" rasa.

I would respond that it can be whichever one likes. The suffix can have a possessive sense, despite the objection. Someone like Rama has rasa, and his speech, since its source lies in his very rasa, may itself be said to be "rasa-laden" or have rasa; when an imitation of such a person is created by a poet, there is a complete identification between the real person and the character, such that the imitation of his speech may likewise be said to be rasa-laden. Or it can have a comparative sense, again despite your objection. Another of that suffix's meanings, "capable of,"[141] is perfectly applicable: a literary text is "rasa-laden" if it is capable of expressing rasas. When the speech of someone like Rama, who has rasa, is being imitated by the poet, it is capable, given the illusion of identity between the real and the imitated speech, of expressing rasas and so can be said to be rasa-laden.

A possible objection: All desirable elements enhance the beauty of a literary work and could therefore be considered "ornaments." Since there would thus be no specificity to "ornament" as such, one should speak only of "combination" or "mixture."[142] My answer is that that would not be possible, for if we did not specify "ornaments," then, since Bharata's *Sutra on Rasa* speaks of a "conjunction of factors," that mixture might be mistakenly taken as the "combination" we intend.[143] This misinterpretation is forestalled by our use of the word "ornament." The aesthetic elements themselves are not ornaments, but rather particular entities that engender "ornaments," which here comprise the emotions, rasas, and the semblances of emotions and rasas.

One might grant this but still object that if "aesthetic elements" and so on are considered qualities of signification, they would still turn out to be "ornaments."[144] True enough, but given that they are appropriated with something else in mind—that is, rasa—they are subsumed under that other thing. In the same way, the constitutive words of a sentence do not individually manifest themselves when we are grasping the meaning of the sentence as a whole.[145] . . .

[628.20] The class of "ornament" is in fact threefold: indirect expression, natural expression, and expression of rasa. The first is present when there is emphasis on "ornament" in the sense of similes and the like; the second, when there is emphasis on language qualities, such as fitness and the rest; the last, when there is the production of rasa by the conjunction just described. . . .

Now, with respect to the last of these, the expression of rasa: "factors" are twofold, "foundational" and "stimulant." The foundational factor is the sight of some loved person in respect of whom pleasure arises, or a hated person in respect of whom pain arises. The experience of such pleasure or pain activates an "innate disposition" that produces recollection, [629] whereas stimulants such as flower garlands, scented creams, and so on stimulate that innate disposition. Once a person has such a memory stimulated by the stimulants, there arise "attributes of the self," i.e., recollection, desire, aversion, and volition, which stimulate actions of mind, speech, intellect, or body. These are termed emotional "reactions" insofar as they are emotionally felt.[146] They intensify a stable emotion, desire and the like, which derives from nothing other than passion. As the stable emotion seeks to attain the desired object or avoid the hated object, it is mixed with the transitory emotions—which include, in the case of desire, pleasurable transitory emotions such as joy, firmness, recollection, reflection, and the like. Ultimately, this stable emotion attains progressively greater intensity[147] and becomes a rasa, such as the erotic enjoyed. When it fails to attain the desired object (or avoid the hated object), the selfsame stable emotion of desire is mixed with disagreeable transitory emotions such as disquiet, longing, panic, profound indifference, and the like, and thereby becomes the rasa called the erotic thwarted, which consists of pain.

An example of the development of the erotic rasa from the stable emotion called desire:[148] "The woman I thought was dead and hoped. . . ."[149] Here, Avanti, that is, Vasavadatta, is the foundational factor. The king of Vatsa feels the stable emotion of desire, which she has given rise to in him. The intensifying factor is her resuscitation. When this intensifies the stable emotion, and when the pleasurable transitory emotions such as joy, firmness, recollection, perplexity, and the like arise, the stable emotion becomes the erotic enjoyed. The king's words, "The woman . . . ," which are his reaction to this, are said to be "rasa-laden" insofar as they are generated by the erotic rasa.

An example of the development of the comic rasa from the stable emotion of amusement: "My friend, you'd better move your blouse. . . ."[150] Here the foundational factor is a woman who is angry with her husband and yet whose breasts are marked with the scratches he has caused during lovemaking with her. The stable emotion of the comic arises in her girlfriend, who here is making fun of her. The intensifying factors include the friend's reminding the woman that she is supposed to be angry, and this intensifies the stable emotion. Hereby arise transitory emotions in the friend, which include doubt, dissimulation, merriment, stammering, and the like. Amusement, the stable emotion here, thereby reaches its full development and turns into the comic rasa. Her words, "Aren't you supposed to be still angry?" and so on are said to be "rasa-laden" insofar as they arise from the comic rasa in her.

An example of the development of heroic rasa from the stable emotion of determination: "Without having conquered land and sea. . . ."[151] Here the stable emotion, determination, arises from the foundational factor constituted by conquest and so on. It is intensified by the speaker's brilliance, firmness, resoluteness, [630] and other intensifying factors; and when his transitory emotions arise—recollection, reflection, perplexity, and so on—the stable emotion is fully developed and turns into the heroic. The speaker is filled with heroic rasa and the words he speaks as a result of this rasa, "Without having conquered . . ." are said to be "rasa-laden" insofar as they are generated by the heroic rasa in him.

An example of the development of the rasa of the fantastic from the emotion of amazement: "On the trees in the garden of the gods. . . ."[152] The physical form of normal trees consists of sprouts, flowers, fruit, and branches, but the trees of Nandana, garden of the gods, have instead silk cloths, jewelry, drinks, and palaces. What a marvel! Thus, these things function as the foundational factor for the speaker of the verse who is visiting the world of the gods. From these arises the stable emotion of amazement, which is stimulated by his seeing the parts of the trees. When the transitory emotions arise (joy, horripilation, perspiration, stammering),[153] the stable emotion is fully developed and turns into the fantastic, and the words spoken as a result, "On the trees . . ." are said to be "rasa-laden" insofar as they are generated by the rasa of the fantastic in him. . . .[154]

[631.18][155] Now, the teacher Bharata holds that it is only these eight stable emotions that receive the names of rasas, that is, the designations "the erotic," "the heroic," and so on, when they reach full development;[156] further that, just as [1] these rasas arise from emotions, and [2] emotions arise from rasas, in the same way [3] rasas arise from rasas. As for [3], here would be an example of the comic arising from the erotic:

"This Shankara,[157] universally acclaimed for abstinence,
now bears his wife with half his body, afraid to be without her.
And people say *he* conquered *us*?" With this, the god of love
squeezed his wife's hand, and laughed—and may his laugh protect you.[158]

An example of the fantastic from the heroic:

"And now listen to what happened at the cattle raid—
I touch your heart,[159] indeed, your own son was a witness:
When armed and massed we attacked, we saw but a single Arjuna,
but then there arose as many of him as us who were waging battle. . . ."[160]

[632.13] This view, however, is wrong. For the emotions such as desire, however fully developed, would themselves then be just emotions and not rasas; otherwise one would wind up having to assume (which Bharata does not do) that the transitory emotions such as joy and the like, which can be as fully developed as desire and so on, could also be rasas (compare memorial verse 11 above). Nor is there any law that there can be only eight rasas. Some people[161] count as rasas also the peaceful, the affectionate, the vainglorious, and the noble.[162] The designations of the four kinds of protagonists, the peaceful, romantic, proud, and dignified, are based on the existence of these additional rasas. An example of the peaceful rasa founded upon a peaceful protagonist:

> "He possesses all treasures who has a contented heart.
> To the man wearing soft leather shoes, the whole earth is covered in suede."[163]

An example of the affectionate rasa founded upon a romantic protagonist:

> "A man who loves a woman. . . ."[164]

[633] An example of the vainglorious rasa founded upon a proud protagonist:

> "So long as I am armed, what need of other arms?
> What other weapon could ever achieve what my weapon cannot?"[165]

An example of the noble rasa founded upon a dignified protagonist:

> "Do not fear I will take vengeance. . . ."[166]

The primary stuff or basis[167] of the peaceful rasa is the stable emotion impassivity; that of the affectionate rasa, attachment; that of the vainglorious rasa, pride; that of the noble rasa, egotism. And the same conjunction of factors, reactions, and transitory emotions can apply to these four rasas no less than to passion.

Others even argue that all forty-nine emotions, arising from this conjunction and fully developed, turn into rasas.[168] And if all emotions are thus equally rasas, it makes no sense to apply the technical terms "the erotic," "the heroic," and so on only to those eight stable emotions, desire and the rest, when fully developed. One may do it, but that would then be only a terminological distinction (compare memorial verse 7 above).

Furthermore,[169] if emotions like desire when fully developed *were themselves* rasas, how could Bharata assert that rasas *come from* emotions? The reverse would then also be illogical, namely that emotions come from rasas. And there do not exist "rasas" in the plural anyway, but only "rasa" singular—that is to say, passion—something we will also argue further below at length.

As for Bharata's postulate that rasas arise from rasas, this can only mean one of two things. It can mean, first, that rasas form the foundational factor for other rasas. But the rule that Bharata gives—"From the erotic arises the comic, from the violent the tragic, from the heroic the fantastic, and from the macabre the fearful"[170]—is not invariable. [634] The comic can be found both to arise[171] from some rasa other than the erotic (such as from the heroic)[172] and not to arise from the erotic (whereas the tragic can arise from the erotic); the tragic can be found to arise from some rasa other than the violent (such as from the erotic), and not to arise from the violent (whereas the fearful can arise from the violent), and so on. . . .

[635.7] The postulate can also mean that one rasa functions as the primary stuff or basis of another rasa. Here also we have to ask whether the comic is *born* from the erotic, or whether the erotic itself *becomes* the comic. The first option is precisely our position, for as we have already stated, no stable emotion, whether fully developed or not, is possible for a person without passion.[173] It is only the man of passion who feels desire, determination, amusement, amazement, revulsion, grief, fear, impassivity, affection, pride, and sense of self. But the second alternative—that the erotic, whose primary stuff or basis is desire, should turn into the comic—makes no sense, given that we never use the term "the comic" in reference to the erotic.

Now, if "The comic may be described as an imitation of the erotic,"[174] we can easily hold, per the above, that an imitation of the heroic can also be comic.[175] The same refutation holds for the argument that the tragic comes from the violent. The former neither derives from the latter, nor does the latter become the former. Last, if it is argued that "the tragic rasa may be understood as an effect of the violent,"[176] we would deny that this is so and admit only that the violent can be *one* of its causes; similarly, the fantastic is an effect of the heroic, though nothing stops the latter from functioning in the production of the former. As for the argument that "from the macabre the fearful" arises, the former rasa would then not differ from the foundational factor.[177]

[636] So the entire doctrine—that rasas come from emotions, emotions from rasas, and rasas from rasas—is just so much chatter. What then is the reasonable position to hold? The one we enunciated above in memorial verse 8 ("The sense of self . . . is what we should understand to be rasa"). Therefore, the following can be taken as established. The first stage of rasa is where ego is prominent. The second stage of this selfsame rasa is when an emotion—and this applies to all forty-nine (the eight stable emotions, eight psychophysical responses, and thirty-three transitory emotions)—is fully developed through the conjunction of factors, reactions, and transitory emotions, and comes to merit the technical name "rasa." The highest phase of rasa is love, which is rasa's ultimate resting point, since Dandin's definition of the affectionate utterance as "an expression of heightened affection" actually indicates

that just as desire transforms into love, so at their full maturation do all other emotions.[178]

Let us explain further these first two developmental stages, starting with the first: [1] In the case of the noble rasa, as in the verse in which the speaker says, "You fear for your crimes, but my sword would never dare to fall upon a retreating enemy,"[179] we perceive a prominent ego. And this ego we can perceive in all of the poems we cited for that stage:[180] "I have gotten Avanti" (the erotic rasa); "Shame on you, your jealous anger is a joke" (the comic); "I could not be king without conquering the earth" (the heroic); "I have never seen such trees" (the fantastic), and so on. . . .[181]

[2] Now, how does "rasa arise from the conjunction of the stable emotions, transitory emotions, and reactions"?[182] [1] The stable emotions are activated in the mind of a person with a deep sense of self when it becomes subject to a given "limiting condition," that is, when the intellect and senses take on the shape of the foundational factor he has encountered. This happens in the same way that a moonstone oozes water in the presence of the moon, or sunstone bursts into flame in the presence of the sun, or crystal dissolves in the presence of camphor.[183] An example with respect to the stable emotions desire and so on:[184]

> "Amazing how when I approached the moon-faced girl with lotus-petal eyes,
> my mind grew numb, and it liquefied like a genuine moonstone."[185]

[637] An example with respect to anger and so on:

> "Then, my lord, from the pain[186] of his harsh words Sita, though gentle by
> nature, grew hard
> and blazed and spat out bright, sharp flames of language, like a sunstone."[187]

An example with respect to grief and so on:

> "Now, here those evil *rākṣasas*, with their trick of the golden deer,
> committed the deed that still brings heartache though avenged in full.
> My brother's half-mad acts when Janasthana was left deserted
> can still make a stone shed tears and break a heart of iron."[188]

[2] Transformations arise in the mind of a person endowed with a deep sense of self[189] when it becomes subject to innate dispositions from earlier experiences, as a result of a given stimulant factor, and these enhance the stable emotions. This happens in the same way that the ocean is agitated when the moon rises, or disease

increases as a result of unhealthy behavior, or a good man is deeply pained in the presence of the wicked. An example of these transformations in the case of sudden agitation of the stable emotion:[190]

> His inborn composure gone, he began to grieve,
> his throat choking with sobs. If even iron melts
> when heated, how much more the human soul?[191]

Or in the case of its increase:

> As she looked at him, she wept even more and beat her breast.
> In the presence of kin, the floodgates of grief are thrown open.[192]

Or in the case of its being counteracted:

> "First the god of love torments my heart with a desire I cannot resist or fulfill;
> and now I have to see mangos sprouting and the south wind ruffling their leaves."[193]

[3] Various reactions and transitory emotions come into being, under given conditions, in relation to one and the same emotion (desire, anger, grief, etc.); both the reactions and the emotions have internal and external aspects, and mingle, functioning either distributively or as a compound. This happens in the same way that one and the same tree has both components (trunk, branches, twigs, etc.) and derivatives (fronds, leaves, flowers, fruits, etc.); or as one and the same mass of water has mutations (swells, whirlpools, bubbles, and waves) and transformations (pearls, foam, salt, and hailstones); or as one and the same sound has timbres (sharp, normal, low, and screechy) and segmentations (phonemes, words, sentences, and animal sounds such as warbling); or one and the same element, air, has courses (the atmosphere, stratosphere, and the like) and continua (inhaled air, exhaled air, circulatory air in the body).[194] [638] With respect to transitory emotions, the internal include disquiet, longing, consternation, and doubt, and the external, perspiration, horripilation, tears, and pallor; with respect to reactions, the internal include recollection, desire, aversion, and volition, and the external, the actions of body, mind, speech, and intellect. Both categories, when they are imitated, receive the technical name "acting," whether psychophysical, physical, verbal, or costuming.[195] An example of transitory emotions and reactions arising from desire:

Revealing her emotions with the down rising on her limbs
like young plantain stalks, the daughter of the Mountain
stood there, her lovely face downturned, with eyes half-closed.[196]

Or from anger:

His anger kindled by the death of Abhimanyu at the hands of his enemies,
Partha's glances, dull with shame and suffused with tears, fell on his bow.
He was nearly faint with grief that the killers were still unavenged
and the words "My child!" flashed through his mind but did not escape his throat.[197]

Or from grief:

"Mother, mother, my heart is breaking, my body's joints are coming undone,
the world seems empty, and I burn inside with a constant fire.
My desolate soul collapses and sinks into deep darkness,
and faintness envelops me. What am I to do in my misfortune?"[198]

[4] The different rasas, then, arise from the stable emotions (desire, anger, grief, etc.) when conjoined with their various factors. This happens in the same way that sap arises from sugarcane and oil from mustard seed; or gold from minerals and iron from ore; or butter from curd and fire from wood, when conjoined with their appropriate causal factors, that is, respectively, a press, a smelting fire, a churn, and a drilling stick.[199] For example, "By chance I came upon my love like a digit of the moon. . . ."[200]

[5] The rasas produced from desire and so on assimilate the causal elements (the foundational and stimulant factors) of different rasas and are thereby strengthened, in the same way that physical tastes such as salty or sour are strengthened by assimilating sweet things such as grapes when these come in contact with them.[201] For example,

[639] "When asked, 'Who are you thinking of?' she said, distraught and weeping,
'Who's left for me to think of?' and made us weep as well."[202]

[6] The factors, transitory emotions, and reactions all become rasa from their conjunction with rasa;[203] in other words, they come to possess a property common to rasa itself. This happens in the same way that, by their conjunction with fire, earth-derived substances such as butter, lac, wax; water-derived substances such as clouds,

snow, hail; and fire-derived substances such as tin, lead, silver all become liquids—in other words, they come to possess a property common to water. For example:

> With this sorrowful composition the king
> of Kosala mourned his wife, and even the trees,
> branches shedding tears of sap, appeared to mourn.[204]

[7] From the various general rasas that appear in a literary work a specific dominant rasa is produced. This happens in the same way that honey is produced from the nectar of various plants, the six-spice drink from different sweet and other substances, or rum from molasses and other substances. For example

> "King Vikramabahu has been made my friend; this treasure of the earth—
> sole source of mastery over land and sea—my beloved Sagarika has been obtained;
> the chief queen is overjoyed to recover her cousin, and Kosala has been conquered.
> With you at my side, great minister, what do I desire that I do not have?"[205]

[8] Finally, for what is thus a single rasa we have various species (the stable emotion, the specific rasa, the semblance forms of both of these), different functions (such as, in the case of the erotic, the feelings of missing the loved one, obsessing about her, or rejoicing in her presence), and different states of being (genesis, growth, or continuity). This happens in the same way that for a single fire we have various species (earthly fire, heavenly fire, digestive fire) with different functions (burning, illuminating, digesting) and different states of being (smoke, flame, coal, etc.).[206]

. . . .[207]

(p. 644) Here an objection might be raised: Let us grant, then, that one may speak of "mixture" in the case of qualities, since these have three subvarieties—qualities of words, qualities of sense, and flaws that, if intentional, can function as good qualities in a poem—and some of these will be either prominent or not.[208] But since you have dismissed the idea that rasa is plural (the heroic rasa, the erotic, and so on), how can this single rasa, passion, allow us to speak of "mixture" when that is something requiring plurality? I would answer: Although passion is indeed the sole rasa, the stable emotions that arise from passion acquire the designation "rasa" too when they are stimulated by the stimulants and, precisely because they are infused with passion, condition the transitory emotions and reactions. Just as the sense of self conditions the stable emotions and becomes rasa when tasted by the mind, so the stable emotions condition the transitory emotions (joy, resolve, disquiet, longing, and the like), and the reactions (the actions of body, mind, speech, or intellect), and by the same infusion with the sense of self are tasted by the mind and so become rasas in the plural. When different stable emotions are enunciated simultaneously, it allows us to speak of "mixture" of rasas. But in fact, a variety of items is mixed in the case of mixture of rasas, since there are various subspecies in rasa: they are called emotions at their origin, rasas when fully developed, semblances of emotions or rasas contrarily,[209] and emotion quiescence or rasa quiescence at the end. So mixture in the case of rasa is actually sixfold, of [1] emotions, [2] rasas, [3] semblances of emotions, [4] semblances of rasas, [5] quiescence of emotion, and [6] quiescence of rasa.[210] An example of [1] the mixture of emotions:

"That insult throbs like a sharp thunderbolt in my heart,
my mind suffused with shame sinks down as if in blinding darkness,
grief at the death of my father consumes me and I can do nothing about it,
and pity for poor Sita cuts at my very vitals."[211]

Here indignation, shame, grief, and love, which we understand as the reactions in the form of a verbalization on the part of the forlorn Rama, are equal (with respect to their mutually independent existence) and mixed together but still separable, like sesame seeds and rice kernels.

[2] Mixture of rasas is found in the poem "Like a husband whose betrayal is still moist,"[212] where in the description of Hara's power the tragic and the erotic, in a relationship of dominant and subordinate, are mixed together[213] inseparably, like earth and water that make up a lump of mud.

[3] Mixture of semblances of emotions is found in the following:

"Oh Sita, this face of yours once lit up with pride at the death of my kinsmen
who stood lost in hopeless confusion before your arrogant husband.
But now I, Ravana, will flood it with tears that pour streaming from your eyes
wide with terror and rolling as your high-piled hair is violently pulled."[214]

Here we see Ravana's semblance of the emotion of desire mixed with a similar emotion of anger like a mirror and the image reflected in it. [645]

[4] Mixture of semblances of rasas:

With one red eye filled with anger she stares at the setting sun
in the sky, and with the other, engulfed in tears, at her beloved.
At the close of day, fearful of separation from her lover,
the *cakravāka* bird displays two rasas mixed, like a skillful actress.[215]

Here anger and grief, in their full development, revealed as semblances given the comparison of the *cakravākī* bird with the actress,[216] are mixed together like the man portion and the lion portion that make up the man-lion incarnation of Vishnu.

[5] Mixture of quiescent emotions:

When she saw her lover, her anger, like her eye,
began slightly to close; when he stood at her side, it was lowered like her face;
like her stiffening down, it rose to go when he touched her; it relaxed
like her belt when he started to speak,
and it fled like her shame when he fell at her feet.[217]

This concerns a woman who had been specifically instructed by her girlfriend to maintain a jealous anger. When she sees her lover (the foundational factor), there arises in her the stable emotion of joy[218] that comes from a powerful erotic attachment; this is stimulated by such stimulants as his approaching her; and as it reaches its highest development through such reactions as her closing her eyes, lowering her face, slipping off her belt, at the same time as pleasurable transitory emotions such as horripilation arise,[219] the stable emotion turns into the rasa of bliss.[220] Because of the inception of this powerful contradictory emotion, and by the very same factors that produced it, her shame and anger diminish moment by moment, and it is the two forms of quiescence of these two feelings that are here equally mixed like milk and water.

[6] Mixture of quiescent rasas:

"Enmity has ceased, and rasa rich with joy flows forth;
my brashness is somehow gone, deference overwhelms me;
at the mere sight of him I am under his power—why so? But then,
like holy places, the great have some greatly precious potency."[221]

In this verse, the rasas of the heroic, the vainglorious, and the autonomous[222] are made quiescent[223] when overpowered by the rasas of the blissful, the quiescent, and the heteronymous, in the same way that white threads of a carpet are overpowered by blue dye. Given this, along with the reaction in the form of a verbalization, the simile, and so on that are produced by the grandeur of the sight of Rama and arise in his son Lava through his impassivity and astonishment, these quiescent rasas are found to be mixed together like the paint colors that make up a painting. . . .[224]

[647.22][225] An objection might be raised: One may speak of the mixture of language qualities, of rasas, or of figures of speech, but how can one speak of the mixture of qualities and rasa? The use of qualities is as obligatory as the avoidance of flaws, and the presence of rasa is as essential as the presence of figures. Occasionally, to be sure, figures may be omitted, but never rasa and qualities. Only those entities that have an entirely contingent relationship with other entities can be conceptualized as "mixed" when they unite, such as sesame seeds and rice kernels, or milk and water, but not those entities that are noncontingently joined, such as parts and wholes, or tokens and types. [648] Here is our answer: We do not speak of "mixture" of qualities and rasa in a passage where we can think of their copresence as *not* resulting from some special effort,[226] that is, when they exist in a part-whole or token-type relation, as in the case of paint colors and a painting, man and lion in the man-lion avatar of Vishnu, earth and water that make up mud. . . .[227] There is no question of mixture in those cases where the language qualities are invariably constitutive of certain rasas or rasas of certain qualities. The sense quality called *aurjitya,* for example, is an expression of "highly developed self-consciousness," the word quality *bhāvikatva* is when an utterance is "prompted by deep emotion"; the sense quality *mādhuryam* is when a character is described as "showing gentleness" even in anger, the sense quality *udāttatva* is "nobility" of sentiment, the sense quality *preyaḥ* is when a character expresses "deep affection" for a thing, the sense quality *kānti* is when the rasa appears with great "brilliance."[228] However, we may indeed speak of mixture in a passage where the presence of qualities and rasas is intentional given their parity in respect of their mutually independent existence, as in the case of sesame seeds and rice kernels, milk and water, image and mirror reflection. There are six varieties of such mixture: where qualities are dominant, rasas dominant, both equally dominant, both equally nondominant, or where either the qualities or the rasas are present in superabundance. . . .[229]

[654.9] With respect to the "mixture of rasas and figures," six types may be distinguished, depending on whether a figure of sound, of sense, or of both sound and sense is predominant over rasa, or whether an emotion, a semblance of emotion or rasa, or a rasa is predominant over a figure. . . . An example of the second type:

> Rama's arrows, shot from hands hallowed by fondling Sita's breasts,
> made Ravana's body thrill with delight even as they pierced him.[230]

Here it is the figure of sense known as "supplying a reason" (he thrilled with delight because he was touched by hands that touched the object of his desire) that overpowers the semblance of rasa of erotic passion (Ravana's illicit desire for Sita) and makes the principal impact on the reader's understanding. . . .[231]

[655.3] In the following, an emotion is predominant over a figure:

"Even the anger in her beautiful face at a lapse in love from me
can steal my heart away, like a spot of musk on the deer in the moon."[232]

Here the god Hari, who possesses the rasa, is speaking, and his words are a reaction in the form of a verbalization, which overshadows the two sense figures in the verse, a "supplying a reason" and a simile. This being the case, the predominant meaning we understand is his state of pleasure at experiencing Satyabhama's anger.[233]

In the following a semblance of an emotion is predominant over a figure:

"Why wouldn't her waist waste away since it will never be beheld
by those dark lotus-petal eyes that her high heavy breasts obstruct?"[234]

The predominant meaning we understand here—since the four figures, "supplying a reason," simile, poetic fantasy, and "transference,"[235] are overshadowed—is a reaction, namely, the verbalization of the semblance of rasa on the part of some character, not the protagonist but rather the antagonist or other.[236] Day by day he himself is pining away, priding himself on his sexual attraction while he experiences the pleasure of his sense of self, which finds expression here by his complaint against the woman he cannot have.[237]

In the following verse a rasa is predominant over a figure:

"Don't be so proud, my friend, to be wearing on your cheek
a flower drawn by your lover with his own hand.
Other women would have the very same thing
if a thrill of ecstasy, that powerful foe, had not intervened."

Here again, the predominant thing we understand, over against the figures of speech "prohibition," "supplying as a reason what is not a reason," and "circumlocution,"[238] is a reaction in the form of a verbalization. This arises from the speaker's fully enhanced rasa of desire, which intimates the transitory feeling of trembling and serves to reveal how deep is the love shared with her beloved, in the face of the boasts of her girlfriend, who is so proud of being loved by her own lover. . . .[239]

(p. 658) So much for "presence of rasa" at the level of the individual passage. Now we treat it at the level of the whole composition. That too manifests itself by the elimination of flaws, the acquisition of language qualities, and the mixing of "ornaments," and becomes thereby a source of intellectual delight for intelligent readers. To give brief definitions of these terms: The "elimination of flaws" is the avoidance of impropriety. . . . [658.21] The "acquisition of qualities" is the artful construction of a composition, achieved through adherence to genre rules pertaining to the different kinds of literary works we will discuss. The "mixing of 'ornaments'" is the careful arrangement of narrative components in these works. . . .

[675.3] There are general and specific language qualities and ornaments, the conjunction with which is the cause for the presence of rasa at the level of the work. . . . [676.11] The fourth of the five "qualities of meaning" of the work as a whole is the "continuous presence of rasas and emotions." The word "rasa" could have been used alone since it includes emotions, which are the cause of rasa (and therefore are invariably copresent with it). But it is used separately in order to emphasize the mutual cause-and-effect relationship of the two. There must be a "continuous presence" or multiplicity of them to be savored—with rasas producing emotions, emotions rasas, and rasas rasas—so that the literary work does not become devoid of rasa, or insipid, like a meal that has only a single taste.

CHAPTER THREE

An Aesthetics Revolution, 900–1000

3.1 FROM RASA IN THE TEXT TO RASA IN THE READER: CORE IDEAS

**Commentary on the* Treatise on Drama, and *Mirror of the Heart* of Bhatta Nayaka (c. 900)

Unquestionably the greatest loss to students of Indian aesthetics is Bhatta Nayaka's *Hṛdayadarpaṇa*, *Mirror of the Heart*; its true title may have been *Sahṛdayadarpaṇa*, *Mirror for the Lover of Literature*, so little do we really know about the work. It was long thought to be a commentary on the *Treatise on Drama*, but it seems likelier to have been a monograph at once modeled on and critical of Anandavardhana's *Light on Implicature*, *Dhvanyāloka*, which was also known as *Sahṛdayāloka*, *Light for the Lover of Literature*. Various citations ascribed to Bhatta Nayaka by Abhinavagupta in his *New* Dramatic Art, however, suggest that Bhatta Nayaka did also write a commentary on the *Treatise*.

Astonishingly for a work of such transformative power, the *Mirror* was lost by the thirteenth century at the latest, and no one who spoke about it thereafter did so on the basis of direct acquaintance.[1] The pitifully few surviving fragments (twelve authentic verses, a few very doubtful ones, three very brief prose passages, and one more extended), most of them transmitted by his critics, and the subtlety of thought these indicate have made it nearly impossible for scholars to make coherent sense of Bhatta Nayaka's doctrine. A close examination of the *Ten Dramatic Forms* and *Observations* (late tenth century), however, reveals that, though never referring to Bhatta Nayaka by name, Dhanamjaya and Dhanika offer a crucially important restatement of the *Mirror*'s key ideas.

Beyond the fact that Bhatta Nayaka wrote in Kashmir sometime between Anandavardhana (c. 875), whom he critiques, and Dhanamjaya and Dhanika (c. 975), we know little about him. Kalhana's chronicle of Kashmir, the *River of Kings*, is almost certainly referring to our author when it states in reference to Shankaravarman (r. 883–902), "The king put in charge of his two new Shiva temples a Brahman named Nayaka, who was at once learned in the four Vedas and himself a veritable temple for poets, the tribe of Sarasvati."[2] As Kalhana is here suggesting, not only did Bhatta Nayaka have a stunningly original voice on literary matters, he was also an astute scholar of Mimamsa, or scriptural hermeneutics. Stray references by later critics confirm what the surviving fragments clearly show, that he had close affiliations with this discipline, which literary thinkers beginning in the middle of the ninth century had begun to utilize to powerful effect.[3] Bhatta Nayaka did not just borrow a term here or an idea there, however, as scholars like Ananda had done; he used that discipline to rethink the entire conceptual scheme of another—aesthetics.[4]

The fundamental thrust of Bhatta Nayaka's theory and the source of its transformative power lay in his directing attention away from the process by which emotion is engendered in the literary text—away, that is, from the formalist analysis dominant across the entire tradition, up to and including the grand synthesis of Bhoja—and toward the subjective experience of the viewer/reader.[5] As a student of Mimamsa, he would have been concerned with one of its core questions: What accounts for the fact that we readers, here and now, find ourselves impelled to reenact scriptural commandments that are shown in the Veda itself to concern other people at other times and places? As a student of literature, he was prompted to pose a related one: What accounts for the fact that we readers, here and now, find ourselves reexperiencing emotions that are shown in the literary work to concern other people at other times and places?

Putting the experience of the reader front and center in his analysis meant that all the earlier questions about the aesthetic experience, which were locked into a linguistic account of literature and hence were text-centric, became largely irrelevant. If the key thing about rasa is one's own subjective experience, it ceases to be interesting, perhaps even intelligible, to argue about whether rasa is engendered, inferred, or "manifested" in the character—indeed, the last theory, that of Anandavardhana, elicited Bhatta Nayaka's sharpest criticism (fragment #10). Talk of engenderment, inference, and manifestation makes sense only in reference to the character; you do not, as reader, "infer" that you are feeling rasa. You begin to ask how literary language transforms a discourse about the emotions of people you do not know (Rama, Sita) into something you as reader somehow come to participate in, and how that process—the term Bhatta Nayaka coins for it is "commonization"—enables an altogether unique kind of experience. And what aids in answering this question is the analytic method already highly developed for scripture. For analogously, scripture gives commandments that, while not directed to you personally (not even "Thou shalt" is used in India, but rather "One should"), are nonetheless meant for you and that you somehow make your own and act upon.

According to Mimamsa, scriptural language, like language in general, is action-oriented: all Vedic statements ultimately resolve into a command to perform (or avoid) some act. The general theory to account for this verbal force is organized around the notion of *bhāvanā*, "actualization," which consists of three parts: every statement can be analyzed as indicating some *thing* to be produced by the action, by means of some *instrument*, and in some *manner*. Thus for the Mimamsaka, the sentence "One who desires heaven should perform the fire sacrifice" signifies "One should actualize, or produce, heaven by means of a sacrifice in the manner required for the fire sacrifice." Insofar as literature is a subset of discourse as such, any adequate theory of literature, as Bhatta Nayaka appears to have conceived of this theory, will necessarily accord with *bhāvanā* analysis and therefore be called upon to specify what literature is "actualizing," whereby, and how. Bhatta Nayaka accordingly proceeded to explain the literary experience as a tripartite process of actualization, and he gives newly coined or reformulated terms for its three components.

The first is "expression," which here comprises all uses of expressive language, including figures of speech with their secondary meaning, so that it is best understood or even translated as "literary language," a form of discourse entirely different from any other.[6] The second is the "capacity for actualization," which is (sometimes confusingly) referred to by the covering term *bhāvanā*, but which Bhatta Nakaya seems to distinguish as something separate: it is, he says, "another order of actualization," and at the same time "unique," utterly different from the scriptural-hermeneutical sort. This actualization capacity consists in the "making common," or "commonization," of the emotional states of the literary text with those of the reader. The third component, "experience," or (yet another coinage) "experientialization,"[7] leads to a kind of absorption in the literary event. These three represent the "what" (experience), the "whereby" (expressive language), and the "how" (commonization) of literary actualization: one actualizes an aesthetic experience by means of an emotional commonization made possible by the unique powers of literary language.[8]

In invoking actualization, Bhatta Nayaka wants to argue that the very same mechanism enabling us to become the subject of a commandment of scripture enables us to become the subject, so to speak, of a literary text. This process constitutes for him the essential or most distinctive trait of literariness.[9] Moreover, just as a scriptural sentence unifies its parts, the words, into a whole that generates action, so the literary text can be thought of as a kind of large sentence that unifies its parts, the aesthetic elements, into a whole that generates its own action, namely, aesthetic experience.

Another way to think of Bhatta Nayaka's theory is to contrast it with Anandavardhana's "manifestation." In fact, the very names of the two works signal the shift in their perspectives. The *Mirror of the Heart* provides a true "reflection," or account, of what is occurring in the mind of the viewer/reader during an aesthetic experience, in contrast to the *Light on Implicature*, which aims to reveal the mechanisms by which aesthetic objects produce their effects. Thus, against the assertion of a new language function for the communication of rasa (and which knows nothing of action, since Ananda was not interested in reception), Bhatta Nayaka reasserts normal language functioning (or, normal literary language functioning), but in an expanded version, where the aesthetic text-event itself is understood as a quasi sentence. As in a sentence, we have a verb, so in the literary text we have the stable emotion; as in a sentence, we have the nominal case forms, so in the literary text we have the aesthetic elements. When these are all "syntactically" construed in the act of reading (or viewing), we have a kind of sentence meaning, which equates with actualization, which in turn explains the experience of rasa.

The point of Bhatta Nayaka's postulating this "discourse" theory of rasa is to lay the foundation for the "action" aspect of rasa. Rasa is not a thing but an action—a uniquely pleasurable experience—and one is prompted to action by sentences;[10] the literary "sentence" meaning functions just like a Vedic sentence meaning: it summons the reader to action. From this new standpoint—a *hermeneutical* standpoint, in the philosophical sense of the term—the rasa experience must be an action on the part of the viewing subject, not a formal feature of the text. But since an action must come about from sentences ("the meaning of a sentence is 'actualization,'" says Kumarila, the seventh-century scholar of Mimamsa), literature as such must constitute a "sentence," or discourse.[11]

The last component of Bhatta Nayaka's grand theory relates to the nature of aesthetic "absorption." "Experiencing" the emotions that have been made "common" by the power of literary "expression" and thus rendered accessible to the reader—horror without the danger of real horror, desire without the impropriety of real desire—is profoundly cathectic, since no phenomenal reality is there to trouble us. This absorptive experience is an event unique to aesthesis, and completely different from normal experience. It is, as a later thinker put it, "a state of rapture that is the true nature of one's consciousness," rendered so completely joyful and luminous that it is akin to the ecstasy of religious self-transcendence, given that "the self-other differentiation has vanished."[12] For Bhatta Nayaka, however, religious experience is in fact inferior: "Nothing can compare with [aesthetic rasa], not even the rasa spiritual adepts bring forth."

Bhatta Nayaka's views of literary response are, clearly, as complicated as the phenomenon itself. But his key move, to redirect attention away from the text and to reception, changed thinking about rasa forever. His victory was so total that many later writers, to say nothing of modern scholars, could no longer grasp even the possibility of a theory of rasa that was *not* reader-centered, and so failed to make intellectual-historical sense of the truly innovative nature of Bhatta Nayaka's contribution. When, for example, in the mid-seventeenth century Jagannatha argued that Bhatta Nayaka's "experientialization" is no different from the doctrine of "manifestation,"[13] he was correct but had things reversed: "manifestation" became no different from "experientialization" once the original doctrine of Anandavardhana, designed to explain the linguistic phenomenon of rasa, had been recoded by Abhinavagupta into something intended to approximate experientialization, thanks to his appropriation of Bhatta Nayaka's own doctrines. If we can move beyond the conceptual and intellectual-historical obstructions that have obscured Bhatta Nayaka's theory and its influence and look as clear-eyed as we are able at the thousand-year history to which he was heir, we can begin to appreciate the revolution he initiated. One early commentator understood this well when he wrote: "When Nayaka argued that, since we experience the stable emotions, we experience rasa itself, did he not touch the very essence, the very core, of rasa?"[14]

In preparing the selections below, I preferred to err on the side of inclusiveness, even where it seemed improbable that the attribution was genuine. For the same reason I have provided every significant restatement and every resonance of Bhatta Nayaka's thought. Nothing that might help us understand better what this remarkable thinker was trying to say should be ignored.[15]

FROM **COMMENTARY ON THE* TREATISE ON DRAMA, OF BHATTA NAYAKA

(#1)[16] In Bharata's statement "I will explain what was declared by Brahma," the word "Brahma" refers to the supreme being, whereas "what was declared" means "what has been offered as an example." That is to say, drama is *exemplary* in enabling us to grasp the barren, dualistic perception produced by our innate nescience. Consider the doings of Rama and Ravana. These are in essence merely imaginary, and precisely for this reason they do not have one single stable form, but rather can all of a sudden produce countless new imaginings. Although they are indeed different from a dream, just like a dream, they can be the source of profound emotional attachment without giving up their illusory character.[17] When produced by an actor—and herein the actor is like the supreme being—these doings, however unreal, seem as if actually coming into existence out of some source, albeit a nonexistent one. And though in this way they remain mere appearance, they can become a means of understanding the true ends of man. The same applies to the universe as a whole, which functions in precisely the same way. It consists of a vast elaboration of nothing but names and forms, and yet, thanks to the capacity we derive from it for "learning, meditating," and so on,[18] it can aid us in reaching the highest end of man. By thus hinting at the supreme, otherworldly human aim of liberation, this opening verse becomes an indicator of the peaceful rasa that will be discussed later (in the verse "The peaceful rasa arises in dependence on its own specific conditions"),[19] and its ultimate purpose is hereby explained.[20]

FROM *MIRROR OF THE HEART* OF BHATTA NAYAKA

Direct (and Possible) Citations

(#2)[21] Homage to Shiva, the poet who creates the whole universe. Thanks to him, people every moment enjoy the rasa of the world's dramatic performance.

(#3)[22] Poetic language, like a cow, brings forth this rasa at the thirsty promptings of her calves, and so nothing can compare with it, not even the rasa spiritual adepts[23] bring forth.

(#4)[24] A "poet" is so called because he produces "poetry," since, although there are all kinds of poets, *poetry* as such remains always self-identical.

(#5)[25] The poet does not pour forth rasa until he himself overflows with it.

(#6)[26] Scripture is distinguished by the fact that wording has primacy in it. Historical narrative is a matter of factual meaning. When both wording and meaning are subordinated and the aesthetic process itself has primacy, we call it literature.

(#7)[27] In the case of literature,[28] what every reader actually does is experience rasa, not gain knowledge or come to be persuaded of some moral precept.

[(#8)[29] We scholars hold that the literary function is threefold: expression, actualization, and experience. Beyond that, we do not accept anything, certainly not what has been called "implicature." Expression is an established fact in the domains of communication;[30] actualization refers to the "commonization" of the aesthetic elements, the factors and the rest; experience refers to the unfettered savoring of rasa.]

(#9)[31] As for the other process called "implicature," which is essentially manifestation, even were it proven to exist as something distinct,[32] it would only be a component of literature, not, as claimed, its essential form.

(#10)[33] [Since implicature is supposed to be found everywhere in discourse,] we would be forced to say that all discourse can be called literature.

(#11)[34] In literature the "three components" are literary expression, a special type of actualization, and experientialization.[35] To the abode of expression belong the figures of sound and sense. Actualization brings into being what we categorize as rasas, the erotic and the rest.[36] If a viewer/reader is a proficient one, the "experientialization" of these rasas will completely pervade him.[37]

(#12)[38] Just as in the Veda, where sentence meaning arises through the syntactic construal[39] of the constitutive words—since that meaning must be a unity, given that it bears a relation to a single result—so in literature we hold rasa to constitute a kind of sentence meaning.

(#13)[40] The purpose of literature is rasa, which is an experience consisting of savoring; it may be said to be "manifested" only by way of a manifestation called awareness, and its domain is the highest consciousness.

[(#14)[41] A precious object may be damaged by vermin yet remain precious. In the same way, imperfect poetry remains *poetry* so long as we derive rasa from it.]

Restatements of Bhatta Nayaka's Doctrine

(#1a, Abhinavagupta)[42]

Bhatta Nayaka argues that rasa can be neither the object of a normal perceptual experience nor some thing that actually comes into being or can be "manifested." [If rasa were perceptible, it would be perceived as either in oneself or in someone else, S.] If rasa were perceived as internal to the viewer himself, then [1] in the case of the tragic rasa, he would feel the actual pain himself [and hence would never again go to see a sad play, S].[43] [2] Such a perception would not even make sense, because a character like Sita cannot function as a foundational factor for the viewer [she is a factor for another character, in Sita's case for her husband, Rama, M]. [3] Neither is the viewer reminded of his own beloved in the course of a description of Sita, [4] nor can she share any properties in common with his Sita [in other words, the notion that a common property of being beloved is shared by Sita and the spectator's wife, producing a foundational factor that can stimulate the spectator's predisposition, is impossible, because Sita is a divine being, DhĀL].[44] [5] Nor could such foundational and stimulant factors [for the spectator's stable emotion, S] as leaping over the ocean[45] and the like ever have anything in common with the viewer. [6] Any putative memory on the spectator's part of Rama's being in possession of such a stable emotion is impossible, because the spectator can never have had the perception of Rama in the first place that is required to ground such memory. [7] Nor can the spectator be said to have "perceived" Rama by some other means of valid knowledge, such as testimony or inference, in order to supply a basis for his memory. Such a mediated perception could no more provide an experience of rasa than would glimpsing with one's own eyes the lovemaking of people in real life, when instead of rasa the spectator would be absorbed in one or another mental state, whether shame, disgust, or yearning.[46]

If, on the other hand, rasa were perceived as external to the perceiving subject, as present in the actor or the characters, it would be something toward which the viewer would be emotionally indifferent [; it could not be a "taste," that is, something experienced, but would be a mere object, like a pot, M].

Accordingly, it makes no[47] sense to say that there is a perception—in the form of an empirical experience or memory or whatever—of rasa. The same criticisms apply to the view that rasa is something that actually comes into being. And lastly, if rasa were something that existed only in potential form [since it has been ruled out that rasa can be conceived of as already existing, like some material object, M] and was subsequently "manifested,"[48] it would be subject both to the gradations of actualizing the object that are inherent in any idea of "manifestation"[49] and to the same dilemmas as before, that is, whether it is manifested in oneself or another, and so on.

[Literary language, however, is different from all other forms of language due to its threefold constitution, comprising an "expressive" function pertaining to the discourse, an "actualization" function pertaining to rasa, and an "experientialization" function pertaining to the sensitive viewer/reader, DhĀL.] "Actualization"[50] is marked in poetry by language that shows an absence of flaws and the presence of language qualities and figures of speech, whereas in drama it is embodied in the four different registers of acting (physical, verbal, and so on), and thereby has the capacity to overcome the resistances of one's deep insensibility.[51] This "actualization," a second component over and above expression, consists in essence in the commonization of the aesthetic elements, the foundational factor and so on. By this process is produced rasa, which comes to be experienced in the form of an "experience" utterly different from empirical activity or memory or anything else; one marked instead by a melting, enlargement, and expansion[52] that depend on the relative degree of volatility and stolidity in the viewer, and marked further by an absorption of the spectator's consciousness consisting of a predominance of sensitivity, light, and bliss, which shares something of the character of savoring supreme being.

(#2a, Mammata)[53]

Rasa is not something cognized, whether as existing in someone external and uninvolved with the viewing subject or as internal to himself. Nor is it something that actually comes into being, or something "manifested." On the contrary, in poetry and drama there is in addition to expression a "process" called "actualization," which consists in the "commonization" of the foundational factor and other aesthetic elements. By this process the stable emotion is actualized and experienced in a third process called "experience," which has the nature of[54] an absorption of consciousness consisting of a predominance of sensitivity, light, and bliss.

(#3a, Ruyyaka)[55]

In Bhatta Nayaka's system, all three positions concerning rasa—that it actually comes into being; that it is the content of a cognitive experience; that it is "manifested"—are critiqued, and his own position, that rasa is "experienced," is established. . . . Against all three he levels a common criticism: if rasa arose in or were perceived as actually existing in oneself, it would have to be experienced in precisely the same way (e.g., sorrowfully in the case of the tragic rasa); if it arose in or were perceived as existing in someone else, one would be indifferent toward it and hence have no taste experience at all; if it were latent and only manifested, it would be subject to the gradations of actualizing the object that are inherent in any idea of "manifestation," and so again one would have no rasa experience. Bhatta Nayaka therefore abandons all three positions and argues in favor of "experience." This consists of relishing rasa and amounts to the same thing as rapture. And it is entirely different from the view that rasa is some thing that actually comes into being, and so on: given that those operations must proceed under the constraints of time, space, and form,[56] they all are subject to the many aforementioned criticisms. "Experience," however, is entirely different, hence has a supermundane quality, and thereby escapes those criticisms.

To be precise: there is a threefold "process" of literature; the three components are called expression, actualization, and experientialization. Among these, the first, namely the language process,[57] is itself twofold by virtue of the distinction between literal and figurative meaning, that is, whether an unmediated or mediated sense is at issue.[58] This twofold process is common to scripture and historical discourse as well, which may be likened to master and friend respectively, insofar as the wording itself has primacy in the former and the meaning in the latter. But the other two components are unique to poetry and drama; whereas, at the same time, literature is differentiated in its language process from scripture and history by being likened to a beloved, since both wording and meaning have primacy.[59]

With respect to those components, we first discuss actualization. Although it is impossible for Sita, for example, ever to be a foundational factor in and of herself,[60] actualization as it comes into being[61] brings about a state of commonality. This is made possible in poetry by the presence of language qualities and figures of speech[62] and by the absence of flaws, and in drama by the use of the four registers of acting. For things derive their particularity from the particularity of their causal factors, just as the moonstone is caused to melt by the proximity of moonbeams. In the same way, from the particular nature of the set of causal elements in poetry and drama there comes about this process of actualization, which may be defined as "commonization." Once the foundational factor and the rest are "commonized," commonization renders the stable emotion an experiential object on the part of the receptive reader. The concluding process, "experientialization," can be defined as making this emotion an object for the reader's relishing. It is precisely because literature has the capacity to delight such a reader that it is likened to a beloved. This experience is in essence a savoring of the highest bliss, and closely approximates the savoring of supreme being on the part of spiritual adepts.

(#4a, Ruyyaka)[63]

When Bhatta Nayaka says that the process of manifestation is a component of literature he is admitting it brazenly, only for the sake of argument.[64] He awards primacy to the aesthetic process as such, with the actual forms of wording and meaning subordinated to this. More specifically, over and above[65] the first two literary processes, expression and "actualization," there exists a third one. This is in essence the relishing of rasa, a synonym for which is "experientialization," and he accepts this as the dominant literary element, insofar as it constitutes the site of "absorption."

(J) (p. 8) Some scholars have argued [9] that "manifestation" is beyond the domain of speech and therefore indefinable.[66] To this view Ruyyaka now turns. "Brazenly," i.e., and not providing a definition. That is why the assertion is brazen: he accepts something only for the sake of argument, which cannot (he says) be defined. "A component of literature," i.e., not its essence, as (Bhatta Nayaka) says, "As for the other process called 'implicature. . . .' "[67] What Bhatta Nayaka means by "process" is poetic creation itself.[68] Otherwise, that is, if literature were not something entirely different—a "process"—it would be impossible to differentiate literature either from the Vedas, where wording itself has primacy, or from historical discourse, where meaning has primacy. As Bhatta Nayaka has said, "Scripture is distinguished by the fact that for it, the wording has primacy." He has declared that literature consists of three components: "Expression, actualization, and aesthetic experience." He sets forth the sphere of the first two components in the verse "To the abode of expression . . ." and the third component in the verse "If a viewer/reader is proficient. . . ." This last component consists of a relishing of the other two that is experienced by lovers of literature. And when he states, "Although this experience is something entirely phenomenal . . ." he accepts this experience as the site of "absorption," being something similar to relishing supreme being.

(S) (p. 9) "Expression," which here includes literal and figurative meaning, is common to literary and nonliterary language. Bhatta Nayaka's two other processes are specific to literature. [10] The one, "actualization," is the generalization of the factors and the other components of rasa; the other, "enjoyment," is a literary process that exists over and above these two, and is described as in essence the relishing of rasa. While both the author of the *Vital Force of Literary Language* and Bhatta Nayaka equally hold the language process to have primacy, the former awards this primacy to expression when artistically qualified, whereas the latter awards it to manifestation as related to rasa, for which a synonym is "experience."[69]

(#5a, Mallinatha)[70]

Bhatta Nayaka's doctrine of aesthetic experience is as follows: the "language process," which pertains to poetry and drama both, assists the "actualization process," whereby the aesthetic elements, the foundational factor and so on, are "commonized."[71] Here the stable emotion is brought to consciousness as something common to the reader, since anything that pertains specifically to the actor and so on[72] is eliminated. And it is thereby experienced by the "actualization" process,[73] also known as aesthetic experience, which consists of an awareness that is pure sensitivity, light, and bliss.

Resonance of Bhatta Nayaka's Doctrine

(#1b, Simhabhupala)[74]

A foundational factor (such as Sita) attains real existence through linguistic communication, its actual external reality being irrelevant.[75] Furthermore, whereas with reference to the historical hero (Rama, for example) such a factor was, originally, wholly particularized (Sita being a specific individual for Rama), the process that in a poem or play is called "actualization" consists of "commonizing" the foundational factor by means of the process of expression,[76] and thereby enables it to be imagined by the spectator as connected with himself. It thereby becomes almost present[77] in the mind of the spectator doing the imagining or "actualizing," without there being any contradiction with its persistence as a foundational factor (that is, for Rama). Thereby, the stable emotion that Rama feels can be experienced by the spectator, and without the least disruption through impropriety,[78] in an experience whose nature is a pure blissful absorption.

3.2. FROM RASA IN THE TEXT TO RASA IN THE READER: ELABORATION

The Ten Dramatic Forms of Dhanamjaya (c. 975) and the *Observations* of Dhanika (c. 975), with *The Lamp* (on the *Ten Forms*) of Bahurupa Mishra (undated) and the *Brief Annotation* (on the *Observations*) of Bhatta Nrisimha (undated)

To some degree the signal importance, in intellectual-historical terms, of the body of rasa theory presented by Dhanamjaya and Dhanika is tied up with the question of their time and place. And attached to that question are two large enigmas, and a small one.

There is no doubt about the date of Dhanamjaya. He was a courtier of the Paramara king Vakpati Munja, uncle of the great Bhoja, who ruled from the city of Dhara (in today's Madhya Pradesh); Dhanamjaya speaks with evident pride of having "participated in the sophisticated assemblies of King Munja."[79] Munja came to the throne in 974 or 975,[80] and ruled some twenty years until he was captured by Tailapa Chalukya, taken to his capital city, Kalyani, and executed by beheading. It is somewhat more difficult to fix the date of Dhanika. The documentary considerations discussed by earlier scholars are inconclusive.[81] The most important fact for establishing his upper limit is that a poem of his is cited (without attribution) by Bhoja in the earlier of his two literary treatises, the *Necklace for the Goddess of Language*.[82] He may well have been a younger brother of Dhanamjaya (their father's name is identical) and was very likely a contemporary. His only surviving work is the *Observations*; his *Analysis of Literature*, assuredly an important work, has been lost.

Munja was succeeded in the kingship by Bhoja's father, Sindhuraja, and then by Bhoja himself, whose long reign extended from about 1011 to 1055. That Bhoja should be ignorant of the literary-critical work of Dhanamjaya and Dhanika would seem to be impossible, but ignorant he is. Their names are never cited in his *Necklace* or *Light*, and their literary-theoretical ideas (in contrast to their poetry, or at least a few verses of Dhanika's) left no trace in either text.[83] The two scholars cannot possibly have outlived Bhoja and written after 1055. It is only slightly less improbable that their works were composed abroad, if as courtier-intellectuals associated with Munja they were not retained by Bhoja (although others, such as the poet Dhanapala, certainly were).

These chronological considerations would not loom so large were it not for the fact that Bhoja's system of aesthetics (chapter 2) stands in such fundamental contradiction to the positions advanced by Dhanamjaya and Dhanika. And we have every reason to expect that Bhoja would at least have acknowledged, if not critically assessed, the very powerful conceptual challenges they present, had he known about them. But he clearly does not, and for all his innovations in technical terminology, categories, and concepts, Bhoja's view of rasa is still essentially the classical one. To understand this view and the frontal assault made upon it by Bhatta Nayaka and, in his footsteps, Dhanamjaya and Dhanika, we need to grasp its two core aspects, the one epistemological, the other ontological, which bear repeating here.

All early theories about the nature of rasa—the "origination" position of Bhatta Lollata, the "inference" position of Shri Shankuka, the "manifestation" position of Anandavardhana—concern epistemological disputes: Do we perceive rasa arising before our eyes? Do we somehow infer it? Is it something "manifested" or "suggested"? This controversy has of course long been noted by scholars, but what has not been sufficiently stressed is the fact that all such epistemological theories at the same time presuppose a particular ontological theory: that rasa is, in the first instance of analysis (though not necessarily exclusively), to be seen as a phenomenon *internal* to the literary work, whether that work is textual ("heard," i.e., poetry) or performative ("seen," i.e., drama). Once this ontology is discarded, the epistemology associated with it must be discarded too;[84] and this is precisely what happened once rasa came to be viewed also, or instead, as a phenomenon largely *external* to the literary work, as a subjective experience of reception. The two ontological positions do not present mutually exclusive truth claims. Viewed phenomenologically, rasa is at once internal and external to the text; which of these one foregrounds is a function of analytical method and theoretical interests.

Consider the view that rasa can only be "suggested." Dhanamjaya and Dhanika leave no doubt they held the very idea to become impossible if rasa is located—as they insist on locating it—in the viewer/reader and not, as earlier (for Anandavardhana himself), in the character:

(Dhanamjaya) Rasa belongs to the spectator experiencing the rasa, and to him alone, because he is alive and present. It does not belong to the character.

(Dhanika) . . . All this being the case, the view that rasa can be "manifested" stands refuted. For an entity can only be manifested by something after it has been brought into being by something else: a pot, for example, can only be manifested by a light when it has already been produced by the clay. It is certainly not possible for an entity to be brought into existence by the very things that are supposed to manifest it, and this at one and the same moment.

Since rasa had become something pertaining to the audience, a new epistemology appropriate to that new ontology was required. Bhoja was entirely innocent of this conceptual revolution[85]—hence our first enigma: how could this be if the text that embodies the revolution had been produced at his uncle's court just a generation earlier?

The Ten Dramatic Forms along with the *Observations* may be said only to "embody" an intellectual-historical revolution rather than "inaugurate" it because of the second conundrum presented by these two works: the fact that, in their discussion of rasa, they present what is not an altogether original contribution, but one that bears the impress of the ideas of Bhatta Nayaka, the early tenth-century Kashmirian author of the *Mirror of the Heart*. Dhanamjaya and Dhanika never mention his name, but their fourth chapter, both base text and commentary, offers a systematic restatement of the main ideas of his lost masterpiece. Since his "hermeneutical turn" transformed Indian aesthetics and provided the basis for Abhinavagupta's reconstruction, the *Forms* with the *Observations* represents the most important extant document—given the disappearance of the *Mirror* itself—in the history of rasa theory between Bharata's founding statement and Abhinava's later synthesis of the hermeneutical school.

The turn is especially clear in the *Observations*, where Dhanika is intent on a radical recentering of the whole discourse—including all the aesthetic elements—onto the viewer/reader. For example, the reactions are now to be considered, not just the effects of rasa displayed by the actor (which, *ex hypothesi*, does not actually exist), but causes of rasa in the viewer (on 4.3ab). Indeed, the aesthetic emotions in general now are said to permeate the mind of the viewer, not the character (on 4.4ab). A new distinction is accordingly required, Dhanika suggests, between "real-world rasa," the rasa of the storyworld, and "drama rasa" (*nāṭyarasa*), the rasa experienced by the viewer of the drama. How far the distance has been opened up from Bhoja's views may be seen in the juxtaposition of their explanation of "rasa-laden" discourse. According to Bhoja, "Someone like Rama has rasa, and his speech, since its source lies in his very rasa, may itself be said to be 'rasa-laden' or have rasa"; for Dhanika, "it can only be the audience members who are the '*rasikas*,' those who taste rasa; the literary text can be said to be 'rasa-laden' only insofar as it brings about the unfolding of that sort of blissful consciousness."

A third, if lesser, enigma about Dhanamjaya and Dhanika's works, to add to those relating to their earlier relationship with Bhatta Nayaka and to their later relationship with Bhoja, is the identity of Bhatta Nrisimha, the remarkable commentator on the *Observations* (and, occasionally, on the memorial verses of Dhanamjaya as well). We have no information about him, and the only question for which we can hope to find an answer on the basis of currently available evidence is whether he is identical with Bhatta Narasimha, author of the important commentary on Bhoja's *Necklace*.[86] There Bhatta Narasimha provides us with the most lucid exposition available of the problem of the locus of rasa (*rasāśraya*) as this relates to Bhoja's aesthetic system.[87] On Dhanika's *Observations* (4.38), however, Bhatta Nrisimha repeats the *Necklace* commentary almost word for word, this time only to reject it. The contradiction in the views of Bhatta Nrisimha/Bhatta Narasimha is undoubtedly a result of the contradiction in the views in the two works upon which he is commenting, and not grounds for postulating the existence of two different, equally brilliant scholars of literary theory who share essentially the same name.[88]

The *Observations*, written by someone who was almost certainly a contemporary of Dhanamjaya, if not his brother, has long had a special claim to authority as an exegesis of the *Ten Dramatic Forms*, and it would have taken a remarkable degree of self-confidence to attempt to displace it. Only one person sought to do this, Bahurupa Mishra, but his egoism exceeded his learning. I have translated from this work only what little it adds to the discussion (he belongs to a different conceptual world from that of Dhanamjaya and Dhanika, sometimes alluding to the rasa of the character, for example, which is precisely what Dhanamjaya rejects). The commentator is later than Sharadatanaya, whom he cites, which would place him after the fourteenth century; his upper limit cannot be determined.

From *The Ten Dramatic Forms* of Dhanamjaya (D) and the *Observations* of Dhanika (Dh), with *The Lamp* of Bahurupa Mishra (BM) and the *Brief Annotation* of Bhatta Nrisimha (BN)

(Dh) (p. 167) Now, then, the varieties of rasa will be described.

(D) (4.1) When, by means of the factors, the physical reactions and psychophysical responses, and the transitory emotions, a stable emotion is brought to the state of being savored, it is said to become rasa.

(Dh) The factors, the physical reactions and psychophysical responses, and the transitory emotions, whose natures will all be described in due course, are presented either in a literary work or through dramatic acting. The stable emotion, the definition of which will also shortly be provided, becomes almost present[89] within the minds of readers and viewers, and when brought within the sphere of savoring—a state of intensely blissful consciousness—it becomes rasa. Therefore, it can only be the audience members who are the "*rasikas*," those who taste rasa; the literary text can be said to be "rasa-laden" only insofar as it brings about the unfolding of that sort of blissful consciousness; it is no more than a metaphorical usage, as in the expression "ghee is life."

(BN) [168.8] The "*rasikas*" are those who actually experience rasa, and when Dhanika identifies them with the audience members, he is refuting the view that it is the literary characters, Rama and the like, who have rasa. . . . By using the expression "ghee is life," he means to say that we can refer to something that is the cause of a thing as that thing itself.[90]

(D) (4.2) The "factors," first of all, enhance the stable emotion by becoming objects of our awareness. They are twofold, foundational factors and stimulant factors.

(Dh) [168] To become an "object of awareness" means to be conceived of in a form given specificity by literary language—that is, tropes such as hyperbole and metaphor—whereby a given man is said to be like this, a given woman like that.[91] A factor is either foundational or stimulant. An example of a foundational factor is the leading male or female character of the work; an example of a stimulant factor is the appropriate time or place. To quote: "'Factor' means making aware."[92] We shall relate factors to rasas duly and as occasion arises.

Now, these factors attain their respective states as factors without reference to any entity actually existing outside the text,[93] but precisely through their embodiment in language.[94] They thereby take on a general form and come to be conceived of by each person actualizing the emotion[95] in such a way that it is connected with himself; they become almost present in his mind and thereby attain the state of being either a foundational or a stimulant factor. Hence, they are not in the least devoid of their own reality. To quote Bhartrihari: "One[96] grasps characters in literature such as Kamsa[97] as causally active, almost as if they were right before one's eyes, when in fact their forms are merely a linguistic construct and they themselves are only objects of thought."[98] [169] And the author of the *Six Thousand*[99] also says, "Rasa arises from these elements in conjunction with the quality of generality."[100]

(BN) [169.21] Just as the actually visible forms of Kamsa and so on are causes with regard to their respective effects, so viewers/readers regard their forms when mediated by literary language as causes of the apprehension of rasa.

. . . .[101]

(D) (4.3ab) A "physical reaction" is a change that intimates an emotion.[102]

(Dh) (p. 171) Things such as weeping, the play of eyebrows, or sidelong glances that enable the audience members to experience the stable emotions[103] and thus bring the rasa experience to full enhancement are called reactions. The reactions accordingly can be said to belong to poetry no less than to dramatic acting.[104] Whether they are called reactions (*anubhāva*) because they are *directly* "experienced" (*anubhūyante*) on the part of the *rasikas*—the viewers/readers actualizing the emotion—or because they are an "*after*-experiencing" (*anu-bhāvana*) by them,[105] the reactions are still something to be *referred to* the *rasikas*. The definition in the memorial verse, "a change . . . that intimates a stable emotion," is given from the viewpoint of real-world rasa;[106] here, by contrast, the reactions are understood to be an actual cause of the rasas.[107] . . . [108]

(BN) [171.71] "After-experiencing" means "after the act of 'actualization.' " . . . We should note that the two etymologies of the word "reaction" have reference to Dhanika's own opinion (the second) and that of the author of the sutras (the first). The final sentence ("The definition . . .") is meant to remove any suspicion that the two are in conflict.

(D) (4.3cd) These two, the one a cause, the other an effect, are empirically given.

(Dh) Factors and reactions, causes and effects respectively with regard to real-world rasa, are empirically given and require no separate technical definition.[109]

(BM) Since the "sensitivities," which are about to be defined, are emotions, the author prefaces this with a general definition of emotion:

(D) (4.4ab) "Emotion" is the permeating of one's feelings by things such as pleasure or pain.

(Dh) (172) "Emotion" is when the pleasure, pain, and the like presented by the poet as belonging to the character "perfumes," or permeates, "one's feelings," that is, the mind of the viewer/reader actualizing the emotion.[110] As Bharata remarks, "People will say, 'Ah, this whole thing is 'caused to be' by this taste or that fragrance,"[111] when what is meant is "perfumed." As for Bharata's more specific uses of the term "emotion"—such as, "Insofar as they bring into being (*bhāvayanti*) the rasas" or "Emotion" (*bhāva*) is also so called because it serves to 'bring into being' (*bhāvayan*) the poet's inner emotion (*bhāva*)"[112]—they are describing the semantic field of the word "emotion" in the context of dramatic acting and poetry.[113] These are the stable and transitory emotions, to be discussed shortly.

(BN) [172.15] "One's" here refers to the audience member.

(D) (4.4cd–4.5ab) The psychophysical "sensitivities" (*sāttvika*), since they are also reactions, are categorized as emotions distinct from the others. They are called sensitivities because they arise from one's psychic sensitivity (*sattva*). They similarly permeate one's feelings.[114]

(Dh) (p. 173) "Sensitivity" is when one's heart is completely amenable to "actualizing" another's[115] sorrow and joy. As Bharata says, "Psychic sensitivity as defined here is something that arises from the mind; it is said to be the mind in a state of heightened awareness."[116] It is precisely because of one's sensitivity that weeping, horripilation, and the like are produced in the presence of sorrow or joy, and because they are produced by this sensitivity, these emotions are accordingly called "sensitivities"; they are emotions since they likewise "permeate one's feelings." Insofar as they arise from this sensitivity, weeping and the like, physical though they may be, are considered emotions; insofar as they are actual transformations that indicate emotions, they are considered reactions.[117] Hence they have a dual nature.

(BN) [173.10] "One's heart" again refers to the audience member.

(Dh) These are:

(D) (4.5cd–4.6) The following eight: paralysis, fainting, horripilation, perspiration, pallor, trembling, weeping, and a broken voice. Here "paralysis" means immobilization of the limbs, and "fainting" loss of consciousness. The rest are clear.

. . . .[118]

(Dh) (p. 174) Now the transitory emotions. First the general definition.

(D) (4.7) Transitory emotions (*vy-abhi-cāriṇaḥ*) are so called because they move (*car*) in especially (*vi-*) close proximity (*ābhi-mukhya*) to the stable emotion. They emerge from and are submerged into the stable emotion like waves on the ocean.

(Dh) Just as waves arise from and disappear into the ocean, which itself remains unchanged, so the transitory emotions, despair and so on, "move," or exist, "in close proximity" by reason of their emergence from and disappearance into the stable emotion,[119] which persists unchanged.

. . . .[120]

(Dh) (p. 196) There are other discrete mental states, but these need not be separately mentioned since they can be subsumed under the basic forms of the factors of, or reactions to, the transitory emotions already mentioned.[121]

Now the stable emotions.

(D) (4.34) A stable emotion is one that is uninterrupted, whether by conflicting or nonconflicting emotions. On the contrary, it assimilates other emotions, as the ocean assimilates rivers.

(BM) Rasas in conflict are the erotic and the macabre; the heroic and the fearful; the violent and the fantastic; the comic and the tragic. Those not in conflict are the comic and the erotic; the tragic and the violent; the fantastic and the heroic; the macabre and the fearful.[122] The stable emotion remains the same throughout the course of the work.[123]

(Dh) A stable emotion is the one presented in such a way that it is not overshadowed by either related or unrelated emotions. In "The Great Tale,"[124] to give an example of the case of related emotions, the protagonist Naravahanadatta's passion for Madanamanjari is not overshadowed by his passion for any of the subordinate female protagonists. For an example of unrelated emotions, take the cemetery scene in *Malati and Madhava*. Here Madhava's passion for Malati is presented in such a way that it is not overshadowed by revulsion, that is, when he thinks:

> For such was the overwhelming earlier impression on my senses, that there remains alive in me as a perpetual memory a perception of my beloved that no conflicting perception can obscure, so that my consciousness takes on the very shape and substance of her.[125]

These instances show us that no actual conflict is caused by the inclusion of other emotions, whether conflicting or not.

(BN) [197.21] In citing the two examples Dhanika indicates that this proposition applies to both traditional narratives (*The Great Tale*) and narratives invented by the author (*Malati and Madhava*).[126]

(Dh) To explain: How could conflict ever arise? Conflict, or contradiction, must be either [1] the impossibility of two things coexisting[127] or [2] the negation of one thing by another.[128] It certainly cannot be both types at once,[129] since in aesthetic experience, which consists essentially of savoring, emotion manifests itself as a unified whole.[130]

(BN) Leave aside for a moment the conflict between two stable emotions. The critical issue is what to do about the potential conflict between the stable emotion and the aesthetic elements that are introduced to enhance it:

(Dh) [1] As for conflict between a stable emotion and an aesthetic element,[131] this cannot be a case of the impossibility of their coexistence, to take that first. It is established in the self-awareness of anyone "actualizing" an aesthetic emotion that the mind can indeed remain imbued with a single stable emotion such as desire while transitory emotions, both those that are in conflict with it and those that are not, are simultaneously presented, after the manner of a variegated flower garland strung on a single thread.[132] Just as this mélange of emotions is proved to exist by one's own self-awareness, so it can apply in the case of the literary character, by means of the full complex of poetic processes [197] and, through a subsequent fusion with the spectator's own awareness, it can bring about the requisite blossoming of that blissful consciousness.[133] Therefore, one cannot argue that the coexistence of a stable emotion[134] can ever be held to be impossible.

Now as for [2], the sort of conflict that consists in the "negation" of one thing by another, that would have to be constituted here by [2a] the overshadowing of one emotion by another. But an emotion that is truly stable cannot conflict in this way with transitory emotions; nor can emotions that are transitory conflict with a stable emotion, for the simple reason that they are subsidiary to a stable emotion: it would be illogical to say that something functions as a subsidiary to a dominant when it is in conflict with it.[135] By the same reasoning,[136] we can also dismiss as impossible [2b] the sequential conflict of a stable emotion and another aesthetic element. Accordingly, in *Malati and Madhava*, even the presentation of the macabre rasa in act 5 after the erotic in the foregoing acts has nothing contrary to rasa about it.

All this being the case, the only real source of conflict could be where a single foundational factor subserves two conflicting rasas. But even that factor[137] will not produce conflict when the rasas are presented with some other, nonconflicting rasa interposed between them.[138] Take the following verse:

> Lucky those women who get to wear fragrance of the finest scent.
> My husband only transfers to me the foul smell of his battle wounds.[139]

Here, the inclusion of the macabre rasa ("foul smell") within the erotic is not in conflict thanks to the interposition of the heroic rasa ("battle wounds"). If such a procedure were not adopted, the conflict arising from having a single locus for two conflicting rasas would indeed be a problem to be avoided.

[199] One might still raise the following objection: Where other emotions, whether conflicting or not, are subordinated to a single purport, there may well be no conflict given that those other emotions are admittedly subsidiary. But how can that be the case where multiple emotions are presented in the narrative as equally dominant? Consider the following poem:

> On one side, his weeping wife, on the other, the blare of war drums.
> The soldier's heart oscillates between love and battle lust.[140]

Here, desire and determination are presented in the narrative as equally dominant. In the following,

> Let honorable men put bias aside, and reflect on what to do, and speak
> forthrightly:
> Is it better to seek out the flanks of a holy mountain or the flanks of woman
> smiling with love?[141]

desire and impassivity are equally dominant. In the following,

> Here that beautiful woman, sole habitation of the world's adornment;
> and there that wretched villain who wronged my sister.
> From one, this wild passion that I feel, from the other, this vast blaze of rage
> and this disguise that I have taken on. How can this be? My mind is perturbed.[142]

[200] desire and anger are equally dominant. In the following,

> With guts for bracelets, and elegant flower chains of hearts,
> and women's lac-painted hands for red lotuses at their ears,
> with thick blood for makeup, the demon women join
> their lovers and drink in skull goblets the marrow wine.[143]

desire and revulsion are equally dominant, and moreover with a single object.[144] In the following,

> One eye is folded like a bud, shut tight in concentration;
> the second, heavy with the weight of love, rests on Parvati's breasts and face;
> the third is ablaze with the fire of anger at the god of love drawing back his bow—
> may Shiva's three eyes, their rasas mixed at that hour of meditation, protect you.[145]

impassivity, desire, and anger are equally dominant. In the following, "With one eye filled with anger . . . ,"[146] grief and anger are equally dominant. How, then, in these instances can there be no conflict?

Because, we respond, in all these instances there is in fact only a single stable emotion. To elaborate: in the poem beginning "On one hand, his weeping beloved," the reference at once to the wife's weeping[147] and the battle drums serves to enhance the heroic rasa and that alone. It does so by expressing the dilemma, which points toward "perplexity," functioning here as a transitory emotion of the heroic. This predominance of the heroic is communicated by use of the word "soldier." Moreover, it is illogical to suppose that two equally dominant rasas—rasas devoid of any relationship of principal-and-accessory between them—could in any way be unified.[148] And last, when a brave soldier heads off to battle, for him to be attending to other matters would suggest indifference toward the aforementioned battle and thereby produce gross impropriety. Therefore, because the husband's passions are directed solely toward battle, his tragic feeling toward his wife[149] serves in the first instance to manifest his bravery and [201] to enhance the heroic rasa.

Similarly, in the poem beginning "Let honorable men put bias aside," an inveterate disposition toward desire is referred to as something reprehensible, and because of this the single dominant stable emotion is quiescence, which is clearly revealed by the words "speak forthrightly." In the same way, in the poem beginning "Here that beautiful woman," the reference to desire and anger points toward the violent as the single dominant rasa, first because Ravana is the antagonist and, being a night-stalker, a creature given to deception; second, because desire and anger occasion perplexity, which can function as a transitory emotion of the violent rasa. In the poem beginning "With guts for bracelets," the single dominant rasa is the macabre. In the poem beginning "One eye is folded like a bud," although Shiva is in a permanent state of impassivity undisturbed by any other emotions, by showing he can achieve a form of meditation unlike that of any other spiritual adept, the poet demonstrates that impassivity constitutes the single dominant emotion. This is made especially clear by the words "at that hour of meditation."

(BN) [202.8] Although Shiva is ever characterized by impassivity, he engages in meditation to distinguish himself from all other dispassionate spiritual adepts, and referring to that here is meant to show that the dominant emotion is impassivity.

(Dh) And, last, in the poem beginning "With one eye filled with anger," the entire sentence concerns the impending mood of the erotic thwarted. Nowhere, then, is there more than a single purport. In verses based on extended puns we may indeed have multiple purports, but there is no flaw in such cases, since the dominance of two significations is based on two separate sentence meanings and their complete independence. . . .[150]

Thus, in accordance with the earlier argument, there can never be conflict wherever the stable emotions are presented in the narrative. As for sentences where no[151] explicit reference is made to desire or any other stable emotion, we shall show in due course that it is still the stable emotion that constitutes the main purport.

[202] The stable emotions are the following:

(D) (4.35) Desire, determination, revulsion, anger, amusement, amazement, fear, grief. Some also include impassivity, but in drama this cannot be enhanced.[152]

(BM) Since impassivity signifies the cessation of all activity, it comprises no reactions and so could never be acted out in drama.

(Dh) With regard to the peaceful rasa, scholars offer a variety of conflicting views. Some say there is no such thing as the peaceful rasa, because the teacher Bharata neither described its foundational and stimulant factors nor even defined it. Others go further and argue that it is an actual impossibility, insofar as passion and hatred flow to us in a stream through beginningless time and cannot be eliminated. Still others claim that it is subsumed under one or the other rasa, the heroic, the macabre, and so on.

(BN) [203.3] An example of the heroic for these scholars would be Jimutavahana,[153] who in his compassion for all beings was at peace regarding their virtues and vices. As for repugnance, a man who feels repugnance despises all creatures as mere corpses, turns away from them all, and thereby attains the state of peace.

(Dh) All these scholars reject impassivity as such as a stable emotion. Be that as it may, drama consists of acting, and by no means can we accept that in drama impassivity can function as a stable emotion. Impassivity signifies cessation of all activity and so cannot have any connection with acting.

[203] Some have countered by arguing that quiescence functions as the stable emotion in a drama like *How the Nagas Were Pleased*. But that stands in contradiction first with the passion of the play's hero for Malayavati, which extends throughout the whole work, and second with the fact that his attaining lordship over the demigods is the end result of the play's action. Moreover, we never find passion for the things of this world and dispassion from them existing simultaneously in one and the same character with respect to the same foundational factor.[154] So the stable emotion that we must accept as present throughout that play is determination, in connection with the rasa of the type "heroic in compassion." There is no conflict in this rasa either with the erotic being a subsidiary component or with the attainment of lordship being a concomitant result. Earlier[155] we made the point that when someone becomes a "conqueror"—that is, in actuality, one who acts in the service of others, on the grounds that he must everywhere do what is desirable—he will as a result achieve other beneficial results concomitantly with conquering. Accordingly, there are only eight stable emotions.[156]

An objection might be raised: In line with the argument that "Insofar as the teachers have identified . . ."[157] [204] other scholars have accepted additional rasas, and accordingly have posited additional stable emotions. But this determination is erroneous. The author now addresses this point:

(D) (4.36) Despair and the other transitory emotions do not have that feature, and therefore cannot be stable emotions and cannot be savored. Their enhancement can lead only to the contrary of rasa. Therefore, there are but eight stable emotions.

(Dh) Despair and the other transitory emotions, given that they are not uninterrupted whether by conflicting or nonconflicting emotions, cannot be stable emotions. Accordingly, were they to be enhanced even though punctuated by other transitory emotions such as anxiety, they would produce a state contrary to rasa. It is not because they have no purposeful end result that they are not stable emotions, for that would entail that the comic[158] and the like would also cease to be stable entities; and in any case, despair can be indirectly purposeful. Rather, it is because they are not stable emotions that they cannot be rasas.

(BN) A "purposeful end result" . . . means a result pertaining to the group of the three ends of man.[159]

(Dh) What, however, is the communicative relation that exists between these stable emotions and poetry per se?[160] It cannot, first of all, be one of direct denotation, since the stable emotions are not expressed by using the actual words for them. We do not, after all, find words such as "desire" or the words for the rasas such as "erotic" [205] used in erotic poetry, whereby the stable emotion (desire) or its heightened state (the erotic) might be directly expressed. Even if the words were in fact to be used, it would only be via the aesthetic elements that the stable emotions become rasas, and not simply because they are expressed by their proper terms.[161] Nor can this relation be one of connotation,[162] because again the words[163] themselves are not used, which would be necessary if they were first to express the emotions or rasas as universals and then connote them as particulars.

(BN) [207.18] A noun that expresses a universal, such as "cow," has the capacity, insofar as the universal itself can have no relationship with a given verbal action, to connote some individual entity that is capable of such a relationship. But in the case of a stable emotion or rasa, no use is made of the actual words ("desire," "erotic," etc.) whereby a universal could be expressed, enabling such connotation to exist.

(Dh) Nor do we comprehend the stable emotions by a secondary connotation produced by a first one.[164] To cite the definition of the sort of connotation at issue here: "A word that cannot properly be construed with its verb is said to 'trip' over its primary meaning and to secondarily connote a meaning that does become construable."[165] Take as an example the phrase "A village on the Ganges." Here, the primary meaning of the word "Ganges," namely a body of water, cannot function as the location of a village. The word therefore trips over its primary meaning and secondarily comes to connote a meaning invariably associated—here by metonymy—with the primary one, namely, "bank." But in poetry, the words for the leading male character and the other aesthetic elements[166] do not trip over their primary meaning, so how could they secondarily connote something else? And no one, when the primary meaning is available, resorts to a secondary usage without any occasion or purpose, as one must, for example, in the metaphorical statement, "the boy is a lion." For the same reason we do not understand the words for the leading character and the other aesthetic elements metaphorically, either.

(BN) [208.6] For secondary connotation to occur [1] the primary meaning of the word must be blocked; [2] there must be some logical relationship with a secondary meaning; [3] there must be a condition (and a purpose) for that usage. Although in a dead metaphor there is no such purpose, there must be one in every other case. In the present instance, however, there is neither condition nor purpose in resorting to secondary meaning. . . . In the collocation "the boy is a lion," the primary meaning of "lion" is impossible; hence it connotes qualities like courage that are invariably associated with a lion, but since those are irrelevant in the present context we are led to understand that it is the boy himself who has these qualities.

(Dh) Moreover, if rasa could be comprehended as something directly denoted, then anyone with a mind capable of grasping direct denotation would be able to appreciate and taste rasa.[167]

(BN) [209.5] Not everyone who understands the meaning of the words will necessarily comprehend the aesthetic elements.

(Dh) But neither is the comprehension of rasa something entirely imaginary, since there is complete agreement that sensitive readers do experience the savoring of rasa. It is for all these reasons that some scholars argue for yet another linguistic function above and beyond the powers posited by others, namely, direct denotation on the one hand and metonymic and metaphorical connotation on the other. They call this function "manifestation" and say it pertains not only to rasa but also to figures of speech and narrative elements.

To explain their position further.[168] If the comprehension of rasa arises from the factors, reactions, and transitory emotions, how could it possibly be directly denoted? Consider a verse such as the following:

The Mountain's daughter revealed her feelings too, the down on her limbs
growing stiff like plantain trees,
standing there with downturned face, her lovely face, with eyes half-closed.[169]

Here the apprehension of the erotic emerges without its ever being literally referred to, merely from the description of the foundational factor—the Mountain's daughter—exhibiting reactions, namely the specific states generated by her passion. The very same procedure can be extrapolated to other rasas. And this applies not only to rasas but also to the bare narrative. Thus in the poem,

[206] You're free to go wandering, holy man. The little dog was killed today
by the fierce lion making its lair in the thicket on the banks of the Goda river.[170]

the fact that we comprehend a prohibition, though not expressed in so many words, is based on the power of "manifestation." The same can apply to figures of speech:

In the presence of your face, which fills all space with the light of its beauty—
this smiling face of yours, woman with such large and darting eyes—
the fact that the ocean doesn't swell, not even for a moment, makes me see
how obvious it is that it should be called a mass of water [or: insensate stuff].[171]

The fact that in this verse we comprehend a figure of speech such as a simile—the woman's face is like the moon—is also brought about by manifestation. In none of these cases is the comprehension derived from the means of valid knowledge known as necessary assumption,[172] because there is nothing in the verses that does not make sense *as things stand.*

(BN) [209.21] We have a case of "necessary assumption" when some fact we encounter that does not stand to reason entails the existence of something else to make it reasonable.[173] Here, however, it is the sentence itself that suggests a second meaning, without this being entailed by something unreasonable in itself.

(Dh) Nor is direct denotation involved here, because manifestation operates at a *third* stage of meaning.[174] That is to say, in the poem "You're free to go wandering," there is another meaning that transcends the first stage (the denotation of the individual words) as well as the second (the sentence meaning, here a command based on the construal of a verb and the nominal case forms) and that clearly manifests itself at the third stage. This is the implied meaning consisting of a prohibition, which is based on the power of manifestation. That new meaning cannot, accordingly, be the mere sentence meaning.[175]

One might counter that in a sentence such as "Eat poison!" where the sentence purport is actually a prohibition though not directly enunciated,[176] it is sentence meaning that is actually in the domain of what is being called the third stage.[177] Even those who accept the concept of manifestation would not wish to deny that the prohibition is the ultimate sentence meaning here, because they argue that this is not a case of implicature but of sentence purport, and implicature and sentence purport are altogether different phenomena.

(BN) [210.3] The opponent of the theory of implicature objects that implied meaning cannot have its domain of functioning at a third stage (beyond the stage of word meanings and that of syntactically generated sentence meaning). In a sentence such as "Eat poison!" where we can determine the purport to have the sense "Do not eat in that man's house" even when this is not enunciated, what the implicature theorist regards as a third stage is actually the stage of sentence purport. Even he would not deny that in the sentence that commands eating poison, the actual meaning, that of a prohibition, falls within the scope of sentence purport. Accordingly, since both positions agree, the prohibition and not the command must be the meaning of the sentence. In other sentences, then, no less than in this one, the meaning that is presumed to be a result of "manifestation" must in fact be simply a function of sentence meaning.

(Dh) But the proponent of implicature would reject this argument, precisely because in the example adduced there is no third stage at all, since the literal meaning of the words does not "come to rest"—that is, does not make sense—at the second stage, that of sentence meaning.[178] It is at that second stage where the prohibition is being expressed, insofar as at that stage the literal verb-object construction would make no sense at all as a commandment, given the context: the speaker is a father, who would never enjoin the addressee, his son, to eat poison.[179] Moreover, with respect to rasa sentences, we do not understand rasa at the second stage, where we comprehend the aesthetic elements.[180] To quote:

> If a sentence does not come to "rest stably"—i.e., if it makes no sense—in its literal meaning,[181] it can hence rightly be said that the meaning where it finally does make sense constitutes its sentence meaning. But where a sentence does indeed come to rest in its literal meaning and thereby attains stability but still proliferates meaning, in all such cases this is something that occurs only through implicature.[182]

[207] Thus, the implicature argument goes, rasa in all cases can only be the object of "manifestation," whereas narrative elements and figures of speech are given sometimes

by direct denotation, sometimes by manifestation. Furthermore, only where the comprehension derived from manifestation is predominant do we have actual "manifestation"; elsewhere, we have "subordinated manifestation."[183]

There are two main types of implicature: (1) where the literal meaning is set aside and (2) where the literal meaning is retained but subordinated to the suggested meaning. The former is of two types: where the literal meaning is completely set aside, and where it transmutes into some other meaning. The latter is also of two types: quasi-instantaneous and gradual. Rasa, when our comprehension of it is dominant, is always the object of a quasi-instantaneous manifestation; when it is subordinate, we have discourse in which rasa functions more as a figure of speech.

[211] To this entire foregoing argument the author now responds:

(D) (4.37) Just as a verb—whether directly expressed or understood as being present by virtue of context or other similar factor—constitutes sentence meaning when construed with the nominal case forms,[184] so a stable emotion constitutes a "sentence meaning" when construed with the other aesthetic elements.[185]

(BM) Just as in the Vedas[186] sentence meaning consists of a verb—whether literally expressed or derived from the context—in a form qualified by nominal case relations, so in literature we likewise have "sentence meaning," namely, the stable emotion qualified by the factors, reactions, and transitory emotions. This proves that, even in the absence of words such as "desire" or "the erotic," we can comprehend a stable emotion and a rasa in a pertinent sentence—which is precisely why sentence meaning where the verb is understood from the context is adduced as an analogy.

(Dh) In everyday sentences, the verb complemented by nominal case forms constitutes the meaning of a sentence, the verb itself being brought to our awareness either because it is directly expressed (i.e., where the verb is actually used, as in "*Bring* the cow!") or because it is understood from the context (i.e., where it is omitted, as in "The door, the door!"). In just the same way, in literature too, the stable emotion constitutes a "sentence meaning." This emotion becomes virtually present[187] in the mind of the viewer/reader actualizing the emotion either from being directly expressed, as it sometimes is (e.g., "My beloved bride becomes even more *beloved* . . ."[188]), or, when it is not directly expressed, from being taken from the context, where it can be understood because it is invariably concomitant with the aesthetic elements when these are enunciated as present.[189] And it is brought to the highest pitch through the stimulation of a chain of innate dispositions in the viewer/reader when the appropriate foundational and stimulant factors, reactions, and transitory emotions for each are presented in the appropriate language.

(BN) [213.22] One particular disposition is brought forward by the factors, another by the physical reactions, yet another by the psychophysical responses or by the transitory emotions. This constitutes the "chain" of dispositions.

(Dh) The counterargument that something like rasa that does not consist of actual word meanings cannot constitute a "sentence meaning" has no real force. For what defines sentence purport is the capacity to issue in some action. To explain: every sentence, whether authored by a human or authorless (like the Veda), is directed toward action; it would otherwise be like the babble of a madman, completely without value.[190] In the case of the language of literature, we must conclude that its "action-outcome" is nothing other than arousing the bliss proper to it,[191] since positive and negative evidence reveals no other performance-oriented purpose with respect to its signified and signifier. As for this outcome, it arises, we come to understand, when the stable emotion is "syntactically construed" with the aesthetic elements. Accordingly, the expressive capacity[192] of such a "sentence" is elicited[193] by a given rasa, and eventuates at last in producing it through communicating the specific aesthetic elements appropriate to its particular character. In this process, the elements may be taken to stand for words, while the stable emotion syntactically construed with them forms a sentence meaning. Thus, literature as such is a *Vākyapadīya*,[194] a work concerned at once with word and sentence, the "words" and "sentences" being those just indicated.

(BN) [214.15] The literary text communicates rasa as its main purpose. It may be thought of as a "sentence," insofar as it communicates rasa acting as sentence meaning. It may also be thought of as "words," insofar as it communicates the aesthetic elements acting as words in relationship to the sentence that is rasa. Therefore, the literary text may be likened at once to both words and sentences.[195]

(Dh) And although it is the case that the literary text produces pleasure,[196] it would assuredly be false to conclude that, in view of this fact, literature has no more use for the signifier-signified relationship than does, say, singing. [212] This is because the savoring of rasa comes about only for those who can actually understand the full complement of the aesthetic elements brought into play in their special way, and who at the same time have the capacity for the "actualization" of the particular stable emotion at issue in the work. This fact negates any overextension of the analogy of song. And last, given the description of sentence meaning that we have provided, we conclude that we understand all such sentence meaning exclusively by virtue of the linguistic capacities posited for everyday language—primary meaning, secondary meaning, and sentence purport—and that, accordingly, it is simply wasted effort to posit any additional capacity.[197]

(BN) The "description of sentence meaning" refers to the argument that rasa constitutes a sentence meaning, insofar as it is the purport or focal point.

(Dh) To quote what I have said in my "Analysis of Literature":[198]

> [1–2] With respect to the sentence in question, "You're free to go wandering, holy man . . . ," which can actually be accounted for by sentence purport, the "manifestation" my opponent assumes, as well as "implicature," need not be posited at all.[199] For what counterargument could be offered against the overextension of implicature to a case such as the sentence "Eat poison!" where the real purport of the sentence is not directly expressed and yet must be something other than what is in fact said?[200] Both the former sentence and this one would wind up being the same in terms of final purport. And since that meaning is the dominant one—and "implicature" is defined as a sentence where the implied meaning predominates over the expressed meaning—how could one deny implicature in the latter case? [3–4] The definition of implicature is when a sentence can come to rest in its literal meaning and still produce further meaning ("You're free . . ."), whereas purport is when it does not come to rest, because to do so would be impossible ("Eat poison"). But what justifies thus restricting the scope of purport's production of meaning? No reckoning has been taken of the fact that purport extends as far as necessary to complete its task. [5] The sentence "You're free . . ." cannot in fact repose in the idea of wandering, as the implicature theorist believes, since it requires further linguistic activity to shift toward a prohibition.[201] [6] Or if the "coming-to-rest" of a sentence is supposed to derive from the fulfillment of the semantic expectation of the addressee, then "coming-to-rest" must be absent in "You're free . . ." insofar as the speaker's intention has not yet been achieved.[202] [7] Human sentences are dependent on intention—and hence it stands to reason that literature should be concerned with purport as intended by the speaker.

Accordingly, the relation between rasa and literature cannot be one of "manifestation," the former being the entity manifested, the latter the means. It is rather one of "actualization," rasa being what is actualized, literature the means. For rasa does not preexist, on its own; it is something that has to be brought into being by means of literature with the particular aesthetic elements of the literary text, for the viewers/readers who "actualize" it.

(BN) [216.4] All speakers use language to achieve particular ends, to be sure. With respect to literature, the intention of the writer in using language is to ensure that the audience savors rasa, and the audience's apprehension of rasa comes from the words of the text. In this act of actualization, accordingly, the audience is the agent, language the means, and rasa the thing to be actualized. Hence, it is the intention of the writer that may be described as the actualizer of the audience's rasa by means of his literary text. No other kind of relationship need be postulated.

(Dh) [213] It would not do to argue that, because this peculiar relation of "actualizer and actualized" does not exist in any other domain of language, there is no reason why it should exist in literature. For it is in fact accepted by those who champion the operation known as "actualization."[203] And even if it were not to exist elsewhere, so be it, since we would have then both positive and negative evidence, namely, that it exists in literature and that it exists nowhere else. . . .[204]

(BN) "Those who champion" argue that in a Vedic sentence such as "He who desires heaven should sacrifice," the thing to be actualized is some end result, such as, here, heaven; the sacrificer is the agent of actualization, while the sacrifice is the means. And hence the operation here is "actualization," namely the relationship of thing actualized and means of actualization that exists in the case of heaven and the sacrifice. . . . By the actor's acting out on stage the pleasure, pain, or other emotion of the character, the rasas are generated, which the spectators then actualize. Hence the emotions can be said to generate the rasas, and the relationship between the rasas and that which generates them can be said to be one of actualizer and thing actualized.[205]

(Dh) But, it might be asked, how do we comprehend intangible things like the stable emotions from words (such as "desire") when no connection can be grasped between the word and the thing itself?[206] Here is our answer: in everyday life, when men and women behave in a particular way, we come to know that they are experiencing emotions such as desire since a given emotion is invariably associated with a given action. In literature, similarly, when we find the same situation presented and hear words that express behavior invariably associated with desire or some other emotion, we have a comprehension of desire that can be understood as a metonymical one, based on an invariable association with the denotative meaning.

In what follows we will explain how the meaning of a literary text "actualizes" rasa.

(BN) Words for a foundational factor such as the hero, and so on, are connected only with their primary meaning, and are not directly connected with emotions such as desire.[207] When in such words as "desire" we do not grasp the relevant connection, how can they possibly express the emotions in question? . . . The words that express behavior and the like have as their final purport the expression of the stable emotions that are invariably associated with them. Thus, the linguistic function of literary language is the metonymical communication of emotion, since we apprehend these emotions as being invariably associated with the behavior that constitutes what is being denoted by that language.

(D) (4.38–39) That same entity is called rasa, "taste," because it is something that is savored. Rasa belongs to the spectator experiencing the rasa, and to him alone, because he is alive and present. It does not belong to the character, because [1] he is no longer alive and present; [2] the ultimate aim of literature cannot pertain to the character; [3] we would otherwise have the absurd situation of the spectator being overcome with shame, jealousy, passion, or hatred—just as if he had seen a man in everyday life in the embrace of his beloved—or else having a merely indifferent apprehension.[208]

(Dh) [217] The referent of "that same entity" is the stable emotion produced to overflowing by the elements of the literary work and existing in the *rasika*, the viewer/reader experiencing the rasa. It becomes rasa when it reaches the state of "being savored," that is, intensely blissful consciousness. It exists in the *rasika* because he is present; not in the character, Rama for example, because he is not. Now, it was said that although the character is not actually present, he appears to be so when mediated by language.[209] But it is only we and others who are experiencing the character's semblance of presence;[210] it is as good as nonexistent as far as the character's own capacity for savoring rasa is concerned. Rama's semblance of presence as a foundational factor *for us*, however, is something we fully accept.[211]

(BN) [218.4] It is has been claimed that only by being mediated by language can the protagonist and so on function as a foundational factor, and in that mediated form he is actually present. . . . Nonetheless, as far as the capacity for savoring rasa is concerned, the protagonist's form is as good as nonexistent. It is only the character's experiencing rasa that is being denied, and which instead is being predicated of the audience. Even if the character can be said to experience rasa while existing in a verbally mediated form, that form serves no purpose with respect to the actual savoring of rasa, but only with respect to constituting him as the protagonist. For of course in that form there can exist no element of conscious awareness.

(Dh) Moreover, literature is not something in which writers engage in order to produce rasa in characters like Rama, but rather in order to make sensitive people feel aesthetic bliss—and rasa is something that all viewers/readers are directly aware of. If the erotic rasa truly did belong to Rama rather than the viewer/reader, the sight in a drama of the erotic protagonist in the embrace of his beloved—just as if one were to have such a sight in everyday life—would produce in the spectators the mere apprehension that the protagonist is having an erotic experience; *rasikas*, however, would not be savoring anything at all. It would also follow that good people would feel shame and the like, and others resentment, passion, or even a desire to take possession of the woman themselves.

All this being the case,[212] the view that rasa can be the object of "manifestation" stands refuted. For an entity can only be manifested by something after it has been brought into being by something else: a pot, for example, can only be manifested by a light when it has already been produced by the clay. It is certainly not possible for an entity to be brought into existence by the very things that are supposed to manifest it, and this at one and the same moment. But that rasa can be "actualized" by means of the factors and the rest in the spectators has already been cogently argued.[213]

(BN) It is precisely the kind of purport we find in everyday communication that is achieved in literature by way of the "actualization" relationship, and so there is no need to admit any additional linguistic capacity in literature such as manifestation.

(Dh) [218] But if rasa resides in the audience, what functions as its foundational factor? Take the case of Sita, who is a goddess:[214] how can there not be something fundamentally wrong in her functioning as such a factor? Here is the author's response:

(BN) [219.3] To restate the main question: Granted that the substratum of rasa is the audience and not the character, why still insist that the form of a foundational factor such as Sita is a purely linguistic construct, and cannot be the actual individualized form?

(BM) If rasa does not arise for us when we see a man in the embrace of his beloved in the real world, why should it arise when we hear about people of the past such as Rama, who most fully experienced the rasa?[215] To this question the author now speaks:

> (D) (4.40–41ab) What characters such as Rama[216] communicate is a particular typological state, such as being a protagonist of the "noble" variety. They thereby "factor"[217] the stable emotions, which are then able to be savored by the *rasika*. Accordingly, it is such states,[218] emptied of all elements of particularity, that are the causes of rasa.

(BM) It is not the specific referent of "Rama" that is the foundational factor of rasa—if it were, rasa could never come into being, since that referent is no longer present. Instead, the word "Rama" loses any intended particularized reference and communicates a typological state represented by the character, in this case that of a "noble" protagonist. And it is this that becomes the foundational factor of the stable emotions such as desire. . . . Accordingly, when the erotic enjoyment of the hero Rama, who most fully experienced the rasa,[219] is communicated, the innate predispositions of the audience members are activated in the highest degree. They shed the distinction between self and other, and with their minds inclined toward the contemplation of the various acts of erotic enjoyment, they experience a pure savoring. And so, although in an ultimate sense Rama does not exist, his form can enter the mind—and precisely when this happens, he becomes the cause of rasa.

(Dh) Unlike a spiritual adept,[220] a poet is not able to behold with the "eye of insight" and to present a character like Rama in a state of sheer individuality, as is the case with historical discourse. Rather, he creates a typological state, such as the "noble" protagonist, which is given presence through the poet's imagination by means of the process of "commonality" that each viewer experiences,[221] the state itself simply providing a substratum for a given rasa. [219] Consider here a word like "Sita": it is emptied of all its particularities, such as being the daughter of King Janaka, and signifies nothing more than "woman"—and how could anything untoward[222] come of that?

(BN) What Dhanika means is this: with respect to the protagonists (e.g., Rama), the true domain of reference of the words signifying them (e.g., "Rama") is the typological state, such as the "noble" hero. That state alone is the object of rasa.[223] It is the audience members who experience the rasa when they "actualize" the rasa upon accessing the states presented in those specific linguistic forms. With respect to being the object of rasa, no use whatever is made of the particularized individualized form. . . . Spiritual adepts behold a past and future form as if it were actually present, but poets are different. Even though they behold particularized forms of the foundational factors and so on, they do not compose poems in the manner of a historical narrative, in order to describe rasa as having its substratum in those forms.

(Dh) Then why are they taken up at all? To this the author now speaks:

(BN) That is, if no attention is paid to the particularized form of Sita and the like, then why should they be "taken up" in those specific forms?

(D) (4.41cd–42ab) When children play with clay elephants, it is their own stable emotion (determination or whatever it might be) that they thereby savor. This is just what readers do with Arjuna and the rest.[224]

(BM) When children are playing with clay elephants, no actual elephant exists; the savor of the game comes from the clay form that participates only in the conception of an elephant. In the same way, Rama, Arjuna, and so on do not really exist but are made almost visibly present in language by the poet's skill. Readers thereby come to focus their minds on the contemplation of these heroes' doings, and are overcome by a dissolution of the distinction between self and other—and thereby rasa comes into being.[225]

(Dh) This is the argument: in literature, the use of such foundational factors as a woman is not like the erotic in the real world. Rather, this use occurs in the manner already indicated, because the rasas of drama are different from real-world rasa.[226] To quote: "The rasas of drama are traditionally counted as eight."[227]

(BN) Dhanika is responding to the following view: if Sita is not used in her particularized form, how can a rasa that has her as its object come into being? For there is no evidence that a rasa like the erotic can have its object in Sita if she is not even held to exist. . . . If [Bharata] had thought of rasa in the same way as its real-world variety, he would not have said there were eight, since real-world rasas—physical tastes—are six in number.[228]

(D) (4.42cd) As for the actor, there is nothing stopping him from savoring the actualization of the subject matter of the literary work.

(Dh) [220] The actor does not experience rasa on the basis of a real-world rasa, for when he is acting the woman he is perceiving as an object of sexual pleasure is not his own wife.[229] But there is nothing stopping him, as he "actualizes" the subject matter of the literary work, from savoring the literary rasa just as the rest of us do.

(BN) The objector holds that this would make sense for the actor since he would have rasa via the real-world rasa in the character, Rama for example.

(Dh) How does the savoring of rasa arise from literature, and what is the nature of rasa? The author now explains:

(D) (4.43–45ab) When there is a fusion[230] of the mind with the meaning of the literary work,[231] there arises the bliss that is the self,[232] which constitutes the savoring of rasa. This fusion is of four sorts: an "expansion" of the mind in the case of the erotic rasa, an "enlargement" in the case of the heroic, a "turbulence" in the case of the macabre, and an "agitation" in the case of the violent. Exactly the same responses pertain, respectively, to the comic, the fantastic, the fearful, and the tragic. Hence, the correct interpretation is that the various (i.e., four pairs of) mental states are produced by the various (i.e., four pairs of) rasas.[233]

(BM) The "meaning of the literary work" refers to the stable emotion "construed with" the factors, the reactions, and the rest. The "fusion" is a mutual interpenetration, as of the waters of the Ganges and Yamuna rivers. Accordingly, the relation between the text and the mind of the audience is thus also one of "actualization," where the text is the object, the mind the agent, it earlier having been argued that the relation is one of communication via the linguistic function of sentence purport.[234] Now, some argue that rasa really exists only in Rama and other characters, and that what is communicated by the literary text and exists in the audience members is a semblance of rasa.[235] We cannot accept this. For one thing, the joy that consists in the awakening of an absolutely blissful consciousness is proved to exist in the experience of all *rasikas*; for another, we have already provided an analysis of literature's final purport as lying in the rasa experience of the audience. . . . The names "expansion" and so on are meant to be actually descriptive of the mental states.

(Dh) The "meaning of the literary work" consists of the stable emotion "construed with" the factors and the rest. When there is a "fusion" between those and the mind of the viewer/reader—that is, a mutual interpenetration, in which the self-other distinction vanishes—we have the genesis of the most powerful form of "the bliss that is the self," namely, savoring. Although in its general form rasa is single, it can occupy one of four different mental planes[236] according to the type of fusion produced by the causes—the factors and the rest—that are invariably associated with a particular rasa. These are: expansion in the case of the erotic rasa, enlargement in the case of the heroic, turbulence in the case of the macabre, and agitation in the case of the violent. The remaining four rasas, the comic, the fantastic, the fearful, and the tragic, [221] once they have achieved a high degree of enhancement by means of their appropriate complement of aesthetic elements, have the same four types respectively (expansion in the case of the comic, and so on). Thus, when Bharata states that "From the erotic rasa arises the comic . . . ,"[237] he means in the first instance to indicate a conditional relationship among these with respect to this fusion, not a causal relationship, since they are actually produced by other causes.[238] When he says, "The comic is an imitation of the erotic,"[239] he makes it clear that each pair is a unity with respect to the types of fusion (expansion and so on). Delimiting the rasas to eight actually stems from the fact that there are only so many types of fusion.[240]

(BN) [222.1] "The bliss that is the self": to say that the bliss is the self, that is, one's own consciousness, is to indicate that there is no distinction between the act of savoring and the object of savoring.[241]

(Dh) The following objection might be raised: The erotic, the heroic, the comic, and some other rasas are in themselves delightful, and so in those cases it is reasonable to say that bliss comes into being from a fusion with the subject matter of the literary work. The tragic and other rasas, however, are in themselves sorrowful, and in those cases, how can bliss be supposed to come into being? To be more specific: when we listen to a tragic work of literature, what is manifested is sorrow; indeed, *rasikas* begin to weep. And this would not make sense if the experience were a blissful one. Now, there is some truth to this objection, but in fact, the bliss in question consists of both joy and sorrow; it is like a woman saying no when she means yes during the spanking and striking that occur in lovemaking. Literary tragedy is different from real-world tragedy. In the former case, *rasikas* cannot get enough of it; if it were the same thing as real-world tragedy and really consisted of sorrow, no one would ever seek it out, and great works like the *Rāmāyaṇa* that consist exclusively of the tragic rasa would have died out long ago. That weeping and the like should appear in the spectators listening to a description of the narrative, just as they do when a disaster like the loss of a loved one befalls them in real life, hardly constitutes a contradiction. Accordingly, the tragic too consists of nothing but bliss, just like the other rasas.

(BN) [223.1] With respect to the *Rāmāyaṇa*, the dominant rasa is in fact the heroic, though there is a great deal of the tragic.

(Dh) [223] Although the peaceful rasa has no place in drama, since it cannot be acted out, there is nothing to prevent its presence in poetry, given the existence of language's capacity for communicating anything whatsoever, however subtle or distant in time. That is why it was said (in 4.35), "In drama [impassivity] cannot be enhanced," and it was settled that with respect to acting there can be only eight rasas.

(BM) An objection might be raised: On what grounds has the determination been made that there are only eight rasas? For some scholars have accepted the view that the full development of the stable emotion called impassivity is a rasa. Even if it cannot be displayed, given the absence of any reactions that might be acted out, still in literature it can function as a rasa. To this the author now speaks:

(D) (4.45cd) At its highest degree impassivity is utterly ineffable. And if it is only joyfulness and other aspects of impassivity that are meant, then in the last analysis that impassivity would consist in one of those four mental states.

(Dh) We lose nothing by insisting that the peaceful rasa cannot exist in dramatic acting. For if it is to be characterized as it is in the following verse,

No sorrow is there in it, no happiness, no disquiet,
no anger or passion, and never any longing—
thus is the peaceful rasa described by the greatest of sages,
which has the same warrant as all the other emotions.[242]

then it is something that manifests itself only in the state of final release, the attainment of the essential nature of the self. And in its essential nature the peaceful is therefore ineffable. That is, scripture itself speaks of it only by way of exclusion of what is other than it, when remarking, "It is not this, not that."[243] Such being the nature of the peaceful rasa, no one who has his heart invested in it would ever want to savor it in performance. Now, even if what is intended is the *means* to the peaceful rasa, namely impassivity—which can be defined as joyfulness, friendliness, pity, and the like—this cannot be "enhanced" in performance and so cannot lead to rasa. If we consider the peaceful rasa in relation to poetry, however, the mind in savoring it will take the form of one of the mental states earlier described, namely, expansion, enlargement, turbulence, or agitation. And this explains the savoring of the peaceful rasa in poetry.[244]

(BN) [224.4] Rasa is directed toward the *rasikas*; they are the ones with an attachment[245] to plays. Such people have no heart for the peaceful rasa and do not savor it; the dispassionate, on the other hand, do not even watch plays. Thus, the peaceful rasa "has no place" in any of the dramatic forms, where it would have to be acted out in performance.

(Dh) [224] The author now offers a capsule account of the chapter so far, after first mentioning the subordinate literary functions as these pertain to the factors and the rest.

(BM) The factors, reactions, and transitory emotions connected with the rasa of the protagonist, Rama, Arjuna, and so on—namely, things like the moon, horripilation, and despair, respectively—have their existence as such heightened, in poetry, by use of the refinements of language qualities (phonic texture and the like) and figures of sense and sound. These elements, each associated with their specific rasa, enable the stable emotion to be "actualized" and savored by the audience—and that is rasa, as the author now states:

> (D) (4.46–47ab) By virtue of literariness, "word meanings" in the form of such things as the moon, despair, and horripilation come to be known as stimulant factors, transitory emotions, and physical reactions respectively. These enable the stable emotion to be "actualized" and hence savored, and that is what is known as rasa.

(Dh) Literary processes like hyperbole and metaphor[246] elevate things like the moon into stimulant factors, a woman or the like into foundational factors, despair and so on into transitory emotions, and horripilation, weeping, the play of the eyebrows, and sidelong glances into physical and psychophysical reactions. These resemble word meanings by reason of their subordinate function, whereas the stable emotion resembles sentence meaning. When the latter is "actualized," that is, brought into actual being, it can be savored—and that is rasa. Such is the purport of the preceding section of the chapter.

(BN) [225.1] Although the foundational factors and other aesthetic elements themselves constitute sentence meanings with respect to the sentences in which they are found, nonetheless, with respect to rasa they have a "subordinate function" and thereby come to resemble word meanings. Rasa therefore can be analogized to sentence meaning, while the factors and so on can be analogized to word meanings.

CHAPTER FOUR

Abhinavagupta and His School, 1000–1200

4.1 RASA AND THE CRITIQUE OF IMITATION

Literary Investigations of Bhatta Tota (c. 975)

What we know about Bhatta Tota (sometimes, Tauta) comes principally from the pen of Abhinavagupta. He refers to him at various places in his writings on literature as teacher, and at the beginning of his commentary on the *Treatise on Drama* explains that he will transmit "the true doctrine of the theory of drama that has issued from the mouth of the goodly Brahman Tota."[1] That Bhatta Tota wrote a work on dramaturgy, if not a commentary on Bharata's *Treatise*, is indicated by Abhinava's later citations in his *New* Dramatic Art. Also ascribed to Bhatta Tota is a treatise, now lost, the *Literary Investigations*, upon which Abhinava himself wrote the *Exegesis* (*Investigations* might have been the name of the dramaturgical treatise).

Bhatta Tota is rarely mentioned in Sanskrit literature after the twelfth century; Hemachandra (d. 1172) may have been the last scholar to have had direct access to his works, though even he was probably only citing citations. Given Abhinava's own coordinates, Bhatta Tota must have lived in Kashmir in the latter half of the tenth century. If the exposition of interpretations of rasa that Abhinava provides in his *New* Dramatic Art is to be understood as a strictly chronological rather than conceptual ordering, then Bhatta Tota would have to be placed earlier than Bhatta Nayaka, though if our interpretation of the reference in the *River of Kings* is correct, Bhatta Nayaka must have lived at the beginning of the tenth century. Thin though the evidence is, the former appears to have known and critiqued the latter. We may contrast the two on the definition of "poet" (Bhatta Tota fragment #1 and Bhatta Nayaka #4), and on poetry and pedagogy (fragments #3 and #7 respectively); also, the term "commonization," closely associated with, if not coined by

Bhatta Nayaka, is used by Bhatta Tota. One problem with this sequence, however, is Bhatta Tota's argument that the character, the poet, and the spectator all have the same experience of rasa (fragment #4). Such a theory would be unthinkable in the wake of Bhatta Nayaka's transformative ideas—unless, of course, it had been offered as stubborn critique.

The fragmentary state of Bhatta Tota's corpus can give us only the merest sense of his views, but they were sometimes as insightful as they were influential. His definition of poetic imagination (*pratibhā*, fragment #1) was to be echoed down the generations. He was the first to draw a radical distinction between the secular poet (*kavi*) and the Vedic "poet" (*kavi*), and to restrict the idea of *kāvya*, literature, to the work of the former (fragment #2). The importance he attributes to "description" in the constitution of literature, rather than, say, narrative action, captures something essential about the specific nature of classical Sanskrit poetry. And the primacy he awards to drama in the conceptualization of rasa (fragment #5) brilliantly recapitulates as theory what was historical fact.

Aside from these tantalizing bits, Bhatta Tota is most celebrated, thanks to Abhinava's extended paraphrase (or quotation?), for his devastating critique of Shri Shankuka's concept of rasa in drama as an imitation of emotion.[3] This critique reveals both a mind skilled in dialectic, sometimes dizzyingly, even facetiously so, as well as the difficulty he and his student Abhinavagupta faced in trying to interpret away the many statements in the *Treatise on Drama* that support the idea of dramatic imitation. The critique itself does not help us determine what his own position on rasa may have been. But his bravura reasoning is a treat in itself, and it was to be taken over almost in its entirety by Abhinava.[4]

FROM *LITERARY INVESTIGATIONS* OF BHATTA TOTA

Direct (and Possibly Direct) Citations

(#1)[5] Wisdom that has ever new insights is called imagination. Imagination is the very life breath of description, and a "poet" is someone who has mastered description. A poet's work is called "poetry."

(#2)[6] There is no true poet who is not a seer. "Seer" comes from seeing, and "seeing" is true insight into the properties of the vast variety of existent things.

Reference made to the word "poet" in the Vedas is based on his true insight, but the meaning of the word that has become conventional in everyday life is based on both his insight and his gift for description. Thus, although his sight was ever clear, Valmiki, the primal sage, did not become a poet until he mastered description.

(#3)[7] Pleasure is constitutive of rasa, and rasa is simply drama, and drama simply knowledge.[8]

(#4)[9] The protagonist, the poet, and the audience, accordingly, all have the same experience.

(#5)[10] [Abhinavagupta: "Rasas are found in drama alone, and in poetry only to the degree that it mimics drama. For as my teacher has argued, with respect to the subject matter of the literary text, rasa comes into being only when a state of awareness simulating perception comes into being. To quote his *Literary Investigations*:]

> To the degree that poetry does not approximate the character of a performance, the possibility of savoring rasa decreases. But when the aesthetic elements—foundational factors such as a beloved woman or stimulant factors like a garden or the moon—are properly made available by the full range of imaginative expression blossoming in the course of description, they can become as clear as actual perceptions.

(#6)[11] The poet, they say, has a vast burden to bear: definitions, figures of speech, language qualities, knowledge of flaws, dramatic modes, and plot elements.[12] Only when all these come together as pleasing virtues in a mutually suitable manner will rasa be manifested, and immediately. A composition that is uncomplicated and engaging, whether with lilting meters or unversified words,[13] in an easily comprehended language—this sort of pure poetry (defined as "verbal acting" within the context of the "general style of acting") facilitates the experience of its rasas and emotions.

From this kind of poetry, whatever may be its narrative content, rasa will emerge from the transfiguration of the full complement of aesthetic elements, when these are neither deficient nor used to excess. The world of the drama is born from everyday life for the enhancement of rasa. Rasa is the be-all and end-all of the creator poet, deriving from his vivid imagination.

Restatements of Bhatta Tota's Doctrine

(#1a, Abhinavagupta)[14]

The position of Shri Shankuka[15] lacks any inherent truth and cannot withstand criticism. To explain: Is the argument that "rasa has the form of an imitation" asserted [1] from the perspective of the apprehending audience member; or [2] from that of the actor; or [3] in reliance on the notions of scholars, who analyze the nature of reality (to quote: "It is scholars, after all, who analyze in this way, and not those who simply engage in the practice")?[16]

[1] Now, as for the first perspective, we cannot reconcile it with Bharata's actual statements if we follow them closely.[17] We can only call something an "imitation" if it has been perceived by some valid means of knowledge. For example, one can only

interpret the drinking of water as the drinking of rum (giving us the idea, "That fellow is drinking rum") if we are actually seeing the water-drinking with our own eyes. And thus in the case under discussion, you need to explain what the spectator is perceiving in the actor that appears as an imitation of desire. For one thing, his body, the headdress, the costume and so on it is dressed in, his horripilation, stammering, the shaking or flailing of arms, the movement of eyebrows, the glances, and so on:[18] none of this appears to anyone as an *imitation* of a mental state such as desire, because all of it differs radically from desire. For one thing, it is material; for another, it is perceived by different sense organs; and last, it is located elsewhere than desire.[19] For another, this cannot be the imitation of a character since such imitation can manifest itself only if we have already seen the actual person. But none of us has ever seen Rama and the desire he feels. The idea, therefore, that the actor is "imitating Rama" can be dismissed as so much empty talk.

Now, suppose you argue that the erotic rasa is an imitation of desire comprehended as simply the mental state of the actor. You still need to explain what the mental state we are apprehending consists of. It consists, you will say, of the everyday mental state—one characterized by causes, effects, and auxiliaries—that we are able to apprehend by signs that prompt an inference: a cause such as a lovely woman, an effect such as sidelong glances, and auxiliaries such as satisfaction and other transitory emotions. But then, unfortunately for you, the mental state we are apprehending *is desire itself*; forget about the argument of its being an *imitation* of desire.

You will reply that there is a fundamental distinction here: the aesthetic elements, the foundational factor and so on, are real only in the case of the character being imitated; in the case of the actor doing the imitating, they are not. So be it, but if these elements are factitious and not really the causes, effects, and auxiliaries of that desire, but are instead something invented thanks to the actor's study of the poetry, his training, and so on, are they or are they not grasped as factitious by the audience? If they are, then how could the audience possibly have any real awareness of desire?[20] That, you will retort, is precisely the reason for claiming that what is being apprehended is an imitation. But, my simple fellow,[21] it is only reasonable to draw an inference about some *second* thing (that is, an *imitation* of desire as opposed to actual desire) when it has arisen as an effect from some *second* cause (factitious elements) *understood to be second* by an observer who knows the difference. But the observer who does not know will only have an inference of the cause itself that is familiar to him (that is, the real desire in the main character).[22] From a particular scorpion, only a knowledgeable observer could make the correct inference that dung is the cause of its propagation; an ignorant observer would make an inference that another scorpion is its cause, and that could be false knowledge.[23] You would not infer an imitation of fire from mist that is actually being perceived as smoke.[24] It is not even correct to say we can infer an imitation of fire from a sign manifesting itself as an imitation of smoke. We do not find that we apprehend the presence of a bouquet of red roses imitating fire from mist actually perceived as an imitation of smoke.[25]

[269] But wait, you will say, the actor who is angry is not really angry but only appears to be so. That is true, he is similar to an angry man, the similarity coming from his frowning and so on, the way a cow's similarity to a wild ox comes from its features[26]—but this in no way suffices to make it an imitation.[27] Given that the audience has no sense of any similarity anyway, and that it believes the actor is certainly feeling some emotion, it is a completely hollow argument to say an imitation must be manifesting itself here.

You make the further argument that the audience has the awareness "This is Rama." Now, if this awareness is certain at the time it arises and not negated[28] at some later point, why does it not count as true knowledge? Or if it is negated later, why does it not count as false knowledge? According to the real nature of things, of course, it is false knowledge even if it is not later negated. It is therefore untrue to say, "We encounter no antithetical ideas. . . ."[29] In addition, we have the same awareness, "This is Rama," when it comes to a second actor too, so there would turn out to be a general class category, a "Ramaness," in which both participate.[30]

You also argue that "A distinct comprehension of the foundational and stimulant factors is gained on the strength of the literary narrative itself."[31] I am not sure what this means. First, the actor does not get the idea "This remarkable woman Sita is mine" as something actually pertaining to himself. And if what you mean by "distinct comprehension" is simply that it is the audience that is supposed to be capable of apprehending the factors, then it should be all the easier for them to "distinctly comprehend" the stable emotion.[32] What the audience chiefly understands, after all, is "This stable emotion is present in this person (the actor)." If we are to be in accord with what the audience is actually apprehending, then, it is false to claim that rasa is an imitation of a stable emotion.[33] (The distinction in the nature of "verbal acting" introduced in the sentence "For *referential* language as such is not at the same time *expressive*" will be considered later at the appropriate place.)[34]

[2] Now, as for the actor, he certainly does not have the idea, "I am imitating Rama or his mental state." For in the first place, if "imitation" (*anu-karaṇa*) is taken in the sense of "making similar" (*sadṛśa-karaṇa*), it is not even something that the actor can accomplish, since he has never seen the original. But if the term means merely "making (*karaṇa*) afterward (*anu*)" (with *anu* understood in a temporal sense), then the definition would be too wide, for this species of "imitation" occurs in everyday life.[35] Then again, if it is not some particular person but rather the emotion (grief, for

example) of a high-status character[36] that the actor believes he is imitating, then you still need to explain what he is using to produce the imitation. It cannot be grief, first of all, for there is no reason for the actor to be grieving.[37] Nor can an imitation of grief be made by shedding tears and the like, because of the radical difference between material teardrops and immaterial emotions that we have already noted. And if you are only prepared to go so far as to say that the actor believes he is imitating the reactions to grief that a high-status character is feeling, we still have to ask: what high-status character are you talking about? If you answer: Just some unspecified character, then how can such an entity lacking all particularity be brought to our awareness? And if you answer: Whoever it is that would be expected to weep the way the actor is weeping, well then, we have the actor's own self barging into the midst of the proceedings,[38] and the whole relationship of subject and object of imitation collapses.

Furthermore, the actor does not feel that what he is doing is an imitation; he just has the sense that he is acting, simply by displaying the physical reactions—first, thanks to his training; next, by reason of his recollecting his own "foundational and stimulant factors" (his own beloved, for example); and last, from the "heart's concurrence" deriving from a "commonization" of the character's mental state—and by reciting the poetry with the proper intonation and all the other appurtenances. [270] For an actor's imitating the actions of Rama is nothing like a woman's imitating the clothing of her lover (as we have shown in chapter 1).[39]

[3] Last, it is also in accordance with the way things really are that we deny that an imitation of the stable emotion takes place. This is so first of all because nothing of which we have no awareness[40] can be said to have any reality. As for what is really the case, this is something we will discuss later. Furthermore, the sage has not directly said anything to suggest that rasa is an imitation of a stable emotion, nor can we find anything in his text that would lead even to an inference of such a thing. In fact, his description of all the things that provide sustenance to drama—the *dhruvā* songs, the variegated rhythms, the components of the preliminary dance—leads us to infer that just the opposite of imitation is taking place, an issue we will enlarge on at the end of the chapter on emplotment in drama.[41] As for the statement in the *Treatise on Drama* itself that drama is "an imitation of everything contained in the seven continents," this is something that can be explained in an altogether different way.[42] And last, if we were to grant for the sake of argument that the sage is indeed speaking of an "imitation" of a stable emotion, why is that new term never applied by him to the woman's actual imitation of her lover's clothes or gait?[43]

Finally, as to your argument about a cow's being "constructed" of yellow and other colors of paint:[44] if the sense meant here is "manifested," that is patently false, because no real cow is being manifested by the paint as though by a lamp. All that is being produced thereby is a particular configuration similar to a cow. The painting is the domain of an appearance, namely, that an entity similar to a cow subsists in a particular arrangement similar to the arrangement of the parts of a cow. The configuration of aesthetic elements, however, is never grasped in a cognition of *similarity* to a stable emotion like desire. Therefore, it is false to assert that rasa is the imitation of a stable emotion.

(#2a, Abhinavagupta)[45]

The peaceful rasa is the most important rasa of them all, insofar as it is based on the highest of the ends of man, because it results in liberation from transmigration. Both my teacher, Bhatta Tauta, in his *Literary Investigations*, and I myself in my *Exegesis* thereon, have carefully and repeatedly analyzed both the pros and cons of this position.

(#3a, Abhinavagupta)[46]

Hence, no one should be confused into concluding that drama is an imitation of things that are *not* particulars. This is what we should understand to be the intention behind the *Literary Investigations* of my teacher, and not that drama may indeed be an imitation of nonparticulars.

(#4a, Anonymous)[47]

Bhatta Tota held that rasa is something both "manifested" and "apprehended" in the literal sense of the terms. It can be said to be something that "arises" only in a figurative sense.

4.2 THE THEORY OF RASA PURIFIED

The New Dramatic Art, of Abhinavagupta (c. 1000)

We know considerably more about the eleventh-century Kashmirian thinker Abhinavagupta (his last work is dated 1015) than any writer discussed so far—about his family, his teachers and students, his religious and philosophical views—in part because so much of his oeuvre has been preserved, in part because he is voluble about his associates, and in part because he left a short poetic autobiography of a kind we have for no other contributor to the *Reader.*[48] Among his extant works are two important texts on aesthetics, both commentaries, one on Anandavardhana's *Light on Implicature*, entitled *The Eye*; the other on Bharata's *Treatise on Drama*, named, punningly, *The New* Dramatic Art or *Abhinava's* Dramatic Art.[49] (Other works on literature that have been lost include his *Exegesis* on the *Literary Investigations* of his teacher Bhatta Tota.) In addition, he is the author of an extensive body of philosophical-theological texts in the tradition of the monist Shaivism of Kashmir. The chronological relationship of his aesthetic to metaphysical works is reasonably clear, and there is no doubt that the former preceded the latter (he tells us he was "greedy for the rich rasa of literature" until he was "seized with devotion" to Shiva).[50]

Abhinavagupta is thus one of the relatively few exceptions to the rule that whereas literary theorists might also contribute to philosophy (and most had affiliations to one or another school), philosophers rarely contributed to aesthetics. These were evidently viewed as more or less separate disciplinary specializations, even discrete realms of thought—until, for a brief moment, Abhinava changed the rules of the game and combined aesthetics and metaphysics, in his own scholarly career at least, if not as fully in his aesthetic theory as some scholars have suggested. On the contrary, his aesthetics seems more autonomous from his theology than what we usually read in secondary accounts; whereas understanding his philosophical treatises may require understanding something of his aesthetics, the reverse is not unconditionally the case. By far the greatest part of Abhinava's theory of literary art fits squarely within the disciplinary formation he inherited, in everything from the central problematics to the principal categories and technical vocabulary. Moreover, while Abhinava is also often viewed as the thinker whose conception of rasa stamped all future developments in the discourse—many later writers (there are numerous exceptions) largely identify their conception of rasa as deriving from his—what is not entirely clear is how much of that conception was in fact Abhinava's.

The two extant works on aesthetics, *The Eye* and *The New* Dramatic Art, the second of which was written later,[51] offer rather different ways of thinking about rasa, no doubt in part as a result of the different concerns of the primary works for which these commentaries were composed. The purpose of *The Eye* is to explain and defend Anandavardhana's conception of implicature, and in the course of executing that task Abhinava does something quite remarkable. Although Ananda consecrated rasa as the very goal of literature in a way no thinker before him (save Bharata) had done, rasa itself remained for him what it was for his predecessors, a phenomenon related to the formal organization of the literary text. And like his predecessors, Ananda was concerned with the textual processes that produce the sense of a feeling. While it is of course the viewer/reader who is ultimately cognizing the feeling, the feeling is that of the characters in the text, once it is "enhanced" and made cognizable by the aesthetic elements. Ananda's only consideration was how to make sense of the linguistic mechanism by which this feeling is created: it can never be directly expressed, he decided, or even figuratively communicated; it can only be implied. In the same way that the more important narrative component or the more powerful figure of speech is the one that is implied, not expressed, so emotion in the character can only be implied by the assemblage of the aesthetic elements, and can never be simply declared. Living as much as a century and a half after Ananda, in a thoughtworld that had experienced the conceptual revolution in aesthetics initiated by Bhatta Nayaka, Abhinava aimed—or at least this seems the unavoidable conclusion—to rescue Ananda from his own obsolescence. He sought to do this by transforming Ananda's linguistic modality (*śabdavṛtti*), whereby rasa was cognized, into a psychological modality (*cittavṛtti*), whereby rasa was experienced. Rasa now became something "manifested" not in the text by means of the aesthetic elements but by the activation of the "predispositions" associated with the stable emotions that preexist in the heart of the sensitive reader.[52] This is undoubtedly a more subtle and interesting theory, but one that Ananda would almost certainly have been perplexed to see presented as his own.

It is therefore at once surprising and unsurprising to realize how rarely Abhinava refers to "manifestation" or its synonym "implicature" in his later *New* Dramatic Art. He only mentions the idea in passing, and nowhere offers anything remotely approaching a full exposition, certainly nothing on the scale found in the synopsis of his theory that Ruyyaka, writing a century and a half later (and almost certainly in ignorance of *The New* Dramatic Art), provides in a text given below.[53] This silence is surprising not only because manifestation/implicature is core to his view in *The Eye* but also because that would be the terminology adopted by all later Sanskrit thinkers for the new reader-centered aesthetics. At the same time, it is unsurprising if we hypothesize, perfectly reasonably, not only that Abhinava found his earlier notions to be of diminished importance for a commentary on the *Treatise on Drama* but also that his own theory had matured, unrecognized though this possibility may be in the secondary literature—and even in the Sanskrit intellectual tradition. For although the theory found in *The Eye* (or in many cases just the précis of it in Mammata's *Light on Poetry*) had the greater effect on the history of aesthetics, this is only the result of an astonishing fact: aside from a group of thinkers all working in late twelfth-century Gujarat (Hemachandra, his students Ramachandra and Gunachandra, authors of the *Mirror of Drama*, and a commentator on another vanished work of literary criticism, *Examination of* The Wishing Vine, *Kalpalatāviveka*), no succeeding writer on aesthetics had access to *The New* Dramatic Art. The work was preserved in what seems to have been a single manuscript (and some late medieval copies of it), and not in Kashmir or even in Gujarat but in Malabar in the far southwest.

The notion of implicature became less relevant for Abhinava's later thinking about rasa, so we may continue to hypothesize, not only because it was less relevant for the work he was commenting on but also because in his mature theory something else, radically different, had come to take its place. What that something else is we can clearly deduce from the inaugural argument of his "critical reconstruction" of rasa theory.[54] Abhinava begins by likening literature to scripture in terms of its capacity to generate in the reader a "surplus comprehension": when we read in the Veda how someone performed a sacrifice and received great benefits from it, we are naturally inclined to apply that story to ourselves. Literature works in precisely the same way, prompting us to apply to ourselves, or to "commonize," the elements of the narrative. "Drama," so runs one of Abhinava's definitions, "is some subject matter that every viewer 'actualizes' as his own by the process of 'commonization,' and thereupon relishes."[55] What is grasped by this new aesthetic apprehension is no longer the character's stable emotion but the viewer's own, and "thus grasped, the stable emotion *is* rasa." The experience of rasa has now become the experience of one's own pure consciousness. Abhinava names this, somewhat obscurely, *anuvyavasāya*, a term that in normal philosophical discourse refers to a kind of secondary, or reflexive, awareness, or knowledge of a knowledge, but which he uses, he tells us, synonymously with "tasting, savoring, rapture, relishing, absorption, 'experience,' and so on"; and he offers an explicit gloss to signal its newly charged meaning: it is "on the order of direct awareness," and "consists of the light of the bliss that is one's own pure consciousness": "In our view, what is being savored is simply one's own awareness, and this is uniformly blissful."[56] (While aesthetic awareness is itself a special kind of pleasure called "bliss," in the course of an aesthetic experience one can also feel what seems to be displeasure, such as pain or fear; but "these are merely one's latent dispositions, of desire, grief, and so on, that serve to add variety to this awareness.")[57] And he is careful at the same time to dematerialize, as it were, the "taste" that is rasa: it is "not some already existent thing but in essence simply this very process of relishing, which exists only as long as the relishing itself exists and does not last beyond it."[58]

If this sounds familiar, it is because many of the same ideas, and much of the same terminology, are found in the earlier theory of Bhatta Nayaka and his disciples, Dhanamjaya and Dhanika, respectively author of and commentator on *The Ten Dramatic Forms*. Bhatta Nayaka based his entire reformulation of aesthetics on a hermeneutical model, borrowing from Mimamsa its central notion of "actualization," or the process embedded in the imperative language of scripture that prompts us to act in the world. All the key terms that Bhatta Nayaka either made his own or perhaps even coined, such as "commonization" and "absorption," were taken over by Abhinava as building blocks of his own theory; he even appropriates his opponent's three-part hermeneutic model.[59] However much Abhinava may criticize Bhatta Nayaka in *The Eye* as well as in *The New* Dramatic Art; however much he may protest—in accordance with a commonplace of Sanskrit intellectual history, that all later innovations are always-already contained *in nuce* in the foundational knowledge—that he is relating "simply what the sage [Bharata] himself has said, and nothing new at all,"[60] his "purified" theory of aesthetics is largely that of Bhatta Nayaka (even the transformation of the idea of "manifestation" may originally have been the latter's).[61] The very fact that he opens his own reconstruction this way shows that he has fully accepted Bhatta Nayaka's grand analogy: that the same mechanism that enables us to understand, and to become the subject or "agent" of, a commandment of scripture and so to actualize by ourselves the action prescribed by its discourse, enables us to understand and become the subject or agent of a literary text, to actualize its affective charge. Even Abhinava's extended reflection on the nature of aesthetic consciousness may owe something to Bhatta Nayaka, who was the first to think about these matters, for we find it already in Dhanamjaya a generation (it seems likely) before Abhinava ("When there is a fusion of the mind with the meaning of the literary work, there arises the bliss that is the self, which constitutes the savoring of rasa"), and in his commentator Dhanika ("The stable emotion . . . when brought within the sphere of savoring—a state of intensely blissful consciousness— . . . becomes rasa").[62] And of course, the very idea of "absorption" or "repose" as the core characteristic of aesthetic cathexis was already enunciated by Bhatta Nayaka, along with the corollary that aesthetic consciousness, when rendered so completely joyful and luminous, is akin to the ecstasy of spiritual self-transcendence, given that "the self-other distinction vanishes" (so Dhanika). Abhinava accepts this fully,[63] though it is noteworthy, in view of his later theological career, how little in fact he has to say in *The New* Dramatic Art about the precise boundaries of aesthetic and religious consciousness.

That said, there is a wide range of astonishingly rich and subtle ideas that are original to Abhinava. He is the first scholar to produce an intellectual history of aesthetics, from Dandin to his own time—indeed, it is his history alone that enables us to produce ours. He is the first to argue out in a philosophical mode that aesthetic rapture is "an apprehension . . . in which only pleasure appears," that all the emotions we experience in an aesthetic event "are primarily pleasant, insofar as the pure homogeneous illumination that takes the form of the relishing of one's own consciousness is in essence blissful,"[64] a point that will be challenged or defended over the next half-millennium (under what description, Jain scholars in particular wished to know, can we claim that the aesthetic experience of violence or horror is really "pleasurable"?). He provides a remarkable account of the "hindrances" that obstruct aesthetic experience, and how these can be removed (that is, by the creators of dramatic art, not the viewer). It is of the nature of human awareness to be constrained by the primary categories of space and time, by our identities, by the phenomena of our everyday lives. Drama is designed precisely to counteract our natural proclivities toward distraction, disbelief, and the like by such strategies as the use of plausible narratives or the neutralization of the actors' space-time constraints through the use of costumes. In fact, Abhinava's phenomenological description of the transformation of the viewer's awareness through the magic of drama as it unfolds step by step offers some of the most penetrating accounts of aesthetic psychology available anywhere (see *On Drama* and *On the Nature of Dramatic Acting*, below). He makes subtle observations on the fact that rasa is a "process of tasting" (*rasyamāna*) and not some substantial thing tasted, thereby attempting to address (or so it seems to a nonprofessional philosopher) what Wilfrid Sellars called "the notorious 'ing/ed' ambiguity of 'experience,' " between acts of experienc*ing* and the contents experienc*ed*.[65]

Abhinava also powerfully (if complexly) reengages with the old question, first mooted by Udbhata, challenged by Shri Shankuka, grappled with by Anandavardhana, and ridiculed by Kuntaka, on the role of words for affective states in generating rasa. For Udbhata, the use in a literary text of the "proper term" or actual word for a rasa was a core factor in engendering it, a notion Shri Shankuka contested by distinguishing expressive from referential uses of language: the erotic rasa cannot be produced simply by way of direct reference, by use of the word "erotic"; it must find *expressive* realization (using the actual word would become an artistic flaw for Mammata). Anandavardhana made this distinction a cornerstone of his theory: rasa cannot be directly denoted, especially not by the actual word for it; it can only be implied by the aesthetic elements. In the important, if difficult passage given below, Abhinava appears, improbably, to be arguing against Ananda, or perhaps more credibly, against someone who offered a stronger formulation of Ananda's position that excluded the entire range of technical emotion words, not just the words for the rasas themselves.[66] Abhinava's position here may have been partly adopted by Mammata,[67] and the problem raised is central: how can you possibly create aesthetic emotion if you are prohibited from using *any* of the vocables in the lexicon of affective states, as a strong reading of the "flaw of using the actual words" for emotions would entail?

On one key question Abhinava does part company with Bhatta Nayaka: the degree to which drama or literature in general can be said to offer social and moral "instruction." Bhatta Nayaka explicitly opposed the idea that the purpose of literature can be anything other than pleasure: although literature and scripture might share similar communicative-conceptual capacities in prompting the viewer/reader to "apply" the text to himself, their modalities were entirely different. Scripture commands us like a master, we are told in an analogy almost certainly originating with Bhatta Nayaka, whereas literature seduces us like a beloved. For Abhinava, by contrast, sharpening his position on the relationship of pleasure and moral instruction in *The Eye*,[68] the focus of aesthetic experience is on those emotions that "pertain to the ends of man," the four life goals of love, wealth, morality, and liberation. It may be that "drama *is* rasa," but "the end result of drama is instruction," something he took from his teacher Bhatta Tota (fragment #3), along with a belief in the primacy of drama both for the rasa experience and for the theorization of rasa (for Abhinava, "rasa exists only in drama—and literature as a whole is nothing but drama," or indeed, just a "mimicry" of drama): "The end result of the savoring is instruction in morality and the other ends of man, expertise in them, and so on." The viewer of drama "comes to possess a certain form of consciousness of the sort conveyed by the deontic language of scripture—that those who do such and such a thing receive such and such a reward . . . so much so that, since his behavior is now interpenetrated by the desire to attain the good and to avoid the bad, he actually comes to do the good and to shun the bad, given that he has now gained an understanding to this end."[69] His brilliant, if anachronistic exposition of Bharata's idea of the four generative rasas is founded squarely on the homology he draws between them and the ends of man ("The most essential aesthetic components are those several forms of consciousness that pertain to the ends of man," etc.).[70] Literature's capacity to refine our moral imagination was thus a central, and newly central, tenet of his aesthetic understanding.[71]

The selections that follow are taken entirely from *The New* Dramatic Art. These begin with the reconstructive portion of Abhinava's account of rasa; his preceding review and critique of earlier theories—those of Bhatta Lollata, Shri Shankuka, Bhatta Nayaka, and Bhatta Tota—are presented elsewhere in the *Reader.* Excerpts from his reflections on other topics germane to the question of rasa follow. Although the space available here even to so important a thinker is limited, I might have included Abhinava's discussion of the peaceful rasa, although it mostly just offers detail, in a highly philosophical mode, on the nature of the stable emotion underlying this emotionless state (it is, he concludes, "true knowledge," which is what "impassivity" or "dispassion," the emotions normally ascribed to it, are taken to really mean), but a careful translation has recently been made available.[72] Similarly, there was no need to translate the discussion of rasa in *The Eye*, since this now exists in an authoritative version.[73]

Two important cautions need to be offered to anyone confronting Abhinava's aesthetics for the first time. His thinking is subtle, sometimes even counterintuitive, and he expresses his thoughts in a style virtually unique among Sanskrit authors for its Hegelian syntactical complexity and Heideggerian semantic idiosyncrasy. Frequently this style is refreshing; sometimes it is turbid as well as turgid; occasionally it is maddening. Added to this (and possibly a result of it), his major work on aesthetics suffered terribly in the course of transmission.[74] In a real sense, it is far too early in the history of Abhinavagupta studies for anyone to presume to describe his theory with any precision, let alone completeness. What follows is an attempt merely to capture in as intelligible a manner as I can some important themes, drawn from Abhinava's principal exposition of his aesthetic doctrine and from more peripheral but still illuminating discussions. I have sometimes left material standing that I do not always fully grasp myself, in the hope of contributing to a better understanding in the fullness of time.

FROM *THE NEW* DRAMATIC ART, OF ABHINAVAGUPTA

(1.272)[75] What, then, is the truth about rasa as purified by critique? It is simply what the sage himself has said and nothing new at all. And what he said is this: "Emotions (*bhāva*) are so called because they bring into being (*bhāvayanti*) the aims of the literary work."[76] Rasa, accordingly, is this "aim of the literary work."[77]

Consider the following analogy: on hearing a sentence of scripture such as "They held a sacrificial session through the night," or "He offered up the oblation into the fire,"[78] a qualified individual—that is, someone who desires a particular reward and meets the other requirements for ritual action—has at first a bare comprehension of the meaning of the sentence, enhanced by the persuasive power of the historical eventfulness[79] it references. But thereupon a certain surplus comprehension arises, of the nature of a transference and the like,[80] whereby the verb tense and person originally used in the sentence are suppressed and the reader thinks, "*Let me* hold a session,"[81] or "*Let me* offer up." This sort of comprehension is identified by various terms of art depending on the philosophical school, such as "understanding," "actualization," "commandment," "undertaking,"[82] and the like. In precisely the same way, from literary language there arises for the qualified individual a surplus comprehension.

[273] Here the qualified individual is the person whose heart is filled with uncontaminated sensibility.[83] When such a person hears verses like the one beginning "The fawn, its neck bent back beautifully,"[84] or "Uma with flowers falling from her long black hair," or "But Shiva, his calmness just barely disturbed,"[85] he first comprehends the literal meaning. There then arises another comprehension in the mind,[86] a kind of direct visualization, in which all the distinctions employed in this or that verse—distinctions of tense, for example—are eliminated. In the case of the fawn and king who appear in the first of the verses as being involved in a state of terror, they are devoid of particularity and ultimately unreal; what appears in the second form of comprehension here is, accordingly, a kind of pure fear—the cognition "afraid"—untouched by time and place.[87] Directly thereafter the fear is grasped[88] in an apprehension free from all "hindrances," differing radically from our usual hindrance-encumbered notions (since those are delimited, giving rise to thoughts of avoidance, acquisition, or indifference caused by pain and pleasure, such thoughts as "I am afraid," or "He—friend, enemy, neutral—is afraid"). And this stable emotion of fear, when it penetrates the heart almost visibly and becomes present before one's very eyes,[89] just *is* the fearful rasa. In this state of fear the viewer's self is neither completely displaced nor prominently referenced, and the same holds for every other person. For this reason, the "commonization" should be seen as not restricted to a single person but as extending beyond him, like the grasping of the invariable concomitance between smoke and fire, or fear and trembling.[90]

The whole assemblage of theatrical components, from the actor onward, conduces to this process of visualization. In this assemblage, all sources of delimitation—time, place, perceiving subjects, both those that really exist and those made available through the literary work—are expunged by canceling each other out;[91] and thereby the commonization just mentioned is enhanced all the more. For this reason, the audience members all share a homogeneous comprehension thanks to the concurrence of their predispositions—everyone's mind being studded with an infinite array of such predispositions—and this supplies even greater enhancement to the rasa.

This unhindered awareness is called aesthetic rapture. The transformations such as trembling, horripilation, and frissons produced from it are called rapture too, as in the following poem:[92]

> Even today Hari is overcome with rapturous wonder that Mount Mandara caused
> not the least harm
> to Lakshmi's limbs,[93] softer though they are than the beams of the crescent
> moon.[94]

"Rapture" is said to be an experience in which one is immersed without interruption, given the absence of any feeling of dissatisfaction: "'Rapture' (*camat-kāra*) is the 'action' (*karaṇa*) of someone 'enjoying' (*camataḥ*)," that is, when one is immersed in a pulsation of a fantastical experience.[95] It may be of the nature of a visualization, a conviction, an imagination, or a memory—though this is memory of a sort that does not emerge as normal memory does.[96] To quote:

> That you can be overcome with yearning, however happy you are,
> when seeing beautiful things or hearing sweet music,
> surely means some memory must be at work, something in your unconscious,
> attachments from former lives enduring in their emotion.[97]

[274] (The memory spoken of in this verse is not the sort described by the logicians, because the subject has never actually experienced the thing he is remembering; it has instead the character of a visualization or pure sensibility.)[98] At all events, this rapture[99] is an apprehension—or, in other words, a savoring—in which pleasure alone appears. Precisely because it is not qualified by any other internal differentiation of time, place, and so on, this apprehension, qua tasting, is not of a normal everyday sort, but at the same time it is neither illusory nor ineffable, neither similar to an everyday apprehension nor a metaphorical or other rhetorical representation of it. You may (with Bhatta Lollata) consider it a state of the enhanced stable emotion,[100] in the sense of its being unconstrained by the spatial or other particularities of the original; you may (with Shri Shankuka) consider it an imitation (*anu-kāra*), since it "produces" (*karaṇa*) its effects by "following after" (*anu*) the stable emotions, that is, by being in conformity with them; you may also regard it as an assemblage of imaginary

objects in the way of the Buddhist idealist school.[101] At all events, what is grasped by this apprehension—which is freed from all hindrances, and is essentially the *process* of tasting—is the stable emotion, and thus grasped, the stable emotion *is* rasa.

What removes the hindrances mentioned here are the aesthetic elements, that is, the foundational factor and so on. The consciousness thus freed from all hindrances is designated by a range of terms found in everyday life—rapture, engagement, tasting, savoring, experience, engrossment, ecstasy, absorption. As for the hindrances to this consciousness, there are seven: [1] "unfitness for comprehension," i.e., lack of plausibility; [2] preoccupation with time-space particularities that comes about by limitations related either to oneself or to another; [3] fixation on one's own states of mind, whether pleasurable or other; [4] deficiency in the means of apprehension; [5] absence of perspicuity; [6] nonessentiality; [7] doubtfulness. To explain in detail:

[1] A person who finds what is being narrated to be implausible cannot fix his consciousness upon it, let alone become absorbed in it. This is the first hindrance, and in the case of narratives familiar from everyday life, it is removed by the heart's natural concurrence with the action. But in the case of exploits entirely unfamiliar in everyday life, the means of removing the hindrance is the use of characters with well-known names (such as Rama), which amplifies a will to believe on our part that is already deeply entrenched, coming as it does from unbroken tradition.[102] For the same reason, in the genre called epic drama, whose purpose is a didactic one—the teaching of the highest moral principles—the use of subject matter consisting of such well-known narratives is a necessity, as we will explain.[103] This is something that should never occur, however, in other genres such as farces. We will address this topic at its appropriate place, so let this suffice for now.

[2] The greatest hindrance is the intrusion of some other state of awareness that might arise when we are savoring the consciousness of pleasurable or painful aesthetic experiences as something pertaining exclusively to ourselves. These other states include a fear that the experience will end, a preoccupation with preserving it, a desire to have (or to avoid) a similar experience, an urge to reveal or conceal it, or some other impulse, as the case may be. By the same token, if one were to have an awareness of the pleasure and pain as being experienced exclusively by some other person, one would at the same time necessarily have an awareness of some corresponding emotion in oneself—pleasure, pain, confusion, mere indifference—which inevitably produces a hindrance.

The means of eliminating this hindrance is the mode of concealment effected by the actor's costume, his headdress and so on, after the viewer had previously been made aware of the actor's actual presence by seeing him during the prologue (per the dramaturgical convention, "The actress, the actor who plays the fool . . . chat with the director"),[104] and the occultation effected by the theatrical preliminaries ("The preliminaries should be carried out according to prescription, but not drawn out too long"),[105] in combination with the theatrical conventions, zones or scenic arrangements within the theater [275], the stage, the preliminary dance, the varieties of unfamiliar languages, and all the rest. When this elimination is effected, there is no particularizing awareness of the pleasure or pain, no thought that the pleasure or pain pertains specifically to this particular person, in this particular place, for this particular reason. This is both because the actor's own person has been concealed and because our awareness does not come to rest on the character's, since in the case of an appearance of an assumed form our awareness can do so only imperfectly. And this is so because the upshot of assuming the character is merely to conceal the real form of the actor.

All such preparations, accordingly, have been required by the sage for their usefulness in promoting the relishing of rasa, by way of achieving the commonization of the aesthetic elements.[106] They will be clarified on the appropriate occasions, and no further attention need be given them here. But this explains the method for removing the hindrance coming from limitations related to oneself or to another.

[3] By the same token, how can the awareness of a person preoccupied with his own states of mind, whether pleasurable or otherwise, ever become absorbed in some other matter? To remove this obstacle, use is made of various modes of "coloration."[107] These reside in all the different components of the drama[108] and are capable of ensuring the "experience" of the whole, thanks to the power of "commonality."[109] These entities consist of words and other properties, and include instrumental music, singing, the enchanting theater itself, and the skilled actresses.[110] To quote: "Drama is something to be both seen and heard."[111] Thereby, the sensibilities of even an insensitive man, by virtue of his acquiring mental clarity, can be rendered completely receptive, so that he becomes a sensitive viewer.

[4–5] Moreover, how can there be any apprehension if the means for apprehension are absent? And when words and inferential signs[112] produce only something unclear, whatever the apprehension, it cannot attain the state of absorption; for that, what is required are ideas as close to perception as possible in the form of clear and distinct apprehensions. To quote: "All valid knowledge ultimately resolves to perception."[113] This is so because, for one thing, it is self-evident that neither inference nor testimony[114] by the cartload can alter something we have seen with our own eyes; and because, for another, a second, stronger perception can displace a first, false one[115] (an everyday example would be the displacement of the notion of a fiery circle upon seeing that it is produced by the swinging of a flaming torch). Thus, the consecrated way of eliminating both kinds of hindrance, that is, deficiency in the means of apprehension and absence of perspicuity, are the various types of dramatic acting, supplemented by social conventions, the theatrical modes, and the costumes. For the process of acting is something completely different from the operations of words and inferential signs;[116] as we shall make clear, it is nearly equal to the operation of perception.

[6] No one's awareness can come to rest upon something that is nonessential, since the moment that the inessential thing is cognized it hastens after something more essential, and cannot come to rest in itself. The inessential pertains to insensate things—the whole class of factors[117] and the physical reactions—but also to the category of the transitory emotions. This is so because these emotions, though conscious processes in themselves, are of necessity always directed toward something else. Accordingly, what stand apart from all that, namely, the stable emotions, is the only object worthy of an aesthetic relishing where awareness can come to rest. To examine this in greater detail:[118]

[276] The most essential aesthetic components are those several forms of consciousness[119] that pertain to the ends of man: love, wealth,[120] morality, and liberation. Thus, the stable emotion of desire pertains to love[121] as well as to forms of wealth and morality that are necessarily related to love; the stable emotion of anger pertains to wealth in those dramatic forms where anger is predominant,[122] and can even eventuate in love or morality; the stable emotion of determination can eventuate in any of the ends of man, morality and the rest; and last, impassivity, when it is the stable emotion and consisting largely in dispassion brought about by true knowledge, is the means of liberation. Hence, these four stable emotions are the most essential.[123] And while they have a certain hierarchy among themselves,[124] any one of these stable emotions can have primacy in the dramatic genre that prioritizes them, and hence, in the succession of dramatic forms all of them can come to have primacy. For one who examines the matter closely, in one and the same dramatic form at different points, a different emotion can have primacy.

Now, all these emotions are predominantly pleasurable, insofar as the pure homogeneous illumination that takes the form of the relishing of one's own consciousness is in essence blissful. To explain: in everyday life, when women relish the consciousness even of pure homogeneous grief, their heart finds repose because such grief itself embodies a repose free from any discontinuities. The absence of repose is the very definition of pain, which is why the followers of Kapila,[125] when describing volatility's mode of existence, state that instability is the life force of pain. All rasas, accordingly, are essentially blissful, though some, depending on the factors coloring them, can have a certain harshness[126] about them. Such is the case with contact with the heroic rasa, whose life force, after all, is, among other things, the capacity to tolerate suffering.

Thus, the most essential components are the four stable emotions: desire, anger, determination, and impassivity. The remaining five, amusement and the others, are essential insofar as they add coloration, with their aesthetic elements being so easily accessible to everyone everywhere—which is the reason the comic and the other four rasas typically pertain to characters other than those of high status. Every unsophisticated person will laugh, grieve, fear, recoil at another's censure, and everywhere be amazed at the slightest well-turned phrase. But these five rasas can also supplement the other four and thereby subserve the ends of man. As we shall argue later, it is precisely this hierarchical relationship among the stable emotions that accounts for the differentiation into the ten dramatic and other literary forms.

These nine emotions, moreover, are the only stable ones.[127] They are the forms of consciousness that encompass a creature from the moment of his birth. In accordance with the maxim that people are "averse to contact with pain and eager to savor pleasure,"[128] every being is pervaded with desire for sex; laughs at others out of a misplaced sense of his own superiority; burns at separation from a loved one; becomes speechless with anger at those responsible, and then, because of his own powerlessness, becomes fearful; is keen for some acquisition but then is overcome with repugnance if the object is unsuitable,[129] thinking it undesirable;[130] feels amazement well up in him at beholding the various things he is about to do;[131] and, last, is prepared to give up something or other. There is no living being devoid of the predispositions latent in such mental states. It is merely the case that in a given person at a given moment this or that mental state predominates, whereas [277] another is diminished; a given person will be constrained by a thing's propriety and another will do just the opposite. Accordingly, only four of the stable emotions—desire, anger, determination, and impassivity—can be taught as subserving the ends of man; and it is this basic division among the stable emotions that leads us to speak in terms of a character's status, whether high, middling, or low.[132]

As for the more particularized mental states, such as those transitory emotions known as fatigue, disquiet, and the like, it is possible for them not to come into existence at all in the course of one's life, when their pertinent foundational or stimulant factor is absent.[133] A sage who uses an elixir, for example, may never be affected by fatigue, torpor, exhaustion, and so on. And even when the power of a foundational or stimulant factor is present and a person is overcome by such emotions, he will find that they diminish in direct relation to the diminution of their cause, and do not for all that necessarily comprise any residue of an innate disposition. By contrast, the stable emotions such as determination, even when they are virtually dissipated after having accomplished their tasks, do not fail to leave the residue of an innate disposition, for the simple reason that they can still have other tasks to accomplish and so cannot be depleted.[134] As Patanjali says, "Just because Chaitra's passion is directed toward one woman does not mean it cannot be directed toward others."[135]

Therefore, the transitory emotions, their existence marked by a myriad of varied stages of coming into being and going out of being, are strung on the thread of those mental states that are the stable emotions. They are like precious stones threaded on a red or blue string[136]—stones of crystal, glass, mica, ruby, emerald, sapphire, and the like, with their thousands of different properties—which can be individually perceived thanks to their interstices. Although these transitory emotions leave no latent impression of their own on the string of the stable emotion, they derive embellishment from the string itself; moreover, themselves dappled,[137] they dapple the string of the stable emotion; and they bring the string, pure though it remains on the very inside of the stones, to the point of manifestation and even while doing so, show themselves to be producing a certain variegation from the luster of the stones—the transitory emotions—that precede and follow. And that is why they are called transitory emotions.

Indeed, their very instability is suggested by the simple fact that, whereas we may ask the reason a particular person feels fatigue (a transitory emotion), we do not ask the reason when someone says, "Rama is prompted by the stable emotion determination." Accordingly, the foundational and stimulant factors that awaken[138] a stable emotion are merely communicating the propriety or impropriety of the emotion, desire or determination or whatever it may be, coloring the emotion with their own particular character.[139] By no means is it the case that in the absence of such factors those stable emotions are nonexistent, since, as we have stated, they are constitutive of living creatures, being in essence their fundamental predispositions. By contrast, a transitory emotion, when the foundational and stimulant factors for it are absent, ceases to exist even in name—something we shall elaborate on where appropriate in the course of our commentary.

Thus, the elimination of the hindrance called "nonessentiality"[140] is achieved by a twofold account[141] of the stable emotion: first, the one that supplements the general definition of rasa, when the sage says, "We shall show how a stable emotion becomes rasa,"[142] and second, the one that pertains to the particular definitions of the individual rasas.[143]

[278] [7] Last, there is no necessary correlation between a given physical reaction, foundational factor, or transitory emotion and a given stable emotion. Weeping, as we see for ourselves, can result from bliss as well as from eye disease; a tiger can cause

anger, fear, and so on, whereas exhaustion, anxiety, and the other transitory emotions are observed to accompany any number of stable emotions: determination, fear, and so on. The *totality* of aesthetic elements, however, does indeed establish an invariable concomitance. In other words, where the foundational factor is the death of some loved one; the reactions lamentation, shedding tears, and the like; and the transitory emotions anxiety, despondency, and so on, the stable emotion in question must of necessity be grief and that alone. And hence, wherever there may be uncertainty, the means to resolve the doubt and hence to remove the hindrance is use of the proper conjunction of aesthetic elements.

With respect to this process: in everyday life we develop through repeated practice the skill of inferring the mental states of others—that is, their stable emotions—by seeing signs betokening causes, effects, and auxiliaries. Now, in the theater, these very elements—a garden, a sidelong glance, the feeling of satisfaction,[144] and the like—transcend the worldly plane where "cause," "effect," and "auxiliary" have their proper significations, and consist solely in the processes of "factoring," "reactionizing," and "colorizing." For that very reason they receive these new, supermundane designations "factor" (whether foundational or stimulant), "reaction," and "transitory emotion," respectively, whose different natures we shall examine in the chapter on emotions.[145] (They are designated by such names in order to call attention to the fact that they derive their existence from the primordial dispositions of cause, effect, and auxiliary to which they are related.) As these aesthetic elements take on their dominant or subordinate status in turn, they attain a "conjunction" (in the *Sutra on Rasa*)—etymologically[146] a correct ("con-") relationship or concentration ("junction")—in the minds of the audience. They thereby bring the aesthetic entity[147] into the domain of relishing, a state of awareness that is supermundane and freed from the seven hindrances. And that entity—which is not some already existent thing but in essence simply this very process of relishing, which exists only as long as the relishing itself exists and does not last beyond it, and which must be something other than the stable emotion itself—is rasa.

Shankuka and others, however, are mistaken to argue that it is the stable emotion itself, apprehended by means of the factors and the rest, that is rasa, and is so called because it is tasted.[148] For not only would rasa then exist in the real world, but also there would be no emotion that would not be rasa: if something nonexistent[149] can be tasted, then why should something that really exists not be tasted? Hence it is only the apprehension of the stable emotion in the form of an inference that is being postulated, not rasa itself. It was for precisely this reason that the sage did not use the term "stable emotion" in the *Sutra on Rasa* itself—indeed, that would have been a red herring.[150] And when the sage states that the "stable emotion turns into rasa," it is merely because of a formal congruity lying in the fact that those things familiar to us as causes when pertaining to a real-world stable emotion take on the designation of "factors" and so on when enabling the act of aesthetic relishing.[151]

That is to say, what kind of rasa can be held to exist in an *inference* of a real-world mental state? On the contrary, the savoring of rasa is in essence a supermundane rapture, completely different from the real-world awareness deriving from inference and memory. To explain:[152] a person predisposed toward an aesthetic event by the practice of drawing real-world inferences does not apprehend a female character on the stage in some neutral manner. On the contrary, without in the least ascending the ladder of inference, memory, and the like but rather on the strength of his aesthetic receptivity (in essence, his heart's concurrence), he apprehends her as the life breath of aesthetic relishing—something congruent with an act of identification—indeed, as the shoot of aesthetic savoring that is about to blossom into fullness. Such relishing does not arise from any other prior act of cognition, [279] whereby some memory might come into play during the aesthetic event; nor is any real-world act of cognition, such as perception, in operation here. On the contrary, the relishing is presented solely by virtue of the conjunction of the supermundane aesthetic elements. Accordingly, it is radically different from [1] awareness of a stable emotion produced by a real-world act of cognition, whether perception, inference, testimony, analogy, or other source of valid cognition; [2] knowledge of another's mental state produced by yogic perception, which remains entirely indifferent; [3] the completely homogeneous experience of his own bliss on the part of a supreme spiritual adept, which is pure because it is free from all coloration of objective reality. The difference lies in the fact that those three forms of consciousness are variously impeded, [1] by the presence of this or that hindrance (such as the desire to actually possess the woman one sees);[153] [2] and [3] by the absence of beauty—in [2] because of the indistinctness that accompanies the indifference, in [3] because one is possessed by the blissful object and thereby overpowered.[154] In the theater, however, because the aesthetic event cannot possibly be restricted to oneself alone, such overpowering cannot take place; because the event cannot be restricted to someone else alone, given one's own participation, that imprecision cannot arise; and because one's congruent predispositions of desire (or other stable emotion) take possession of one when activated by force of the "commonization" of the aesthetic elements, none of the hindrances can come into play—this is something we have stated repeatedly.

In view of this radical difference, the aesthetic elements cannot be viewed as normal phenomena. They cannot be causes for an actual "arising" of rasa,[155] for that would lead to the absurdity that rasa could exist even after cognition of the aesthetic elements has ceased. But neither can they be causes of "knowing" rasa—which would entail their being numbered among the valid means of cognition—since rasa is not a cognizable object given that it is not a concrete entity.[156] What, then, do we mean by "aesthetic elements"? It is a term we use to refer to something supermundane that enables aesthetic relishing to take place. The fact that we find these elements nowhere else than in the theater actually enhances our argument for proving[157] their supermundane character. It is exactly like saying that the savor of a mixed drink cannot be located in any one of its ingredients, brown sugar, black pepper, etc.[158]

But then, one might object, does rasa not thereby cease to be a cognizable object? This is in fact logically the case. The very essence of rasa, or "taste," is a *state of being tasted*; its nature is not that of a cognizable *object*. Then what does "arising" in the *Sutra on Rasa* refer to? Not to rasa itself, but to the aesthetic tasting directed toward rasa. There is no harm if, in referring to the arising of such tasting, we also speak of the arising of the rasa whose existence depends entirely on it. As for this tasting, it is a process neither of production nor of cognition, and for all that it is not itself without cognitive basis, because it is proven to exist by our reflexive consciousness. Aesthetic tasting is, to be sure, a form of awareness, but utterly different from any kind of real-world awareness, since its means, the aesthetic elements, differ utterly from real-world means. Hence, since it is from the conjunction of the aesthetic elements that aesthetic tasting arises, rasa itself, which comes under the domain of this unique kind of tasting, must be a supernormal entity. Such is the gist of the aphorism.

Here is a synopsis of the whole matter: first of all, the idea that it is an actor we are seeing on stage is obscured by his costume—the crown, the headdress, and so on. But the notion that he is Rama, however much stimulated by the power of the literary text, does not come to rest on the actor because of dispositions of our consciousness that are old and deeply implanted.[159] For this very reason[160] the dimensions of time and space pertaining to both actor and character are eliminated. The sight of the physical reactions in the actor, the horripilation and so on, that serve to produce the convincing apprehension of desire when we observe them in the real world, gives us to understand the presence of desire in a way that is, as a result of the foregoing, unrestricted by time and space, and in which the viewer himself comes to participate thanks to his own predispositions toward desire. The understanding we have of such desire cannot, therefore, be one of indifference. Moreover, since we do not understand the desire as being brought about by a cause specific to oneself[161]—a particular woman, say—there is no possibility of our wanting to possess her, embrace her, or the like; and since we do not understand it as exclusively concerning someone else, there is no possibility of hatred arising toward that person, or sorrow, or any other emotion.[162] [280] The desire is thus "commonized" and, when brought within our consciousness (whether consciousness is conceived of as a sequence of moments or as a unity),[163] *is* the erotic rasa. This "commonizing actualization," for its part, comes about through the aesthetic elements.[164]

. . . .

[281] The ultimate savoring of rasa, however, occurs only when there is equal prominence of the aesthetic elements, something that takes place only in an extended narrative,[165] though in actual fact only in one of the ten forms of drama. As Vamana states, "Among all the varieties of literary composition the best is drama in any of its ten forms. For the drama, like a painted canvas, is multifaceted, by virtue of the full complement of its particular components."[166] In the case of an extended narrative, one or another such dramatic form is being transferred, thanks to the reader's capacity for imagining the proper speech, costume, regional customs, and the like. In the case of an isolate verse, it comes to be understood only by being ultimately enlivened by such narrative—that is to say, by receptive readers' ability to imagine what is appropriate in view of the sequence of events, and to establish a contextual foundation by conjecturing for the verse the appropriate speaker on the given occasion.[167] Thus, for those who are receptive readers thanks to, among other things, their study of literature and their good karma from past lives, the "aim of a literary text"[168] manifests itself with absolute clarity, as if before their very eyes, even when only a limited number of aesthetic elements is disclosed. And hence for them, literature alone, without any reference to dramatic spectacle, can bring at once pleasure and instruction. Drama can be an additional source of mental clarity for such people too, of course, on the analogy of radiant moonbeams falling.[169] But for those lacking in receptivity, drama alone can produce such clarity, because it is only there that the apprehension of singing, music, and the courtesan actresses does not lead to vicious behavior, since they are simply features of drama.[170]

In this connection we may note that the actor is an object of meditation analogous to that used by meditators. In the latter case we do not of course have the apprehension that it is the very Vasudeva Krishna before us, painted with vermillion, whom we are to call to mind; the apprehension is rather that the particular deity, when come within the ambit of a conceptualization made especially vivid thanks to the physical medium, will reward those who meditate on him. In the same way, the content of a drama can become the object of an identification made especially vivid thanks to the actor's procedures, while remaining completely untouched by any particularization of time or space pertaining to actor or character. The content is thus comparable to a Vedic commandment in providing moral instruction to the effect that such and such a reward comes from such and such an act; and comparable as well in view of the fact that in neither case does a subsequent perception ever arise to negate it, whether with respect to the law that something must be either what we are seeing or something else, or in the spectator's subsequent mental state.[171] Quite the contrary, the apprehension is veridical and complete. Accordingly, we have the bare apprehension "Rama," and never later the idea, "This person before my eyes was not Rama but someone else." We will clarify this in due course.

On the Homology of Physical Tasting and Rasa

(1.283) The author of the *Treatise on Drama* shows that there is a homology between tasting and rasa with respect to the object and agent of the experience and the end result. Just as there is something being savored in the food prepared with condiments; an agent of savoring in the agent of the gustatory experience when he is single-minded (since a person who has the experience when his mind is elsewhere will have no sense of savoring anything); an end result of the savoring, namely, pleasure, weight gain, vitality, nourishment, strength, health, and the like, so it is in the case of rasa: there is something being savored when rasa in the form we refer to as the stable emotion is manifested by the various forms of acting; there is an agent of savoring in the audience when they are single-minded, that is, when they identify with the drama; and there is an end result of the savoring, namely, instruction in morality and the other ends of man, expertise in them, and so on, in a way that is predominantly pleasurable. Thus, because of the similarity of act, agent, and outcome, we can refer to the specific kind of apprehension produced by the aesthetic elements as an act of tasting. Such is the gist of the matter. . . .

When Bharata speaks of "joy and the like,"[172] some scholars believe that "and the like" includes grief and other such emotions. That is unreasonable. The outcome of drama for spectators is joy and that alone, not grief or other such feeling. This is so, first, because there is nothing to cause such grief, and second, because if there were, people would simply avoid the theater. With this in mind, some scholars actually believe the text should read, instead of "joy and the like," the plural "joys."

. . . .

[284.15][173] With the words "they savor," the author shows that "savoring" is a mental process far superior to eating, the process of physical tasting. The basic idea here is that "savoring" is not the physical process of tasting but a mental process. And in this case it is a complete, or whole, process. The usage here is figurative, since it is well known that in everyday life the mental follows immediately upon the physical process of tasting. . . . The stable emotions, which are beyond the reach of thought as such, are "conjoined" with the aesthetic factors. Here "con-joined" means properly joined, that is, becoming identically grounded in the viewers who all enter gradually into a state of identification[174] through the heart's concurrence. When this occurs, the "learned" "fully savor" them. Here "fully" indicates that this happens by virtue of an apprehension free from all "hindrances" thanks to total commonization. "In their heart" means free from the possibility of being hindered through any of the senses; "savor," that is, enjoying by "relishing," in other words, a state of consciousness of ultimate joy afforded by the wide variety of dispositions that punctuate it: pleasure, pain, and so on.[175] Given this state of rapture-savoring to which one feels virtually subjugated owing to the absence of the self-other distinction, this consciousness is of a sort entirely different from everyday apprehension, since that is crowded with hindrances, such as acquisitiveness and the like,[176] but also from yogic apprehension, since that is so to speak harsh, owing to its repudiation of any savoring of objects.

On the List and Order of Rasas

(1.261.15) Insofar as love is readily accessible to all creatures and thus entirely familiar, and thereby pleasing to all, the erotic is named first. The comic follows in the wake of the erotic. The opposite of the erotic, insofar as it is a state of hopelessness,[177] is the tragic. Next comes the violent, which is the cause of the tragic, and concerned primarily with wealth.[178] Then the heroic, insofar as love and wealth have their ground in morality and the heroic is concerned primarily with morality, consisting as it does essentially in providing security to those who are afraid. The fearful is next, followed by the macabre, because it can be argued that they share the same foundational and stimulant factors; both are implied by the heroic. The fantastic is mentioned next since it appears at the conclusion of the heroic. (Bharata will state that the fantastic is the rasa that must always be used at the end of a play.)[179] Thereafter comes the peaceful, whose ethos is in essence the cessation of all acts in contrast to the ethos of engagement in the group of three ends of man, love, wealth, and morality; its end result is spiritual liberation.

. . . .

[335.7] There are accordingly only nine rasas, for only so many have been taught either as serving the purpose of instruction or as adequately pleasurable. Thus, the argument that others have made, that although other rasas are possible, the number is restricted by scholarly convention, is refuted. . . .[180] It is false to claim that affection, with tenderness as its stable emotion, can be a rasa.[181] Affection is simply attachment, and attachment always resolves into desire, determination, or one or another of the standard stable emotions. To explain: the affection a child feels for his mother or father amounts to fear; that of a young man for his friends, desire; Lakshmana's affection for his brother Rama is in fact the "heroic in morality," and the same logic applies to an elder's affection for his son. This line of reasoning can be followed in rejecting a rasa of avarice with a stable emotion of greed—it resolves into amusement or desire. The same can be said of devotion too.

[The Number of Transitory Emotions]

(1.373) When Bharata states, "There are thirty-three transitory emotions," all others are meant to be included in this set: deceit in dissimulation, for example, distress in despair, hunger, thirst, and the like in fatigue. Other examples are easily supplied. Some scholars, however, wonder how anyone could possibly number[182] all the various states of mind. And they ask with respect to their enumeration how any given number could capture this totality, whether the nine attributes of the self logicized by logicians; the eight properties of the intellect numbered by Samkhya numerologists, or their four types of apprehension (error and the like); or the duality "mind" and "mental activities" broadcast by Buddhists.[183] If one argues that, if it was for the purpose of teaching poets and actors that these few have been described, then others could certainly have been enunciated—well, others will in fact be enunciated by the sage in his discussion of the "general style of acting"[184] when describing the emotions, behavior, and ornamentation of men and women. And in the present chapter too, they have at least been intimated in the enumeration of foundational and stimulant factors and reactions, such as when hunger and thirst are mentioned as factors in fatigue. They have not been literally defined only because their definition, perfectly well known to begin with, would not be all that useful to playwrights and actors.

Others argue that it is in the performance of these few emotions that beauty arises. For when the auxiliary emotional states are displayed in performance in this finite number and no more, the stable emotion becomes fit for relishing. Some believe that these are to be known first and that such knowledge allows one to extrapolate to the definition of others.

On Drama

(1.260.12) By "drama" is meant a particular species of literature that comprises the whole range of genres beginning with the epic-derived play. It constitutes a homogeneous conviction in the mind that produces a visualization on the strength of the registers of acting on the part of the actors. Although a drama consists of innumerable aesthetic elements, given the fact that all these insensate things can be reduced to the consciousness of them, and consciousness to the class of people experiencing them, and that class to the principal person experiencing them, drama can be said to consist essentially of the stable mental state of that principal person, whom we call the protagonist. Now, this single mental state is differentiated from the countless other mental states that are understood as belonging to oneself or another; thanks to . . . the employment of the power of poetry, perfected and beautified by the singing and instrumental music, the figures of speech, language qualities, adherence to the thirty-six "characteristics" of dramatic poetry, and appropriating the enlivening force of the ten components of the preliminary dance (the recitative and the rest), it is utterly disconnected from any particular locus;[185] and insofar as it is "commonized," it can invest the audience members with its own presence. And precisely by reason of this identification,[186] it appears as different from any mundane mental state that is felt to belong to some separate person, which is based on inference or testimony or yogic perception and where the agent and object of cognition are entirely neutral; [261] and because it is free of any appearance of being located in one's delimited self, it is incapable of producing the kind of mental state—attraction,[187] for example, or repulsion—that comes into being in the case of feelings of desire or grief arising from a mundane source of knowledge. It can therefore be grasped by a "process," otherwise known as "tasting," that can be defined as repose in one's own unhindered consciousness, and thus comes to be expressed by the term "rasa," or taste. Hence, drama *is* rasa, whereas the end result of drama is instruction.

. . . .

[NS 6.31+ (p. 266): "We will explain the rasas first, for no *artha* of drama will be achieved without attention to rasa"][188]

(1.265.14) By *artha* is meant: [1] "aesthetic element," such as the foundational factor, which except for rasa would never be "achieved," or enter the mind, as an analytical category; [2] "purpose," that is, instruction through literary pleasure, which without rasa would never be "achieved," or take place; [3] "entity" and the like, for when the audience is absorbed in the rasa experience—a homogeneous apprehension that consists of tasting—no entity is "achieved," or is individually present[189] to their minds, because the whole class of aesthetic elements, all insensate themselves, appears as subsumed under the principal mental state, namely the stable emotion, which all other mental states subserve. Hence, rasa is listed first in the contents of the *Treatise on Drama* and defined first, since it has primacy for all three readerships: the scholar, the actor, and the audience.

. . . .

(1.284.25) When Bharata speaks of "drama rasas,"[190] he may mean the "rasas *that arise* from" the composite artistic enterprise that is "drama." Or he may mean "rasas *are* drama," for drama is a composite of rasas. Or finally, he may mean that "rasas *are found in* drama alone," and in poetry only to the degree that it mimics drama. For as my teacher has argued, with respect to the subject matter of the literary text, rasa comes into being only when a state of awareness simulating visual perception comes into being. . . .[191] [285] Whereas some scholars assert that the relishing of rasa can occur in poetry no less than in drama, produced by the exceptional beauty of its language qualities and rhetorical figures, our view is as follows: first of all, "literature" is comprised chiefly of the ten dramatic forms. For it is there, thanks to the appropriate languages, cultural modes, intonations, costumes, and so on, that the presence of rasa achieves plenitude. In a poetic work like a courtly epic, by contrast, we even have female protagonists speaking in Sanskrit, one of many improprieties that find place in the narrative simply because it is not possible to do otherwise[192]—however much it may not seem inappropriate, in view of the maxim that you like whatever you are given.[193] This is precisely the reason it has been argued, as noted earlier, that "Among all the varieties of literary composition, the best is drama in any of its ten forms." Other poetic genres, from the courtly epic to the isolate verse, come into being by borrowing structures such as acts and scenes from the ten forms. As for the meaning of the phrase "ten forms," it simply refers to drama, as the author will later say (when speaking of language), "It constitutes the body of drama."[194]

Now, given the varying degree of their heart's concurrence, those who hear a reading or watch[195] a play can have a highly differentiated appreciation, depending on its clarity or obscurity to them. Someone whose heart is by nature like a spotless mirror[196] has, for that very reason, a mind no longer subjected to the anger, confusion, craving, and so on typical of this phenomenal world; for such a person, on the occasion of hearing a play with its various appropriate components, the cluster of rasas—the defining feature of drama—will be entirely clear and cognized by a relishing that is essentially a tasting of their commonality.[197] Someone else, by contrast, who lacks these traits will require the procedures of actors and the rest of stagecraft in order to attain that sort of perception-like relishing; for such a person the sage—on the maxim that a work of systematic thought must seek to fulfill everyone's needs—has made further provision in the procedures of singing and so on, to loosen the knot of the viewer's heart, hardened as it is by the anger, grief, and so on he bears inside.

Thus, rasa exists only in drama—and not in the world—and poetry as a whole is nothing but drama. For the same reason, rasa is not in the actor.[198] And if you were still to demand, Where then is it? I would say in reply: What[199] a forgetful reader in need of constant reminding! I have already explained that rasa is something completely unconstrained by time, space, and perceiver in any way, shape, or form—why then this question? If you were then to ask, What then is there in the actor? I would answer: a means of savoring. That is why the word used to refer to an actor etymologically signifies "vessel": there is no savoring of liquor that remains in the vessel; the vessel is the means of savoring. When we therefore use the term "actor" it is in the sense of "chief vessel"[200] for our savoring rasa. But enough digression. I would only add that from the drama, again—that is, from its meaning portion—are painting, sculpture and the like distilled, just as courtly epics and so on are distilled from its wording portion. We will address this at length in our commentary on NŚ 7.10.[201]

Others have explained the term "dramatic rasas" as "rasas that come from drama," where the word "drama" (*nāṭya*) is taken to mean "a property of an actor" (*naṭa*), namely his action,[202] drama being an externally visible aggregation of the various registers of acting. . . .

[285.26] Those who hold rasa to be an imitation of desire or other stable emotion respond to the critique of the view that something like grief can be a source of pleasure by arguing that the emotions of the theater are unique. But the critique itself is unfounded. Since when did it become a hard and fast rule that the perception of grief always produces pain in the perceiver's heart? When the pain you are perceiving is that of your enemy, the perception produces joy, and in the case of someone who is neither friend nor foe, mere indifference. And their answer is a sheer postulate on the nature of the theatrical emotions. None of this has an ounce of truth. [286] In our view, what is being savored is simply one's own awareness, which is uniformly blissful, so why would we have any worries about its comprising pain? The fact that one and the same awareness can appear emotionally multiform is simply a result of the operation of latent predispositions of desire, grief, and so on—which are themselves awakened by the operation of the various registers of acting.

The Causal Relationship of Rasa and Emotion

(1.286.8) The rasas in the actors would seem to be the source of the emotions in the audience, such as their feeling grief from seeing the tragic rasa. Yet the tragic rasa comes to exist in the audience only when it is enhanced by the emotions and other aesthetic elements.[203] Hence the doubt arises whether emotion comes from rasa or rasa from emotion. A third position is accordingly also on offer, namely that rasas and emotions are mutually generative at different moments in the process. Then again, one could analyze the three positions as follows: first, the emotion is in the actor alone, or in the character alone, Rama for example; second, when this is enhanced, it becomes rasa; third, when it is diminished, it becomes emotion. But actually, that analysis would be false, since we have already refuted the suggestion that such can be the proper assessment of rasa's nature.

There is yet another view of the matter, that of Shri Shankuka.[204] It, however, is falsified by the simple fact that the viewer actually perceives no distinction whatever between character and actor. And in any case, the doctrine of imitation itself has already been refuted.[205]

Therefore, the correct analysis is that there are three questions: Do the emotions derive from the rasas, or rasas from the emotions, or are they mutually generative? . . . Now, first of all, the author has stated[206] that rasa arises from the emotions and other aesthetic elements, and hence the second view has already been vindicated. But how is this possible? In the real world there exist no aesthetic elements—no "foundational causes" or "stimulant causes," no "reactions," no "transitory emotions"; there, such things have the status simply of real causes and effects. But these are the very things that become aesthetic elements so as to make aesthetic tasting possible. It can therefore be said that the "emotions"—that is, the aesthetic elements—arise by virtue of rasa.[207] But then it might well be objected that if the author has already stated that rasa arises by virtue of the aesthetic elements, whereas it is now being claimed that it is by virtue of rasa that the aesthetic elements become such, we have a circularity, and as the *Great Commentary on Grammar* declares, "Operations based on a circularity do not work."[208]

Bharata's conclusion is as follows. Upon being apprehended, an aesthetic element—a foundational cause, as for example the female object of desire—affords a savoring of rasa, as previously stated. Hence the emotions here cannot be said to derive from the rasas. And from an examination of the etymological meaning of the word "emotion" itself this makes perfectly good sense [287], as the sage states: they are called emotions (*bhāva*) because they "bring into being (*bhāvaya-*)," or produce, the rasas "when they are fully," i.e., properly, "configured with the various registers of acting," in other words, when the emotions[209] come to be lodged in the heart.[210] [. . .] Hence, the author summarizes the position he adopts by saying, "There is no rasa devoid of an antecedent emotion." Given that the opponent would argue that the reverse is also true, that there is no "emotion devoid of an antecedent rasa"—in view of the fact that the aesthetic elements are not part of everyday life[211]—the author responds by saying, "Their production is mutually effected in the course of acting." In other words, it is only with the presence of acting, or full aesthetic visualization, that aesthetic elements *can be referred to as such*, insofar as they only then function in support of acting. When they are conceived of in this way, their mutual causality becomes reasonable, and there is nothing vicious about this sort of circularity. Here the author provides the analogy of the "conjunction of condiments and spices." Just as condiments and food make each other savory, so emotions and rasas bring each other into being—emotions "bring the rasas into being," that is, produce them, and rasas "bring the emotions into being," that is, make them "emotions" in the first place—in other words, make them identifiable as aesthetic elements.

The point is that circularity becomes vicious when two things are simultaneously produced in one and the same action, not when there are two actions. For example, food is only made tasty when conjoined with condiments and spices, whereas condiments and spices only become pleasant to eat when they are incorporated into food. Similarly, it is thanks to the emotions that the experience of rasa arises, whereas it is the rasas that enable the causes [288] to be identified as aesthetic elements. To draw an analogy: threads can only be referred to as a cause in reference to a piece of cloth; the cloth, however, can be considered an effect only in reference to the threads. There is no more circularity than this in the case at hand.

One might object that, if rasa arises from emotion, why did Bharata state, "We will explain the rasas first, for no aim will be achieved without attention to rasa"?[212] Surely it is emotion that should have been addressed first. In response to such an objection, the author uses the analogy of the seed.[213] Rasa is just like a seed functioning as the source of a tree. [1] From its source in rasa, instruction arises mediated by pleasure, and it is for this reason that the rasas principally merit comment first.[214] [2] The actions of the actor, for his part, because they depend upon the literary text, have their ultimate source in the consciousness of the author that has been commonized—a consciousness that in the final analysis is rasa. [3] The audience members too are captivated first by the apprehension of rasa, and only afterward, by an act of analytical understanding, come to apprehend the various aesthetic elements. Thus the same source, namely rasa, pertains to the work itself,[215] to the performance of a drama, and to the audience's awareness.[216] It can also be the rasa in the author that corresponds to the seed in the simile, the author being in this identical with the audience; this is why Anandavardhana has said, "If a poet is filled with passion, the whole world of his poem will consist of rasa";[217] the literary work would then correspond to the tree, with the various actions of the actor, his registers of acting, corresponding to the flowers and the like, and the savoring of rasa on the part of the audience to the fruit. Thereby the whole world consists of rasa.[218] . . . [219] Hence, the gist of this discourse is that all three positions can somehow be accommodated, depending on the particular perspective one adopts.

[289] [The *Treatise on Drama* states: "Among the rasas four are generative causes. . . ."][220]

(1.289.13) There are four "causes"—that is to say, indicators—of the engendering of a rasa. In other words, the full range of causal relationships among the rasas can be indicated by reference to just four of them. To explain the four relationships: [1] When we are told that the imitation of the erotic rasa is the comic, the erotic in the form of an imitation is meant to indicate that any rasa presented as a "semblance" is a cause of the comic.[221] When we have a semblance of all the aesthetic elements—the foundational and stimulant factors, the reactions, and the transitory emotions—we apprehend a semblance of desire; when this happens, we have a semblance of the erotic rasa that leads in turn to what is essentially a semblance of relishing. Here desire functions not as a stable emotion but only as a transitory one in the form of mere lascivious craving, even though it will seem in the man's own eyes (i.e., the eyes of the antagonist) as if it were indeed stable;[222] as a consequence, all the aesthetic elements here become semblances. As a result, desire becomes a semblance of a stable emotion.[223] After all, the idea never enters Ravana's mind[224] that Sita must either hate him or be completely indifferent to him, and were it in fact to do so, Ravana's illusion[225] would vanish utterly. Instead, he never has done with[226] the certainty that she loves him, since his feelings are in essence a delusion produced by sexual passion—exactly like the semblance of silver that can appear where only mother-of-pearl is actually present.

Now, it is true that in all of Ravana's utterances,[227] as for example,

> Hearing her name is like a magnet or a bewitching spell.
> My heart cannot bear her absence a fraction of a second.
> These limbs of mine are tortured by love, my desire itself is tormented . . .
> and I see no clear way to ever have the joy of having her.

[290] we find only the semblance of desire; the comic rasa does not manifest itself. Nonetheless, a foundational factor in the shape of Sita;[228] a host of transitory emotions (anxiety, despondency, confusion, and the like) that are at odds with Ravana's character and his maturity; the array of reactions, weeping, lamenting, and the like—all this, since it is entirely out of character in him, becomes a *semblance* of the erotic and thus a foundational factor for the comic (Bharata will define this later, in the passage beginning "Wearing incongruous clothing and jewelry that belong to someone else").[229] The erotic rasa is referred to above only to indicate this type of semblancing; we should understand that the semblances of all other rasas, the semblance of the tragic and so forth, also lead to the comic. For to be a foundational factor of the comic amounts to nothing more than such "improper" or out-of-character usage (and this can be extended to the foundational and stimulant factors and the reactions of all the rasas; the same holds true for the transitory emotions). This is why the ancients, who were well versed in the true nature of human consciousness, spoke here and there of "the rasas, the emotions, and the *semblances* of both."[230] We similarly have a semblance of the peaceful rasa leading to the comic when something is

not actually a source of liberation but a mere semblance of one. The dramatic form of the farce in particular provides the instruction that impropriety with respect to all the ends of man must be avoided—something that will be enunciated in the definitions of the individual rasas.

Among these eight semblances of rasas, the following is an illustration of the semblance of the comic, a poem of Vamanagupta, my father's brother:

His deeds are otherworldly, and if this world
does not honor them, well then, what to say?
But the fact that the world is raucous with laughter at him . . .
who wouldn't burst into sidesplitting laughter at that?[231]

Similarly, the tragic rasa that arises when someone grieves for a person with whom they do not have a kinship bond is itself comic.[232] The same reasoning applies to the other rasas. The above can suffice as an example, and others can be inferred from it (I have simply followed here the sage's formulation).[233]

[2] A second rasa inevitably follows upon the end result of a first. Bharata offers as an example the violent rasa with the tragic as its result. The end result of violence is killing someone, taking him captive, and so on, and with this foundational factor the tragic rasa will inevitably come about. Here is an example from the *Tying Up the Braid*:[234]

This very day the two of us went to the battlefield after seeing our father and
  mother.
They kissed me on the head as I bowed, and did the same to Duhshasana.
Now that his enemy has reduced their child to this state,
how I can approach our parents, cruel man that I am? What am I to say?

Similarly, the fearful will necessarily follow upon the violent, and the tragic upon the erotic.[235] Of course, no effect of the erotic leads necessarily to the tragic, but the erotic can contribute as a subordinate factor to engendering the tragic. This is so in the case of Udayana, king of Vatsa, as a result of the supposed immolation of his queen, Vasavadatta, in the play *The Ascetic King of Vatsa*. It would be wrong to argue that what we have here has nothing to do with the erotic but is simply grief occasioned by a loved one's death after desire has been interrupted. For we find instances where anger is interrupted even at the moment that the tragic is arising,[236] as the author of the other play says: "Let Pandu's sons rejoice, the fires of enmity be quenched by their quelling their foes."[237] Nor in fact is the cause of the tragic rasa simply Udayana's being married to Vasavadatta, with desire for her no longer present. Were that the case, in the following verse [291],[238]

You were trembling, with your garment slipping off in terror,
casting those two eyes of yours distressed in every direction,
as the cruel fire burned you without pity—was it so
engulfed by smoke that it could not see who you were?

the word "those," which bears the life force of the verse, would serve no purpose whatever. In the "Mourning of Rati" a similar sort of memory of the erotic gives life to the tragic:[239]

I now see those intimacies—"You dwell in my heart"—were tricks, mere figures of speech.
How otherwise could your body be gone,[240] and your Rati survive?

In the same sense, the fearful can be said to arise from the heroic, as in the verse, "The whole world stood in fear of Arjuna as he killed Karna's son before his very eyes."[241] Shri Shankuka, by the way, is wrong to assert that determination, the stable emotion of the heroic, is not at work in the above verse.[242] Determination has no scope anywhere if it is not present here, since its prerequisite requires no deep searching: in "the heroic in war," which is at issue in the verse, this prerequisite is what is known as martial ardor, which produces[243] the enemy's defeat and brings burning pain to their hearts. And what this ardor gives life to is the fearful rasa, among their wives and so on, as in the following verse:

May he protect you who slaughtered the demons,
the few survivors being overcome with terror
just to look into their wives' eyes, lovely eyes though they were,
that were darkened by kohl as dark as him.[244]

That there is a *necessary* relationship between the one and the other rasa is expressed in Bharata's text by the word "and" used directly after the ablative case ("of violence"), intimating *immediate consequentiality.*

[3] Every rasa can aim toward another as its end result. Bharata offers as an example the heroic rasa, with the fantastic as its result. For a great man's determination is exercised with the aim of amazing[245] the world as its end result, as for example in the verse, "He was set on breaking the bow of Shiva as he spanned it in

his iron-rodlike arms. . . ."[246] The case is different from [2]: the violent rasa does not *aim* toward the tragic as its end result, but only aims toward destroying the enemy. As for the laughter of the jester in a drama, it has no other aim than provoking the laughter of the leading lady.[247]

[4] One rasa will as a rule strongly imply another because the aesthetic elements[248] are common to both. Bharata offers as an example the macabre rasa implying the fearful, for its foundational factors—streams of blood and the like—are necessarily causes of fear;[249] so too its transitory emotions, dying, confusion, possession; and its physical reactions, the leering mouth and so on. An example from the *Tying Up the Braid*:[250] "Call back the armies breaking in retreat from the battlefield, dropping their weapons in terror at the macabre sight of Bhimasena spattered with the blood left from what he had drunk from the chest of the dead Duhshasana."[251] . . .

[292.20] These four rasas (the erotic, violent, heroic, and macabre) as generative causes are furthermore intimately related, through their specific properties,[252] to the four ends of man: love, wealth, morality, and liberation, respectively.[253] The reason is their capacity to produce extraordinary beauty. The other rasas, the comic and so on, insofar as they provide coloration for these, should be presented in dramatic genres as complements to the four.

As we stated earlier, this is the total number of rasas. To claim, as Bhatta Lollata does, that rasas are in fact numberless but that only this many should be used, in conformity with the norms of scholarly assemblies, is simply unthinking arrogance.[254]

[294.5] [The *Treatise on Drama* states: "Now . . . we shall show how a stable emotion becomes rasa."] In everyday life the stable emotions are the states of mind that are the sources of all manner of cares, and bespeak the unbroken series of obligations to which we are subject. And it is these, to be sure, that "we shall show becoming rasa" by becoming the sole basis for the state of absorption, as the teachings declare.[255] And they become rasas when poets or actors introduce the aesthetic elements as appropriate. (To quote: "The poet's new vision, preoccupied with enabling the rasas to be tasted"[256]—here the word "new" is used of poets alone because actors are dependent on poets and have no "new vision" themselves that sees and makes the tasting possible.) Thus, when the author states that, by teaching the proprieties of the aesthetic elements and how they make tasting possible, he will show how the stable emotions become rasa, he is making clear the goal of the account of definitions he is about to offer.

Since desire is the goal of aesthetic experience and is something with which everyone's heart concurs, and the erotic is predominantly desire, the author defines the erotic first. . . .[257] [296.4] He now clarifies the portion of the aphorism "The erotic . . . has its origin in the stable emotion of desire" by the following exegesis: "Its cause is a woman and a man. . . ." With the words "a woman and a man" he means to suggest that the desire that takes the form of a stable emotion and becomes the cause of the erotic rasa is entirely different both from such everyday notions as "This man possesses this woman," which is marked by the experience of mutual craving, and also, accordingly, from the transitory emotion that persists only during the stage of passion and is essentially nothing more than craving.[258] For this stable emotion perdures from the beginning of their relationship to the attainment of the final goal, i.e., the plenitude of pleasure. Predispositions of real-world desire pervade the poet, but when he deploys the aesthetic elements—and the actor the physical reactions—he does so in such a way that the savoring of desire turns into the erotic rasa. And for the person who experiences the savoring too, some experience of real desire in the stage prior to the aesthetic experience is of service to it, as we have already stated.

Here is the main point: desire is a game that is fundamentally possible only for two lovers, for it is only with lovers that the stream of pleasure comes to its resting point.[259] Everything else, the beauty of physical objects, flower garlands and so on, is manufactured by the poet and merely imaginary. The supreme experience of desire is a fusion that consists in a mutual interpenetration and is accompanied by awareness, for consciousness is the all-important element; everything else[260] is only an insensate thing that forms the object of an experience. To quote:

> It is merely the vexatious effort of respiration
> that goes on in my body. My true life breath is Janaki.[261]

This is why the objection raised by some—that, since there are different kinds of desire depending on the object of desire, the erotic rasa cannot be a single, self-same thing—is based on ignorance. No matter how many forms it takes, desire remains one and the same wherever there is no possibility of separation, thanks precisely[262] to this mutual consciousness. And that is why the author specifies that in the erotic rasa "the characters are a young couple of high status."[263] . . . "High" refers to consciousness, not bodily properties, for it is to sentience that the attributes "high" and "young" actually apply. . . .[264] And it is this awareness that, as a result of its being fit for savoring, turns into the erotic rasa. In the case of characters who are not of high status or who are not young,[265] we do not find the element of persistent stability, and so we do not have this awareness of desire, precisely because there is an expectation of separation, whereas the very life breath of the erotic rasa is awareness of inseparability.[266] . . .

[297.7] When the author speaks of the two "states" of the erotic rasa, he means two conditions . . . not two different species of the erotic, as the dappled and the black form two species of cow. Rather, in both situations desire is continuously present as a bond of mutual care, and the erotic consists of savoring this[267] form of desire. To quote:

> They say absence makes the heart grow less fond—but in fact the rasa
> for the beloved grows from enjoyment's lack, and it turns into a mass of love.[268]

This is why even in the state of the erotic enjoyed we can imagine the state of the erotic thwarted and become fearful, whereas the latter can be permeated with dreams of enjoyment—out of such things is the body of the erotic rasa formed.[269] Craving, jealousy, absence from home, and other situations are subsumed under these two, so long as desire in the form of that bond of mutual care is present. Thus the term "the erotic enjoyed" can be figuratively applied even in the absence of enjoyment, whereas we have the highest form of beauty when the two situations are combined, as in the following verse:

> They lay upon the bed, each turned aside and suffering in silence;
> though love still dwelt within their hearts each feared a loss of pride.
> But then from out the corner of their eyes the sidelong glances met
> and the quarrel broke in laughter as they turned and clasped each other's neck.[270]

Here the rasa experience consists precisely of a combination of the erotic enjoyed and the erotic thwarted (of the subtype "jealousy"); it breathes one and the same spirit. It is brought about by the foundational factors, reactions, and transient emotions being mutually shared—all of which make this the highest aesthetic experience possible.

On the Nature of Dramatic Acting

(1.35.12) The idea we come to have about the characters in a dramatic performance is not of some real thing; nor of a similarity, as one twin is similar to another; nor of a cognitive error, like the silver for which we mistake mother-of-pearl as a result of a memory of silver when we see the shell; nor of a superimposition, like the silver brought about by a cognition eventually known to be false once it has been negated by a correct cognition;[271] nor of an identification of two things, as in the case of a metaphorical statement like "The man from Balkh is an ox"; nor of a "poetic fantasy" about two things, as in the trope of a woman's face being the moon; nor of their being a copy, as is the case in a painting or clay sculpture; nor of their being an imitation, like the natural desire of a student to imitate the exposition[272] of the teacher; nor of a momentary fabrication, as in the case of a magic act; nor of an illusion produced by a stratagem, as in the case of sleights of hand. In all those instances, viewers would remain indifferent because they have no *commonality* with such objects, and hence they would never be able to savor rasa; or[273] they would wind up being subject to mundane feelings of lust, anger, and the like, just as if in the presence of a couple making love in real life, and because of this, whether they thought they were beholding the main character or the performer (since those feelings could be grounded in either), they could never experience the "repose of consciousness" necessary for rasa. Moreover, with respect to the poet, if he were set on describing that sort of particularized being, he could never successfully produce poetry, because he would be rendered incapable of avoiding the kind of impropriety just mentioned.[274]

What then is drama?[275] The answer is as follows: Rama and other such characters are never brought into any such cognitive sphere as those produced by the processes mentioned above.[276] Although a sense of their particularity may well issue from a received text—an extended work[277] along the lines of the *Rāmāyaṇa*—such particularities amount to real individuality, in the sense of the capacity for causal efficacy for the purported deeds, only where they are actually present, and from such texts we do not have a [36] notion of particularity based on actual presence.[278] In literary works generally speaking, first of all, the aesthetic elements do come to be generalized in the heart; but among these, with respect to the bare story, although indeed it makes such generalization possible, one's mental state, because of the absence of any deep pleasure, never experiences true conviction, any more than from the bald statement, "Whoever commits such and such an act suffers such and such a consequence."[279]

With poetic works, whose body consists of stylistic features, figures of speech, and beautiful words and meanings, and whose life breath is supermundane rasa, it is true that one can have this kind of mental absorption by virtue of the heart's concurrence. But in poetry not everyone can experience the awareness that everything is, as it were, happening before one's very eyes.

With respect to drama, however, that is the true state of things.[280] The viewer is never predisposed to believe that some quotidian task awaits him; he is only predisposed to believe that he is about to hear and see something supermundane and precious because of its boundless rasa, a pure pleasure he shares in common with all the other audience members. This state renders everyone's heart as spotless as a mirror, and as he relishes the apposite vocal and instrumental music he forgets all phenomenal reality. He begins to identify with the joy or grief that emerges from watching the various registers of acting, from the simple gesticulation[281] onward. As other actors enter or their recitations reach his hearing, he gains a kind of "ascertainment" regarding Rama, say, or Ravana, one not penetrated by any particularities of time and space and free from any assessment of the normal cognitive categories of truth, falsehood, doubt, or conjecture. He thereby becomes[282] predisposed toward the aforementioned ascertainment about Rama, one accompanied by predispositions activated by the experience of the many beautiful accompanying things—the vocal and instrumental music, the beautiful actresses—which are the causes of the continuity of those earlier predispositions.[283] So that for five or six moments[284] each spectator is filled with rapture[285] and has the idea that he himself has entered into the life story of Rama, and thereby beholds the universe as such while still in his own form; and he comes to possess a form of consciousness of the sort conveyed by the deontic language of scripture—namely, that those who do such and such a thing receive such and such a reward—but without any assessment of the specifics of time and space; a consciousness that is of a general sort but that delights as if particular to him alone,[286] which is like the love of one's life,[287] and where one's predispositions are activated by the beautiful vocal and instrumental music accompanied by the savoring of rasa; a consciousness implanted into one's very heart in such a way that a hundred cleansings[288] could not cause it to fade away; so much so that, since the viewer is now suffused with the desire to attain the good and avoid the bad, he actually comes to do the one and shun the other, given that he has now gained an understanding to this end.

Another name for drama is thus, as the text puts it, "re-narration,"[289] in other words, a particular kind of reflexive consciousness. There should be no confusion about this being an imitation, since we do not have any sense that the prince or whoever has been "imitated" by a process of mimicry.[290] For in fact, imitation is parody and for that reason a source of mere amusement for onlookers. As the sage later says: "The comic arises from *imitating* someone else's actions."[291] . . .

[37] One might wonder why, although drama may not, for all that, be an imitation of a particular individual, it cannot still be imitation as such. No reason—aside from the fact that it is impossible. "Imitation" means "making similar," but in our case similar to what? Not Rama, first of all, since technically he cannot be imitated.[292] And the same reasoning disqualifies the imitation of all the other foundational factors, the heroine and so on. Nor can it be an imitation of mental states, grief, anger, and so on; the actor does not make his own grief similar to Rama's for the simple reason that he has no grief at all to begin with—and if he did, he would not be producing an imitation. Nor is there anything else he could produce that would be similar to grief. It is true that he produces physical reactions; these are not *similar* to the others, however, but, precisely, *homogeneous* with them. And what sense would it make to say one thing is "similar" to another when the two things have the same

properties? As for a universal property, it cannot simultaneously be "similar" to a particular instance; only a discrete thing can be imitated, and then, only in stages. What, in short, would be the meaning of imitation with respect to a thing that exists as a generality? Hence, no one should be confused into concluding that drama is an imitation of things that are *not* particulars. This is what we should understand as the intention behind my teacher's *Literary Investigations*, not that drama may indeed be an imitation of nonparticulars.[293]

Hence, drama is a rendering of something as an object of a particular kind of reflexive consciousness. To explain:[294] the costumes and other theatrical props neutralize belief that one is actually perceiving particular actors, Chaitra, say, or Maitra, who exist in a given time and place. But since it would be impossible for perception to function without any trace whatsoever of particularity, a name like "Rama" has its special functionality in this context, communicating as it does a reputed tale as connected with this celebrated name, and thanks to its capacity for thereby eliminating our basic sense of implausibility,[295] the viewer's reflexive consciousness takes on the character of a direct perception.[296] The play, because it is a site of aesthetic rapture, becomes an appropriate locus for emotional absorption insofar as it is permeated by pleasing vocal music and the rest. The actors' identities are concealed by means of the four registers of acting; the prologue and the other theatrical preliminaries assist the viewer's predispositions produced by knowledge about the actors. Thereby, as he comes before our eyes, the performer enters into the center of the complex of enchanting aesthetic elements, his own identity being concealed; armed with predispositions produced by earlier mundane perceptions and inferences, he is assisted by other predispositions derived from his knowledge of actors and receptive viewers, and he can thereby function as an auxiliary to the process of aesthetic identification through the heart's concurrence. Through him there comes into being this special kind of reflexive consciousness that consists of the light of the bliss that is one's own pure consciousness; it is "laden"[297] with this or that mental state, pleasurable or painful, as the case may be and hence multifarious; something that is given many different names—tasting, savoring, rapture, relishing, enjoyment, experience. The thing that reveals itself in this reflexive consciousness is what we call "drama." It hardly matters whether this "thing," as I call it, is a mere mental construct, a superimposition,[298] a generality, a temporary artifact, or whatever.[299] We have no desire to impose upon the sensitive reader by impeding the analysis of the matter at hand with irrelevant disquisitions that only serve to put on display the author's intimacy with discourses from other philosophical traditions.

Hence, drama is a "narration"[300] that consists of a reflexive consciousness "laden" with conceptual sense experience of the sort earlier described; for drama is made known by this kind of awareness. What drama is not is an imitation. There is no harm, of course, in saying that it is "imitation" (*anu-karaṇa*) in the sense that it "accords with" (*anu-sāri-*) the "doings" (*karaṇa*) of the real-world characters, since the use of such terminology is not a source of controversy so long as the actual distinction is kept securely in mind.

On "Verbal Acting"

(2.221)[301] Some scholars have argued that the actual words for the aesthetic-emotional elements[302] are themselves external to the creation of the mental state of rasa,[303] but this is erroneous. To explain: they argue that rasa cannot be communicated by the words because the negative concomitance[304] is invalid. But the invalidity of the negative concomitance is itself unproven to apply to any and all such words. For[305] as we explained in the seventh chapter, the fourfold form of general acting must indeed be involved where any clear apprehension of rasa is present.[306] But then, they retort, we actually do apprehend the erotic and other rasas even in the absence of such words as "the erotic" that directly express them, as in the following poem:

> Your cheek is pale as a ripened *śara* reed;
> like a lotus folding its petals in wintertime
> is your eye; and your lips, wilted with hot breath lingering,
> slender girl, bring the god of love to life.[307]

And that, they say, is surely an instance of the "absence of the negative concomitance." But their argument here too is flawed, since it would be easy to identify some other cause for the apprehension of rasa here.[308] The same reasoning applies in this case as in that of, say, scorpions: those born of dung are of one sort, those born of other scorpions are of another.[309] And if that is acceptable, as it should be, our situation would be analogous. We may not have precisely the same kind of apprehension of rasa when the word "erotic" is used as we do under other circumstances; that said, it is not true that we do not have *some* apprehension of rasa from the word "erotic," for if that were the case it would turn out that a statement like "The erotic, comic . . . are the eight dramatic rasas"[310] would be as meaningless as the cawing of crows. When words are used in their conventional meaning, what is to stop them from denoting things, whether substantive or verbal? And hence the fact of something's being a verbal form is no source of discomfort for our theory: what are we to say about the semantic capacity on the part of such forms as "one eroticizes," or "one is amused," "one tragicizes"? It is essential that such words be expressive of rasa, for otherwise, if your argument were valid, in poems like the following,

> When Krishna left for Dvaravati the pining Radha embraced
> the reeds on the bank of the Kalindi bent over from his footfall,
> and the song she sang—shrill and broken by deep convulsive sobs—
> made even the creatures in the water start to moan with yearning.[311]

[222] the restatement of the transitory emotions by the emotion words "pining" and "yearning" would be completely useless: they would have no capacity for enhancing the physical reactions because they could never actually convey those bodily forms.[312] And when we apprehend the variety of transitory emotions pertaining to a given stable emotion, as in the following poem,

> As she receded, she kept turning her face toward me,
> bending round like a lotus upon the stalk of her neck,
> her long-lashed eyes implanting in the depths of my heart
> a glance that was barbed at once with nectar and with poison.[313]

it would be virtually impossible to comprehend the physical reactions, to say nothing of the rasa itself, since we would have no understanding of the actions of those things that enliven the woman's glance—"turning," "bending," "implanting," "barbed." The same arguments apply to a verse like "Absorbed, or mirrored she seems, or painted."[314] Indeed, they apply to a whole host of poems: "With a laugh they flung themselves into a close embrace"; "Lakshmi's body, her arms slack with torpor"; "Only for a few days did she show some torpor in her eyes";

> When you see something beautiful or hear sweet sounds
> and grow melancholy even though you are happy,
> it's because you are remembering unknowingly
> attachments from a former life lodged in your being.

[223] "Her eyes closed in sleep, languid with passion"; "The Mountain's daughter too was revealing her emotions with her limbs":[315] in all these poems—themselves the very image of the full moon rising over the ocean that is the hearts of sensitive readers—if the laughter, torpor, longing, sleepiness, intoxication, craving, and so on,[316] the very things that enliven them, were *not* able to be conveyed by the words themselves, the poems would be as stolid as men whose natures cannot be swayed

by any foundational cause,[317] and resemble nothing so much as the meaningless play of crows and cranes. . . .

4.3 POTENTIAL FLAWS OF RASA

Light on Poetry of Mammata (c. 1050) with the Commentaries of Shridhara (c. 1225), Chandidasa (c. 1300), Vishvanatha (c. 1350), and Paramananda Chakravartin (c. 1500)

The analysis of literary aesthetics in general and rasa in particular had from the beginning been provided in one or another specialized treatise: works on dramaturgy in general (such as the *Treatise on Drama*), or on figures of speech (such as the *Looking Glass of Poetry*), or linguistic modalities (such as *Light on Implicature*), or general literary criticism (such as the *Vital Force of Literary Language*). There was clearly a need for a more comprehensive assessment of literary art, and it was provided by Mammata in his *Light on Poetry.* I find no compelling reason to think that Mammata did not write both the memorial verses and the exegesis (his reference in the latter to himself as "the author" is typical of the genre), though others have raised doubts. Mammata begins with a definition of literature, one that would be repeated, and contested, down the centuries, and goes on to investigate its linguistic modalities, the nature of rasa, language qualities, literary flaws, figures of sound and of sense—the whole range of literary topics outside of dramaturgy. No other work on the subject has been remotely as popular or influential. The *Light* has been preserved in thousands of manuscripts all across India, and has attracted scores of commentators beginning as early as the mid-twelfth century, one of whom, as late as the eighteenth, refers to Mammata in all sincerity as an "incarnation of Sarasvati, goddess of language."[318]

We know next to nothing about Mammata. Given whom he mentions (including Bhoja, unexpectedly in a northern work such as this) and the date and place of appearance of the earliest commentaries, he must be placed in the second half of the eleventh century and in Kashmir. We have only one other work of his, the brief *Introduction to Linguistic Modalities* (*Śabdavyāpāraparicaya*). It is clear that Mammata studied Abhinavagupta's *Eye for* Light on Implicature with great care. His analysis of rasa is the quasi-chronological one borrowed from Abhinava, and he has nothing of his own to add; direct access to the works treated there had by his time clearly become difficult, if not impossible. Mammata's analysis ends triumphantly with Abhinava and the theory he developed in *The Eye*—and not, significantly, the more mature one in *The New* Dramatic Art, which Mammata appears not to know. And that earlier theory, given the extraordinary impact of the *Light*, would henceforth dominate the discourse.

If Mammata has nothing of his own to add to the concept of rasa, he does provide an innovative and systematic analysis of one aspect that had previously been treated in a piecemeal fashion: the range of flaws to which rasa is liable. Much is borrowed from Ananda's *Light on Implicature*—in terms of both argument and illustration—though Mammata introduces greater order into this material and, on occasion, addresses it with greater insight. What obstructs the creation of the aesthetic experience obviously at the same time tells us a great deal about what makes such experience possible. If we are given insufficient information in the literary text, for example, something especially important in short works as the isolate poem; if we are given misleading information; if a rasa is introduced at the wrong moment (the erotic in the context of the horrors of war, for example), the aesthetic experience will be defective. We already learned from the *Treatise on Drama* that affective states and social states (and gender) are related: male characters of high status feel erotic desire, but not fear, whereas amusement is felt by characters of low status and women. Misaligning emotional and social state, accordingly, also disrupts the rasa.

An overriding concern of Mammata is "propriety," which comprises both verisimilitude (with respect to "time, place, age, gender, and caste") and moral correctness—the two in fact being coextensive. These had been concerns of Sanskrit criticism for centuries, but Mammata again adds systematicity to the discussion. And he reexamines, in a concentrated and insightful way, the thesis on the use in literature of the "proper terms" of rasa (employing the word "erotic" in an erotic passage, for example) put forward by Udbhata three centuries earlier, restated by Pratiharenduraja, critiqued by Shri Shankuka and Anandavardhana, and defended by Abhinava:[319] there is a domain, he argues, where the words for certain emotional states must in fact be used, since they give an apprehension of the emotion that no description suffices to do. And last, Mammata reengages with the question of conflict of rasa, already introduced by Ananda and Dhanika, where like his two predecessors he is able to demonstrate how acutely perceptive "practical criticism" could be.

I preface this selection with Mammata's account (and later interpretations of his account) of the peaceful rasa and "emotion poetry," early and influential discussions of two important issues in aesthetic response: how one responds emotionally to a (supposed) absence of emotion, and why an emotional response to poetry about love for God cannot be rasa—and indeed, what "emotion poetry," introduced by Udbhata in the early ninth century and largely ignored afterward, actually is. A selection from the long tradition of interpretation is added, including remarks by Ruyyaka (c. 1150), Shridhara (c. 1225), Chandidasa (c. 1300), Vishvanatha (c. 1350), and the genial Paramananda Chakravartin (c. 1500). While some commentators question the very possibility of emotion poetry on theoretical grounds, strikingly, none of them observes that it renders the idea of the "devotional rasa" a pure contradiction in terms. The imminent arrival of a full defense of that rasa (chapter 6.3) would radically challenge the whole discourse.

FROM *LIGHT ON POETRY* OF MAMMATA (M), AND SELECTIONS FROM COMMENTARIES

Chapter 4: The Peaceful Rasa and "Emotion Poetry"

(M) (35ab): An additional rasa is the peaceful, its stable emotion being dispassion.

(Shridhara) (p. 780):[320] By "dispassion" is meant true knowledge. The view that the stable emotion of the peaceful rasa is "impassivity," or the cessation of all mental states, is quite mistaken. To quote:[321] "If absence meant absolute negation, there would be an absence of all mental states and hence no emotion at all. Our view, accordingly, assumes specific negation. . . ."[322] [781.4] The argument has been made that while everyone can apprehend the peaceful rasa, not everyone will appreciate it, and hence it cannot be a real rasa.[323] But if that were true, other rasas that are not appreciated by everyone would also cease to be rasas. The erotic, for example, is not appreciated by the lower social orders, the miserably dressed villagers, who are gripped only by the brute feelings of desire common to all creatures;[324] nor the heroic by the cowardly. . . . As for the "heroic in compassion," it differs markedly from the peaceful. It is characterized by a developed sense of self, since its stable emotion is determination of the sort that blazes forth with energy, satisfied with nothing less than conquest of the three worlds. That sense of self finds expression in such thoughts as "It is I who am doing such and such," or "By doing such and such I will gain such and such a reward." Where, by contrast, one performs an act required by scripture with no expectation of reward, and with all sense of self eliminated, we have the peaceful rasa. The author, however, understands the heroic in compassion as another name for the peaceful . . . but the fact is that it is only where the sense of self is utterly extinguished, whether in the heroic in compassion or the heroic in munificence, that they may be counted subspecies of the peaceful rasa.

(M) An example:

A snake or necklace, a flower-strewn bed or stone,
a jewel or clod, strong enemy or friend,
straw or women—may I regard them as all the same
and pass my days in a holy forest chanting "Shiva, Shiva, Shiva."[325]

(Ruyyaka) (p. 779): Here the highest truth (expressed in the chanting of Shiva's name) constitutes the foundational factor; the holy forest the stimulant factor; the unchanging views the reaction; the anxiety detectable in the prayer the transitory emotion, with constancy and others also implicit. These "manifest" the peaceful rasa. (This procedure of analyzing the various aesthetic elements, here shown for the first time, will be used again elsewhere for the purposes of instruction; sensitive readers should consider it carefully.)

(M) (4.35cd–4.36ab): When desire is directed to a deity or comparable figure, or when what is *principally* manifested is a transitory emotion, we have "emotion" rather than rasa.[326]

"Comparable figures" include a sage, a teacher, a king, and a son. By contrast, when it is desire directed toward the beloved that comes to manifestation, we have the erotic rasa. An example of the first type of "emotion":

> World-destroying poison I would take as nectar were it lodged within your
> throat, dear Lord,
> and spurn nectar within my very grasp were it separate from your body.[327]

(Shridhara) (p. 790): Desire and so on, when directed toward a deity and the like, as in the case of devotion or panegyric, is not a stable emotion and hence becomes specifically a transitory emotion. Thus, although the desire can be manifested by the aesthetic elements, it is not a rasa.

(Chandidasa) (p. 790): It is because the desire lacks the seed of full enhancement in conformity with a situation of mutuality that it does not become rasa. Were the enhancement to be fully realized, desire for a deity would be a subspecies of the tranquil rasa, such is the basic idea. . . . Amusement and the other stable emotions as well, when they are not enhanced, are also understood by sensitive critics as simply "emotions." In those cases too we find both traits, the awakening of latent predispositions as well as a composite form of awareness,[328] that we found to be present in rasa in accordance with our foregoing analysis; we call the one "emotion" and the other "rasa" in acknowledgment of the difference in their natures.

(Vishvanatha) (791): At the moment of savoring we have no sense that some elements are dominant, others subordinate, since literary meaning is always grasped as a unity. It is only subsequently that analytical thinkers have this distinctive experience of the predominance of an "emotion." . . . In some cases stable emotions remain just "emotions"[329] due to the absence of full enhancement through mutual affection, once we consider the whole context. An example is "Hara, however, lost his composure. . . ."[330]

(Paramananda Chakravartin) (793): The argument has been made that any stable emotion lacking the full enhancement produced by the aesthetic elements and simply awakened counts as "emotion"; the example given is "Hara, however, lost his composure." Since here we find desire awakened in Shiva but lacking full enhancement (given that he is about to burn the god of love and abandon the company of the woman), it is supposed to remain "emotion" and does not become rasa. But this argument is false. That there is a savoring derived from this verse, which is fully enhanced by all the aesthetic elements, can be ascertained by our actual experience. The imminent burning of the god of love and the other impediments to rasa have no effect on this, since they have yet to occur.[331] And one cannot argue that the impediments are at that very minute descending upon those audience members who may indeed be familiar with the larger context [794] without at the same time admitting that a full enhancement of desire must derive from the vast empire of pleasure recounted in the poem's eighth canto detailing the joy of Shiva and Parvati's marriage. In fact, the very experience of savoring brought about and manifested by the verse in question shows that no obstacle[332] to rasa is presented by reflecting on the larger context of the literary work—otherwise in a drama where the heroic, for example, is the dominant rasa, no other rasa could ever play a contributing role, since a consideration of the context would always render the heroic all-powerful. . . .

In the above verse "World-destroying poison . . . ," Shiva is the foundational factor; his infinite lordliness, signaled by the word "Lord," the stimulant factor; the eulogy itself the reaction; constancy, remembering[333] the Lord's greatness and the like, the transitory emotions. The desire here, which the aesthetic elements awaken in the audience—who infer from these elements the desire in the eulogist—and which is self-manifesting and a composite form of awareness, is said to remain "emotion." Why, one might object, is there in this case no rasa? There is no evidence that the desire in question is not pleasurable; it is no different from rasa with respect to the totality of aesthetic elements; and surely in one way or another it can be savored, if only like relishing a dry coconut—though in fact, if one proceeded more thoroughly, the way sugarcane stalk is relished, one would have an experience of full homogeneous bliss.[334] If one adduces as proof of this being "emotion" poetry the evidence provided by the heart of the sensitive reader,[335] well, is the person making this argument the one and only sensitive reader? In actuality, it is only a result of the fact that the sage Bharata has arbitrarily established that there are nine and only nine rasas, just as Gotama established there to be five and only five logical fallacies:[336] "There are only nine rasas," said the sage, "and the rest is simply 'emotion.'"

(M) (*elucidation*) Here is an example of when the transitory emotion is principally manifested:

I saw my love in a dream last night, turning her back in anger
and crying "Don't touch me!" and starting to walk away,
but I swear to you, brother, I am sure
I could have taken her in my arms
and calmed her with a hundred sweet nothings
if wretched fate had not gone and robbed me of my sleep.

Here the transitory emotion that is principally manifested is resentment directed toward fate.

(Shridhara) (801): While it is undoubtedly the case that we have here implicature of rasa—of the erotic thwarted, made beautiful by the stable emotion of desire, which itself is stimulated by the dream vision—the real point of the poem is the resentment toward fate prompted by the man's anger.

Chapter 7: The Flaws of Rasas

(M) (7.60–62) The flaws that can afffect rasa are the following: [1] employing the proper term for a stable emotion, a transient emotion, or a rasa, or the word "rasa" itself; [2] manifesting a reaction or foundational factor in a way grasped only with difficulty; [3] making use of an antithetical aesthetic element; [4] repeatedly arousing a rasa;[337] [5a] unfolding a rasa at the wrong moment[338] or [5b] terminating it at the wrong moment; [6] excessively describing a subsidiary component of the rasa; [7] ignoring a dominant component; [8] misassigning rasas to dramatic characters; [9] describing something nonessential.

An example of [1]:

Parvati's glances in all their variety—ashamed before the face of her beloved,
tragic before the elephant hide, frightened before the serpent,
amazed before the moon flowing with nectar, jealous before Ganga,
and despondent before the hollows of the skulls[339]—
may these glances, when she first found delight
in Shiva's embrace, bring you welfare.

In this verse, it is a flaw that the words "shame" and the rest are employed. The poem would have been correct, however, had "lowered" been used (for "ashamed"), "shut tight" (for "tragic"), "trembling" (for "frightened"), "unblinking" (for "amazed"), "frowning" (for "jealous"), "saddened" (for "despondent"). In the case of "rasa," the flaw occurs when the proper term itself ("rasa") is used or the terms for any of the individual rasas, such as "erotic" and so on . . . ;[340] and when the proper terms for the stable emotions are used, e.g., "determination." . . .

An example of [2]:

As the moon flooded the sky with streams of luster white as powdered camphor,
the arrangement of her veil revealed to the young man's gaze her heaving breast.

Here we have a stimulant factor (the moon) and foundational factor (the woman) entirely appropriate to the erotic, but they do not lead naturally[341] to the requisite physical reactions.[342] In this next example,

He avoids all pleasure, stops thinking, trips over himself or wanders in circles—
his wretched state overpowers his body, and there's nothing to be done
for it.[343]

because avoiding pleasure and the other reactions can also occur in the tragic rasa, it is only with effort we come to comprehend the foundational factor here, namely, the man's beloved (and the rasa, the erotic thwarted).

An example of [3]:

My love, be gracious, show your favor and put your anger away;
my body is withering away, sprinkle the nectar of your words upon it;
show me, if only a moment, your face, the source of all delights.
My simple girl, time is a fleet deer that, once fled, never returns.[344]

Here in an erotic poem the poet has used a stimulant factor of the peaceful rasa—the disclosure of the transience of life—which is antithetical to the erotic, as well as an antithetical transitory emotion disclosed by that factor, namely, dispassion. Another example:

When her paramour appeared before her in the midst of her in-laws
the young wife was ready to give up everything and leave at once for the forest.

In this poem, giving up everything and leaving for the forest are reactions of the peaceful rasa. Had the poet indicated that under the guise of collecting firewood she left for the forest to make love, there would have been no flaw.

An example of [4] occurs in the lamentation of Rati in the fourth chapter of the "Birth of the War God."[345]

An example of [5a] is found in the second act of the *Tying Up the Braid*, when, after countless brave warriors have been slaughtered, we have a description of the erotic rasa of Duryodhana and Bhanumati;[346] an example of [5b] occurs in the second act of the *Life of the Great Hero* when, as the heroic rasa of Rama and Parashurama is reaching a climax, Rama announces that he is going off to untie Sita's marriage bracelet.[347]

An example of [6] are the descriptions of Hayagriva in the *Slaying of Hayagriva*.[348]

An example of [7] is found in the play *Ratnavali* when, with the arrival of Babhravya, Sagarika herself is completely forgotten.[349]

[8] The dramatic characters are gods, humans, and demigods, and are further subdivided into the four types of protagonist, the dignified, proud, romantic, and peaceful, that are fundamentally related to the heroic, violent, erotic, and peaceful rasas, respectively; and yet further into high, middle, and low status. With respect to these characters, desire, amusement, grief, and amazement may be ascribed to gods as well as humans of high status,[350] but desire in the form of the erotic enjoyed is not to be actually described in the case of gods of high status. It would be something entirely inappropriate, like describing the lovemaking of one's own parents.[351]

Anger of the sort that carries immediate consequences but without there being any physical transformation in the subject, such as knitting the brows, is to be ascribed to gods alone. An example:

"Restrain, dear Lord, restrain your anger"—with the wind gods' words echoing in
the sky
the fire that flashed from Shiva's third eye reduced the god of love to ash.[352]

The same restriction to gods holds also for the stable emotion of determination when it comprises such acts as journeying to heaven or hell, or leaping over the ocean. With respect to humans, however, the literary composition should describe a great act only so far as tradition or propriety permits. Exceeding these limits in composing the narrative winds up creating false appearances that inhibit the communication of the central moral, namely, to act like the protagonist and not like the antagonist. This applies, on both counts (that is, of tradition and propriety), to demigods[353] as well. . . .

[9] The description of something "nonessential" means the description of something that does not contribute to the rasa. An example is found in *Karpuramanjari*, where the king discusses the description of springtime given by the court bards while ignoring his own description and that of the female protagonist.[354] "Such" in the memorial verse indicates that there are other kinds of impropriety, as, for example, describing a lover who becomes angry when spurned by his beloved. To quote the author of the *Implicature*: "The one thing that can impair rasa is impropriety. . . ."[355]

The author now goes on to argue that in some instances even such things do not become flaws:

(63ab) In some instances[356] there is no flaw when a transitory emotion is referred to by its proper term.

For example, in the verse "Gauri, rushing in her *longing*,"[357] the use of the proper term of the transitory emotion gives us an apprehension of a sort that any physical reaction associated with the emotion alone would not. Thus, in the verse[358] about a mistress's eyes upon seeing her errant lover, "Filled with *longing* when he was at a distance, downcast when he drew near . . . brimming with tears when he bowed at her feet," it is clear that we do not derive the same comprehension of longing from its physical reaction (suddenly hurrying out or the like)[359] as we do of shame or attachment[360] from their respective physical reactions (being downcast and weeping). And that is why the poet has used the proper term for the transitory emotion, "longing," in reference to Gauri.

(63cd) The use of a transitory emotion or other aesthetic element pertaining to a *conflictual* rasa, when it is referred to as being negated, enriches the work.

When an aesthetic element is referred to in such a manner that it is negated, it is not only not a flaw but actually enhances the rasa at issue. Take as an example the following verse:

What has the royal lunar line to do with moral lapses?
When might I see her again?
My education was meant to check such failings.

Even in anger her face is beautiful.
What will those virtuous wise men say?
Not even in my dreams can I attain her. . . .
Oh mind, get a grip on yourself! I wonder
what lucky lad is sipping at her lip?[361]

Here, although expression is given to a range of transitory emotions such as perplexity—these are in each odd-numbered line and pertain to the peaceful rasa, which conflicts with the erotic in the even-numbered lines—our minds come to rest on anxiety ("I wonder . . ."), in such a way that the primary rasa[362] is enhanced. An example with respect to reactions:

Your face is wan and drawn, your heart filled with chyle [or: passion],[363] your body torpid—
all signs, dear friend, that in your heart some illness has come that can't be cured.

Here, since a wan complexion and so on are common to several rasas (the tragic and the erotic in particular), there is in fact no conflict at all.[364] An example with respect to foundational factors:

Women are charming, true enough, and, true enough, riches are grand.
But the only thing more unstable than a woman's glance is life itself.[365]

The idea in the first half of this verse (the erotic) is presented only to be negated in the second (the peaceful). It is of course universally understood that it is the woman's glance that is more unstable than life, and hence using the glance only as a standard of comparison for instability serves to enhance the peaceful rasa and it alone: we have no apprehension here whatever of the erotic, because no other aesthetic elements (such as the glance acting as physical reaction to desire) are available to enable us to comprehend it as such. One cannot say that there is a conflict here between the two rasas and resolve it by arguing that the erotic is used to catch the attention of young students who need to understand the importance of the peaceful rasa, because the erotic and the peaceful cannot exist in immediate proximity to each other. Nor can the presence of the erotic here be justified by claiming it is a way of "beautifying" the poem, because beautification can come about by means of the other rasa alone (i.e., the peaceful), or simply through the figure of sound in the verse.[366]

(64) A rasa that conflicts with another by being located in one and the same substratum should be moved to a different one; a rasa that conflicts with another from immediate proximity with it should be separated by a third rasa.

The heroic and the fearful are in conflict when located in the same substratum, and hence the fearful should be located in the antagonist. The peaceful and the erotic are in conflict when in immediate proximity, and so must be separated by a third rasa. Thus, in the drama *How the Nagas Were Pleased*, between Jimutavahana's peaceful rasa at the start and his erotic rasa directed toward Malayavati, the fantastic rasa is interposed (in the scene where he says, "What amazing singing! What amazing music!").[367] This procedure applies not only at the level of the work as a whole but even in a single passage: the conflict between two rasas can be resolved by the interposition of a third, as in the following passage:

Befouled with dust from the ground—while perfumed with pollen
from heavenly coral tree garlands;
held tightly by jackals—while embraced
by the women of the gods;
fanned by the wings of carrion birds flashing crimson with blood—
while refreshed by silken celestial vines scented with sandalwood essence:
the heroic warriors, seated in heavenly chariots,
gazed down upon their own dead bodies
as beautiful goddesses pointed them out with intense curiosity.[368]

Here, between the macabre and the erotic rasas, the heroic is interposed.

(65) There is no flaw [1] when a conflictual rasa is the object of a memory; [2] when it is intended as a comparison; or [3] when rasas that conflict with each other become subsidiaries to a third, dominant rasa.

[1] Consider the following verse:

This used to loosen my belt and untie the knot holding up my skirt, and fondle
my heavy breasts and touch my navel and thighs and mound—this very
hand.[369]

The wife of Bhurishravas addresses these words to her husband, lying dead on the battlefield, when she catches sight of his severed hand. Here, the recollection of a former state of affairs, though a component of the erotic rasa, does not conflict with the tragic but enhances it. An example of [2]:

The bites and nail wounds on your body,
left by the lioness in her lust for blood [or: in her passion for you]
and your hair everywhere stiffening with pleasure—
even the monks observe all this with longing.[370]

Here, the bites and the rest on the Buddha's body are described as being as wonderful as those on a lover's; and just as a susceptible bystander might observe the lover and long for such an experience himself, so do the monks when they see the Buddha's wounds. Here a comparison is intended between the two rasas.

An example of [3]:

As they wander the sharp-grass thickets, their soft toes cut and the dripping blood
coloring their feet as though with lac, their faces washed with tears of fear,
their hands held in their husbands' hands and circling the forest fires,
today the wives of your enemies are reliving their wedding day.[371]

What we apprehend in this verse of flattery to a king is the poet's own desire,[372] and because both the tragic and the erotic are equally subsidiary to it, there is no conflict between them. Consider this analogy:

"Come, go, sit down, stand up, speak, be quiet"—This is how
the rich will play with the poor possessed as they are by the demon Hope.[373]

Here, each of the verbs is used only with reference to "play," so any contradiction between them in themselves—between coming and going, and so on—is only apparent. A second example of [3]:

Like a husband whose betrayal is still moist,
it was driven away when trying to clutch their hand,
it was mercilessly struck when grasping their hem,
shaken off when stroking their hair, and spurned
in a panic when falling at their feet,
and when attempting an embrace forcefully rebuffed
by the women of the Triple City, tears brimming in their eyes:
may this fire of Shiva's arrows burn away your sins.[374]

In this poem, the tragic is subsidiary to the dominant meaning, namely, the grandeur[375] of Shiva, enemy of the Triple City, whereas the erotic in turn is subsidiary to the tragic; since our minds do not come to rest on the tragic, however, it too remains subsidiary.[376] Alternatively, we can say the erotic becomes subsidiary by enhancing the tragic—with the god's fire being likened to the behavior of the women's lovers who had strayed in the past—which in turn strengthens that same principal meaning. To quote: "Once developed, a subordinate element becomes more dominant and thereby assists the true dominant all the more."[377]

One final point: since rasa, given our earlier description,[378] cannot ultimately conflict with another rasa or exist in a principal-subsidiary relationship with it, the word "rasa" here may be taken as referring to the stable emotion.

4.4 THE PURIFIED THEORY IN ABSTRACT

Short Explanation of Light on Poetry, and *Commentary on* Analysis of "Manifestation" of Ruyyaka (1150)

Ruyyaka was a leading intellectual in Kashmir in the first half of the twelfth century. We have already encountered the work of his father, Tilaka, on Udbhata's treatise. Aside from Ruyyaka's commentaries excerpted below—he left one of the earliest on Mammata's treatise, and the only one on Mahima Bhatta's—he wrote an account of figures of speech, the *Compendium of Tropes*, that stands as one of the most penetrating in the long history of reflection on the topic, as well as a short treatise on qualities of the leading female character (*The Connoisseur's Sport, Sahṛdayalīlā*).

Ruyyaka's significance for the history of aesthetics lies in part in being an early witness of the emergent consensus on some key elements of the rasa discourse. One is the basic outline of Abhinavagupta's theory of rasa, which Ruyyaka offers in his commentary on Mammata. This outline is derived entirely from Abhinava's *Eye for* Light on Implicature; Ruyyaka appears to know nothing of *The New* Dramatic Art. Another is the recoding of the notion of "manifestation," on which Ruyyaka provides the first explicit reflection. As we saw, this concept was introduced by Anandavardhana to make sense of how literary texts produce the idea of an emotion (and other sorts of meaning, whether narrative or figurative). Abhinava transformed Ananda's manifestation of emotion in the text into a manifestation of emotion in the heart of the sensitive reader. Ruyyaka explains and defends this new signification vigorously, and, strikingly, does so in his commentary on a book, *Analysis of "Manifestation,"* that not only seems to know nothing of this transformation but actually leveled a full-scale critique against Ananda's original conception.

FROM *SHORT EXPLANATION OF* LIGHT ON POETRY OF RUYYAKA

(p. 577) According to Abhinavagupta, in keeping with the doctrine of implicature, rasa is something "manifested" and the aesthetic elements are the medium of manifestation, the relation between them therefore being one of object and agent of manifestation. It is the stable emotion[379] that appropriately turns into rasa.[380] The relation is expressed in the *Sutra on Rasa* by the word "conjunction," and the word "arises" means "manifested." Rasa belongs to the audience, not to the character or the actor. . . . The fact that the aesthetic elements are common to both the character and the viewer/reader entails that the object of cognition too, namely, the stable emotion, should be common. And this entails a commonality of the cognition itself. Accordingly, acts such as Hanuman's leaping over the ocean, prompted by emotions common to both the character and the viewer/reader, can become objects of aesthetic experience, precisely because the latter apprehends himself as identical with the former. There would indeed be a logical problem if this were reversed and the commonality of the cognizer were predicated upon the commonality of the object cognized. But that is not the position we take, and hence our view of manifestation is perfectly sound.

To explain: no one devoid of the pertinent predispositions can savor rasa. Thus, Vedic ritualists and desiccated theologians, even when they are in the theater, sit like logs because they have no capacity for aesthetic sublimity; ascetics and religious celibates are similarly excluded from the savoring of the erotic rasa; men of deep passion are incapable of savoring the tranquil rasa, whereas men who have never experienced the touch of grief are like stones when the opportunity of savoring the tragic rasa is afforded them. Hence, [578] the very capacity to relish rasa is a sign of one's predispositions. And what becomes rasa by virtue of the aesthetic elements is that primordial predisposition, which is in fact the stable emotion (and never a transitory emotion, given the technical definition of the term "rasa"). And it is through "manifestation" alone that the stable emotion becomes rasa by means of the aesthetic elements, since there obtains between emotion and the elements a relationship of object and agent of manifestation. To explain briefly: manifestation is of two sorts. In one kind, the effect exists in subtle form in the cause, and "manifestation" signifies the acquisition of its gross form, as in the case of the white substance that exists in the milk state and then takes on the form of yogurt. This sort of manifestation is independent of any cognition and is simply inherent in the thing itself. The second kind, however, is a cognition of the thing when mediated via the cognition of the medium of manifestation, as in the case of a pot and a lamp: we cognize the pot only in association with the cognition of the lamp, because the lamp is the medium of manifestation. To quote: "Manifestation produces a cognition of something else—if that something is an already existing entity—by the cognition of itself, as in the case of a lamp. Were the situation other than this—i.e., were the object not an already existing entity—there would be no difference between manifesting a thing and actually making it."[381]

With respect to these two types, in the present case we accept that rasa and the aesthetic elements have a relationship of object and agent of manifestation of the second sort, because rasa is cognized in association with the cognition of the elements, on the analogy of the taste of the mixed drink. This is why the author of the *Light on Implicature* spoke of manifestation with reference to rasa as one where "no succession is registered," and has used the example of the pot and lamp.

FROM THE *COMMENTARY ON* ANALYSIS OF "MANIFESTATION" OF RUYYAKA

(p. 62) The reasoning of the advocate of "manifestation"[382] . . . is as follows. . . . [63] It is incorrect to attempt to vindicate inference instead of manifestation, or to claim that if the notion of manifestation is used it can only be in a figurative sense, by resorting to the idea that the aesthetic elements and the stable emotions are actually factitious.[383] It is relishing that actually animates rasa, and it is the sensitive viewer/reader alone who relishes rasa; hence, when we characterize rasa's essence, it must be as something that exists in the viewer/reader. Rasa does not exist in the character or the actor, because we can only apprehend rasa through commonization, which requires eliminating all the character's (or actor's) particularities, those of space, time, status, and literary type. It is not of course completely incoherent to ascribe rasa to a character such as Rama or the actor portraying him, since they participate in rasa.[384] But it is altogether incorrect to classify rasa as *existing* in them, given the authoritative statement of the sage himself that "The stable emotion itself is rasa."[385]

Since, accordingly, it is the stable emotion that is rasa, and since those who lack rasa themselves cannot relish it, the stable emotions really and truly exist in the form of our predispositions, and they become rasa when they are made accessible to the act of relishing—such is our position. There is nothing factitious here about the rasas, desire and the rest, nor indeed, even about the causes, effects, and ancillary causes that come to be designated "factors" ("foundational" and "stimulant"), "reactions," and "transitory emotions" when apprehended by the viewer/reader as common to him, because these actually do exist: they are called "foundational factors" and so on in the primary sense of the terms only when apprehended by a sensitive viewer/reader; otherwise they remain "causes" and the like. (This was the intention of the sage in giving these things their supermundane designations in the *Sutra on Rasa*.) Therefore, the truly existing stable emotion in the form of a predisposition is manifested by the aesthetic elements without the interposition of any recollection of some connection[386] among them. Given this, rasa is "manifested" in a quite literal and not figurative sense, while its being something that must be inferred is refuted. The same holds for the emotions.

As for the four different kinds of manifestation that have been recognized,[387] depending on whether the object of manifestation is real or not, that subject is quite irrelevant here, because we accept for our theory of manifestation the model of the lamp and the pot. It is also false to raise the specter of the absurdity that, if the manifestation were real, the rasa would have to become visible. We do not refute our opponent's view by way of his own definition of manifestation as "coming to visibility"; and in fact no one has defined the term this way. It can be defined generally (according to the statement, "Manifestation produces a cognition of something else . . .") as "coming to awareness." There is accordingly no objection whatsoever to the application of "manifestation" to rasa.

CHAPTER FIVE

Continuing the Controversies Beyond Kashmir, 1200–1400

5.1 WHERE IS RASA? IS RASA ALWAYS PLEASURABLE?

Mirror of Drama of Ramachandra and Gunachandra (c. 1200)

Ramachandra and Gunachandra were students of the celebrated Jain scholar and cleric Hemachandra (d. 1172). The former was a prolific and strikingly inventive playwright, to judge from his six extant dramas and their dizzyingly complex plots of mistaken identity. Of the latter we know nothing. The important and innovative treatise on dramaturgy they jointly wrote (with Ramachandra's contribution making this the first such text composed by a working playwright) is extant, surprisingly, in only four manuscripts; even more surprisingly, not a single commentary on it has been identified, and the sometimes uncertain state and sense of the text present a challenge. The *Mirror* must have been more widely disseminated, however, than the current paucity of manuscripts would suggest; it exerted palpable influence on Rudra Bhatta, an almost-contemporaneous writer on aesthetics far to the south (in today's Karnataka).[1] As for the influences on them, the impact of Hemachandra (his *Manual of Poetry*) is naturally apparent, though our authors do not hesitate to disagree with him on occasion; so too that of Abhinavagupta (especially and surprisingly the *New* Dramatic Art), whom they critique both by name and anonymously.[2] They know the writings of Bhoja,[3] something unusual for northern scholars (explained no doubt by the fact that Bhoja's library had been looted and removed to Gujarat by Jayasimha Siddharaja, Hemachandra's patron), and had closely studied Mammata's *Light on Poetry*.[4] Equally important, they had access to a wide range of literature no longer extant. They refer to dramas by Shri Shankuka, for example, and quote from several celebrated lost plays.[5]

One of the main questions addressed in the portion selected here is prompted by Abhinavagupta's strong claim (advanced also, though less forcefully, by Dhanika) that rasa must be essentially pleasurable, "insofar as the pure homogeneous illumination that takes the form of the relishing of one's own consciousness is in essence blissful."[6] But are all the experiences we have over the course of an aesthetic event pleasurable, or only some of them, and if some, which ones? And in order to resolve that question, do we need to more carefully define "pleasurable," or to specify whether the "course of an aesthetic event" includes its end? These refinements are what Ramachandra and Gunachandra offer when they draw a new differentiation between two phenomena that Abhinava had identified, the rasa experience itself and the "rapture" that, they argue, only *follows* the experience and registers its wondrous character. The pain we experience from stories we still somehow find pleasurable is surely real pain, and felt by readers far beyond medieval India. Think of Dr. Johnson's remarks on *King Lear*: "I was many years ago so shocked by Cordelia's death, that I know not whether I ever endured to read again the last scenes of the play till I undertook to revise them as an editor."[7] But it is an especially sensitive problem for scholars belonging to the Jain tradition, where supreme value attaches to nonviolence. It is entirely understandable for them to argue that depictions on the stage of violence, anger, and associated feelings would be *a priori* morally distressful no less than affectively painful.

Of additional interest is the writers' view on the endlessly engaging problem of the location of rasa. They seek a compromise between the old and new paradigms—natural in thinkers familiar with the conflicting viewpoints of Bhoja and Abhinava—though the one they achieve appears, and perhaps must inevitably be, somewhat confusing at times. Their synthesis prompts them to offer a subtle analysis of all the aesthetic elements as they pertain, on the one hand, to the characters in themselves ("the men and women of the [story]world"), and, on the other, to the reader or viewer ("when the characters are narrated in a poem or acted out on the stage"). Thus, in the case of a character, a reaction functions as a consequence of rasa; in the case of the viewer/reader, as a cause of rasa;[8] at the same time, the viewer/reader also has his own reactions and transitory emotions. The authors conclude by covering all their bases: rasa is everywhere, in the principal character, the spectator, the auditor or reader of a poem, and even, on occasion, the actor (though no longer in the author).

Noteworthy, finally, is the rejoinder given to the critique of imitation that Abhinava received from his teacher, Bhatta Tota, and made integral to his own theory of the aesthetic. Ramachandra and Gunachandra allow that there can indeed be no imitation of a thing if the original has not been perceived, as in the case of a playwright writing about Rama or an actor portraying him. But while actual perception can err, perception transmitted by tradition can be inerrant: the sages who crafted dramaturgy knew everything about Rama and passed this down through the generations, and this is what the skilled actor reproduces—in his imitation.

FROM *MIRROR OF DRAMA* OF RAMACHANDRA AND GUNACHANDRA

(109) (p. 158) Rasa is a stable emotion intensified by the factors and the transitory emotions, and made evident by clear and distinct reactions. Its nature may be either pleasurable or painful.

A "stable emotion" is so called because, whereas all the many transitory emotions have the characteristic of constantly coming into and going out of being, the stable emotion necessarily retains a continuous existence. Or it may be so called because its existence is essential to the transitory emotions, for the latter exist only when a stable emotion exists and are absent[9] when the latter is absent. When strengthened, the stable emotion comes to exist in the form of a rasa. Such is the basic idea.

To explain further. The stable emotion is "intensified," first, by being brought to manifestation—given that it must already be in existence—thanks to the "factors" that are the external causes (foundational factors such as a beautiful woman, stimulant factors such as a garden), [159] and, second, by being enhanced by the transitory emotions that exist in the mind and body of the *rasika,* the person experiencing the rasa.[10] Here "intensified" means reaching a state able to be experienced as providing a direct awareness of itself.[11] The stable emotion is then "tasted," or savored, and so becomes rasa. Rasa is by nature either pleasurable or painful, depending on the case. Five of the rasas, the full development of whose nature comes about through desirable foundational factors and the rest, are pleasurable (the erotic, comic, heroic, fantastic, and peaceful); the remaining four (the tragic, violent, macabre, and fearful), however, which come into existence by way of undesirable foundational factors and so on, are painful.

The argument that all rasas are pleasurable[12] is falsified by what we actually find to be the case.[13] Even when they are strengthened by foundational factors presented in a poem or acted out on the stage—to say nothing of when this occurs in the foundational factors in the form of the main characters[14] themselves—the fearful, macabre, tragic, and violent bring those savoring the rasa into a state of perturbation that is almost indescribable. The audience, we must conclude, is distressed by those rasas, and it is hardly reasonable to maintain that such distress can derive from a pleasurable aesthetic experience. That the four rasas produce rapture is something that happens only *after* the savoring of rasa has itself ceased, and is the result of acknowledging the genius of the poet or the skill of the actor in showing things as they really are. For those who have an appreciation of courage are filled with amazement at the martial skill of a hero, even when he has decapitated someone. And in the same way sophisticated people, beguiled by the rapturous response that the power of a poet or actor can elicit, whereby the whole body is suffused with a kind of ecstasy, are led to believe that a state of pure bliss is found even in the tragic and other painful rasas. It is because of their thirst for savoring this experience that viewers repeatedly subject themselves even to such spectacles. As for the poets and playwrights, they compose their *Lives of Rama* and works of that sort in conformity with the nature of worldly existence, which is indeed both pleasurable and painful, and thereby of necessity produce texts that are shot through with both pleasurable and painful rasas. They also know full well that a painful experience makes pleasure all the more pleasurable, as the sweetness of a drink is enhanced by a touch of bitters.

Moreover, in what sense can it really be said to be a pleasurable experience for sensitive viewers to see Sita's abduction being acted out, Draupadi dragged by the hair and disrobed, Harischandra reduced to servitude to an untouchable and his son Rohitashva dying, Lakshmana wounded by a lance, or Malati being prepared for slaughter? It is clear enough that the tragic and other such rasas in the characters are painful, inasmuch as they result from lamentation and the like.[15] If it were argued that it is in the *performance* that these rasas are pleasurable, the performance would be flawed, since it would be presenting just the opposite of what is actually the fact of the matter.[16] Moreover, the savoring of pleasure we appear to get from the tragic rasa of people pained by the loss of a loved one, when it is narrated in poetry or acted out on the stage, is in reality a savoring of pain. It is only a man who has been pained himself who takes pleasure at the news of another man's pain and finds the news of another man's joy distressful. Thus the tragic and the other three rasas are, in actual fact, painful. In the case of the erotic thwarted, however, while it is indeed painful since it results from such things as an inner fire, it is actually pleasurable in that its very core lies in fantasizing the erotic enjoyed.

As for the rasa itself, it is located in the main characters, in the spectator in the case of drama, and in the listener and reader[17] both in the case of a work of poetry.

When we describe the reactions as "clear and distinct," we mean that they must be properly ascertained, because for a sign to prompt a correct inference, it must be indubitable. They are called "reactions" because they *enable reaction* to a rasa, [160] that is, they make it known, even though located in another person.[18] These reactions include paralysis, perspiration, horripilation, weeping, the play of the eyebrows, and so on. By means of these a rasa is determined to be present.

Now, with respect to these reactions, it is familiar to everyone that understanding[19] rasa means in the first instance understanding something existing in someone else. And that kind of understanding cannot be a direct sense perception, given that mental events of other minds are not perceptible to us. It must thus be nonsensory, but nonsensory understanding can only derive from one thing invariably concomitant with another.[20] With respect to rasa, it has to be the effects of rasa that are concomitant with it, since nothing else is possible.[21]

One cannot challenge this argument—that the reactions are *invariably* connected with rasa—on the grounds that when an actor, in order to entertain the audience,[22] engages in the imitation of the factors and the rest that pertain to the character, he shows the reactions of paralysis, perspiration, and the like when he himself does *not* have rasa. For the actor's reactions are not effects of rasa at all; they are merely meant to generate rasa in the audience. That is to say, the paralysis and so on that appear to be present in the actor function as the cause of rasas in the viewers, whereas the paralysis and the rest in the audience are effects of *their* rasas.[23] If one aims to know some nonsensory thing, one must be attentive to the nature of the inferential sign that is invariably concomitant with that thing.

That said, those reactions may also be making known a rasa that exists in the actor himself, should it be *his own* rasa that brings them about, since there is no hard and fast rule that an actor cannot feel rasa. Courtesans, in their desire for monetary gain, make a display of sexual pleasure and the like in order to please someone else, but they can sometimes experience the highest degree of pleasure themselves. Singers too are sometimes themselves delighted while they are seeking to delight someone else. In the same way an actor, imitating the rasa of the erotic thwarted in Rama, for example, may well on occasion come to identify with him completely. The horripilation and so on in the actor, therefore, can indeed make known a rasa in himself. That is why the memorial verse speaks of "clear and distinct reactions."

Now, the horripilation and so on that are reactions present in the female and male characters, in the actors,[24] or when narrated in poetry should actually be classified as foundational *factors* for their capacity to produce rasa in the audience. Insofar as they come to exist also in the spectator, however, and in the listener and reader and so on, they become again diagnostic of rasa, being its effects.

With respect to the "foundational factors" mentioned in the memorial verse: when these really exist,[25] what they cause to transform into rasa is a stable emotion in relation to some specific object, and in that case, the apprehension of the savoring of rasa makes reference to that specific object. A young man savors as the erotic rasa the stable emotion of desire that he feels for a specific young woman who feels passion for him as well. But where the desire arises with respect to a woman in love with someone else, and thus has a generalized object[26] as it comes to be strengthened into rasa, there will be no savoring of the erotic rasa toward a specific object, since what the foundational factors are manifesting is in fact a stable emotion with respect to a general object. Likewise, when one observes a woman weeping in grief for some beloved one, one will be savoring the tragic rasa of a generalized object.[27] This distinction between general and specific object is applicable to the other rasas too.

In the case of the foundational factors narrated in a poem or acted out on the stage, which are presented as if they really do exist when they do not,[28] it can only be the viewer/reader's stable emotion toward a general object that is being transformed into rasa by these factors: in this case, the apprehension of savoring rasa is independent of any differentiation of the object.[29] After all, when Rama's erotic rasa with reference to Sita is being imitated, what presents itself to the audience is not erotic rasa for Sita per se, but rather for woman in general. (However, should our stable emotion come to be directed toward a particular object by virtue of our remembering [161] such an object,[30] then our savoring of rasa could indeed be said to have a particular object.) Accordingly, the foundational factors, which really exist in the case of the character and are only brought to life for the viewer/reader when narrated in poetry or acted out in drama, are common to many. Hence, one person's savoring of rasa does not confute it[31] for others,[32] and the relationship is accordingly one of broad inclusiveness, not of narrow exclusiveness.[33] Thus, the savoring of rasa, in the storyworld (for the characters) and in the artwork (for the viewer/reader), is the same for all *rasikas*, but not, for all that, totally without reference to some specific ground.[34] No mental state arises without reference to some ground, and rasa is after all a mental state.

As for the transitory emotions mentioned in the memorial verse,[35] these enhance a stable emotion once it is manifested by the foundational factors and are to be understood as belonging to anyone experiencing rasa. For when a stable emotion is revealed to be on the point of becoming rasa thanks to some foundational factor—the female character, say, in herself[36] and when she is presented in a literary text or acted out on the stage[37]—the transitory emotions, in a way appropriate to a given rasa, also become manifest. For no rasa can become manifest without its accompanying transient emotion: anxiety about the woman, say, in the case of the erotic, or satisfaction in the comic, depression in the tragic, vindictiveness in the violent, joy in the heroic, fright in the fearful, disquiet in the macabre, longing in the fantastic, despair in the peaceful. Just as[38] rasa cannot come into existence, even if you grasp the meaning of the literary text or see the woman on the stage, if you are not paying attention or have given up all worldly attachments, so it cannot come into existence in the absence of the appropriate accompanying transitory emotion, anxiety or whatever the case may be. The fact that we sometimes do not perceive these transitory emotions because they are so subtle or fleeting is no counterargument to the above statement. Being manifested and enhancing the stable emotion that is on the point of becoming rasa, the transitory emotions turn it into rasa. It is for this reason we say that the transitory emotions *accompany* stable emotions when they are on the point of becoming rasa, whereas the foundational factors *precede* them.

As for the transitory emotions in the female and male characters when narrated in a poem or acted out on the stage, as these reveal a stable emotion on the point of becoming rasa, they, like the reactions[39] previously mentioned, become *foundational factors* in the case of the audience,[40] insofar as these transitory emotions can produce rasa. The term "transitory emotions" and "reactions" refer both to what pertains to the characters themselves and, when narrated in a poem or imitated on the stage, to the reader and viewer.[41] Similarly, in Bharata's *Sutra*, "Rasa arises . . . ," the reactions and transitory emotions are to be understood as referring both to the characters in themselves and to when these reactions and emotions are narrated in a poem or imitated in a drama.

To conclude, then, rasa belongs to the character,[42] the actor, the listener or reader of poetry, and the viewer of drama; it is pleasurable or painful in nature; and it is directly cognizable[43] when it is a personal experience, and indirectly when it is the experience of another. Only in the case of the principal male and female characters does the rasa have a clear and distinct form, since the foundational factors actually exist for them; for the same reason, the transitory emotions and reactions existing in them, which are produced by rasa, also have a clear and distinct form. Elsewhere, that is, in the viewers and so on, rasa exists only in an "impure" form, since the foundational factors do not actually exist at all but are only made to appear via the poem or drama. For the same reason, the transitory emotions and reactions in the audience that arise in conformity with the rasa are also indistinct. It is for this reason that the rasa in the audience, listener, and reader is said to be supernormal.[44]

The literary artwork can be said to "have rasa" or be "rasa-laden"[45] only insofar as it *possesses the factors* that bring rasa to light; the work is not itself rasa, of course, but neither does rasa exist in the work [162] as in a vessel. For rasa is a stable emotion in the form of a mental state that is "intensified." How then could it be the "self" of an insensate thing like a literary work,[46] or be contained within it? Accordingly, we say that it is upon understanding the subject matter of the literary work that rasa is manifested to the understanding subject. The subject savors rasa in himself as a kind of pleasure, and does not apprehend it as something external to him, like a piece of candy. The savoring of candy is one thing, the apprehension of rasa another altogether. The notion of our merely apprehending rasa as something existing outside ourselves cannot be reconciled with our savoring rasa as a kind of relishing. For it is the fear and grief that exist as events in the mind of the understanding subject that get transformed into the fearful and tragic rasas through the corresponding foundational factors and other elements of the literary text. If it were not precisely the stable emotion of the subject that comes into being as rasa, then rasa would be something external, and it would make no sense to speak of its being apprehended, since rasa does not exist as such in the literary work, or in the actor, or in any other such thing. And only on the absurd assumption that we could apprehend something nonexistent could we apprehend a rasa not present in our own heart. Therefore, what becomes rasa is the understanding subject's own stable emotion upon understanding the literary work that communicates the foundational factors, and it is only because the work is itself the source of those factors that it is said to "have rasa," or be "rasa-laden."

On the Nature of Dramatic Acting

(p. 188.8) Acting (*abhinaya*) is that whereby the subject matter of the drama is brought (*nīyate*) visibly before the eyes (*ābhi-mukhyena*) of the audience. . . . Writers compose their works out of particular actions that reveal the emotions of the characters. A case in point is verbal acting, to take that register, for this does not consist of one person (the actor) merely repeating imprecisely what another person (the character) has said. Now, the imitation that makes up the various kinds of acting comes from a *conviction*,[47] not from the presence of some really existing thing, since neither the actor nor the viewers have themselves ever actually seen the character, Rama, say, who is the object of imitation. And any subject doing the imitating who has never seen the original is certainly not capable of imitating it. Nor is a viewer who has not seen the original capable of accepting that the imitator is producing an imitation. Accordingly, the actor studies the story of Rama presented by the poet and, accepting the poet's vision gained through extraordinary application,[48] consciously decides to present an imitation. In actual fact, however, he is simply following real-world behavior. Even though he himself may be happy, he weeps when Rama is supposed to weep, and does not laugh; though he himself may be sad, he laughs when Rama is supposed to laugh, and does not weep, and so forth. The viewers too, once they hear the word "Rama" and grasp its conventional meaning, at the same time becoming enthralled by the beautiful music, become convinced[49] that the actors are Rama and the other characters,[50] who, distinguished though they are from those characters by a host of differences of time, space, and nature, approximate them by concealing that distinction through the fourfold process of acting. As a consequence, such viewers come to be fully absorbed in Rama's different states, whether happy or sad or whatever. Other thinkers, however, hold that, whereas the registers of acting, the conventional meaning of "Rama," the music, and all the rest may convince us that the actors are the characters, the didactic element is foremost, and they focus their minds completely on the dimension of instruction, on affirming what is right and rejecting what is bad.

An alternative way to understand the question of imitation is as follows: the sages with their wisdom and insight into past, present, and future determined every single one of Rama's traits without exception—his precise features, the way he walked and talked, his moments of anger, his graceful movements, and so on—and poets present them in their dramas. And the actor, because of his confidence in the sages' knowledge in these matters, is able to display this right before our eyes. Moreover, [189] whereas those who see with physical eyes can sometimes err with respect to the true nature of a thing, those who see with the eye of wisdom cannot. And since the actor is truly imitating what the sages' wisdom has revealed, which we understand to be even more valid than the sight of the thing itself, on what grounds should the poor fellow be reproached by the half-educated? The spectators, whether or not they have their own views in this matter, most decidedly come to believe that the actor is Rama; otherwise, they would realize that it was pure artifice and could never come to be fully absorbed in Rama's happiness and sadness. And indeed, the erotic and other rasas can certainly arise from a pure illusion: how otherwise could a man behold in a dream his beloved, an enemy, a thief, or the like and exhibit the various reactions, paralysis and so on, that are the first shoots of the rasa plant?

THE SINGLE STRAND OF VIDYADHARA (C. 1300) WITH THE *CENTRAL GEM* OF MALLINATHA (C. 1400)

That the *Single Strand* is the work of a poet is evident in almost every line, but the author also tells us at the start that he has conceived his treatise as a new poetic genre: the handbook on rhetoric that at the same time, through the poetry examples it provides, functions as an encomium on a king, in this case, Narasimha of Utkala/Kalinga (today's Odisha), for whom Vidyadhara worked as court poet:

> From among the three types of discourses of instruction[51] I, Vidyadhara, will provide an account of the discourse that has been likened to a beloved, while offering as examples poems of praise in honor of King Narasimha.
>
> No one but King Narasimha is worthy of my literary craft. Who but the moon-crested Shiva can bear the waters of the Ganges?[52]

The genre of praise poem as poetics manual that Vidyadhara created in his treatise was to be imitated repeatedly over the coming centuries in both Sanskrit and vernacular works.

The one place the poet does not use his own compositions as examples is in his analysis of rasa in the third chapter. "In discussing the rasas," he writes, "I adduce only poems written by others in order to demonstrate the type of implicature where rasa is dominant, for if I were to adduce my own praise poems to the king, the poet's feelings—that is, my own feelings of desire—would be dominant, not the rasa."[53] As we have seen, the idea was first hinted at by Udbhata in the early ninth century and more fully developed by Mammata in the second half of the eleventh that poetry where the stable emotion of desire is directed toward a "deity or comparable figure," that is, a sage, a guru, or indeed, one's king, cannot develop into a rasa. The desire is obviously of a different order from the sexual, and the object of affect does not fulfill the requirements laid down in the *Treatise on Drama* for the erotic rasa (a man and a woman, both young, both of high status). The sentiment cannot be "enhanced," and will thus remain "emotion." But in addition to these formal constraints, in a eulogy to a patron (no less than in a prayer to a god), the emotional attachment of the poet (or suppliant) is the poem's overriding concern—the "dominant" feeling—and in turn subordinates to itself any other emotion described in or generated by the poem.[54] Vidyadhara could therefore never successfully illustrate rasa were he to have used, as he does throughout the rest of the work, poems written in honor of his king.[55]

Vidyadhara was a careful student of the *Light on Implicature*, the *Ten Dramatic Forms*, and the *Light on Poetry*, for whose views he provides a good précis. This is especially the case in his discussion of the incapacity in the face of rasa of the different means of valid knowledge or linguistic modalities (by this date, most thinkers simply accept the implicature of rasa and do not bother to argue it out). The *Single Strand* merits attention for such small amplifications and modifications, no less than for its style. Other innovations include the argument that when animals are the subject of a literary work, they are indeed "receptacles of rasa," and not, as earlier writers had asserted, of "semblance of rasa." The core question here is: What do we experience when we read a poem or see a play about an animal shown to feel desire or fear? Do we have an experience of rasa, or of the semblance of rasa? If we can only "actualize" the feeling that the original character experienced, our answer depends on whether an animal can be a "receptacle" of rasa. But what does it mean, cognitively, to be such a receptacle? For earlier writers such as Kuntaka, animals, unlike higher beings, do not possess the requisite emotional apparatus for rasa, but have only "impulses."[56] Bhoja defines the very category of "semblance" in his *Necklace* as "the presence of rasa in characters of low status, animals, antagonists, or entities referenced in a merely metaphorical manner," and in the introduction to his *Light on Passion* denies that an animal can be the locus of rasa.[57] Abhinavagupta, by contrast, places at the very start of his "reconstruction" a verse on the fearful rasa where the subject is the stable emotion of fear felt (he makes clear) by the deer chased by King Dushyanta in *Shakuntala*. So

Vidyadhara's question was a live one, and in its own way, expressive of some large issues about rasa.

For earlier writers, judgment about the nature of rasa in the literary representation of animals was tied up with the question of the analytical locus of rasa. If this was squarely the literary character, as held by Kuntaka and Bhoja, it would seem to make no sense to attribute rasa to an animal; for Abhinava, by contrast, for whom the analytic had shifted entirely to reception, the original character did not really experience rasa anyway, and hence it was entirely reasonable for the viewer to have a rasa experience in the presence of such a representation. Vidyadhara's account itself is too brief to give us a nuanced sense of his position. He only affirms that "animals *can indeed have* rasa" (though in the précis he took from the *Light on Poetry* he asserts that only the audience, not characters, can have rasa).[58] This strong position would be ridiculed by Singabhupala later in the century. He would deny that animals have an emotional life, and accordingly insist that the viewer/reader's experience of such poetry must be a "semblance of rasa"—because such is precisely the experience of the animal itself.

The high status of *The Single Strand* in the tradition of poetics in south India is indicated by the presence of a detailed exegesis provided by Mallinatha (c. 1400). This notable scholar wrote commentaries on all the major courtly epics, but on no other nonliterary treatise. By his act of homage he affirmed the judgment on the work that the later history of its influence would render.

FROM *THE SINGLE STRAND* OF VIDYADHARA (V) WITH *THE CENTRAL GEM* OF MALLINATHA (M)

(V) (p. 85) With respect to the type of implicature by which rasa is manifested, namely, where the succession from the expressed to the implied is not registered, there is no scholarly dispute. For after all, rasa is not simply the factors, the reactions, and the transitory emotions; [86] instead, it *arises from* them. And thus while a succession does indeed exist, it happens too quickly for us to register when we apprehend the factors and so on, any more than we register the succession when a hundred lotus petals are all pierced by a needle.[59] And hence this type of manifestation receives the apposite name "where the succession is not registered."

There are eight types of this sort of implicature: rasa, emotion, semblance of rasa, semblance of emotion, cessation, emergence, conjuncture, and oscillation of emotion. Where one of these eight achieves predominance, it becomes the object toward which any figural elaboration is directed; where, however, no predominance is achieved, the eight types themselves become figures, the "rasa-laden" expression and the like. First we shall describe the essential nature of rasa.

When a stable emotion like desire and so on starts to sprout thanks to the foundational factors such as a beautiful woman; branches out owing to the stimulant factors such as the moon, the cuckoo's call, the Malabar breeze, a pleasure garden; becomes apprehensible because of the reactions, such as the sidelong glances of the woman's eyes, her smiles, her enfolding her lover in the vines of her arms; [87] begins to blossom with the transitory emotions such as anxiety and the like; in a way not to be experienced through direct denotation, nor conveyed to the ear through sentence purport, nor made the object of secondary meaning, nor brought into the sphere of sensory perception, nor led into one's cognitive precincts by inference, nor carried along its path by memory, nor affected by being an effect,[60] nor known as some thing to be made known, nor schooled in limitation, since all other objects of cognition vanish in its presence; existing in the tight embrace[61] of a unique function called implicature, as a predisposition in the audience, having nothing to do with character or actor: when the stable emotion achieves this state, it is termed the erotic or other rasa. [88] It is something that exists only so long as the aesthetic elements exist; that is savored on the analogy of the mixed drink of many ingredients, the savoring itself being its sole mode of existence; that flashes forth as a veritable soulmate of the savoring of supreme being, and effects a transcendent amazement.[62]

(M) (p. 88.18) Just as the bliss of supreme being, though ever existent, illuminates itself for spiritual adepts only so long as the current of their meditation flows in a stream, but neither before nor after meditation, so in the case of rasa too. It is an exudation of the bliss of the self—which is also an ever-existent entity—and reveals itself, all other objects of cognition vanishing in its presence, as the removal of the heart's obscurations[63] assisted by the implicature function, for those whose minds are skilled at comprehending literature.

(V) [89] Not even in one's wildest dreams would it be possible to argue that rasa can be directly expressed. To explain: rasa in that case would have to be expressed either by the word "rasa" or by such words as "the erotic" and so on, but neither is possible. Even if the word "rasa" is not employed, rasa can become a traveler on the path of our apprehension only if the aesthetic elements are communicated; and rasa does not enter onto the path of apprehension even if the word "rasa" is employed so long as the aesthetic elements themselves are not employed. From this positive and negative concomitance we conclude that it is the aesthetic elements that are directly expressed, and only thereby does rasa become available to our apprehension—and that therefore, rasa itself must be something that is implied.[64]

Now, if you should imagine that rasa falls instead into the domain of sentence purport, this can hardly withstand scrutiny. Rasa is not a locus of direct expression, whereas sentence purport exercises its power in what is directly expressed. When predicate and subject are enunciated together, the subject is taken up for the sake of the predicate; the predicate is what is not otherwise given. Consider the sentence [90], "The priests move about wearing red turbans." The movement of the priests is already given from some other source of knowledge (in this case, the context); what is being predicated is the fact of their wearing red turbans.[65] Thus elsewhere, we can conclude, the verbal function we call the purport of a sentence exercises its power with regard to the signification so far as it has been directly expressed and is otherwise not given, but not with regard to any and every implication. Were sentence purport to have power to express what is implicit as well, then in a sentence like "The former man is running," the purport would issue in other meanings such as "The latter man is running." But sentence purport does not in fact function to tell us whether the other man is running or not.[66]

Nor can the argument be sustained that rasa is conveyed by secondary meaning. That arises only when the primary meaning is blocked, but the primary meaning of the aesthetic elements is never in fact blocked when they manifest rasa. As for the possibility of rasa's being grasped by perception, it would have to be grasped through either nonconceptual or conceptual sense experience. It cannot be the former, since only a distinct comprehension of the aesthetic elements enables rasa to be invested with existence, [91] whereas nonconceptual sense experience isolates merely the thing itself, the percept, devoid of all qualification. But neither can rasa be the object of conceptual sense experience, since that always follows directly upon nonconceptual sense experience, and if an effect could arise in the absence of a cause one would never go to the trouble of providing one.

One might ask why rasa cannot be understood to be something we infer: an actor skilled in portraying a foundational factor like Rama, who responds with pleasure or pain when he is together with or separated from Sita, exhibits his feelings, and as the audience member observes these and reflects upon the various feelings arising in himself that he had previously experienced, he infers Rama's own condition and [92] thereby experiences pleasure or pain himself. But that view too is false. The aesthetic elements are not real *causes* of these feelings, such that they are rendered capable of establishing a relationship of invariable concomitance known to all; they have merely the capacity for suggesting it, and hence cannot be actual inferential signs. Since the aesthetic elements do not have any real function as causes and so on with respect to rasa, the inferential capacity concomitant with that causal status must also be abandoned. In the real world we do not have factors, reactions, and transitory emotions, but rather things called causes, effects, and ancillary causes.

(M) Moreover, no matter how beautiful something may be, if it were in the possession of someone else and only inferred, it would in effect be entirely indiscernible. Hence the very idea that it could be present as savoring, that it could bring about supermundane rapture, as rasa actually does, would be utter nonsense.

(V) [93] How, lastly, could rasa be something in the realm of memory? When an external object arises in the self by means of contact with the senses in the course of our experience of it, the object deposits a subliminal impression, and through that a memory arises at some later time. It is thus a previous experience, by way of a deposit of a subliminal impression, that functions as the cause of a memory. But there is no actual previous experience with respect to rasa; there is only an experience of the aesthetic elements that is figuratively taken as an experience of rasa. Then again, if we were to admit that rasa had once been really experienced, it would contradict the tenet that rasa is "manifested." Since there is no relevant prior experience of rasa, there can be no memory of it, and hence rasa cannot be an object of memory, but instead must be "manifested."

Moreover, when I say here that rasa is not some thing that is effected, I mean that it is not some thing actually brought into being by the aesthetic elements located in the actor. [94] And when I assert that rasa is not some thing made known to us, my point is that, since Rama's real desire is long gone, it cannot possibly be made known to us in the standard ways, such as by contact of a sense organ with something temporally and spatially present, or by inference or testimony.

(M) Rama's desire is used here merely as an example of the fact that rasa is beyond sensory perception. For present desire could no more be made known in the rasa process than past desire. If we took our author's words literally and held that *present* desire can be made known, this would be in contradiction with the entire foregoing and succeeding section of the book, and it would at the same time negate the impossibility[67] of knowing past desire through verbal testimony or inference.

(V) Hence, the aesthetic elements, since they neither bring about anything nor make anything known, can be considered a cause only insofar as they enable relishing; in other words, they are a supermundane cause, and thereby make manifest the fact that rasa itself must be supermundane. [95] To quote: "With what can rasa be compared? It is at once of this world and beyond; proved to exist thanks to causal factors yet not an effect; a conceptual sense experience and yet nonconceptual."[68]

Some have argued that "rasa is the savoring of supermundane pleasure in the hearts of viewers of literature that is seen, and of those capable of fully imagining literature that is heard."[69] And one might then wonder on what grounds one can justify the claim that the tragic and the like, given that they are painful, can be rasas.

But such an objection would be wrong. The state of bliss referred to is that which arises when all other objects of cognition have vanished. And if that bliss should flash forth when listening to poetry, by virtue of a proper presentation of factors, reactions, and transitory emotions, how could one claim there is any feeling of pain even in the case of the tragic rasa?

[96] "When there is a fusion of the mind with the meaning of the literary work, there arises the bliss that is the self, which constitutes the savoring of rasa. This fusion is of four sorts: an expansion, enlargement, turbulence, or agitation of the mind":[70] expansion as of a flower, enlargement as of a tree crown, turbulence as of the ocean, agitation as of the wind.

The erotic is "conditioned by"[71] expansion, the heroic by enlargement, the macabre by turbulence, and the violent by agitation. These "conditions" are the different mental planes.[72] The comic, fantastic, tragic, and fearful have the same conditions, expansion and so on, respectively, and thus the erotic and so on stand to them in relation of affinity, not causality,[73] since we see that each of the pairs (the erotic and the comic, and so on) is distinctive in its causes, the aesthetic elements and so on.

Some say there is a ninth rasa, the peaceful . . . [98] and we accept this and agree that there are nine and only nine rasas. The king, however, in his *Light on Passion*, has accepted only one rasa, namely, the erotic.[74]

(M) Insofar as Bhoja's work is fatally impaired by its contradictions with the foundational works of Bharata and so on, simply ignoring it, as Vidyadhara does, is the best critique.[75]

. . . .

(p. 103) We call it "emotion" rather than rasa when [1] desire is directed toward a deity, a Brahman, a teacher, a son, a friend, and the like; or [2] when a transitory emotion is completely endowed with all the aesthetic elements.[76] As for [1], all authorities agree on restricting the erotic rasa to desire directed toward a beloved. An example of "emotion" toward a deity:[77]

Even if he severs the head of Brahma, rejoices in friendship with the dead,
gets drunk and plays with the Mothers, delights in cremation grounds,
creates beings only to destroy them—still, in deep devotion
I serve him, what else? He is the only lord; the rest of the universe is empty.[78]

[104] We could also cite an example where the object is a Brahman and so on;[79] when the object is a son, however, some have identified this as a separate rasa called tenderness.

(M) "And so on" is meant to include also kings worthy of description, for which the author's own eulogistic poems may be adduced as examples.

(V) Now as for [2], although it is true that the literary work as a whole lives from rasa—which is in essence homogeneous rapture—it still sometimes happens that we derive even greater rapture from a given transitory emotion. When this occurs we call it "emotion" too, the emotion being manifested by the factors and the reactions. An example:

Foolish moon, do you really think the mind of Bhima's daughter
would be absorbed in *you* now that she has no need of life?
The great scholar, Love, rightly explained the relevant holy text to me
by saying the moon intended is the moonlike face of Nala.[80]

[105] Here we apprehend Damayanti's deep resentment toward the moon.[81] And although this is a poem of the erotic thwarted, a greater degree of savor comes from the rapture produced by the transitory emotion here known as resentment.

"Semblance of rasa" is as in the following verse:

Brahma, now is no time for Veda recitation, stand outside in silence;
cease your chattering, silly Brhaspati, this is not Indra's court;
silence your vina, Narada, and you too, Tumbara, your eulogies:
the lord of Lanka is unwell, his heart pierced by the arrow of longing for Sita.

There is no possible way [106] for anyone other than the goodly Rama ever to be a receptacle for the love of the princess of Mithila. Accordingly, Ravana's desire for her is something that operates entirely through impropriety, and hence here the rasa of the erotic thwarted has become "semblance of rasa." The gist of the matter is as follows. Rasa arises only where the stable emotion surges over a young couple to their *mutual* satisfaction; where only one of them feels passion, however, the stable emotion is operating through impropriety, and we have semblance of rasa.

Some assert that in the case of animals there can only be semblance of rasa, but that position cannot withstand scrutiny, since the aesthetic elements can function in the case of animals too. It is wrong to argue that since animals are devoid of awareness of the foundational factor and other aesthetic elements they are not an appropriate receptacle of rasa. For some human beings can be equally unaware, and we would then be forced to deny that they too can be loci[82] of rasa. Here again, it is the sheer presence of the aesthetic elements that actuates the rasa, not awareness of them *as* aesthetic elements. So animals can indeed have rasa.

(M) The objector's doubt is whether animals can be the substratum of rasa since, even though the aesthetic elements are present, animals are incapable of registering them. . . . The awareness that actualizes rasa, the author argues, must pertain to the aesthetic elements either *as* aesthetic elements or merely as things in themselves. He excludes the first option. . . . Being "loci" of rasa means being the substratum. . . . "Presence" means presence of an awareness of the things in themselves, and not awareness of the aesthetic elements, that is, the distinctive awareness that they *are* aesthetic elements. For otherwise, if you deny the role of awareness as such, it would turn out that actions and the like, even were they to go completely unperceived, could still be stimulant factors.

(V) For example:

The cow elephant gave the bull a trunkful of water fragrant with lily pollen;
the *cakravāka* bird honored his mate by means of a half-eaten lotus filament.[83]

[107] Here the bull elephant is the foundational factor that engenders the stable emotion desire; the springtime and so on are the stimulant factors that stimulate it; the giving of the fragrant water from the cow elephant's trunk is the reaction that manifests it; the joy and so on are the transitory emotions that enhance it. Thereby the desire achieves the state of the erotic rasa enjoyed.

ORNAMENT OF THE FAME OF KING PRATAPARUDRA OF VIDYANATHA (C. 1320) WITH *THE JEWEL STORE* OF KUMARASVAMIN (C. 1430)

Like Vidyadhara, Vidyanatha produced a treatise on poetics that at the same time functioned—as loudly proclaimed in the title itself—as an encomium to his patron, Prataparudra, king of Warangal (in today's Andhra Pradesh) in the first decades of the fourteenth century. Like Vidyadhara too, Vidyanatha was lucky in attracting a brilliant commentator: Kumarasvamin, the son of Mallinatha, Vidyadhara's exegete.

Vidyanatha himself does not add much to the history of rasa theory.[84] All his key ideas are taken from Dhanika: the "commonization" of the foundational factor, for example, and even the notion that rasa and the aesthetic elements can be homologized to sentence meaning and its constitutive words. And there is a kind of imprecision to his restatements that renders Vidyanatha's Dhanika considerably less perspicuous than Dhanika himself. For example, Dhanika's (and Bhatta Nayaka's) analogy between stable emotions and aesthetic elements on the one hand and sentence meanings and word meaning on the other is completely recast so as to conform with the idea of "manifestation." The notion of "actualization," *bhāvanā*, moreover, is no longer the commonization of the foundational factor like Sita or Malati into woman as such, leading to a reexperiencing in distilled form of the experience of the fictional character; it now refers, in a way more explicitly stated than when the idea was first presented in the *Mirror of Drama* (and subsequently in Rudra Bhatta's *Bud of Rasa*) to an *imagining* of *one's own beloved* (here Kumarasvamin seems to say both that it is one's own beloved being imagined and that the factor is being imagined as one's own beloved).[85] Such imprecision, or perhaps more charitably redefinition, is especially evident in the case of Vidyanatha's understanding of the locus of rasa. In intellectual-historical terms, the fact that the topic is raised yet again, and contested—how little Abhinavagupta seems to have settled the matter for these southern writers—is significant in itself. But Vidyanatha's conclusion remains somewhat ambiguous. "The substratum of rasa is the character and the character alone," he insists at the start of his exposition; what the viewer/reader experiences, by contrast, is "bliss." Yet at the end of his account he states that rasa "exists, with respect to the real world"—the world inside the narrative—"in the character alone, and with respect to the drama, in the audience." Vidyanatha's basic idea seems to be that rasa actually and truly is something that occurs only in the character; it is by hermeneutical actualization that the viewer/reader experiences it, and in that case the rasa cannot be called real but rather transcendent of reality, or "supermundane," for which "bliss"—*ānanda*, with its Upanishadic resonances—is the signifier of choice.[86] Kumarasvamin sharpens the distinction between rasa and bliss by repeatedly stressing that the former is mundane, the latter supermundane, a distinction that would be further modified by the theorists of devotional rasa (see chapter 6.3). He nicely captures the difference between the character's rasa and our experience of it by the analogy of the happiness a father feels upon seeing his son's happiness. Kumarasvamin's own views, however, are far more radical.

We have seen the homology repeatedly drawn between the experience of rasa and the experience of supreme being since the idea was introduced by Bhatta Nayaka in the early tenth century: rasa experience "shares something of the character of," "is something similar to," or "closely approximates" the experience of *brahma*.[87] For Kumarasvamin, for whom "the final doctrine is that rasa has no location at all," rasa is held to be "*identical* to the bliss of supreme being." The only difference is that in the rasa experience, the cognizing subject preserves an awareness of objects, i.e., the aesthetic elements, whereas the spiritual adept does not.[88] For this view Kumarasvamin draws on innovative thinkers who have almost completely vanished from intellectual history, including one Naraharisuri (from whom nothing is extant) and Amaranandayogin, whose *Lamp for Spiritual Discipline of the Inner Self* was nearly lost.[89] His formulation represents another step in the Vedanticization of rasa discourse, which was first intimated by Dhanika and further developed by Vishvanatha (in the next selection, the *Mirror of Literary Art*), and which would come into full flower in the early seventeenth century.

FROM *ORNAMENT OF THE FAME OF KING PRATAPARUDRA* OF VIDYANATHA (V) WITH *THE JEWEL STORE* OF KUMARASVAMIN (K)

(V) (p. 205) Here we would note that the substratum of rasa is the character and the character alone. There is nothing contradictory, however, about the fact that rasa should be visibly "actualized" for the audience by the actions of a talented actor or from listening to a great work of poetry; and that accordingly rasa, albeit located in one person (the character), might generate pure bliss in another (the viewer/reader) through proper "actualization." Another way to put this is as follows: there is nothing contradictory about the fact that, although on hearing the name "Malati" the audience members have an apprehension of woman in general, the character enables them to call to mind some particular woman so that the audience can also become the substratum of rasa.[90] As for the actor, being concerned exclusively with the process of imitation, he is not fit to be regarded as a substratum of rasa. And if one were to argue that he too experiences rasa,[91] it would only be because he was for the moment being regarded as an audience member.[92] The fact that he manifests reactions and so on is to be explained as a result of his training, practice, and talent, and not because he is experiencing rasa.

(K) (p. 203.15) Literary rasa is of two sorts, mundane and supermundane. The former is like the pleasure derived from savoring a plantain or mango, and is something produced and hence transitory. The latter is the veritable soulmate of the bliss of supreme being, and is permanent.[93] It is the former the author is discussing when he says, "The substratum. . . ." The hero who is being portrayed, Rama for example, is the substratum of rasa. The adverb "alone" is meant to exclude anyone or anything else. If, however, this were really the case, the audience's repeated eagerness to watch dramatic acting and listen to literature would resemble the behavior of a madman. The author accordingly says, "There is nothing contradictory. . . ." "'Actualized'" means regarded as connected exclusively to oneself.[94] In literature there comes about, accordingly, a blissful happiness like that of a father seeing his son's happiness. This is what is meant by the following verse in the *Light on Emotion*: "To feel contentment in the presence of contentment, grief in the presence of grief, anger in the presence of anger, fear in the presence of fear is to be the ideal spectator."[95] But there is also a difference between what the character and the viewer feel, which the author refers to with "albeit located in one person." It makes perfectly good sense that there should be a difference in bliss as a result of a difference that comes from this process of actualization. The author turns to supermundane rasa with "Another way to put this. . . ."[96]

"On hearing the name Malati" one has a notion of woman in general, with no particular reference to the woman Malati herself. . . . "The character enables them to call to mind": since it is clear that calling to mind a particular on apprehending some general is rooted in the concomitance of the two. [204] There is no need to demand proof that a viewer eliminates all particularity in characters like Malati when they are mentioned in a play or poem, and thereby can call to mind his own beloved. Particularities are not what is intended in a poem. It is not the states of sheer individuality[97] of characters like Rama that great poets like Valmiki perceive in their moments of inspiration and describe in their poems, but rather states common to everyone, which the poets grasp by the power of their creative genius while using Rama merely as a substratum. To quote the author of the *Six Thousand*, "Rasa arises from these elements in conjunction with the quality of generality."[98] One might then ask why poets do not simply eliminate all particularity and make use only of generality. But savoring is possible for readers only if particularity is made use of. To quote: "When children play with clay elephants, it is their own particular will they thereby savor. This is just what readers do with Arjuna and the rest."[99] (Note that when the author writes "some particular woman," we are meant to understand as well her reactions—her sidelong glances at the hero, and so on—and transitory emotions, despair and the rest, since rasa cannot arise from woman as such.)

One might be willing to admit that a particular man or woman is indeed called to mind by the viewer, but still wonder how rasa can thereby arise, and how the viewer can become the substratum of rasa. In response we offer the following considerations. The hearts of the viewers are first prepared by certain inferences they make about the passion and so on of the real-world male and female protagonists; thereupon, by the power of literary language, they "actualize" Rama and so on as connected to themselves in a generalized form; thus actualized, Rama and the others appear as if fully present in the courtyard of the mind of the actualizing viewer/reader. As Bhartrhari says, "One grasps characters in literature such as Kamsa as causally active."[100] There is nothing improper about "actualizing" characters like the lordly Rama and Sita as one's own husband or wife. For, as we have said, they lose all their particularities—as the son of Dasharatha or the daughter of Janaka—and correspond to man and woman as such. This man and woman are real-world beings who are consecrated in the position of aesthetic element by way of literary representation or dramatic acting, and as they are "actualized" by the sensitive viewers they are reflected in their hearts, on the analogy of a seal stamped by a signet ring, and come to be located in the audience. In the same way, Rama and Sita's desire and so on are real-world feelings, but they are consecrated into the emperorship of the supermundane stable emotions. The aesthetic elements too, more generally, are completely supermundane, since they are the object of a verbal apprehension that is itself supermundane, which we indicate by using terms like "relishing." This relishing is entirely different from other kinds of apprehension; whereby we do not ask, any more than in the case of a realistic painting of a horse, whether it is truly that, is not that, may be that, or is similar to that.

Arising from this set of factors, the *supermundane* sort of rasa has its substratum in the audience as a result of its being[101] a transformation of the stable emotion reflected onto the hearts of the audience. On this matter, as the author will remark at the end of the chapter, there is unanimity among the ancient authorities. And it is with this in mind that he says, [205] "The audience can thereby also become the substratum. . . ." Indeed, it is impossible for there to be any other substratum of supermundane rasa; whoever maintains the contrary would have to answer whether this other substratum is the character or the actor. It cannot be the character since he is dead and gone. Nor can it be the actor, as the author proceeds to show. . . .

(p. 206) The author summarizes the nature of rasa in three verses for ease of comprehension.[102]

(V) (4.136) Assisted by the beauty of language qualities and figures of speech, the power of a stable emotion—at whose sudden emergence thoughts of all other objects of cognition gradually vanish—transforms into the full weight of rasa in the heart of the receptive reader, so as to consist of pure bliss, whatever the pain or pleasure it may cause to congeal in the young lovers in the story.[103]

(K) (p. 206) First of all, as the viewer's attention is focused on the poetry or the dramatic acting and at the moment rasa begins to emerge,[104] he develops a firm apprehension that the actor is Rama. Next, the viewer apprehends that his own heart and the character's are identical. Then, the viewer's heart is submerged in the various properties of the play, the dance, the song, and so on, and thereupon thoughts of all other objects of cognition vanish. At that point, supermundane rasa, which is comparable to the bliss of supreme being known to spiritual adepts, becomes itself the locus of relishing.[105] To quote: "When rasa has reached plenitude. . . ."[106] The author has all this in mind when he says, "All other objects of cognition gradually vanish." There is this difference, however: when one is experiencing the bliss of supreme being, no empirical object whatever appears, whereas in savoring rasa, all objects of cognition are eliminated except for the aesthetic elements. . . .[107]

[209] The author now responds to the query how this kind of rasa is actually apprehended in a poem:

(V) (4.137) Rasa acts like sentence meaning; the aesthetic elements are like word meanings, finding in sentence meaning the point where apprehension properly comes to rest.[108] It is, accordingly, the stable emotions, empowering each other as they gradually arise,[109] that bear within themselves the coming-into-being of rasa, as threads bear the coming-into-being of cloth.[110]

(K) (pp. 207–9) "Rasa . . . sentence meaning": This is so formulated because it is rasa that has primacy among the poet's ultimate aims. To quote: "Authorities regard as 'sentence meaning' whatever is conceived of as having primacy according to the poet's intention."[111] This "sentence meaning" cannot be either primary or secondary meaning, depending on whichever doctrine one accepts, like the sentence meaning that emerges from the various linguistic processes (such as syntactic construal and so on),[112] since there is no question of direct or indirect signification in this analysis. As for the specific notion of "sentence purport," it has already been set forth in the chapter on poetry[113] that this is subsumed under "manifestation." Hence, what we must understand here by "sentence meaning" is precisely "manifested meaning."[114] Those aesthetic elements, by contrast, that manifest rasa—the foundational factor and so on—are "word meanings." Although each element does indeed constitute a word meaning with respect to its own sentence (to quote the *Light on Emotion*: "A stable emotion, a psychophysical response, or a transient emotion can under different circumstances become a sentence meaning as a result of its predominance"),[115] nonetheless they are referred to as "word meanings" because they perform a subordinate function with regard to rasa. The upshot of the matter is that rasa can be likened to sentence meaning since it flashes forth only after we apprehend the factors and so on,[116] which can therefore be likened to word meanings. . . . When the author says, "bear within themselves the coming-into-being of rasa," he means the following: at first the stable emotions exist only as predispositions, but by virtue of the aesthetic elements they transform into rasa—indeed, become something we only then are able to refer to as "rasa."

(V) (4.138) As the power of desire or other stable emotion slowly swells like the ocean, additional emotions, wavelike, continuously arise and disappear.[117] Rasa is a deep self-savoring brought about by the experience of these transitory emotions, despair and the rest, and, as we have said, exists, with respect to the real world,[118] in the character alone, and with respect to the drama itself, in the audience.

(K) (p. 209) "Self-savoring": This is formulated thus because, although rasa is not some *thing* that can be separated from itself, it can make itself its own object of cognition[119]—as when the poet speaks of "beholding the self in the self."[120] . . . Regarding rasa "with respect to the drama," it has been argued in *The Eye for* Light on Implicature, "This apprehension of rasa requires no other basis than the actor. But the actor must be thought to be the character portrayed in order for the audience to savor the experience. . . . Therefore, rasa exists only in the drama and not in the characters to be portrayed or anyone else."[121] To quote Sharadatanaya:

By the literary process or dramatic acting a stable emotion is turned into rasa and made available for savoring. The audience alone is the substratum of this rasa. Because rasa is something happening in one's presence, it cannot belong to the character, because a character, Rama for instance, is known to belong to times past. And a poet does not compose a poem in order to reveal the rasa of a character belonging to the past. For that reason the substratum of rasa must be the audience.[122]

Some scholars hold that the audience is the substratum of rasa only in a metaphorical and not a literal sense. To quote the arguments of the learned Naraharisuri:[123]

Rasa can be described as supermundane if one accepts that it inheres in the audience. [210] But in actual fact, why bother conceiving of a locus of rasa, which is a bliss that is full, whole, uniform[124]—indeed, synonymous with God? One surely would not identify a single place for the true, infinite, blissful supreme being. In the same way, the poets from the beginning of time who have achieved insight into the matter have considered rasa to be without any location; it is merely something relished by the members of the audience, merely manifested by the aesthetic elements. We tolerate as a figure of speech the notion that it is located in the audience only for the same reason that we concur that the Lord dwells in the minds of spiritual adepts by the mere fact that He is apprehended by them.

Thus the final doctrine is that rasa has no particular location at all. And for this reason it is held to be identical to the bliss of supreme being, but with one distinction: the latter is apprehended through spiritual practice, and the former through complete engagement with the factors and other aesthetic elements. The same scholar has also said the following:

The manifestation of bliss that remains the same in all circumstances is referred to as worldly happiness; it is called supermundane rasa when manifested by the supermundane aesthetic elements in simple conformity with literary convention; it is termed "supreme being" or "the highest self" or "the Lord" when manifested in the nonconceptual sense experience of spiritual adepts, when their hearts are purified by virtuous actions, when they have attained impassivity, self-restraint, and so on, and are focused on learning, reflection, and concentration.

To quote the *Lamp for Spiritual Discipline of the Inner Self*:[125]

The stable emotion of desire that, depending on causal conditions, turns into one or another of the nine dramatic rasas, the erotic and the rest, and brings bliss to the audience of sensitive viewers, the actor, and the character as well—identical with that desire am I myself, with my innate plenitude of rasa.[126]

5.2 A PHILOSOPHICAL PRÉCIS OF THE RASA PROBLEMATIC

Mirror of Literary Art of Vishvanatha (c. 1350) with *The Eye* of Anantadasa (c. 1400)

As we can deduce from stray remarks in his extant works, Vishvanatha hailed from a family of poet-intellectuals who had long served the royal house of Kalinga, and can be confidently dated to the mid-fourteenth century. It is therefore curious, given his time and place, that Vishvanatha appears unfamiliar with the treatise of his compatriot Vidyadhara, and that his own work circulated north, in Bengal, rather than south, like the *Single Strand*. Most of Vishvanatha's creative writing—he was a poet and playwright in both Sanskrit and Prakrit—including a large-scale multilingual encomium and a courtly epic on his patron, King Narasimha, has disappeared except for a romantic comedy (*nāṭikā*) called *The Girl Named Digit-of-the-Moon* (*Candrakalā*), a short poem on an epic theme ("The Quest for the Golden Flowers," *Saugandhikāharaṇa*), and a couple dozen quotations he drew from his works in the two scholarly texts of his that have been preserved, the *Mirror of Literary Art* and a commentary on Mammata's *Light on Poetry* (a later work).

Vishvanatha shows familiarity with many of the authors already encountered. He knows Dhanamjaya's *Ten Dramatic Forms* and Dhanika's commentary on it; *The Eye for* Light on Implicature of Abhinavagupta; Bhoja's *Necklace for the Goddess of Language*; and of course Mammata's *Light on Poetry*, but he also intriguingly cites authors no longer available to us. These include one Dharmadatta, and his own grandfather, Narayana (who he says defeated Dharmadatta in a debate at the court of the king of Kalinga), as well as other material whose authors' names we do not even know (see the quotations adduced in his remarks on 3.28).

The *Mirror* is essentially a compendium of earlier views about literary art in general, both "heard" and "seen," or poetry and drama. In fact, though not the first work to treat the two great divisions together (Vidyanatha had done so a generation earlier), Vishvanatha's is the most complete up to his time; this comprehensiveness, presumably, led him to use the seemingly more capacious term "literary art," *sāhitya*, and this is the first extant treatise in which it appears.[127] Despite the conventional nature unavoidable in such an exposition, Vishvanatha's treatise displays considerable independent thinking and a mind given to strong opinions. He is, for example, the first to declare in so many words that rasa is "the soul" of poetry (1.1); he refines the conception of commonization, calling it an "imagined sense of commonality";[128] and most notable, he is far more concerned with the philosophical problems of rasa than most other Indian aestheticians. Consider his argument on why rasa cannot be some thing that is made: if that were the case, "the factors and so on would have to be considered its cause. But then the factors could not be apprehensible at the moment we apprehend rasa (as they indeed are), since we never have perceptual knowledge simultaneously of both a cause and its effect."[129] He also, subtly and without fanfare, redescribes the "manifestation" of rasa: it is not the revealing of something already existent, like a pot by a lamp (so Anandavardhana and Ruyyaka), but a transformation, like yogurt from milk.

Vishvanatha's philosophical bent makes the development of his argument somewhat convoluted, so that a brief outline is called for. After offering a general and a specific definition of rasa (chapter 3, vv. 1, 2–3), Vishvanatha turns to the problem of rasa and pleasure (4–5) and the peculiar nature of aesthetic sadness (6–8). (His analysis of the nature of commonization [9–12], the supermundane character of the aesthetic elements [13], their unity [14–16ab], and how we are able to fill in the blanks, so to speak, when any of those elements is lacking [16cd–17ab], as well as the location of rasa, which cannot be either the original character imitated or the actor doing the imitating [17cd–20ab], is already familiar to us, and omitted here.) The more complicated part of the exposition concerns the peculiar ontology of rasa: it is not an *object* of consciousness, not some *thing* that is effected; it is not eternal, not future, and in an important sense not even present; it is a form of neither conceptual nor nonconceptual awareness. In short, rasa is something without parallel in our everyday reality (20ab–26ab). The only proof of rasa's existence is our experience of it, and this experience is "self-revealing" like one's self-awareness, and a unity that subsumes the parts of which it is made. The similarity to the ontology of the self and supreme being as presented by Vedanta is something to which Vishvanatha himself calls our attention, though without elaboration; the deeper implications of that analogy would not be drawn for another three centuries, by Vishvanathadeva.[130]

In addition to Vishvanatha's general account of rasa given here (chapter 3), he reverts to the topic in his discussion of manifestation (chapter 5). In that section, which could not be included, Vishvanatha is the first to admit the logical problems of applying the linguistic notions of Anandavardhana for a reception theory of rasa. As we have seen, once the concern with rasa had shifted from formal questions about the text to phenomenological questions about the reader, "manifestation" had to be recoded as a psychological rather than linguistic term of reference. Although Vishvanatha accepts that rasa can be said to be manifested, he does so hesitantly, employing the language of "manifestation" despite its obvious inapplicability in order to underscore the unique process by which aesthetic experience arises: "This linguistic function is called 'manifestation' by scholars. But when it comes to the 'manifestation' of rasas, others"—including Vishvanatha?—"say that the function is called 'tasting.' "[131]

Vishvanatha's work circulated little outside of eastern India before the nineteenth century and attracted only a few commentators. One of these is Anantadasa, who appears to have been the author's son; he makes no such claim in the introduction of his commentary, but remarks offhandedly in reference to a citation from a work of Vishvanatha that it is by his father. The commentary is not always as reliable as one might expect, given its lineage, but in a few places it does contribute to the exposition.

FROM *MIRROR OF LITERARY ART* OF VISHVANATHA (V) AND *THE EYE* OF ANANTADASA (A)

(V) What, then, is literature? Here is our answer:

(1.1) Literature is discourse whose soul is rasa.

We will later describe the essential nature of rasa. "Soul" here means that which endows something with life, insofar as it is the essence. Nothing lacking rasa can be accepted as being "literature." The etymology of rasa, "taste," is from the passive verb form ("it is tasted") or the impersonal passive ("a taste is had"),[132] and as a result, I include in my definition of literature, in addition to rasa itself, emotion as well as the semblances of both rasa and emotion.

. . . .

Now to the question, What is rasa?

3.1. A stable emotion, desire and so on, when manifested by the factors, reactions, and transitory emotions, becomes rasa for the responsive viewer/reader.

These aesthetic elements will all be discussed in due course (since the "sensitivities," or psychophysical responses, are in essence reactions, they have not been separately mentioned). To say that rasa is "manifested" is meant to indicate that it has undergone a formal transformation, on the analogy of yogurt transformed from milk.[133] Rasa is something brought into being through manifestation; it is not something already existing and then manifested, like a pot by a lamp. Thus, as the author of *The Eye for* Light on Implicature has averred, "When we say, 'A rasa has been apprehended,' it is just a manner of speaking, as in 'One is preparing cooked rice.' "[134]

In addition, the term "stable emotion," although obviously implicit in the phrase "desire and so on," is mentioned separately in v. 3.1 in order to indicate that desire and the rest can function as *non*-stable emotions for other rasas—in other words, that amusement, for example, or anger can become *transitory* emotions for the erotic and the heroic respectively. To quote: "An emotion comes to be called stable only when it stays fixed in the rasa."[135]

We now offer an account of the mode of savoring rasa, which amounts to an account of its essential nature.

(3.2–3) What we call rasa is an indivisible whole,[136] self-revealing,[137] and consisting of blissful consciousness,[138] completely insulated from any other object of perception, and thus akin to savoring supreme being. Its life force lies in supermundane rapture. It is savored by certain special people when they cognize it through a superabundance of sensitivity, as being something identical to themselves, like their own body.

"The mind untouched by volatility and stolidity is here called 'sensitivity.'"[139] According to this definition, sensitivity is an internal property that renders one impervious to things external to the aesthetic event. "Superabundance" refers to the emergence of sensitivity once volatility and stolidity have been eliminated, and the basis for this emergence is a state of absorption in the subject[140] of supermundane works of poetry or drama. Rasa is an "indivisible whole" because it is a unity, consisting of a feeling of rapture that brings pleasure by illuminating the aesthetic elements and the stable emotions; we will shortly explain the grounds for this claim.[141] It is "self-revealing," in a manner also to be shortly explained;[142] and in the phrase "consisting of consciousness" the suffix denoting "consisting"[143] should be taken to connote "*is* consciousness."[144] "Rapture" is essentially an expansion[145] of consciousness; a synonym for it is "amazement." That amazement is the life force of rasa has been argued by my grandfather Narayana, that great aesthete, salon eminence, and chief scholar-poet. As Dharmadatta stated in his treatise:

> Rapture is the essence of rasa, since it is experienced in every instance. Given this, it follows that in every rasa is to be found the fantastic rasa—which, according to the learned Narayana, can therefore be considered the sole rasa.[146]

When we speak of "certain special people," we mean people possessing merit acquired in a former existence. To quote: "It is only those with merit who, like spiritual adepts, can apprehend the continuum of rasa."[147]

(Anantadasa) (p. 72): Just as spiritual adepts have a direct realization of the pure supreme being in the form of self-revealing, blissful consciousness, so people of merit directly realize rasa, dappled though it may be by its various components, the stable emotions and so on. To quote: "Rasa has the form of self-revealing and blissful amazement, albeit dappled by the stable emotions, components fused with the factors and other elements, which are not eliminated from the viewer's consciousness."[148] Other thinkers, however, hold that after the direct realization of bliss fused with the stable emotions there comes about a manifestation of the actual principle of supreme being consisting of blissful consciousness, whereby all external reality becomes quiescent, and which approximates the state of dreamless sleep or deep meditation. To quote: "When rasa attains plenitude. . . ."[149] My teacher,[150] nonetheless, holds that there is nothing more than the experience of what is necessarily a variegated event and the presence of the recognition, "I am experiencing pleasure." . . . What the author is intimating by "continuum of rasa" is that rasa, being akin to savoring supreme being, flows in a current unbroken by our awareness of it.

(V) Furthermore, even though it has been demonstrated that rasa is not some *thing* separate from the savoring of it (compare such statements as "When there is a fusion of the mind with the meaning of the literary work, there arises the bliss that is the self, which constitutes the savoring of rasa"),[151] I still must make it clear that when I say it "is savored," the usage is based upon a merely hypothetical sense of differentiation; or it can as easily be taken as a reflexive or impersonal passive usage.[152] To quote: "Insofar as rasa is in essence merely a state of being tasted, it can be nothing other than consciousness as such."[153] Comparable usage elsewhere in this treatise, in similar contexts,[154] is to be taken in this figurative sense, and not literally.

One might raise the following objection: if it is indeed the case that rasa is not some thing different from the experience of it, then one winds up arguing that rasa is not an object of knowledge. And since manifestation, which you accept as the mechanism for knowing rasa, is the making known of some particular object, rasa and manifestation would wind up being one and the same thing, since both are forms of knowledge and not objects of knowledge. And how then could rasa possibly be some thing that is manifested, as you claim in verse 1, when the source of manifestation and the thing manifested must be absolutely separate entities, like a lamp and a pot? To quote: "Manifestation produces a cognition of something else."[155] This objection is entirely valid. And for this reason it has been argued that "Rasa must be completely distinguished from all acts of making and knowing. It is a unique function, something we can call 'savoring.' "[156] And that is why scholars use distinctive terms for it, such as "tasting," "savoring," "rapture," and so on.[157] It is only because we are keen to establish the process as such, and to differentiate it from all other language functions,[158] that we have said that rasa is something "manifested."

One might object that, if rasa is supposed to consist of bliss, then the tragic and other painful rasas would not in fact be rasas at all. The response is as follows:

(3.4) That in the case of the tragic and similar rasas there eventually comes about pleasure requires no other proof than the experience of the responsive viewer/reader.

"And similar" is meant to include the macabre and the fearful. Still, in order to permanently silence hostile critics, I offer a second postulate:

(3.5ab) Moreover, if they really felt pain, no one would be so eager for it.

No rational person ever seeks to bring pain upon himself, and yet we see everyone keenly seeking out literary works featuring the tragic and other such rasas. And still another illogicality would result:

(3.5cd) And then, the *Rāmāyaṇa* and other such works would be a source of pain.

That is, if the tragic rasa were a source of pain, we would face the absurd conclusion that works in which that rasa predominates would themselves be sources of pain. But how, one might still object, can pleasure arise from things that cause pain?

(3.6–7) From things that become causes of grief and joy by being based in the real world, real-world grief and joy do indeed arise in the real world. But from those things that become supermundane "factors" by being based in literature—and indeed, from all of them—only pleasure arises. There is no logical problem here.

The very things that can indeed be described as causes of pain in the real world—Rama's departure into forest exile, for example—become, when consigned to poetry or drama, part of a process of supermundane "factoring." They thereby cease to be describable as causes and take on the new supermundane descriptor, "factor." And like the bites and scratches made in lovemaking, they give rise only to pleasure. Accordingly, it is a hard and fast rule that real-world grief and joy arise from the causes of real-world grief and joy, whereas in literature, only pleasure arises from all the factors and other aesthetic elements. There should be no conceptual difficulty with this.

One might still ask why stories about Harischandra[159] and so on, whether seen in a drama or heard in poetry recitation, cause weeping and other signs of pain. The response:

(3.8ab) The weeping and so on, similarly, must be understood to be a result of an aesthetic "melting" of the heart.[160]

It might be asked[161] why this sort of rasa manifestation is not found in everyone as a result of listening to poetry. Here is the response:

(3.8cd) The relishing of rasa cannot arise without some predisposition toward the various stable emotions, desire and the rest.

Predispositions are acquired both in the present existence and in former ones, and make the savoring of rasa possible. If the former were not causal factors, then even dry theologians and ritualists would savor rasa; if the latter were not, then it would never be the case that some men keen to savor rasa[162] turn out to be incapable of doing so. To quote Dharmadatta, "Savoring rasa is possible only for audience members[163] with the requisite predispositions. Without them, people are like the walls and wooden posts and stone floor inside the theater."[164]

. . . .

(3.20ab) Rasa is not an *object* to be known, because it stands in an invariable relationship with our apprehension of it.

An object that is knowable, something like a pot, can exist without our knowing it. This is not the case with rasa, however, since it does not exist unless it is apprehended.

(3.20cd–21a) Rasa also cannot be considered something made, insofar as it is essentially embedded in the assemblage of aesthetic elements, the factors and so on.[165]

If rasa were "something made," an effect, then the factors and so on would have to be considered its cause. But then the factors could not be apprehensible at the moment we apprehend rasa (as they indeed are), since we never have perceptual knowledge simultaneously of both a cause and its effect. We cannot simultaneously touch a cooling cream and have an awareness of the pleasure we derive from touching it.[166] The idea here is that because we apprehend rasa as something "essentially embedded in the assemblage of aesthetic elements," the factors and so on, it cannot be caused by an awareness of the factors, etc.

(3.21b) But rasa is not, for all that, something always existent, because we lack prior awareness of it[167]—that is to say, it has no continuous existence at the time we have no consciousness of it.

And it is assuredly not the case that a thing that really is permanently existent would cease to exist on the occasions when we have no consciousness of it.

(3.22–25a) Nor again is it something that comes into being later (after the performance), since it has a form of self-revelation and the blissfulness of some direct awareness; but neither can it be said to be a present entity because of its utter difference from anything made or brought to awareness. Insofar as rasa has as its object the particularized reflection on the aesthetic elements on the part of the responsive viewer/reader, and is clearly something of which we are conscious as consisting of pure bliss, it cannot be nonconceptual sense experience that grasps rasa.

But neither is rasa brought to our consciousness by conceptual sense experience, because it is not something fit for connection with linguistic expression.[168]

Things brought to consciousness through conceptual sense experience are captured in linguistic usage. And this is not the case with rasa.[169]

(3.25b–cd) Insofar as rasa is a direct awareness, it cannot be thought of as something supersensory, but neither is the cognition of rasa strictly[170] sensory, because it is possible for it to arise through language alone.

Tell us, then, the true nature of rasa, which seems to fall under a description of something never before seen or heard of.

(3.26ab) Accordingly, rasa is truly supermundane and brought to consciousness by receptive readers/viewers.

But what proof is there for its existence? Here is our answer:

(3.26cd) The learned hold[171] the act of relishing to be the proof of rasa—which is in fact nothing other than the act itself.

Relishing means savoring; its nature has already been described as follows: "When there is a fusion of the mind. . . ." But here one might object: if rasa is not something brought about as an effect, how can the sage have defined it thus: "Rasa arises from the conjunction of factors, reactions, and transitory emotions"? Here is the response:

(3.27ab) The "arising of rasa" is used in the secondary sense of the arising of the relishing of rasa.[172]

Relishing, since it is identical with rasa, can no more be some effected thing than rasa itself. Yet it can be figuratively referred to as an effect because of its episodic nature (relishing passing into and out of existence); and thereby a figurative sort of effectedness can be attributed to rasa itself.

. . . .

One might object: if it is the stable emotion when combined with the other aesthetic elements that becomes rasa, how can rasa be said to be either "self-revealing"[173] or a "unity" (3.2)? Here is the response:

(3.28) Insofar as desire or any other stable emotion becomes a rasa precisely because it is transformed into a state of awareness, the fact of rasa's being both self-revealing and a unity is proven as a matter of course.

If desire and the rest were entirely different from consciousness as such, then rasa could indeed not be proven to be self-revealing. But far from being different, they in fact become identical, as we have maintained. To quote:[174] "Although relishing too is not something effected, since it is nothing other than rasa itself, nonetheless, because of its episodic nature we figuratively refer to it as an effect, just as we refer to a stable emotion as an effect though it is identical to savoring, being a transformation of the viewers' beginningless predispositions." Moreover, "And since we maintain that pure pleasure, amazement, and so on are identical to rasa, one may make one's bed on our tenets and sleep in peace for a thousand heavenly years."[175] And again, "Although rasa is nothing other than itself—that is, than the experience of it—it comes to be objectified in the act of cognition as being identical to the stable emotions present in the predispositions." Should anyone not accept the view that cognition is self-revealing, the Vedantins will come and lower the boom on him.[176] Finally, because again rasa is identical to cognition, it is a unified "whole." The stable emotions and so on are first apprehended individually, but then all appear as a unity and turn into rasa. To quote: "The factors, the reactions, the sensitivities, and the transitory emotions are first apprehended part by part, but then become a whole." And last: "But in actual fact rasa should be understood to be a unity, just like supreme being as understood in Vedanta."

5.3 RETHINKING "SEMBLANCE OF RASA"

The Moon on the Rasa Ocean of Singabhupala (c. 1385)

Singabhupala was king of a small principality in today's western Andhra Pradesh, and by caste a Velamanayudu, a subcaste of Shudras. His *Moon on the Rasa Ocean*—and it is virtually certain that it is his, not written by one of his court scholars (the most famous of whom was Vishveshvara, author of the *Moonlight of Rapture*, a work on poetics)—is in the main a treatise on dramaturgy. Aside from the vast amount of Sanskrit (and Prakrit) literature he cites, some of which is extant nowhere else, Singabhupala shows himself to be a subtle and delightful reader of Sanskrit poetry and writer of Sanskrit prose. These traits are illustrated especially well in his reflections on the problem of "semblance of rasa."

Consider Singabhupala's discussion of the poem, "The bond of his affection broken . . ." (see below), about a woman mourning the death of passion in her marriage. How does rasa theory explain the impact of such a verse? The question is raised nowhere else in the tradition, and Singabhupala has an interesting and shrewd point to make. The rasa cannot, he says, be the erotic, certainly not the erotic enjoyed but also not the erotic thwarted, since there is no chance of "reunion." Yet the poem undoubtedly has a powerful emotional-aesthetic force. How is it to be categorized according to rasa theory? Singabhupala calls it "semblance" of the erotic, whereby he is clearly not making a judgment on the quality of the poem—indeed, Singabhupala goes out of his way, here and elsewhere, to adduce as illustrations verses from the finest works of Sanskrit poetry—but specifying the nature of the experience it produces. A great poem like the *Rāmāyaṇa* is unthinkable without such semblance—since it is unthinkable without Ravana and his "semblance of the erotic rasa" for Sita—but understanding precisely what the aesthetic power of this semblance is, within the confines of the rasa theory, requires deep reflection. If rasa is the ultimate literary value, how are we to assess the value of a literary work where rasa *as such* is not—indeed, must not—be present?

Equally interesting, if more complicated still, is Singabhupala's treatment of the question of rasa in respect to entities who themselves may be thought incapable of understanding rasa, such as animals and the "uncultured." Singabhupala engages this issue with a direct attack on the views of Vidyadhara in his *Single Strand*. The difficulty in grasping Singabhupala's argument is tied up, as noted already on Vidyadhara's work, with the more primordial question of the locus of rasa. Is the point that animals or the uncultured have no "discrimination," thereby entailing that rasa—which implicitly, on this view, is located in the character—cannot be located *in these characters*? Or is it rather that they cannot be an appropriate source of rasa located *in the viewer/reader*? When Vidyadhara asserts that "the aesthetic elements can function in the case of animals too," that animals "can be foundational factors," he would appear to mean, in the first instance, they can be factors for other animals, not for us. A verse like Kalidasa's "A bee drank honey from a flower cup, after his beloved had drunk" then would be taken to indicate that animals are capable of emotion, that is, self-aware feeling—to which readers can also respond (though Vidyadhara does not explicitly raise this last point). For much of Singabhupala's discussion, this latter step, the viewer/reader's response, is uppermost in his mind. Thus, with respect to another verse of Kalidasa's that Singabhupala cites, it is not the discrimination of the woman and man *themselves* in the poem (Arundhati and Agastya) that does or does not permit them to function as foundational factors for the erotic rasa, but the discrimination of the viewer/reader, who knows they cannot so function because they are in fact ascetics. If in the end the two poles of the rasa phenomenon—certainly by this point in the history of the discourse—form part of a single continuum, there remains a confusing oscillation, given the varying analytical focal points. Vidyadhara is concentrating on the character when disputing the idea that lack of discernment disqualifies animals from *experiencing* rasa; Singabhupala is concentrating on the audience when arguing that the lack disqualifies animals from *being* foundational factors of rasa for the viewer. But of course the case of the audience is logically connected with that of the character: you cannot have a rasa experience from the representation of an entity that cannot have one itself; you are instead experiencing a semblance of rasa—because that is what the entity itself is experiencing.[177]

FROM *THE MOON ON THE RASA OCEAN* OF SINGABHUPALA

(p. 292) Now to semblance of rasa:

(265cd–266ab) The principal rasa becomes a "semblance" when a subsidiary rasa is amplified by willfulness,[178] just as a king becomes a semblance of a king because of an undisciplined minister.

To quote the *Light on Emotion*:

> The erotic becomes semblance of the erotic when overwhelmed by the comic; the comic, semblance of the comic when overwhelmed by the macabre; [293] the heroic, semblance of the heroic when overwhelmed by the fearful; the fantastic, semblance of the fantastic when associated with the tragic; the violent, semblance of the violent when associated with grief and fear;[179] the tragic, semblance of the tragic when overwhelmed by the comic; the macabre, semblance of the macabre when possessed of the fantastic and erotic; and the fearful, semblance of the fearful from contact with the violent and the heroic.[180]

The erotic rasa, to take that case, becomes predominantly a semblance in four different ways: from unrequited passion; from passion for more than one person; from passion being represented between animals; or from its being represented between the uncultured.

"Unrequited passion" is when passion is absent in one member of the couple. Thus there is semblance of the erotic in the case of Sita and Ravana because of her complete lack of passion for him. . . .[181] [294] One might object that the absence of passion in one member cannot logically make for semblance of the erotic, because then we would have semblance of love at first sight, as in the case of Ratnavali, who feels passion for the king of Vatsa before he feels it for her.[182] I would reply that "absence" is of three types: [1] the absence of something before it comes into being; [2] absolute absence; [3] the absence of something after it ceases to exist. [1] In the first, because passion can be expected to arise once its cause (such as seeing the love object) is present, we have no semblance of the erotic; we do, by contrast, in the latter two types, because passion does not arise even in the presence of its cause. Other scholars [295] hold that it is only with reference to absence of passion in the woman that semblance of the erotic arises, but this is mistaken. For rasa is unable to be savored when there is no passion in the man too. Consider the following poem:

> The bond of love is broken, the respect due to affection has trickled away,
> trust has come to an end, and he passes strangely before me like a stranger.

I think about this over and over, my friend, and all the days gone by,
and I can't see why my heart doesn't break into a hundred pieces.[183]

Here the woman's passion, although manifested by such transitory emotions as despair, remembrance, and the like—we infer these from her thinking about "all the days gone by" prior to the time when her heart was broken—fails to attain beauty because [3] the man's passion has ceased to exist (this is indicated by the breaking of the "bond of love" expressed in the verse). We can also have semblance of rasa by reason of [2] the absolute absence of passion in a man, as in the following verse:

"What woman are you thinking of with your eyes closed a moment,
pretending to be meditating?
Look at the person standing here before you, wounded by love's arrows—
you are a savior, can you not protect her?
Your compassion is a sham, is there any other man
more pitiless than you?"
So Mara's daughters-in-law, jealous of Enlightenment,[184]
addressed the Victor—and may he protect you.[185]

Here we have semblance of rasa because of the Buddha's complete absence of passion.

[296] There is semblance of the erotic rasa when passion for one and the same woman is represented in more than one man. Take for example the following verse:

When the fighters struck each other, their life breaths simultaneously departed,
and they carried on their dispute—now in heaven—in quest of a single nymph.[186]

Here two warriors attain divine status by dying in battle without retreating, and the passion both have for a certain heavenly nymph, which is conditioned by their incomparable heroic qualities,[187] is semblance because it appears as equally distributed between them. We also have semblance when passion for one and the same man is found in more than one woman. In the following verse,[188] an antagonist has gone to heaven when slain by the hero's sword, and since the passion for him is equally distributed among Menaka and other courtesans of the heavenly world, it is semblance of passion.

One might object that, if this were so, then the passion of a "playboy" and similar types of protagonist would always be semblance. But that would be incorrect. The fact that a playboy behaves uniformly toward multiple women is a function of his comportment, not [297] his passion. His passion is intense only for one of them, and middling or weak for the others—and hence it is not a semblance. But in the above case of the warriors we are right to posit semblance because the workings of the passion are equally distributed over multiple partners.

Here is an example of semblance of the erotic rasa when passion is represented between animals:

> A bee drank honey from a flower cup, after his beloved had drunk,
> and with his horn a black buck scratched his mate, who closed her eyes at his touch.[189]

Here is an example of semblance of the erotic rasa when passion is represented between the uncultured:

> She fainted at orgasm. "She's dead!" the bumpkin thought, and ran,
> and the cotton stalks with half-opened pods seemed to laugh out loud.[190]

In this poem we deduce the bumpkin's uncultured character from his inability to distinguish between death and fainting from orgasmic sex.

The proponent of the view that rasa does indeed exist in the uncultured might here object: passion in animals or the uncultured should not be classified as semblance, "since the aesthetic elements can function in the case of animals too,"[191] and we apprehend their capacity for savoring rasa. Poor fellow, I can see you are an intimate of the poet Vidyadhara, that obsequious attendant of Narasimhadeva, King of Utkala, self-styled master of the literary erotic.[192] [298] Here is how Vidyadhara has justified his view in the *Single Strand*: . . .[193] In response, first of all, it makes no sense that animals can be foundational factors. The sage has decreed that, in the case of the erotic rasa, a foundational factor can only be something brilliant, pure, and beautiful,[194] and it is, as everyone knows, completely inconceivable for animals to be thus, since they engage in none of the requisite practices: lathering their bodies with fragrant unguents, performing ablutions, decorating themselves with ornaments, and so on. And it is mistaken to argue[195] that a bull elephant can be a foundational factor for a cow elephant by virtue of properties innate to the species, because on that argument the bull would be functioning as an actual *cause* of the cow's passion, not a foundational *factor.* Moreover, something becomes a foundational factor thanks not to properties specific to its species, but to things that expand the mind of the viewer/reader who "actualizes" the experience, properties that have something desirable about them. Again, what Vidyadhara calls "awareness of the foundational factor and other aesthetic elements"[196] can really signify only discernment of propriety,[197] and since animals are devoid of such discernment, they cannot be foundational factors.[198] If this entails that for people[199] who have no such knowledge of foundational factors and the other aesthetic elements [299] there can only be semblance of rasa, then so be it, for it supports our view that rasa in someone uncultured[200] can only be a semblance, given that "uncultured" is meant to stand for a person devoid of discernment.

Furthermore, it is false to claim that "it is the sheer presence of the aesthetic elements that actuates the rasa, not awareness of them as aesthetic elements."[201] To explain: there are two options here. The first is that rasa is actuated by the presence of an aesthetic element *distinguished as such.* If you accept that the actuating capacity belongs to a thing distinguished in this way, you are simultaneously accepting that there is a role played by discernment—and thereby accepting our position. You cannot respond that "being distinguished" here means simply possessing properties that distinguish one thing from another, without discernment playing any role. This is because there is no set number of distinctions: they are what enable us to register the strong points in the entity in question, and are not mutually exclusive either.[202]

The second option is that rasa is actuated by the presence of some thing *as such.* But then in a poem like "Arundhati sat behind her husband like the goddess Svaha behind the sacred fire,"[203] it would turn out that the erotic rasa was being savored, for after all we have the presence of both a foundational factor in the two individuals, a man and woman plain and simple, and a physical reaction, here that of sitting behind.[204] And again, in a poem like the one above, where the country bumpkin thinks the woman has died, we have the presence of a foundational factor in the two individuals, a man and woman plain and simple . . . well, my opponent can rush forward if he wishes and try to rescue an erotic rasa here—a rutting elephant sinking in the mud!—from the comic rasa produced from the man's lack of discernment. But really, enough of his trying to talk his way out of these being cases of semblance of rasa.

But wait, he might ask one last time, it is a foundational factor such as Sita, i.e., the thing as such—and not the thing as differentiated[205] in any way—that enables an apprehension of woman as such, and when that comes about rasa arises in the audience members. How do you explain that? Well, I would respond, as foundational factor,

"Sita" relinquishes the various specific properties—being the daughter of Janaka, the wife of Rama, and so on—that would inhibit the arising of rasa, and is taken as[206] differentiated by other properties—being graceful, brilliant, pure, beautiful. It is as such that the factor is able to communicate that sense of "woman" in general, not because of its being a mere species of woman herself. In this way all is in order.

CHAPTER SIX

Rasa in the Early Modern World, 1200–1650

6.1 A READER READING FOR RASA

Elixir for the Rasika, of Arjunavarmadeva (c. 1215)

A king in the lineage of Bhoja of Dhara—he calls himself "lamp to the family of Bhoja"[1]—Arjunavarmadeva shared his ancestor's passion for poetry, put on full display in his only known work, *Elixir for the* Rasika, a commentary on the seventh-century collection of erotic lyrics ascribed to the poet (or, likelier, anthologist) Amaru.

Aside from insisting that rasa is the central concern of Amaru's oeuvre, Arjunavarmadeva is concerned in his commentary on the first two poems to distinguish between rasa poetry and "emotion" poetry.[2] In the first poem, an invocation to the mother goddess, the predominant element is not any emotional charge the verse may deliver to the reader, but rather the "subject matter" itself. The subject matter, or express sense, however, is at once the goddess's heroic capacity to destroy evil in the world and the celebration of that power on the part of the poet, that is, his own emotional attachment to the goddess. The subject matter in both aspects is the dominant theme of the poem; the heroic rasa becomes, as it were, an ornament enhancing its impact, an assessment of rasa when subordinate that goes back, through Anandavardhana, to the beginnings of rasa theory.

The same is true, though in an even more complex way, in the second poem, a prayer addressed to Shiva as destroyer by fire of the Three Cities, which according to ancient myth had been constructed by cosmic demons. Arjunavarmadeva builds on earlier interpretations (of Anandavardhana and Mammata) but has something of his own to add.[3] In this poem the erotic rasa—the fire is represented as a wayward and repentant lover—and the tragic rasa—the wives of the demon king are seeing their husband being burned alive in a cosmic conflagration—would appear to stand in tension with each other. There is a further complication from the conventions of Sanskrit poetry, for the tragic rasa occurs when the beloved is dead, never to return, and in such circumstances the erotic is impossible. Here, however, the tragic and the erotic are both subordinated to the heroic rasa, embodied in Shiva's determined act of righteousness, which neutralizes the contradiction between them. But even that rasa is subordinate to the "subject matter" of the poem, which is at once the grandeur of the god and the expression of wonder and devotion on the part of the poet,[4] and for this matter, the rasa can again be thought to function as an "ornament."

FROM *ELIXIR FOR THE* RASIKA OF ARJUNAVARMADEVA

(p. 1) The first of Amaru's poems is an invocation to the goddess:

> Bathed in rays of light from her gleaming nails
> as her hand takes the pose called "drawing a bowstring,"
> may the mother's sidelong glance protect you, her eyes
> two bees hungry for the blooming flowers at her ear.

[2] The poem has a higher meaning beyond the literal, and in quest of this sensitive readers will seek to make sense of the poem's secrets as follows. First of all, the rasa that the poet has set out to create in his collection undoubtedly rises to its highest pitch when it is swelling with the waves of the mutual and truly felt love between a man and a woman. Yet the predominant component therein is the female character, and hence the poet has put in the first position of his work an invocation written to the goddess, his chosen deity—as represented appropriately by her glance—in order to indicate that predominance. Only in the second position comes a poem about Shiva. Then too, what other treasure house is there of love—which among the ends of man is superior to wealth and morality and only barely inferior to spiritual liberation—than woman, who by presenting a man with a son provides the means to set him free from the debt owed to his ancestors? . . . Moreover, there is nothing wrong even if the erotic rasa in a poem concerns the wife of another man,[5] for in the end such poetry is providing a kind of instruction: "This is how a woman's character can be destroyed," we are being told, "so she must be carefully guarded." Why else, in fact, would the great sage Vatsyayana[6] have written about the procedures for seducing a married woman? As has been said: "If a man becomes familiar through an authoritative work with the ways of adultery, he will never be deceived about his own wife."

Now, although the "pose" mentioned in the verse is discussed in the science of archery, what is meant here is the hand gesture used as a refinement in dance—and hence an important distinction is being drawn: we come to understand that the goddess can destroy the almost invincible forces of evil in the world merely by her erotic dance, and we thereby grasp her extraordinary power. . . . Some pseudo-critics have chosen to debate finer points of archery here: which among the five kinds of bow grips this might be, which among the five styles of fighting, and on and on.[7] Well, here is our position: Amaru is concerned with one and one thing only, the erotic rasa; indeed, when in another poem he writes, "The face of a woman making love on top / . . . will save you. Who needs Vishnu or Shiva or Skanda or any other god!" he goes so far as to suggest that the very invocation of a deity is beside the point. So who except someone immune to sex would bother to dilate upon archery? . . .

[3] In the subject-standard relationship of the simile in the poem, the subjects are the glance and the light rays from the gleaming nails, the standards the bees and the blooming flowers respectively. The charm of the darting glance dappled by the soft lacquered hands and spotless nails communicates the beauty and allure of the goddess that serve to delight Shiva. That poets are preoccupied with describing the beauty of goddesses is purely out of the desire to communicate why their husbands should love them so much; any other desire would be immoral. . . .

[4] Perhaps precisely because the simile indicates none of the physical transformations expected when preparing to destroy the demons (frowning, reddened eyes, and like), the figure here communicates the high resolve of the goddess that crowns her beauty and allure. Hence the figure would be expected to be subordinate to the rasa "heroic in war" (the heroic rasa, defined as consisting of determination and of three types [the heroic in war, munificence, and compassion or morality], is further manifested by the dense nominal compounding and other signs of the "Eastern" style). But what is dominant in this poem is not in fact the rasa but the subject matter: the goddess's power as such, when she resolves upon a task impossible for any of the other three hundred and thirty million gods to accomplish. Accordingly,[8] the simile functions as an ornament not for a rasa but for a "rasa-laden" statement. . . .[9]

(*Amaru* 2)
Like a husband whose betrayal is still moist. . . .[10]

In this poem the blessed Shiva, bow in hand, is burning to death the exalted lord of demons with his fiery arrows, and hence the rasa rendered the principal one is the heroic, suggesting the lord's preeminent power. Subsidiary rasas are the erotic thwarted, here in the form of wives' jealousy ("driven away when trying to clutch their hand," etc.), and the tragic, consisting of grief for their husband ("tears brimming," etc.). There is no conflict between these two subordinate rasas, the erotic and the tragic, because both are in service of something else—like those proverbial enemies the snake and the mongoose when they find themselves in a great sage's ashram. To quote: "When the intended rasa has been fully enhanced, there is no harm in giving expression to conflictual rasas if they are blocked from full development or are made subsidiary."[11] That is especially the case when, as here, the subsidiary rasas enhance the principal one. The erotic thwarted (in the form of jealousy), first of all, enhances the tragic, and does so to a high degree given that [5] "Things beautiful by nature that have become a source of sorrow make us even more sorrowful when their charms, now past, are called to mind."[12] For here we come to grasp that the demon king's wives had once been angered and placated by their beloved with all the different overtures and tactics at his disposal, and are now putting on the same display of jealous anger as they once did even in the midst of a tragedy,[13] and are overcome by a blazing fire. And the resulting tragic rasa, though[14] it pertains to the antagonist, enhances the heroic rasa of the protagonist—Shiva, enemy of the Triple City, whose triumph is a source of rejoicing and veneration. Resentment and weeping (transitory emotion and psychophysical response, respectively) suit the rasa[15] to a marked degree. . . . In this poem as well, however, it is the subject matter that is dominant, whereas the mixed rasas are subsidiary to it; hence, as in the prior example, we have a case where we have a "rasa-laden statement," which functions as an ornament to that subject matter.[16] Our earlier claim that the heroic is principal was made only with reference to the erotic and the tragic.[17] . . .

[6] No other work aside from this one collection of lyrics is ascribed to this poet, and hence he no doubt intends with the book's first two poems to demonstrate his ability to compose in mixed rasas, since all the remainder of the work is exclusively in the erotic. The ability to compose in mixed rasas is the touchstone of a poet—and indeed, we have in these poems as full a complement of stimuli of rasa as we have in complete works. Hence the declaration of the commentator on *Bharata*:[18] "A single verse of Amaru is worth a hundred whole works."

(*Amaru* 3)
The face of a woman making love on top—
hair mussed and swaying, earrings swinging, makeup
running from her sweat, eyes rolling in ecstasy—
will save you. Who needs Vishnu or Shiva or Skanda or any other god!

. . . In this poem it is not, by contrast, the subject matter that is dominant, but rather the rasa itself. And thus there is no question here of the "rasa-laden statement" being an ornament; instead, it is rasa itself that is ornamented by the figures of speech.

6.2 A POET WRITING OF RASA

The River of Rasa of Bhanudatta (c. 1500)

A northeast Brahman poet who worked at a southwest Islamicate court, Bhanudatta is principally known to historians of Sanskrit literature—and of Indian painting—as the author of the highly influential *Bouquet of Rasa* (*Rasamañjarī*). This was both an early example of a subspecies of aesthetics devoted to a close analysis of the "foundational factor" of the erotic rasa, namely the leading female character, and an important stimulus to the nascent painting tradition of seventeenth-century Rajasthan, which found inspiration in attempting to turn into line and color the extraordinary beauty of his poetic examples.

The *River of Rasa* is at once and paradoxically an innovative and a conservative book. It is the first independent treatise, in the millennium-long discourse, devoted exclusively to the subject of rasa, in the sense of providing a complete analysis of the topic in eight chapters (dealing with the stable emotions: the factors, the reactions, the "sensitivities," the transitory emotions, the rasas themselves, and miscellaneous matters such as dominant and subordinate rasas, flaws of rasas, and the like). In accordance with older tendencies that were to prove even more consequential in the early modern period, Bhanudatta seeks not only to define and explain rasa and its components but also to illustrate them with poetry, often very high-quality poetry, of his own composition.[19] Although by no means an innovation of Bhanu's (Vidyanatha and Vidyadhara composed most of their illustrations themselves for their eulogy textbooks, though Singabhupala followed the older format and took his from canonical poets), this style of exposition was to become, because of his artistry, a model not only for later writers like Jagannatha but also for vernacular poets, especially in classical Hindi.

Bhanudatta's conservatism, by contrast, relates to his actual understanding of rasa, which seems to affiliate him with the oldest traditions of aesthetic analysis. At the beginning of the sixth chapter of the *River of Rasa* he provides three definitions of rasa, whose differences are certainly subtle (and the argument is not always perspicuous). The first emphasizes the process of tasting the "fully matured" stable emotion; the second foregrounds the state of mental "repose"; the third focuses on the awakening of predispositions. All three—rasa as process, repose, and awakening—reference the viewer/reader's experience as Abhinavagupta would have understood it. Yet elsewhere Bhanu has something else in mind. He describes every rasa as the "fully matured" stable emotion, or its "full development": "The fully matured mutual pleasure of a young couple, or the properly matured feeling of desire, is the erotic" (6.10); "fully matured anger—or a state of intensification of all the senses—is the violent rasa" (7.21), and so on. With this, Bhanu is aligning himself to the most archaic concepts of all. As Abhinavagupta puts it: "The view of the most ancient authorities is that it is the stable emotion alone that, once intensified by the causes, reactions, and the rest, becomes rasa."[20] Such was the position clearly enunciated by the first extant commentator on the *Treatise on Drama*, Bhatta Lollata ("Rasa in the primary sense of the term exists in the character; it exists in the actor only by force of his complete identification with the part").[21] And it was this that Abhinava, following Bhatta Nayaka, sought to completely overcome.[22]

Not only is Bhanu's understanding of rasa archaic, but so too is the location presupposed by that understanding. Bhanu nowhere openly addresses this matter, but his view is suggested throughout. When he states, for example, that "A rasa is the trace memory of a stable emotion when this trace has been awakened," he implicitly explains whose memory is in question when noting that his definition of rasa can encompass people who fall in love at first sight (an assessment that will surprise readers of Abhinava, who first introduced the issue of predisposition in elaborating his theory of *reader* response). And when he asks, with reference to the physical reactions, "why there should be any need for something that shows rasa being reacted to," and answers that the reactions are the instruments to make rasa known (3.1), he is clearly talking about the character's experience of rasa, not the reader's. For Bhanu, then—and nothing in the *River of Rasa* militates against this—rasa is first and foremost a phenomenon pertaining to characters; he nowhere directly concerns himself with viewers or readers. Both rasa as "the stable emotion in a heightened state" and its location in the character would be preserved beyond Bhanu into the vernacular future, for example by the important eighteenth-century Hindi poet-intellectual Dev, who fully concurs with the *River of Rasa* on the question of definition.[23] The intellectual revolution initiated in Kashmir in the tenth century by no means displaced all earlier conceptions everywhere; the theological aesthetics that was to blossom in the generation or two after Bhanu offers abundant evidence of their preservation.

Bhanu did seek on occasion to extend his analysis of rasa beyond the doctrines of the old scholars, in rather original ways. He analyzes anew the dual nature of physical reactions (as a means of identifying a rasa and a stimulant factor producing it), and the notion of the "sensitivities." He offers a new account of why affection for a child cannot be a rasa, or even the stable emotion for a new rasa (as it was for many other thinkers), but must be the transitory emotion of the tragic rasa. His distinction between "mundane" and "supermundane" rasa does not reference the earlier theorists who had made use of it, and only with difficulty can be mapped against their views (let alone the redefinitions of the theological aesthetics that was to come). Mundane rasa is produced by "mundane sense contact," or everyday tangible sense experience, supermundane by the more intangible experience of "dreams, imagination, and representation." Since "representation"[24] includes poetry and drama, it is presumably here (and only here, and very quietly) that Bhanu is bringing the viewer/reader back into the analysis—which would entail that the "mundane" variety comprises the rasa of the characters. Yet "supermundane rasa" includes the subcategory called "rasa occurring in the imagination," which, in view of his example, must refer to what happens inside the narrative. (It is the character, or more precisely the literary "I"—and not the reader—who is experiencing the rasa, which in this case arises not from a sensory perception of a concrete foundational factor but from imagination.) At all events, that subtype does capture a real phenomenon that Sanskrit literary theory to date had ignored. Being fully aware of the reluctance to multiply categories that marked a millennium-old Sanskrit discourse, Bhanu is careful to adduce a classic poem by Bhartrihari (rather than a new one of his own) in support of his claim and to demonstrate precisely how "we are actually reading about an erotic *fantasy*." Similarly, in attempting to account for the existence of the peaceful rasa, Bhanu posits a new "rasa of phenomenal reality" (*māyārasa*, 7.63) to encompass worldly engagement parallel to the peaceful rasa of disengagement. It is hard to see how this would be anything more than a covering term for the eight standard rasas, though this is something Bhanu himself anticipates and denies.[25]

These gestures at renovation had few historical effects. What counts for intellectual history is Bhanudatta's new affiliation to the oldest tradition of aesthetic analysis coupled with his interest in, and talent for, illustrating this with new poetry of his own making. And it was this analysis and poetic practice, descending directly from Bhanu—for his influence was enormous, among not only classical Hindi writers but also those working in Marathi, Telugu, and Persian[26]—that would continue to shape the thinking of wide sectors of both the Sanskrit and the vernacular tradition for the next two centuries.

FROM *THE RIVER OF RASA* OF BHANUDATTA[27]

(1.5) Since a cause must always precede its effect, it is entirely appropriate to first turn our attention to the cause of rasa, which lies in the emotions and the like. Thus the emotions will be described prior to the rasas. An emotion is a transformation conducive to rasa. "Transformation" refers to a modification and is of two sorts, bodily or internal. The internal is also twofold: stable and transitory. A bodily transformation is a psychophysical response. We reject the argument that "emotion" refers exclusively to a mental transformation and that therefore the use of the term in reference to bodily transformations such as perspiration must be purely figurative. Since the word "emotion" is found in use equally in both cases, it is impossible to decide the matter one way or the other. After all, one does not decide about the nature of a thing by making it fit with a definition.[28]

The first, or "stable," emotion is defined as one that is not displaced by other emotions whether similar (that is, stable) or dissimilar (that is, transitory), insofar as it has the capacity to subordinate other emotions to itself; or more simply, as a mental transformation that is not displaced by any other stable emotion; or better yet, as a mental transformation dominant over all others. The definition is not so wide as to include either transitory emotions or physical reactions, because neither has the capacity to subordinate all other emotions to itself. It is referred to as "stable" since it remains stable up to the climax.[29]

Among these, desire is a mental transformation, not fully matured,[30] produced by longing for some wished-for object. It can arise from seeing, hearing, or remembering. . . .

Humor is an incomplete mental transformation produced by an incongruity of speech or dress that is meant for amusement. The definition is not so wide as to include fear or anger brought about by a peculiar type of speech or dress, since the element of amusement is absent there. . . .

(3.1 ff.) Next, the physical reactions will be described. Things that show a rasa being "reacted to"—in other words, that make rasa an object of reaction—are called "reactions." These include sidelong glances and so on. Their being a "reaction" derives from the fact that they are a means, a means being something directly connected with an effect.[31]

One might well ask why there should be any need for something that shows rasa being reacted to. True enough, rasa is defined as a fully matured stable emotion, but since it is an internal phenomenon we can have no knowledge of it without something else to make it known, hence the necessity of a physical reaction.

But one might also ask why sidelong glances and the like are not reckoned stimulant factors since, when a sidelong glance is seen, a mental transformation in the two lovers becomes fully matured—this is proven by experience and so cannot be denied. Moreover, there is a consensus of the ancients on this point. . . .

This is all true. Insofar as a sidelong glance is a means, it can be classified as a reaction; insofar as it is an object of perception, it can be classified as a stimulant. That is, a sidelong glance directed toward the protagonist is a reaction insofar as it is a means of showing the rasa being reacted to in the female protagonist herself. When the glance itself becomes an object of perception, it brings about a mental transformation in the two lovers and hence acts as a stimulant factor. . . .

(6.1) The rasas will now be described. When a stable emotion is represented by the factors, the physical and psychophysical responses, and the transitory emotions and thereby becomes fully matured, it is "tasted" and thus becomes a rasa. Another definition: rasa is that upon which the mind is brought to focus by the emotions, the factors, the physical reactions, and the transitory emotions. Yet a third definition: a rasa is the trace memory of a stable emotion when this trace has been awakened, and what awakens it are the factors, the physical reactions, and the transitory emotions. This last definition is not so narrow as to exclude the love at first sight of two young people, on the grounds that they have no previous experience (and hence no memory). For even in their case there exists an earlier experience—namely, in a former life.

Rasa is of two sorts, mundane and supermundane, the former produced by mundane contact, the latter by supermundane contact. Mundane contact is of six types[32] and depends on a material object; supermundane contact is mental. That is, the mental state itself supplies the contiguity, either directly, when its causes and so on have actually been experienced, or by way of latent memories, when the causes have been experienced but not in the present life.

Supermundane rasa is of three sorts: occurring in a dream, in the imagination, or in a representation. The last is found in the beauty of drama as well as in the beauty of the words and themes of poetry; both forms consist of bliss that is pure and unmixed.[33] While it is fair to object that "rasa occurring in the imagination" has no traditional standing, consider a poem such as the following:

> Fortunate are those who dwell in mountain caves and contemplate the highest light
> as birds alight in their laps without fear and drink their flowing tears of joy.
> As for me, my life wastes away in endless pursuit of diversions in pleasure groves
> or on the ledges of pools or palaces imagined only in my dreams.[34]

In this verse we are hearing about what is actually an erotic fantasy; moreover, the bliss here, one of the three reckoned in authoritative texts,[35] cannot come into being without rasa.

. . . .

(6.7) One might wonder why affection for a child, covetousness, devotion to a god, or even avarice are not rasas, given the presence in them of the stable feelings of attachment, craving, faith, and greed, respectively. The answer is that affection for a child and so on are not stable feelings but instead transitory emotions, all of them aspects of desire. One might then well ask what rasas they are supposed to be transitory emotions of. The answer is that in the case of affection for a child, the rasa is the tragic; in the case of covetousness, the comic; in the case of devotion to a god, the peaceful; in the case of avarice, likewise the comic. But why, in the case of love for a child, shouldn't desire as a transitory emotion alone be in operation—why is it necessary to bring in the tragic rasa? For in the former case the phenomenon is actually in existence, whereas in the latter it has to be postulated through there being an emotion that is transitory for it, and it is more parsimonious to postulate a property (in this case, desire) than an entity (in this case, the sorrowful rasa). The reason is that the desire expends itself in producing grief, since grief comes from desire. . . .[36]

(7.63) Now, there are two basic states of mind, engagement and disengagement. In the case of disengagement we have the peaceful rasa, and analogously in the case of engagement we would appear to have a "rasa of phenomenal reality," for we cannot argue that rasa arises in the former case but not in the latter. . . .

Furthermore, this rasa of phenomenal reality cannot be purely the genus of which the other rasas are species, for the peaceful would have to be excluded and thereby turn out to be a semblance of rasa. Instead, like flashes of lightning, desire, along with amusement, grief, anger, determination, fear, revulsion, and amazement, arise and vanish in this rasa of phenomenal reality, and hence all these stable emotions function for it as transitory emotions. The definition of the rasa of phenomenal reality is this: it is a latent impression, consisting of nescience, that comes to be awakened. This nescience is its stable emotion; its foundational and stimulant factors are good and bad karma, which underwrite experience in the world; whereas its reactions are such things as a child, a wife, success, or preeminence.

6.3 DEVOTEES EXPERIENCING RASA

Pearls of the Bhāgavata, of Vopadeva (c. 1300) with the *Lamp for Transcendence* of Hemadri (c. 1300)

Pearls of the Bhāgavata, a now little-studied but historically influential work from late thirteenth-century Maharashtra, was composed by a scholar known principally for his elementary Sanskrit grammar. Basically an anthology of citations from the *Bhāgavatapurāṇa*, the late tenth-century masterpiece of religious poetry, the *Pearls* is arranged so as to illustrate, on the basis of selected verses from the *purāṇa*, core themes in Vaishnava theology: the nature of the deity, the character of devotion and its subsidiary practices (learning the deeds of Vishnu/Krishna, singing hymns about him, and so on), and the definition and illustration of the kinds of devotee. What is significant is that the various emotional attitudes the devotee can have toward Vishnu are now all conceived of by way of rasa theory. The canonical rasas are redefined as simply nine aspects of a single "devotional rasa," a concept mentioned in passing in earlier texts but developed for the first time in the *Pearls*.[37]

More valuable for our purposes here than the text of Vopadeva is the commentary of Hemadri, who appears to have been his teacher.[38] He is known to us principally for his work on law, the massive *Philosopher's Stone of the Four Ends of Man* (*Caturvargacintāmaṇi*), but also as chief minister of the Yadava kings of Devagiri in their last decades of autonomy before absorption into the Delhi Sultanate (1294). Hemadri's account is a spirited and innovative defense of the new rasa, a concept that in the following centuries was to be elaborated far beyond the *Pearls* and that found wide resonance in Bengal with the rise of new religious movements in the sixteenth century.

The devotional rasa in the *Pearls* is not one thing but a category that covers the whole spectrum of emotions that devotees experience when confronted with the deeds of Krishna. But here again is the ambiguity that has persisted, in one form or another, throughout the long history of the discourse on rasa. Is the rasa Vopadeva and Hemadri are analyzing something they think is located in the characters who are themselves in their multifarious ways devoted to the god? Is it instead, or in addition, located in everyday devotees listening to or watching the stories—or indeed, such devotees who thereby become themselves veritable characters in the Krishna story? The *Pearls* never raises the third possibility—that would be the great innovation of Bengali theological aesthetics—and its exposition of the first and second gives no decisive answer. Vopadeva's base text itself is decidedly in favor of the first option. In the illustrations of the erotic provided below, the author makes clear he is interested in the devotional erotic of the women, in its four principal aspects: the aristocratic women of Hastinapura, who are *seeing* Krishna as he leaves the city; the village women of Vraja, who are described (by the Hastinapura women) as *touching* Krishna; the women freed by Krishna from a demon's captivity and then betrothed to him, who have *intercourse* with Krishna; and again the women of Vraja, who have the enjoyment of *conversing* with Krishna. It is undoubtedly the reactions of the various classes of women that are key for Vopadeva; even in the absence of explicit comment, their juxtaposition is enough to make the argument.

It may be that the illustrations are sometimes adduced to show us not the devotees in the original Krishna storyworld experiencing the various rasas, but instead the various kinds of poems that produce the nine rasas experienced by real-world devotees. And this seems to be Hemadri's understanding. While he himself reviews, if only parenthetically, the different possibilities of the location of rasa and declines to assert his own view, his defense of the devotional rasa is in part based on "The very fact that the audience comes to have the devotional rasa with its full complement of aesthetic elements." And he is more emphatic elsewhere: "What exists in the characters, Janaki, the goodly Rama, and so on is only desire or other such emotion, not rasa," which must, accordingly, exist in the viewer/reader alone.

It would not do to conclude that author and commentator disagree, not only because we have so little evidence about the former's view but also because the two aspects of rasa are, as we have frequently noted elsewhere, in the end inseparable. The longer-term historical development of the devotional rasa, however, would largely render the older dichotomy irrelevant.

FROM *PEARLS OF THE* BHĀGAVATA, OF VOPADEVA (V) WITH THE *LAMP FOR TRANSCENDENCE* OF HEMADRI (H)

(Chapter 11)

The Section on the Devotee of Vishnu. First, the definition of "devotee," and the various types.

(V) (11.1) Whoever in this world find their thoughts directed to Krishna just once, if only to his lotus feet, and thereby become enamored of him, if only of his qualities, will become devotees. They will have undergone all expiation and so will never, even in their dreams, behold Yama, god of death, or his noose-bearing minions.[39]

(p. 164) There are nine kinds of devotee, precisely because the experience of the devotional rasa has nine forms: the comic, erotic, tragic, violent, fearful, macabre, peaceful, fantastic, and heroic.

Such are the general definition and the varieties of devotee in the *Pearls.*

(H) Devotion may arise either from scriptural injunction or spontaneously,[40] but at all events, when it reaches the highest pitch it becomes rasa. To quote: "Emotions when fully developed become rasa."[41] One becomes a devotee from the experience of devotion, in the same way as one becomes a satisfied person from the experience of satisfaction. There are nine sorts of devotee by virtue of the nine modalities of rasa. In other words, the comic and the rest, when employed with respect to the Blessed One, achieve the state of being rasa, given that all those emotions are encompassed by the definition of devotion, as the scripture tells us ("Therefore, one must by some means or other direct one's thoughts to Krishna").[42] The comic[43] and the rest will be defined in due course. The nine rasas arise from particular combinations of the three constituents of reality: pleasure, pain, and insensibility.[44] To explain: the first three (the comic, erotic, and tragic) are based on volatility; the second three (the violent, fearful, and macabre) on stolidity; the last three (the peaceful, fantastic, and heroic) on sensitivity, for rasas are derivatives of these three constituents (which are discussed in BhPu 11.25). . . .

As noted, the violent, fearful, and macabre rasas consist of stolidity, hence are inauspicious, and for that reason are not mentioned first in the above list (those rasas are themselves listed in order of least to most objectionable). One might still wonder why the erotic is not placed at the head of the list here ("the comic, erotic," etc.), for at least two reasons. For one thing, the erotic is the leading rasa, according to the doctrines of the teacher of dramaturgy,[45] since everyone knows that a person in love is enviable. For another, the very etymology of the term "the erotic" (*śṛṅgāra*)—"what goes to" (*iyarti*), i.e., attains, the "peak" (*śṛṅga*), i.e., the primary position—betokens its primacy. Why then should the comic have been placed at the head here?

There is some truth to this objection, but in fact the teacher[46] did not mention it first precisely in order to indicate that in the *Bhāgavata*, a sacred work concerned with spiritual liberation, the erotic is subordinate to [165] devotion and as such cannot be predominant. In view of this, and the fact that something must of necessity be listed first, the comic is mentioned since it is the least complex.[47] . . .

The devotional rasa is thus experienced in these nine varieties, the comic and so on. But how, one might ask, can devotion be a rasa at all when it is not defined as such—as for example in the *Ten Dramatic Forms* and its commentary—with its specific factors and reactions? . . . [48] [167] But surely, whenever there is a conjunction with all these, rasa must arise. (On one view, rasa in the primary sense of the term is something that exists in the character, Rama for example, thanks to the power of the actor; on a second view, it exists in the actor alone; on a third, in the audience; on a fourth, in the actor as well as in the audience since the consciousness of rasa finds equal footing in both. For some, rasa is something produced; for others, it is something made known or experienced or manifested. The curious can get details from the treatises themselves; I refrain from dilating on the matter here lest this work grow too long.) The argument some make that devotion cannot be a rasa because it lacks the full complement of aesthetic elements has been rejected by others who aver that this can very well be posited of devotion. Hence the author gives his reply:

(V) The "devotional rasa" is the rapture produced from hearing or otherwise experiencing the deeds of Vishnu, as described by Vyasa and others, or of his devotees, and is of nine different sorts.

(H) (. . . The "devotees" of Vishnu are the cowherd women[49] and so on. "Otherwise experiencing" means that the rapture can be a matter of seeing, chanting, remembering, or dramatic acting.)[50] The very fact that the audience comes to have the devotional rasa with its full complement of aesthetic elements shows that its existence cannot be denied. The full complement of aesthetic elements is as follows: the stable emotion consists of the directing of one's mind to Vishnu by one means or another; the stimulant factors are hearing or otherwise experiencing his deeds; Vishnu or his devotees are the foundational factor; the reactions, shortly to be detailed, are paralysis and so on, as appropriate to the situation, and the transitory emotions, satisfaction and so on. The "means" just mentioned are desire, amusement, and the other stable emotions. "As described by" poets: this implies that the term "rasa" pertains only to matters conveyed by great poets in their compositions. (Accordingly, what actually exists in the characters themselves, Janaki, the goodly Rama, and so on, is only desire or some such emotion, not rasa, since the true form of rasa is transcendent rapture. Moreover, while sometimes rapture exists in the erotic or other such rasas, it is not found among the fearful and related rasas, and hence we should not in fact use the term "rasa" in reference to them.) And that is why the qualifications "if (the principal causes, ancillary causes, and effects of the stable emotion) are used in poetry or drama"[51] are provided. I would add that when rasa is conveyed by literary compositions, it tastes much sweeter than when it is displayed through dramatic acting. To quote: "The means of rasa are twofold: a poet's speech and dramatic acting. The former is superior, since it comes about through the grandeur of the narrative's power."[52]

Now, Abhinavagupta and Hemachandra are wrong to argue that "the same thing can be said of devotion."[53] For we have demonstrated that devotion is indeed a rasa, and to deny it, despite the presence of the full complement of factors, is merely the last resort of stubbornness. And there is no point objecting that, although devotion may conform to a rasa formally, it fails to achieve the status of rasa because it is not something universally accessible. For if that reason really proved anything, [168] then all rasas would be cease to be rasas.[54] For when ritualists and bloodless interpreters of the Veda enter into the theater they are nothing but boors, given their incapacity for aesthetic rapture. Similarly, men who have attained spiritual peace, religious celibates, and others like them are outsiders to the savoring of the erotic rasa. Men of intense passion are incapable of relishing the peaceful rasa, while people who have never felt the sting of grief sit stone-faced when they should be savoring the tragic. Since, accordingly, only people with the relevant predispositions are capable of relishing rasa, the view that devotion is a rasa is quite unobjectionable.

Nonetheless, one might contend that we are minimizing the number when we say the rasa of devotion is "of nine different sorts." For did King Bhoja and others not argue that there are many other rasas?[55] Thus, we are told there is an "affectionate rasa," whose stable emotion is attachment, as in the following poem: "A man who loves a woman. . . ."[56] Here we have a romantic protagonist of tender[57] nature; the foundational factor is his beloved; the stimulant factors are the beauty of the female object of his affection[58] and so on; confusion, sagacity, satisfaction, and the like are the transitory emotions; thereby the attachment is apprehended as love. There is also said to be a "noble rasa" whose stable emotion is sagacity,[59] as in "Any other man, however lowborn, / would not hesitate to ask for this girl's hand // let alone a world conqueror, / the great grandson of Brahma."[60] Here we a have a dignified protagonist, Rama, exercising his sagacity—"This Sita is fit for me to marry." When stimulated by seeing her wooed by Ravana and by goading from Lakshmana, and combined with the transitory emotions that are then generated (anxiety, perplexity, shame, dissimulation, remembrance) and those that can be inferred as appropriate for what follows (discernment, adroitness, firmness, and so on), this sagacity arises in the form of the noble rasa. Again, there is said to be a "vainglorious rasa," whose stable emotion is pride, as in "So long as I am armed. . . ."[61]

The entire foregoing argument is false, however, because one or another of the primary stable emotions themselves is present in each of the above cases. Moreover, Bhoja himself classified "attachment" and so on among the transitory emotions ("pride, attachment . . . are the transitory emotions"),[62] and "transitory" and "stable" are antithetical terms, like "mother" and "barren woman." Should one nonetheless persist in this argument, the number of rasas would turn out to be the same as the number of transitory emotions, which is precisely why Bharata and other authorities have not broached this. And for the same reason, [169] the argument for yet another rasa called lustfulness, with pride as its stable emotion, can be rejected. Therefore what the teacher has said, that there are "nine sorts," is indeed correct.[63] . . .

(V) (p. 171) The erotic rasa is of two sorts, the erotic enjoyed and the erotic thwarted.

(H) "En-joyment" is the joy the comes about from the "en-gagement" of a man and a woman. This engagement is of four types: seeing, touching, conversing, and intercourse. All other subtypes can be included in these. . . . The enjoyment experienced by the female is superior to that of the male, given the predominance of affection in her, and this is what the author shows as he introduces the enjoyment of seeing.

(V) The erotic enjoyed is illustrated in the following verses spoken by the women of Hastinapura:[64]

(v. 7) "There he is, the Primal Man, they say, who was one and alone when his self—
the Lord himself, the world's self—lay enfolded, without distinctions,
in cosmic night, his powers slumbering
before nature's three constituents began their work. . . .[65]

(v. 14)[66] In a past life they must have been married to the Lord and worshipped him
with vows, ablutions, offerings and the like, dear friend,
that those women of Vraja can now drink in the nectar of his lower lip
again and again, and grow faint at the very thought of it.[67]

(H) In the above verse he illustrates the enjoyment of touching.[68] . . . One cannot say that this is a case of semblance of rasa on the grounds that, whereas the city women are longing for Krishna, the Blessed One is indifferent to them (and one defines semblance of rasa as the absence[69] of mutual responsiveness).[70] For in the very next verse reference is made to his own affection for them ("As the city women spoke these words, Hari greeted them with a smiling glance as he went by").[71] . . .

(v. 17) The women,[72] having obtained Shri's husband as their own—
whose ways even Brahma and the other gods cannot fathom—
loved him unceasingly, with boundless joy, though still too bashful
to speak when in his presence, with a look filled with love and laughter.[73] . . .

(H) In the above he illustrates intercourse, which follows upon touching.

(v. 21) Blessed indeed are the women of Vraja that the Primal Being,
hidden in the guise of a mortal—decked with a wildflower garland,
tending the cows with brother Bala, playing the flute—
came to play among them, he whose feet are worshiped by Shiva and his wife.[74] . . .

(H) In the above he illustrates the enjoyment of conversing. . . .[75]

DIVINE JEWEL OF ORNAMENTATION OF KAVIKARNAPURA (C. 1550) WITH THE *COMMENTARY* OF LOKANATHA CHAKRAVARTIN (C. 1690)

Kavikarnapura—Paramanandadasasena Kavikarnapura, to use his full name—was a poet, dramatist, and poetician from Bengal active in the late sixteenth century. He was the son of a direct disciple of the charismatic religious figure Chaitanya (1486–1533), a fact that stamped his creative work profoundly. His poetry and drama as well as his poetics are all concerned directly with Chaitanya or indirectly with the doctrine of Krishna devotionalism that he promulgated. Kavikarnapura's fame rests upon his *Divine Jewel of Ornamentation*, a full-scale account of literary theory modeled on Mammata's *Light on Poetry* ("divine jewel," *kaustubha*, a generic title suffix for comprehensive surveys of knowledge systems in the early modern era, is especially apt in the present case since the word refers to the chest ornament of Vishnu).

The ideas about rasa that Kavikarnapura proposes stand in a complicated relationship to the pioneering works of Vaishnava aesthetic theology, those of Rupa Gosvamin and Jiva Gosvamin, examined in the following section. While chronologically a decade or two later and participating in the same religious movement, Kavikarnapura seems to have been influenced by neither. This is most certainly not the case with the author of the sole printed commentary on the *Divine Jewel*, one Lokanatha Chakravartin (likely late seventeenth century), who goes to considerable lengths to reconcile their divergent views.[76]

The *Divine Jewel* is a curious work, occasionally hard to follow owing to apparent inconsistencies. It is also, occasionally, rich with new insights. Kavikarnapura differentiates between "latent" and "patent" rasa,[77] terms he invented to account for why (as he believes) the character does not feel rasa—the question of the location of aesthetic emotion being as alive as ever; provides a new typology of semblance of rasa ("commonly acknowledged," "artificial," and "axiomatic") and insists that Krishna's love for the married women of Vraja is not "improper" and hence not a semblance of the erotic; and distinguishes "ordinary" from "extraordinary" rasa.[78] These last terms are introduced to address a new problem: how to preserve within a single analytic both secular and religious rasa, so to call it, for now the latter is constituted as a new, *complementary* category of its own (the *Pearls of the* Bhāgavata had paid no attention to nonreligious poetry, and while subsuming all devotion under rasa implicitly subsumed all rasa under devotion). And there are other innovations Kavikarnapura makes, or perhaps remakes. One is the apparent reduction of the multiplicity of affective states in the rasa experience to one: the "particular property of the mind" that constitutes "the root of the sprout of savoring" is, he declares, "single, but it becomes multiple given the multiplicity of the objective factors." And from reducing all emotions to one, he goes on to reduce all rasas: "In fact, all rasas are contained in the rasa of love."[79] This might suggest a knowledge of Bhoja's *Light on Passion*, and in fact Kavikarnapura mentions Bhoja (as Hemadri did before him) when noting that the king proposed eleven rasas, adding parental affection and love to the canonical nine. But there is no evidence that scholars in late-sixteenth-century Bengal had access to Bhoja's *Light*, where the singularity doctrine is fully expounded,[80] and in any case Kavikarnapura's overall grasp of his views (like Hemadri's) is flawed: Bhoja does add those rasas but does not cap the number at eleven (in fact, all the emotions can become rasa); his notion of love or passion has nothing whatever to do with the love that lies at the root of the *Divine Jewel*; and most important, his concept of the locus of aesthetic response is at odds with that of Kavikarnapura.

Consider for this last point the argument made at the end of the verse just cited: "And this mental property belongs to the audience members." For Kavikarnapura, the stable emotion that is the source of rasa belongs exclusively to the viewer/reader—and it is one and one only because rasa as such must always consist of pleasure, regardless of the specific rasa of the aesthetic object. (This argument, deriving ultimately from Dhanika and/or Abhinavagupta, was long debated, as we have seen, especially in such works at the *Mirror of Drama*.) It is largely (though not exclusively) because rasa must be pleasurable that it cannot apply to the character—who obviously feels pain as well as pleasure across the various rasa contexts—or does so only in a conventional sense. The author is far from clear here, however, and the new terminology he uses does not always succeed in attaining the requisite precision.

Thus, Kavikarnapura speaks of rasa as being "self-evident" or "given" or "normal" in the case of the characters while at the same time flatly asserting that rasa "cannot be located in the character." With regard to an example of the heroic, contrarily, he characterizes rasa in the character as "latent" and in the viewer/reader as "patent." The tragic, however, cannot exist in the character even in latent form, since in the character the tragic cannot be a feeling of pleasure and hence cannot be rasa.[81] Arjuna's fear at the sight of the cosmic form of Krishna does become rasa in the character (Arjuna), but only because of his joy at the presence of Krishna, the foundational factor. In the end, the many considerable tensions of the exposition reach the breaking point when we learn that eight rasas exist in drama, whereas only a few rasas, such as the erotic, exist in the viewer's world; the macabre is accordingly a rasa in the storyworld though it is not pleasurable, but not a rasa in the viewer's world, though it can be as pleasurable in its own way as any other rasa.

We might illuminate some of the obscurities in Kavikarnapura's account by distinguishing between the two analytics at work. Rasa is pleasure; it is felt in a real way by the viewer, across all rasas; it is felt by the character in a "latent" or occluded way, and only in the case of the rasas that are inherently pleasurable or where Krishna himself is present to transform an unpleasant experience into a pleasant one. More generally, a better sense of the challenge Kavikarnapura was facing might produce a more charitable interpretation of his effort. He was poised between two models of aesthetic response. One was the theory, by then dominant, of Bhatta Nayaka/Abhinavagupta, which understands literary rasa as exclusively an experience of the spectator and, crucially, of secular literature. The other was the new Vaishnava theological aesthetics in the air, and taking concrete shape among theorists such as Rupa Gosvamin and especially his nephew Jiva. They regard the rasa of the "character" as predominant, indeed, essential, and religious literature as its only vehicle. For it is the real devotee in the real world, just like the character devotee in the storyworld, who experiences rasa when participating as "characters" in the play of Krishna that is their actual lives.

Here, however, we confront the problematic chronological and intellectual-historical relationship earlier noted. Rupa was some forty years senior to Kavikarnapura, while Jiva was almost an exact contemporary, give or take a decade (Jiva is counted an immediate disciple of Chaitanya, while Kavikarnapura as noted was the son of an immediate disciple, Shivanandasena). Kavikarnapura cites none of Rupa's or Jiva's treatises in his *Divine Jewel* (though he does mention Rupa in his play, the *Moonrise of Caitanya, Caitanyacandrodaya*), and knows none of their specific doctrines.[82] And of course the uncle and nephew lived in Vrindavana, while Kavikarnapura was 1,500 km away in eastern India (probably Puri). Resonances between the *Divine Jewel* and Rupa and Jiva's theories are superficial and no doubt derive from a common source (perhaps the *Bhāgavatapurāṇa* itself).[83] It is highly unlikely, then, that Kavikarnapura was aiming to revise Jiva's and Rupa's works, however much his otherwise unmotivated insistence that "in this work on rasa the analysis exclusively concerns literature" might be seen as directed against Jiva, who wants to leave behind the rasa of secular poetry entirely.[84] It is more reasonable to hold that he was familiar only indirectly with the remarkable theological-aesthetic innovations they were offering, which were to completely supersede his own, but toward which, in his own way, he was groping.

FROM THE *DIVINE JEWEL OF ORNAMENTATION* OF KAVIKARNAPURA (K) WITH THE *COMMENTARY* OF LOKANATHA CHAKRAVARTIN (LC)

(LC) (p. 118) The characterizations of the factors, stable emotions, rasa, and so on that we find in this work differ from those found in the *Ambrosial River of the Rasa of Devotion*. [119] They are enunciated in deference to the literary-critical tradition and hence on occasion are analytically deficient. Nonetheless, [120] when the author describes the chief rasa, of the "extraordinary" sort, the characterization is identical in both works, and hence nothing is really amiss.[85]

> (K) (5.63) There is a particular property of the mind free from volatility and stolidity and endowed with sensitivity that is the root of the sprout of savoring.[86] The learned call this the stable emotion. It is single,[87] but it becomes multiple given the multiplicity of the objective factors. And this mental property belongs to the audience members.

The stable emotions of the characters, on the other hand, are inherently[88] various:

> (5.64) Desire in the case of the erotic rasa, determination in the case of the heroic . . . :

[123] There are, according to some, these eight stable emotions, pertaining to eight associated rasas, in drama. Others, however, argue for a ninth rasa called the peaceful, whose stable emotion is dispassion. Bhoja asserts that there are eleven, adding parental affection and love, for which the stable emotions are possessiveness and tenderness respectively.[89] These eleven rasas, in both literature seen and literature heard, are prized by the assembly of sensitive viewers/readers.

[124] First, regarding desire:

(5.65–67) Desire is a mental state of delight that inclines one to the enjoyment of pleasure. It comprises three additional emotions: affection, friendship, and companionship. Desire strictly speaking pertains to an intimate relation, which must be the relation of a man and a woman. A nonintimate relation is termed affection, such as that between (from the man's viewpoint) the wife of one's friend and (from the woman's) the friend of one's husband, as in the case of Krishna and Draupadi. Friendship pertains to two females or two males for each other. Affection is a purely mental state, whereas friendship allows for physical contact. Companionship is a steady state that manifest no changes.

This last pertains to the relationship between male and female friends of the hero and the heroine respectively.

(5.68) When this mental state of delight pertains to a deity or the like, it is called "emotion."[90]

"Or the like" means a guru and so on. . . .

(LC) Insofar as Krishna is the supreme lord, who is characterized by such traits as omnipresence, the stable emotion of the devotee singing his praises can never *not* be in intimate relation with him, and hence it must[91] be termed "desire." Nonetheless, this stable emotion must be given an independent designation, "emotion" as such. . . . This "emotion" is what the author will define as the "devotional" rasa, and it has to be distinguished from the emotion that is a transformation of desire, the stable emotion pertaining to intimate relations.[92]

(K) The author now describes the precise nature of rasa, for whose manifestation the aesthetic elements function as direct and ancillary causes and effects:

(5.70) Rasa is a pleasure so rapturous that it occludes all other cognitive functions, internal as well as external, comprising only the causal and related elements.[93]

Rasa may self-evidently pertain to the high-status characters, but in the case of literature [130] it belongs exclusively to the audience members.[94] Theirs is the stable emotion aforementioned, that particular mental property at the root of savoring, which alone is susceptible to the manifestation of any rasa. A logical argument is offered:

(5.71) Because rasa consists only of bliss, it must be singular; it is in fact that one stable emotion.[95] Rasa seems to be multiple only because of the multiplicity of its conditioning factors, which are desire, amusement, grief, and so on.

For example, however much or little water may be contained in a vessel of whatever sort, there is always only a single image of the sun reflected in it. In the same way, any variety that rasa may appear to have in fact relates to its conditioning factors, not to the bliss that rasa consists of.[96]

The multiple stable emotions earlier listed can be located either in two characters, in one, or in two and/or one:[97] thus, desire must be located in two, disgust in one, whereas anger can be in two or one. But these all pertain to the characters; as already noted, the audience members have only a single stable emotion.

(5.72) Rasa is of three types: ordinary, extraordinary, or semblance.

Rasa is ordinary, that is, worldly, when it concerns literary characters such as Malati, Madhava, and so on. It is extraordinary when it concerns the divinities Krishna, Radha, and the like.

(LC) The fact of the matter is that rasa in the case of an "ordinary" character does not really exist, and so when the author describes the three types of rasa he is only doing so in conformity with the views of others. Those who believe that rasa can exist in the case of an ordinary character are in error. There can be no rasa in perishable beings like ordinary protagonists, who come to an end in worms, feces, and ash, because we apprehend upon reflection that the foundational factors (like the female protagonist) are degraded beings; on the contrary, what arises is the opposite of rasa, pure aversion. So the description of rasa must be restricted to the extraordinary character. In fact, this is why the author has adduced not a single poem to illustrate the ordinary rasa, and all his illustrative verses pertain to the extraordinary.

(K) The semblance of a rasa is occasioned by such things as social impropriety.[98] It too is of three sorts: commonly acknowledged, artificial, and axiomatic. The first is when a relationship between two characters is commonly acknowledged to be deficient from the start and does not attain consummation; and semblance though it may be, it does enhance the rasa. An example in the case of an ordinary rasa is the commonly acknowledged character of the relationship of Malati to Nandana and how this enhances her desire for Madhava; in the case of an extraordinary rasa, the commonly acknowledged character of the relationship of Rukmini and Shishupala, [132] which enhances her desire for Krishna.[99] An example of artificial semblance is when Madhava's friend Makaranda disguises himself as Malati and manifests petulance toward Nandana. The axiomatic sort of semblance is occasioned by impropriety as such, as for example if a woman were to have multiple lovers. To quote [133]: "Although a poem may constitute a semblance of rasa by representing desire for a married woman, it can still constitute great poetry if it shows mastery of implicature."[100] That is to say,[101] in accordance with my earlier statement that "Rasa, emotion, semblance of rasa and emotion, cessation of emotion, and so on are all implicature of the sort that is without succession" (3.10), we may agree that "Although a given rasa may be a semblance, it can participate in implicature at the moment of aesthetic rapture."[102] Thus, in the case of the ordinary rasa, what constitutes the limiting condition of a poem's greatness is implicature and that alone, not whether or not it violates propriety.[103]

For extraordinary rasa, by contrast, it is precisely desire for a married woman that is taught[104] as desire's highest form of all. This is not occasioned by impropriety, both because it is proven to be something supermundane—which, as the maxim goes, is not only not a failing but also a strength—and because it is beyond the capacity of reason to understand. [134] To quote: "One cannot grasp by logic entities that are supermundane."[105] The daughters-in-law of Vraja were singlemindedly given over to Krishna, and hence were no longer concerned with their husbands; their husbands had physical contact with them only by fixating on the women's shadow form created by cosmic maya.[106] For these two reasons, far from there being anything improper, the women's mental state of delight was, on the contrary, completely innocent, since it was conditioned by nothing more than pure love.[107]

[135] In this work on rasa, the analysis exclusively concerns literature, both the seen and the heard.[108] In the former, the aesthetic elements are conveyed both by language and by actors' acting and the things acted out; in the latter, only by language. Now, how could rasa be located in the character? Nor can it be in the actors, for they [136] are only skilled in displaying what they have learned by training and practice, and have no privileged capacity for savoring rasa. Should they too ever appear to be in that state where all objects of cognition have vanished, it would simply mean that they have become members of the audience; that they continue to act is simply a consequence of their innate dispositions, as an adept who is "liberated in life" continues to eat food and engage in worldly affairs. Accordingly, it can only be the audience members who have rasa.

(LC) The question in this prima facie statement is this: since the characters, that is, the devotees,[109] do not actually exist then and there,[110] who is it that experiences rasa on seeing a drama or hearing a poem?

(K) (p. 137) To explain: When viewers/readers see or hear the deeds of the characters being imitated by the actor, an intense rapture is produced, and this rapture is accompanied by a vision wherein all objects of cognition vanish for them, except for the aesthetic elements themselves. By virtue of this, and following upon the experience of rapture, they have an intense vision of the fantastic rasa, whatever other rasa may be at issue, in accordance with the view that "Rapture is the essence of rasa—rasa cannot be rasa without it. Given this, it follows that in every rasa is to be found the fantastic rasa."[111] That is, they think, "How fantastic is Rama and Sita's skill in the arts of love," or "How fantastic is this battle of Rama and Ravana," or "How fantastic are the doings of the hungry ghosts." This leads to a special kind of apprehension entirely separate from any that can be said to be either true, false, doubtful, or similar.[112] Thereby the aesthetic elements, factitious though they be, are not apprehended as such—they are like images perfectly painted in a picture, so that one thinks, "These two are Rama and Sita"; "This is Rama overwhelmed with grief for Sita"; "These two are Rama and Ravana"; "This is the tiger sowing terror among the people"; "This is the cremation ground, crowded with dancing ghouls drunk on the entrails and flesh of the masses of corpses they have eaten." As a result of this process, the minds of the audience members, their stolidity and volatility cleansed by their innate predispositions for rasa, are rendered as pure as possible, and a self-identical bliss is engendered.[113]

It is not possible for *all* the various stable emotions, desire and the rest, to inhabit one and the same mind of the viewer; [138] being mutually dissimilar, they cannot possibly coexist at the same time in the same location. Moreover, desire could not possibly be a stable emotion in the mind of an ascetic, nor fear or grief in those who have achieved inner peace. On the contrary, we are led to posit in the viewer a special mental property, a *single* root of savoring that allows one to experience the rapture that underlies all rasas. That is why the fearful, the macabre, and the like can be rasas in poetry and drama, and only there and not in the world.[114] That is why it has been said [139], "There are held to be eight rasas *in drama*";[115] that is, some rasas exist in drama alone, whereas only a few rasas, the erotic and some others, can be said to be rasas in the viewer's world too, insofar as they are covered by the aforementioned definition of rasa.[116] . . .

(p. 140) [An example of the heroic, where Krishna fights Jarasandha, an enemy king]: Here the stable emotion is determination, and it is located in both warriors. The foundational factor for Krishna is Jarasandha, and Jarasandha for Krishna. Their threatening each other is the stimulant factor; the reactions are such things as their handiwork in showering each other with arrows; the transitory emotions are pride, ferocity, vindictiveness, recklessness, and the like. The stable emotion, enhanced by these elements, becomes rasa. The rasa in the character, in the present case Krishna, is latent, but it is patent in the audience member upon hearing the poem. This distinction should be understood to apply everywhere in the following analysis. . . .

(LC) The rasa in Krishna is "latent" because all his divine play and its objects are at present occluded from our view; for the audience members, however, it is the inconceivable power of their own stable emotion—root of the sprout of aesthetic savoring—that it is able to manifest that play of Krishna's, occluded though it may now really be, when it is presented in a play or poem. And it manifests itself as if right before one's eyes.

(p. 141) [An example of the tragic, where a woman mourns the death of her child in the flooding of Dvaraka, and calls on Krishna for aid:] Here the stable emotion is grief, which is located in a single individual. The foundational factor is the death of her child; the stimulant factor is her possessiveness over the child; the reactions are her breast beating and so on; the transitory emotions are depression, despondency, fatigue, and the like. This rasa is in the audience members alone, not in the character, not even in latent form. And although the rasa is in the audience, it is of the extraordinary type, since it relates to Krishna. . . .

(LC) The sorrow at the death of her son obstructs in her the manifestation of rasa, which after all is pure bliss.

(p. 144) [An example of the fearful, where Arjuna has just glimpsed the cosmic form of Krishna:] Here the stable emotion is Arjuna's fear, and it is located in the single individual. The foundational factor is Krishna displaying his cosmic form; the stimulant factor the fangs and so on appearing in that form; the reaction the fright indicated by his calls for help, and the transient emotion the despondency in his cry ("I have ceased to be Partha / I have become *'apārtha,'* " that is, useless). Since all the requisite elements are present, the stable emotion has already attained the state of rasa, even in the character Arjuna, given that Krishna is the foundational factor. Even though the emotion is fear, there is bliss present, connected as it is with the vision of Krishna, and hence it is an entirely "extraordinary" rasa. But in the case of Makaranda[117] confronted with the foundational factor of the tiger threatening Malati and the others, there can be no bliss but only fear. If he were to take some heroic action, of course, the stable emotion would then be determination, whereby bliss might perhaps come about—but certainly not from fear. There cannot, accordingly, be any ordinary rasa of the fearful.[118] . . .

(p. 147) Just as in the case of despair, which, though a transitory emotion, takes on the function of a stable emotion so as to become the peaceful rasa, so desire directed toward a god, which, as earlier noted, is technically termed "emotion" as such, becomes the "devotional rasa" when endowed with the full complement of aesthetic elements. This makes twelve rasas. When the object of the devotional rasa is Krishna, the devotional rasa itself has ten subvarieties, thanks to the ten different stable emotions.[119] These can easily be adduced from other works. . . .

[148] Now the rasa of love:

"You love me and I love you," we tell each other,
"You are my life and I am yours," we prattle,
"You belong to me and I to you." . . . It's just not right, Radha.
We should never use "you" and "I" when we talk.[120]

Here the stable emotion is tenderheartedness,[121] which is located in both. The foundational factor is each partner for the other; the stimulant factor is the perfume of each other's excellences; the reaction is the absence of any need to specify these; the transitory emotions are sagacity, longing, and so on. The rasa is latent in Krishna and Radha, it is patent in the audience members.

In fact, all rasas are contained in the rasa of love. It would require a very detailed exposition to show this, and I therefore only offer it as a proposition lest the book grow inordinately long.[122]

[149] Some scholars argue that the rasa of Krishna and Radha is always the erotic, but even on that view the present example is not inapposite: one could say that here the erotic is the dominant and the rasa of love the subordinate, with the subordinate rasa overshadowing, as sometimes happens. But for us, love is actually the dominant rasa here and the erotic is subordinate. To quote: "Rasa is an undivided whole, and all rasas and emotions arise in love and vanish in love, like waves on the ocean."[123]

[150] Now the devotional rasa.

Victory to you, glorious lord, son of Nanda, who delights Vrindavana;
lover of divine women in the form of the village girls, crestjewel of the gods;
the nectar of your lotus feet surpasses even the flow of mental bliss.
Homage, homage to you, Govinda, great root of all the worlds.

Because this poem pertains to a deity, desire (the mental state of delight) is here "emotion" as such, which now functions as a stable emotion.[124] The foundational factor is Krishna; the stimulant, his greatness; the reaction, tenderheartedness; the transitory emotions despair, despondency, and so on. The rasa in the devotees[125] is latent, and patent in the audience members.

AMBROSIAL RIVER OF THE RASA OF DEVOTION OF RUPA GOSVAMIN (1541) WITH THE *PASSAGE THROUGH THE IMPASSABLE* OF JIVA GOSVAMIN (1541), AND *TREATISE ON DIVINE LOVE* OF JIVA GOSVAMIN (C. 1550)

Rupa Gosvamin (c. 1470–1557) was a remarkable figure whose life and work embodied many of the new social, cultural, and religious possibilities of the early modern era in India. Born in Karnataka, he migrated to Bengal, where he received a traditional Sanskrit education from the celebrated logicians of Navadvip before entering the service of Nawab Husain Shah as private secretary. His encounter with the religious reformer Chaitanya prompted him to leave political life. Along with Sanatana, his elder brother, and later Jiva (b. 1513 or 1523), the son of his younger brother, he eventually settled in Vrindavana, legendary site of Krishna's childhood, and devoted himself to Vaishnava theology.[126] Rupa was a leading theoretician of one of the most remarkable religious movements of early modern India, and in particular, a striking innovator in the aesthetic turn in theology. Although he knew Vopadeva's *Pearls*, he moves far beyond him;[127] at the same time, by what is only a superficial contradiction, he hearkens back to a much older conception of rasa at variance with the notions ascendant since the reformulation of Abhinavagupta five centuries earlier. In his works and those of Jiva, many of the complexities of rasa theory achieve their greatest intensification.

The system of theological aesthetics that Rupa created is complex, and we must leave aside here many of the finer distinctions he introduced. (In the taxonomy of rasas, for example, he recognizes twelve, adding to the classical eight the peaceful, the affectionate, the friendly, and the servile. These four and the erotic constitute the five principal rasas, the remaining seven taking on a subordinate status, almost as transitory emotions enlivening the primary five, which are all now considered, as in Vopadeva, species solely of the rasa of devotion.) More consequential for our purposes are the issues that flow from Rupa's definition of rasa: "The stable emotion . . . becomes itself the supreme state of rasa through the full development of the full enhancement of the aesthetic elements . . . [and] comes to be savored in the hearts of devotees." While the language of savoring may faintly recall Abhinavagupta (it is of course part of the foundational metaphor in the *Treatise on Drama*), Rupa's overall understanding is decidedly nothing like Abhinava's, in which rasa is "emotion that is grasped [by the spectator] when he is in a state completely unencumbered by the impediments of phenomenal existence (and that remains in essence a process of tasting)." Rupa argues that rasa is nothing other than a stable emotion in a state of full development through the work of the various aesthetic elements, which affiliates him not only with Bhoja but also with the classical tradition, beginning with Bhatta Lollata in the early ninth century, that Bhoja crowned.

The recentering in rasa discourse of the stable emotion of the character is fully spelled out later in this selection. "The view of authorities on drama—and it is entirely correct—"

Rupa argues, "is that the desire that exists in the characters cannot be rasa, because, among other reasons, it is mundane. But this desire for Krishna is supermundane, and more fantastic than all fantastic things." All interactions of characters with God in the storyworld of the drama or poem are blissful, and hence cannot but satisfy the final definition of rasa. This becomes even clearer in the work of Jiva. Of course, Jiva must first establish, in view of the continuing resistance by "ordinary *rasikas*"—the discourse of "normal" aesthetics—that devotion can even be a rasa. He does this by arguing that "divine love"[128] can be a stable emotion no less than any of the other nine; that Krishna can be a foundational factor in and of himself, without the mediation of poetry; and that the viewer/reader—that is, the devotee—most certainly has a capacity for experiencing such a rasa. Then he must go on to establish the locus of this new rasa, whereby he shows how the discrepant positions reappraised so many times in the past were still very much alive in the mid-sixteenth century. But the "primary sense of the term 'rasa,'" he concludes, is the oldest one of all: the rasa that arises in the characters. Indeed, how could rasa—defined as a supermundane phenomenon of bliss—*not* exist in those actually experiencing the full presence of God as Krishna in Vrindavana, Mathura, Dvaraka, and elsewhere? (Whether or not Krishna himself experiences rasa, the way Rama, for example, did, is a theological-aesthetic question of considerable interest to Jiva.) But the most startling conceptual move of this theological aesthetic, though only obliquely expressed in these selections, is that the characters of God's drama are not restricted to the diegetic world; they exist in this world too. People here "imitate" the original characters by participating in the ongoing drama of Krishna. The devotee himself becomes a character, and an "actor" as well, one who really experiences rasa in the primary sense of the term.

Accordingly, although only poems of the original source narrative are analyzed in these works, the narrative was now meant to be understood not in the perfect tense of myth, so to speak, but in the future tense of real life: it offers roles that the living disciple could adopt. The Vaishnava devotee who becomes a character in the divine drama of Krishna takes on the role of servant or friend or lover, even entering onto the scene, so to speak, by visiting Mathura;[129] indeed, "the entire world becomes a divine stage."[130] As is abundantly demonstrated in the history of Bengali Vaishnavism and corroborated in the lives of its greatest exponents—not only Rupa, whom his followers identified as an avatar of Rupamanjari (an attendant on Radha), but also Chaitanya himself, whose multiple roles in the divine play of Krishna are on full display in the classic Bengali biography, *Immortal Life of Caitanya* (*Caitanyacaritāmṛta*)—a true devotee is no spectator at all, but an actual participant in the drama of Krishna that is life on earth. Rasa thus belongs, as Jiva puts it, to "the original characters and their attendants, whose hearts are ever endowed with absolute rasa," and "transfers over to those who imitate them" or take on their roles in their everyday lives.

Abhinavagupta (following Bhatta Nayaka) had drawn an analogy between savoring rasa and savoring supreme being, but this was only an analogy. He forcefully and repeatedly denies that the two experiences could ever be identical. Just as the aesthetic elements exist only in the theater, so rasa exists only in drama, and never in actual reality.[131] Rupa and Jiva inhabit a profoundly different thought world, in which the very idea of aesthetic distance has been obliterated. Furthermore, all rasas other than the devotional have been relegated to the mundane sphere, and hence cannot really be rasa at all, since none, in the end, provides rasa's true bliss. In fact, secular literary experience as such cannot possess the supermundane quality of religious experience. The conclusions to which this logic leads are entirely unanticipated: that divine love is always-already a state of rasa experience, and that literature itself is in the end irrelevant—in fact, Jiva can do away with it entirely: "For one already filled with divine love, anything can cause rasa, even turning one's mind randomly toward the Blessed One—indeed, even hearing the notes of a flute. For such people, accordingly, the emotion of divine love alone suffices to generate the full complement of aesthetic elements." Whereas "mundane" literature had once been thought to produce "supermundane" rasa—Abhinava's great insight—the new theological rasa made an exclusive claim to that status (real rasa existing only in the religious experience of God)[132] and thereby demoted the old rasa of nonsacred texts to the mundane.[133] In a further irony, religious consciousness, which had once been exiled from the world of rasa—religious works were never considered part of literature, or could only be accommodated as "emotion" poetry and never fully rasa[134]—eventually succeeded in exiling literature itself, henceforth deemed incapable of producing real rasa.

Put differently, "literature" was now redefined to mean exclusively Vaishnava poetry. Whereas many Vaishnava writers, including Jiva, cite only scripture (namely, the *Bhāgavatapurāṇa*) in their discussions of theological aesthetics,[135] Rupa exemplifies his arguments about the devotional rasa with poetry, but only Vaishnava poetry, whether established classics (*Gītagovinda*, *Śrīkṛṣṇakarṇāmṛta*) or his own compositions. This is true both in the work translated here and in the *Blazing Sapphire* (or *Sapphire of the Erotic*, *Ujjvalanīlamaṇi*, on which Jiva wrote a commentary in 1540), an anthology of poetry that provides an exposition of the "erotic" rasa (the term is used here in the most esoteric of senses)[136] in reference to Krishna. Yet, the point of Rupa's practice remains uncertain. Is the viewer/reader/devotee/character supposed to *experience* the devotional rasa through his poetry? Does his poetry only *illustrate* the kinds of situations and factors that in the real world would give rise to rasa? Are both phenomena meant to occur simultaneously?

What is certain is that in these treatises the discourse of rasa is not just being transferred from poetry to theology, it is being restricted to theology. Rupa and Jiva are not arguing for yet another new interpretation of aesthetic response but for a new aesthetics of religion, a new understanding of religion as aesthetic action, which encompasses and transcends what had hitherto been thought of as the aesthetic. Rasa as an aesthetics of literature has been replaced by rasa as an aesthetics of religious life.

FROM *AMBROSIAL RIVER OF THE RASA OF DEVOTION* OF RUPA GOSVAMIN (R) WITH THE *PASSAGE THROUGH THE IMPASSABLE* OF JIVA GOSVAMIN (J)

(R) (2.1.4–5) We now describe how the stable emotion of desire—which as defined[137] pertains only to Krishna—becomes itself the supreme state of rasa through the full enhancement of the aesthetic elements. Thanks to the foundational and stimulant causes, the psychophysical and physical reactions, and transitory emotions, this stable emotion of desire for Krishna comes to be savored in the hearts of devotees who listen, understand, remember, etc.,[138] and thereby becomes the devotional rasa.

(J) "Desire" is meant to stand for all the stable emotions, since it is the dominant one.

(R) (2.1.6–11) This savor of the devotional rasa can arise only in the heart of the person who has predispositions to devotion that have been acquired both in this life and in earlier ones. When devotees have been rendered free of faults by their devotion, and their minds have become clear and brilliant; when they take delight in the *Bhāgavatapurāṇa*, are keen to associate with other *rasikas*, enjoy the pleasure of devotion to the feet of Govinda, who is their whole life, and hence do all their duties as subordinated to their love of God—then that desire in the form of bliss blazes forth in their hearts, made brilliant by the two sets of innate dispositions.[139] It is brought to the point of becoming rasa by the foundational factors, Krishna and the others, when these have entered into the devotees' experience, and it reaches the highest state of rapture or profound bliss. Love, however,[140] when brought even to a minimal state of "factoring" by the foundational factors and so on—and however sparse these may be—can be savored almost instantly.

(J) Here are described the means (ending with "do all their duties"), the accompaniment (the two sets of innate dispositions), and the manner ("It is brought"). . . . "Entered into the devotees' experience": the idea is that here, in contrast to the case of mundane rasa, there is no actual need for any literary composition, however good it may be.

. . . .

(R) (2.5.79–85) This desire, in either literal or figurative form,[141] becomes rasa in devotees when Krishna and the others become aesthetic elements as a result of being brought to consciousness in poetry recitation or grasped through dramatic acting. Just as a substance such as yogurt becomes the taste known as lassi by the specific admixture of sugar, pepper, and the like, so here too devotees come to taste the full rapture of bliss, the fantastic rasa[142] of experiencing Krishna and the others as if right before their eyes. While one may become conscious of this or that particularity as it comes to manifestation during the course of aesthetic rapture, the rapture itself constitutes a unity of the different stable emotions and aesthetic elements.[143] To quote: "First the aesthetic elements are cognized individually, but as they become rasa they are assembled and become a whole. Just as one or the other ingredient of a mixed drink—the pepper, sugar, or whatever—can become individually apparent although they form a unity, so too the aesthetic elements in the whole that is a rasa."[144] The causes of desire are Krishna as aesthetic object and his beloveds as aesthetic subjects. . . .

(2.5.90–91ab) The principal factor in making these aesthetic elements what they are, according to connoisseurs of drama and poetry, is constant dedication to poems and plays about the Blessed One. But actually the most important cause is the power of desire for him, with its fantastic wealth of sweetness beyond the reach of reason. For reason cannot negate the fact that this emotion called desire is the play of a cosmic power, and possessed of an inconceivable character.

(J) "The play of a cosmic power" is meant to counter the objection that this desire is really like that for any other deity: even if the latter were to be the object of a great poetic composition, let alone anything lesser, it would still be unable to become rasa.[145]

(2.5.92cd–100) The ancients themselves have cited this statement from the *Mahābhārata*, from the "Book of Effort": "Entities that are in fact inconceivable cannot be grasped by reason. The very definition of the inconceivable is to exist beyond all the elements of nature."[146] When this beautiful desire succeeds in turning Krishna and the others into aesthetic elements (the foundational factors and the rest), it dramatically intensifies itself by means of these very elements—just as in the case of the jewel-rich ocean, which, after filling the clouds with its own waters, winds up bearing yet more water when those same clouds rain down. When desire freshly sprouts in a devotee of Hari, poetry or drama about him becomes a source of the aesthetic elements. Even when simply hearing stories of Hari, devout people can relish rasa. Such is the power of desire to cause this transformation in the aesthetic elements. Desire transforms Krishna and the rest of the characters into a locus of the erotic rasa, and they in turn, as they come to be experienced, heighten the desire all the more. Hence desire and the four aesthetic elements clearly require unabated assistance from each other. But desire's power too can be blunted when there is any deformation—"deformation" in the case of the aesthetic elements being impropriety.

(J) This sort of desire "commonizes" the emotions of today's devotees with those of the devotees of old whereby an identical sort of rasa state can come about. This is the argument of what follows.

(2.5.101–108) It is through some supermundane capacity that rasa attains this improbable state where those emotions appear as perfectly held in common. The inability here to discern any necessary distinction in these emotions between self and other is the "commonality" that has been described by earlier teachers. To quote Bharata:[147] "The aesthetic factors have a certain power for 'commonization' whereby the observer comes to think of himself as identical with them." Moreover, although sorrow and the like might appear in the heart as one's own, they really only produce a relishing of profound aesthetic rapture. And pleasures, though they may appear as if present in someone else, will produce the deepest bliss in one's own heart. On those occasions when only some of the aesthetic elements are merely present, they imply the rest and at once achieve plenitude. The view of authorities on drama—and it is entirely correct—is that the desire that exists in the characters cannot be rasa, because, among other reasons, it is mundane. But this desire for Krishna is supermundane, and more fantastic than all fantastic things. When Krishna is present the desire becomes a unique species of rasa in someone filled with love for him.

(J) But Krishna's absence is a source of sorrow, and how can there be any rasa then if rasa is supposed to be pure bliss? To this the author speaks:

(2.5.109) When Krishna is absent, the desire takes on the character of an apparent transmutation of fantastic bliss, and being so intense, it produces the semblance of a profound weight of pain.

(J) The separation will produce a "transmutation of fantastic bliss" because, first, this desire is itself in essence supreme bliss, and second, the foundational factor is the Blessed One, source of all bliss. It is a "semblance . . . of pain" because the pain that develops out of the knowledge of separation is superimposed upon the desire. But the actual cause of that pain is the desire, and the pain itself is overpowered by the hope of reunion.

(2.5.110–11) More specifically, where the foundational factor for the desire is Krishna appearing as the son of a cowherd chieftain, we hold that the ultimate horizon of blissful aesthetic rapture is reached. For here,[148] however small the drops of pleasure, one becomes a veritable Agastya with the power to drink in the vast ocean of bliss that comes from actually seeing with one's own eyes the sweetness of Shri's husband.[149]

FROM *TREATISE ON DIVINE LOVE* OF JIVA GOSVAMIN

Para. 110 (p. 65.17) Now, divine love itself, accordingly, may be called a "stable emotion" since it too becomes rasa—in no way less than the erotic desire or other stable emotion known to students of mundane literature—once it is combined with the principal and ancillary causes and effects, which for their part come in turn to be designated "foundational and stimulant factors," "reactions," and "transitory emotions." Given its very character, divine love must be considered an "emotion," and one that is "stable" in accordance with the definition given in the science of rasa.[150] We shall demonstrate in due course that all the remaining components[151] that make divine love a rasa become foundational factors and the other aesthetic elements by virtue of their capacity for "factoring" and so on. When conjoined with these components, love for God, with its specific degree of vividness being manifested in dependence on the vividness of the causes, comes to be designated the rasa of divine love. Given that it is a rasa consisting of devotion, it is also referred to as the "devotional rasa." (To quote: "It is the individual emotions themselves, as they present themselves, that become individual rasas.")[152]

That ordinary *rasikas*[153] do not accept devotion as a rasa, in view of what they see as a lack of the "full complement" of elements required for rasa, could only be true where the object of the rasa is some ordinary deity or other being. For "full complement" in reference to rasa's coming into being has three "capability" requirements: the capability of [1] the stable emotion itself; [2] the participants; [3] the person experiencing the rasa. With respect to [1], whereas desire and the other stable emotions are in themselves capable of producing mundane rasa precisely because they are stable emotions and held to be identical with pleasure, we have already shown not only that divine love is a stable emotion but also that it far transcends even the pleasure of supreme being, an ocean whose waves are all just pleasures of that sort. As for [2], the participants and the causal factors, in the case of mundane rasa, are actually incapable of "factoring" in and of themselves, and become capable only when they are rendered *supermundane* thanks to the literary craft of a skillful poet; in the case of the rasa of divine love, by contrast, the participants are capable in and of themselves of appearing in a fantastic, supermundane form, and have in fact been seen as such. As for [3], the capability of the person experiencing the rasa consists of his possessing the appropriate predispositions, such as those possessed by Prahlada,[154] without which even mundane literature cannot be held to produce rasa.[155] . . .

[66.9] Furthermore, the existence of the devotional rasa accords with the views of ancient scholars of supermundane rasa. This has been demonstrated in a general way by Shridhara, author of the *Moonlight Commentary* on the *Bhāgavatapurāṇa*, and with particular reference to such verses as BhPu 10.43.17, where he has discussed the five types of rasa, the peaceful and four others, that arose in Mathura when Krishna appeared there: women felt the erotic rasa; his cowherd companions felt the rasa of friendship (the stable emotion in this case being amity consisting of the kind of playfulness indicated by the word "comic" in the designation of the traditional rasa; in Shridharasvamin's view, the cowherds meant here are Shridhama and other friends of Krishna); his mother and father felt the rasa of compassion, or in other words, parental affection; spiritual adepts felt the peaceful rasa consisting of knowledge-devotion; and his Vrishni kinsmen, the rasa of pure devotion.[156] Last, men are shown to have felt a rasa consisting of a general divine love; that it is designated in the *Bhāgavatapurāṇa* verse as the fantastic is due to the fact that all rasas feed off the fantastic, and can therefore be so named when no other specific designation (such as "the peaceful") is used.[157] (The violent and remaining rasas that the wrestlers and others are said to have felt and that were accepted by Shridharasvamin[158] are in conflict with the rasa of divine love, and so can be ignored here.)

Such is the view of the authorities of supermundane rasa. But even some scholars of mundane rasa, such as King Bhoja, have similarly accepted additional rasas, those of love and parental affection.[159] . . . [67]

Another point: the capacity of mundane rasa to offer pleasure is highly inconsistent; indeed, if the matter is carefully considered, this pleasure in fact ends in pain. . . . [160] And even those who accept mundane rasa reject the very notion that stable emotions like revulsion can produce pleasure. Such rasas are furthermore denounced by the divine sage Narada, who at the same time praises the rasa of the Blessed One.[161] . . . One should therefore put no credence in the possibility of mundane foundational factors and the rest producing real rasa at all. On the contrary, it is a proven fact that what they do produce is, in every case, sheer repugnance. The rasa of the Blessed One, by contrast, can transform anyone, from the material hedonist to the spiritually liberated—indeed, even those without eyes to see or ears to hear, even the insensate man—so how could it be disbelieved?[162] . . . It is with the intention of making this clear that the *Bhāgavatapurāṇa*, which is concerned with manifesting divine love for the Blessed One and nothing else, explicitly characterizes itself as consisting of rasa in the verse that begins "A fruit fallen from the wishing tree of scripture."[163] . . .

Para. 111 [p. 68.25] Thus, we have demonstrated how, through "conjunction" with the aesthetic elements, the rasa of divine love manifests itself. Now, scholars of mundane dramatic rasa have maintained four different positions about it: [1] rasa in the primary sense of the term exists in the characters, that is, the original protagonists, and in them alone; it exists in the actor only in a secondary, figurative, sense; [2] because rasa in the characters is in fact mundane, limited to them alone, and punctuated by fear and the like,[164] rasa must exist only in the actor; [3] since actors imitate the original protagonists as it were mindlessly, simply as a result of their training, rasa must exist only in the audience; [4] if, however, actors are conceived of as acting mindfully, there would be no objection to rasa existing in them no less than in the audience.

The devotees of the Blessed One, however, hold that the rasa of divine love exists in all of these, since none of the reasons cited—that the rasa in the original character is "mundane" and all the rest—is cogent. This pertains especially to the original characters and their attendants, whose hearts are ever endowed with absolute rasa, a rasa, moreover, that transfers to those who imitate them.[165] In the case of those characters it is self-evident that the love of God is supermundane and infinite, and utterly unlike the mundane desire or other stable emotion depicted in worldly literature (something we established earlier when describing the true nature of that love).[166] And it is perfectly clear, from the stories of Prahlada and the goddesses of Vraja, that this rasa is never interrupted by fear or other negative emotions, nor even by later rebirth, as the story of Vritra or the elephant king or Bharata shows; indeed [69], the story of Shuka proves that it is not interrupted even by the bliss of supreme being.[167]

Moreover, the foundational causes of this rasa, its effects, and so on are all supermundane. This is proven in the case of the foundational cause, the Blessed One himself, precisely because he is the Blessed One, incomparable, transcendent, and surpassing; and in the case of his attendants because they are equal to him, as the constant drumbeat of scripture and ancient lore proclaims. As for their stimulant causes, they are supermundane precisely because they pertain to them.[168] . . . And like the clouds and so on that function as stimulant causes, so the effects too, the horripilation and the rest, are supermundane. . . . Similarly, the ancillary causes, dispassion and the others, must be understood to be supermundane, among which we might cite the madness and other feelings brought about by separation from the Blessed One, despair over him, and so on, that are likewise completely different from their mundane counterparts. In some cases, indeed, the entire assemblage of aesthetic elements is supermundane in their very nature. To quote the *Collection of Brahma*: "The beloved ones were the goddesses of wealth, the lover the Supreme Person, the trees the wishing trees of heaven, the ground a heap of magic wishing stones, the water the drink of immortality. . . ."[169]

When, accordingly, the power is present to make the rasa, even in the characters, truly rasa by virtue of the fact that these elements, the causes of divine love and so on, are all supermundane, unlimited, and unpunctuated, they are given the technical names "foundational factor" and so on—to be sure, that is precisely why they receive this or that new designation.[170] Moreover, just as scholars of mundane rasa hold that the causes and the rest, mundane though they may be, acquire a supermundane power through poetry and are given the names "foundational factor" and the like, whereby pleasure arises even from grief and real rasa comes about, we ourselves similarly hold that, given the inherently supermundane character of the elements here, the same thing may be held to occur. This is so even in the case of separation from God: whereas outwardly there may appear to be pain of separation from him, the heart throbs with the Blessed One and deep feeling for him, both rich in ultimate bliss. For neither of these two riches can ever be lost, and hence their existence as rasa can never be annulled—it is like sweet warm milk for those parched with thirst. In the state of separation, this deep feeling for God, though supreme bliss in itself, may become a source of pain, but only the way[171] moonlight seems to burn lovers when they are separated. And because the pain is engendered by that blissful feeling and nourishes [70] a sense of pleasure at the coming union, it can be classified[172] under pleasure. The same is proven to apply even to the tragic rasa in reference to the Blessed One since, given the hope of attaining the Lord certified by the Omniscient One's own words,[173] the tragic must have a residue of reunion. Hence, it is proven that rasa does arise in the characters. And that is in fact the primary sense of the term "rasa," since the passion produced in the characters from actually seeing the Lord is superior to that produced by hearing about him. . . .

In supermundane rasa, the actor too who imitates the Blessed One will understandably be a devotee, because no one else is capable of properly imitating him. Hence, rasa must arise in the actor too.

However, when a rasa has as its *object* a devotee as a result of his or her devotion, that rasa cannot, generally speaking, exist in God himself, since it would be contrary to the logic of devotion. Nor, consequently, can it be imitated. The experience of such rasa occurs only as something *related to* God, not as actually existing in him. It fulfills its purpose by functioning as a stimulant factor for the devotional rasa. Hence, while it might sometimes occur that especially pure devotees may imitate the Lord's physical reactions, they are "actualizing" it as connected with themselves, not with him—this is how we would reconcile the apparent contradiction. Where there is no contradiction with the logic of devotion, as in the equally shared feelings of people like Gada for people like Vasudeva,[174] rasa can most definitely arise. As for the audience members, they will certainly be devotees, and hence rasa in them is a proven fact.

Such is the manner of the actualization of rasa in "literature seen," that is, drama. In the case of "literature heard," or poetry, the manner of actualization must be similarly understood, but here pertaining properly to the object of description, the describing subject, and the listener/reader.[175] Moreover, generally speaking, there is a need for one or the other component—the object or the narrator—only for someone still at the early stage of spiritual desire. For one already filled with divine love, *anything* can cause rasa, even turning one's mind randomly toward the Blessed One—indeed, even hearing the notes of a flute.[176] For such people, accordingly, the emotion of divine love alone suffices to generate the full complement of aesthetic elements.[177] Even scholars of mundane rasa admit that if one or the other rasa component is lacking it will be extrapolated as a matter of course, in order for rasa to arise. . . .[178]

[71.7] Having now proven that love for the Blessed One has the possibility of becoming rasa, we may conclude that this occurs once it is fully provided with the aesthetic elements.[179] This rasa is at once the *act* of savoring and the *thing* savored, the former by virtue of the stimulant factor that forms one of its components—here a savoring that may be identified as an experience consonant with[180] the Blessed One's sweetness; the latter by virtue of the foundational factors—here the Blessed One himself, his devotees, and so on. This is why the term "rasa" can be used in both senses.

6.4 VEDANTICIZING RASA

The Nectar Ocean of Literary Art of Vishvanathadeva (1592)

Virtually unknown to Indian intellectual history until his principal work was edited and published in 1978, Vishvanathadeva was the son of Trimal[l]adeva and identifies his ancestral town as Dharasura. The name of his father suggests, and that of his village makes likely, that he hailed originally from today's Andhra Pradesh.[181] He later migrated to Varanasi and composed, in addition to his *Nectar Ocean of Literary Art*, a four-act drama (*The Moon's Crescent*, *Mṛgāṅkalekhā*).

The most striking fact about the *Nectar Ocean*, from the point of view of intellectual history, is the number of close parallels it shows with Jagannatha's *Bearer of the Ganges of Rasa*, and sorting out their relationship is therefore necessary. The *Nectar Ocean* dates itself precisely to VIKRAMASAṂVAT 1649, that is, 1592 C.E. As discussed in the next section, Jagannatha's literary activity commenced at least twenty or thirty years after that of Vishvanathadeva; he was a young man at the court of Shah Jahan, where his presence is recorded in imperial chronicles in 1635. Accordingly, either Jagannatha borrowed from Vishvanathadeva, or both borrowed from a common source.[182] Neither author refers to a literary treatise presenting the Vedantic epistemology and ontology at issue in both works, and no author prior to Vishvanathadeva is known to have used precisely the philosophical terms he does. The one exception might be the *Examination of Literature* of Shrivatsalanchana, where Vishvanathadeva's key Vedantic paragraph is repeated nearly verbatim. But Shrivatsa's discussion is manifestly an eclectic assemblage, comprising quotation from and exegesis of other works (Mammata's summary of Abhinavagupta, the *Mirror of Literary Art*, and so on), which strongly suggests that he borrowed from the *Nectar Ocean*.[183] However improbable the conclusion, then, given their radically unequal reputations today, it seems to have been Jagannatha who took from, though much expanded upon, the work of Vishvanathadeva.

In most respects Vishvanathadeva's exposition is conventional, raising all the themes rehearsed so often before (and to a great extent the book is an anthology of his own poetry illustrating the rasas).[184] What marks his general theory as important is his attempt to rethink rasa according to a specifically Vedantic worldview. This is hardly surprising for an era that saw an astonishing proliferation of writings on that philosophical system, which virtually colonized other, previously independent forms of thought (such as Mimamsa).[185] Especially important in Vishvanathadeva's revision is the role of the self (*ātman*) in cognition, and the notion of the "bliss component" (*ānandāṃśa*) of the self, borrowed from a celebrated passage in the *Taittirīya Upaniṣad* describing the last of the forms of the self as "consisting of bliss" (2.5).

Rasa was characterized as "the bliss that is the self" as early as the *Ten Dramatic Forms*,[186] but here the idea is worked out more expansively. The true nature of the self is the bliss found in the state of pure consciousness, but the processes of phenomenal life work to obscure it completely. Vishvanathadeva is the first to speak of aesthetic experience as a "removal of the veil of unknowing," followed by a state of pure, joyful awareness. This is the core idea Jagannatha picks up,[187] attributing it not to Vishvanathadeva but to Abhinavagupta, though Abhinava's notion of "manifestation" never explicitly refers "to the consciousness of the viewer from which obscuration has been removed."[188]

Given the conceptual linkage to the Upanishads, it may seem entirely natural to juxtapose the aesthetic process and the nature of scriptural revelation, which is of course central to the Vedanta vision, but Vishvanathadeva is the first to actually do so, and by a striking and entirely original analogy. Both literature and scripture are in the end linguistic phenomena, providing "direct awareness derived from the meanings of words," but both are unlike any other such phenomena in their capacity to confer a supermundane result.[189]

A useful summary of Vedantic rasa theory to supplement Vishvanathadeva is offered by the eighteenth-century polymath Nagesha Bhatta:

> The essence of the matter is as follows. When listening to a poem or seeing a drama, we encounter the aesthetic elements. These are properties of the mind and have an ontological status that is "undecidable"[190] as to whether they are real or unreal. A desire for these properties, which is directly apprehended by the witnessing self,[191]

arises when the elements are artfully presented. When the desire comes to be relished, the obscuration in the bliss component of the self is removed, and the self, whose true nature is the bliss that is pure consciousness, comes to light there. (It should be noted, first, that although the self actually has no parts, a bliss "component" and an awareness "component" may be postulated of it hypothetically; and, second, that the bliss component is hidden by an obscuration.) The seed to all this is hearing a work of poetry or seeing a drama, aided in both cases by the receptivity of the viewer or reader. The end result is rasa, which is the desire or other stable emotion directly apprehended by the witnessing subject in conjunction with the bliss component of the self, commingled with the aesthetic elements. That is why even in the case of rasas like the tragic, which are based on grief and consist of pain, there is no inconsistency in the fact that pure bliss should arise: for the tragic rasa is nothing but the consciousness specific to grief when obscuration is removed in its bliss component.[192]

FROM *THE NECTAR OCEAN OF LITERARY ART* OF VISHVANATHADEVA

[3] In this world, literature can produce the kinds of benefits ascribed to it (heaven, spiritual release, and the like)[193] only when it has been carefully analyzed by the audience members. It is in service of such an analysis that I have written this book.

. . . .

[81] The author[194] now discusses the nature of rasa, and the means of knowing it.

(3.24) Rasa is said to be a stable emotion brought to manifestation by causes, effects, and auxiliaries when used in literature.

[85] The causes are beings like Rama, Sita, and so on; they can be mutually causal factors when, as in the case of the erotic, their passion is mutual; the effects are such things as sidelong glances; the auxiliaries are transitory emotions such as shame, the comic,[195] and so on.[196] [86] "Used in literature" implies that these elements acquire new designations to distinguish them from their mundane variety: that is, "factors," "reactions," and "transitory emotions." . . . [88] One might ask why, given the existence of the terms "cause" and so on, these new designations should be required. My response is as follows. Consider the case of Sita. She is regarded as a being to be worshipped, and thus does not arouse sexual desire in the audience in such a way as to merit the name "cause."[197] [89] The aesthetic elements, the foundational factors and the rest, acquire their particular designations by executing a threefold process of what we may call "factoring," "reactionizing," and "emotivizing." These

three processes have the effect of making the stable emotion manifest (in the case of the factors), more manifest (in the case of the reactions), and most manifest (in the case of the transitory emotions). The result is a condition in which all other, quotidian objects of knowledge vanish, and there comes into being a sense of rapture before the flashing forth of rasa.

Now, a stable emotion like desire is a particular mental state.[198] How can the awakening of rasa with its supreme bliss lie precisely in the revelation of that stable emotion? [90] The fundamental idea is this: in literature, the aesthetic elements reveal the stable emotion,[199] and in this revelation, which takes the form of a mental state, the self also appears, which is in essence the bliss that is consciousness. According to the Vedantins' view, the self necessarily appears in every cognitive act because the full complement of the self's luminosity—formed of the conjunction of the self and mind—is always present.[200] This being the case, under the power of a literary text, when we watch or listen to it, the obscuration of the bliss component of our consciousness is removed by the aforementioned process of revelation. The basic notion, in other words, is that rasa is this consciousness specific to a stable emotion like desire when transformed into bliss with the obscuration of the bliss component removed.[201] [91] Scripture speaks to this matter too, in the *Taittirīya* corpus: "It is verily rasa, for having obtained this rasa one grows blissful," where "one" refers to the individual soul.[202]

This "obscuration" is nothing but unknowing. But note that there is no other form of cognition that enables the obscuration to be removed, and rasa thereupon to be awakened, for the simple reason that cognition of the aesthetic elements would be lacking there. Hence, we will argue that rasa's life span is set by the aesthetic elements, and that in the revelation of rasa a fusion with the aesthetic elements is as essential as the presence in a syllogism of the middle term (e.g., smoke) for the knowledge of the major term (e.g., fire). [92] This is why Bharata stated that "When there is a fusion of the mind with the meaning of the literary work, there arises the bliss that is supreme being, which constitutes the savoring of rasa."[203] Here "meaning," or subject, means the foundational and stimulant factors and the rest, while "fusion" is knowledge. The upshot is that rasa's essence lies in the assemblage of aesthetic elements, which is why the *Light on Poetry* uses the analogy of the mixed drink to explain it.[204]

Now, an objection might be raised: rasa is, we agree, the awakening of an emotion, say desire, located in the audience. But how can that come about with reference to someone like Sita, who is known to be related to Rama but with whom the audience itself has no relationship? The answer depends on the essential "commonization" of the aesthetic elements. Commonization refers to the fact of something's being recognized as related to oneself through some particular relationship despite the fact that it is not recognized as such in actuality. [93] In the case of our recognition of Sita, this sort of commonization means that we recognize her as nothing more than woman as such, eliding, thanks to the power of the aesthetic process, the notion that she is in fact Sita. This is the reason, again, why it makes sense to have different technical terms in aesthetic discourse for causes and the like, and why, furthermore, the causes of rasa elide all particularities, as we have stated. We should also note that the modality[205] for the direct visualization of rasa is "manifestation," while the proof for the existence of such revelation is nothing more or less than the heart of the receptive viewer or reader. And for this reason it has been declared, "The phenomenon called rasa is defined as sense of self, or ego, or passion, and it is the presence of rasa that makes literature beautiful."[206]

. . . .

[98] Rasa is not some thing that can be said to be *made*, since it is essentially a mental event. Nor is it some thing that can be said to be *made known*, the way a pot, for instance, is made known, because rasa is not some *thing* illuminated by some other consciousness.[207] [100] Rasa can be said to be made known only insofar as it is something invariably registered through a cognitive process. As was said in another context: "Although consciousness is self-illuminating, it is subject to a cognitive process like any other thing. What the teachers have denied is that it is *objectivized*. . . . But a cognitive process is indeed required to destroy ignorance regarding the identity of one's consciousness with supreme being."[208] [101] In literature, recall, this cognitive process is grounded in manifestation. Precisely as happens in scripture, with the statement "That art Thou," for example, the process in literature too has the form of a direct awareness derived from the meanings of words.[209] [102] And like the "supreme being that is directly known and not hidden,"[210] it is something of which we are directly aware in the consciousness portion of our self.

THE BEARER OF THE GANGES OF RASA OF JAGANNATHA (C. 1650)

We know, relatively speaking, more about Jagannatha than about almost any other author in this sourcebook aside from Abhinavagupta. Jagannatha was a Brahman from Telangana, the son and student of Peru Bhatta, who had himself been trained by the greatest scholars of early seventeenth-century Varanasi. From this community Jagannatha acquired not just learning but also something of his style, which echoes the precise but often rebarbative idiom of the New Logic (a strident "banging of pots in the halls of debate," as one contemporary observer put it).[211] Jagannatha "passed his youth," he says of himself, "under the care of the emperor of Delhi," Shah Jahan (r. 1627–1658), where a

Persian-language history places him in 1635. This and other data make it reasonable to accept the dates of 1620–1665 for Jagannatha's literary activity.[212]

Jagannatha is remembered in royal chronicles of the time as a singer (other Hindi-language accounts associate him closely with the celebrated musician Tan Sen), and also as the "Emperor of Poets" (*mahākavirāy*); he claims to have received the title "King of Scholars" (*paṇḍitarāja*) from the emperor himself. He was patronized by several princely houses, for whom he wrote political praise poetry, and according to a historical account attributed to a grandnephew, married a Muslim woman. He was a poet of renown, whose *Ways of a Lovely Woman* (*Bhāminīvilāsa*) circulated widely and from which he took many of the illustrations for his literary treatise. Unlike most other Sanskrit authors, but again resembling Abhinava, something of Jagannatha's highly opinionated, highly distinctive personality comes through in his writing. *The Bearer of the Ganges of Rasa*, composed later in his life and left incomplete, is his most important work and, while predominantly concerned with rhetoric, is at the same time an important contribution to aesthetic theory—in fact, the tradition's last creative contribution.[213]

In his work as in his life, Jagannatha was a curious mixture of modernity and tradition. He was a man of his times in adopting Vedanta as the new-old explanatory framework of his aesthetics. By contrast, he was a traditionalist in reasserting the authority of the discipline of aesthetics against the revolutionary innovations of aesthetic theologians like Rupa and Jiva Gosvamin. This would seem to be the case too—though the claim is more speculative—in his discussion of the "semblance of rasa." The category, invented by Udbhata (4.5, 4.7, above), comprised narratives that violated (through "impropriety") core features of the definition of rasa; in the case of the erotic, for example, the requirement of mutual affection would be violated by the use of force. Such narratives were not only not themselves improper, they were essential to literature—without Ravana's forcible abduction of Sita there could be no *Rāmāyaṇa*. Jagannatha, however, seems to be using the rubric almost as a mark of censure, and to be intent on proscribing, almost as if they would be aesthetic failures (and perhaps thereby shaping the later, negative understanding of "semblance") narratives concerning such things as "martial determination on the part of a lowborn man," or "laughter directed at one's father." It was precisely such transgressive material that elsewhere in the world—and not in Sanskritic India—would move to the very center of literary creativity and help make modern literature modern (for example, Jagannatha's near contemporary in France, Corneille, with his *Cid*).

Jagannatha's view of rasa is basically that of Abhinavagupta, but now inflected by Vedanta epistemology. In this he very likely borrowed from his predecessor (and fellow Andhra Brahman) Vishvanathadeva. The core idea is the Upanishadic notion that the self is in essence bliss, which is "veiled" or obscured by the phenomena of quotidian life. The aesthetic is the only human experience, aside from spiritual liberation, that offers the opportunity for glimpsing this quality of the self, when the spatio-temporal constraints of life are eliminated, the obscuration is removed, and the joy of pure unadulterated consciousness emerges.

Like many earlier thinkers, Jagannatha situates his theory within an intellectual history of the discipline, much of it derived from Abhinavagupta, though Jagannatha abandons, or no longer grasps, its chronological order. Several aspects of his account merit particular notice. His extended examination of the views of Bhatta Nayaka is marked by several mischaracterizations, several inherited from earlier scholarship. For example, one of Bhatta Nayaka's principal objectives had been to overturn the new paradigm of Anandavardhana, which postulated the linguistic notion of "manifestation" as the explanation of rasa. Jagannatha, however, simply accepts Abhinava's critique, or better, misappropriation, and argues that what Bhatta Nayaka offers instead—namely, "experience" or "experientialization"—is "really . . . indistinguishable" from manifestation.[214] What Jagannatha, like others, failed to grasp is the *historical* transformation that the language of aesthetics had undergone between Anandavardhana and Abhinavagupta, which had turned the former's linguistic phenomenon into the latter's psychological phenomenon. This becomes especially clear when Jagannatha characterizes the "manifestation" that pertains to the rasa experience as a removal of "the veil," or obscuration, of the viewer's consciousness.

More interesting than Jagannatha's inherited errors and what they say about the historical accuracy of his survey is his report on the view of the "New Scholars."[215] Thinkers who identified themselves (or were branded by others) as "new" (*navya*) have only recently become the object of scholarly research, and as yet no other information has come to light about those discussed by Jagannatha. But their notion of rasa is indeed new and noteworthy. In the eyes of the tradition beginning with Abhinavagupta and reaffirmed (and Vedanticized) by Vishvanathadeva and Jagannatha, rasa is a *positive* revelation of the true nature of the self. For the New Scholars, by contrast, rasa depends upon cognitive *error*, misidentification with the hero. Whereas many of the other positions Jagannatha reports were almost certainly never actually defended by anybody, but just extrapolations generated to fill out every conceptual possibility, this seems unlikely in the case of the New Scholars, and it remains a mystery that their works should have vanished without a trace.

Also notable is Jagannatha's attempt to refute the postulation of a rasa of devotion, rather odd in a scholar who (if the biography previously mentioned is authentic) was a committed Vaishnava by confession. However, the claims he advances against the new rasa were based on the *disciplinary* authority of aesthetics, and the coherence of that system—indeed, preserving the traditional framework of literary analysis is an overriding feature of his work. In the mid-seventeenth century this may well have constituted a new move,[216] but in historical terms, Jagannatha's attempt at closure was to prove no match for the brilliance of such expositors as Rupa and Jiva Gosvamin, let alone for the actual experience of countless devotees in the presence of Vaishnava poetry. The domain of rasa, as Bhoja had shown in the past and as history was to show in the following centuries, is inherently expandable, no less so than the domain of literature itself.

FROM *THE BEARER OF THE GANGES OF RASA* OF JAGANNATHA

(p. 25) There are five different sorts of implicature, but the most beautiful of them all is the implicature of rasa. For this reason rasa, the very soul of implicature, will be treated first.

A well-constructed literary work, one that is graceful in its aesthetic appropriateness, is able to convey the aesthetic elements in such a way that they enter the heart of a receptive viewer or reader. By the power of a special kind of "actualization" aided by the viewer's own receptivity, the individual characteristics of these elements—being the beloved of King Dushyanta,[217] for example—vanish. The elements, accordingly, come to be referred to by the supermundane terms "foundational and stimulant factors," "reactions," and "transitory emotions," which represent, respectively, foundational causes such as Shakuntala and stimulant causes such as moonlight; effects such as weeping; ancillary causes such as anxiety. When these are experienced in combination, a supermundane process unfolds whereby the unknowing that obscures the bliss component of the self is, for the time being, removed from the cognizing subject, who thereby finds himself freed from all personal characteristics such as the normal spatiotemporal limitations on his cognitive agency.[218] Thereupon, along with the bliss that constitutes his true nature—the ultimate real, insofar as it reveals itself directly—[26] the subject brings into his sphere of awareness the stable emotion (desire or one of the others) in the form of a predisposition long implanted in him.[219] It is this emotion that constitutes rasa.

[1] This view is in agreement with the following formulation:[220] "The stable emotion, manifested by the aesthetic elements, is known as rasa." "Manifested," or being made an object of manifestation, refers to the consciousness of the viewer[221] from which obscuration has been removed.[222] When a lamp has been hidden under a bowl and the bowl is removed, the lamp brings to light the objects within range as well as itself. In the same way, the self's consciousness, when its obscuration is removed, brings to light the viewer's desire (or other stable emotion) that is commingled with the aesthetic elements, as well as itself.[223] For it is acknowledged that the aesthetic elements are in reality properties of the mind that can be "directly apprehended by the witnessing subject."[224] This fact of direct apprehension is no more incompatible in the case of the aesthetic elements than in the case of a horse seen in a dream or silver perceived where there is actually only tin.[225] Given that both the viewer's

stable emotion and the bliss that is the self are permanent,[226] when we refer to the appearance and disappearance of rasa we are doing so in a figurative sense, in view of the appearance and disappearance of either the relishing of the aesthetic elements that manifest the rasa, or the obscuration's removal. (Analogously, despite the fact that phonemes exist permanently, we refer figuratively to the appearance and disappearance of, say, [27] the phoneme *g*[227] from the appearance and disappearance of the articulatory processes of the palate and so on that manifest it.) The obscuration's removal lasts only as long as the relishing of the aesthetic elements; when the relishing ends, the illumination is extinguished, and so even though the stable emotion of course continues to exist in the viewer, it is not illuminated.

Here is another way to state the matter: the power of relishing the aesthetic elements,[228] quickened by the receptive viewer's very receptivity, engenders a specific mental state, which is in essence bliss (and the subject's true nature)[229] conditioned by this or that stable emotion—in short, a state of identification. This can be likened only to the mental state of a spiritual adept in the course of meditation, for this kind of bliss is not comparable to any other mundane pleasure, because it does not take the form of a normal mental state.[230] Such is the position that accords with the most natural interpretation of the texts of Abhinavagupta, Mammata Bhatta, and others, namely, that rasa is a stable emotion qualified by a consciousness from which obscuration has been removed.

In truth, however, in accordance with the most natural interpretation of the scriptural passage cited below, rasa is not the stable emotion itself but rather consciousness delimited by a stable emotion when obscuration has been removed.[231] But in either case, it is a fact, first, that rasa—the entity ultimately being qualified in all this[232]—can be considered permanent and self-revealing with reference to its consciousness component, whether consciousness qualifies the stable emotion or is qualified by it; and, second, that rasa can be considered impermanent and revealed by something outside itself with reference to its stable emotion component. As for the relishing of rasa, this is either nothing more than the removal of the obscuration of consciousness, or, as previously stated, a mental state consisting of nothing but rasa itself. And it is to be differentiated from the savoring of supreme being in meditation, first because the bliss of consciousness that is the basis of rasa [28] remains commingled with objects (the aesthetic elements), and second because it is brought into being by purely literary processes.

If one were to demand proof for the element of pleasure appearing in aesthetic savoring, one might equally demand proof for the element of pleasure appearing in meditation. And if one can offer as proof for the latter the single statement, "Where one knows absolute pleasure, supersensual, grasped only by the mind,"[233] we can offer two sources of proof for the former: both a scriptural statement, "It is verily rasa, for having obtained this rasa one grows blissful,"[234] and the actual perception of every receptive viewer. Now, the savoring of rasa that we have posited, which on the second interpretation is defined as a mental state consisting of rasa itself, is a linguistic phenomenon, since it is something brought into being by a verbal process. At the same time, it is a transcendent phenomenon, since it constitutes the basis for a transcendent pleasure. In these two features it may be likened to the notion produced by the Upanishadic statement, "That art Thou."[235]

[2] Now the view of Bhatta Nayaka. If the viewer/reader were entirely detached from the aesthetic process, there would be no savoring in the act of apprehending rasa. Yet, it is very difficult to make sense of the contrary, namely, the apprehension of rasa as something happening in the viewer's own self: after all, Shakuntala *herself* cannot be a foundational factor for the audience members,[236] and without such a factor the erotic rasa and the underlying emotion of desire would lack any foundation and hence could not be comprehended. Nor can it be argued that the general trait[237] of being a beloved woman could delimit the category of foundational factor even in Shakuntala's case. For what is further required for delimiting it (in the case again of the erotic rasa) is the *absence* of an awareness that the beloved woman is an *illicit* sexual partner (there can be no hint of the possibility that this judgment is unwarranted, and the countercorrelate—i.e., the absence of illicitness—must be inherently connected with the woman thus qualified).[238] Otherwise, one's sister would wind up being a foundational factor since she too is beloved. Similarly, in the case of the tragic rasa, we would require a comparable absence of awareness that the foundational factor is a lowly man or someone who has renounced all claim to our grief.[239] But it is impossible to deny that such assured awareness must remain unavailable in the absence of some further explanation for restricting the category of foundational factor. To suggest that some sense of identity with the character, Dushyanta say, that arises in the viewer could provide that restriction is absurd: the hero being a resolutely kingly figure [29], the viewer a common man of the present day,[240] and other such differences make the distinction between them crystal clear and the notion of their identity impossible to sustain.

Moreover, what is this apprehension of rasa[241] supposed to be? If it were thought to be normal verbal apprehension, on the grounds that no other cognitive operations apply, then it could sometimes turn out to be disconcerting, like learning about an actual couple's doings through other, ordinary language. But the apprehension of rasa cannot be purely mental, since as we can plainly see, there is a vast difference between it and the mental apprehension of the very same objects when they are conveyed to us in later reflection. And it certainly cannot be memory, since there cannot have been any prior experience of the sort necessary to ground the memory.

Therefore, says Bhatta Nayaka, we must conclude that the entities, communicated to us by denotation,[242] come to be qualified by properties that are in accordance with rasa (the female protagonist's being a beloved woman, for example) by means of an "actualization" process that blocks any notions contrary to the rasa (such as the female protagonist's being an illicit sexual partner). Thereby Dushyanta, Shakuntala, their time, place, age, and condition of life are all "commonized," the power of the former process of denotation being crippled[243] before it could go any further. There then arises a third process, "experientialization," through which the following occurs: with the elimination of the viewer's volatility and stolidity, his sensitivity predominates and engenders a direct awareness that can be defined as "absorption," a state of rapture that is the true nature of one's consciousness. Desire or other stable emotion, which has been presented by "actualization" and thereby in essence turned into something common to the viewer, is rendered the object of this direct awareness, and thus becomes rasa. Rasa can accordingly be considered either the object (like desire) that is being experienced or the cognitive experience of desire, or both. And this experience is said only to "share something of the character of savoring supreme being,"[244] because of its being commingled with external objects.[245]

Thus, according to Bhatta Nayaka, there are three components to the literary text: "denotation, actualization, and experientialization."[246] [30] This doctrine, however, differs from the previous one of Abhinavagupta only in accepting the process that he calls "actualization"; his "experience" is really nothing but manifesting, while his "experientialization" is indistinguishable from manifestation.[247] In all the rest the approach is the same.

[3] The New Scholars, however, argue as follows: when the aesthetic elements are brought to light by the author of a poem or the actor in a drama, and the stable emotion—say, Dushyanta's desire for Shakuntala—is grasped by the process of manifestation, a particular kind of "actualization," which the New Scholars understand as the cognitive *error* of superimposition, emerges thanks to the viewer's or reader's receptivity, and by virtue of this erroneous superimposition, his self is veiled by the illusion of being Dushyanta. In the self delimited by this kind of unknowing there arises a desire for Shakuntala, apparent only to the witnessing subject and ontologically undecidable as to its reality,[248] just like the illusory appearance of a piece of silver in place of what is actually a shard of mother-of-pearl. This is rasa. It is thus the effect of a certain kind of error, and vanishes when that error vanishes. The New Scholars say the term "pleasure" can be used in reference to rasa because nothing distinguishes rasa[249] from the transcendent joy that follows in its wake; and also that rasa can be described as "manifested" and "relished"[250] either because no distinction can be grasped between rasa and the desire or other stable emotion that pre-

cedes it, or because we identify it as being one and the same thing as that desire. The sense of being Dushyanta too, which veils the self, is likewise ontologically undecidable.[251] By this reasoning, the New Scholars resolve the dilemma that, whereas the desire in Dushyanta himself cannot be rasa because it cannot be relished by the viewer/reader, the desire in one's own self, since it has no connection with the actual Shakuntala, [31] cannot be "manifested,"[252] since any sense in oneself of identity with Dushyanta is negated at once by the antithetical sense that one is not, in fact, Dushyanta. The "commonality" of the aesthetic elements posited by the ancients, they add, is unwarranted unless we admit some conception of cognitive error in respect to Shakuntala, who after all is communicated to us in a literary work by the word "Shakuntala" that produces, among other ideas, the fact of her being the particular woman of that name. Hence, some conception of error must be admitted, which would make it easy to justify the sense in oneself of identity with Dushyanta.

With reference to rasa as pleasure, the objection might be raised that while desire, to be sure, might produce a particular pleasure in the receptive viewer/reader as it does in Dushyanta, in the case of the tragic and some other rasas, stable emotions like grief are known to produce pain, and they could hardly then be a source of joy for the receptive viewer. On the contrary, it is only reasonable that they produce pain in the viewer no less than in the protagonist. Nor can it be argued that only real grief is capable of producing pain, not fictive grief, and hence only the original protagonist feels pain, not the viewer. Accepting such an argument would entail, for one thing, that an illusion like a rope being taken for a snake could never produce fear, trembling, and the like, when in fact it clearly can; or, for another, that the desire in the viewer could never produce pleasure since the desire too would be fictive.

Now, all that may be true, say the New Scholars, but if it is proven, as it surely is in the heart of a receptive viewer or reader, that joy pure and simple comes from a predominantly tragic work of literature no less than from a predominantly erotic one, then we would have to conceive of a cause consistent with such an effect. And, accordingly, we would have to postulate that one and the same transcendent literary process blocks pain no less than provides pleasure.

One might rejoin that the very same mode of proof establishes the existence of pain no less than joy, and so one cannot postulate such a blocking function; joy and pain must each come about from its appropriate cause. But then it would be unclear why authors would engage in creating such literature and receptive viewers engage in viewing it. It would be only be reasonable for them to refrain from such literature, since it would be a source of something unpleasant. But on the contrary, it makes perfectly good sense to engage in such literature since its pleasant aspects far outweigh its unpleasant ones—in the same way that the pleasant aspects of sandalwood cream far outweigh its unpleasant ones.[253] And of course for those who argue that aesthetic experience is one of pure joy, there is nothing whatever to stand in the way of engagement with such literature. [32] The weeping and so on that accompany it are not a result of pain but a natural response to the blissful experience of one or another rasa. A perfect analogy for this[254] is the weeping on the part of devotees of the god Vishnu when hearing a description of his deeds, since that behavior comprises no experience of pain whatever.

Still, one might further object that, if one could really feel joy when identifying oneself with the grieving Dasharatha,[255] then one should feel joy when making that sort of identification while dreaming or delirious. It is an empirical fact that in those cases one feels only pain, however, and it is reasonable to suppose that precisely the same applies in literature. Such an objection would be incorrect, however, for the greatness of the transcendent literary process lies precisely in the fact that things like grief, however unpleasant in themselves, lead to the production of supermundane joy when used in literature. The exquisite savoring produced by the literary process is altogether different from the experience produced by any other cognitive instrument. And incidentally, there is no harm in saying that the savoring of rasa is "produced" by the literary process, since by "being produced" we actually mean that it has as its object the desire or other stable emotion produced by the "actualization" that is itself produced by literature. As for the idea arising in the viewer that Shakuntala is an illicit sexual partner, it would be blocked by his sense of identity with Dushyanta.

[4] Others argue as follows:[256] while not admitting either the process of manifestation or the ontological undecidability of the cognitive event, one can agree that there exists cognitive error as previously described.[257] By virtue of this error, literary "actualization" gives rise to a purely mental[258] sense of nondifference from someone feeling desire for Shakuntala, eventuating in identification with Dushyanta; and it is this sense, with its unique object-directedness, that constitutes rasa. When such a sense occurs in a dream, it cannot be rasa since it is not produced by reflection on the subject matter of the literary work, and for this reason we do not find the same kind of joy in the dream state. And it would be mistaken to still ask how one can possibly experience desire or other stable emotion when it is not present in oneself. For this is not the mundane direct awareness [33] of desire, of the sort that necessarily presupposes the existence of an external object, but rather cognitive error. These scholars also assert that in speaking of this savoring as referring to rasa they are relying on the fact that it refers to desire or another stable emotion. And for them, finally, it is an awareness of one of three different sorts that must be acknowledged as the entity called rasa. It must be an awareness in the viewer/reader's self that eventuates either in a particular kind of desire where the object is Shakuntala and the subject Dushyanta; or in an

identification with Dushyanta, who is qualified by a desire for Shakuntala; or in a state of being qualified by being Dushyanta and by desire toward Shakuntala.[259] In all three forms of awareness, the desire or other stable emotion that functions as a qualifying property cannot be apprehended through language, whether literal or figurative; and since these scholars do not accept the existence of a third linguistic function known as "manifestation" to enable the apprehension, they say that we must admit from the first, if we are to gain knowledge of the emotion, the role of inference made on the basis of the dramatic gestures or other signs.[260]

[5] Some[261] hold that in the primary sense of the term, "rasa" refers exclusively to the stable emotion in the character, the desire in Dushyanta for Shakuntala, for example; we have direct awareness of this desire when it[262] is superimposed upon the actor who is imitating Dushyanta and is skilled at beautifully acting out the aesthetic elements.[263] [34] On this view, the direct awareness "This is Dushyanta, who feels desire for Shakuntala" is, as in the previous case, purely mundane with respect to the referent (the actor), but supermundane with respect to the character superimposed (the desirous Dushyanta).

[6] Others[264] hold that rasa is desire or another stable emotion in a character like Dushyanta when it is *inferred* in the actor. The actor becomes the locus of the inferential thesis that he is Dushyanta thanks to the aesthetic elements, which are pure artifice but not grasped as such. In the case of an object cognitively unavailable to us, such as another's emotion, inference is efficacious, whereas perception is not.

[7] A few hold rasa to be the three categories of aesthetic elements taken as a whole.

[8] Many hold rasa to be the element of aesthetic rapture in the three categories, without which the categories themselves cannot even exist as such.

[9] Others hold that rasa is only the factors, foundational and stimulant, when they are being actualized.

[10] Others posit this only of the reactions.

[11] Yet others, lastly, hold that rasa is only the transitory emotions that transform into rasa.[265]

The *Sutra on Rasa*, "Rasa arises from the conjunction of factors, reactions, and transitory emotions," has been interpreted variously so as to support each of these positions. In (1) "conjunction" means "manifestation," "rasa" the stable emotion qualified by the bliss that is consciousness or the bliss that is consciousness conditioned by the stable emotion, and "arises" means bringing to light in its essential form; in (2) the "con" (*sam*) in "conjunction" (*saṃyoga*) means "proper" (*samyak*), [35] that is to say, in the form of commonality, whereas the "junction" means "actualization" by way of the actualizing process; "rasa" is the bliss that is the true self brought to light by the predominance of sensitivity when conditioned by the stable emotion, and "arises" means made into an object of direct awareness, which is termed "experience"; in (3) "conjunction" means cognitive error in the form of a particular kind of "actualization," "rasa" the ontologically undecidable stable emotion (desire in Dushyanta, say), and "arises" means comes into being; in (4) the "conjunction" of the aesthetic elements means awareness of them, and "rasa" a specific type of awareness, while "arises" means to come into being; in (5) the aesthetic elements are related rather than conjoined,[266] "rasa" is the stable emotion, and "arises" means superimposition; in (6) the aesthetic elements, though pure artifice, are not grasped as such; "conjunction" means inference; "rasa" is the stable emotion, and "arises" means "is inferred"; in (7) the "conjunction" of the three categories of aesthetic elements means their totality; "rasa arises" means that it becomes capable of being referred to by the word "rasa"; in (8) the "conjunction" among the aesthetic elements means their correct junction, that is to say, rapture. The remaining three views are in contradiction with the aphorism.

Any individual aesthetic element among the three categories can be common to other rasas and so cannot manifest a specific one, which is why all three are referenced collectively in the aphorism. Hence, since it is a valid fact[267] that the elements have the capacity for manifesting rasa only as a collectivity, in those few cases where rasa is awakened by an individual element that is exclusive to the rasa, elements from the other two categories will be simultaneously implied. So the general rule remains unconditional.

Thus, while according to these heterogeneous lucubrations rasa has been conceived in multifarious ways, what is beyond dispute is that rasa is inseparable from pure joy, as knowledgeable people fully realize, and furnishes the greatest experience of beauty in the world.

[36] Rasa is ninefold: The erotic, tragic, peaceful, violent, heroic, marvelous, comic, fearful, and macabre are the nine rasas.

In this matter the sage's declaration is authoritative.[268] Some, however, hold that "The peaceful rasa is produced by impassivity, and that stable emotion cannot possibly exist in the actor. Hence there can only be eight rasas in drama; it makes no sense to include the peaceful among them." Others dispute this, arguing as follows: the reason adduced for rejecting the peaceful rasa—namely, that there can be no impassivity in the actor—is irrelevant, since no one admits that rasa is manifested in the actor anyway. But the audience members can feel impassivity, and hence there is nothing standing in the way of the peaceful rasa awakening in them. Nor is it any retort to say that if the actor lacks impassivity himself, he cannot possibly manifest it through acting. He equally lacks anger and the other stable emotions and hence does not produce the effects of anger—murder or other violence—in actuality; but there is nothing stopping him from producing artificial effects of anger through his training and practice. This is perfectly evident, and can be extended to the case at hand. One might argue further that in drama the presence of singing and instrumental music would keep the peaceful rasa from achieving predominance even in the audience members, since after all that rasa consists of turning away from the objects of the senses. But those who admit the possibility of the peaceful rasa in drama do not conceive of music as an impediment to it precisely by virtue of the fact that the rasa does produce its effect. To admit that, as a general rule, preoccupation with sensory objects is an impediment to the peaceful rasa would entail that the foundational factor of the peaceful rasa—the impermanence of life—and its stimulant factors—listening to the recitation of the *purāṇas*, [37] religious fellowship, visiting sacred groves or holy rivers, and the like—would all be impediments since they are all sensory objects. This is why in the last chapter of the *The Jewel Mine of Symphony* the author has concluded that the peaceful rasa exists in drama no less than in literature: "Some have urged that in drama there are only eight rasas. That is unacceptable, since the actor never savors rasa at all anyway."[269]

Those who hold that the peaceful rasa cannot exist in drama must in any case accept its existence in poetry since there is nothing to hinder its presence, and everyone has experienced the predominance of the peaceful rasa in works like the *Mahābhārata*. It is for this reason that even Mammata Bhatta can say when introducing the rasas, "There are eight rasas in drama," but declare in conclusion, "and also a ninth rasa, the peaceful."[270] . . .

[56] But how, one might ask, can one assert that these are the only rasas that exist? For example, when devotees of Vishnu are listening to the *Bhāgavata* or other similar *purāṇa*, it is difficult, given their reaction, to deny the existence of "the devotional" rasa: its foundational factor is Vishnu, it is shown being reacted to by horripilation, weeping, and so on, and it is enhanced by joy and other transitory emotions. Here the stable emotion would be devotion, or love for Vishnu. Nor can the devotional rasa be subsumed under the peaceful, since love conflicts with dispassion,[271] which is the stable emotion of the latter.

Our answer is that devotion is only really desire for a deity or other such exceptional being, and hence it must be included among the emotions and cannot reasonably be considered a rasa.[272] [57] This is indeed the settled conclusion of the ancients: "When desire is directed toward a deity or comparable figure, or when what is *principally* manifested is a transitory emotion, we have 'emotion' rather than rasa."[273] One might ask why, desire being desire, it should not be held to remain an "emotion" rather than developing into a rasa even when it is directed toward an amorous woman. Or conversely, why devotion itself should not be a "stable emotion" and desire only an "emotion" even when it is directed toward an amorous woman, given that it is not possible to decide for certain one way or another in any of these cases. This would not do, however, for only the declarations of Bharata and the other sages are capable of differentiating among rasas and emotions and so on; they alone can exercise independent judgment.[274] Otherwise, why would desire directed toward a son or the like not be considered a "stable emotion" capable of developing into rasa,[275] or revulsion, grief, or other stable emotion not remain a "pure emotion"? In short, the whole scholarly discourse would be thrown into chaos. It is far preferable to follow the authoritative texts and devote oneself[276] to the fixed series of nine rasas according to the limitations set by the declarations of the sages.

On Semblance of Rasa

(p. 119) "The property 'semblance of rasa' is caused by there being an inappropriate foundational factor."[277] Some critics hold that the impropriety of the foundational factor is something people understand from social practices, the sense that it is wrong. Others disagree, on the grounds that, whereas that definition would cover such cases as desire for the wife of a sage who is an inappropriate love object, it would not include desire for more than one lover or desire not shared by both partners in a relationship. In the latter two cases, there is no impropriety in the foundational factor as such.[278] Therefore, for there to be semblance of rasa, it must be the primary emotion itself (in this case, the emotion of desire) that has to be characterized by impropriety. And in this way both desire for an inappropriate object, as well as desire for more than one lover or desire not shared by both partners, would be included. "Impropriety" would remain as defined above.[279] . . .

[123] A father's grief for a son who is querulous and wicked, or grief on the part of ascetic who has given up all attachments; spiritual disenchantment with life on the part of an untouchable, who is not authorized to participate in spiritual Vedic knowledge; martial determination on the part of a lowborn man; anger on the part of a timorous man or directed toward someone like one's father; amazement in response to a mere magic trick; laughter directed at one's father; fear in a hero; disgust felt for the fat or flesh or blood of a sacrificial animal—all these produce the semblance of, respectively, the tragic, the peaceful, the heroic, the violent, the fantastic, the comic, the fearful, and the macabre.

English-Sanskrit Glossary

RASAS, STABLE EMOTIONS, AESTHETIC ELEMENTS

aesthetic elements	*vibhāvādi*
the affectionate	*preyaḥ/preyān*
amazement	*vismaya*
amusement	*hāsa*
anger	*krodha*
attachment	*sneha*
the comic	*hāsya*
desire	*rati*
determination	*utsāha*
dispassion	*nirveda*
emotion	*bhāva*
the erotic	*śṛṅgāra*
the erotic enjoyed	*saṃbhogaśṛṅgāra*
the erotic thwarted	*vipralambhaśṛṅgāra*
factor; "factoring"	*vibhāva*; *vibhāvana*
the fantastic	*adbhuta*
fear	*bhaya*
the fearful	*bhayānaka*
foundational factor	*ālambanavibhāva*
grief	*śoka*
the heroic	*vīra*
the heroic in war, munificence, compassion (or morality)	*yuddha-*, *dāna-*, *dayā-* (or *dharma-*) *vīra*
impassivity	*śama*
the macabre	*bībhatsa*
motherly love (sometimes, parental affection)	*vātsalya*

the noble	*udātta* (sometimes *ūrjasvin*)
the peaceful	*śānta*
psychophysical responses (sometimes, "sensitivities")	*sāttvika[anu]bhāva*
reaction (physical); "reactionizing"	*anubhāva*; *anubhāvana*
revulsion	*jugupsā*
stable emotion	*sthāyibhāva*
stimulant factor	*uddīpanavibhāva*
the tragic	*karuṇa*
transient (emotion)	*saṃcāri*
transitory emotion; "emotivizing"	*vyabhicāribhāva*; *vyabhicāribhāvana*
the vainglorious	*uddhata*
the violent	*raudra*

THE THIRTY-THREE TRANSITORY EMOTIONS

anxiety	*cintā*
attachment	*sneha*[1]
confusion	*moha*
depression	*viṣāda*
despair	*nirveda*
despondency	*dainya*
dissimulation	*avahittham*
dreaming	*suptam*
dying	*maraṇa*
exhaustion	*śrama*
fatigue	*glāni*
ferocity	*ugratā*
fright	*trāsa*
intoxication	*mada*
jealousy	*īrṣyā*[2]
joy	*harṣa*
longing	*autsukya*
madness	*unmāda*
numbness	*jaḍatā*
panic	*āvega*
perplexity	*vitarka*
possession (sometimes, misrecollection)	*apasmāra*
pride	*garva*
recklessness	*capalatā*
remembrance	*smṛti*
resentment	*asūyā*
sagacity	*mati*
satisfaction (sometimes, constancy)	*dhṛti*
shame	*vrīḍā*

sickness	*vyādhi*
sleepiness	*nidrā*
torpor	*ālasya*
waking	*pra(vi)bodha*
disquiet	*śaṅkhā*
vindictiveness	*amarṣa*

THE EIGHT PSYCHOPHYSICAL RESPONSES

broken voice	*svarabheda (-bhaṅga)*
fainting	*pralaya*
horripilation	*romāñca*
pallor	*vaivarṇya*
paralysis	*stambha*
perspiration	*sveda*
trembling	*vepathu*
weeping	*aśru*

THE FOUR KINDS OF LEADING MALE CHARACTER

the dignified	*dhīrodātta*
the peaceful	*dhīrapraśānta*
the romantic	*dhīralalita*
the vainglorious	*dhīroddhata*

THE TEN FORMS OF CHARMING BEHAVIOR

adornment	*lalita*
coquetry	*vilāsa*
coyness	*moṭṭhāyitam*
disarray	*vibhrama*
giving the cold shoulder	*bibboka*
mimicry	*līlā*
negligence	*vicchitti*
reticence	*vihṛta*
saying no when meaning yes	*kuṭṭhamitam*
turmoil	*kilakiñcitam*

THE TEN STAGES OF THE EROTIC THWARTED[3]

anxiety	*cintā*
craving	*abhilāṣa*
death	*nidhana*

distress	*udvega*
glorification	*guṇakīrtana*
madness	*unmāda*
raving	*pralāpa*
remembrance	*smṛti*
sickness	*vyādhi*
stupor	*jaḍatā*

OTHER TECHNICAL TERMS

absorption (sometimes, repose)	*viśrānti*
acting	*abhinaya*
(its four registers: physical, verbal, psychophysical, costuming-makeup)	*āṅgika, vācika, sāttvika, āhārya*
actualization	*bhāvanā*
affectionate utterance	*preyaḥ* (*preyasvat* in Udbhata)
cessation (of a rasa or emotion)	*śānti*
charming behavior	*hāva*
coloration	*uparañjana*
"commonize," "commonization"	*sādhāraṇīkṛ, sādharaṇīkaraṇa*
complete identification with	*anusandhāna* (*-dhi*) (in Bhatta Lollata)
conjuncture (of two rasas or emotions)	*sandhi*
connotation	*lakṣaṇā*
costume (sometimes regional customs)	*pravṛtti*
denotation	*abhidhā*
direct awareness; aesthetic visualization	*sākṣātkāra*
distinct comprehension	*anusandhāna* (in Shri Shankuka)
dramatic mode	*vṛtti* (*bharatī*: verbal mode; *sāttvatī*: serene/sublime mental mode, pertaining to the heroic in particular; *ārabhaṭī*: energetic physical mode, pertaining to the violent in particular; *kaiśikī*: graceful, pertaining to the erotic in particular)
ecstasy	*laya*
ego	*ahaṅkāra*
emergence (of a rasa or emotion)	*udaya*
emotion poetry	*bhāvakāvya*
ends of man	*puruṣārtha*
enhance	*pari + puṣ*
experience, experientialization	*bhoga, bhogakṛti, bhogīkṛttva, bhogakṛttva*
expression; sometimes, literary language	*abhidhā* (in Bhatta Nayaka)
figure of sense or sound; ornament	*alaṅkāra*
full complement (of aesthetic elements)	*sāmagrī*
haughty utterance	*ūrjasvi* (in Dandin)
heart's concurrence	*hṛdayasaṃvāda*

identification with	*tanmayībhāva*
immersion	*samāveśa*
implicature	*dhvani*
impulsive utterance	*ūrjasvi* (in Udbhata)
indirect expression	*vakrokti*
innate disposition	*saṃskāra*
instruction in, knowledge of (the ends of man)	*vyutpatti*
jealous anger	*māna*
language quality	*guṇa*
leading female character	*nāyikā*
leading male character, protagonist	*nāyaka*
liberation	*mokṣa*
love	*kāma*
love	*prema* (in Bhoja = *śṛṅgāra*, passion)
manifestation	*vyakti, vyañjanā, abhivyakti*
morality	*dharma*
narrative element	*vastu*
natural expression	*svabhāvokti*
object (of affect) (rarely, subject)	*viṣaya*
oscillation (between different rasas or emotions)	*śabalatā*
passion	*śṛṅgāra* (in Bhoja)
"paths" or styles of literature	*rīti*
predisposition	*vāsanā*
preliminary dance	*lāsyāṅga*
process	*vyāpāra*
proper term, actual word	*svaśabda*
propriety	*aucitya*
purport	*tātparya*
quality (of language)	*guṇa*
quiescence (of a rasa or emotion)	*samāhita* (in Udbhata; = *śānti)*
rapture	*camatkāra*
rasa-laden statement	*rasavat*
receptive, responsive viewer/reader	*sahṛdaya, sacetāḥ*
receptivity	*sahṛdayatā*
relishing	*carvaṇā*
to savor	*(ā)svad*
secondary knowledge, of a knowledge	*anuvyavasāya*
semblance of a rasa, of an emotion	*rasābhāsa, bhāvābhāsa*
sense of self	*abhimāna*
sensitivity (sometimes, psychic sensitivity)	*sattva*
stolidity	*tamaḥ*
to strengthen	*upa + ci*
subject matter	*tātparya*
substratum, subject (of affect) (rarely, object)	*āśraya*

supreme being	*brahma*
types of heroine	*nāyikābheda*
typological state	*avasthā*
vainglorious, proud (sometimes, impetuous)	*uddhata*
verbalization	*vāgārambha*
viewer/reader	*bhāvaka (bhāvuka), śrotṛ, anusandhāyaka*
volatility	*rajaḥ*
wealth, power	*artha*

Notes

PREFACE

1. Preeminently Ingalls et al. 1990.

2. In the first category are KM, KD, *Bhaktirasāyana*; in the second, *Agnipurāṇa* (now known to be a late, probably eleventh-century, compilation), and *Candrāloka*, among others. BhP occupies a place apart: unlike the *Agnipurāṇa*, it was occasionally cited, but it is both derivative and too diffuse to properly excerpt.

3. The now-standard edition shows these traces everywhere. Chapter 6, for example, ends, "Such are the eight rasas" (6.83); Abhinavagupta had a different text before him ("There are thus nine and only nine rasas," he comments ad loc., ABh 1.335.8).

4. After long clinging to the translation "reproduction," I was convinced by Andrew Ollett of the greater applicability of this term. For an extended consideration (sometimes at odds with the analysis offered here), see Shulman 2012.

5. An onomatopoeic word, "making the sound *chamat*," a smacking of the lips that seems especially apposite for "aesthetics," or "feeling" (for a Shaiva etymology see IPVV v. 3 p. 251). No one before Ananda had used the term, and he only once (DhĀ 4.16).

6. See Dhanika on DR 4.4cd–4.5ab, below.

7. Literally, "the erotic deceived" (SKĀ 5.56–58; ŚP pp. 1172–73; RAS p. 276).

8. For the eighth-century southerner Dandin, *ūrjasvi* is slightly deprecatory ("haughty declaration"); for the ninth-century northerner Udbhata, it indicates a moral lapse (the "impulsive").

9. *The New* Dramatic Art 3.273.

10. For the former see Shridhara on KP 4.30; for the latter, NŚ 1.111.

11. *Nyāyasūtra* 1.1.17; for Bhasarvajna see *Nyāyasāra* p. 12.

12. The rasa *raudra* exemplifies the difficulty. It is typically translated, vaguely, as "rage" or "the furious"; NŚ 1.313–314 indicates that "the violent" is closer to what is intended (see Abhinava ad loc.: "'*Raudra* is based on anger,' and the domain of anger is, generally speaking, unlawful action," and RAS 2.131: "The locus of *raudra* is savages [*krūrajana*]").

13. The editions of the ŚP and KP principally used here are continuously paginated.

INTRODUCTION

1. Feagin and Maynard 1997, compare Korsmeyer 1998. Many of their questions derive from Beardsley 1981 [1959].

2. Treatises on painting simply list the rasas and their associated colors (see for example *Viṣṇudharmottarapurāṇa* 3.30).

3. Shri Shankuka fragment #1a, below; on music and rasa, DhĀ pp. 405, 417; VV p. 100, Anantadasa (p. 72), SRĀ 7.1351 ("The learned hold that the principal element of the triple symphony is rasa"). Thus, while classical Indian aesthetic theory may well apply to all the "fine arts," it never was in fact applied before the modern period (contrast M. Hiriyanna in Raghavan 1975: xv, among many others).

4. Bhatta Tota's definition of creative imagination would be invoked repeatedly (see fragment #1, below).

5. Pollock 2014.

6. The term *rasaśāstra* is found only once (in Jiva Gosvamin p. 110 [65.17], below), and may be peculiar to the Bengali Vaishnava tradition.

7. For this assessment of what is currently missing in literary theory, see Harpham 2005: 24.

8. For Weber, see Gerth and Mills 1946: 340–43; the ideological reading is found in Eagleton 1990: 3. Hegel's *Lectures on Fine Arts* (1835) is structured, deeply if with no self-awareness, by the inequity of colonial judgment. For Arnold's assertion a generation before Weber (1880),"Most of what now passes with us for religion and philosophy will be replaced by poetry," see Muldoon 2006: 349.

9. Neill 2003: 423.

10. Additional detail and argument are offered in Pollock 1998a, 2001c, 2010, 2012a, 2012b.

11. See DhĀ pp. 87–88.

12. DhĀ p. 498.

13. NŚ 7.2.

14. KĀ 1.51.

15. Bhatta Tota fragment #4; Bhatta Nayaka fragment #5.

16. Especially problematic is the absence in the *rasasūtra* of the key term "stable emotion" (compare Bansat-Boudon 1992a: 109–11).

17. For the NŚ it is the *sattva* of the actor that is at issue, for he cannot weep or sweat without *intentionality.*

18. Pollock 2012a.

19. NŚ 1.11.

20. Cited in Solomon 2002: 122 (emphasis added).

21. Pollock 2012a: 202.

22. Krishnamoorthy 1968: 45 (few later scholars have appreciated this insight).

23. NŚ 1.282; 6.32–33. A "traditional verse" to the same effect is added.

24. Rudra Bhatta, *Śṛṅgāratilaka* 1.5. The statement makes better historical sense if the author is identified with Rudrata (early ninth century), rather than another scholar of the late tenth/early eleventh century (on their dates and possible identity, see Kane 1971: 158).

25. RKA 12.2, below.

26. The three mentioned here (*rasavat*, *preyaḥ*, and *ūrjasvi*) are discussed by Dandin, KĀ 2.273, below.

27. Perhaps anticipating Anandavardhana's later distinction between rasa and "subordinate implicature" in his brief remark on the "elevated" figure (Krishnamoorthy 1979b: 305).

28. KASS 4.3–4.

29. Pratiharenduraja p. 50, below.

30. See McCrea 2009.

31. VJ p. 144, below.

32. The *Candrāloka* (c. 1250) simply adds to the four emotion tropes given by Udbhata the remaining three stages of rasa as tropes in their own right (5.117–118). This conception continued into the seventeenth century (KD p. 291).

33. See *Avaloka* p. 206, below, for a classic example. "Narrative element" here and passim translates *vastu*, a fact, situation, or other component of the narrative (see Ingalls et al. 1990: 82).

34. There is dispute over which of the many types of "manifestation" is at work in literature. Contrast Ruyyaka, *Kāvyaprakāśasaṃketa*, p. 577, and Vishvanatha, SD 3.1, both given below.

35. DhĀ 2.1–2 and DhĀ 3.3; *Ekāvalī* p. 85, below. Few later thinkers make this categorization an object of analysis; a rare exception is KD p. 149.

36. For Bhatta Nayaka see further below; for Dhanika, *Avaloka*, p. 211, below; for Mahima Bhatta, VV p. 70, 78, below, and passim.

37. KASS 4.3–4; Pratiharenduraja on 4.2, below.

38. Pollock 2007: 42–44 (inadvertently omitting Udbhata); see also MM 5.28, cited in ŚP p. 625, below.

39. One Chakravartin Bhattacharya cited by Jhalkikar in his edition of KP, p. 434.

40. VJ p. 146; Shri Shankuka, both below.

41. DhĀ pp. 80–83, below.

42. See "On Verbal Representation" below.

43. Bhatta Tota fragment #5; ŚP p. 3, both below.

44. Shridhara in KP p. 77.

45. See Dhanika's introductory remarks on DR 4.36, below.

46. See ŚP vv. 7 and 11, below.

47. Raghavan 1975 charts this expansion (though without explaining it). For the devotional rasa, contrast Hemadri p. 167 and RG p. 56, both given below.

48. Compare RG pp. 35–36, below. At late as the turn of the fifteenth century, Singabhupala was denying the very existence of a peaceful rasa (the idea that spectators could experience such a rasa is like "parrots tasting bananas painted in a picture," RAS p. 206).

49. Some emotions we might expect to see included but are not were evaluated as components of other emotions that are. The absence of hatred, for example, from the canonical list can be explained by the fact that it was thought of as "a mental state of harshness, whereas anger is the manifestation of hatred" (Prajnakaramati on *Bodhicaryāvatāra* p. 82.15). Darwin himself suggests that hatred expresses itself as anger or terror, whereas Ekman curiously defines it as "non-emotional" (Gross 2010: 51).

50. ABh 1.266.11–15; for the citations see KĀ 2.279, 281.

51. See Bhatta Lollata fragment #1a, below.

52. Wimsatt and Beardsley 1949: 51.

53. I find no conceptual difference in the distinction *upacita/paripoṣa*.

54. *Harṣacarita* v. 8.

55. ŚP p. 616, below. SKĀ is centrally concerned with *āśrayaprakṛti*, the nature of the substratum of rasa, i.e., the main character.

56. *Śatapatha Brāhmaṇa* xiii.5.4.1.

57. The distinction is not drawn in the Sanskrit, and cannot always be captured in translation.

58. Gadamer 2004: 283, and pp. 306–307 for the *subtilitas applicandi* of Pietistic hermeneutics.

59. A precise analogy works at the micro-level too: literary language, commonization, and pleasure parallel the "means" (sacrifice), "procedure" (recitation of mantras, inter alia), and "outcome" (heaven, inter alia), respectively, of ritual "actualization" (Pollock 2010: 151–57).

60. *Avaloka* pp. 171, 173; ND p. 160, both below.

61. *viśrānti*, a concept that was to become central to Abhinavagupta's theory.

62. Bhatta Nayaka fragment #3, below.

63. He had already appropriated his opponent's three-part hermeneutic model (DhĀL p. 189).

64. Hemachandra, a close reader of Abhinava, incorporates this into his definition of rasa: what is "manifested" by the aesthetic elements is the stable emotion existing in the form of the predispositions *of the viewer/reader* (KA 2.1 *vṛtti*, p. 88).

65. DhĀL p. 188.3 (and compare pp. 52.7–8 and 189.4).

66. *Avaloka* pp. 212 and 217, and n. 217, below.

67. Ingalls et al. 1990: 37. It may have been Bhatta Nayaka himself who first suggested the enlarged notion of "manifestation," fragment #14, below.

68. See for example PR, ed. Raghavan, introduction p. 27.

69. ABh 1.285.17; DhĀL p. 155.5–6, ABh 1.278.11, 278.20 (*alaukika*).

70. Bhatta Tota fragment #2, below.

71. Fragment #6, below.

72. Perhaps first with Bhatta Narayana (ninth century); see Stainton 2013: 175–78.

73. The earliest reference in poetics literature, that of KASS, strikes me as an interpolation (chapter 1, n. 131), which is not to say it cannot have been borrowed from a lost work of Udbhata's (compare Krishnamoorthy in NŚ vol. 1, p. 4). For an exhaustive history of the rasa see Raghavan 1975.

74. See p. 226.

75. Ruyyaka, on KP p. 779, below.

76. Masson and Patwardhan 1969; Gerow 1995.

77. KP 35ab, below.

78. KASS 4.2, below. This is a forerunner to what comes to be called emotion poetry (*bhāvakāvya*) in contrast to rasa poetry (*rasakāvya*), though in fact the terminology is rarely used.

79. See especially the commentary of Paramananda Cakravartin on KP p. 793, below.

80. For these three points see, respectively, BhPu 1.1.3 (Vishvanatha Chakravarti and other commentators ad loc. adduce Bhatta Nayaka's theory); BhPu 10.43.17 (Shridharasvamin ad loc. refers to "ancient authorities on supermundane rasa" when analyzing the passage); in his commentary on BhPu 1.1–3, Madhusudhana Sarasvati (c. 1600) calls the work a *mahākāvya* (*Ślokatrayaṭīkā* fol. 14r).

81. ABh 1.335.14 (bhakti is mentioned in connection with rasa nowhere else in the ABh or in the DhĀL), KA p. 106.15. We do not know whose position they were opposing.

82. Others complicate this picture. In his *Bhaktirasāyana*, Madhusudana Sarasvati uses the language of aesthetics to explain the psychology of actual religious experience; when he reverts in chapter 3 to the standard literary conception, the gap between aesthetic and religious experience remains unbridged (he makes no reference to earlier bhakti rasa theory).

83. PS p. 70, below; for the denial of "secular" rasa, see Lokanatha on AK 5.72, below.

84. Lokanatha Chakravartin on AK 5.72, below.

85. I pass over statements such as *Taittirīya Upaniṣad* 27.2 *raso vai saḥ*, though cited by later thinkers like Jagannatha.

86. Bhatta Nayaka #1a; DR 4.43 and *Avaloka* there and on 4.1, below. Abhinava reports on a Vedanta position in ABh 1.37.21.

87. ABh 1.286.1, 37.19, 271.5, 276.7–8. His concept of aesthetic "hindrances," for example (ABh 1.274, below), has little in common with the *vighnas* of Kashmir Saivism (though compare ABh 1.284 with IPVV v. 2, p. 178), while his formulation of aesthetic awareness as "repose in one's own *unhindered* consciousness" (1.261.7; compare 273.8, 278.12, 284.20) differs from what was to come.

88. Vidyaranya's *Pañcadaśī* (c. 1350).

89. The key term is *āvaraṇabhaṅga* (or *bhagnāvaraṇatva*). Jagannatha is merely seeking a time-honored lineage for this innovation when he associates it with Abhinava (RG p. 26, below); it is terminology Abhinava himself never uses (see chapter 6 n. 188).

90. For the first see SSS p. 101, for the second (derivatively), RG p. 27, both given below.

91. SKĀ 5.8; ŚP p. 628 (*alaṅkāra* is to be taken in the widest possible sense).

92. Dufrenne 1973: 455.

93. Ruyyaka employs the technical term *prayoga*, analytical operation, used in both grammar and logic, for his dissection of the peaceful rasa (above n. 75).

94. See especially chapter 24 (where "nature," "role," and social status are complexly intertwined); see Abhinava's restatement in ABh 1.276–77, below.

95. On humor, see NŚ 6.51; Abhinava discusses fear at ABh 1.325.14.

96. If the loved one is not lost forever, we have the "erotic thwarted" (NŚ 1.304; compare RG p. 32, though contrast *Śṛṅgāratilaka* 2.1, 93).

97. NŚ 6.62 and 1.311 (*iṣṭa*, *iṣṭajana*), ABh 1.290 (*bandhu*). Abhinava dismisses (the Buddhist?) Shri Shankuka's idea that *karuṇa* has anything to do with *dayā*, compassion (ABh 1.311). On semblance and the comic, see ABh 1.289.14, below.

98. The same occurs with "heroic perfection" (*vīryapāramitā*), where *utsāha* is determination not for martial victory but for spiritual merit (*kuśalotsāha*, *Bodhicaryāvatāra* 7.2).

99. The standard list of topics is found first in KASS 4.7, below, which provides the model for DhĀ 2.3 (which, however, only mentions "semblance" in passing and offers no detailed account).

100. KASS 4.5–4.7, below.

101. Narayana Rao and Shulman 2012: 163; see also Ingalls et al. 1990: 37 (contrast, for example, the explicit statement of AK p. 133, given below). As Abhinava notes, Ravana's desire for Sita is not illicit under his own moral regime. It is no less real than Rama's, and a semblance only for us, not for him (ABh 1.289).

102. Implausibility is the first of Abhinava's hindrances (ABh 1.275), and one of the last of Mammata's "flaws" (KP 7.62, below). Someshvara ad loc. discusses revisions in the *Rāmāyaṇa* required to meet social normativity, see chapter 4 n. 353). Anandavardhana insists on the poet's obligation to alter a narrative in the interests of rasa (DhĀ p. 334, below).

103. RG, p. 123, below. The semblance or otherwise of rasa in animals is another topic heatedly discussed, especially by Vidyadhara (*Ekāvalī* p. 106, below) and Singabhupala (RAS p. 297, below), and it is not trivial. Abhinava begins his reconstruction of rasa theory with a discussion of the fear in the doe in AŚ (ABh 1.273, below), which Kuntaka adduces to prove the very absence of rasa (chapter 1 n. 308, below).

104. For *rasodaya*, *-śānti*, *-sandhi*, and *-śabalatā*, see for example RT chapter 8.

105. DhĀ 3.17–19; *Avaloka* pp. 196–201; KP 7.64, all given below.

106. KP 7.62, below. The poem is cited first in this context by Abhinavagupta (DhĀL p. 362). Compare also Arjunavarmadeva on AmŚ v. 30.

107. *Elixir for the* Rasika, p. 4, below. See also DhĀ p. 195; *Avaloka* 4.65; ŚP 11.38; KP 7.6 v. 340.

108. Unattested, however, prior to the mid-seventeenth century.

109. In fact, the NŚ itself alludes to this (1.113).

110. KASS 4.3–4, below

111. DR 1.6; Bhatta Nayaka fragment #7, below.

112. DhĀL pp. 40–41.

113. DhĀL pp. 335–36.

114. ABh 1.261;1.36, below.

115. ABh. 1.292.20; ABh 1.276, below.

116. Rorty 1989: xvi; 141.

117. As in Aristotle; see Cohen 2004.

118. SD 3.3, 3.8cd, below. Two centuries earlier Ruyyaka offered a similar if less developed rationale; see his comment on KP p. 577, below.

119. ABh 1.281, 285, below. Other thinkers like Bhoja make the same argument on the basis of a Samkhya psychology where *sattva*, or sensitivity, is a personality variable.

120. The long list of vanished masterpieces includes, besides all the commentators on the *Treatise on Drama* before Abhinava (Udbhata, Bhatta Lollata, Shri Shankuka), Udbhata's *Exegesis of Bhamaha* (*Bhāmahavivaraṇa*), Bhatta Lollata's *Exegesis of Rasa* (*Rasavivaraṇa*), Bhatta Nayaka's *Mirror of the Heart*, Dhanika's *Analysis of Literature* (*Kāvyanirṇaya*), Bhatta Tota's *Literary Investigations* and Abhinava's commentary on it, Kashishvaramishra's *Inquiry Into Rasa* (*Rasamīmāṃsā*), Naraharisuri's *Exposition of Rasa* (*Rasanirūpaṇa*), Dharmadatta's work (its title is unknown), and the authors (whose names are not even known) cited in VV, *Avaloka*, *Ekāvali*.

121. ND (four mss.); ŚP (three); ABh (possibly just two, with seven fragmentary parts); VK (only partly preserved); ABh in many places is deeply corrupt; NŚ mss. in their profusion and disagreement defy synthesis.

122. ŚP, ABh, and ND are prominent instances.

123. Anandavardhana wrote on Buddhist logic, Abhinavagupta on Shaiva theology, as did Bhoja in addition to his work on yoga philosophy; Hemachandra on epistemology, logic, and yoga; Ramachandra on logic; Mallinatha on logic and Mimamsa; Rajacudamani Dikshita on a wide variety of systems.

124. There is little doubt that Vijnanavadins participated in rasa discourse; see ABh 1.274.6, and ABh 1.37.21, below (four positions on aesthetic experience belonging apparently to Buddhists, logicians, Prabhakara Mimamsakas, and Vedantins).

125. ŚP p. 374.

126. For Jagannatha's affiliation to Pustimarg Vaishnavism see Pollock 2001a: 409.

127. There is an apparent misrepresentation in the case of Bhatta Nayaka's core idea of the four "mental planes" of reader response; see ABh 1. 271.4, DhĀL p. 183.3 (Mallinatha on

Ekāvalī p. 96 also misunderstands). DR 4.43 and Dhanika ad loc., below, offer the correct analysis.

128. Jayaratha on AS p. 12. Ruyyaka's own father, Tilaka, shows a less committed attitude toward chronology, indifferent as he is to the fact that Udbhata could have known nothing of a theory of implicature in aesthetics formulated at least a half-century after he lived (on KASS 4.2).

129. Elsewhere Jagannatha does show some interest in historical distinctions (Tubb and Bronner 2008: 623–24).

130. Hemachandra, his students Ramachandra and Gunachandra, and an anonymous commentator on a lost treatise on rhetoric (KLV) knew the ABh, but none of their works circulated outside of Gujarat. A commentator on DhĀL (Krishnamoorthy 1988) may represent a fifth case, but his time and place are unknown. I have been unable to confirm Kavi's claims about an ABh "epitome" by Purnasarasvati (c. 1400) and two other echoes (NŚ, ed. Kavi 1926: 10).

131. See e.g., ABh 1.36.21; 37.11, 18, 24; 173.15.

132. Note that *anuvyavasāya* is not used in the DhĀL at all; in Abhinava's philosophical writings it has the sense familiar from epistemology (see, e.g., IPVV v. 1, p. 39).

133. Though see SD 5.5 (p. 271 ed. NSP), and Pollock 2012: 248–49.

134. Of a piece with this oversight is Jayaratha's assessment of Bhatta Nayaka; see n. 128 above.

135. See ABh 1.275.6 (*sāmānya* in NŚ 1. 342 has an unrelated meaning), 1.270. Similarly Dhanika (on DR 4.2, see n. 100 there).

136. Pollock 2006.

137. Pollock 1998a: 141 (citing also Eagleton 1990). More generally, literary fiction is currently being studied for its contribution to Theory of Mind (identifying and understanding others' mental states); see for example Kidd and Castano 2013.

138. Narayana Rao et al. 1992. His "logicization" of rasa's intellectual history leads to numerous errors: there is no evidence Bhatta Lollata was aware of the application of rasa theory to narrative poetry (KD p. 140); nowhere in our extant materials does Shri Shankuka ascribe the "relishing of rasa" to the audience (p. 145, the very phrase *carvyamāṇo rasaḥ* is Abhinavagupta's); "the notion that rasa is 'revealed' in the audience's self" is not the Anandavardhana doctrine of "manifestation" against which Bhatta Nayaka argued—he saw that doctrine as pertaining to a verbal process, not the psychological one Abhinava later proffered in its stead (p. 146).

139. I am thinking of *Rasacandrikā* of Vishveshvara (c. 1700) and *Rasamīmāṃsā* of Gangarama Jade (c. 1800). The *Rasamahārṇava* of the celebrated logician Gokulanatha Upadhyaya (c. 1700) has in fact to do not with rasa at all but rather with *dhvani*.

140. Venidatta's *Rasakaustubha* (c. 1700) is a good example of poetry without analysis, despite the intellectual brilliance Venidatta shows in his commentary on Bhanu himself (RT, ed. Pollock 2009: xl). The same is even truer of Vishveshvara, and to some extent, Gangarama; see ibid. pp. xxxix–xl.

141. Ollett 2012; Behl 2012; Busch 2014.

142. From the portions available to me, the *Rasasindhu* of Paundarika Ramesvara (post-Bhanudatta, probably seventeenth century, *pace* Gode 1934), for example, seems like a primer for an elementary rasa exam—which may be exactly what it was.

143. RT 6.1; DhĀ pp. 24–26, for example.

144. *pārṣadaprasiddhi*.

145. RG p. 56, below.

146. See for example Narayana Rao and Shulman 2013: 70. Note that the *Naiṣadhīyacarita* itself is adduced by Vidyadhara in his discussion of the "erotic thwarted" (see *Ekāvalī* p. 104), and read by commentators on the poem accordingly (see, e.g., Narayana on 18.3). The rise of the phenomenally popular *nāyikābheda* genre in Brajbhasha and other languages—where poets read rasa theory and wrote along its lines—offers even more persuasive counterevidence.

147. Although little studied, plays in Sanskrit continued to be written and performed at royal courts in both north and south India well into the seventeenth century.

148. Hume cited in Cohen 2004: 168.

149. Paramananda Cakravartin, on KP p. 793, below.

150. Gadamer 2004: 35.

151. Danto 1981: 96.

152. Korsmeyer 2001; 2008: 128–29.

153. ABh 1.283, below.

154. Gadamer 2004: 31 (I thank A. Ollett for the reference).

155. Specific questions could of course provoke disagreement. There were continued debates about the principal rasa of a literary work, even in the case of the *Rāmāyaṇa* (see Bhatta Nrisimha p. 223.1, below).

156. "Of the Standard of Taste"; "Of the Delicacy of Taste and Passion."

157. ABh 1.36, below.

158. Additional material is offered in Pollock 2001c.

159. Bourdieu 1984, in particular p. 6. The more overtly Marxist work of Della Volpe (1991) is curiously uncritical of taste itself as a social category.

160. Wellek 1974 (1942): 57.

161. Wimsatt and Beardsley 1949: 48, 44.

162. This was true of Beardsley himself (his description of aesthetic experience could have been written by Abhinava, 1981: lxii).

163. See for example Thrailkill 2007 (the novel); Robinson 2005 (music); Clough and Halley 2007 (the social); Plamper 2010 (the history of emotions); Rosenwein 2005 (emotion in history); Leys 2011 (new cognitive theories).

1. THE FOUNDATIONAL TEXT, C. 300, AND EARLY THEORISTS, 650–1025

1. P 4.3.110; Kalidasa, *Mālavikāgnimitra*, Act 1, v. 15+.

2. RG pp. 34–35, below.

3. Shrinivasan 1980.

4. The first mention in the scholarly tradition outside the NŚ is in the early ninth century with Udbhata (4.4; possibly an interpolation, see n. 131 below). Dhanika (on DR 4.35) observes that the NŚ does not mention it. (For early references outside *alaṇkārśāstra*, see Raghvan 1975: 24.)

5. ABh 1.333.

6. Krishnamoorthy 1968: 45.

7. NŚ 6.51, p. 308.

8. NŚ 1.342 (compare n. 46 below on the use of *abhivyakti*).

9. NŚ 1.282.

10. One may well wonder whether the prose elaborations concerned with "discerning viewers" and the "traditional verse" that substantiate their antiquity are later than the main compilation. It is above all in chapters 6 and 7 that prose commentary and *ānuvaṃśya* verses are found; their historical provenance awaits serious text-critical scrutiny (for an interpretation, see Varma 1958).

11. I am not persuaded of the reality of a commentary attributed to Mātṛgupta (early seventh century?). For the evidence, see Kane 1971: 54–55.

12. Abhinava takes these to mean definitions and their analysis respectively.

13. Here follow the definitions of compendium of topics, summary verse, and etymology, and lesser components of dramatic art.

14. A legendary predecessor of Bharata.

15. Here follows a discussion of dramatic conventions, styles, modes, costumes, music and singing, and the theater structure.

16. Elsewhere in rasa discourse *artha* can have the sense "meaning," "purpose," "subject matter." Its very vagueness has much exercised thinkers, especially Abhinavagupta (see ABh 1.265, 272, below).

17. The celebrated *Sutra on Rasa*. The use of *utpad* in reference to rasa has been analyzed by Dwivedi 2005: 124–27. For Bharata it is the stable emotions that become rasa (*sthāyino bhāvā rasatvam āpnuvanti*, NŚ 1.282; see also 1.349.10 and 377.14).

18. "Condiment," *vyañjana*, is related to *vyañjita*, "manifested," below.

19. *vyañjita-*. The term is not to be connected with the linguistic theory of Anandavardhana; here, inner states are—and must be—made "manifest" by reactions and the like (the term is, however, found elsewhere in the NŚ in connection with rasa only on 1.343, prose following 7.7; see also n. 30 below).

20. In accordance with Abhinava's gloss (or: "with the acting out of emotions").

21. In what follows *bhāva* refers also to *vibhāvādi*, the aesthetic elements.

22. The following verses, presenting views denied in the preceding prose passage, apparently seek to allow them by differentiating the analytical framework in which one determines cause and effect. Thus, "emotion" could be taken as referring to what is experienced by another character (Sita's emotional reaction to Rama's erotic rasa) or by the spectator (whose own emotional reaction comes from rasa); on another analysis, the technical signification of *bhāva* comes into play *only after* rasa has turned the emotion or element into an aesthetic object. For later interpretations and critiques of Bharata's view, see ŚP p. 631.18 (and n. 155) and ABh 1.286, both discussed below. Abhinava and Hemachandra attribute to Shri Shankuka the view that rasa precedes emotion (see Shri Shankuka selections #2 and #2a, below), which might suggest that this passage of the NŚ postdates 850, Shri Shankuka's likely *floruit*.

23. I read *saṃbaddhā* (with Dwivedi, for *saṃbaddhān*).

24. *vyañjana* as "condiment" is impossible here—a condiment is not itself produced by the substances; my translation agrees essentially with Abhinava ("'condiment' here means a particular postprandial drink, in effect, taste"). The verse may have been inherited by Bharata and uses a terminology slightly different from his.

25. And food of course makes spices edible.

26. Abhinava understands this verse in a schematic as opposed to a literal sense: rasas in general can stand in four different kinds of cause-effect relationship with each other (the pairs given are illustrative only, not exhaustive): (1) one rasa can function as the cause of another insofar as it imitates the other, as a "semblance" of a rasa; (2) one rasa can be seen

as a necessary consequence of the end result of another; (3) one rasa can be seen as aiming toward another as its end result; (4) one rasa can necessarily imply another insofar as the two share the same foundational factor (see ABh 1.289–291, below). That this interpretation reflects Bharata's intention, however, may be seriously doubted.

27. Analyzed by Bhoja, ŚP, p. 635, Dhanika, p. 221, and Abhinava, ABh 1.289.13, below.

28. Abhinava identifies this sentence as a sutra. Unlike the names for the other rasas, which correlate with their referents (*vīra*, for example, means "hero"), the meaning of the word for the erotic, *śṛṅgāra*, is obscure, hence the need for etymology (*nirukta*). Presumably because the word *śṛṅgāra* also refers to decorative clothing (especially for dressing the deity's image), it can be related to the erotic, as English "lovely" is related to "love." For the later etymology, see Hemadri on BhM p. 164, below.

29. The reactions and registers of acting seem less sharply distinguished in the early period than they are later (see also Induraja on KASS, p. 47 n. 116; p. 49 n. 129, both below).

30. The text is dubious, since these are of course transitory emotions, not reactions. But the reading was known to Abhinava, who tries to defend it (ABh 1.301.24).

31. See "the ten stages of erotic thwarted" in the glossary.

32. NŚ 24 ("homogeneous acting," Bansat-Boudon 1989–1990, following Abhinava).

33. Later thinkers postulated a "tragic erotic thwarted"; see RAS p. 275 and Venkatacharya's n. there.

34. The erotic is subject to all emotions because it includes the erotic thwarted—which, however, is to be distinguished from the tragic.

35. The verse would appear to indicate all three aesthetic elements: foundational and stimulant factors, transitory emotions, and reactions, though the second phrase, "feeling . . . ," is vague. Abhinava restricts the verse to the factors.

36. According to Abhinava, these are meant to stand for the transitory emotions as such (*pramoda* presumably doing duty for *harṣa*). But the two verses do not provide a systematic account of the elements of rasa: the first verse mentions only the stimulant factors; the second, bodily and verbal representation, the transitory emotions (presumably), and more bodily representations.

37. Bharata continues in the same vein with respect to the remaining seven rasas.

38. For Abhinava, at issue in these rasa subtypes are the various shades of emotion appropriate to the underlying factor in question. One can easily see in the case of the comic how language, behavior, and dress would constitute three different types, less so in the case of the erotic and the violent.

39. Abhinava notes that "grief" here refers to loss of a loved one and the like (rather than to the stable emotion as such); the NŚ is cataloging these tragedy types according to the three ends of man.

40. "It would be false to claim that even persons of high status can truly be stricken with fear in the face of a transgression they may have made against a parent, teacher, or other guru. For fear consists of the dread of one's own death, and this cannot arise among such persons. This is why fear will be defined generally as relating to women and persons of low status" (Abhinava; for the definition, see NŚ 1.347).

41. An interpolated prose passage on the peaceful rasa follows.

42. Or, purpose ([*kāvya-*]*artha-*); contrast n. 16 above. The compound is found only once elsewhere in this chapter (p. 343), and in 19.69 (and the term *kāvya* itself is rare).

43. The three different definitions are meant for the instruction of three different kinds of audience of the NŚ: playwrights, actors, and spectators (Abhinava).

44. That is, makes available to the viewer.

45. Repeating 6.34 above.

46. *-abhivyakti-*, which is used only here in connection with rasa (see also above n. 8); the phrase "literary rasa" (*kāvyarasa*) is used only once elsewhere (18.93).

47. *sāmānyaguṇayogena* (used only once elsewhere, NŚ, 22.194). The term probably refers to the qualities shared by a *bhāva* and its respective rasa; it most certainly does not have the significance we find in the Bhatta Nayaka tradition (compare *Avaloka* n. 100, below).

48. The glosses here (cited in NŚ 4th ed. and Krishnamoorthy 1988: xxiv) do not pertain to this verse in the context of the NŚ.

49. What Bharata proceeds to offer seem in fact to be definitions of the specific categories of emotions.

50. Here follows the definition of the eight stable emotions, their factors and reactions.

51. Here follows the definition of the thirty-three transitory emotions, their factors and reactions.

52. With the real emotions.

53. I read in desperation *aduḥkhitena asukhitena* (with Kangle, for *duḥkhitena sukhitena*).

54. Bharata goes on to name the psychophysical responses, their causes, and their "function in bringing about the rasas and the emotions."

55. Bronner 2011.

56. We have of course seen *kāvya* used of drama in the NŚ itself (see n. 42 above).

57. See above, p. 9.

58. Udbhata (4.7, below) fits *samāhita* into the category of affective utterance by redefining it as the "evening out" or "quiescence" of a rasa or emotion, and that is how it will be treated in the later tradition (e.g., *Candrāloka* 5.117–18).

59. See Kuntaka, VJ 3.11, below.

60. Contrast Krishnamoorthy 1979b: 304.

61. KĀ 2.280. The rest of Dandin's illustrations are not so clear, though the commentator Ratnashrijnana certainly takes them this way.

62. A list of seventeen additional semantic figures of speech follows.

63. A citation from an unknown *Mahābhārata* play (a portion of the verse is interpolated after MBh 5.87.23; it possibly refers to Krishna's visit with Vidura in 5.89–90). Vidura is the wise half-brother of King Dhritarashtra and a well-wisher of the Pandavas and their counselor, Krishna, also known as Govinda. (The verse is cited also in KĀ 2.274, DhĀ 2, and many later treatises.)

64. On the example, see the headnote.

65. From an episode in the *Mahābhārata*, where Karna's first shot at his enemy Arjuna misses; Shalya is Karna's (reluctant) charioteer. (Bhamaha conflates two passages, MBh 8.66.8 and 8.1104*; I thank Y. Bronner for the reference.)

66. The three following tropes are provided only here, and ignored in KĀ.

67. The machinations of the jealous king Shishupala against Krishna are detailed in the *Mahābhārata*. The *Ratnāharaṇa* mentioned is not extant.

68. The *Rājamitra* is lost, and the episode mentioned is otherwise unknown.

69. Chanakya was the wily advisor of Chandragupta Maurya, and enemy of Nanda (the episode is not known in the extant literature). Moonstones ooze liquid when struck by moonbeams.

70. For the former, see Dimitrov 2014; for the latter, Pollock 2006: 344 (on p. 422 I misidentified him as a Jain; the incipit of his commentary shows him to be a Vaishnava).

71. Subsequent authorities will define the latter differently: for Bhoja, for example, the *arthaguṇa mādhurya* is when a character is described as showing gentleness even in anger (ŚP p. 502.16; Tarkabagisa on KĀ is wrong to say that this is merely the manifestation of the stable emotion, p. 49.7).

72. SKĀ 5.4–6 deals with rasa as sophisticated expression; "word rasa" is ignored.

73. KĀ 2.273. See Ratna's comment ad loc., and Bhoja's full exposition (ŚP p. 624.18–626.6; see also SKĀ p. 704.12).

74. ABh 1.266, where KĀ 2.279, 281 are adduced.

75. See Ratna's extended note on 2.279, below.

76. See chapter 2 headnote, and notes 17 and 73 there.

77. Presumably, their own poetry; and thus perhaps an echo of the "expression theory" of poetic creation (see the introduction, section 2), if the reference is to rasa taken generally.

78. *priyatara*. The examples below use the derived substantive *prīti*, which signifies both pleasure and affection.

79. *yuktotkarṣam*. Here I follow the explanation of Ratna and Bhoja (contra Böhtlingk and Tarkabagisa ad loc., and Raghavan 1978: 420; compare KĀ 1.76: *utkarṣavān guṇaḥ*, "an intensified quality," and the Kannada *Kavirājamārga* 3.199, where the definition of *ūrjita* is given: *ārūḍhanijamanōhaṃkārōtkarṣaprakāśam ūrjitasadaḷaṃkāram*, "an intensification of the sense of self").

80. I read *īyasunādibhir . . . uktaḥ. yuktotkarṣa iti pratyāmnāto 'bhivyaktyartham iti* (with the Nepal ms., for *ayam u[p]amādibhir . . . ukto yuktokarṣa iti*). The "and so on" comprises the *matup* suffix in both *rasavat* and *ūrjasvi*.

81. BKA 3.5, above.

82. Ratna is correct in taking this verse as Dandin's explanation of the example, not a continuation of it. The following illustrative verse adheres to the same pattern.

83. The verse is addressed to Shiva, who is embodied in the eight forms listed.

84. A scion of the Raghu clan, according to Ratna (V reads *rāmavarmanaḥ*; the correct reading may, however, be *rājavarmanaḥ*, referring to Narasimhavarman II, alias Rajasimha, very likely Dandin's patron).

85. The two examples are probably not meant to illustrate objective and subjective aspects of the "affectionate utterance" (how it affects the listener in the first example and the speaker in the second), since it is the speaker's emotion that should be at issue, as in all later discussions. It may well be that Dandin wanted simply to reference the two principal deities, Vishnu and Shiva. And given that both verses are addressed to a god, they clearly represent what in later discussions is called emotion poetry (first in Induraja on Udbhata 4.2, below), which typically concerns the stable emotion of desire for a god.

86. Bhoja provides an exegesis of Dandin in ŚP pp. 629–31, below.

87. Source unknown. King Udayana speaks in reference to his beloved, Vasavadatta, who had been thought dead but has just been revealed as present in disguise.

88. That is, the two male deities.

89. "Highly strengthened": *(aty)upacaya*, a term of art of the early commentators on the NŚ such as Bhatta Lollata.

90. "Inner principle": *antastattva*. I find no precise definition for the term elsewhere.

91. I read *vācika*- (with the Nepal ms., for *nāṭikā*).

92. From a lost Mahabharata poem. Draupadi is the wife of the heroes, the Pandavas (one of whom is Bhima); Duhshasana is one of the antagonists, the sons of Dhritarashtra.

93. I read *kāruṇyākhyānaviśeṣāśrayaḥ* (with the Nepal ms., for *kāruṇyākhyarasaviśeṣāśrayaḥ*).

94. I read *abhivyaktim* (with the Nepal ms., for *abhivyaktam*). The term was not necessarily borrowed from DhĀ (though Ratna knows the work); see above, n. 119.

95. I read *mānāyā* (with Vadijhangala and ŚP p. 679), for Ratna's *mālāyā* (where the girlfriend is amused at the *nāyikā*'s boldness in the first days of her marriage, the uncrushed garland, *mālā*, indicating the top position in lovemaking).

96. I read *kāvyābhidheyasya vastunaḥ* (with the Nepal ms., for *kāvyādheyavastunaḥ*; correct the printed edition to *sāgrāmyatā sabhyatā*; and in the final line, *sambandhinī* [*sambandhinā* Nepal ms.; *sambandhinaḥ* printed ed.]).

97. From a lost Ramayana play or poem.

98. Ravana is the demon king who abducted the wife of the hero, Rama.

99. This and the following example may well be Dandin's ad hoc creations; they are not found in extant literature.

100. Bronkhorst 2008.

101. "Only the small-minded ask whether one is kin or stranger. To the high-minded the whole world is family." The poem ascribed to Udbhata in *Subhāṣitavalī* no. 498.

102. For Pratiharenduraja, see the colophon to his commentary; for Tilaka, Jacobi 1908: 291; Ramaswami Sastri (in his edition of KASS), pp. 39–41.

103. For a general reassessment of Udbhata, see Bronner forthcoming.

104. However implicitly in BKA 3.6.

105. The apparently redundant form *preyasvat* does not of course indicate ignorance of the analysis by which both the comparative (*preyas*) and the possessive (*vat*) signify *atiśaya* (see Ratnashrijnana on KĀ 2. 237, above), but its precise function is unclear to me (it may pertain to Udbhata's redefinition of the figure as referring to any emotion; thus, it seems, Krishnamoorthy 1979b: 306, and compare DhĀL p. 192).

106. Abhinava is the first we know of to add *udaya*, *sandhi*, and *śabalatā* to Udbhata's typology (DhĀL on 2.3). Bhoja will use different terminology (SKĀ 5.9–10).

107. A good example of Udbhata's combination of conservativism (honoring the old template of *alaṅkārśāstra*) and innovation (introducing a new affective one); see n. 152 below. I omit from the translation his verses on double entendre and two other rhetorical figures (n. 46).

108. KASS p. 54. If Induraja really thought Udbhata himself had resolved this question, he would have ascribed to him the verses he cites later anonymously (KASS pp. 80, 83; contrast Krishnamoorthy 1979b: 307). That Udbhata's framework of rasa analysis was taken as fully rhetorical was precisely what provoked the critique of Kuntaka (VJ 3.11–13).

109. For the early eighth-century playwright Bhavabhuti, see Pollock 2007: 42–44 (compare his verses cited in ŚP p. 624, below).

110. See "On Verbal Representation" (chapter 4.2).

111. By contrast Tilaka, the second commentator, inhabited a conceptual landscape radically discontinuous with this tradition (see for example his comment below, n. 112.

112. I omit from the translation below the disingenuous statement and double entendre.

113. The normal understanding of "emotion poetry" (see KP 4.35cd, and n. on *Ekāvalī* p. 103). The example (motherly love) supports Tilaka, though Udbhata's definition and Induraja's explication do not, and clearly represent an earlier conception.

114. Induraja lists them, citing NŚ 6.17–22 (with a v.l. that notably includes *śama*).

115. The reactions and the other three categories are usually said to intimate the eight (or nine) stable emotions (as below), not all fifty emotions (contrast Banhatti p. 98).

116. These are typically taken to be the four registers of acting, not four types of reactions. Yet note that the four kinds of *anubhāva*, i.e., the *ārambhas*, are correlated with the four kinds of *abhinaya* elsewhere (e.g., *Agnipurāṇa* ch. 341). There may well be two parallel traditions, the one, *abhinaya*, referring to drama, the other, *ārambha*, referring to poetry.

117. The term *viṣaya* is usually used for the object of emotion, not as here *āśraya*, which refers to the subject.

118. *sādhāraṇyena*. This recalls Bhatta Nayaka, though for him the object of affect, not the affect itself, is "commonized" (*Avaloka* pp. 218–19, below); see also n. 122 below.

119. Udbhata cannot have known the theory of suggestion in aesthetics (Anandavardhana's innovation was some three generations later), though he might be said to have anticipated it.

120. *svalakṣaṇasvabhāva-*, like *svalakṣaṇasvarūpa-* later on, is not a *dvandva* (so Banhatti) but a *bahuvrīhi*. For Buddhists, language refers only to constructed universals, not unique particulars, but the idea is found elsewhere too (see Abhinava's IPVV v. 1, p. 117). And in Bhatta Mimamsa semantics, "proper terms" denote a universal.

121. I conjecture *anubhava* (suggested by L. McCrea, for *anubhāva-* in all printed editions).

122. *sāmānyarūpatayā* (or perhaps, in view of the preceding Buddhist terminology, "in the form of a constructed universal").

123. Note the absence of the stable emotion, which is required for the rasa to be clearly displayed and defines the figure as the "rasa-laden."

124. Source unknown, but probably from Udbhata's commentary on the NŚ (so with other Udbhata citations below). By "emotions" is presumably meant emotion poetry (see below); contrast the five different elements of rasa poetry (Induraja on 4.4, below).

125. Not all elements need be present; those absent are supplied by implication (thus many later thinkers, for example SD 3.16cd–17ab).

126. *tayā* (sc., *ratyā*) *sāhacaryāt*.

127. It is probably going too far to take this as "given that desire is the necessary accompaniment to all of them," and so seeing a prefiguration of Bhoja's view (ŚP p. 613; Bhoja seems to echo Induraja's account of *preyaḥ*, see ŚP p. 625, below).

128. I read *nirviśeṣa-* (clearly indicated by P, so T and Jacob, for NSP, BSPS *nirviśeṣā-*), and *-vāllabhyāt* (implied by P, so T, BSPS, and Jacob, for NSP *-vātsalyāt*).

129. This refers to the physical register of acting.

130. The stable emotion is only "hinted at," not "clearly indicated."

131. If genuine, this would be the first mention of the peaceful rasa in Sanskrit theory (the few references in the NŚ are later additions, though undatable). But the verse seems to be an interpolation that has crept into the text, being irrelevant to Udbhata's discussion of narrative rather than dramatic poetry. It may of course still be Udbhata's, perhaps borrowed from his NŚ commentary.

132. The symmetrical relationship between the rasas and the ends of man—the erotic relating to love, etc.—will be detailed first by Abhinavagupta (see ABh 1.276, below).

133. Induraja goes on to contrast the "special" savoring of rasa from the "mere" savoring of the transitory emotions, linking the former to the sphere of the four ends.

134. RKA 12.4, see below. Induraja's interpretation conflicts with that of Rudrata's commentator ad loc. (and that of ŚP p. 683, below).

135. Jacob and NSP identify this as a *kārikā* of Udbhata's, but this is mistaken, as Induraja's treatment shows (Tilaka omits).

136. Contra Jacob, NSP, and BSPS, the words *prāpya parihāryau* must be read in compound.

137. Source unknown. The verse offers early evidence of the discursive turn away from formalist analysis of rasa to reader response (see introduction, section 6).

138. Source unknown.

139. When a poem has five elements as its basis it can "clearly" manifest the rasa.

140. Induraja will call this view into question in what follows.

141. The view of the late ninth-century scholar Anandavardhana.

142. *hāsādisamatvaṃ ca kāvyasya prāpnoti.* Presumably this refers to the descriptive portions of a poem devoted to prompting the inference of the stable emotion.

143. The subdivisions are listed first in DhĀ 2.12 (p. 217), with *abhilāṣa* as the first stage.

144. Or even "being factored": *vibhāvyamānā* (T clearly read *bhāvyamānā* in P).

145. *abhivyajyate*; see n. 94 on KĀ 2.285, above.

146. The Sanskrit term is the same as in the "haughty" declaration of Dandin, but it is translated as "impulsive" here in accordance with Udbhata's redefinition.

147. Udbhata follows the traditional order of figures found in Dandin and Bhamaha, and thus discusses the figure *paryāyokta* between *ūrjasvi* and *samāhita.* But in Udbhata's treatment, unlike Dandin's and Bhamaha's, the figure *samāhita* is defined in terms of rasa, thereby linking it to the first three figures of the group (*preyas, rasavad, ūrjasvi*) but not to *paryāyokta.*

148. I read *-vṛtteḥ* (with T, for *-vṛttaiḥ* Jacob, NSP, and BSPS).

149. The predisposition in the *character,* as clearly indicated in what follows.

150. I read *dṛṣṭyā vibhramāṃś ca* and *romāñcaṃ* (with T, for *dṛṣṭvā vibhramāc ca* and *romāñca-*, Jacob, NSP, BSPS).

151. Presumably by the cupped hands raised to his face in greeting.

152. The v. is critically analyzed in VJ pp. 159–61, below. Udbhata retains the old sense of the figure (BKA 3.11, KĀ 2.298), while expanding it (at least in terms of subordination) in accord with his new rasa template.

153. Three of the traditional eight sources of pearl. I read *sūkara-* (for *sūkare*).

154. The reading *puṣṭa* (P), *puṣya* (T) is uncertain; the word is unattested in the sense given by both, "a particular type of precious stone."

155. Udbhata's novel refinement of the second type of *udātta* seems comparable to Anandavardhana's *guṇībhūtavyaṅgya*, but the idea is not developed beyond what we have here. Note that Anandavardhana will turn this schema upside down, arguing that it is precisely when subordinated to some other sentence meaning that rasa functions as the figure *rasavat* (DhĀ 2.5, below; this raises yet further problems of categorization; see KLV p. 280).

156. SRĀ 1.11. The omission of Bhatta Nayaka is even more startling.

157. KA 5.3 (33); also cited by Namisadhu on RKA 3.59 and KM p. 45.3 (attributed to the otherwise unknown Aparajiti, perhaps a patronymic of Bhatta Lollata). Bhatta Lollata

is also credited by Kshemaraja with a commentary on the *Spandakārikā* (Pandey 1963: 196–97).

158. Manikyachandra, KP (ed. Mysore, 1st. ed.), p. 147.

159. For the former see ND p. 160, or RT 4.3, both below); for the latter, Dhanika (possibly) on DR 4.3ab, p. 171 (see note 104 there), and RG p. 55. It is an anachroniism on the part of Someshvara Bhatta, the earliest KP commentator, to take Bhatta Lollata to be referring to audience reaction (KP p. 535).

160. NŚ 1.299 (see n. 29 on the conflation of the reactions and acting registers), and compare Kangle 1973: 126.

161. See Vishvanatha's comment on KP p. 536.

162. See NŚ 1.266 and n. 17 above.

163. ABh 1.266; KA p. 89.

164. I read *vibhāvāś* (with KA, for *vibhāvaś*).

165. Those produced by rasa are in another character (e.g., Sita's in the presence of Rama).

166. I read *bhāvānāṃ ye 'nubhāvāḥ* | (with KA, for *bhāvānāṃ eva* | *nanu ye 'nubhāvāḥ*). Manikyachandra confusingly reads *rasakāryatvena* (for *rasakāraṇatvena*).

167. Both stable and transitory emotions are states of mind, and should occur sequentially, not simultaneously (so Dhanika on DR 4.34; Manikyachandra on KP p. 534).

168. I read *vāsanātmatā tasya* (sc., *sthāyinaḥ*) *vivakṣitā* (with KA, for *vāsanātmaneha tasya vivakṣitāḥ*). The syntax is still hard, but Manikyachandra leaves no doubt about the sense.

169. I conjecture *'pi vyañjan-* (for *'py abhivyañjan-*)

170. Bhatta Lollata is playing on the etymological meaning of *vāsanā* (from the root *vās*, to perfume).

171. This would seem to refer to emotion poetry (see Induraja on KASS 4.2, p. 48, above).

172. *mukhyayā vṛttyā*. It is unclear whether this pertains to reference ("literal sense," so, e.g., Bhatta Gopala, KP, p. 537) or ontology ("in actual fact," so, e.g., Maheshvara, KP, p. 540).

173. Abhinava identifies this as "the view of the ancients," and cites KĀ 2.279, 281, above.

174. ABh 1.292.22.

175. Abhinava adds, "This little bit of arrogance on Lollata's part can be safely ignored." As he elaborates in ABh 1.335.8, Bharata's list was exhaustive not by convention but because "only those nine rasas are taught as subserving educational needs and as adequately pleasurable."

176. ABh 1.258.

177. *anusandhi-* (= *anusandhāna* above), and contrast Kangle 1973: 57.

178. Ruyyaka, KP, p. 534.

179. *apuṣṭas tu sthāyī* recapitulates *sthāyī bhavaty* [KA *-tv*] *anupacitaḥ* (ABh 1.266.11–12; Shridhara's *aparipuṣṭas tv asthāyī* p. 536 is false).

180. *Rājataraṅgiṇī* 4.705 (*abhyudaya* normally is predicated of a king, but no Bhuvana is known from this period).

181. See *Subhāṣitāvali*, p. 127; *Śārṅgadharapaddhati*, pp. 564 (son of Mayura) and 591; Nagesha Bhatta seems to name him Shankukarna, KP (BHU ed.) p. 611.

182. ND 1.53 (*vṛtti*); 2.28 (*vṛtti*, on the question of the social class of the protagonist of a farce).

183. A fortiori does this apply to later elaborations of Shri Shankuka's thought in the RG p. 28, below.

184. Gupta 1963.

185. Fragment #4a, and see the introduction, section 8. Note also his use of the Buddhist locution *bhāvanāprakarṣaja* in fragment #5a.

186. See for example 1.66, 74; and 1.212, 213.

187. DhĀ pp. 83–84; ABh 2.221.

188. VJ 3.10+.

189. ABh 1.266–267; I supplement this very condensed account with KA pp. 90–93 and KLV pp. 303–305. Abhinava also discusses Shri Shankuka's view in ABh 1.278. The positions detailed in DhĀL pp. 185–86 combine parts of Shri Shankuka's theory, but it is impossible to sort out which are his and which not.

190. I.e., that rasa arises from a "conjunction *of the stable emotion* with the aesthetic elements."

191. That is, to speak of "enhancement" is necessarily to speak of the "enhancement" of something, and the rules of discourse tell us that this "something" has to be stated first, or known from context. (I thank A. Ollett for this observation.)

192. It remains unclear how Shri Shankuka himself reconciled the two different discussions (of rasas and of *sthāyibhāvas*) in the NŚ.

193. NŚ 1.318 and 1.347.

194. I read *-mandatvādi-* (with KLV, for *-mandamādhyasthyādya-*).

195. Each having its own degree of intensity of the comic. KA cites NŚ 6.51–52.

196. KA cites NŚ 22.170–172.

197. I read *prāgavastho bhāvaḥ* (with Manikyachandra KP p. 543, for KA's *prāgavasthābhāvaḥ*).

198. KA here inserts selection #2b, noting that, given these phenomena, rasa cannot be thought of as being preceded by or dependent on the stable emotion, but just the reverse.

199. I read *sahakāri-* (with KP p. 543, for *sahacāri-*).

200. Presumably, an effort on the actor's part.

201. The question the following discussion seeks to answer concerns the peculiar nature of the stable emotion, why it cannot be taken in Bhatta Lollata's sense, why it can only be represented or imitated, and perhaps also why inference is required.

202. *anusandhāna-* (contrast the usage of Bhatta Lollata, for whom the term means something like "identification").

203. As #3a below indicates, the narration recited by the actor can communicate the factors, but presumably there will be many cases when the factors appear in physical form on the stage. KD makes it seem that it is the actor who is referred to as comprehending the factors, pp. 143–44; 145.1–2 (and the audience, 144.4). But this makes no sense here, if in fact the question is how and why inference is required for apprehending the stable emotion. The criticism of Bhatta Tota (p. 185 below) shows that the uncertainty was old.

204. A critique of Udbhata's notion that the stable emotions can be communicated by their "proper terms."

205. The verse is from a lost Ramayana play (*Kṛtyāravaṇa*, according to KLV p. 304). Rama is speaking about the abduction of Sita.

206. The fire inside the ocean that burns up the incoming waters and keeps them from overflowing.

207. KA's readings (*kṛtastambhaḥ* for *kṛtaḥ stambhaḥ* and *yena vardhitā-* for *yo 'navasthitā-*) are confirmed by the edition of the *Tāpasavatsarāja* (2.7) itself. Vinitideva is describing King Udayana's grief.

208. *Ratnāvalī* 2.11.

209. Not only is "stable emotion" not included by Bharata in the principal compound (*vibhāva-*, etc.), it is not even mentioned in the instrumental ("by means of the stable emotion") or the nominative ("the stable emotion becomes rasa"), thus KLV (p. 305.1). Better, however, is the genitive, as understood by Bhatta Lollata (*arthāt sthāyinaḥ*).

210. And cannot be directly equated with the stable emotion strengthened, as in Bhatta Lollata's view.

211. Bharata says of other rasas that they "consist of" the stable emotion (e.g., *hāsya* is *hāsasthāyibhāvātmaka*, NŚ 1.305). KLV errs in pointing to NŚ 1.294.

212. I read *dṛṣṭā* (with KA, for *adṛṣṭā*).

213. *Pramāṇavārttika* 2.57. Both knowledge episodes are "false," since Buddhists hold that the class category involved in such an inference (as the universal "fire" from a particular smoke) is a conceptual fiction. But in one case the false knowledge does enable one of the men to find the real gem (see further in McCrea 2011).

214. Mammata restates this as "This actor is in fact Rama, and Rama is in fact this actor" (KP p. 543).

215. The punctuation around the clause *ayam eva rāma iti* in both NŚ and KA is misleading. The correct interpretation is indicated by KP, *auttarakālike bādhe rāmo 'yam iti*. The sense here is: *ayam eva rāma iti pratītyāṃ bādhitāyāṃ na cāpy ayam [rāmaḥ] na [ca] sukhīti pratītiḥ iti na)*.

216. "The actor is really Rama" is not true because that is not the apprehension we actually have, but rather "Here is Rama."

217. It is precisely *not* the identity of actor and character that is being inferred (so Ingalls et al. 1990: 229), which would be self-canceling anyway, since for the aesthetic inference to work the actor must vanish completely. It is just as in the case of a pictorial representation: we think, not, "This is *actually* a horse" (*turaga evāyam*), but "Here is a horse" (*turago 'yam*). In KD (p. 142) this is called *nirgalitāvadhāraṇarūpā pratītiḥ*, an apprehension where the very determination [or restriction, *eva*] that underlies it vanishes.

218. There is no reason not to take this as a direct quotation from Shri Shankuka.

219. Such as doubts (KLV).

220. *-saṃplava-* (*-anekarūptatāpratibhāsaḥ*, KLV).

221. ABh 1.286. In Abhinava's view, the actor "contains" rasa like a vessel (ABh 1.285), and how far his idiom of "relishing" accurately represents Shri Shankuka's views is unclear.

222. *loke*, the storyworld; see also Manikyachandra's gloss on the passage in KA cited in the next section (*laukikasya . . . rāmādigatasya rasasya*, p. 206). Compare Dhanika's use of *laukika* (on DR 4.3ab, see n. 106, below) and Abhinavagupta's discussion, ABh 1.286, below.

223. And thus his emotion. For the purpose of the present argument (see ABh 1.286–287 and especially n. 203), the dramatis persona or foundational cause stands for all the aesthetic elements, which of course include the emotions more narrowly conceived.

224. Given the context in which Abhinava adduces this citation—a discussion of whether emotion precedes rasa or the reverse—the first position would seem to indicate that rasa can be said, if not to precede emotion, then at least to be simultaneous with it, and the second, that emotion can be said to precede rasa.

225. Presumably, that rasas and emotions are mutually constitutive (Bharata's third position, see NŚ 1.286). Abhinava dismisses this argument on the grounds that the viewer makes no distinction between character and actor. But aside from the fact that this is Shri Shanku-

ka's own view (as the analogy of the painting of the horse shows), what he is here offering is an analytical, not a phenomenological, account.

226. KA p. 91. This is Hemachandra's reworking of Shri Shankuka's interpretation of NŚ 1.286. The quote attributed to the "sage"—presumably Bharata—is not found in NŚ, and the second sentence is of course the position of Shri Shankuka.

227. That is, again, the aesthetic elements, which include the *foundational cause* that is being seen (compare ABh 1.286.21: *tarhi rasaprasādād bhāvā vibhāvādayaḥ*, "It can therefore be said that the 'emotions'—that is, the aesthetic elements—arise by virtue of rasa").

228. KP p. 543 (supplemented by KA pp. 91–92).

229. The syntax is *naṭe . . . anumīyamāno . . . ratyādir bhāvas . . . rasaḥ*. This might seem to be at odds with Abhinava (#2a) (*anukartari rasān āsvādayato 'nukārye bhāvapratītiḥ*) though confirmed by (#1a) (*anukartṛsthatvena liṅgabalataḥ pratīyamānaḥ sthāyī bhāvo mukhyarāmādigatasthāyyanukaraṇarūpaḥ*). The emotion we infer in the actor is an imitation of the emotion of the character, and that inferred emotion is rasa.

230. Both untraced (the latter is cited also by Rudrata). In the monsoons travelers return home to enjoy the company of their beloved.

231. There is a *yathāsāṃkhya* relationship between the elements here, *-balāt* going with *kāraṇa-*, and *prakāśitaiḥ* with *kāryasahakāri-*.

232. *saṃbhāvyamānaḥ*.

233. Note that KP reads *-vilakṣaṇo sthāyitvena* (KA *-vilakṣaṇasthāyitvena*).

234. It is unclear whether Mammata and Hemachandra, neither of whom had independent access to Shri Shankuka's work, are fairly representing his thought when they refer to viewers tasting the rasa by way of their "predisposition," the latter term being introduced into rasa theory by Bhatta Nayaka (or perhaps Dhanika, on DR 4.37) several generations after Shri Shankuka.

235. ABh 1.311.17–19.

236. *sadayāhṛdayatā*.

237. Abhinavagupta remarks: "This is the blathering of someone who forgets the first thing when he says the second. For he holds *karuṇa* [read thus for *karuṇā*] to be the simulation of grief, whereas [he just defined it as] compassion, which is the desire to rescue someone. How can that be an imitation of grief? And I haven't the faintest idea what the spectators are supposed to feel 'compassion' for."

238. ABh 3.150–151. There are uncertainties in the text and translation.

239. NŚ 1.22.1, 3.

240. Should we read *ahetukatvam*? The question is not whether *sattva* is caused or uncaused, but whether its manifestations can be.

241. Aside from arguing, among other things, that Shri Shankuka confuses us on the location of the psychophysical element (it is in the actor rather than in the character), Abhinava has a radically different understanding of the NŚ verses (1.151–152).

242. Vallabhadeva (early to mid-tenth century) refers in his commentary on *Śiśupālavadha* (4.21) to an exegesis he wrote on Rudrata (I thank L. McCrea for the reference).

243. Literally people "filled with or fond of rasa," and below, treatises "devoid of rasa."

244. Namisadhu reads *nīrasebhyas te*; I see no need for the awkward *nīrase 'bhyaste* in the printed text, which also violates the caesura that falls before *te*.

245. This verse is unmetrical and probably corrupt. I conjecture: *tat kāvyaṃ kartavyaṃ*.

246. *sarasa-*.

247. *vakrokti* (the first "word figure" treated, 2.14) and *vāstavokti* (the first "sense figure," 7.10, synonymous with *svabhāvokti*).

248. Compare Namisadhu on RKA 1.7; 10 (*sphuṭārthaṃ na varam*), 12.5, etc.

249. I conjecture *mati-* (for *rati-*, which is the basis of a rasa, so its presence here is impossible).

250. Paralysis is numbered among the *sāttvikabhāvas*, which are viewed as partly reactions, partly emotions; see DR 4. 4cd–5ab, below.

251. NŚ 6.32–33, given above.

252. Namisadhu's candor about the uncertainty of the canonical list is uncommon.

253. Or perhaps, "to win over critics." Compare Bhatta Lollata's argument (as reported by Abhinavagupta) based on the *pārṣadaprasiddhi*, or norms of the scholarly community (above, Bhatta Lollata fragment #2a, and ABh 1.335.7; see also Raghavan 1975: 128).

254. Rudrata goes on to consider the nature of the protagonist, and to briefly define the other rasas.

255. *Rājataraṅgiṇī* 5.34.

256. DhĀ p. 364. For the larger question of the rise of a literary teleology, see McCrea 2009, passim, but in particular p. 442.

257. Ananda nowhere discusses *rasodaya*, *-śānti*, *-sandhi*, or *-śabalatā*, while *rasābhāsa* is mentioned only twice, in passing.

258. The keyword of reception theory, *sāmājika*, audience, never is used in the work. The "sensitive reader" does not experience (taste, savor, etc.) rasa; rasa "appears" to him (DhĀ p. 402).

259. *rasādīn bandhum, rasavanti hi vastūni*, DhĀ 2.17, 2.16 (pp. 221–22); *vaktā kaviḥ kavinibaddho vā, kavinibaddhaś cāpi rasabhāvarahito rasabhāvasamanvito vā; raso 'pi kathānāyakāśrayas tadvipakṣāśrayo vā*, DhĀ 3.6 (p. 318).

260. Ingalls et al. 1990: 413 (the important distinction surprisingly plays no role in their analysis of Ananda's theory).

261. H. P. Grice's term "implicature" seems to me both to capture at least the linguistic (if not the aesthetic) phenomenon Ananda sought to describe, and to provide a neologism comparable to Ananda's innovative use of *dhvani* (literally, "sound").

262. DhĀ 1.2, 2.3. A good summary is offered in *Avaloka* pp. 205–206, below.

263. Compare DhĀ pp. 78–82, below, with Shri Shankuka fragment #1a, p. 267, above.

264. In technical terminology, *guṇībhūtavyaṅgya*, "where the manifested sense"—here rasa—"is subordinate" to another meaning.

265. Ananda's expression may be a little loose, but I fail to understand why Abhinava adds *tātparyaśakti*, the position that Ananda rejects. The aesthetic elements themselves are indeed directly expressed, and they in turn indirectly express—i.e., suggest—rasa.

266. The second is Ananda's position, and will be vindicated later.

267. Or perhaps we should in fact read *'kāvye* (for *kāvye*, see *akāvyam* in, e.g., DhĀL p. 497.19): "In what is not poetry," such as a list of rasas in a textbook.

268. A reference to Valmiki's creation of poetry (*Rāmāyaṇa* 1.2.39).

269. Rather than as a (quasi) figure; the distinction is argued out in what follows.

270. *anyatra* = *anyasmin*; see VJ p. 149 (*anyo vākyārthaḥ*).

271. Ananda is fundamentally redefining the idea of the "rasa-laden": it is not actually a figure at all, but rasa itself when playing a subordinate role.

272. Literally, the "affectionate utterance figure," but figures cannot themselves be the subject matter, a problem that Abhinava sought to deal with in his commentary ad loc.

273. Kuntaka will insist that the verse also conveys the erotic rasa (VJ 151.2).

274. Perhaps to hide his transgression (so Ingalls et al. ad loc.).

275. To the expressed sense of flattery of the king's power.

276. Presumably Ananda is using the term *rasavat* in the redefined sense, as he will continue to do in what follows.

277. The dispute here seems to lie in the difference between the earlier conception of rasa as simply another figure of speech, and Ananda's asserting its independence from and primacy over rhetoric. The distinctive feature of rasa viewed as a figure, i.e., as *rasavat*, is not the fact that its subject is animate (a view attributed to Udbhata by Shridhara; see Krishnamoorthy 1979b: 306): since anything can in some way be connected with an animate being, that criterion would leave all the other figures with no scope of operation, for they could simply be folded into the category of *rasavat*. The distinctive feature is whether or not rasa plays a subordinate role in the poem. Note also that the entire discussion that follows presupposes rasa's being located in the character.

278. That is, as a stimulant factor (as explained below).

279. VU 4.52.

280. I omit the *kārikās* (they are recapitulated in the *vṛtti*) and purely grammatical points.

281. That is, part human, part divine (as below).

282. A reference to the Prakrit romance *Līlāvaī* (which is, according to a standard classification that the text itself refers to, *divyamānuṣī*, an observation I owe to A. Ollett).

283. Compare the discussion of Abhinavagupta on the first of the "hindrances" (ABh 1.274, below).

284. The reference is to Kalidasa's portrayal of the lovemaking of Shiva and Parvati in KS 8 (see DhĀ pp. 316–18).

285. Possibly from Yashovarman's eighth-century play *Rāmābhyudaya* (Pollock 2007: 58).

286. That is, zeal.

287. A likely echo of Bhatta Lollata (see the headnote to his section).

288. The rasa is clearly posited of the character, not the audience; hence "experienced" below is likely to refer to the character as well.

289. I read *pravṛddha-* (with KM ed., for *pravṛtta-*), and in the next line *devaprāya-* (with KM ed., for *rāmadevaprāya-*).

290. I read *svapravṛtti-* (with KM ed., for *pravṛtti-*).

291. Discussed in DhĀ 1.9 (p. 99), which Ananda quotes here.

292. Ananda here offers another interpretation of the term *vṛtti* in the *kārikā*, pertaining to either the dramatic modes or forms of alliteration.

293. Ananda is not referring to the subjective experience of rasa, let alone claiming that all living beings experience the erotic rasa in their everyday lives; the "erotic" here is only pointing toward the desire that underlies it (so correctly *Didhiti*; compare the statement of Mammata cited in chapter 3 n. 123).

294. Ananda has been discussing *citrakāvya*, which includes verbal puzzles, picture poems (*technopaegnia*), and so on.

295. Abhinava attributes this and the following verses to Anandavardhana (the former is quoted also in SKĀ 5.3 and ŚP p. 706). The context of the verse requires the construction *kāvye*...

jagat ("the world of the poem"); contrast Ingalls et al. 1990: 639. Abhinava understands the verse differently here (it is filled with rasa in view of [the readers'] submergence in it) and in his analysis of NŚ 6.38 (1.288).

296. That this tendency was clear to the tradition itself is shown by the intellectual history Ruyyaka provides in AS pp. 3–12.

297. VJ p. 141 (see below, n. 308); ABh 1.273, below. "Semblance of rasa" in animals is first clearly enunciated by (the formalist) Bhoja (SKĀ 5.8).

298. I conjecture *pradhāna-* (for *pradhānaṃ*; see p. 140, *apradhānacetana-*).

299. *pratyagratā-*; for the usage see VJ p. 45.6.

300. VU 4.2. King Pururavas has fallen in love with the divine nymph Urvashi.

301. Compare p. 158.5.

302. *samanvaya-*, translation uncertain (a favorite word of Kuntaka's, used some forty times; see e.g., pp. 96.4 and 111.15).

303. VU 4.6.

304. As a divine being Urvashi would never actually touch the earth.

305. In *Tāpasavatsarāja* King Udayana, neglecting statecraft in his infatuation with his queen Vasavadatta, is tricked by his ministers Yaugandharayana and Rumanvat into believing she has died in a fire; whereupon he becomes an ascetic, only to be reunited with her at the end. The dominant rasa of the play is the erotic, but here there is the subordinate rasa of the tragic (rather than the erotic thwarted), since as far as Udayana is aware, there is no hope of recovering the queen. In this verse, the king is addressing the queen's pet deer.

306. *Tāpasavatsarāja* 2.11.

307. *Tāpasavatsarāja* 2.13.

308. After adducing as an example a naturalistic description of a lion, Kuntaka cites the opening verse of AŚ, in which the deer hunted by King Dushyanta looks back at him in terror (p. 141). He goes on to point out that animals, as well as insensate things such as trees, enhance literary beauty especially when they are functioning as stimulant factors.

309. I conjecture *-sarasatvarūpam* (for *-sarasaṃ svarūpam*; compare 2.35).

310. The second (more technical) point is discussed on p. 147.15–24, which I omit.

311. Kuntaka, citing BKA 3.6, proceeds to show, by an analysis of the compound "rasa-laden," that must in fact refer to the poem itself, not the ornament.

312. KĀ 2.278.

313. KASS 4.3.

314. *udāracaritair*; or perhaps conjecture *uccāritair*, "just by pronouncing the words."

315. That is, and not to be put on a par with regular figures of speech.

316. DhĀ 2.5, above.

317. I add this (and "he concludes" below) in order to indicate that this constitutes Ananda's view, which Kuntaka will reject.

318. Given Kuntaka's important revision of Ananda, I include this section, though it bristles with uncertainties, with which I must take liberties in order to clarify for the reader. He wants to make two points: first, the rasa here cannot be an ornament but must be the main point of the verse; second, the erotic is also present in the verse, as either an equal or a complementary component.

319. DhĀ p. 193, above.

320. Ananda specifically cites the verse to illustrate the case where the rasa is "unmixed" with any other rasa or figure.

321. The husbands.

322. For the nature of conflictual rasas, see Mammata's analysis in chapter 4.3.

323. And hence, have survived. The erotic thwarted is possible only when the lovers are alive; if one is dead, the rasa is the tragic.

324. I conjecture *-cārutvasvarūpa-* (for *-cārutvaṃ tatsvarūpa-*).

325. The first of Ananda's examples was omitted here.

326. It is not reasonable according to Ananda's own theory that rasa can only be implied, not expressed.

327. I am uncertain of both the text and my translation.

328. KASS 4.5, above.

329. DhĀ p. 330, above.

330. The context concerns the god Shiva. Rasa requires propriety in order to be a rasa, but subsequently some element of impropriety enters into it and transforms it into something else (or so Kuntaka seems to be framing his opponent's argument).

331. KS 6.95.

332. By Kuntaka's new definition, *rasavat* refers to figurative language in general, which as such is "equal to [*vad*] rasa" both in ensuring that the literary work is endowed with rasa and in delighting receptive readers (*kārikās* 3.14–16).

333. See n. 340 below; *adṛṣṭadarpaṇa-* (VV v. 4).

334. Anandavardhana claimed that manifestation/implicature was at work in these cases as well.

335. Like that of a light and an object, both of which are manifested quasi-simultaneously (so Ananda, cited VV p. 66).

336. It is the figurative use of "manifestation" (and not of "implicature") that is at issue; see VV pp. 70, 78 (*vyaṅgyatvopacārasya* [*prayojana-*]).

337. This is largely based on the statements of Ananda himself that the cognition of the aesthetic elements and the cognition of rasa are successive (DhĀ p. 67).

338. Which when illuminated by a lamp can produce an experience of sublimity (Ruyyaka).

339. Mahima Bhatta rejects the category of "manifestation" throughout his work; he is only prepared to accept its usage in a figurative sense, to describe the uniqueness of the rasa experience (so Ruyyaka, p. 71).

340. Abhinava cites the verse in the context of his critique of Bhatta Nayaka (see fragment #13 and n. 40), and it is possible that it should be attributed to Nayaka himself despite the fact that Mahima Bhatta claims never to have seen his work (Pollock 2012b: 241–44). Ruyyaka comments:

> "'Manifested' is meant [literally] by the supporter of the implicature theory, but on [Mahima Bhatta's view] the manifestation is taken as a figurative expression. . . . Although it is some 'experience' that actually cognizes rasa, the statement [that rasa is an experience] is a figurative expression of their identity, meant to indicate that rasa is something indissociable from its apprehension."

341. NŚ 6.34 is cited.

342. I compress here and omit the citations from the NŚ adduced to support the argument.

343. Source unknown. In rasa discourse the term "identification" (*tanmayībhāva*) is post-Abhinava.

344. Source unknown.

345. Of the emotions in the real characters. This is in part the position of Shri Shankuka (see p. 81), with the addition of Abhinava's ideas of relishing and the "heart's concurrence."

346. Compare *Avaloka*, p. 217 below, for a related argument.

347. DhĀ 1.13.

348. DhĀ 1.5 is cited.

349. Ruyyaka understands the two uses of *viśeṣa* in these two different senses (as "kind" and "excellence").

350. One cannot have greater or lesser degrees—that is, better and worse degrees—of rasa.

351. This is meant to refer to the two types of literature, poetry and drama (so Ruyyaka).

352. Source unknown. The verse illustrates the unqualifiable nature of rasa, the fact that there cannot be degrees of excellence.

2. THE GREAT SYNTHESIS OF BHOJA, 1025–1055

1. ŚP p. 382.2. For additional detail see Pollock 1998a, from which some of what follows here is adapted.

2. The fifth chapter of CC (c. 1385, court of Singabhupala of Andhra), for example, follows the SKĀ closely, and supplements Bhatta Narasimha. The work was read closely by Vishvanathadeva (also originally from Andhra) in the late sixteenth century (see chapter 6.4).

3. Of Bhatta Narasimha (who commented on the entire SKĀ, contrast Raghavan 1978: 406 n., and see Kamimura 1976) we know nothing beyond his name, but he is certainly identical to the Bhatta Nrisimha who wrote on the *Avaloka* (see further in chapter 3.2). A second complete commentary by one Ājada (the ms., from Jaisalmer and now in Kobatirtha, Gujarat, Patasanghvi 102–1, is incomplete) came to my attention too late to be of use in this book.

4. Raghavan, for example, frequently found it "very difficult to understand what Bhoja is driving at," postulated nonexistent affinities between him and Bhatta Nayaka (1978: 469), misunderstood Bhoja's differentiation of *tātparya* and *dhvani* (1978: 154), failed to grasp his sense of the relationship of *guṇas* and *svabhāvokti* or his interpretation of a key passage in KĀ (1978: 40), and buried his idea of rasa under an anachronistic hodgepodge of theories (1978: 423, 454, 467).

5. SKĀ 5.9–12; ŚP p. 3.

6. See for example Bhattacharyya 1963: 106.

7. On *Ekāvalī* p. 98, below.

8. ŚP p. 377.6.

9. Desire was foundational for Spinoza (*cupiditas est ipsa hominis essentia*, *Ethica* III; see Pollock 2012a: 199 n. 35); for a contemporary assessment, see Robinson 1983.

10. ŚP p. 613, below.

11. Vachaspatimishra, *Sāṃkhyatattvakaumudī* on *Sāṃkhyakārikā* v. 24.

12. *Tattvaprakāśa* v. 53 (there is no compelling evidence to deny Bhoja's authorship, in the sense discussed earlier; see also Gengnagel 1996: 18–21). The ego is also analyzed according to the predominance of the *guṇas* (v. 54), which Bhoja uses in his account of the *prakṛti* of the *nāyaka*: Rama as *sāttvika*, Agnivarma as *rājasa*, Bhīma as *tāmasa* (see SKĀ 5.108, ŚP pp. 862–63, with illustrations).

13. ŚP v. 10; p. 615, both given below. Bhoja's conception of *bhāvanā* has nothing to do with Bhatta Nayaka's (hence the anodyne translation "production" rather than the charged term "actualization"). Other apparent affinities between the two (the taxonomy *śabdapradhāna*, *arthapradhāna*, *ukti*- or *ubhayapradhāna* in ŚP p. 355.4–5, or Bhoja's *Yogasūtravṛtti* 1.17, to which Gnoli and others have drawn attention, Gnoli 1968: 47–48 n.) need not presuppose Bhoja's direct familiarity with the latter's aesthetic theory.

14. ŚP p. 625.19, below.

15. Bhoja's disagreement with Bharata becomes most explicit in ŚP p. 631.18–19.

16. RKA 12.4, above.

17. See SKĀ p. 704; ŚP p. 624 (see also Induraja on KASS pp. 56, 58, 90).

18. From the text in Raghavan 1978: 412.16 ff. (from GOML, Madras: R 2499, a transcript of the Paliam ms.).

19. I conjecture *saṃvidhānaucityavaśena* (against the ms. and Raghavan's apparent conjecture *saṃvidhānena (au)cityavaśena*); *tasyānvayāt* (for *tasmād anvayāt*); *sāmājikahṛdayānuhlādī* (for *sāmājikahṛdayānukārī*).

20. See DR 4.38–39, below.

21. *rasikāḥ syuḥ . . . rasabhājaḥ*.

22. Bhatta Narasimha frames the objection as that of Abhinavagupta; see DhĀL p. 158 (the *vibhāvas*, etc. are neither *kāraka* nor *jñāpaka* of rasa).

23. The *rasasūtra* is here cited (omitted by Raghavan).

24. That is, the real Sita, the foundational factor that really produced passion in Rama, is not actually present to the audience.

25. The text of the omitted passage is uncertain (Raghavan's emendations, with the one exception noted, are unwarranted). See Pollock 1998a: 133 n. 34.

26. That is, as opposed to what is taken to be the factual plot of a work like the *Rāmāyaṇa*.

27. *rasānvaya* = *rasāviyoga* in ŚP p. 613; see n. 93 below.

28. See Raghavan 1978: 413.18–19.

29. The verse is cited in (or perhaps original to) DhĀ p. 498, above.

30. Hence the verses that follow address the nature of literary language, for it is that which enables the poet to transmit the character's rasa.

31. What is addressed here is vulgarity and its opposite at the level of word selection, whereas the following two examples concern meaning. (In vv. 4–6 Bhoja borrows from KĀ 1.62–64.)

32. *śruti* (translation uncertain).

33. I read *-arthayuktiś* (with Bhatta Narasimha, for *-arthā yuktiś*). He glosses *arthavacana*; see Abhinava on NŚ 9.164 (*arthasya upapattiḥ*).

34. *vāṅmaya*. Usually the term refers to all textual genres (*śāstra* and *kāvya*; see KM p. 2), but it is here used in a more restricted sense.

35. *vakrokti* refers to the presence of figures of speech, *svabhāvokti* to direct, unadorned description where language qualities take precedence (see also ŚP p. 628, below).

36. Nos. 13–22 concern elements of the subgenres of the erotic (the paradigmatic rasa for Bhoja), including the erotic thwarted, the erotic enjoyed, the etymologies of these terms (compare ŚP p. 1173), the qualities of the leading male and female characters, and so on.

37. For the existence of rasa *prior* to its emotion in Bhoja's system, see headnote.

38. Bhoja replaces *apasmāra* (possession) and *maraṇa* (dying) with *sneha* (attachment) and *īrṣyā* (envy) (and reads *saṃbhrama*- for *āvega*- and *gada*- for *vyādhi*-).

39. The transitory emotions and psychophysical responses, according to Bhatta Narasimha.

40. They persist by virtue of the *saṃskāras*, latent memories (Bhatta Narasimha; KD p. 183); "adjuncts," *anubandhibhiḥ*: according to Bhatta Narasimha and KD, the transitory emotions and psychophysical responses (see below, 5.25) "amplified," *pravṛddhāḥ* (so KD); v. l., *prabuddhāḥ*, "when awakened."

41. Bhatta Narasimha: *kāye viśeṣeṇābhitaḥ saṃcāraṇān manovāgbuddhiśarīraṃbhājām anubhāvānāṃ jananaṃ praty api yogyatāpādanam* (fol. 152).

42. A second meaning of the word is "inconsistent." The first etymology is drawn from the causative derivation (*vyabhicārayanti*); the second, from the simplex (*vyabhicaranti*).

43. *prema* is a synonym for *śṛṅgāra* in the sense of primal affect (so in ŚP).

44. In the case of desire when it transforms into the erotic, all the other stable emotions, from amusement onward, can function as transitory emotions (Bhatta Narasimha). See ŚP p. 664, below, where Bhoja argues that stable and transitory emotions are shifting categories.

45. On these four additional rasas see also ŚP p. 632.19, below. They are used again by Hemadri, BhM p. 168, below, and will be critiqued in RAS 2.159–160, below (on the grounds that *sneha* is a subdivision of *rati*, and cannot form the basis of a separate rasa, whereas the three others cannot be "enhanced").

46. *āśraya*, the feeling subject (*kāmitṛ*, Bhatta Narasimha); see 5.35. Other authors confusingly use the term for the object of emotion, i.e., the *ālambana* (for which, as here, the more usual term is *viṣaya*); see Induraja on KASS 4.2, and n. 117; so too CC 5.13, 5.19 (though it normally follows SKĀ).

47. The apparent illogicality here, that rasa is generated when it generates, is resolved by Bhoja's conception of a primordial rasa of passion giving rise to specific rasas.

48. I read *-atiśayāc* (with SKĀ, BHU ed. p. 431 last line, for *-atiśayaiś*); compare CC 5.19.

49. Compare CC 5.22.

50. *anyadrāgāc* glossed *anyasmin rāgaḥ* (so to be read) by Bhatta Narasimha (see P. 6.3.99), though I am unsure I catch the true implication; he also reports a variant *anyodrekāc*, "by its being overpowered by," but this seems redundant.

51. I conjecture *āśraya-* (for *āśrayāt*; see CC 5. 26: *rasasya vāsanāsthairyād āśrayaprakṛter uta*).

52. Bhoja interrupts his list of the twenty-four powers to discuss the components of the "supplements."

53. Shiva has three eyes.

54. KS 3.67.

55. But not that a rasa has been "generated."

56. RV 7.22.

57. RV 7.23.

58. RV 6.80.

59. This glancing is considered a reaction, unlike that of Shiva in the above-cited verse from the KS, because it is contextualized as such by the transitory emotion mentioned in the preceding RV verse (Bhatta Narasimha).

60. Fuller annotations are available in Pollock 1998a.

61. The reference is to the androgynous form of Shiva.

62. On the referent of *rasika*—the main character—see the headnote above, and ŚP p. 616 and n. 148, below.

63. "The 'source of intensification' of the various attributes of the self, i.e., intellect, pleasure, pain, predilection, aversion" (ŚP p. 614.12, below); see *Vaiśeṣikasūtra* 3.2.4 for the signs (pleasure, pain, etc.) establishing the existence of the self.

64. See ŚP p. 624.25, below; the phrase is used in reference to the character, as the examples show.

65. The *vatsala* or *vātsalya* rasa is found first in RKA 12.3.

66. Bhoja will cite this verse in arguing that indifference and even pain bring pleasure to the man of passion (p. 614.1; see also Bhatta Narasimha's explanation of rasa: *yena anukūlavedanīyatayā duḥkham api sukhatvena abhimanyate* [text in Raghavan 1978: 412]).

67. Just as the element of fire is manifested by the flames, so passion is manifested by the stable emotions (p. 616.18, below).

68. We do not experience the "sense of self" directly, but only in the transfigured form of an emotion.

69. For the definitions of "substratum" and "object," see SKĀ 5.35; the preeminence of the latter and the nature of the former both condition the arising of the predisposition, see ŚP p. 615.12, below. On the functioning of predispositions, see further below, ŚP p. 637.11–14, below.

70. I conjecture *yathāvat* (for *yāvad*).

71. I follow the text of Kulkarni 1989: 43. Bhoja's sentiment is nearly quoted by Shridhara on KP p. 77. He also cites anonymously a verse to the same effect: "Poetic language and dramatic representation are the two ways [of expressing rasa]. The former is superior in this because of the range of its narrative power"; he adds that one cannot show sexual intercourse on the stage, but it can be imagined through description in poetry. Contrast Vamana (KAS 1.3.30), reasserted by Abhinava and his teacher Bhatta Tota, that the paradigmatic form of literature is drama (see ABh 1.285, below).

72. BKA 1.16.

73. In a move central to his doctrine of the "combinations" that make literature what it is, Bhoja often uses the word *alaṅkāra*, ornament, in the sense of anything that makes literature beautiful, as well as in the narrower sense of a figure of speech (what later scholars call *vācyopaskāraka*). This wider meaning is familiar already from Dandin (KĀ 2.1, cited below by Bhoja); Bhoja is explicit about it at ŚP p. 624.2–3, below.

74. Bhoja's comments on *kārikās* 3 and 4.

75. I take *arthavāda* in the Mimamsa sense of accounts, descriptions, etc. (all contrasting with commandments), not in accordance with Bhoja's later definition (p. 458.6).

76. Compare DhĀ p. 49, which likens *dhvani* to *lāvaṇya* and takes the latter as a feature of physical beauty. Yet Bhoja's correlation of *tātparya* and *dhvani* as "internal" and "external" qualities of speech respectively remains unclear to me.

77. ŚP p. 333; compare *kārikā* 5a.

78. Bhoja now explains his understanding of the stages of meaning in ordinary discourse by adducing his own introductory verses as examples.

79. Namely, the discussion of the third stage of meaning begun on ŚP p. 366.

80. On Raghavan's analysis of *tātparya* in Bhoja, see Pollock 1998a: p. 148 n.

81. Received knowledge (or authoritative testimony), perception, and reasoning (necessary assumption).

82. That is, the second stage of meaning.

83. And Samkhya is unique in accepting only those three.

84. That is, the third stage of meaning, which here lies in the implication of Samkhya conclusions about the ontology and epistemology of rasa.

85. I read *trividhapramāṇāśrayaḥ* (for Raghavan's *trividha[pramāṇāśrayaḥ] śreyān*, which led to Dwivedi's impossible *trividhapramāṇāśrayaḥ śreyān*). Compare Dhanika on the "manifestation" of rasa (especially *Avaloka* p. 217), where despite the apparent critique of a Samkhya view, it is clear that Dhanika's main opponent is Anandavardhana; Bhoja is unconcerned with the *vyaṅgyatva* of rasa in Ananda's sense.

86. Bhoja is quoting his own observation from ŚP p. 3.

87. Bhoja's combination of Shaivism and Samkhya is on display in his *Tattvaprakāśa*, chapter 4 in particular, which provides a Samkhya evolutionary account of the world. See also the tripartite division of ego discussed in the headnote.

88. I read *utpannaś ca sarvasyā ātmaguṇa-* (conjectured by A. Aklujkar, for *utpannasya sarvasyātmā ātmaguṇa-*).

89. Compare Ratneshvara ad SKĀ p. 79: "When under the right causal circumstances memory traces manifest themselves, consciousness awakens as if in places where darkness, or stolidity, is breached. On its first appearance it is unmixed with any stable emotions and is called *ahaṅkāra*."

90. In chapters 18–21 Bhoja discusses the four subtypes of *śṛṅgāra* (*dharma-*, *artha-*, *kāma-*, and *mokṣa-śṛṅgāra*), where it is the psychological state of the character in the literary work enabling him to achieve his ends that is at issue.

91. The ŚP itself.

92. That is, language qualities.

93. The litotes (*aviyoga*) produces a strong positive (according to the maxim *dvau nañau prakṛtārthaṃ draḍhayataḥ*), "the *necessary* presence of rasa"; note the rephrasing, *rasānvaya*, in SKĀ 5.1.

94. Source unknown. One might have expected: if there does not exist, in the lover, a heart filled with passion [for his beloved]; i.e., if one has no feeling for a woman, all her outward adornments mean nothing. This is impossible, however, if the simile is to construe with the preceding prose (*prema* is for Bhoja a synonym of rasa). While the reader (the lover) cannot be ignored, Bhoja's first concern is rasa's existence in the work (the lovely woman).

95. Source unknown. A literary work must be able to represent powerful human emotion, and this requires (on the part of the character) "pride" or "self-confidence," elsewhere "sense of self," which for Bhoja is the same as rasa.

96. And hence, according to standard theory, would become rasas.

97. All these different emotions are in the last analysis resolvable into "love" or emotional intensity. The verses that follow are meant to show the fundamental nature of passion.

98. URC 5.17.

99. Source unknown.

100. URC 2.19.

101. *Sattasaī* 1.100. The three verses again indicate that all other emotions—pleasure, indifference/impassivity, even pain—are epiphenomenal upon *śṛṅgāra*. Passion ensures that even something like anger can be, in some sense, pleasurable (thus one can "*love* anger").

102. Bhoja's opponent is arguing that to equate fully developed emotions with love and love with rasa should mean that we can equate those emotions with rasa.

103. Bhoja is speaking here about characters who are "men of feeling" or not, especially since this rasa, per the next sentence, is the source of the "emotions" characters feel.

104. In his list of the transitory emotions, Bhoja includes jealousy and impassivity (here presumably not reckoned a stable emotion) and excludes death and possession (see above, SKĀ 5.14 and n. 38). Missing is *sneha*, attachment (the stable emotion of the affectionate rasa, *kārikā* 6), which should perhaps be read for *śama*.

105. The four verbs connote four stable emotions, which themselves are related to four rasas: the erotic, comic, heroic, and affectionate.

106. I conjecture *sukhaduḥkhādiṣu* (for *sukhādiṣu*).

107. See *kārikā* 10, and the headnote.

108. What follows is a restatement of *kārikā* verse 12.

109. I conjecture *-saṃskāratvāt* (for *-saṃskārāt*).

110. The former is invariable; and the variations in the latter do not affect the question whether the emotion is "stable" or "transitory."

111. This was already the position of Rudrata (RKA 12.4, above); and compare Abhinavagupta: "Some have noted that while Bharata enumerates all the other components of aesthetic affect—eight rasas, thirty-three transitory emotions, eight physical responses, four forms of acting—the stable emotions are not explicitly enumerated. This suggests that these transitory emotions can also be counted as stable" (ABh 1.262).

112. Compare SKĀ 5.20. This would seem to contain a quotation, but I cannot locate it (for the preceding, see NŚ 1.373.6).

113. Bhatta Lollata fragment #1a, though he knew nothing of the later idea of "manifestation" in its technical sense (for the general sense, see NŚ 1.342 and n. 46).

114. Presumably, however improbably at first sight, the storyworld, since the stable emotion is activated by an *aesthetic* factor (and not by a real person) and in the next paragraph the emotion will be ascribed to a character.

115. Compare *kārikā* 4.

116. Compare *kārikā* 9.

117. That Bhoja is defining *kānti* here is clear from the discussion beginning on p. 497 (compare also KAS 3.2.15). For *dīptarasa*, see also Ratneshvara ad SKĀ p. 77: "[This signifies] the highest development of rasa, that is, when passion or sense of self becomes intensified by means of the stable emotion when fully furnished with its aesthetic elements."

118. For this enlarged sense of "ornament," see n. 73 above and n. 122 below.

119. Bhoja has a special category of ornament wherein sense is inseparable from its expression (*ubhaya* or *bāhyābhyantara*), which comprises what are elsewhere considered pure figures of sense (see also Raghavan 1978: 379).

120. The sets of four in the similes before and after this require this addition; see next n.

121. The *upameya*, which also must be fourfold, consists of the *guṇas*, *śabdālaṅkāras*, *arthālaṅkāras*, and *ubhayālaṅkāras*.

122. Having defined rasa, Bhoja turns now to his main objective in the chapter, which is to show that language qualities, rasa, semblance of rasa, and emotions are all "ornaments" of a poem, and, in accordance with the above, that the "presence of rasa" consists in their "combination." The discussion is found also in SKĀ beginning on p. 703.

123. The reference must be to p. 617.3.

124. Bhoja here cites KĀ 2.1, 3.

125. Bhoja quotes KĀ 2.273, above. Bhoja's purpose here is to show that when these three qualities are "intensified" they become rasa, or rather, three "stages" of rasa, while at the same time they are "listed as ornaments" (contrast Raghavan 1978: 297).

126. *adṛṣta* here refers to *dharma* ("property") in *kārikā* 4.

127. Bhoja is again glossing *kārikā* 4.

128. Source unknown, as is the next. Note that rasa is attributed to the *speaker* here and below.

129. See *kārikā* 9.

130. MM 1.29 (Madhava is speaking).

131. MM 5.28 (Madhava is speaking). In the two examples, the stable emotion, the transitory emotions, and the reactions are all shown to be present.

132. Bhoja is quoting *kārikā* 10. He may also have in mind Induraja on KASS p. 48, above.

133. I conjecture *premarūpeṇa* for *rasarūpeṇa*, or at least understand it as such, in view of the parallel passage, p. 636.11 (see n. 178 below). Bhoja's interpretation is confusing given Dandin's express differentiation between *preyaḥ* as characterized by *prīti* or nonerotic affection, and *rasavat* as characterized by *rati* (etc.) (so Ratnashrijnana, Tarunavachaspati, and *Hṛdayaṃgama* ad KĀ 2.281 [= 2.279]), but he may have in mind KASS 4.2, and perhaps even Induraja's remarks ad loc., p. 48, given above.

134. See ŚP p. 613, above (it cannot be confirmed whether this is intended as a direct quotation of a character).

135. URC 1.40.

136. See Pollock 1998a: 165.

137. After discussing the different meanings of the three terms when they are regarded as *guṇas* and as *alaṅkāras*, Bhoja returns to the question of rasa.

138. "Possessive," *matup*; "comparative," *vati*.

139. Compare *Mahābhāṣya* 5.2.94, *bhūmanindā-*, etc.

140. P 5.1.115–16.

141. P 5.1.117.

142. Since any given verse would, given the definition of *alaṅkāra*, always consist of various "beautifying" features. The target of the critique is such a phrase as "mixture of various ornaments"; see p. 623.27, above.

143. That is, when he spoke earlier (p. 617.3) of the "presence of rasa" in a poem at the level of a passage (as distinct from its presence at the level of the work) as coming about especially by the "combination of various ornaments."

144. Bhoja has already shown that language qualities can also be considered ornaments, and one category of quality is that of the signification (*arthaguṇa*, p. 502).

145. Bhoja is only offering an analogy (although he accepts the principle he is enunciating; see p. 449.22). Nothing indicates an echo of Dhanika's *vākyapadīya* argument about the literary text (*Avaloka* p. 211, below). Contrast Raghavan 1978: 165, 522.

146. Bhoja will distinguish the first set as internalized reactions and the second as externalized, p. 638 (without any suggestion of serial correlation; see note there). See also SKĀ 5.38–40.

147. I suspect the correct reading here is *-ottarottaro* (for *-ottarottara-*).

148. In what follows we are given the entire series of rasas as they are produced, and the *rasavad alaṅkāras* that arise from the rasa and embody it. All examples are borrowed from Dandin (KĀ 2. 278 onward), but the analysis of what rasa is and how it works in a literary text

is Bhoja's own. In each case, it is the speaker of the verse (or, in the case of the fearful, the main character) who experiences the stable emotion, the conditions that enhance it, the predispositions that underlie it, and the rasa that results, and who "has" or "tastes" the rasa (compare SKĀ p. 728, cited below at ŚP p. 655.3). Bhoja reconsiders all eight examples on p. 636.

149. KĀ 2.278–79, above.

150. KĀ 2.287, above.

151. KĀ 2.282, above.

152. KĀ 2.288, above.

153. These are externalized transitory emotions for Bhoja (ŚP p. 637, above).

154. I omit the remaining examples (the violent, the fearful, the tragic, and the macabre).

155. Bhoja's critique of Bharata's complex observations on the relations of rasas and *bhāvas* (NŚ pp. 286–88, above, and n. 22 there) is even more complex. Bharata is said to hold that, just as rasas can arise from *bhāvas* (postulate 1) and *bhāvas* from rasas (postulate 2), so a second rasa can arise from a first rasa (postulate 3), for which Bhoja gives the examples of *hāsya* from *śṛṅgāra*, etc. (see NŚ 6.39). Bhoja refutes postulate 3 by saying (apparently) that the first rasa does not exist as such at the time the second arises, since it remains a *bhāva*. Bharata's restriction to eight rasas is also false; some people add four more, *śānta, preyaḥ, uddhata*, and *ūrjasvin* (wherein the same process of conjunction of factors is present), whereas others say all 49 *bhāvas* can become rasas. As for postulate 1, that rasas arise from *bhāvas*: rasas do not find their origin in *bhāvas* but rather are *bhāvas* in full development. As for postulate 2: *bhāvas* do not arise from rasas plural, because there exists in fact only a single rasa. As for postulate 3: for a second rasa to arise from a first entails that the first constitutes either the foundational factor for the second rasa or the prior state (*prakṛti*) out of which it develops, but there is no causal or terminological regularity that shows this to be true.

156. Dwivedi and Raghavan have both arranged the lines so as to exclude the statement "it is only these eight stable emotions," etc., from Bhoja's critique (it is true that the statement echoes the end of Dandin's account of *rasavad alaṅkāra*, but he is quoting Bharata too). The ensuing discussion requires that it be included, however; Bhoja will refute the idea on p. 632.19, and see *kārikā* 11.

157. Shiva, in his androgynous form.

158. Source unknown, as is the next poem.

159. The idiom (swearing an oath?) is unfamiliar to me.

160. Bhoja goes on to cite MVC 2.20 as an example of the tragic rasa coming from the violent, and MVC 1.35 as an example of the fearful rasa coming from the macabre.

161. Bhoja himself; see SKĀ 5.23, above.

162. *Preyas* ("affectionate") in the context of a rasa typically refers to nonsexual, especially parental, love (the example given below is not this, but neither is it erotic), and *ūrjasvin* to what Bhoja elsewhere calls *udātta* (e.g., SKĀ 5.23).

163. *Pañcatantra* (ed. Hertel), v. 79. Bhoja nowhere interprets *śānta* as the renunciant's peace.

164. ŚP p. 625, above.

165. VS 3.46.

166. KĀ 2.291, above.

167. *prakṛti.*

168. Bhoja here cites RKA 12.4, above.

169. Having refuted Bharata's view that there are only eight rasas, Bhoja now addresses the other two components of his theory.

170. NŚ 6.39. Bhoja goes on to show that no strict concomitance is found: other rasas arise, and sometimes the aforementioned rasas do not.

171. Bhoja is speaking hypothetically, since he does not actually accept that rasas arise from other rasas.

172. The example here and those in the rest of the paragraph are omitted.

173. Raghavan observes that Bhoja here "mixes up" the foundational passion and the rasa (1978: 500 n. 2), but theirs is a kind of type-token relationship, and is constitutive of the ŚP.

174. NŚ 6.40.

175. Precisely Abhinava's position (see ABh 1.289, below).

176. NŚ 6.41 (perhaps understood by Bhoja as "*the* effect").

177. Which is position (1), and that has already been refuted.

178. Given that desire is the paradigmatic emotion. While for Bhoja rasa and *prema* ultimately signify the same thing, the logic of the argument indicates that we should read *premarūpeṇa* for *rasarūpeṇa* in the parallel passage, p. 625.21 (see n. 133 above).

179. Here and below, Bhoja paraphrases rather than quotes the earlier citations.

180. That is, we can see how the speaker's or character's sense of self constitutes the rasa principle and underlies the individual rasas.

181. Bhoja adduces partial quotes for the violent, the fearful, the tragic, the macabre, the peaceful, the affectionate, and the vainglorious.

182. Since for Bhoja rasa does not "arise" (let alone "rasas"), his interest in provisionally accepting Bharata's dictum (in the *rasasūtra*) is to demonstrate the singular rasa upon which the conventionally conceived plurality of rasas is epiphenomenal.

183. The three similes are for *śṛṅgāra*, *vīra*, and *karuṇa* respectively. For this last poetic convention I am unable to find a parallel.

184. The triadic grouping of the *sthāyibhāvas* (*rati*, etc., *raudra*, etc., *śoka*, etc.) throughout this passage derives from their correlation with *sattva*, *rajaḥ*, and *tamaḥ* (discussed in *Tattvaprakāśa* v. 54). The categories are explained first by Hemadri, BhM p. 164, below.

185. MM 3.5.

186. The verse puns on the word *ātapa*, which means both pain and sunlight.

187. *Rāmacarita* 19.89.

188. URC 1.28. The three poems cited both illustrate and corroborate the explanation of the mental transformation in the presence of the objective condition (Madhava seeing his beloved Malati; Sita reacting to Ravana's advances; Lakshmana's description of Rama's madness at the abduction of Sita). Bhoja's citations and brilliant analyses demonstrate throughout the deep relevance of his analysis of rasa to actually existing literature.

189. I conjecture *abhimānimanasaḥ* (for *manasaḥ*; compare p. 636.23).

190. The three examples are the sudden shock of King Aja on seeing his dead wife; the increase of already existing feeling when Rati sees Vasanta while mourning for Kama; the emotional contrariety of Pururavas's feeling the south wind while longing for Urvashi.

191. RV 8.43.

192. KS 4.26.

193. VU 2.6.

194. The former set of items in each comparison is meant to indicate the interior and less distinct entities, the latter set the exterior and more distinct.

195. Compare NŚ 6.23.

196. KS 3.68. SKĀ p. 431 calls horripilation a psychophysical response (*sāttvika*), rather than an external transitory emotion as in ŚP here, and "dissimulation" (*avahittha*) a transitory emotion ("half-closed," *paryasta-*, in accordance with Bhoja's interpretation). ND (pp. 162–63) draws a similar distinction between external and internal reactions and feelings: "'reactions,' i.e., firmness [or satisfaction, *dhairya*], etc., and perspiration, etc.; 'transitory emotions,' i.e., despair, etc., and sickness, etc. That is, each of these [including the *vibhāvas*] can be either mental or physical features."

197. Source unknown. The reactions are the glances and the words, the transitory feeling is shame (compare SKĀ p. 440). Mourning is inappropriate for heroes so long as vengeance has not been exacted (see ŚP p. 363, with reference to this v.).

198. MM 9.20. The transitory feeling is faintness.

199. The three broad categories of emotional states (typified as above by desire, anger, and grief) produce rasa by three different kinds of processes, which the similes effectively suggest (contrast Raghavan 1978: 646, the process of producing rasa "cannot be said to have been sufficiently explained by these similes").

200. MM 5.28, cited above.

201. A key to this passage is provided by DR 4.34 (n.b., *ātmabhāvaṃ nayaty anyān* [*bhāvān*] *sa sthāyī* and here, *ātmarūpatāṃ nayante*), and the discussion of Dhanika and Bhatta Narasimha (a stable emotion is not interrupted by the presence of [other] emotions whether contradictory or otherwise; it assimilates them and thereby becomes a source of [even greater] beauty). Bhoja is showing how the erotic rasa can assimilate the transitory emotions and other factors associated with the tragic, which enhance it, as a salty mixture takes on a heightened intensity when a drop of sweetness is added (note the close parallel with his earlier example, p. 634.7).

202. *Sattasaī* 4.69.

203. Bhoja here turns Bharata's formula upside down (or perhaps adopts the counterintuitive assessment; see NŚ p. 286, above, and n. 22): rasa *precedes* the elements that are conventionally taken to produce it through their conjunction, and transforms them into itself. The example he cites, however—the trees of the garden where King Aja had walked with his queen, which are a stimulant of the tragic rasa, are themselves affected by it—seems rather too literal for the large conceptual argument he is making.

204. RV 8.70.

205. *Ratnāvalī* 4.19. Bhoja appears close to Abhinava in his understanding of the higher-order unity of rasas (*śṛṅgāra* and *vīra*, or at least the concerns of *kāma* and *dharma*) in the *Ratnāvalī*. See Ingalls et al. 1990: 511, as well as *Avaloka* on DR 1.33.

206. Bhoja illustrates the species of stable emotion by Shiva's first passionate look at Uma (KS 3.67; see above SKĀ 5.138); the species of a specific rasa by Uma's realization that she and Shiva are equally in love (KS 5.85, compare SKĀ p. 431, where the verse is cited as an example of the *niṣpatti* of rasa); the species of the semblance of emotion (not "the semblance of rasa," per Raghavan's note ad loc.; see below on p. 644.27, where Bhoja repeats and comments on the verse) by Ravana's semblance of desire for Sita and semblance of anger at her (from the *Udāttarāghava* of Matraraja/Mayuraja).

207. Having established that language qualities, rasas, stable emotions, etc., are all "ornaments," that is, "factors of beauty in a poem" (compare the discussion beginning on p. 624), Bhoja goes on to identify six varieties of mixture of elements: mixture of language qualities, of

rasas, of figures of speech, of qualities and rasas, of qualities and figures, and of rasas and figures. The selection picks up the discussion as Bhoja returns to the question of rasa.

208. *sollekha, nirullekha* (compare Raghavan 1978: 303).

209. That is, when full development of the emotion is not possible (in the case of the erotic, when desire is felt by the antagonist for the heroine, or by an animal for an animal).

210. Varieties of "mixture" are generally distinguished as to whether the elements remain "manifest" or not. Here the pertinent condition is whether the mixed elements are *constitutive* of some end product (painting, man-lion, mud) or not (rice-sesame, mirror-image, milk-water); see p. 648.

211. MVC 5.32.

212. See KP 7.65 v. 340, and Arjunavarmadeva, p. 4, both below (and see DhĀ p. 195).

213. The tragic is *prakṛta* and hence dominant, so the two compounds are not *yathāsāṃkhya*.

214. *Udāttarāghava*. I read *-trāsa-* (with SKĀ p. 717, for*–tryaśra*). Ravana is speaking and referring to himself in the third person.

215. *Sūktimuktāvalī*, p. 249 (attributed to Chandra, a legendary Kashmir dramatist; see p. 32). *Cakravaka* birds are condemned to be separated from their mates each night.

216. This would seem to overdetermine the semblance, since for Bhoja animals cannot experience true emotions anyway; see SKĀ 5.8, above, and ŚP p. 616, below (contrast *Ekāvalī* p. 106, below).

217. AmŚ 160.

218. This is technically and usually considered a transitory feeling, but (per *kārikā* 11 and elsewhere) Bhoja explodes all these categories.

219. Recall that horripilation is an externalized transitory emotion (see p. 638, above).

220. *ānanda*. Referred to as a rasa only here in the ŚP (see also Raghavan 1975: 137).

221. URC 6.11.

222. *svātantrya*, identified a rasa only here, like *pāravaśya* in what follows.

223. I read *praśamā[ḥ] . . . saṃkīryamāṇāḥ samupalabhyante* (with SKĀ pp. 719–20, for *praśame . . . -āṇaḥ . . . -ate*).

224. A discussion of mixture of figures follows.

225. This closely follows SKĀ p. 720.

226. That is, where qualities and rasas are mutually constitutive, or where the former is a natural byproduct of the poet's concentration on producing the latter (compare DhĀ 2.17).

227. Bhoja here cites KĀ and DhĀ to show that certain rasas and certain qualities always will be copresent if each is to exist as what it is (e.g., *raudra* and *ojas*).

228. While apparently just repeating the definitions of certain *śabdaguṇas* and *arthaguṇas* given previously, Bhoja has in fact selected those qualities characterized by a constitutive relationship with the expression of affect. This is clear from the kinds of examples adduced in the discussion of qualities in chapter 9, beginning on p. 498.

229. Examples of the mixture and relative dominance of language qualities and rasas follow.

230. *Setubandha* 15.66 (correct the Prakrit to *-pphaṃsamahagghavia-*).

231. The following discussion of the last three types, which alone have a bearing on Bhoja's conception of rasa, closely follows SKĀ (p. 728), where the analysis is introduced with the following general remark: "The type of mixture in which a rasa is predominant over a figure comes about when it is the person experiencing the emotions who describes the situation,

for the actual sentence containing the figure is then in fact his or her *reaction* in the form of a verbalization." Contrast the example just cited ("Rama's arrows . . ."), where the sentiment, insofar as it is not being expressed by the one who experiences it, is submerged by the figure of sense.

232. Source unknown, but likely Sarvasena's lost *Harivijaya* (Kukarni 1991: 8).

233. The anger of Satyabhama, a wife of Hari/Vishnu/Krishna, was provoked by seeing the bouquet of the divine coral tree he had given to Rumini, another of his wives.

234. Source unknown.

235. Bhoja defines this as the transference to one thing of the features of some other thing (p. 598). In the present case, the wasting away of the speaker through the woman's indifference to him is transferred to the woman's waist; the "reason supplied," the "obstruction" of her shapely breasts, applies in both cases.

236. This last condition explains why this is a semblance of rasa.

237. My translation of the second clause is uncertain. Note that the man of passion (*abhimānin*, etc.) finds pleasure even in the experience of neglect and pain (see *kārikā* 8 and n. 66).

238. "A reason that is counteracted and fails to produce its effect despite the presence of all the causal conditions, is the figure 'nonreason'" (ŚP p. 571.21): the ability of the lover to produce decorations is in fact evidence of *insufficient* love between the couple; "a circumlocution is [effected by] the use of a pretext, a turn of speech, or a special occasion" (ŚP p. 607.10), here presumably of the second variety, where what is meant—"my lover and I actually share a deeper love than you and your lover"—is expressed in a roundabout way. (In SKĀ p. 77, where the verse is also cited, Bhoja observes that the two women are rivals for the same man, but his use of *priyavayasyā* here instead of *sapatnī* suggests he understood the verse slightly differently on this occasion.)

239. "Trembling" is typically categorized as a psychophysical response.

3. AN AESTHETICS REVOLUTION, 900–1000

1. This was already with case with Mahima Bhatta in the mid-eleventh century, who regrets "never having seen the *Mirror*" (VV v. 4). No commentator on the famous précis in KP 4 after Someshvara Bhatta (and Manikyachandra, who borrows from him) and Ruyyaka—all twelfth-century Kashmir—appears to have had direct access to the text. Jayaratha (1200, Kashmir) is the last writer to quote independently from the work, but probably through an intermediary. I include below a citation from the *Kaumudī*, Uttungodaya's thirteenth- or fourteenth-century commentary on the DhĀL, but this can hardly be authentic. (I omit the one from Prabhakara Bhatta's sixteenth-century *Kāvyapradīpa*, p. 4, which clearly presupposes the definition of poetry in the KP, although he gracefully summarizes Bhatta Nayaka's system: *kāvyārthaparyantābhidhā ratyādiviṣayā bhāvanā sahṛdayaviṣayaś ca bhoga iti, Rasapradīpa*, p. 26.)

2. RT 5.159. A verse is attributed to him in the *Śārṅgadharapaddhati* (#1020).

3. Vedantic leanings seem likely from his commentary on the *Treatise on Drama* (below), though missing from other fragments.

4. For details see Pollock 2010; also Rajendran 2004.

5. If I understand him correctly, Krishnamoorthy seems to be the first scholar to have appreciated this (1979a: 215). Bhatta Nayaka had important observations to make about poetic language too, which shows his abiding interest in literary form.

6. "Literal meaning" and "denotation" (Ingalls et al. 1990: 221, Gnoli 1968: 45, respectively) are imprecise; see also n. 30 below. Chintamani's critique of De (1927: 271 n. 1) is also incorrect, and the true reading of the *Locana* passage is in fact *abhidhā vilakṣaṇā eva* (p. 183): literary language is "completely dissimilar" from the language of science [*śāstra*; or, just possibly, Veda] or everyday discourse, and it is the process of *bhāvakatva* that renders it so. See also Someshvara Bhatta on KP p. 44.15, and n. 57 below.

7. Often *tadbhogīkṛttva*, i.e., of the "commonized" emotional complex (*tad*). Some later writers such as Jagannatha render this (oddly) as *bhogakṛttva*.

8. Abhinava reappropriates this triad for his own view (DhĀL 2.4; Ingalls et al. 1990: 225).

9. *vyāpāra*, one of Bhatta Nayaka's important terms (see *vyāpārapradhānye kāvyagīr bhavet*, #6 below), is often used in Mimamsa to define *bhāvanā*.

10. So *Avaloka* on 4.37, below.

11. *bhāvanaiva hi vākyārthaḥ*, *Ślokavārttika Vākyādhikaraṇa* v. 330.

12. RG p. 28, below.

13. KM ed., pp. 29.9 and 30.2.

14. Manikyachandra (ed. Mysore, 1922), p. 147 (the verse is absent from Mysore 2nd ed. and the Ananadashrama edition; cited also by Bhattacharya 1964: 32 n., who misquotes and interprets differently).

15. Dubious citations have been enclosed in brackets. For full annotations see Pollock 2010.

16. ABh 1.5, explaining the first verse of Bharata's NŚ.

17. I read *-svālambanaṃ* (for *-svālambana-*); compare also Karnakagomin on *Pramāṇavārttika*: *svālambanam eveti vikalpapratibhāsam eva* (p. 170).

18. The phrase "learning, meditating, and so on" references Vedantic interpretations of *Bṛhadāraṇyaka Upaniṣad* 2.4.5.

19. The quote is NŚ 1.329 (the reading here, *śāntād utpadyate rasaḥ*, disagrees with the printed text in chapter 7, *śāntād bhāvaḥ pravartate*). A corrupt citation from Bhatta Nayaka's NŚ commentary, NŚ 3.305 (Abhinava also quotes him briefly and obscurely in his refutation, pp. 309–10), suggests his acceptance of *śāntarasa*. Dhanika, Bhatta Nayaka's most fervid disciple, argues forcefully against the possibility of *śāntarasa* in drama (*Avaloka*, p. 202, below).

20. Abhinava adds that the foregoing interpretation underlies a verse in Bhatta Nayaka's *Hṛdayadarpaṇa* ("Homage to Shiva . . ."), which he goes on to cite.

21. ABh 1.6. Probably the first verse of the treatise.

22. DhĀL pp. 91–92 (v. l. *ekaṃ* for *etaṃ*). "At the thirsty promptings of," *-tṛṣṇayā*; "in affection for" (Ramasaraka).

23. Spiritual adepts achieve "rasa"—in the sense of ultimate reality (*Taittirīya Upaniṣad* 27.2)—only with enormous effort; literature, however, provides her "calves," the lovers of art, with rasa unbidden.

24. Ruyyaka on VV p. 101 (I am uncertain about the translation of *pāda* d, *bhede 'pi hi tad asti yat*).

25. DhĀL p. 87. Abhinava cites this in support of his view that Valmiki, the first poet, did not create poetry directly out of experience but only once that experience was processed through creative genius.

26. DhĀL p. 87; ABh 2.298 (which reads *arthe tattvena yukte tu*; so too Someshvara KP p. 3]); KA p. 5; Ruyyaka, KP, p. 1, introduction; Jayaratha, AS, p. 9 (reading *-dhīr* for *-gīr*, "we have what we think of as literature"). Abhinava's criticism here turns on the meaning of "process" (*vyāpāra*): if this refers to the relishing of rasa based on implicature, then Bhatta Nayaka is saying nothing new; if it refers to signification or expression as such (*abhidhaiva*), then this has already been shown not to have primacy (DhĀL p. 87). Both objections seem odd: Bhatta Nayaka rejected implicature, as Abhinava well knew, and he also defined "process" far more broadly than expression, as the three-part unity expression, actualization, and experientialization (Abhinava, however, repeats the narrow interpretation in NŚ 2.298.9: *bhattanāyakenāpi kuśalaśikṣitābhidhāvyāpārapradhānaṃ kāvyam*; see also Kulkarni 2003: 38).

27. DhĀL p. 39. See DR 1.6, which echoes this verse. Uttungodaya (and independently Ramasaraka) understands that the capacity to experience rasa constitutes the *qualification* for literature: "every person who experiences rasa is qualified for literature, every person who seeks knowledge . . . is not" (p. 78). But Uttungodaya had no firsthand knowledge of the *Hṛdayadarpaṇa* and cannot be regarded as an unimpeachable interpreter (pace Ingalls et al. 1990: 73); the only independent "citation" of Bhatta Nayaka in the *Kaumudī* is #8 below, but unlikely to be his *ipsissima verba*. Another interpretation: every process in literature offers rasa (like a beloved); it does not offer knowledge (like a friend) or give commandments (like a master). Abhinava cites the verse to show that Bhatta Nayaka agrees that *rasacarvaṇā* is the principal matter in literary experience. But the point of contention between Anandavardhana and Bhatta Nayaka is not whether rasa is the telos of literature, but how rasa works.

28. Bhatta Nayaka may have been the first to fully formulate the idea concerning the three aims of formal discourse: enjoyment (literature, correlated with the beloved), advice (correlated with the friend), moral precepts (correlated with the master). (The full analogy is available only in DhĀL p. 40).

29. *Kaumudī* on DhĀL p. 79 (compare Krishnamoorthy 1979a: 221). Aside from the doctrinal issues (see next note), the art meter of the verse speaks against its authenticity.

30. That is, "all domains." But to the degree that the definition of *abhidhā* in #11 demarcates literary language as a particular form of language, per n. 57 below, this definition would be too wide (though see also Samudrabandha in fragment #4a).

31. DhĀL p. 39; Jayaratha on AS p. 9. Abhinava cites the verse to indicate that the position represented by Bhatta Nayaka has been rejected by the DhĀ. (De 1988, vol. 2: 183 misunderstands the DhĀL when he writes that Bhatta Nayaka "accepts the suggestion of rasa as the essence of poetry").

32. Presumably, distinct from literal and figurative meaning (not expression and actualization, per Ramasaraka, since implicature is not of the same order as actualization and so is not to be distinguished from it).

33. DhĀL p. 88. I omit Bhatta Nayaka's specific criticisms ad loc. of Anandavardhana's analysis of two famous verses, "You're free to go wandering" (see *Avaloka* p. 206, below, and n. 170 there), and "Here sleep I" (DhĀL pp. 68 and 72; see Ingalls et al. 1990: 90–91 and 99); and his downgrading of *dhvani* in DhĀL pp. 171 and 172 (see Ingalls et al. 1990: 209 and 211).

34. ABh 1.271; KA pp. 96–97 (vv. 1–2); Jayaratha on AS p. 9. In the original text the verses may not have been consecutive.

35. I read *-kṛtir* with Jayaratha (for Hemachandra's *-kṛtam*).

36. I read *mataḥ* (with Jayaratha, for *hi yat* with Abhinavagupta and Hemachandra, which would seem to take *tad-* in c as correlative, when it is part of the compound that is a technical term, as v. 1 indicates); and again with Jayaratha *-kṛti-* for *-kṛta-*.

37. Jayaratha includes hereafter a half-verse that is difficult to interpret without further context: "Or, just by virtue of being perceived, this clearly becomes an aid to spiritual release."

38. KA p. 97. Hemachandra adds that the view expressed here has (Abhinava's? KLV: Bhatta Tota's) full endorsement. In DR, the idea of rasa as a *vākya* is clearly part and parcel of the argument *against vyañjanā* and in favor of the *tātparya* position (*Avaloka* p. 211, below; Bahurupa Mishra's *avataraṇikā* seems to allude to this verse of Bhatta Nayaka's), a linkage that will be misunderstood later in the tradition (Kumarasvamin on PR 4.137 and RG p. 30.2, below; see Pollock 2012b).

39. "Veda": *śāstre* (compare KLV p. 307.24, who otherwise misunderstands the verse). I conjecture *saṃsargād dhi* (for KA's *saṃsargādir*; note that Dhanika on DR 4.37 offers *saṃsṛṣṭa*, and refers to no other linguistic operations). For the idea here compare PMS 2.1.47: *arthaikatvād ekaṃ vākyam* (and see *Vākyārthamātṛkā* 11.5, p. 378: *ekakāryatvād vākyam apy ekam*). The Bhatta Mimamsakas hold that sentence meaning is a *saṃsarga*, or conglomeration, of word meanings, or more precisely, that the class properties denoted by words take on specific meanings through conjunction with other words in sentences (see TV [Chowkhamba ed.] p. 429). See also ŚP p. 418: *vākyārthaś ca kriyākārakasaṃsargarūpaḥ*.

40. ABh 1.271. For variants and the problems of ascription and interpretation, see Pollock 2012b: 241–44.

41. SD p. 11, and ascribed to the HD by a sixteenth-century author who cannot possibly have had access to it (Prabhakara, *Rasapradīpa*, p. 4). (This certainly looks like yet another attack on Mammata's definition of poetry as *adoṣa*, and thus long postdating Bhatta Nayaka, *pace* Kane 1971: 224).

42. ABh, pp. 270–71 and KA, pp. 96–97, supplemented by the version in DhĀL pp. 180–83, the précis of Someshvara (S) (RORI ed. v. 1, pp. 43–44) and of Manikyachandra (M) (Mysore ed. vol. 1, pp. 216–21), and KLV (p. 306). As in the case of Shri Shankuka, the terseness of the ABh account requires exegesis based on these supplements, which I have incorporated into the translation.

43. In DhĀL (p. 182.1), this criticism is linked with the *utpattipakṣa*, not as here with the *pratītipakṣa*.

44. Reason 3 seems dependent on 4, but they are independent in all versions (they are reversed in the DhĀL, but still unconnected). Both ABh and KA read *sādhāraṇīkaraṇāyogyatvāt* (notably missing in DhĀL), but taking it in Bhatta Nayaka's technical sense is awkward, for precisely in such circumstances is "commonization" supposed to work (as Dhanika clearly shows, on DR 4.40–41ab). DhĀL's *pūrvapakṣin* gives the right sense: *kāntātvaṃ sādhāraṇam*, implying something like *sādhāraṇyāyogyatvāt* in the *siddhānta*, which is what I adopt in the translation (this also construes well with *asādhāraṇyāt* in the next line).

45. An act typically ascribed to Hanuman; DhĀL replaces with "Rama's bridging the ocean." The odd variation is found elsewhere as well.

46. The clause *pratyakṣād iva*, etc., is found here in all sources, but the argument belongs at the end of the following paragraph, since it concerns the problem with perceiving rasa externally (this is how DR, which undoubtedly had direct access to the original, presents it, 4.39, *pratīti-*[= *tātasthya*]*vrīḍerṣyā-*, etc.; things are not helped by reading, as does Gnoli,

pratyakṣād iva. nāyaka-, which is anyway contradicted by DhĀL, p. 182.1). Its current position is mystifying, and suggests an old corruption dutifully reproduced.

47. I read *tan na* (with Someshvara, for *tatra* in both texts).

48. On "manifestation" as a linguistic phenomenon, which Bhatta Nayaka rejects (see fragment #8), as distinct from the psychological phenomenon that it will later be held to be, see the introduction, section 4.2, and Pollock 2012b.

49. So that one would never be said to have a full rasa experience (see Ruyyaka below, Pollock 2012b: 250–51, and contrast Ingalls et al. 1990: 221).

50. What follows are features of the *expression* process, not of actualization. Ruyyaka on KP below assimilates them to actualization as contributory elements, but I suspect he is making the best of a corrupt text (expect *abhidhāvyāpāreṇa abhidhīyamāno* after *-abhinayarūpeṇa*).

51. Like the play's music, literary language has a transformative mental impact (see ABh 1.285.16: *svagatakrodhaśokādisaṅkaṭahṛdayagranthibhañjanāya gītādiprakriyā*, and compare DhĀL p. 189.6).

52. *druti, vistāra, vikāsa* (H reads *vistara*, which is authenticated by DR 4.43; see also Mallinatha on *Ekāvalī* p. 96; Ingalls et al. 1990: 36, like KLV p. 307.3, seem to have misread *vikāsa* as *vikāśa* and hence translated as "radiance"). The fourfold analysis given by Dhanika (on DR 4.43–45ab, below, and n. 230) is irreconcilable with what we find here, and indubitably authentic. Abhinava's criticism—that limiting the "apprehensions" or experiences of rasa to these three alone makes no sense, since there should be as many responses as there as rasas (ABh 1.271.15–18)—is actually preempted by Dhanika's exposition of what seems to be Bhatta Nayaka's actual position.

53. KP p. 560.

54. I read *-satattvena* (with Shridhara, for *-sattvena*).

55. From Ruyyaka's commentary on KP p. 563.7 (ed. Bhattacharya p. 16). Confusions in this précis lead one to doubt the manuscript or the ascription to Ruyyaka.

56. The specific traits of a character like Sita.

57. *śabdavyāpāra*. Ruyyaka is using this as a synonym of *abhidhā* (this more expansive sense is found also in Mukula Bhatta, *mukhyena lākṣaṇikena vābhidhāvyāpāreṇa*, *Abhidhāvṛttamātṛkā*, p. 1, and comes from Udbhata; see DhĀL p. 32 and Bronner ms.).

58. Since for Bhatta Nayaka, per the above extract, it is the figures of sound and sense that are involved rather than direct and indirect meaning, we must assume that "indirect meaning" (*sāntarārtha*) is another way of characterizing figures of speech (recall that for thinkers from Dandin to Bhoja, *vakrokti* was a synonym of *alaṅkāra* as such). Vishveshvara (*Rasacandrikā* p. 45) takes the two terms to refer to *śakti* and *lakṣaṇā* respectively.

59. In the standard distinction, perhaps introduced by Bhatta Nayaka himself, scripture is like a master in that it commands; historical discourse is like a friend in that it advises; literature is like a beloved in that it seduces.

60. That is, for anyone other than her husband Rama, such as the spectator.

61. The reading *bhavad bhāvanam* is dubious, but is found in both editions and in Shridhara's KP commentary, which essentially reproduces Ruyyaka.

62. I conjecture *guṇālaṅkārayogāt* (for *guṇālaṅkāratvād*, see *guṇālaṅkārayoga-* in Shridhara KP p. 565; compare also *guṇālaṅkāramayatva-* in ABh 1.271.1 and KA p. 96.19 cited above).

63. AS of Ruyyaka (R), p. 9, with the commentaries of Jayaratha (J) and Samudrabandha (S).

64. The text has been imperfectly transmitted, with Jayaratha alone preserving the truth: *kāvyāṃśatvaṃ bruvatā* (Vidyachakravartin falsely reads *kāvyātmatva*, for *kāvyāṃśatva*, ed. Janaki pp. 11–12; Samudrabandha is adrift). The "brazen" admission refers to #9 above (and/or possibly to #13).

65. *-uttīrṇa*, borrowed from DhĀL p. 52. Since *bhoga* is the *result* of *bhāvakatva*, it cannot be "far beyond" it (Ingalls et al. 1990: 81).

66. The reference is to DhĀ 1.1c.

67. Fragment #9. I conjecture *rupatā* (for *rūpitā*).

68. *kavikarmaṇaḥ*. This is confusing, since *vyāpāra* is not itself the literary *work* (the normal meaning of the term *kavikarma*), but the work's *capacity* to produce an experience of it.

69. For this mischaracterization, compare n. 247 on RG 29.10–11, below.

70. From Mallinatha's "Central Gem" (c. 1400), p. 85.

71. I conjecture *-kṛta-* (for *-kṛtena*).

72. That is, most importantly, the character.

73. Here Mallinatha draws a distinction not previously noticed: the final process, perhaps the process as such (which Bhatta Nayaka has in mind when he says literature is *vyāpārapradhāna*, #5) is distinguished here as *bhāvanā*, whereas the second component, the subordinate element of commonization, is called *bhāvakatva*. Bhatta Nayaka himself above uses *anyā bhāvanā* for *bhāvaka(tva)*.

74. RAS, p. 251.

75. See *Avaloka* p. 168, below.

76. I read *-vyāpāreṇa* (for *-paryāyeṇa*). For Bhatta Nayaka, *bhāvanā/bhāvakatva* is a second function, different from *abhidhā*, see #11 (and *abhidhāto dvitīyena*, ABh 1.271.2–3).

77. *viparivartamāna-*. See n. 89.

78. The impropriety would stem from the fact that Sita is another man's wife.

79. DR 4.87.

80. Munja's first extant charter was issued in 974–75 (*Corpus Inscriptionum Indicarum* vol. 7, part 2, pp. 10ff.). The last of his predecessor, Siyaka, was issued in 969 (pp. 8 ff.), however, and thus Munja could well have been king as early as then.

81. De 1988: 125, for example.

82. Noted first, I believe, in Kane 1971: 248.

83. See also Raghavan 1978: 667–68 (correcting his earlier statement, p. 89). I suppose some of Bhoja's thinking about *tātparya* (ŚP pp. 366–90) could have been informed by Dhanika's restatement of Bhatta Nayaka (*Avaloka* on 4.37, below, and the selections from his *Kāvyanirṇaya*, p. 212, below), but the case is hardly decisive (*pace* Venkatacharya 1969: lviii).

84. No doubt the process could be seen as the reverse one too: what must rasa *be* (the ontological question) in order for our experience of it to make sense (the epistmological question)?

85. Bhatta Nayaka, the source of Dhanamjaya's and Dhanika's theory, is also unknown to Bhoja; see Pollock 1998a n. 57 (*pace* Raghavan 1978: 469) and Pollock 2009.

86. See headnote to chapter 2. Until recently it was the only known commentary on that chapter.

87. Pollock 1998a: 132–33; Raghavan 1978: 412.

88. As I have earlier observed (1998: 137 n. 40); contrast Venkatacharya 1969: lxv. See also Kamimura 1976.

89. *viparivartamāna-*. For the use of this word in apparent reference to Bhatta Nayaka, see ABh 1.273.8, and RAS (Bhatta Nayaka #1b). The term including the nominal form *viparivṛtti* is used by earlier writers with reference to the psychological process whereby words form sentences in the mind (for Prabhakara Mimamsa it is a synonym of *saṃnidhi*; see *Prakaraṇapañcikā* p. 389: *atha sannidhiḥ kaḥ? yasyārthasya śravaṇānantaram ākāṅkṣāyogyatābhyām arthāntare buddhiviparivṛttiḥ*). Compare *Śābarabhāṣya* 4.3.11 [BI ed. p. 498].

90. The literary text, which is described as "rasa-laden," only causes rasa to arise in the viewer/reader.

91. *Prabhā* brings out the implication of this vague formulation: "As, for example, when a poet says, 'This man is the god of love himself,' or 'The woman is Rati herself, wife of the god of love.'" It is literary language as such that, for the viewer/reader, transforms quotidian things into aesthetic elements; see Dhanika on 4.46–47ab, below, and Bhatta Nayaka fragment #10.

92. NŚ 1.340.

93. *-bāhyasattva-*; compare Helaraja: *cirakālātītatvāt kaṃsādināṃ bahirasattvād* . . . (*Vākyapadīya* v. 3 part 2, ed. Sharma, p. 99). As Helaraja makes clear, the problem at issue is verbal narrative, where in contrast to painting, sculpture, or drama, there is no actual physical image or likeness (*pratikṛti*). Presumably, in the case of the poem about Urvasi (the illustration cited from VU p. 170, omitted here), while the physical "nymph" has an existence on the stage, she only can be said to become a foundational factor for the viewer when she is described in literary language.

94. *śabdopadhānāt*. Given Bhatta Nayaka's new response theory of rasa, Dhanika must ask how the factors work for viewers/readers, for whom they do not exist in the same way they do for the actual characters. (Improbable is Bhatta Nrisimha's notion that the question is how figuratively constituted factors can be efficacious, since they correspond to nothing in the real world.)

95. *bhāvaka*, an early (if not the first) use of the term. It refers exclusively to the viewer/reader who "actualizes" the experience of the main character, the term referencing *bhāvanā*, actualization, as described here and in 4.38.

96. As Dhanika's earlier restatement shows, he thinks the subject of the verb is the listener, not Patanjali (so Helaraja; this indicates that, n. 93 above aside, no conclusions can be drawn regarding Dhanika's knowledge of Helaraja).

97. Krishna's evil uncle and king of Mathura, whom he eventually slays.

98. *Vākyapadīya* 3.7.5. The point of the verse seems to be the purely mental status of syntactical relations, of which storytelling is a sort of limit case: storytellers create a reality of their own, and when in their story they "have Krishna kill Kamsa," those narrated characters can seem to have an agency of their own. See also Filliozat 1963: 344–45.

99. Bharata's NŚ is traditionally said to contain six thousand verses (Dhanika's reference appears to be the first). The citation is NŚ 1.342.10.

100. *sāmānyaguṇena*. While the original usage in NŚ is unclear, it would appear that Dhanika's understanding of the phrase is an anachronism, meant to provide a deeper historical pedigree to Bhatta Nayaka's concept of "commonization." Similarly in the case of Abhinava; see ABh 1.275.6, below.

101. I omit the examples of the foundational and stimulant factors given by Dhanika (which also show how hyperbole and metaphor respectively create the factors, as he notes earlier).

102. *bhāva-*, which Bahurupa Mishra takes to refer to any of the 49 emotions (the position of Induraja, on KASS 4.2, above).

103. The novelty of Dhanika's thought has engendered much confusion in the manuscripts, and as a result the precise reading is uncertain. Presumably the reactions enable viewers/readers to experience their own stable emotions as well as the character's. Dhanika's remarks on the "sensitivities" in what follows suggests that the reactions might even be those of the viewer/reader (so ND, see p. 160, below and n. 23 there, and RG p. 55).

104. "Reactions" are not only the visible physical effects in the character of his rasa but also causes of rasa in the viewer/reader, and can therefore pertain to narrative no less than performance. (Bhatta Nrisimha comments, rather unhelpfully: "Things that enhance the rasa can be considered reactions, and since both poetry and dramatic representation enhance the rasa, reactions can be said to belong to both.")

105. I.e., of what the characters experience on the stage/in the poem.

106. "Real-world" (*laukika*), that is, of the storyworld. This is Dhanika's term for the rasa experience of the character (see Bahurupa Mishra's introduction to 4.46), and is differentiated from "the rasa of drama" (*nāṭyarasa*) and "the rasa of poetry" (*kāvyarasa*, on 4.42cd), that is, the rasa experience of the viewer/reader (Dhanika on 4.41cd; he can thus differentiate "real-world tragedy" and "literary tragedy," see 4.43–45ab), though for Dhanika the "real-world" variety is no longer rasa in the full sense. See also ND pp. 160–61, below (which makes the exact same distinctions); PR 4.138, p. 210, below. Note also Nagesha's gloss of "character under description" as "the substratum of [i.e., the character who experiences] real-world rasa" (*varṇanīyaśabdena ca laukikarasāśrayādir ucyate*), KP p. 141. The use of the term in NŚ 1.283.2 and 6.33 may be related (and suggests further the revisionist nature of the passage).

107. "Here," that is, in the realm of aesthetic response (the commentator's remark below notwithstanding). In the storyworld, reactions are an *effect* in the main character of his own emotion; in the world of aesthetic response, the character's reactions are a *cause* of rasa in the audience. The same distinction is drawn in ND p. 160.8–9, below.

108. Dhanika illustrates Dhanamjaya's definition with a poem of his own (omitted).

109. Dhanika takes the phrasing from NŚ 1.342, which he cites.

110. The antecedent of *tad* (in *tadbhāva*) is obscure, but I see no alternative to Dhanika (and Bhatta Nrisimha).

111. NŚ 1.338–339.

112. Ibid.

113. Whereas Dhanika's definition pertains to the context of response.

114. Generally the *sāttvika (anu)bhāvas* are thought to be psychophysical—being both bodily reactions and mental states, e.g., the perspiring that arises from fear, in contrast to the perspiring that arises from heat—and hence requiring special treatment (see especially Namisadhu on RKA 12.3, above, and Bhanudatta, RT 1.5, below).

115. Presumably the character's (thus *para* consistently in ND). That Dhanika is referring to the viewer/reader would seem to be indicated in what follows.

116. NŚ 1.373. "Concentration" indicates single-mindedness. Whereas the psychophysical responses presuppose some mental engagement, the purely physical reactions are automatic, and cannot, as Bharata says, "be produced when one's mind is elsewhere," i.e., not concentrated (as usual, Bharata has the actor uppermost in mind here).

117. The "sensitivities" can be considered reactions (*anubhāvas*) in the case of a character, and emotions (*bhāvas*) in the case of the viewer/reader.

118. The illustrations that follow have been omitted.

119. Bahurupa Mishra understands differently: "'especially favorable' for the transformation of the stable emotion into rasa."

120. The list, definitions, and illustrations of the transitory emotions that follow have been omitted.

121. Presumably all other mental states beyond the thirty-three transitory emotions need to be included under either the factors or the reactions—both of which are open categories. But it is not clear how transitory emotions can be subsumed under factors.

122. Bahurupa Mishra here cites two verses, one of which is often ascribed to Bharata but not found in the NŚ, the other a variant on NŚ 6.39 (see *Śṛṅgāratilaka* 3.21–22, where both verses appear in the quoted form).

123. The *kārikā* speaks of conflicting emotions, not rasas, but both Bahurupa Mishra and Dhanika imperceptibly slip from one to the other. Mammata directly addresses this slippage in his discussion of the conflict of rasas (*rasavirodha*, see KP [BHU ed.] p. 442, *rasaśabdenātra tatsthāyibhāva upalakṣyate*), though whether the ideas in play there (derived from Abhinavagupta) are also here remains uncertain.

124. The *Bṛhatkathā* is a lost work ascribed to Gunadhya. It is unclear which of the later adaptations Dhanika would have used.

125. MM 5.9+ (trans. Coulson); see also MM. 5.10, cited in DR 4.20 p. 185.

126. I see no propriety for *anyat . . . anyat*, which appears to be the editor's conjecture (n. 182).

127. Like heat and cold.

128. Like the perception of a snake negated by a subsequent perception that the object is in fact a rope.

129. The passage is somewhat obscure and has been subject to much corruption. The Jaipur Pothikhana ms. gives *ubhayarūpo 'pi na tāvat* (fol. 62r), which strikes me as sound (the reading *ubhayarūpeṇāpi na tāvat tādātmyam asya ekarūpatvād āvirbhāvāt* in GPP ed. pp. 142–43, accepted by Kundu 2000: 349, makes little sense to me).

130. In the rasa experience emotion is a unified mixture, which axiomatically does not permit of any sort of contradiction (*Prabhā*).

131. Adyar's reading is corroborated here by the Jaipur Pothikhana ms. GPP ed.'s *ca bhāvādinām* for *vibhāvādinām* is an attempt to correct a loose usage on Dhanika's part since he goes on to discuss only one class of these elements, the transitory emotions.

132. See *Pradīpa* on KP (BHU ed.) p. 154.

133. The sentence reproduces what is essentially Dhanamjaya's definition of rasa; see 4.43.

134. That is, "with another aesthetic element."

135. This may seem slightly circular, since in arguing that a stable emotion cannot be blocked by a transitory emotion precisely because it is stable, Dhanika is assuming what the *kārikā* may be thought to be trying to prove. But the *kārikā* is offering not a proof but a stipulation: stable emotions are indeed stable precisely because they are not or cannot be interrupted.

136. Namely, that something in conflict with the dominant element cannot be subsidiary to it (so Bhatta Nrisimha). Dhanika has already dealt with simultaneous conflict; he now turns to sequential conflict.

137. I understand the antecedent here to be *-ālambanatva*, attracted into the gender of the predicate, *-hetu*, in the preceding sentence (i.e., *vidheyaprādhānyāt*).

138. See DhĀ 3.26–27.

139. Source unknown. The single foundational factor is the husband.

140. Source unknown; cited also at DhĀ 3.24, as a case where two rasas are equally developed.

141. *Śatakatrayam* 2.66.

142. From the unpublished *Udāttarāghava*. Ravana speaks, referring in the penultimate line to the Brahman dress he adopted to disguise himself in *Rāmāyaṇa* book 3.

143. MM 5.18 (trans. Coulson).

144. *ekāśrayatvena* (expect *ca* here), and note that *āśraya* typically refers to the "substratum" of rasa, the subject experiencing the emotion, not the *viṣaya* or *ālambana* (see n. 223 below for its use in the latter sense; and KASS 4.2 n. 117; SKĀ 5.24 n. 46, both above). In the other illustrative verses in this passage, the multiplicity of rasas is based on a multiplicity of foundational factors; here the female ghouls appear to be the foundational factor of both desire and revulsion (though for whom is unclear: the male ghouls do not feel revulsion, and the audience does not feel desire). Dhanika will identify the dominant rasa as the macabre.

145. Source unknown (but note the awareness of Udbhata's arguments about "proper terms").

146. See ŚP p. 645, above.

147. I read *rodana-* (v. l. reported in Adyar ed., for *karuṇa-*).

148. That is, united in a single sentence (other texts in fact read *ekavākyabhāvaḥ*, including the Jaipur Pothikhana fol. 64a).

149. According to Anandavardhana, the conflict is between desire and determination in the soldier, and Dhanika is therefore subtly correcting him here by identifying the emotions as grief and determination, a far more powerful reading (Abhinava claims her weeping enhances his desire, but that seems off the mark). The husband's *tragic* feeling toward his wife (and it must be he who is feeling, not she, otherwise there would be no question of equipollence) stems from the fact that he knows he is going to die.

150. DhĀ p. 237 (Anandavardhana's own composition) is cited in illustration.

151. I understand *vāśrūya-* (for *vā śrūya-*), in accordance with Bhatta Nrisimha. Dhanika discusses this on DR 4.37, p. 213.8, below (Bhatta Nrisimha refers to the discussion of the KS verse below, but that is in a *pūrvapakṣa*). For *Prabhā* this means that in those cases the stable emotions are implied by the other aesthetic elements.

152. That is, to the point of becoming rasa.

153. The protagonist of the *Nāgānanda*, a drama ascribed to King Harshavardhana (c. 640). See Dhanika's discussion below.

154. *vibhāvālambanau*: improbable but attested in all editions.

155. Dhanika on DR 2.4cd–5ab.

156. I read *-avirodhāt. īpsitam eva ca sarvatra kartavyam iti paropakār-*, etc. (with GPP, for *-avirodhād abhīpsitam. evaṃ ca sarvatra draṣṭavyam iti*), which Dhanika on 2.5ab confirms: *rāmāder api jagat pālanīyam iti duṣṭanigrahe pravṛttasya nāntarīyakatvena bhūmyādilābhaḥ*. Bhatta Nrisimha's comment shows he had a corrupt text before him.

157. RKA 12.4, above.

158. It would be easy to read *hāsa-* (with GPP ed.) for *hāsya-* (Adyar ed., Bhatta Nrisimha, Kundu 2000: 361, Jaipur Pothikhana fol. 65r), but the variant would remain unexplained. And note that Bhatta Nrisimha above (see n. 123) refers to rasas themselves as "stable entities."

(Compare n. 123 on the terminological slippage between rasas and stable emotions, but in the present context such slippage is obviously problematic.)

159. The omission of the fourth end, liberation, is unexpected.

160. That is, how does poetry communicate emotion, or how is emotion "apprehended"? (The question is not how readers *experience* rasa, since that is the result of "actualization" and "experientialization," though this distinction is muddied by the fact that Dhanika refers to stable emotions and rasas indiscriminately in the discussion that follows.) Dhanika emphasizes poetry (*kāvyenāpi*) because the relation in drama is clearer, being visual rather than purely verbal. Strictly speaking, *kāvya* of course includes drama, but the two are often distinguished in rasa discourse (by Dhanika himself, e.g., p. 223.3–4, and others such as Ruyyaka and Mallinatha on Bhatta Nayaka, #3a and #5a respectively).

161. Dhanika is echoing Anandavardhana's analysis of the positive and negative concomitance (DhĀ p. 83, given above: the word "erotic" without the aesthetic elements does nothing, whereas the aesthetic elements without the word can convey the rasa; hence, the word itself is not a causal factor).

162. The Mimamsa notion of connotation: a noun, which naturally denotes the universal, can be said to "connote" a particular once construed in a sentence (since [1] its denotation of a universal is blocked and [2] that general meaning is invariably joined with some particular).

163. I assume the antecedent to *tat-* and *tal-* to be *śṛṅgārādiśabdāḥ* (so *Prabhā*); less probable is a reference to the aesthetic elements (so Bhatta Nrisimha, though later in his comment here he focuses the discussion on the words for the stable emotions and rasas).

164. The first, or bare, connotation would be the one just explained (*lakṣaṇā* in the Mimamsa sense), and the second, what we think of as normal connotation through metonymy or metaphor. This is close to what Mammata will call *lakṣaṇalakṣaṇā* (KP [BHU ed.] p. 58; at the same time he rejects the Mimamsa variety insofar as it is constitutive of language as such and not figurative), and should be distinguished from Abhinava's use of *lakṣitalakṣaṇā* in DhĀL p. 61 (there it is the coolness that is connoted by the bank's propinquity to the river, while the bank is itself connoted by the "blockage" of the primary meaning of the word "Ganges"; in Dhanika's usage, that second level of meaning, coolness, etc., is not at issue). The matter is also closely examined in ŚP chapter 7.

165. Source unknown.

166. That is, we do not come to understand words for the aesthetic elements—for the foundational factor such as the hero, Rama for example, or for the stimulant factor, such as "battlefield"—by some negation of the direct meaning of the words expressing them (so Bhatta Nrisimha below [p. 216.19]; *nāyakādiśabda* here does not mean "such words as '*nāyaka*,'" even though *nāyaka* in itself is occasionally used in literature instead of the proper name of a dramatis persona, as in the case of Jimutavahana in *Nāgānanda*). Mukula Bhatta (*Abhidhā*. 8.2) does attribute secondary meaning to a name, "Rama" for example, but the context there is not rasa.

167. See DhĀ 1.7.

168. Dhanika will reject (on 4.37) the theory he now proceeds to explain, that rasa is communicated by implicature.

169. KS 3.68 (a verse that also figures prominently in ŚP chapter 11; see, for example, p. 638.7, below).

170. *Sattasaī* 2.75. The example and analysis are taken from DhĀ 1.4. A woman aims to dissuade a mendicant from going to the place where she meets her lover (see also Pollock 2001c: 202-205).

171. *jala/jaḍa*. DhĀ 2.27 (identified by Anandavardhana as his own composition).

172. Mimamsakas sometimes thought of secondary meaning not as *lakṣaṇā* (metaphor and metonymy) but as *ākṣepa* (implication), which they equated with *arthāpatti* (*Nyāyaratnamālā Vākyārthanirṇaya* v. 38; see also Kunjunni Raja 1994).

173. E.g., "The stout Devadatta does not eat during the day" does not make good sense as it stands, and thus logically entails the conclusion that he eats during the night.

174. Note that Abhinava speaks of *dhvani* as appearing at a fourth stage of comprehension, since he includes *tātparyavṛtti* as the second stage (DhĀL pp. 59.8, 65.1).

175. See DhĀL pp. 55–56. The occasional similarity in Dhanika and Abhinava suggests both were drawing on the same source for the arguments here, given that Dhanika's work almost certainly antedates Abhinava's. (Abhinava might be thought to cite Dhanika as the proponent of *tātparyaśakti* at DhĀL p. 70.3, and as *kenacit* at p. 61.5, depending on how we understand the phrase *lakṣitalakṣaṇā* [see above, n. 164], but there is no conclusive reason to believe this, and in general he seems not to know Dhanika's work.)

176. The full sentence is usually given when the example is adduced (see, e.g., ŚP p. 366): "Eat poison but do not eat in that man's house," implying: better to eat poison than to eat in that man's house. The true meaning can only be gotten from the full context of the utterance, namely, that a father is speaking to his son. The whole point for Dhanika (and no doubt for Bhatta Nrisimha) is that sentence purport (*tātparya*) suffices to explain such a sentence; implicature is superfluous.

177. The meaning of this sentence is termed *pratīyamāna*, "understood," by Bhoja, ŚP p. 366, 476 (see also KD p. 326, though there the question concerns the relationship of the two parts of the sentence, "eat poison, and do not eat in his house").

178. In implicature, the meaning of the second stage is entirely acceptable (the holy man is indeed free to go wandering); it is simply that additional meaning is generated at the third stage—which in fact makes the hypothesis of a third stage necessary. But in the case at hand, the meaning of the sentence, which can only be generated at the second stage, cannot be the literal command to "eat poison"—since that makes no sense in the context—but must be instead a prohibition against going to the enemy's house.

179. Hence, since the literal meaning is impossible, it is the second stage of comprehension that produces the prohibition against eating in an enemy's house. And since we understand this prohibition at the second stage, there is no scope for a third stage, and hence it is only implicature that comes within the scope of the third stage (*Prabhā*).

180. But only at the third stage, that of implicature.

181. That is, at the second stage, of normal syntactical construal (Bhatta Nrisimha).

182. Source unknown, though the definition of *dhvani* here conforms to what Dhanika attributes to the *dhvanivādin* in his *Kāvyanirṇaya*, cited below (v. 3). The verses are also cited in BhP 6 (p. 149), which would seem to rule out Venkatacharya's conjecture *dhvanitā-* (p. 345), though such is the reading of Bahurupa Mishra (p. 124.15). (BhP also reads *tāvad āgatam* for *tāvatā gatam* in 2b, and *tat tasmāt* for *tatra syāt* in 2c.)

183. Dhanika cites DhĀ 1.13 and 2.5, adducing "The reddening moon . . ." as an example of the latter (DhĀ 1.13, p. 109; Ingalls et al. 1990: 137).

184. Compare *Ślokavārttika Vākyādhikaraṇa* vv. 330–331: *bhāvanaiva ca vākyārthaḥ sarvatrākhyātavattayā | anekaguṇajātyādikārakārthānurañjitā.*

185. This *kārikā* elaborates on Bhatta Nayaka #12 (which offers a far more pertinent refutation of the *dhvani* interpretation of the "*bhama dhammia*" verse than what Abhinava reports as Bhatta Nayaka's critique in DhĀL p. 68).

186. Bahurupa Mishra likewise seems to be alluding to the Bhatta Nayaka verse; hence I translate *śāstra* as Veda. Dhanika, however, speaks of *laukikavākyas* as the comparative element, suggesting that *śāstra* in Bahurupa Mishra may mean "scholarly discourse."

187. *sākṣāt . . . viparivartamāno* (see above, n. 89).

188. *Nāgānanda* 3.4.

189. GPP ed. reads *niyatābhihita-*, "which are necessarily enunciated" (for *saṃnihitābhihita-*; Bhatta Nrisimha reads *saṃnihita-*).

190. For the argument here, see Pollock 2010: 150.

191. I read *-ānupalabdheḥ svānand-* (with GPP, for *-ānupalabdheḥ. kāvyaśabdānāṃ ca svānand-*), and take *niratiśayasukhāsvādavyatirekeṇa* as a gloss that has crept into the text.

192. *abhidhā*, which for Bhatta Nayaka comprises all signifying aspects of language, both literal and figurative. See Bhatta Nayaka fragment #11, and notes 6, 30, and 57 above.

193. *ākṛṣyamāṇā*. *Prabhā* glosses the unfortunately vague word by *svānukūlīkṛtā.*

194. The title of a celebrated work on the philosophy of grammar by Bhartrihari (c. fifth or sixth century).

195. Compare Bhatta Nrisimha on DR 1.9: "The aesthetic elements, being communicated as they are by such things as figures of speech—hyperbole, for example [see Dhanika on DR 4.2]—are of course themselves sentence meanings, not word meanings. But since rasa arises from a 'construal' with these elements, they take on the character of words in respect to rasa, and for its part rasa, inasmuch as it is generated by these 'words,' takes on the character of a sentence meaning."

196. Bhatta Nrisimha's comment on this passage is misleading, suggesting that the "case" concerns the production of rasa, when it is the production of pleasure that is clearly at issue.

197. Such as implicature.

198. The work is not extant, and the extract here has been imperfectly transmitted. Bhatta Nrisimha's exegesis is incorporated into the translation.

199. I find the GPP reading here, *tātparyānatirekāc ca vyañjanīyasya* ("Since 'manifestation' is nothing other than sentence purport, there can exist no such thing as implicature") to be superior to Adyar's, despite the apparent authority of Bhatta Nrisimha for the latter, but the two texts transmit much the same sense.

200. That is, this sentence would turn out to be a case of implicature, which the implicature theorist would reject because it makes no sense for it to occur at the second stage.

201. Literally, "If it did repose . . . without further . . . it could never shift."

202. Bhatta Nayaka's own analysis of the verse in question seems to be based on other criteria, at least as reported by Abhinava (DhĀL p. 68), but the proponent of *tātpāryaśakti* and *vivakṣāsūcakatva* (DhĀL p. 70) must be Bhatta Nayaka or a follower (see also n. 185).

203. The scholars of Mimamsa.

204. Dhanika cites NŚ 6.34 (see n. 22 there; I make no sense of Venkatacharya's *bhāva-* and so adopt the standard reading *nānā-*). While the verse would seem to validate the simple notion of "production," it does not provide evidence for the more complicated concept, the process

of "actualization" by the audience member. Bhatta Nrisimha addresses this in his comment that follows.

205. Bhatta Nrisimha's literal reading of "actualization" fails to do justice to either Bhatta Nayaka's original formulation or Dhanika's elaboration.

206. Unlike, say, the words for the foundational factor (such "Rama"), which are connected with actual entities.

207. See Dhanika on 4.36 above, and n. 166.

208. This passage is cited in BhP (p. 152.18–21) and ascribed (oddly) to Sadashiva. It is of course pure Bhatta Nayaka; see #1a.

209. Dhanika on DR 4.2, above.

210. GPP ed. reads *ananubhūyamānatvād* (for *anubhūyamānatvād*), which would seem to mean: We experience the character as a foundational factor, not as a living being (real or unreal) who can experience rasa.

211. Dhanika is referring to the foundational factor in reference to the audience. If rasa is experienced by the viewer/reader, the factors must, in the last analysis, be factors for him, not for any other character in the narrative.

212. This seems to be the conclusion of the whole argument on the location of rasa that is the subject of Dhanamjaya's verses. And it indicates how intimately any given position on the location (or ontology) of rasa—whether in the text or in the reception—is connected with a particular modality of its cognitive genesis (or epistemology)—such as here, whether implicature or actualization.

213. Dhanika's argument here is crucial, though its logic is elusive. Bhatta Nrisimha seems to take it as rather general (words simply cannot both create and manifest rasa at one and the same moment), but it must be more closely related to what Dhanika has been saying about the substratum of rasa: if rasa existed in the character, it would have to be both produced and manifested by the same words, with the two processes happening simultaneously, but something can only be manifested after it has been produced, and by something other than what produces it. If rasa exists in the audience, however, it can first be communicated by the discourse (*tātparya*) and subsequently actualized by the viewers/readers.

214. Or, queen (*devī*). Both were thought of as mothers, and thus not objects of sexual desire.

215. *paramarasika*. Bahurupa Mishra would seem to misunderstand the problem at issue, as Dhanika shows. Dhanamjaya is concerned with the question, at once aesthetic-psychological and quasi-ethical, how a foundational factor for Rama, namely, his wife Sita, can be a foundational factor for another man, the spectator. He is not concerned with the difference between seeing real-life emotions and fictional emotions.

216. Both the subject (Rama) and object (Sita) of emotion in the storyworld become aesthetic factors for the viewer, though it is easier to understand how this works in the case of the object, hence Dhanika's redirection below.

217. *vibhāvayati*, which seems to be used almost as a denominative of *vibhāva*, in the sense of providing a foundational factor for the emotion of the viewer/reader.

218. The pronoun *tā* must refer to *avasthānām* in 40a, but Dhanika takes it to refer to *sītādiśabdāḥ*, which is not quite the same thing (Bahurupa Mishra does not comment on the line).

219. Again Bahurupa Mishra, cleaving to the old model, radically misunderstands the text he is commenting on (though compare his remarks on 4.43–45ab below).

220. If there are not two separate comparisons here (though this seems likely) and we are actually meant to connect the yogin with historical discourse, the only candidate would be Vyasa, author of the MBh.

221. With this term (*sarvalokasādhāraṇya*) Dhanika seems to be making the point that every viewer thinks the characters "common" to himself (compare ABh 1.43: *lokasya sarvasya sādhāraṇatayā svatvena bhāvyamānaś carvyamāṇo 'rtho nāṭyam*), not that the process of "commonality" (or more usually, "commonization," *sādharaṇīkaraṇa*) is available to all people, though Dhanika may well have assumed this.

222. The spectator would be feeling desire toward "woman" as such, not toward the queen (or the goddess)—and married woman—Sita.

223. *rasāśrayaḥ*. This normally means the substratum of rasa, the subject who feels it, though it sometimes refers to the object (see above, n. 144), which is how Bhatta Nrisimha is using it here and on 41cd. If we take *rasāśraya* in its normal sense, Bhatta Nrisimha will not be speaking to Dhanika's concern, which pertains to the problem that arises when the substratum becomes the viewer/reader.

224. The historical character is merely a typological state providing a substratum for a given rasa, the way the toy elephant is simply a *point d'appui* of the child's own imagination, and it is the reader's own stable emotion that is savored, not the character's. (The context of the argument is about historical particularity, not ontological truth, as Bahurupa Mishra takes it.)

225. Bahurupa Mishra (or his editor) loses his way in the syntax of this sentence. "Overcome," *pratipannaiḥ*, is also uncertain.

226. *laukika-*. Again, the storyworld of the play or poem (there is no rasa in the real real world, only emotion). See n. 106 above.

227. NŚ 6.15.

228. Bhatta Nrisimha's comment is odd. Dhanika cites Bharata to draw a distinction between the character's "real-world" emotional experience and the spectator's experience of rasa (and the analytical, even categorical, and therefore numerically limited aspect of such rasa), not between everyday "taste" and aesthetic experience.

229. Again, Dhanika is speaking of the "real world" of the drama itself, where Rama has rasa when perceiving his own wife, Sita (so Bhatta Nrisimha).

230. This shows Abhinava's account of Bhatta Nayaka (#1a) to be erroneous. I construe *manasaḥ* here as well as in v. 44b (so Dhanika and Bhatta Nrisimha). The four states arise when the rasas are present (they are produced by the rasas, per Bhatta Nrisimha, not conditions for their production, per Bahurupa Mishra).

231. Probably alluding to NŚ 1.266, above (see n. 16 there), though I understand *artha* here differently.

232. See Dhanika and Bhatta Nrisimha below for this Vedantic interpretation (so too Mallinatha on *Ekāvalī* p. 96, *ātmaivānandaḥ*).

233. So Bhatta Nrisimha (Bahurupa Mishra understands, "Hence, the latter four rasas are viewed as being produced by the former four rasas"). See also Venkatacharya pp. 305–306.

234. Bahurupa Mishra appears to take the two positions as complementary, not contradictory.

235. The term *rasābhāsa* is used nowhere else in this sense.

236. The term *cittabhūmi* is found first in Buddhist thought (*Abhidharmakośa*) and then in yoga, where the mind is said to have five *bhūmis*, which bear some faint relationship to these

aesthetic states: *kṣiptaṃ mūḍaṃ vikṣiptam ekāgraṃ niruddham iti cittabhūmayaḥ* (*Yogasūtrabhāṣya* 1.1.3; Bhoja on *Yogasūtra* 1.2 explains these as particular configurations of *guṇas*, but they are decidedly not symmetrical with Bhatta Nayaka's four: *vikṣiptam*, for example, contains a predominance of *sattva* and is a property of the deities for Bhoja, whereas here it is connected with the violent rasa). The notion of *cittabhūmis* is found nowhere else in aesthetic discourse save for a brief echo of Dhanika's remarks here in *Ekāvalī* (p. 95, see below, misunderstood by Mallinatha).

237. See NŚ 6.39, above.

238. "Conditional" (*hetuhetumadbhāva*) as in smoke and fire, not "causal" (*kāryakāraṇabhāva*) as in a pot and clay. The erotic and the comic are both "conditioned by," i.e., inferred to exist from the presence of, "radiance"; as Bhatta Nrisimha puts it: just as the presence of *vikāsa* "indicates" (*sūcaka-*, contrast Abhinavagupta, ABh 1.289.13) the presence of the erotic, so its presence indicates that of the comic. The two rasas are related by this *hetuhetumadbhāva* (so correctly Venkatacharya p. 305).

239. NŚ 6.40, above.

240. Although there are only four types of fusion, each rasa produces its own specific one (Bhatta Nrisimha). Dhanika below observes that there are eight and only eight "drama rasas"; this is corroborating evidence that Bhatta Nayaka held this to be the case too (though see n. 19 above).

241. The nondifferentiation here is based on the identity of rasa and blissful experience rather than on the identity of self and bliss (so SSS and RG; and see *Vijñapriyā* on SD p. 72).

242. Source unknown.

243. *Bṛhadaraṇyaka Upaniṣad* 3.9.26.

244. Venkatacharya suggests that Dhanika's position is ambiguous, and can be taken as either restricting the peaceful rasa to nondramatic literature (implied by the last sentence of this section) or denying it altogether.

245. I conjecture *saṃsargin* (for *saṃsārin*).

246. I read *atiśayoktirūpakādikāvyavyāpāra-* (for *atiśayoktirūpakāvyavyāpāra-*) in view of Dhanika's use of the phrase on 4.2 (confirmed in Kundu 2000: 389) and Bhatta Nrisimha on p. 169 line 5 (Dandin's remarks on *atiśayokti*, KĀ 2. 212, 218, notwithstanding).

4. ABHINAVAGUPTA AND HIS SCHOOL, 1000–1200

1. ABh 1.1, v. 4 (*sadvipra-* may simply mean Bhatta).

2. DhĀL p. 374.

3. For later reflections on this question, compare ND p. 188. No later writer shows awareness of Bhatta Tota's critique—since none had access to the ABh, in which alone it was reproduced.

4. See ABh 1.35, given below.

5. Kshemendra, *Aucityavicāracarcā*, p. 151, KA p. 3, and later writers quote all or part of this fragment, and ascribe it either to Bhatta Tota (the first) or to *Kāvyakautuka* (the rest). KD p. 7 and others begin and end the fragment with the following two verses of uncertain origin: "Memory's domain is the past, forethought concerns the future, intelligence the present, but wisdom is transtemporal"; "The goddess of speech has two paths, scripture and poetry. The first is the creation of wisdom, the second comes from imagination."

6. KA p. 432. An important (and, for cultural history, entirely valid) differentiation between the Vedic *kavi* and the *laukika kavi*.

7. DhĀL p. 336 (*tad eva nāṭyaṃ*: compare p. 402: *nāṭyaṃ ca rasa eva*).

8. Knowledge, that is, of the four ends of man, something clear from the context of Abhinava's citation.

9. DhĀL p. 92. I do not see how this can be reconciled with Abhinava's position (Ingalls et al. 1990 also note this ad loc.). It clearly is a step back from the insights of Bhatta Nayaka.

10. ABh 1.284.26–285.4.

11. ABh 3.78.5–16. My translation of parts of this passage is uncertain. The last verse embodies a conjecture on the part of the editors.

12. Compare BKA 5.4.

13. For *cūrṇapada*, see NŚ 14.40.

14. ABh 1.268–270, supplemented by KA pp. 93–95 and Manikyachandra on KP pp. 213–16 (2nd ed. Mysore). This section may well be taken directly from the lost work of Bhatta Tota, despite the fact that Abhinavagupta occasionally interjects observations about matters he himself, and not Tota, will later address (e.g., ABh 1.269.14; 1.270 3, 5).

15. Chapter 1.4 above.

16. I add, to complete the text, *na tu vyavahārtāraḥ*. Scholars are *tattvacintakā nyāyānusāriṇaḥ* (Dharmakīrti, *Pramāṇavārttika*, p. 39 [ed. Gnoli]).

17. Bharata, according to Bhatta Tota/Abhinava, could not have meant that rasa is an imitation (see also ABh 1.35, below).

18. The psychophysical responses, the main and subordinate physical representations (KLV p. 305).

19. "The actor's body is a material entity and visible to the eyes, desire is nonmaterial and invisible; the body is the locus of the headdress and so on, whereas the mind is the locus of desire" (Manikyachandra).

20. And if Shri Shankuka denies they are grasped as factitious, he contradicts his own theory, that rasa is an imitation of a stable emotion.

21. I read *mugdhabuddhe* (with Manikyachandra, for *mugdhabuddheḥ* of ABh and Kangle); and I read the rest of the sentence with KA.

22. KA adds a gloss here: The imitation of desire is a cause different from the familiar cause, desire itself. Only if the reactions arising from this imitation of desire are understood as such (i.e., as imitations) by the discriminating observer would it be correct to posit an inference of some second thing, i.e., imitation-of-desire. But this is not the case, so how can one argue that there is an apprehension of the *imitation* of desire? When the nondiscriminating observer sees those kinds of reactions, he infers desire itself to be present—and that is false knowledge (KA p. 94.15; so KLV p. 305.13).

23. Conventionally it was thought that scorpions were produced from cow dung as well as from other scorpions, the different provenance accounting for the differences in their virulence, though not in their natures. Abhinava uses the image again in ABh 2.221, below.

24. In the same way, we do not infer an imitation of desire from artificial reactions mistaken for real ones.

25. It is hard not to believe that the mindbending complexity here is not tongue-in-cheek; it is certainly a *reductio ad absurdum*.

26. The standard example of similarity, or analogy, in Indian philosophy.

27. The actor is not an imitation of an angry man, nor is there some actually existing violent rasa that is an imitation of anger (KLV p. 305.20).

28. ABh, KA, and Someshvara (KP p. 547) all read *-vaidhuryābhāve*. Manikyachandra correctly rephrases as *yadi na bādhakodayaḥ*, which makes it likely that *-abhāve* was a gloss on *-vaidhurye* that crept into the text.

29. Shri Shankuka #1a (end).

30. Which, the argument presupposes, Shri Shankuka would reject (further evidence that he may have been a Buddhist, since Buddhists deny the reality of class categories; see Gupta 1963).

31. Shri Shankuka #1a.

32. Which Shri Shankuka denies; ibid.

33. This sentence and the next are reversed in ABh; I follow KA.

34. Presumably chapter 14 (I do not locate the precise phrase, but in any case it is Abhinavagupta, not Bhatta Tota, who is making the argument; see above, n. 14). Shri Shankuka's distinction is offered in ABh 1.267. I make no good sense of the compound *bhedābhidhānasaṃrambhagarbhamahīyān* (and find Kangle's emendation radical), and omit it from the translation. Hemachandra omitted it too.

35. All of us are "doing" things "later" than Rama.

36. Unlike the erotic, where the locus of rasa must be a person of high status, no such restriction is placed on the tragic in the NŚ, though it is discernible in literary practice.

37. Compare ABh 1.37.4–5 (*na hi naṭo rāmasadṛśaṃ svātmanaḥ śokaṃ karoti, sarvathaiva tasya tatrābhāvāt*). Manikyachandra glosses *uttamaprakṛteḥ śokābhāvāt*, which I assume means: because of the absence of the high-status character's grief, sc., in the actor.

38. It would turn out that the actor is imitating himself (Manikyachandra).

39. I read *-vad dhi* (for *-vṛddhi*). Presumably ABh 1.37 is the earlier passage meant (but *kāntaveśānukāra* is not discussed there). There is a feminine "charm" known as "mimicry" where a woman dresses up in her lover's clothes for the amusement of her girlfriends. But as we see below, even that does not get the name "imitation" in the NŚ. The NŚ (1.112) unambiguously proclaims that drama is *lokavṛttānukaraṇaṃ*, an "imitation of worldly events," so Bhatta Tota and Abhinava have to admit it in some measure.

40. I read *asaṃvedyamānasya* (with KA, for *anusaṃvedyamānasya*); compare ABh 1.271.14: *na cāpratītaṃ vastvastitāvyavahāre yogyam*.

41. NŚ 19 (*sandhyaṅgas*).

42. NŚ 1.117; see ABh 1.35.1, below.

43. I conjecture *-gatyanukaraṇādau* (for *-gatyakaraṇādau*).

44. This part of the critique is directed at a proposition of Shri Shankuka's nowhere exactly preserved. Only his analogy of the painting of a horse is extant; see #1a.

45. DhĀL p. 394.

46. ABh 1.37.9–10.

47. KLV p. 303.11, who goes on to say that "like teacher, like student," Abhinava accepts Bhatta Tota's view and for that reason did not bother to set it forth after his refutation of Shri Shankuka in ABh chapter 6.

48. *Tantrāloka* 37.33–82 (he tells us, for example, that his mother died when he was still a child, thereby consigning him to a life of detachment, 37.56–57). There are several other accounts of his life elsewhere in his works.

49. Abhinava uses the pun elsewhere; see for example *Tantrāloka* 37.85d. In the Malayalam mss. the title is regularly prefaced by the descriptor *Nāṭyavedavivṛti*, "Exegesis of the Veda on Drama."

50. *Tantrāloka* 37.58; he also refers in IPVV v. 2, p. 179 to his ABh commentary and the rasa theory he expounds in it. See also Ingalls et al. 1990: 32–33. Note there is no echo of his work on *śānta* rasa in his understanding of *mokṣa* (Gerow 1994: 192). The most recent assessment of the order of the philosophical works is Sanderson 2007: 352–82, but he does not address the two literary-critical texts.

51. See for example Abhinava's reference to DhĀL on ABh 1.337.

52. DhĀL p. 51.

53. On ABh 1.337, Abhinava notes that he has explained in DhĀL how Anandavardhana showed that rasas could not be communicated through their own words, but beyond this and a few other simple references there is no extended account of the crucial concept of implicature. It is entirely absent from the core presentation of his reconstruction (ABh 1.272–287).

54. ABh 1.272.18.

55. ABh 1.43.11.

56. ABh 1.37 for the synonyms ("experience" is one of Bhatta Nayaka's terms of art); *sākṣātkārakalpānuvyavasāya*, ABh 1.173, 174; 3.294; pure consciousness, ABh 1.37 and 1.286.

57. ABh 1.286.5; 1.43.11. See n. 297 below. (IPVV v. 3 p. 251, *cittavṛttyantarodaya . . . -virahita eva āsvādo*, however, would seem to stand in tension with this).

58. ABh 1.278.

59. Already in DhĀL, p. 189.

60. Abhinava, like others, anachronistically ascribes the very idea of commonization to Bharata (ABh 1.275).

61. This appropriation began already in the DhĀL, where Abhinava assimilates Bhatta Nayaka's *bhoga* to the (reformulated) notion of *vyakti/vyañjanā*, which misled later writers, such as Jagannatha (RG p. 30 and n. 247, below). See also Bhatta Nayaka fragment #14 for what may well be the first psychological interpretation of "manifestation."

62. DR 4.43, Dhanika on 4.1, above.

63. ABh 1.278.20–21, below.

64. ABh 1.274, 276, below. I say "philosophical" mode since even here Abhinava was anticipated by Dhanika, though his position is more general. See *Avaloka* on 4.43–45ab, above.

65. Sellars 1963: 154.

66. Which appears to have been Ananda's concern (Shri Shankuka included the terms for the stable emotions, see there, #1a, p. 267, above; Induraja, all affective terms, see KASS 4.3–4 and commentary, above).

67. KP *kārikā* 63ab, below (not evidence he knew the ABh, and I find no other). Abhinava's discussion pertains to all the aesthetic elements; Mammata permits the use of a proper term only in the case of transitory emotions not associated with particular physical reactions.

68. DhĀL p. 336; pleasure subserves instruction.

69. ABh 1.261 and 1.36, below.

70. ABh 1.276, below.

71. Or, again, "newly" to a degree. Udbhata (4.3–4) had already made the argument, but offered no detailed exposition.

72. Gerow 1994; for the text, see ABh 1.326–335.

73. Ingalls et al. 1990.

74. As noted, the work is extant in only a few fragmentary manuscripts from Kerala (three, containing successive sections and so basically constituting one manuscript, have vanished, only transcripts of them remaining; four other fragments, whose relationship to these missing mss. and to each other is unclear, are available in Trivandrum). For the exasperation of the editor of the *editio princeps*, see NŚ ed. Krishnamoorthy, p. 69. Several later scholars, confronted with difficult readings, simply rewrote the text (Visvesvara Siddhantasiromani, Kangle).

75. For further reflection on this passage (and references to other reflections) see now Ollett 2015.

76. See NŚ 1.336, above. Abhinava (in KA's version) glosses *bhāva* as stable and transitory emotion. On *artha*, see NŚ 1.266, above and n. 16.

77. KA p. 97.26 adds Abhinava's gloss from ABh 1.337.19, on which see further below.

78. The first example is untraced, but recalls many well-known *arthavādas*; the second is an imprecise quotation of *Taittirīya Saṃhitā* 2.1.1.4. The Jain Hemachandra replaces the reference to Vedic sacrifice with the following: "'Śāmba [Sāmba] once sang a hymn of praise to the sun, and was cured of his illness.' With respect to the poem beginning thus, the reader first understands the bare meaning. Then to this first comprehension he indubitably adds another, whereby the tense and so on of the original are elided, so that he thinks, 'Whoever sings praises to the sun is cured, so I too will praise the sun, so as to be free of disease.'" (KA p. 98.6–12; I have no idea why the verses should be attributed to Bhatta Nayaka, as the editors of KA ad loc. and Gnoli [1968: 53] believe.)

79. *itivṛtta(prarocita-)*, referring to the *arthavāda* itself (not *itikartavyatā*, KLV); compare TV p. 241, *arthavādaprarocita-*.

80. I read *-svabhāvā* (with Triv., for *-svābhāvā*) and delete the *daṇḍa*. I take *-ādi* as referring to the interpretative techniques "supplementation" (*adhyāhāra*), grammatical transformation (*vipariṇāma*), and the like (see, e.g., Śabara on PMS 1.2.1), though I do not find *saṃkramaṇa* to be attested elsewhere in the sense I give it here.

81. I conjecture *āsai* (for *āste*; Triv. mss. read *āstai*, and more rightly read *pradadāni*, for *saṃ-*).

82. For *pratibhā* and *udyoga* see *Nyāyamañjarī* vol. 2, pp. 140–41.

83. *pratibhāna*.

84. Kuntaka cites this to illustrate the "impulses" of animals in contrast to the stable emotions of higher-order beings (VJ p. 141). See also the introduction, section 8.

85. AŚ 1.7; KS 3.62 and 3.67. KLV notes that the nature of aesthetic apprehension in the second two examples (the desire of Uma and Shiva) is not detailed, having already been explained in the case of fear (p. 308.24), but this does not explain why extra examples are provided (let alone why Abhinava chose to begin his exposition with fear rather than desire).

86. Presumably as opposed to the *buddhi*, where linguistic knowledge arises.

87. I follow the exegesis of KLV for this convoluted sentence.

88. I read *-grāhyaṃ* (with Triv., KA, for *-nigrāhyaṃ*).

89. *cakṣuṣor iva viparivartamānam*, possibly one of Bhatta Nayaka's technical terms (see DR 4.1, 2, and n. 89, above.

90. ND p. 161, below (on the "broad inclusiveness" of rasa) suggests it is the *capacity* for commonization; see also ABh 1.36.8 (*sarvapariṣadsādhāraṇa-*); for KLV, it is the commonization itself captured in an inference.

91. The actually existing particularities are those of the actors on the stage; the literary ones are those of the characters (see the "synopsis" in ABh 1.278, below).

92. Source unknown. I read *'pi* (with Triv., KA, for *hi*) and *camatkāraḥ* | (for | *camatkāro*).

93. The goddess of wealth, consort of Vishnu (Hari), was produced at the churning of the cosmic milk ocean, when Mount Mandara was used a churning stick.

94. In *pāda* a, read *camakkai* (for *camakkaī*).

95. I accept Pandey's conjecture *camataḥ karaṇam* (for *ca manaḥkaraṇam*; see also Kangle 1973: 160) to account for the *ca*, despite the fact that, first, the recorded reading, "the activity of the mind of one [immersed]," repeats the reference to the *manas* as the place of *camatkāra* emphasized in the preceding and following lines, and, second, no etymology as conjectured is found elsewhere in Abhinava's works (contrast IPVV v. 3, p. 251; see also Bansat-Boudon 2011: 321). KA (p. 99.5) deletes the whole compound (as well as the preceding sentence), indicating that the textual uncertainty is old.

96. I read *tathātvenāsphuranty* (with KA, see also Triv., for *tathātvena sphurann*).

97. AŚ 5.2.

98. The parenthesis is found only in KA (and certainly seems like an early comment that has crept into the text).

99. I assume that *eṣā* refers back to *camatkāra* and is attracted into the feminine of the predicate (rather than: "this apprehension is . . .").

100. I read *-avasthāstu* (i.e., *-avasthā astu*, with KA, *for avasthāsu*).

101. Presumably, in thinking of the whole dramatic experience as a mental construct of the viewer (hence my addition of "imaginary"). (This position is discussed, obscurely, at ABh 1.170.14, where it is associated with Samkhya.) Kangle perceptively notes that Abhinava does not mention Bhatta Nayaka's position here because he accepts it (1973: 161).

102. Compare DhĀL p. 331.8–9, and Someshvara on KP 7 v. 329+ (ed. Parikh p. 182).

103. On NŚ 18.10 (so Kangle).

104. NŚ 20.30. In the prologues to Sanskrit dramas, the director and actors appear in their own person, not in the guise of the characters that they will represent.

105. NŚ 5.157–158.

106. Bhatta Nayaka's insight is anachronistically attributed to the author of the NŚ (compare Dhanika on DR 4.2, and n. 100, above).

107. *uparañjana-* (or *rañjana-*) refers to the theatrical elements—poetry, singing, instrumental music—that provide "color" to the drama. A tragic drama, for example, requires substantial "coloration," a farce none (ABh 2.447); music is "the life breath of coloration" (ABh 4.399).

108. KLV: such as different components of the *lāsya* dance (the seated recitation, *āsīna*, the *puṣpagaṇḍika*, etc.).

109. Both quoted words are Bhatta Nayaka's terms of art.

110. I read *-maṇḍapavidagdha-* (with KA, for *-maṇḍapapadavidagdha-*); improbable is Kangle's *-maṇḍalapada-*, "circle dancing" (unattested). "Actresses," *gaṇikā*; the term means courtesans, but such women also typically performed as actresses.

111. NŚ 1.11. I have shifted this citation to where it logically belongs.

112. Or "linguistic signs" (so KLV p. 309.20, and see KA cited in n. 116, below).

113. *Nyāyasūtrabhāṣya* 1.1.3. The received text actually reads *sā ceyam* (instead of *sarvā ceyam*).

114. Two additional forms of valid cognition.

115. I read *tatpramity-* (with KA, for *taptam ity*).

116. For *saśabdaliṅga-* KA gives *śabdalakṣaṇaliṅga-*.

117. The factors must be restricted to the stimulants, since the foundational can of course be and typically are sensate.

118. Abhinava will not return to the question of the hindrances until ABh 1.278, below.

119. That is, the stable emotions.

120. Or, in many of its aspects, "power." For the linkage between rasas and ends of man, see also ABh 1.261, below.

121. I read *kāma-* (with Kangle, for *kāmaḥ* or [KA] *kāme*). The editors of both NŚ and KA mispunctuate the passage as a whole.

122. So KLV p. 309.27 (see ABh 1.276.4 below).

123. The addition of the ninth rasa, and of course the homology with the ends of man, force Abhinava to abandon Bharata's own scheme; see NŚ 1.289, given above.

124. The hierarchy among the stable emotions is nowhere discussed, but the ends of man with which they are associated are indeed hierarchically related (morality takes precedence over wealth, wealth over love), and that may be what is intended here.

125. The reference is to Samkhya philosophy, and its doctrine of the three constituents of reality: stolidity, volatility, and sensitivity.

126. *kaṭu kiṃnā* is a misprint for *kaṭukimnā*, but which is itself difficult to construe (the true reading may be *kaṭukimā*, but the corruption would be hard to explain).

127. KA moves the following discussion (to p. 277.21), with substantial modifications, to his formal discussion of the *sthāyibhāvas* in 2.18 (p. 124).

128. Cited in IPVV v. 3 p. 174 (with the reading *-āsvādarasādaraḥ*).

129. The reading *anucita-* (for *aparicita-*) seems further corroborated by 1.277.1, *ucitaviṣayaniyantritā*, and by KA, *ayuktatayā* (De and Kangle, perhaps overcleverly, *-jigiṣuḥ* [for *ārjijiṣur*, or perhaps better *arjijiṣur*] *api jita-*). (KLV construes this qualification with fear, thereby mistakenly deleting *utsāha*, p. 310.2.)

130. The participial phrase is otiose (perhaps a gloss that has crept into the text).

131. The formulation is as vague in the Sanskrit as in the translation, and the exact nuance is unclear to me (and KA's *tattatsvaparakartavyavaicitryadarśanāt* is not much help).

132. For example, only characters of high status can be the subjects of an erotic or heroic literary work, only characters of low status can be the subjects of a humorous or disgusting one.

133. I read *-vibhāvābhāvāt janmamadhye* (with Triv., KA, for *-vibhāvāt jaganmadhye*).

134. More clearly KA: "for the simple reason that desire and so on will (always) have yet additional objects and so cannot be depleted" (p. 125.13).

135. *Yogasūtrabhāṣya* 2.4 (p. 60; cited also in IPVV v. 2, p. 178; Caitra = John Doe), where the discussion concerns the punctuated but persistent nature (*vicchitti*) of the disturbances (*kleśas*): even though discontinued under the force of a conflictual disturbance, or concentrated on a single object, a disturbance can in the one case reappear and in the other be simultaneously directed toward some other object.

136. The same image is used in 1.334.27–28, where the string corresponds to the self.

137. I read *vicitrārthāḥ* (with Gnoli, for *vicitrārtha-*).

138. I.e., and not engender (KLV).

139. Or: coloring the particular character of the stable emotion. The reading *svarūpoparañjakatvam* (though also given by KA) seems dubious; the correct reading may well be *samuparañjakatvam* (see 1.278.8).

140. That is, by stipulating the method of elimination as concentration on the stable emotion.

141. I read *-nirūpaṇayā* (with KA, for *-nirūpaṇāyā*). KA also adds, "on the part of the sage [Bharata]."

142. NŚ 1.293.13, above.

143. For KLV, the general definition runs from the *rasasūtra* to p. 288.2; and the particular, from p. 289.1 through the account of the various rasas.

144. I read *-dhṛtyādi-* (with KA, for *-vīkṣādi-*), despite the fact that transitory emotions are typically not held to be signs for inferring but rather what is inferred (the reading *katākṣavīkṣa-* ignores the *vyabhicāribhāva*, is redundant, and appears to be *hapax*).

145. NŚ 7.

146. Abhinava is glossing the word *saṃyoga*, "conjunction," in Bharata's *rasasūtra*.

147. *artha*. KLV glosses "stable emotion in the form of a predisposition" (p. 310.14).

148. For Shri Shankuka, rasa is actually an imitation in the actor of a stable emotion in the character cognized by the viewer through inference; for Bhatta Lollata, rasa is the stable emotion in an intensified state. In DhĀL pp. 155–57, Abhinava ascribes some of the views that follow to a Mimamsaka (which Shri Shankuka was not, see headnote, chapter 1.4), while at the same time accepting them in a qualified way.

149. The imitation of an emotion on the stage.

150. Insofar as that would produce the impossible notion that rasa is simply the stable emotion (KLV p. 310.16).

151. The NŚ passage in question is 1.282. In DhĀL p. 157, Abhinava explains the congruity as twofold: we relish the predispositions of our mental state in a way congruent with the aesthetic elements pertaining to the character's mental state; and when we come to understand the mental states of others in the real world (which forms the basis of our aesthetic sympathy), it is their stable emotion (such as desire) that we become aware of through the causes (like gardens) and effects (like horripilation).

152. Another version of part of this passage is found in DhĀL pp. 155–56.

153. KLV agrees that the ablative here is parallel with following two instrumentals.

154. As Ruyyaka (glossing Mammata's précis) puts it, the mental states of such adepts "are in the end focused exclusively on their inner self" (*svātmamātraparyavasitāni*, KP p. 579). That said, Abhinava has just stated that the spiritual adept is "free from any coloration of objective reality," and hence the reading in both NŚ and KA (KLV) here and below *viṣayāveśavaivaśyena* strikes me as dubious. We might wish to conjecture *-vaiṣamyena* ("harshness toward the lure of objects") in view of *yogipratyayād viṣayāsvādaśūnyatāparuṣād* (ABh 1.284.22, below), and IPVV v. 3, p. 233: *amī sukhādyā vicitravaiṣamyabhājaḥ* (see also *Mokṣopāya* 1.28.13: *viṣaṃ viṣayavaiṣamyaṃ na viṣaṃ viṣam ucyate*).

155. That is, making or producing as a concrete thing (essentially Bhatta Lollata's view).

156. This is basically Shri Shankuka's position.

157. Kangle notes that Mammata reads *-siddheḥ* (for *-siddhau*), "our argument, since we have proven."

158. The analogy hardly seems "exact," since in the one case it is the super-phenomenal nature of the elements that is at issue, in the other, the composite nature of the drink.

159. Presumably our deeply implanted intuitions prevent us from seeing Rama himself as completely superimposed on the actor. How such an awareness would function with respect to a fictional character, such as Madhava, is unclear.

160. I read *tata* (with KA, KLV, for *ata*). The elimination is a result of a mutual cancellation—of the true belief in the actor by the false belief in the character, and vice versa (KLV).

161. So KLV (for this sense of *niyata-*, see ABh 1.35.17, 273.13, 338.22).

162. "Sorrow" (*duḥkha*) presumably stands for *īrṣā* (envy), which appears in other occurrences of this argument (e.g., ABh 1.35.18). Both in respect to these three states (of indifference, self-involvement, and involvement of a specific other; see also 1.273.6) and in the discussion of commonization that follows, the magnitude of Abhinava's debt to Bhatta Nayaka will be obvious.

163. The term "sequence of moments"(*santānavṛtti*) is Buddhist in inspiration (see IPVV v. 2, p. 128, where Dharmottara is discussed).

164. Which can have various relationships of predominance and subordination among themselves (KLV). I understand *sādhāraṇībhāvanā* (for *sādhāraṇī bhāvanā*).

165. The extended narrative (*prabandha*) is typically distinguished from both drama and the isolate verse, but obviously Abhinava is including it in the former. (Kangle's deletion is contradicted by KLV.)

166. KAS 1.3.30–31 (reading with the editions *tad dhi citram* [for *tad vicitram*]). The "particular components" are mentioned in what follows (the dialects used in drama, etc.).

167. Isolate verses do not identify the speaker, who therefore, along with the dramatic situation, needs to be inferred from hints in the poem itself.

168. That is, "rasa"; see ABh 1.272.20, given above.

169. Which illuminate everything, however already bright and pure.

170. Compare above, ABh 1.275.9–12, on the third hindrance.

171. My understanding of the phrase ("whether . . . mental state") is imperfect; the text *dṛśyānyaniyamādau* in particular is almost certainly corrupt.

172. NŚ 1.283.2, above.

173. Abhinava is glossing NŚ 6.33, above.

174. That is, with the protagonist.

175. Compare ABh 1.37 and n. 297, below; and especially IPVV v. 2, p. 179: "When one is tasting honey and the like, physical contact with the object is interposed [between the tasting and the consciousness]. In the case of poetry or drama, however, although such interposition is absent, one's latent dispositions do remain interposed and penetrate [the consciousness]."

176. The Shaiva hindrances; compare, e.g., IPVV v. 2, p. 178.

177. Whereas the erotic thwarted preserves the hope that the lovers will be reunited.

178. I understand *tannimittaṃ* (see KLV p. 311.27) *raudraḥ, sa cārthapradhānaḥ* (for *tannimittaṃ cārthapradhānaḥ raudraḥ, sa cāmarṣapradhānaḥ*). For the linkage of anger with wealth/power, see ABh 1.276, above, where the other ends are linked with other rasas.

179. NŚ 18.43.

180. See Bhatta Lollata fragment #2a.

181. We have no record of this position in earlier literature (see also Raghavan 1975: 123).

182. I read *gaṇayitum* (conjectured by L. McCrea, for *gamayitum*).

183. Normally Nyaya speaks of eight *guṇas* (among the twenty-four) that pertain to the *ātman: buddhi, sukha, duḥkha, icchā, dveṣa, prayatna, dharma, adharma*; presumably Abhinava here adds *saṃskāra*. The Samkhyas' eight are *dharma, adharma, jñāna, ajñāna, vairāgya, avairāgya, aiśvarya, anaiśvarya*, and the four types of apprehension, *viparyaya, aśakti, tuṣṭi,* and *siddhi* (Kangle 1973: 438).

184. NŚ chapter 22.

185. I read *viśeṣāśrayāt* (with Kangle, for *viśeṣāśrayatvāt*), but the text of the preceding compound is dubious (and hence marked with an ellipsis).

186. I am not entirely certain this refers to "commonization."

187. I read *abhiṣaṅga-* (Kangle's conjecture, for *ṣaḍja-*).

188. *artha*, taken as "enterprise" in NŚ 1.266 above, is here left untranslated given Abhinava's exegesis.

189. Abhinava is glossing *pra + vartate*.

190. NŚ 6.33.

191. For the citation omitted, see Bhatta Tota fragment #5, above.

192. Presumably because of the genre constraints of the courtly epic (not the "incapacity" of the poet to become a playwright, Kangle, p. 196).

193. *tāvatīva hṛdyam*, translation uncertain.

194. NŚ 14.2. "It" in the v. refers to language, not "[the group of] ten forms," and hence the force of the quote is dark to me. Perhaps Abhinava is simply saying that Bharata uses the word *nāṭya* to refer to what others call *daśarūpakam*.

195. *śrotṛpratipattṛ-*. I see no reason to emend the text (*pratipatti-* is easy but does not explain the corruption; Kangle's *-prītipari-* is a mere guess), though the collocation appears nowhere else in Sanskrit, and it is accordingly uncertain that Abhinava actually means to contrast listener/listening (*śrotṛ/ākarṇana*), that is, to a recitation of a play, with watching a performance (*naṭaprakriyā*), as I translate.

196. *-mukurahṛdaya-*, the sole use of the simile in Abhinava. Quite different is the figure *hṛdayadarpaṇa* in Bhaṭṭa Nāyaka; see headnote to chapter 3.1.

197. I take *sādhāraṇa-* almost in the sense of *sādhāraṇya* (Kangle reads *'sādhāraṇa-*).

198. More or less the view of Shri Shankuka, at least insofar as he takes rasa to be an imitation in the actor (of an emotion in the character).

199. I read *nanu* (with Kangle, for *na*).

200. I read *-pātre* (with Visvesara, for *-mātre*).

201. The section is not extant.

202. The emendation *naṭakarmarūpam* (for *naṭadharmaḥ karmarūpam*) has been proposed (see Kangle ad loc.).

203. The aesthetic elements include the transitory emotions as well as the psychophysical responses, which are classed as emotions.

204. Shri Shankuka fragment #1, above.

205. This earlier refutation (ABh 1.35.10) is translated below; see also Bhatta Tota, #1a, above.

206. In the *Sutra on Rasa*.

207. "To say that rasas cause emotions to come into being is to say they make them, that is, enable them to be identified as aesthetic elements" (ABh 1.287.21–22). The standard example is that the son is the cause of his father being a father.

208. *Mahābhāṣya* 1.1.1.4, and elsewhere.

209. It is the *bhāvas*, not the rasas, that are configured with forms of representation. I therefore read *-baddhāḥ* and *gatāḥ* (for *-baddhān* and *gatān*). See above on NŚ 6.34.

210. NŚ 6.34; see above.

211. And hence it is only the creation of rasa that allows us to identify its causes as emotions in the aesthetic sense, as Abhinava goes on to explain.

212. Abhinava's understanding of NŚ 1.266, given above.

213. See NŚ 6.34–38, above.

214. I conjecture *vyākhyānārhāḥ* (for *vyākhyānārhāt*, so too Kangle).

215. I rearrange the first two items to correspond with the preceding exposition.

216. I read *prayojye . . . -dhiyi ca tad eva mūlam | bīja-* (for *prayojane . . . -dhiyi ca | tad evaṃ mūlabīja-*).

217. See DhĀ p. 498.

218. Abhinava is subtly reinterpreting the verse to conform with his new reader-reception aesthetics. See DhĀ p. 497 and n. 295, above; contrast Gnoli 1968: xlviii–xlix.

219. Several false interpretations rejected here by Abhinava are ignored.

220. See NŚ 1.289 (6.39–45), above.

221. In other words, any rasa when imitated becomes, in the end, comic (KLV p. 312.7). See also above both Bhoja, ŚP, p. 635, who takes this conclusion as a reductio ad absurdum, and Dhanika, *Avaloka* p. 221, who offers an analysis from within Bhatta Nayaka's system.

222. The text here is unclear, and my assumption that it is to the subject himself that the emotion is supposed to seem stable is not entirely certain.

223. "First, the lust was the cause of the desire being a semblance, and as a consequence the aesthetic elements were semblances. Now he shows it is the aesthetic elements being semblances that is the cause of the desire being a semblance" (KLV).

224. DhĀL p. 178.8 gives *veti pratipattir hṛdayaṃ* (for *veti hṛdayaṃ*).

225. KA confirms *abhimāno*; or read *abhilāṣo*, "craving," with DhĀL p. 178.9 (and possibly *vilīye-* for *-pi līye-*).

226. Though the reading *anupayogī* is given also by KA, I derive no sense from it. Whatever may have been the true reading (Kangle's *ābhāsatvayoniḥ* is a guess; perhaps better is *'py anapāyī*), the meaning required is given in the DhĀL p. 178.9, *na . . . niścayena kṛtam*, which I offer here.

227. Or reading *-kāvye* (for *vākye*, see DhĀL p. 178.1): "throughout the poetic narrative of Ravana" (or: the *Poem of Ravana*). The source of the verse itself is unknown.

228. I read *sītālakṣaṇo vibhāvaḥ* (with Raghavan, for *sītāvibhāvalakṣaṇam*).

229. NŚ 1.306.

230. The reference to the "ancients" is unclear, given that Bharata nowhere speaks of the "semblance of rasa." The first use of the phrase in question is Udbhata 4.7, above.

231. Characteristically, Abhinava chooses a complex example, of the comic negated by the comic. Hemachandra comments: "The world's raucous laughter toward something that is in fact praiseworthy is itself a 'semblance' of the comic" (KA p. 149). But as KLV adds, the semblance of the comic is itself comic (p. 312.14).

232. Bharata restricts the tragic emotion to the loss of a loved one (6.62). For reflections on the "tragic" in Indian aesthetics, see the introduction, section 8.

233. Uncertain.

234. VS 4.15 (Duryodhana speaks).

235. KLV (p. 312.16) suggests a problem with the text, and seems to point toward a missing line indicating that there is no *essential* relationship between the erotic and the tragic. I add this to the text for ease of comprehension.

236. That is, the interruption of desire no more rules out the presence of the erotic than the interruption of anger rules out the presence of the violent that gives rise to the tragic.

237. VS 1.7.

238. *Tāpasavatsarāja* 2.16 (King Vatsa is thinking of the "dead" Vasavadatta).

239. KS 4.9 (the wife of the god of love mourns his death).

240. A pun on the love god's name, the "bodiless one."

241. VS 5.5.

242. And hence that there is no heroic rasa. The work of "determination" is conquering an enemy in a way that conforms with the rules of engagement (the application of peace entreaties and so on) (KLV).

243. I read *-janitā* (with Kangle, for *-janitaḥ*).

244. Source unknown. The reference is to Vishnu, whose complexion is blue-black.

245. Determination is the stable emotion of the heroic rasa, and amazement that of the fantastic.

246. MVC 2.54 (a description of the young Rama).

247. Is this an exception to the rule that every rasa aims toward another as its end result?

248. We might wish to read *-bhāva-* (for *-vibhāva-*), given what follows; *bhāva* can connote *vibhāvādi*, though the latter may in fact be the true reading (see 1.292.17).

249. And thus imply the fearful rasa.

250. VS, beginning of Act 4.

251. Abhinava goes on to examine the same phenomenon with the other rasas.

252. I read *yathāsvam* (with Kangle, for *yathāsvayam*).

253. See ABh 1.276, above.

254. The same point is made in ABh 1.335.9 (see also Lollata #2a, above).

255. I conjecture *-tvenopa-* (for *tvepa-*).

256. DhĀ 3.43.

257. I omit Abhinava's analysis of the word *śṛṅgāra* (1.294.16–296.3); see NŚ 1.294 and n. 28, above.

258. I read *-lakṣaṇāyā . . . dhiyās tena . . . -rupāyā api . . . -paryantavyāpinī* (for *-lakṣaṇayā . . . dhiyā. tena . . . -rupāṇīti yā . . . -paryantā vyāpinī*; see also KA p. 108.5 and 108.22).

259. And rasa is itself a "resting point" or state of absorption.

260. I read *anyasya* (with Kangle, for *anyatra*), though without full conviction.

261. Source unknown.

262. I read *eva* (for *eka-*).

263. A grammatical point is omitted here.

264. I omit the next sentence, which is unintelligible to me (and may be corrupt).

265. I read *ayuvatve* (with Visvesvara, for *ayuktve*).

266. I omit the corrupt illustrative verse and series of glosses that follow.

267. I read *tasyā āsvādya-* (with KA, for *tasyāś cāsvādya-*).

268. *Meghadūta* 2.45.

269. KA adds: "The hope for enjoyment remains uninterrupted in the state of the erotic thwarted; were there absolute despair, we would have the tragic rasa. And if there were no fear of separation even during the course of enjoyment, a woman would never show respect for a compliant and submissive husband—such is the perversity of love" (p. 108.6–8).

270. AmŚ 23 (trans. Ingalls 1965: 223).

271. Or: brought about by a false cognition when the correct cognition has been negated.

272. One expects reference to the student's emulating the Vedic pronunciation of his teacher, but *vyākhyā* seems nowhere to have this sense. For *hevāka*, see ABh 3.187.14.

273. The following clauses cannot construe as given in the received text since such considerations always refer to the *viewer.* Hence my transposition.

274. That of describing, for example, the lovemaking of a real individual. (I read *anaucityāvarjanayogāt* with T 566a fl. 48, for GOS *anaucityavarjanāyogāt.*)

275. For the remainder of this section (especially the next few sentences) the original is riddled with textual problems, and the translation as a result is uncertain.

276. Or perhaps: by the actors.

277. *mahāvākya*, uncertain.

278. The ablative *-paryavasānāt* is hard for me to construe.

279. I read *cittavṛttir nirṇayagatā* (with GOS correction; there is no need for Visvesvara's conjecture *nimagnatā*).

280. T 566a fl. 55 adds a *daṇḍa* here.

281. For *sūcī*, see NŚ 9.279.

282. I conjecture *bhavan* (for *bhavat*).

283. The exposition here is unclear to me.

284. "Five or six moments," *pañcaṣair divasaiḥ*: I follow *Madhusūdhanī*. I doubt one can feel rapture for "five days" since the aesthetic experience ends, for Abhinava, as soon as one leaves the theater. (Sanskrit plays may have been performed over many days, like today's Kuttiyatam, but I know of no evidence for this.)

285. I read *sacamatkāras* (with Gnoli, for *sacamatkāra-*)

286. I read *–rañjakaṃ . . . -pratimaṃ . . . -saṃskāraṃ* (with Gnoli, for *rañjaka- . . . -pratima- . . . -saṃskāra-*).

287. Recall the Bhatta Nayaka likened literature to the beloved, because it seduces one to action (i.e., enjoyment), in contrast to scripture, which commands, or history, which advises.

288. I read *evotpuṃsana-* (for *evanutpuṃsana-*).

289. *anukīrtana-*, NS 1.107.

290. I conjecture *anukṛtam ityādi-* (for *anukṛte 'nyādi-*).

291. NŚ 7.10.

292. No actor has ever actually seen him, and imitation presupposes experience of the original.

293. Bhatta Tota fragment #3a; see his #1a, from which much of the preceding is derived.

294. The syntax of the following five lines in the text is uncertain.

295. The first of the "hindrances"; see ABh 1.274.13, above.

296. I read *-kalpatā* (with Gnoli, for *-kalpanāṭye*).

297. *rūṣita*: a Shaiva technical term, it seems, for the "laden" consciousness of phenomenal life, as opposed to the unladen nature of truly transcendent consciousness (see Jayaratha on *Tantrāloka ahnikā* 4 v. 125; compare *-kāluṣyānārūṣitaṃ svātantryam* in reference to *saṃvid*, IPVV v. 1, p. 49, etc., whereas by contrast the embodied self is *-cittavṛttirūṣita-*, ABh 3.124.11). Aesthetic consciousness, while pure pleasure, is "punctuated" by one's dispositions of pleasure, pain, and the like (ABh 1.284.23, a close parallel).

298. I read *āropitasvarūpaṃ* (with *Madhusūdhanī*, for *āropitaṃ svarūpaṃ*).

299. The four positions are essentially those of the Idealist Buddhists, the Vedantins, the Logicians, and the Prabhakara Mimamsakas.

300. *kīrtana*, uncertain, given that *anukīrtana*, "re-narration," had just been used.

301. This section builds on arguments in DhĀ (and DhĀL) pp. 79–84, above.

302. The discussion concerns not language in general but the technical terms used in aesthetic theory: the names of rasas and of the stable and transitory emotions and physical reactions.

303. As Abhinava elsewhere explains, the bringer of the good news "A son has been born to you" is said to "produce a mental state" (*cittavṛttiṃ janayati*); but literature is a process of verbal meaning production totally different from this everyday sort (DhĀL p. 80.6–7).

304. The negative concomitance is: "Where we do not have the actual word for the rasa we do not apprehend it." These scholars (like Anandavardhana) argue that we do indeed apprehend rasas without any of the actual words being used.

305. The force of *bahiḥ* escapes me here (a dittography for *hi*?).

306. "Acting" includes verbalization. The discussion in ABh on chapter 7 is not extant.

307. Source unknown.

308. Presumably "some other cause" actually related to the aesthetic terms themselves.

309. See n. 23 above.

310. NŚ 6.15, above. Abhinava uses this in the DhĀL to show that citing the terms does not produce a rasa experience (p. 83.8).

311. Source unknown. The verse is cited by Abhinava (DhĀL p. 82) to show that when technical terms *are* used, they have some other purpose than simply restating the transitory emotion.

312. *tadrūpāsparśe*; uncertain, but see *-aspṛṣṭatva* (2.223.3) and other uses below.

313. MM 1.29 (trans. Coulson).

314. Ibid., 5.10.

315. Respectively AmŚ 19, VS 1.3, VU 5.7, AŚ 5.2, *Caurapañcāśikā* 36 (ed. Solf), KS 3.67c.

316. That is, the transitory emotions (Abhinava once again including craving, anomalously).

317. I hesitantly read *-svabhāveṣu* (with *Madhusūdhanī*, for *-svabhāve*).

318. The oldest commentaries are the *Kāvyādarśa* of Someshvara Bhatta (see Parikh's introduction to his edition) and the *Saṃketa* of Ruyyaka, both c. 1150, and both in Kashmir. For the deification of Mammata see *Sudhāsāgara* of Bhimasena Dikshita (1723 C.E.; Pollock 2005: 39 and n.).

319. Mammata shows no clear awareness of ABh 2.221, or of any other part of the work, but the question awaits systematic study.

320. He expands on Someshvara, *Kāvyādarśa*, who differentiates the cessation of material desires (the actual stable emotion of the peaceful) from the cessation of all mental states.

321. Someshvara remarks, "As Bhatta Tota argued in his *Literary Investigations* and Abhinavagupta too, in his commentary thereon," but the only extant source is DhĀL p. 390.

322. That is, nonattachment understood not as absence of attachment but as the presence of a rejection of attachment.

323. Someshvara, whom Shridhara is again following here, refers to the potential absence of *hṛdayasaṃvāda*.

324. With "miserably dressed," Shridhara is alluding to the "lovely" nature of the erotic (see NŚ 1.295, above). I am uncertain about *sarvaprāṇiṣu kāmabhāvaniṣṭhānām*, which seems corrupt.

325. Ascribed to Utpaladeva by Kshemendra (*Aucityavicāracārcā* v. 45 [*Kṣemendralaghukāvyasaṃgraha* p. 29]) but not found in mss. of his *Śivastotrāvalī* (it is attributed

to Munja in *Saduktikarṇāmṛta* v. 2300). Ruyyaka clearly read in *pāda* c *yāntu* (for *yānti* of most KP eds.).

326. In the one case, some condition necessary for rasa development is absent (e.g., the mutuality required for the erotic); in the other, a transitory emotion is highlighted rather than a stable one. But the two situations may not in the end be analytically separable; hence the conflation in some of the commentaries.

327. Utpaladeva, *Śivastotrāvalī*, 13.17.

328. *samūhālambanātmakatva-*, i.e., synthesizing the multiple aesthetic elements.

329. I read *-rāhityād bhāvataiva* (for *rāhityābhāvataiva*).

330. KS 3.67, translated in SKĀ 5.138, above.

331. I conjecture *ajātatvāt* (for *jātatvāt*).

332. I conjecture *apratibandhāt* (for *pratibandhāt*).

333. I read *-māhātmyasmṛtyādhayḥ* (for *-māhātmyādayaḥ*) with Nagesha's *Uddyota*, which borrows from Paramananda (p. 164).

334. If we "chewed" over the verse long enough, the way one eats sugarcane, we would get the full rasa.

335. That is, Mammata.

336. See Gautama, *Nyāyasūtras*, 1.2.4.

337. First in RKA 11.14.

338. First in RKA 11.12.

339. The various attributes of Shiva; the goddess Ganga, who resides in Shiva's headdress, is conventionally viewed by his wife, Parvati, as a rival. While the example was chosen for its naming of the transitory emotions—shame, jealousy, despondency—it also uses words for rasas (the tragic) and stable emotions (amazement).

340. Here and below, the ellipses signal omitted examples.

341. I read *-aparya-* (with *Kāvyādarśa* and *Pradīpa*, for *-parya-*).

342. Such as the man's paralysis. Unless we are given some sense that the man is reacting erotically, we do not respond to this as an erotic poem.

343. Commentators disagree about the subject in the first two lines, and the precise meaning of the verbs.

344. Adduced first in this context by Abhinavagupta (DhĀL p. 362).

345. Rati, the wife of the god of love, laments when he is destroyed by Shiva, in *Kumārasambhava* 4.

346. The example is borrowed from DhĀ p. 340.

347. MVC 2 (untying the bracelet is a ceremony held on the tenth day after the wedding). Breaking off the battle suggests Rama's inability to win.

348. The demon Hayagriva is the antagonist of the (lost) *Hayagrīvavadha* (Vishnu is the protagonist), and the overlong descriptions risks reversing the roles.

349. In the *Ratnāvālī*, Babhravya is the chamberlain of the king of Simhala, and his conversation with King Udayana displaces the centrality of the heroine, Ratnavali (disguised as Sagarika).

350. The sociology of the comic in Bharata is more complex than this: it is "most often" found among women and low-status characters, with a few subvarieties only found among characters of high and middle status (NŚ 6.51–52).

351. A point first raised by Anandavardha, DhĀ, pp. 317–18.

352. KS 3.72.

353. Such as Arjuna in the *Mahābhārata*, as Someshvara notes. He adds that even well-known stories like the *Rāmāyaṇa* should be altered in the interests of propriety, such as occurs in the *Udāttarāghava*, where Lakshmana, not Rama, chases the jeweled deer, and Rama is sent to save him (thus avoiding the impropriety of an inferior protecting a superior).

354. *Karpūramañjarī* 1.16.3 (ed. Konow).

355. DhĀ p. 330, given above.

356. That is, where the transitory emotion is not unambiguously associated with some unique physical reaction (so Jhalkikar).

357. *Ratnāvalī* 1.1.

358. AmŚ 49.

359. Which can indicate a number of other emotions, such as fear or anger.

360. I am assuming Mammata is using *prema*, which is not a transitory emotion, as a synonym of *sneha*, which is.

361. The source of the verse is disputed (it is cited earlier in KP 4.53), but it clearly depicts a prince or king (ruling lineages in India traditionally traced their descent to either the moon or the sun) who is mad with passion for a woman he cannot have.

362. Technically not the erotic but the "oscillation between emotions" (*bhāvaśabalatā*).

363. The pun on the word *sarasa* embodies the "commonness" Mammata refers to in what follows.

364. This answers DhĀ 3.20 (p. 368), which had argued that there is a conflict in this verse between the tragic and the erotic, but it is eliminated by the tragic elements functioning as subordinate components of the erotic.

365. Cited in DhĀ 3.20 (p. 399).

366. The alliteration *mattāṅganāpāṅgabhaṅgalolaṃ*. These last two points are meant to refute DhĀ 3.30.

367. *Nāgānanda* 1.14+. Contrast *Avaloka*, p. 203, above.

368. Source unknown.

369. MBh 11.24.17.

370. Source unknown. The verse is addressed to the Buddha, who out of compassion offered up his body to a lioness with starving cubs. The poet uses the word "even" of the monks feeling longing (that is, feeling compassion) because they are supposed to be dispassionate beings. The two rasas in conflict here are the erotic and, for most commentators, the "heroic in compassion" (for others, the peaceful). The comparison is not between the rasas themselves but between their stimulant factors (the animal bites and mistress's bites, etc.).

371. Source unknown. Brides paint their feet with lac (and the marriage arena is spread with holy *darbha* grass), weep at having to leave their family, feel fear from being without kin while holding their husband's hand, and walk seven times around the marriage fire.

372. Per KP 4.35cd–4.36ab, the stable emotion of desire when directed by a devotee to a god, a child to a parent, or, as here, a client to a patron, differs from its sexual variety. It cannot be "enhanced," so the poem remains "emotion," not rasa.

373. *Hitopadeśa* 2.23.

374. AmŚ 2.

375. Some commentators, including the oldest, Someshvara Bhatta, read (or imply the reading) *-bhāv-* (instead of *prabhāv-*, or understand it as *prakṛṣṭabhāva*), so that it would (as for the former verse) be the *poet's* feeling about god's power that has primacy in the verse,

not god's power itself, with the result that this is *bhāvakāvya*, not *rasakāvya*; this is Arjunavarmadeva's interpretation (see chapter 6.1). Other ancient commentators suggest that there is in fact a dominant rasa here, whether *raudra*, *vīra*, or *adbhuta*.

376. So we indeed have a case where the dominant-subsidiary relationship is itself subordinate to something else—the glory of god (or the poet's desire for god), on which the reader's mind "comes to rest." Moreover, the erotic, which is conveyed by the figure of speech (see below), is "more distant" from this than the tragic, so the former is subordinate to the latter (Someshvara).

377. Cited in DhĀL 3.22 (likely borrowed from *Nyāsa* on *Kāśikāvṛtti* 1.1.5).

378. Mammata (KP p. 574) follows Abhinavagupta in understanding rasa as an experience in which all other contents of consciousness disappear and that in the last analysis is self-identical and singular.

379. That is, the stable emotion of the viewer/reader.

380. The phrase at the start of this sentence, *teṣām sthāyinā saha*, appears to be corrupt.

381. *Pramāṇavārttika* of Dharmakīrti, *kārikā* 262 (ed. Gnoli, p. 137).

382. The position of Ruyyaka himself, as becomes clear in what follows.

383. The position of Shri Shankuka, with which Mahima Bhatta, the author of the text on which Ruyyaka is commenting, in fact agrees.

384. *anupraveśa-*. It is unlikely that the term is used here in the technical sense it has in Kashmir Shaiva philosophy (something like "contemplative absorption").

385. As in the preceding selection, Ruyyaka clearly takes "stable emotion" to refer to the actual feelings of the viewer/reader.

386. Such as would support Mahima Bhatta's rival doctrine of inference.

387. VV p. 80.

5. CONTINUING THE CONTROVERSIES BEYOND KASHMIR, 1200–1400

1. Compare, for example, ND p. 161.21 (*lokasya naṭasya kāvyaśrotranusandhātroḥ prekṣakasya ca rasaḥ*) with RK p. 101.10 (*rasāḥ . . . nāyakanaṭasāmājikāśrayā ity eke*); ND 160.28–161-.1 (*niyataviṣayasmaraṇa-*) with RK 101.19 (*tena sāmānyena smṛtyārūḍho yoṣidādiḥ sāmājikānām ālambanatvaṃ bhajate*), and see also PR p. 205 (*tattadyoṣidviśeṣa-*).

2. Aside from Hemachandra and the author of the contemporary KLV, they are the only scholars who evince knowledge of the text of the ABh. They directly criticize Abhinava's etymology of *nāṭaka* (p. 28; see ABh 3.80.15) and indirectly his theory of rasa as always pleasurable (p. 159.6, below); they also make reference on p. 164 to ABh 1.297.7 (why the erotic enjoyed and the erotic thwarted are not two different species of the erotic), and echo the text elsewhere (see, for example, n. 34 below); Raghavan notes two cases of probably borrowed citations (1963: 861, 890).

3. They rely on the SKĀ and/or the ŚP in their enumeration of the *uparūpakas* (Raghavan 1978: 530, 689).

4. They largely follow him in their assessment of rasa conflicts and faults, pp. 171–76. On the looting of Bhoja's library, see Pollock 2006: 181.

5. Including *Devīcandragupta* of Vishakhadatta and the *Pārthavijaya* of Trilochana; see Raghavan 1978: 574.

6. ABh 1.276, above.

7. Davies 1965: 295. The play was actually long performed with Nahum Tate's happy ending.

8. A distinction first drawn by Dhanika (on DR 4.3ab, p. 171, above).

9. I understand *vābhāvāt* (for *vā bhāvāt*).

10. The term here pertains to both the character and the viewer/reader.

11. I construe *svīkṛta-* with *-avasthaḥ*, assuming it is glossing *śrita-* in the *kārikā*. Note that *sākṣātkṛ* is typically used in reference to the response of the viewer/reader.

12. ABh 1.276.7 and Dhanika on DR 4.43–45ab, above

13. I conjecture *pratīti-* (for *pratīta-*).

14. *mukhya-*; see p. 159.27 (and compare ABh 1.35.19).

15. I conjecture *paridevitādikāryatvāt* (for *paridevitāni[nu]kāryatvāt*).

16. In the actual—painful—lives of the characters.

17. *anusandhāyaka*, unattested in this sense and uncertain; possibly "composer," i.e., author, but the ND does not elsewhere ascribe rasa to the poet.

18. Reactions in the character experiencing the rasa make the rasa known, but so do the reactions in the viewers; see below.

19. "Understanding," *pratipatti-*, here used as a synonym of *pratīti*, "apprehending."

20. It can only derive from some perceptible thing that is invariably concomitant with some imperceptible thing.

21. There should be a *daṇḍa* after *-kṛtaṃ*.

22. The text here and in what follows confusingly speaks only of "others" in reference to both the audience and the character. I try to clarify by expanding the translation.

23. That "reactions" pertain also to the audience seems to have already been suggested by Dhanika (on DR 4.3, see n. 104 there).

24. *strīpuṃsanaṭa-*, not "female and male actors" (compare, e.g., p. 161.16). Rasa exists (necessarily) in the characters, as the authors said at the start, as well as (potentially) in the actors.

25. As they do for the original characters.

26. This refers to the viewer, for whom the specific foundational factor in the case of the character becomes a generalized one (as Dhanika argued, *Avaloka*, pp. 218–19, above).

27. Whereas the woman herself experiences it in reference to a specific object.

28. They only really exist for the other characters in the play.

29. "Differentiation" into general and particular; it is always general.

30. Presumably as when one remembers one's own beloved in the course of experiencing the drama or reading the literary text, though both Bhatta Nayaka, according to Abhinavagupta's account, and implicitly Abhinava (for whom the intrusion of the viewer's real life would seem to fall under his third "hindrance") deny this possibility (see Bhatta Nayaka fragment #1a; ABh 1.275.9; contrast Kumarasvamin, PR, p. 204, below).

31. I read *so 'nyāpratikṣepātmā* (for *so 'nyā[n] prati kṣepātmā*).

32. Literally, "exclusion of nonconnection," i.e., affirmation of connection. The spectators can jointly experience rasa in connection with the same factors.

33. This seems to echo Abhinava's view on the generalized capacity for commonization (p. 273.9–10, above).

34. (*na*) *ādhārānullekhī*. Compare Abhinava's argument that in the state of aesthetic response "the viewer's self is neither completely displaced nor specifically referenced" (*nātmātyantatiraskṛto na viśeṣata ullikhitaḥ*, ABh 1.273.9, above).

35. I conjecture *tatra* (for *atra*); compare p. 160.19.

36. In the storyworld, where she functions as a factor for another character.

37. Where she functions as a factor for the viewer/reader.

38. *vā* in the sense of *iva* (compare 161.17, 162.1).

39. *anubhāvā vā*. See p. 161.19.

40. *parasmin*; compare *pareṣām*, p. 161.19.

41. My translation brings out what I understand to be the implication of "when narrated . . . or imitated" here and in the next sentence: not only do the characters themselves have transitory emotions, so also do the viewer and reader.

42. *loka*, short for *mukhyaloka* as above (p. 159.27).

43. I conjecture *gamyaḥ* (for *gamaḥ*).

44. Rasa in the character is "normal"; that in the audience—foregoing as it does the requisite real object—is "supernormal." The distinction derives ultimately from Dhanika's; see *Avaloka* p. 171, and n. 106, above.

45. *sarasatvam*.

46. The position *kāvyasyātmā rasaḥ* is associated specifically with Vishvanatha in the following century, but Pratiharenduraja knows the *pakṣa*: *rasānāṃ . . . kāvyajīvitatvam* (KASS p. 50, above).

47. On the part of the audience, of the reality of the representation.

48. I.e., on the part of the poet.

49. I conjecture *adhyavasyanti* and *tanmayībhavanti* (for *adhyavasyati* and *tanmayībhavati*)

50. Literally, "they determine Rama . . . to be in the actors."

51. According to Bhatta Nayaka's typology: Veda, which commands like a lord; history, which instructs like a friend; poetry, which seduces like a beloved.

52. *Ekāvalī* 1.7–8.

53. *Ekāvalī* p. 100.

54. Compare for example Mammata's illustrative poem "As they wander the sharp-grass thickets . . ." (KP 7.65, above, chapter 4.3).

55. He could, however, have used his own royal encomia to illustrate "emotion poetry," as Mallinatha observes (see *Ekāvalī* p. 104, below).

56. See VJ 3.7, p. 138, above.

57. ŚP v. 8; SKĀ 5.30, both above.

58. *tiraścām apy asty eva rasaḥ* (p. 106); *anukāryānukartṛgatatvaparihāreṇa sāmājikānāṃ . . . bhāva eva . . . rasaḥ* (pp. 87–88).

59. Usually *utpaladalaśatasūcīvyatibhedanyāya*.

60. If rasa were an effect, it would continue to exist after the disappearance of its causes (the aesthetic elements), the way a pot continues to exist when the potter is no longer there. But it does not (Mallinatha).

61. Mallinatha wishes to tighten the very loose syntax of *-parirambhanirbharatayā* by construing with *samullasan* (88.2), but this seems to me a stretch.

62. Here Vidyadhara is restating Abhinavagupta's views as given in the précis of the KP.

63. This appears to be the first occurrence of the quasi-Vedantic term *āvaraṇa* in the rasa context (compare also p. 91.13). See further on Vishvanathadeva's SSS below.

64. Derived from DhĀ p. 78–83, above.

65. A standard example in Mimamsa (Śabara on PMS 3.8.12).

66. Borrowed in part from KP (ed. Jhalkikar, pp. 225–28), while ignoring *Avaloka* pp. 206–12.

67. I conjecture *-ajñāpyatva-* (for *-jñāpyatva-*).

68. Source unknown.

69. Source unknown.

70. DR 4.43. The second part of the quote is Vidyadhara's own addition.

71. That is, "its presence is indicated by."

72. In the viewer's experience. For *bhūmikāśrayaḥ* here we must understand *cittabhūmikāśrayaḥ* (see Dhanika on DR 4.43–45ab, and n. 236, above; in a rare slip, Mallinatha mistakenly glosses *śṛṅgārādibhedāśrayaṇena*).

73. This is in accordance with the view of Dhanamjaya and Dhanika; see DR 4.43–45ab, *Avaloka* p. 221, and n. 238, above.

74. Vidyadhara cites ŚP 1.6.–7 (in reverse order).

75. Vidyadhara hereafter provides definitions of each rasa.

76. This distinction was systematized by Mammata KP 4.35 (above), which is Vidyadhara's source here.

77. Ascribed to Umapatidhara in *Saduktikarṇāmṛta* 1647.

78. A description of Shiva.

79. I read *dvijādi-* (with Mallinatha, for *dvijāti-*).

80. *Naiṣadīyacarita* 4.52. In death, according to scriptural texts, the mind reverts to the moon. But the moon erroneously takes this to refer to himself, rather than to the moonface of Nala, Damayanti's lover. The god of love provides the correct exegesis.

81. Whose gentle moonbeams she finds fatal in the absence of Nala.

82. *viṣayabhāva-*: translated in accordance with Mallinatha, though strictly this should mean "object" of rasa, not subject (normally *āśraya*; for the terminological instability, see chapter 3, n. 144).

83. KS 3.37.

84. Filliozat 1963: iv–vi.

85. See especially Vidyanatha's remarks on the *bhāvikālaṅkāra* (v. 251): "*bhāvanā* is a visualization that comes from bringing something repeatedly before the mind's eye: a traveler, for example, through the process of *bhāvanā* on his beloved will come to visualize her." For the ND, see p. 160.28–161.1; for the RK, p. 101.

86. On this he is close to Abhinavagupta's *alaukikacamatkārakārī . . . rasaḥ* (see e.g., DhĀL p. 155.5–6; KP. ed. Jhalkikar, p. 93).

87. Bhatta Nayaka fragment #1a; Jayaratha on AS p. 8; Ruyyaka on KP p. 563.

88. Raghavan points out that Kumarasvamin may be the first to argue thus. For earlier theorists the key difference was that, whereas the aesthetic experience comes to an end, the experience of supreme being does not (PR introduction, p. 34).

89. The *Svātmayogapradīpa* appears now to be published in Chitambaran 1998, but is inaccessible to me.

90. The idea here is borrowed in part from Dhanika on DR 4.40–41ab and ND 160.28–161.1, both above, but more directly from RK (p. 101), with the important addition of *tattadyoṣidviśeṣa*.

91. *bhāvuka* (a word used elsewhere in the text [see after 251, *bhāvikālaṅkāra*, "*bhāvukānāṃ hṛdi bhāvanodayāt*") is a common variant for *bhāvaka* in (perhaps only in) south Indian texts; among the earliest occurrences are those in the BhPu (e.g., 1.1.3; PS p. 68 cites a commentarial gloss, *rasaviśeṣabhāvanācatura*).

92. Compare for example DR 4.19, above.

93. Kumarasvamin elaborates on this type below.

94. Bhatta Nayaka's view; see in particular the précis thereon of RAS #1b, above.

95. BhP p. 288.

96. Kumarasvamin's construction does not seem to me to capture the force of Vidyanatha's words or argument.

97. Compare Dhanika on DR 4.40–41ab.

98. NŚ 1.342.10.

99. See DR 4.41cd–42ab, above (Kumarasvamin reads *svecchā hi*, for DR's *svotsāhaḥ*). We use a particularized form to imagine something else, indeed, something within us. Children do not play with clay as such, but with particularized forms of clay; literature in the same way makes use of particularized beings, such as Arjuna.

100. See Dhanika on DR 4.2, from whom much of this paragraph is adopted.

101. I read *pariṇāmatvāt* (with the Balamanorama ed., for *pariṇāma-*).

102. These verses are written in art meters different from the simple verse form of the rest of the treatise, and are therefore meant to carry special significance.

103. I am assuming *pariṇamati* is used almost in the sense, and with the predicative syntax, of *bhavati*. It is possible that *bhāvavibhāvaḥ* is a *bahuvrīhi* modifying *rasabharaḥ* (so Kumarasvamin), but this is a more awkward construction.

104. *rasaprādurbhāvasamaye* glosses *sphuratprādurbhāvaḥ* in the verse (and is not a *bahuvrīhi* with *naṭe*).

105. For an explication, see below 4.138 and n. 119; the idea is similar to Abhinavagupta's (ABh p. 279, above).

106. See Anantadasa on SD 3.23, below.

107. I omit here Kumarasvamin's remarks on a range of traditional questions treated elsewhere in the *Reader*: the unity of rasa though composed of multiple ingredients; the pleasure of sad stories; the multiplicity of rasas despite the rasa experience itself remaining always the same.

108. Compare DR 4.37 and Dhanika thereon, though there it is the stable emotion, not rasa, that is analogized to sentence meaning. Vidyanatha's emendation renders the idea considerably less perspicuous, as does Kumarasvamin's gloss (it is always the viewer/listener's apprehension that is said to "come to rest," not the playwright/poet's).

109. Kumarasvamin here alludes to the *Ekāvalī* (upon which his father had commented): "gradually the stable emotion starts to sprout, branches out, begins to blossom" (*Ekāvalī* p. 86, above).

110. The analogy is found in BhP p. 58.17 (unrelated is the usage in ABh 1.288).

111. BhP p. 159.18.

112. See Bhatta Nayaka fragment #12 and n. 39.

113. PR *Kāvyaprakaraṇa* 5+ (*tātparyo 'pi vyaṅgyārtha eva na punaḥ pṛthagbhūtaḥ*).

114. This radically revises (or, more accurately, confounds) the original view of Dhanika, who in agreement with Bhatta Nayaka rejected the idea that rasa can be "manifested"; it is instead "actualized."

115. BhP p. 305.11 (correct *bhāve* in Kumarasvamin to *bhāvo*); my translation of the last compound is uncertain.

116. I read *-vibhāva-* (for *-bhāva-*).

117. See DR 4.7, above.

118. The storyworld. The idea is Dhanika's (on DR 4.3ab, above).

119. Rasa, like "taste," is not some thing other than the tasting itself, but it can be the object of a second-order cognition, as in the case of self-consciousness.

120. KS 3.50.

121. DhĀL pp. 185–86; trans. Ingalls et al. 1990: 223 (slightly emended). I fail to see how the citation can support, and not contradict, Vidyanatha's argument.

122. BhP p. 153, borrowing from DR 4.38–39, above.

123. The scholar is otherwise unknown; his *Rasanirūpaṇa* is not extant.

124. *ekarasa-*.

125. See n. 89 above.

126. Presumably spoken by a spiritual adept who has had a vision of the divine principle within himself (the original is not available to me). Note the echo of Bhoja's doctrine in viewing desire as the fundament of all particularized rasas.

127. The *Sāhityamīmāṃsā* has been misattributed to the twelfth-century poet Mankha; it is a much later work.

128. *sāmānyakalpanā*, 3.10.

129. 3.20cd–21a.

130. See, however, Kumarasvamin on PR 4.138.

131. SD 5.5. Compare VV p. 59, above.

132. Since Vishvanatha will argue (on 3.2–3 below) that rasa is not a thing but a process, the etymology must be either the passive used in a nonliteral sense (since there is no actual object), or the impersonal passive.

133. Recall that Ruyyaka had explicitly ruled out the yogurt analogy: "This kind of manifestation is independent of any cognition and is simply inherent in the thing itself" (KP p. 570, above). The pot/lamp analogy is Anandavardhana's.

134. DhĀL p. 187. That is, a proleptic expression: it becomes rasa *by being apprehended*. Rasa does not preexist the experience of it (any more than the cooked rice preexists the cooking); on the contrary, it becomes rasa only upon being tasted.

135. Source unknown.

136. The aesthetic elements do not appear as individual components but rather are merged into a whole (later, as in Chandidasa, referred to as *samūhālambātmaka-*, composite cognition).

137. That is, not apprehended as a separate *object* through a second act of thought (apperception), but rendering itself knowable to the subject by its very occurrence: rasa *reveals itself* (as is argued out in what follows). The term here (and elsewhere in SD), *svaprakāśa*, which Vishvanatha was the first to use in the context of rasa theory, has a Vedantic resonance; Abhinava had earlier employed *svasaṃvedana*, which seems to me identical but carries a (Yogacara) Buddhist tone.

138. Or: consciousness that is bliss.

139. SKĀ 5.20.

140. *kāvyārtha-*, that is, the aesthetic elements, the foundational factors and so on. The phrase bears the sense here that it has in DR 4.43, which is cited below (and not Abhinava's, e.g., ABh 1.337.15).

141. See 5.9.

142. See 5.28.

143. See P.5.4.21–22 for the two senses of the *mayaṭ* suffix, *prācurya* and *prakṛta*.

144. Consciousness is not a "predominant part" of rasa but its most "essential" part: rasa and consciousness are identical.

145. *vistāra* [*sic*], a term likely referencing Bhatta Nayaka (Dhanika on DR 4.43). The phrase *vyāpāramātra* below also hearkens back to him (*vyāpārapradhānya-*, fragment #5, above), though Vishvanatha could not have known his writings directly.

146. The source is unknown, as are the two authorities mentioned. Here *camatkāra* is being equated with *vismaya*, the stable emotion of the fantastic rasa.

147. Source unknown.

148. Source unknown. Recall that Kumarasvamin notes that all objects vanish in the experience of rasa except for the aesthetic elements themselves (see above, p. 259).

149. See VV p. 100, above (where *dhruvāgānāt* is found, for *dhruvākhyānāt*). The reference is to drama generally, not to the aesthetic response to music (compare with Ruyyaka ad loc.).

150. Or perhaps, "[other] teachers."

151. DR 4.43. Aesthetic taste, like everyday taste, is no *thing*, but only a pleasurable experience, not an object different from the act.

152. See v. 1.1, n. 132, above. There the commentaries take *rasyate* as impersonal passive ("a taste is had"). Here they offer the standard examples of the reflexive, "The rotten branch breaks of its own accord," or better, "Honey tastes sweet." In all cases, the subject-object split is purely formal and not real.

153. Source unknown, though the phrase *rasyamāntāsāra* is Abhinava's (in DhĀL, e.g., p. 84.8; the term never appears in ABh). "Consciousness as such" (*prakāśaśarīra*, literally "the body which is light"); the phrase is common in Kashmir Shaiva discourse. See also below after v. 3.28.

154. See, for example, vv. 8 and 12.

155. *Pramāṇavārttika* of Dharmakirti, cited by Ruyyaka, *Short Explanation*, p. 578, above.

156. Source unknown. Again, the reference to "function" (*vyāpāra*) echoes Bhatta Nayaka (see above, n. 145).

157. Commentators and manuscripts are in disagreement on this passage. Anantadasa construes the whole passage from *vilakṣaṇa* to *bhavatīti* (which he thus reads) as the direct discourse introduced by *āhus* (whom he calls the ancient authorities). I read *iti* after *vyāpāraḥ* and omit it after *vyapadeśāḥ*. The last line seems to me Vishvanatha's defense (*asmābhiḥ*) of *vyañjanā* despite its logical irrelevance to a theory based on a hermeneutic *vyāpāra* (recall that Bhatta Nayaka firmly rejected *vyañjanā*).

158. On Vishvanatha's hesitations about the *vyañjanāpakṣa*, see the headnote.

159. A king who was forced to give up his kingdom and family.

160. Abhinavagupta, erroneously it appears, attributes the term *druta/druti* to Bhatta Nayaka (see Bhatta Nayaka fragment #1a, above); in DR's classification of Bhatta Nayaka's system, the reaction to *karuṇarasa* is *vikṣepa* (agitation).

161. I read *nanu* (for *tarhi*). A new problem is raised, not a further objection to the preceding one.

162. *rāgīṇām* (not "men passionate about literature," *pace* some commentaries, since this assumes a difference between literary passion and the experience of rasa).

163. *sabhyānām* (not, I think, "people of refinement," which adds an additional and unnecessary conditional).

164. Source unknown.

165. This appears to be a critique of the theory of rasa as something "produced" and "enhanced," and has nothing to do with *sukhajñāna* as *kārya* (so commentators).

166. The touch and the pleasure cannot be the object of one and the same act of cognition (Tarkavāgīśa).

167. Prior, that is, to our awareness of the aesthetic elements. Continuously existing things are continuously available to our awareness, and rasa is not thus available prior to our arrival at the theater.

168. The phrase *abhilāpasaṃsargayogya-* is Dharmakīrti's (*Nyāyabindu* 1.5).

169. Rasa cannot be denoted or connoted by language (the invariable concomitant of conceptual sense experience). It can only be suggested by the aesthetic elements.

170. The author has shown only that rasa awareness is different from other sense perceptions, not that it is not itself a sense perception (Tarkavāgīśa).

171. Or: It is held that the act of relishing on the part of the learned is. . . .

172. The idea comes from Mammata's summary of Abhinavagupta (KP p. 574).

173. Desire and the other emotions may be thought to be insensate (*jaḍa*) and not forms of consciousness, and hence cannot be thought to reveal themselves (like self-awareness).

174. The five following quotations are untraced, and the lack of context makes their interpretation difficult.

175. The author has claimed that rasa consists of "bliss" (3.2) and "sublimity" (3.3).

176. Since the self-manifesting quality of awareness is a basic tenet of Vedantic thought. This is rejected by the proponents of Nyaya, who believe awareness requires an act of second knowledge, or apperception, to be cognized.

177. This is essentially Abhinava's view; ABh 1.289.16 (*carvaṇābhāsasāra*).

178. From what Singabhupala goes on to say, the term *svecchāvṛtti* seems to have a moral sense, referring to a character's "willful," self-willed or improper, behavior (a standard explanation of "semblance of rasa," as in Vidyanatha, p. 106, above; originally Udbhata 4.5, see Induraja ad 4.7, above), yet the BhP quotation points toward a formal sense, where a subsidiary willfully predominates over a principal rasa.

179. This is the only one of the definitions where the primary rasa is associated not with a conflicting rasa (or rasas) but with conflicting stable emotions, which in this case must be those in the mind of the principal character experiencing the violent rasa. (The sole illustration I can locate, SD p. 233, concerns illicit violence, of a brother, Arjuna, against an elder brother, Yudhishthira.)

180. BhP p. 132 (with variations; the author is no doubt quoting from memory).

181. The verse cited (*Hanumannāṭaka* 10.12) is evidence only of the absence of passion, and is not itself an example of *rasābhāsa*.

182. Illustration omitted.

183. AmŚ 43.

184. I read *bodhau* (with Ganapati Sastri, for *buddho*).

185. *Nāgānanda* 1.1. Mara, the god of desire and death, sent his daughters-in-law to seduce the Buddha-to-be and thereby keep him from reaching enlightenment, *bodhi*, which is feminine in Sanskrit, hence their jealousy.

186. RV 7.43.

187. The thought here is unclear (the reading of the text is uncertain).

188. Omitted (source unknown).

189. KS 3.36.

190. *Sattasaī* 4.60. In classical Indian literature, laughter is by convention white. Here, of course, the white teeth are supposed to be showing (presumably the source of the convention), which is also a sign of vulgarity.

191. See *Ekāvalī* p. 106.4–9, above.

192. I may be mistakenly reading negative connotations into the terms *cittam anuvartamānena* and *-abhimāninaḥ*.

193. See *Ekāvali* p. 106.4–9, above.

194. NŚ 1.294–295, given above.

195. As Vidyadhara does by his example, p. 106.

196. *Ekāvalī* p. 106.8–9.

197. Foundational factors (such as a woman) *become* foundational factors only if they are appropriate and known to be such by the subject (e.g., the man who is a potential lover).

198. Presumably: for another animal and hence for the audience. Singabhupala here and in the next sentence seems to be shifting the focus of the argument: from the character (and whether the animal can be a foundational factor for another animal) to the viewer (and whether that animal can be a foundational factor for him).

199. The spectator watching a play about an uncultured person, not the uncultured person himself.

200. The uncultured person in the play.

201. *Ekāvalī* p. 106.8, above.

202. While the two qualifications are somewhat opaque to me, the author seems to be arguing that "distinction" is not some natural property, but exists only in the act of *discerning* an entity's distinctive features.

203. RV 1.56 (*anvāsitam* v. l. for *anvāsīnam*).

204. An act of discernment, however, would show that these cannot be foundational factors of the erotic, given that the man and woman are both ascetics.

205. That is, not as the object of any particular discernment.

206. I conjecture *śrutaḥ* (with Ganapati Sastri, for *śabdataḥ*, which seems itself to be a conjecture).

6. RASA IN THE EARLY MODERN WORLD, 1200–1650

1. Introduction to the commentary, v. 5.

2. The second poem in particular had been the object of bravura analysis by Anandavardhana (DhĀ 3.20), Bhoja (ŚP 9.370, 11.117; SKĀ 5. 499, p. 731; so 1.146, p. 133), and Mammata (KP 7.65, given above), and would continue to elicit comment for centuries, among Mammata's commentators and elsewhere.

3. See DhĀ p. 196, and KP 7.65, see notes 375–76.

4. Someshvara Bhatta on the KP actually reads *bhāvātiśayasya* (for *prabhāvātiśayasya*). See chapter 4.3 n. 375, and n. 13 below.

5. A number of the Amaru poems are about adulterous love affairs.

6. Author of the *Kāmasūtra*.

7. Possibly a reference to the view of the commentator Vemabhupala (though he does not enumerate gestures, he takes the figure of the bow literally).

8. The straightforward translation in what follows, "the simile becomes the rasa-laden ornament," is impossible, since as the following quotation, as well as the comments on the next two poems, make clear, it is rasa itself that in such circumstances becomes an ornament, not an ornament that takes on traits of rasa. (I find no v. l. in the mss. consulted.)

9. And the rasa-laden statement itself is functioning as an ornament to the subject matter. Arjuna cites DhĀ 2.5, above.

10. See KP 7.65, above.

11. DhĀ 3.20 (correct *vācyānām* to *bādhyānām*).

12. From Someshvara Bhatta on KP (p. 2227). Arjuna also cites as an example the famous verse on Bhurishravas's hand from the MBh (11.24.17), see KP 7.65, above.

13. The text here, *ananubhūtānyaviṣayatayā*, is probably corrupt (though mss. offer no good alternative). Chandidas, a later commentator on KP (7.65), notes that the figure "like a lover" can be interpreted either as a poetic fantasy (*utprekṣā*) (the women react as if it were the case, which it cannot be, that this fire is a husband), or as a simile (they react as was actually the case in the past when their husbands misbehaved). Arjuna is apparently pointing to the latter.

14. Understand *api* (as *bhinnakrama*) with what follows.

15. I read *rasasaṃgatau* (with Jaipur Pothikhana ms. #525, for *rasatāṃ gatau* of all editions).

16. In Arjuna's mind is no doubt Someshvara Bhatta: "The (poet's) emotion of desire, consisting of the ornament called the 'affectionate utterance,' is here rendered the subject matter that functions as dominant element" (KP p. 2227).

17. I conjecture *aṅgitvam* (for *aṅgatvam*) and *-āpekṣayaiva* (for *-āv eka eva*).

18. Abhinavagupta. The v. is not found in the ABh, but the idea is expressed in DhĀ 3.7, p. 325. But it is interesting that Arjuna refers to Abhinava as the author of a work he most certainly never saw (rather than as author of *The Eye*).

19. All of these illustrations have been omitted here, but they are available in RT, ed. Pollock.

20. ABh 1.266.11–15 (reading *tv* for *bhavati* with Hemachandra). The citations are from KĀ 2.279, 281, above.

21. Fragment #1a.

22. ABh 1.278.13.

23. *Bhāv Vilās* 3.2 (in the definition verse, 3.1, he speaks of rasa as a "fully developed *vāsanā*" of the *sthāyī*: *thiti kī pūrana vāsanā sukavi kaha rasa soi*; I thank Allison Busch for the reference).

24. Bhanu uses the rare term *aupanayika*.

25. The later critique of Bhanu's position is charted in Raghavan 1975: 155–58.

26. See Pollock, ed., 2009: xix and n.

27. The numbering is according to my edition; see there for further text-critical annotation and interpretation.

28. Compare Vachaspatimishra: *na ca svalakṣaṇānurodhena lakṣyasyānyathākaraṇaṃ yuktaṃ parīkṣyakāriṇām* (*Nyāyavārttikatātparyaṭīkā* in *Nyāyadarśana* p. 137).

29. Of a scene or the work as a whole.

30. *aparipūrṇa*. In other words, it has not reached the state of a developed rasa.

31. Unclear; perhaps what is meant is that "reactions" are not actually reactions, but the visible means by which characters react to rasa.

32. Contiguity, inherence, and the rest (*Tarkasaṃgraha* p. 22).

33. If we are to be consistent—though I am unsure about the accuracy of this interpretation—the third form of supermundane rasa would be the character's experience of a play (within the play), which is normally (for the actual viewer) considered a purely pleasurable experience. The rasas of dream and the imagination can obviously have an admixture of sorrow.

34. *Śatakatrayam* 3.14.

35. See *Pañcadaśī* 11.87, *pratibimbānanda*, referring to a joy "reflected" or even imagined (the other two are *brahmānanda* and *vāsanānanda*). The "bliss" is what is experienced by the speaker in the poem, and bliss and rasa are essentially coextensive.

36. It is unclear why affection should be a transitory emotion of the tragic in the case of a child (unless the child's very "disappearance" as it grows up is implied). Note that Jiva Gosvamin concurs; see PS p. 66.14, below ("rasa of compassion, or in other words, parental affection"). Compare also ABh 1.335 above.

37. For the twelfth-century commentator Shridharasvamin see the introduction, n. 80. The first mention of the term *bhaktirasa* is found in the tenth-century Shaiva *Stavacintāmaṇi* of Bhatta Narayana (v. 50), but whether it is used in an aesthetic sense or nontechnically ("nectar of devotion") cannot be determined (Stainton 2013: 175–78).

38. There is some uncertainty, due to assertions in the work itself, about its real author: Hemadri asked Vopadeva to allow the *Pearls* to pass under his own, Hemadri's, name, though it was actually the work of Vopadeva (BhM pp. 2, 321). Perhaps this was simply a kind of compliment.

39. BhPu 6.1.19.

40. The distinction (*vihita/avihita*) corresponds to the later *vaidhi/rāgānuga* pair (see BhRAS 1.2.6, 270): bhakti that derives from a scriptural commandment (preeminently the BhPu) and bhakti that "follows the trend of devotion and attachment of the people of Vraja who stood in actual relation to Krishna" (De 1932: 651).

41. *Śṛṅgāratilaka* 1.16.

42. BhPu 7.31.

43. Below Hemadri explains this new ordering (rather than "the erotic and the rest").

44. Synonyms of sensitivity, volitility, and stolidity.

45. Bharata.

46. Vopadeva.

47. *alpaparikaratvāt*; uncertain.

48. Hemadri cites DR 4.1 and Dhanika ad loc. and goes on to list the *vibhāvas* and *anubhāvas* from DR 4.4–8 and 4.26.

49. Lovers of Vishnu in his Krishna avatar.

50. I conjecture *-nayebhyaś* (for *-nayaś*).

51. KP 4.17; the sequence of Hemadri's thoughts seems to require that we understand the preceding two sentences as parenthetical, as I have done.

52. Source unknown, but perhaps borrowed from Shridhara; Bhoja defends the same idea, see ŚP 1.12+, above, and n. 71 there for Shridhara. Jiva Goswami, given his theology of practice, rejects the superiority of poetry to "drama" (see PS p. 70, below), as does Bhatta Tota (fragment #5, above) but for intellectual reasons.

53. I.e., that it is not a separate rasa but rather is to be categorized under one of the nine canonical rasas. See KA p. 106.15 and ABh 1.335.14 (the one time bhakti is mentioned in connection with rasa in the ABh; the passage parallel to KA, 1.261, is silent about bhakti, as is

DhĀL). Hemadri shows no other knowledge of the ABh elsewhere, and it is unclear how he would have been aware of Abhinava's position.

54. An argument made already by others; see, for example, Shridhara on KP 4, above.

55. See ŚP p. 632; SKĀ 5.23, 33.

56. ŚP p. 632.25; see also SKĀ 5.23, and the verse on p. 598.

57. While *vatsala* usually concerns parental affection, Bhoja cites the poem in the context of *śṛṅgāra*.

58. *viṣayasaundarya-*, compare SKĀ 5.8 (prose).

59. For Bhoja the stable emotion is actually *ahaṅkāra* (ŚP p. 683; Hemadri throughout appears to be citing SKĀ rather than ŚP, though in any case his understanding of Bhoja is imperfect).

60. MVC 1.31.

61. See ŚP 633, above.

62. SKĀ 5.16,18.

63. And hence there are nine species of the devotional rasa that arises when a devotee hears or reads the stories of Krishna (the devotion rasa thus being conceived of as the overarching category and not a separate rasa).

64. The women are watching as Krishna leaves the capital.

65. BhPu 1.10.21 and the six verses that follow are omitted here. This illustrates the enjoyment of seeing (a clarification omitted by Hemadri, or lost).

66. The women of Hastinapura are still speaking.

67. BhPu 1.10.27.

68. The following eight verses are omitted.

69. I (rather desperately) conjecture *-ānubhāvābhāvāt* (for *-ānubhāvāt*).

70. Here it is evident that the distinction between rasa in the viewer/reader and rasa in the character (the latter of which Hemadri claims, as we have seen, not to accept) almost vanishes.

71. BhPu 1.10.31.

72. The demon Bhauma's captive women, whom Krishna set free and married.

73. BhPu 10.59.44 (I follow Hemadri's syntactical analysis, rather than Shridhara's, and omit v. 45). The following verses, omitted here (BhPu 10.41.27–28), pertain to intercourse with the women of Mathura.

74. BhPu 10.44.13, vv. 10.44.14, 10.29.31–32 are omitted.

75. Only very occasionally in the remainder of the commentary is there explicit discussion of *bhaktirasa* as such. Thus on 19.1 (p. 299), the presentation of the heroic rasa, Hemadri notes that "With these three types of heroic rasa in mind, the author believes that the experience of the devotional rasa is impossible in the form of the 'heroic in battle,' and so begins with the 'heroic in munificence.'"

76. The commentary, published as anonymous by its first editor, was attributed to Lokanatha by De 1988: 257, though without providing evidence (a commentator of that name wrote also on the *Vālmīki Rāmāyaṇa*). Several other commentaries are known, including a *Sārabodhinī* by Vishvanatha Chakravartin, but the commentary recently printed under his name is in fact identical with that of Lokanatha.

77. *parokṣa* and *pratyakṣa*.

78. *prākṛta* and *aprākṛta*.

79. AK 5.63 (p. 122), and p. 141.

80. It is of course also mentioned in SKĀ, and Jiva shows he knew this text (PS p. 66).

81. See Lokanatha's comment, p. 141.

82. Such as the doctrine of five primary and seven secondary rasas (see next selection, n. 149).

83. See n. 90 below on the stable emotion named, simply, "emotion." Similarly Kavikarnapura's discussion of the charge of impropriety of Krishna's love affairs with the married women of Vraja; see n. 106, and PS pp. 119–21, both below.

84. The opposition was clear to Lokanatha, who was familiar with Jiva's writings. See his comment on v. 72.

85. The "supernatural" rasa is described on AK p. 131. As Bhattacharaya points out, Lokanatha's concern lies in the fact that Kavikarnapura holds rasa to belong solely to the audience, rejecting the reality of the rasa in the characters, which for Rupa and Jiva Gosvamin constitutes the primacy of *bhaktirasa*. Kavikarnapura's "deference" to the literary-critical tradition lies in his accepting that rasa must be pleasurable and hence can only pertain to the audience, and not the characters.

86. "The root": quoting SD 3.174.

87. I conjecture *eka* (for *eṣa* in both printed eds.) in 63c, in accordance with the *vṛtti* and the later reference *eka eva . . . sthāyī* (p. 130.1). The aesthetic mental state is always pleasurable, regardless of the particular mood of the aesthetic object.

88. *svatantra*, literally, "independently" various, whereas the stable emotion of the viewer is *dependent* on the characters' emotions.

89. Bhoja's views are more complicated than Kavikarnapura appears to know, though it is true that both *vātsalya* and *prema* are added in ŚP (*kārikā* 6 et passim).

90. A technical use of the term (AK p. 147 below), deriving ultimately from Pratiharenduraja (on KASS 4.2) and affirmed for religious poetry in KP 4.35cd–4.36ab.

91. Reading with the editor's conjecture.

92. As the editor points out, Lokanatha's view is that of theological aesthetics, not that of literary theory. In addition, the emotion that Lokanatha here reckons a species of desire will later be distinguished from it (PS p. 100, below).

93. Lokanatha first claims that the aesthetic elements are not cognized (*abhānam*) when one is experiencing rasa, but in his conclusion he suggests that for Kavikarnapura the elements had to remain cognizable (*-sahitasyaiva*, etc.). See also the discussion of Kumarasvamin, PR p. 206, above.

94. Lokanatha takes "characters" to refer the "supernatural" characters mentioned below, which he further identifies as the "devotees," presumably those in the literary texts (compare Jiva Gosvamin on BRAS 2.5.100, below). The characters of high status will be the hero and heroine of the narrative, those to whom the "principal" (*aṅgi-*) rasa of the work refers.

95. Lokanatha understands, "'It is the stable emotion,' sc., that undergoes change." But in the following *vṛtti* it is the multiplicity of rasa that is at issue.

96. Lokanatha doubts the authenticity of the passage offering the analogy, and indeed, it is amiss (the example should illustrate the appearance of diversity of an entity through its conditioning factors, not its unity despite the conditioning factors).

97. Or in many, as in the case of the comic (p. 142).

98. For Rupa, there would appear to be no *rasābhāsa* of this sort. The only impropriety he recognizes is the ascription of emotion to insentient things or animals (BhRAS 2.4.228).

99. Malati was betrothed by the king to his brother-in-law in the MM, Rukmini by her elder brother to Shishupala in the MBh.

100. The text (source unknown) appears to be discussing a specific example, but I translate as a more general declaration.

101. I conjecture *tathā hi* (for *tathāpi*).

102. Source unknown.

103. *anaucityarītyā*. The reading *aucityarītyā* would certainly be easier.

104. *śrūyate*, or "given in scripture," as Lokanatha implies with his gloss: "in the poems and plays of great adepts (*mahānubhāva*)."

105. MBh 6.6.11 (variant). Also cited by Rupa Gosvamin, BSAS, 2.5.92cd, but in a different context.

106. For Rupa, the women of Vraja never had actual sexual intercourse with their husbands (De 1932: 676); for Jiva, the women, seen from the transcendental perspective, are not women at all but *śaktis* of the deity (PS p. 121). See also *Ujjvalanīlamaṇi* p. 99: "The fact that a married woman is not permitted to be involved in the principal rasa in a drama is a rule promulgated only with respect to ordinary vulgar heroines. To quote: 'That a married woman is not permitted by poets to be involved with the dominant rasa does not apply to the women of Gokula, whose very avatars were instigated by Krishna, enemy of Kamsa and crestjewel in the circle of *rasikas*, in the hope of enjoying rasa.'"

107. "Pure love," *kevalānurāga*, a technical term, like *kevalaprema* in BhRAS 4.6.14. I read *cetorañjakatāyāḥ* (with Haridasasastri, for *cetorañjakatayā*).

108. Kavikarnapura is distinguishing his work not so much from those concerned with the rasa of real-life devotees as from those concerned in other ways with the spiritual dimension of rasa (so the editor ad loc.).

109. The characters in the Krishna story (the cowherd women, Uddhava, and so on) are also considered devotees (BhM, p. 167 with Hemadri, above). Kavikarnapura's argument suggests we are still at some historical remove from the view that the audience members are not only devotees but actual characters in the living pageant of Krishna.

110. When we are watching a play about them, the real characters—Rama, Sita, and so on—no longer actually exist (see Bhatta Nayaka's position, as explained by Dhanika, DR p. 210, above).

111. Compare SD 3.2–3, above.

112. Borrowed from Shri Shankuka fragment #1a, above (as is much else in the paragraph), mediated most likely through DhĀL or KP.

113. The argument that follows presupposes that the stable emotions exist only in the characters, whereas the audience feels only pleasure no matter what the nature of the stable emotion represented (fear, repugnance, etc.) may be.

114. The world of the viewer/reader.

115. KP 4.44 (ed. Jhalkikar, p. 98).

116. I.e., since all the viewer's rasas are pleasurable.

117. The hero's friend who saves the heroine Malati when she is attacked by a tiger in MM.

118. A mundane character cannot feel joy in the face of fear and so cannot truly have a rasa experience; by contrast, the audience does have a joyful experience of the fearful rasa.

119. The twelve rasas are the standard eight and the peaceful, plus three described earlier (AK p. 123) and again in what follows: the rasas of parental affection, love (*prema*), and devotion, with their stable emotions possessiveness (*mamakāra*), tenderness (*cittadrava*)

(p. 122), and desire understood asexually as "a mental state of delight." It is unclear why there should be ten and not eleven forms of the devotional rasa (not twelve, of course, since the devotional cannot be a subvariety of itself), unless this has something to do with the relationship of "love" and "the erotic" discussed on AK pp. 148–49. (The ten listed by the editor, p. 148 n., are not the "stable emotions" that Kavikarnapura specifically names.)

120. He means: because we are really one. The v. is presumably the author's own.

121. *cittadrava*, a new stable emotion.

122. See headnote for the unlikely connection with Bhoja's doctrine.

123. Source unknown.

124. The argument is convoluted, but this is inevitable in reworking the older notion of "emotion" poetry (especially in relationship to a deity), where the stable emotion cannot be fully developed, into the new devotional rasa. The parallel with *Ujjvalanīlamaṇi* (*sthāyibhāvaprakaraṇa* 142, p. 459, "emotion" as love, *anurāga*) may not indicate borrowing but only shared understanding.

125. The original characters imagined to be speaking in the verse.

126. Further detail in Haberman 2003: xxxi–xxxiii.

127. BhM 12.72 (p. 212) is cited in *Ujjvalanīlamaṇi* p. 450 on *premavaicitrya* (love that leaves a woman unsatiated). He knows nothing of Kavikarnapura.

128. *bhagavatprīti*.

129. De 1932: 652–53.

130. Haberman 2003: lxvii.

131. ABh 1.271.5, 279, 285, above.

132. See PS pp. 68–70, below; see also De 1932: 656 n.

133. This is made clear by Lokanatha on AK pp. 118, 131.

134. Jiva takes on the latter issue directly in PS 110 [65.17], below. On the explicit exclusion of the Vedas from "literature," see Bhatta Tota fragment #2, above.

135. See again Lokanatha on AK p. 131, above.

136. The "erotic" was described only synoptically in the BhRAS, Rupa tells us, because it is "secret doctrine" (*rahasyatvāt*) and hence reserved for a second, esoteric text, namely, the *Ujjvalanīlamaṇi* (see 1.2).

137. It is unclear what earlier portion of the work is meant (but see the later echoes, 2.5.2 and 2.5.72).

138. *śravaṇādibhih*. Compare 2.5.63.

139. Those produced by past lives and in the present.

140. I.e., as distinct from desire.

141. So Jiva.

142. The reading *-anubhavādbhutaḥ* strikes me as dubious.

143. The original confusingly reverses the concessive clause ("One may become aware . . . although the rapture. . . .").

144. The first verse is untraced; the second is SD 3.261.

145. See also PS110 [65.17], below, and BhR 2.75–76.

146. MBh 6.6.11 (actually, the "Book of Bhishma," not the "Book of Effort"); the "ancients" include Shankara, who cites the verse in his commentary on *Brahmasūtra* 2.1.6 (as noted also by Jiva).

147. There is no such verse in the NŚ; the idea is Bhatta Nayaka's.

148. That is, when the character is separated from Krishna.

149. Krishna showed his virtues in the fullest plenitude (the third of the three stages of the plenitude of his earthly manifestation, BhRAS 2.1.220–223) when he was a boy in Vraja, something equal to (or even greater than, see BhRAS 1.2.58, cited by Jiva) his grandeur as universal lord (in the case of Shri) or actual husband (in the case of Rukmini, both likely indicated by *ramā*; see Jiva). Rupa goes on to discuss primary and secondary types of the devotional rasa.

150. *rasaśāstrīya-*, a neologism. Jiva here cites DR 4.34, above.

151. That is, the Blessed One, his attendants, the sound of his flute, and so on.

152. Source unknown.

153. Here used in the sense of scholars, rather than people who experience the rasa. He may have in mind Hemachandra or even Abhinavagupta (see BhM p. 167, above).

154. The son of the antigod Hiranyakashipu, he resisted his father's admonitions and remained firm in his devotion to Vishnu (BhPu 7.8).

155. Jiva cites SD 3.2, 3.8, above. He goes on to briefly contrast the difference between mundane and supermundane rasa in their origin and the mode of aesthetic experience, citing SD 3.2 for the former and BhPu 4.3.23 for the latter, which also is said to exceed the experience of *brahma* (BhPu 4.9.10).

156. Jiva apparently sees the last two as subtypes of one rasa.

157. Jiva here cites Dharmadatta from the SD 3.2, above.

158. On BhPu 10.43.17.

159. Jiva cites SKĀ 5.23 and illustration v. 74, perhaps borrowed from BhM.

160. Jiva cites BhPu 11.19.41 and 36.

161. Jiva cites BhPu 1.5.10–11, as well as Rukmini's statement in 10.60.45.

162. Jiva cites BhPu 10.21.19 and 10.17.15.

163. BhPu 1.1.3. Jiva here offers an extended exegesis of the verse.

164. Whereas the real rasa experience must by definition be entirely pleasurable. See SD 3.17, above, from which Jiva borrows some of his ideas here.

165. That is, present-day devotees.

166. Presumably the arguments on, e.g., PS p. 1.

167. The "goddesses" refer to the cowherd wives; Vritra was a demon beheaded by Indra and merged with Narayana (BhPu 6.7–13); the elephant king called upon Narayana to rescue him from a crocodile (BhPu 8.2–4); Shuka is the narrator of the BhPu; Bharata (Jadabharata, Bharata the Mute) was reborn as a deer for ignoring Narayana, and then as a Brahman who sought divine wisdom, and thus is the only case that seems to illustrate Jiva's point.

168. Jiva here (and below where ellipses are provided) cites various descriptions from the BhPu of, for example, Krishna's eyes and his flute.

169. *Brahmasaṃhitā* 5.67–68, a description of Shvetadvipa, home of Vishnu. Jiva notes that, when the verse goes on to list song as something "relished," it shows that "like drama, singing is also productive of rasa," one of the few explicit references to the existence of rasa in domains other than literary.

170. Jiva here cites SD 3.13.

171. I conjecture *iva* (for *eva*).

172. I conjecture *antaḥpāta* (for *antapātaḥ*).

173. Presumably a reference to *Bhagavadgītā* (e.g., 18.68). Technically, the tragic rasa requires that the separation of the lovers be permanent; this feature alone distinguishes it from the erotic thwarted.

174. Vasudeva was Krishna's father, Gada, Krishna's brother.

175. Rather than the character, the actor, and the viewer.

176. Krishna's principal accoutrement.

177. Jiva cites various proof texts in the course of these arguments, including BhPu 7.4.36–41.

178. The idea, implied already by Pratiharenduraja (on KASS 4.2, above; see n. 125), is explicitly formulated first in SD 3.16cd–17ab.

179. Jiva here cites SD 3.15.

180. I conjecture -*anukūla* (for -*anukūlya*-).

181. Dharasura is located in Andhra in the Telugu *Jaiminīya Bharatamu* (see Ramaraju 2002: 520; I am unable to confirm this).

182. So Pratap in his edition; see 1978: 33 (where the key parallels are also listed).

183. Important variants from the *Kāvyaparīkṣā* are included in the notes to the translation that follows. In an earlier publication I tentatively placed Shrivatsa in the 1560s (Pollock 2005: 22). That date should now be revised upward at least a generation.

184. The standard nine plus *preyān*, *dānta* (*sic*, for *udātta*), and *uddhata* (taken from Bhoja).

185. See Minkowski 2011.

186. DR 4.43, above.

187. The key term is *āvaraṇabhaṅga* or *bhagnāvaraṇatva* (*āvaraṇa* had already been used in rasa discourse in Mallinatha's commentary on the *Ekāvalī*, p. 88.21).

188. *Pace* Tubb and Bronner 2008: 625. Abhinava's actually terminology (*nirvighnasvasaṃvedana*, ABh 1.261; *nirvighnapratīti*, 1.273, 284) does not necessarily aim at the same thing.

189. It is not entirely clear, despite the origins of the idea in a mystical treatise, that anything particularly mystical adheres to this notion of "removing the veil" of ignorance in Vishvanathadeva's (and later Jagannatha's) treatment. A general epistemological sense is suggested as early as Shankara's commentary on the *Bṛhadāraṇyaka Upaniṣad* 1.5.18.

190. The term is used in Vedanta to describe phenomenal reality as such.

191. *taddharmarateḥ sākṣibhāsyāyāḥ* (referring to the viewer/reader's emotion, as in the *sākṣibhāsyo ratyādiḥ* that follows). *sākṣibhāsya*, a technical term common in Vedanta, refers to the ontological status of the object of affective states, erroneous cognitions, and other internal events. In other cognitions, consciousness in conjunction with the mind (*antaḥkaraṇa*) illuminates external objects.

192. *Uddyota*, pp. 119–20.

193. A reference to KP 1.2.

194. Vishvanathadeva is referring to himself.

195. *hāsya* (expect *hāsa*) appears also in Shrivatsa's version. See also above, chapter 3 n. 158.

196. Vishvanathadeva here adds a note attempting to explain the two spellings of the term, *sahacāri* and *sahakāri*.

197. The author defers but will return in due course to the specific question of Sita's status as a foundational factor.

198. A state or modification of the mind where it assumes the form of—that is, possesses as internalized content—the object it is cognizing.

199. That is, of the viewer/reader; see p. 92.

200. Shrivatsa adds: "The self, which itself remains unknown, shines forth, and were that lacking, perception and the other cognitive instruments would not be capable of providing cognition, i.e., knowledge of something that is unknown" (*Kāvyaparīkṣā* p. 15).

201. Compare RG pp. 25, 27, below.

202. *Tattirīya Upaniṣad* 2.7.1. The passage itself has nothing to do with the rasa of aesthetic discourse, but a long history of etymological speculation in the Vedas authorized this sort of equivalence (see *Taittirīyopaniṣadbhāṣyavārttika* 2.422–426; also Gangadhara Sastri, ed., RG p. 40 n.).

203. Not NŚ but DR 4.43 (with *ātmānanda-* instead of *brahmānanda*). Others also cite as "Bharata" Dhanamjaya or Dhanika (thus Shrivatsa quoting Dhanika; see KP p. 602.29 and DR p. 219.1), or even Bhatta Nayaka (see n. 147 above).

204. KP (BHU ed.) p. 130, in restating the position of Abhinavagupta.

205. *vṛtti* here refers to the psychological, not the linguistic modality (compare RG p. 26).

206. SKĀ 5.1, above (Vishvanathadeva cites 5.2–4 as well, and an untraced Prakrit verse, "To the nature of the poet corresponds the charm of his literary composition"). This is followed by a more or less accurate summary of Abhinava's theory from KP.

207. That is, it is itself a form of consciousness and hence self-revealing. (Here follows a sentence that seems to be an insertion, since it interrupts the argument: "It can be said to arise only metaphorically, from the arising of relishing.")

208. *Pañcadaśī* 7.90cd, 92ab. The two verses enunciate, in the case of consciousness itself, at once the necessity of cognition and its limits. As Vidyaranya goes on to add, "To see a pot we indeed need both eyes and light; to see light, however, we need only eyes, not a second light." Rasa is a form of consciousness, and like consciousness it is cognized by the mind—that is, the mind removes anything obscuring rasa or consciousness—but again, like consciousness, it is not an object illuminated but rather is itself illumination. For a thing to be illuminated by a lamp, anything covering the thing needs to be removed, and this is what the "cognitive process" achieves. But whereas normal objects then require consciousness to illuminate them, rasa, or consciousness itself, does not.

209. As Jagannatha shows (RG p. 28, below) and Vedanta discussions of the *mahāvākya* confirm, the point of the parallel is that both rasa and scripture are phenomena of human language, but unlike any other, since they produce a superhuman, transcendent effect.

210. I read *yat sākṣād aparokṣād brahma* (see *Bṛhadāraṇyaka Upaniṣad* 3.4.1, for *yaḥ sākṣād aparo brahma*).

211. Pollock 2011: 40.

212. See *Bhāminīvilāsa* 4.32; Pollock 2001a: 404–12 for other references in what follows.

213. The title makes reference to Shiva, its planned five chapters (only two were completed) being called "faces" in a play on *pañcānana śiva*, the "five-faced" aspect of the deity.

214. See below, n. 247.

215. See in general Pollock 2001b; with particular reference to Jagannatha, Tubb and Bronner 2008.

216. Or perhaps not so new, given the view Abhinavagupta attributes to Bhatta Lollata (and ridicules); see Bhatta Lollata fragment #2a and n. 175, above.

217. Shakuntala, in the drama of that name by Kalidasa.

218. In Vedanta the self is conceived as having three aspects: existential (*sat*), cognitive (*cit*), and affective (*ānanda*). Nonaesthetic insight may remove the cognitive obscurations of

the self, but not necessarily the affective ones. As Jagannatha will note, the unveiling that occurs in an aesthetic experience is transitory ("for the time being," that is, so long as "actualizing" insight lasts), unlike the unveiling that occurs in a mystical experience.

219. Not all readers have the dispositions that make them sensitive to literature. See Dharmadatta, cited SD 3.8cd+, above.

220. Much of the following recapitulates Mammata (the actual quote is from KP 4 *kārikā* 28), though Abhinava nowhere mentions the unknowing that obscures the "bliss component" of the self (see SSS n. 188 above). In the midst of this exposition Jagannatha introduces a second analysis of Abhinava (*yad vā*, p. 26.10), followed by his own correction (*vastutas tu*, p. 27.3).

221. I add the genitive phrase here and below for the sake of clarity. Jagannatha is most decidedly not referring to the stable emotion in the character.

222. Abhinava nowhere defines *vyakta/vyakti/vyañjanā* in this way. For the history of the transformation of "manifestation" see sections 4.2 and 4.6 of the introduction.

223. Nagesha formulates the question to which the following section is intended as the response: "It may be that the aesthetic elements can be said to be illuminated insofar as they are considered predispositions in the observing subject, but how can the elements in themselves be illuminated by one's consciousness, with which they have no collocation and hence no connection?"

224. On this technical Vedanta phrase see above, n. 191.

225. The two different examples highlight two different processes: the former accounts for the purely internal, imaginary existence of the aesthetic elements, whereas the latter explains how, for example, a foundational factor like Shakuntala can be "perceived" in the actress (Ojha p. 72).

226. The clause is added in accordance with Ojha (p. 72).

227. The mention of the *tālu* (palate) would seem to require *jakāra-* (for *gakāra-*), though *gakāra* (referring to the first phoneme in the word for cow, *gauḥ*) is normal in such contexts (see also *Nyāyamañjarī* vol. 2, p. 151).

228. I translate the printed *vibhāvādicarvaṇā-*, but Madhusudhan Shastri's conjecture *bhāvanāviśeṣa-*, "the power of a particular kind of 'actualization'" (see 25.11, 30.6, which he may also be right to attach to *-tattatsthāyi-*) is required, though it lacks ms. support and leaves the origin of the variant unexplained (perhaps an old dittograph; see line 1).

229. Compare *sthāyyupahitacidānanda-* in the summary (34.12).

230. "This is because the aesthetic state is not a form of consciousness delimited by a mental state" (as normal states are), according to Nagesha (I do not see the corruption in this gloss that Ojha finds). See below, p. 27.12; the experience of rasa is *tad*[i.e., *rasa*]*ākārāntaḥkaraṇavṛtti*.

231. The subtle distinction between the stable emotion and consciousness of the emotion was made first, it would appear, in the SRĀ 7.1352–1356 (perhaps parallel is BhR 3.12–13, which defines rasa as either the "sensitive mentality" produced by the aesthetic elements or the pleasure that results).

232. I read *asya viśiṣṭātmano* (with mss., for *asyā*, in all printed editions).

233. *Bhagavadgītā* 6.21, in a description of yoga.

234. *Taittirīya Upaniṣad* 2.7.1 (a *śruti* text, and hence, normatively, more directly probative than a *smṛti* text like the *Bhagavadgītā*).

235. *Chāndogya Upaniṣad* 6.8.6. The analogy with the Upanishadic passage was first drawn by Vishvanathadeva (p. 101, above); see also *Kāvyaparīkṣā* p. 17.

236. Since she is King Dushyanta's mistress and later wife.

237. I read *sādhāraṇaṃ* (with mss., for *sādhāraṇa-*; see also Ojha).

238. The style here is that of the crabbed "new logic," originating in about the thirteenth century, and Jagannatha's implicit ascription of it to Bhatta Nayaka is a breathtaking anachronism.

239. Such as an old man or one who has withdrawn from all worldly concerns.

240. I read *dharādhareya- . . . adhunika-* (with the majority of mss., for *dharādhareyatva- . . . adhunikatva-*).

241. See *rasapratitau* p. 28.9 (less likely, the apprehension of a foundational factor like Shakuntala in oneself).

242. Here not the expected (and necessary) "literary language" (see chapter 3 n. 6) because in the next sentence Jagannatha misunderstands Bhatta Nayaka's use of the term *abhidhā*.

243. *abhidhā* for Bhatta Nayaka is literary language (especially figurative language), which *disarms* normal referentiality; it is not referentiality itself.

244. Compare Abhinavagupta on Bhatta Nayaka #1a; Ruyyaka on #3a.

245. That is "but not *equal*, because of the commingling." Commentators like Shrivatsa state that the difference between the state of *mukti* and the rasa experience is the continued fusion in the latter with the aesthetic objects (KP p. 602; Nagesha speaks of *vibhāvādisaṃvalitānandāṃśa-*, KP [BHU ed.] p. 120); see also Kumarasvamin p. 210, above, and KD p. 152.4.

246. Jagannatha misquotes here, reading *caiva* for *cānyā* (see above, Bhatta Nayaka fragment #10).

247. "Manifesting," *vyakti*; "manifestation," *vyañjanā*. The claim that *bhoga* is in essence *rasadhvani* is made repeatedly by Abhinavagupta himself (DhĀL pp. 189.4, 52.7–8, 188.3).

248. If the desire were real, it would continue to exist even when the actualization through the aesthetic elements was not taking place; if it were unreal, it would never be experienced (Ojha).

249. Both here and in the clause the follows, Ojha and Madhusudan Shastri take the referent of *sva* to be *rati*, which makes no grammatical sense to me.

250. I read *carvaṇīya-* (with mss., for *varṇanīya-*); compare *vyañjitaś carvaṇīyaḥ* in KP p. 574.

251. Jagannatha adds, "the 'veiling' being specified as the object of qualification when one has the sense of being qualified by desire or other stable emotion," from which I derive little sense.

252. Again, the term is being used in the experiential as opposed to the linguistic sense.

253. Presumably either the trouble of acquiring the cream in the first place (harvesting it from snake-infested sandal trees) or its crusting as it dries (Mathuranath Sastri).

254. Literally, and awkwardly: "For this reason the weeping . . . makes sense."

255. The father of Rama, grief-stricken when forced to send his son into exile.

256. It is unclear who is meant (only the rejection of implicature pertains to Mahima Bhatta).

257. In this interpretation, it is the viewer's awareness (e.g., of being Dushyanta, who feels desire for Shakuntala) that is rasa, not his stable emotion; rasa is identical with the savoring of rasa. It is never made clear how, in the absence of the Vedantic analysis of ontological undecidability, these scholars justify the cognitive error (Ojha).

258. That is, not based on perception or other reliable cognitive instrument (Ojha).

259. More simply: the sense in the reader that (1) "I, who am filled with desire for Shakuntala, am Dushyanta"; or (2) "I am Dushyanta, who is qualified by a desire for Shakuntala"; or (3) "I am qualified by a sense of being Dushyanta and by a desire for Shakuntala." Although the upshot is the same in all three cases, the first takes the form of "I am Dushyanta," where "being Dushyanta" is predicated of "I"; the second takes the form of "Dushyanta is me," where "I" is predicated of "Dushyanta"; in the third, "being Dushyanta" and desire are both posited as qualifications of one's self (Mathuranath Sastri).

260. One infers the existence in Dushyanta of desire for Shakuntala; cognitive error conceals the difference between the viewer and Dushyanta, and effects an identification between the viewer and the desirous Dushyanta. This purely mental sense of identity with the desirous character, then, for these "other" scholars, is rasa (Mathuranatha Sastri). In this part of the argument, "manifestation" refers (as in Anandavardhana) to the linguistic process, not (as in post-Abhinavagupta thought) to the mental state.

261. Largely the ancient view, associated with Bhatta Lollata, though there is no evidence that Bhatta Lollata viewed rasa as an object of awareness on the part of the audience.

262. The expression is loose: the desiring Dushyanta is superimposed, not just the desire.

263. Literally, "representations of the foundational factor and other aesthetic elements," but this is an imprecise formulation: Dushyanta may be the foundational factor for desire in Shakuntala, but the point of this discussion is *his* desire for *her*.

264. Shri Shankuka.

265. Theories 7, 10–11 are probably borrowed from DhĀL p. 186 (Raghavan 1975: 138 also noticed the connection); the source of the other two is unknown, and may in fact have no historical antecedents but be purely speculative.

266. The point of this distinction escapes me (perhaps related to the actor/performance, rather than to each other).

267. Presumably: because the *rasasūtra* says so.

268. Ironically, this is not the original reading of NŚ 6.15, given above.

269. SRĀ 7.1360.

270. KP 4.29 and 35 (*sūtras* 44 and 47).

271. *vairāgya*, which Jagannatha is equating with *nirveda* (dispassion).

272. The middle step in this argument ("and since it is desire that is not normative—not being that between a young heterosexual couple—and hence cannot be consummated in the normal way, it cannot fully develop into a rasa and so must remain an emotion") is the unspoken assumption in the defense that follows.

273. KP 4.35.

274. Madhusudan Shastri's *-ayogāt* (for *-yogāt*) may be correct.

275. Jagannatha is clearly unfamiliar with the arguments of Bhoja, e.g., ŚP p. 615, above.

276. Pun intended.

277. This is less a *sūtra*-like definition (as formatted in the printed editions) than simply an older position under examination.

278. In the first case, the cause is the fact of many lovers, all of whom may be appropriate love objects; in the second, the cause is the attitude, not the social status, of one of the partners.

279. That is, established by social convention.

ENGLISH-SANSKRIT GLOSSARY

1. Bhoja's substitution for either *apasmāra* or *maraṇa*.

2. Bhoja's substitution for either *apasmāra* or *maraṇa*; DR's substitutution for *asūyā*.

3. The progression is: lust, anxiety, remembrance, glorification, distress, raving, madness, sickness, stupor, death.

Bibliography

PRIMARY SOURCES

Abhidhāvṛttimātṛkā of Mukula Bhaṭṭa. Ed. Rewa Prasad Dwivedi. Varanasi: Caukhamba Vidyabhavana, 1973.

Abhinavabhāratī, Oriental Research Institute and Manuscripts Library, Trivandrum, ms. T 566a, b, c (abbreviated Triv.). See also s.v. *Nāṭyaśāstra*.

Agnipurāṇam. N.e. Pune: Anandasrama, 1909.

Alaṃkārakaustubha of Kavikarṇapūra, with the commentary [of Lokanātha Cakravartin]. Ed. Sivaprasad Bhattacharya. Rajshahi: Varendra Research Society, 1926.

Alaṅkārasarvasva of Rājānaka Ruyyaka, with the commentary of Jayaratha. Ed. Durgaprasad and Kashinath Pandurang Parab. Bombay: Nirnaya Sagar Press, 1893; with the commentary of Samudrabandha, ed. T. Ganapati Sastri. Trivandrum: Travancore Government Press, 1915; with the commentary of Vidyācakravartin, ed. S. S. Janaki. Delhi: Meharchand Lachhmandas, 1965.

Aucityavicāracarcā. Ed. Shrinarayana Mishra. Varanasi: Chowkhambha Orientalia, 2006.

Bhaktirasāmṛtasindhu of Rūpa Gosvāmin, with the *Durgamasaṃgamanī* commentary of Jīva Gosvāmin and the *Bhaktisārapradarśinī* commentary of Viśvanātha Cakravartin. Ed. Shyama Das. Vrindavan: Vrajagaurav, 1981.

Bhaktirasāyana of Madhusūdhana Sarasvatī. Ed. Gosvami Damodara Sastri. Varanasi: Jnanamandal Press, 1984 V.S. (1927 C.E.).

Bhāvaprakāśana of Śāradātayana, 2nd ed. Ed. Yadugiri Yatiraja and K. S. Ramaswami Sastri. Baroda: Oriental Institute, 1968.

Bhāv Vilās of Dev. *See* Dindayal.

Bodhicaryāvatāra of Śāntideva, with the commentary of Prajñākaramati. Ed. P. L. Vaidya. Darbhanga: Mithila Institute, 1960.

Camatkāracandrikā of Viśveśvara. Ed. Pandiri Sarasvati Mohan. Delhi: Meharchand Lachhmandas, 1972.

Çṛṅgāratilaka of Rudraṭa [*sic*] and *Sahṛdayalīlā* of Ruyyaka. Ed. R. Pischel. Kiel: C. F. Haeseler, 1886.

Daśarūpaka of Dhanaṃjaya, with the *Avaloka* commentary of Dhanika and the *Laghuṭīkā* thereon of Bhaṭṭa Nṛsiṃha. Ed. T. Venkatacharya. Madras: Adyar Library and Research Centre, 1969; with the commentary of Bahurūpa Miśra, ed. A. N. Pandey. Varanasi/Delhi: Bharatiya Vidya Prakasan, 1979; with a gloss *Prabhā*, ed. Sudarsanacarya Panchanadiya. Bombay: Gujarati Printing Press, 1927; Jaipur Pothikhana ms. of the *Avaloka* #352. (*See also* Kundu below).

Dhvanyāloka of Anandavardhana, with the *Locana* of Abhinavagupta and the *Bālapriyā* of Rāmaṣāraka, ed. Pattabhirama Shastri. Varanasi: Chowkhamba Sanskrit Series Office, 1940; with the *Kaumudī* of Uttuṅgodaya, ed. Kuppuswami Shastri et al. Madras: Kuppuswami Sastri Research Institute, 1944; with the *Locana* of Abhinavagupta, ed. Durgaprasad and Wasudev Laxman Sastri Pansikar. Bombay: Nirnaya Sagar Press, 1928; with the *Dīdhiti* commentary, ed. Badari Nath Sarma. Varanasi: Jaya Krishna Das Haridas Gupta, 1937.

Ekāvalī of Vidyādhara, with the commentary of Mallinātha. Ed. Kamalasankara Pranasankara Trivedi. Bombay: Government Central Book Depot, 1903.

Gāthāsaptaśatī with the commentary of Gaṅgādharabhaṭṭa. Ed. Durgaprasad and Kasinath Pandurang Parab. Bombay: Nirnaya Sagar Press, 1889.

Īśvarapratyabhijñāvivṛtivimarśinī of Abhinavagupta, 3 v. Ed. Madhusudan Kaul. Bombay: Nirnaya Sagar Press, 1938–1943.

Kalpalatāvivekaḥ. Ed. Murari Lal Nagar and Harishankar Shastry. Ahmedabad: L. D. Institute, 1968.

Kavirājamārga. Ed. M. V. Seetha Ramiah. Bangalore: Karnataka Sangha, 1968; reprint, Bangalore, 1994.

Kāvyadarpaṇa of Rājacūḍāmaṇi Dīkṣita, v. 1 Ullāsas 1–6 [all published]. Ed. S. Subrahmanya Sastri. Shrirangam: Shri Vani Vilas Press, 1926.

Kāvyādarśa of Daṇḍin, with the commentaries of Vāḍijaṅghāla, Taruṇavācaspati, and Hṛdayaṃgama. 1936. Ed. D. T. Tatacharya. Tirupati: Shrinivas Press; ed. Premachandra Tarkabagisa. Calcutta: Baptist Mission Press, 1863.

Kāvyalakṣaṇa [= *Kāvyādarśa*] of Daṇḍin, with the commentary of Ratnaśrījñāna. Ed. A. Thakur and Upendra Jha. Darbhanga: Mithila Institute, 1957.

Kāvyālaṅkāra of Bhāmaha. Ed. Raman Kumar Sharma. Delhi: Vidyanidhi Prakasan, 1994; ed. C. Sankara Rama Sastri. Madras: Shri Balamanorama Press, 1956; ed. B. N. Sarma and Baldeva Upadhyaya. Varanasi: Chowkhamba Sanskrit Series Office, 1928.

Kāvyālaṅkāra of Rudraṭa, with the *Ṭippaṇī* of Namisādhu. Ed. Durgaprasad and Wasudev Laxman Sastri Pansikar. Bombay: Nirnaya Sagar Press, 1928.

Kāvyālaṅkāra[sāra]saṃgraha of Udbhaṭa, with the *Laghuvṛtti* commentary of Pratihāharendurāja. Ed. M. R. Telang. Bombay: Nirnaya Sagar Press, 1915; ed. N. D. Banhatti. Poona: Bhandarkar Oriental Research Institute, 1925.

Kāvyālaṅkārasārasaṅgraha of Udbhaṭa, with the *Vivṛti* of Tilaka. Ed. K. S. Ramaswami Sastri Siromani. Baroda: Oriental Institute, 1931.

Kāvyālaṅkārsūtravṛtti, with the commentary *Kāmadhenu* of King Govindatippa. Ed. Ratna Gopal Bhatta. Varanasi: Vidya Vilas Press, 1908; ed. K. S. Vatsyacakravarti. Shrirangam: Shri Vani Vilas Press, 1909.

Kāvyamīmāṃsā of Rājaśekhara. Ed. C. D. Dalal et al. 3rd. ed. Baroda: Oriental Institute, 1934; ed. Madhusudhana Misra. Varanasi: Chowkhamba Sanskrit Series Office, 1931–34.

Kāvyānuśāsana of Hemacandra. Ed. Rasiklal C. Parikh and V. M. Kulkarni. 2nd ed. Bombay: Shri Mahavira Jaina Vidyalaya, 1964; compiled by Tapasvi S. Nandi. Patan: Hemachandracharya North Gujarat University, 2007.

Kāvyaparīkṣā of Śrīvatsalāñchana. Ed. P. L. Vaidya. Darbhanga: Mithila Institute, 1956.

Kāvyaprakāśa [of Mammaṭa], *solah ṭīkāoṃ sahit*, 6 v. Ed. Jotsna Mohan. Delhi: Nag Prakashan, 1995-; with the *Viveka* commentary of Śrīdhara, 2 v. Ed. Sivaprasad Bhattacharyya. Calcutta: Sanskrit College, 1959; with the commentaries *Pradīpa* of Govinda Thakkur, *Uddyota* of Nāgeśa Bhaṭṭa, and *Prabhā* of Vaidyanātha Tatsat. Ed. Visvanath Bhattacharya and Jayasankarlal Tripathi. Varanasi: Banaras Hindu University, 2003; with the *Saṅketa* commentary of Māṇikyacandra and the *Madhumatī* commentary of Ravi Bhaṭṭācārya. Ed. N. S. Venkatanathacharya. 2 v. Mysore: Oriental Research Institute, University of Mysore, 1974 (1st ed., 1922); and by Vasudevsastri Abhyankar, Poona: Bhandarkar Oriental Research Institute, 1921; with the *Saṅketa* commentary named *Kāvyādarśa* of Someśvara Bhaṭṭa. Ed. Rasiklal C. Parikh. Jodhpur: Rajasthan Oriental Research Institute, 1959.

Kāvyaprakāśasaṃketa of Rucaka [*sic*]. Ed. Siva Prasad Bhattacharya. *Calcutta Oriental Journal* 2 (1935): 1–72; in *Kāvyaprakāśa solah ṭīkāoṃ sahit* (see above), (v. 2, p. 563.7 ff.).

Kṣemendralaghukāvyasaṃgraha. Ed. Aryendra Sarma. Hyderabad: The Sanskrit Academy, Osmania University, 1961.

Mīmāṃsādarśanam. 6 vols. Ed. Vasudev Abhyankar. Pune: Anandashrama Press, 1970.

Mokṣopāya. Das Erste und Zweite Buch. Ed. Susanne Krause-Stinner. Wiesbaden: Harrassowitz, 2011.

[*Bhāgavata*] *Muktāphala* of Vopadeva, with the commentary of Hemādri, rev. ed. Ed. Durgamohan Bhattacharyya. Calcutta: Calcutta Oriental Press, 1944.

Nāṭyadarpaṇa of Rāmacandra and Guṇacandra. Ed. G. J. Shrigondekar. Baroda: Oriental Institute, 1929 (text unchanged in 2nd ed., Baroda, 1959).

Nāṭyaśāstra of Bharata, with the *Abhinavabhāratī* of Abhinavagupta, v. 1, 4th ed. Ed. K. Krishnamoorthy. Baroda: Oriental Institute, 1992; 2nd ed., ed. K. S. Ramaswami Sastri, 1956; 1st ed., ed. Manavalli Ramakrishna Kavi, 1926; v. 2, 3rd ed., ed. M. V. Kulkarni and T. Nandi; v. 3, 2nd ed., ed. M. V. Kulkarni and T. Nandi, 2003; v. 4, 2nd ed., ed. V. Kulkarni and T. Nandi, 2006 (reference is to chapter and verse, or volume, page, line); with the *Abhinavabhāratī* of Abhinavagupta and the *Madhusūdanī* and *Bālakrīḍā*, 2 v. Ed. Madhusudan Shastri. Varanasi: Banaras Hindu University, 1971–1975; see also s.v. Nagendra.

Nyāyadarśanam, with *Bhāṣya* of Uddyotakara, *Tātparyaṭīkā* of Vācaspati, and *Pariśuddhi* of Udayana. Ed. Taranatha Nyayatarkatirtha et al. Calcutta: Metropolitan Printing and Publishing House, 1936.

Nyāyamañjarī of Jayanta Bhaṭṭa, 2 v. Ed. K. S. Varadacharya. Mysore: Oriental Research Institute, 1969–1983.

Nyāyaratnamālā of Pārthasārathi Miśra. Ed. Gangadhara Sastri. Banaras: Chowkhamba, 1900.

Nyāyasāra of Bhāsarvajña. Ed. K. Sambasiva Sastri. Trivandrum: Government Press, 1931.

Pañcadaśī of Vidyāraṇya. Ed. Devasvarupa Misra. Varanasi: Caukhamba Amarabharati Prakasan, 1984.

Pañcatantra. Ed. J. Hertel. Cambridge, Mass.: Harvard University Press, 1915.

Pātañjalayogasūtra, with the *bhāṣya* of Vyāsa. Ed. K. S. Agase. Poona: Anandasrama, 1904.

Prakaraṇapañcikā of Śālikanātha. Ed. A. Subrahmanya Sastri. Varanasi: Banaras Hindu University, 1961.

Pramāṇavārttika of Dharmakīrti with the *Commentary* of Karṇakagomin. Ed. Rahula Samkrtyayana. Reprint, Kyoto, 1982; *The First Chapter with the Autocommentary.* Ed. R. Gnoli. Rome: Istituto Italiano per il Medio e Estremo Oriente, 1960.

Pratāparudrīya (= *Pratāparudrayaśobhūṣaṇa*) of Vidyānātha, with the Commentary *Ratnāpaṇa* of Kumārasvāmin. Ed. V. Raghavan. Madras: Samskritvidyasamiti, 1987; ed. C. Sankara Rama Sastri. Mylapore, Madras: Balamanorama Press, 1931.

Rājataraṅgiṇī of Kalhaṇa. Ed. Aurel Stein. Bombay: Education Society's Press, 1892.

Rasacandrikā of Viśveśvara. Ed. Vishnu Prasad Bhandari. Banaras: Chowkhamba Sanskrit Series Office, 1926.

Rasagaṅgādhara of Jagannātha Paṇḍitarāja. Ed. Mathurnath Sastry. Bombay: Nirnaya Sagar Press, 1947; v.1, ed. Kedarnath Ojha. Varanasi: Sampurnanand Sanskrit University, 1977; ed. Madhusudan Shastri. Varanasi: Banaras Hindu University, V. S. 2020 (1963 C.E.); Baroda ORI ms. no. 5208; Jodhpur Fort mss. no. 2878 and 2879.

Rasakalikā of Rudrabhaṭṭa. Ed. Kalpakam Sankaranarayanan. Madras: Adyar Library and Research Centre, 1988.

Rasamīmāṃsā of Gaṅgarāma Jāḍe. Ed. Rudradeva Tripathi. New Delhi: Lalbahadur Sastri Kendriya Samskrta Vidyapitham, 1973.

Rasapradīpa of Prabhākara Bhaṭṭa. Ed. Narayana Sastri Khiste. Varanasi: Tara Printing Works, 1925; ed. Prabhata Shastri. Allahabad: Devabhasha Prakashanam, 1983.

Rasārṇavasudhākara of Siṃhabhūpala [Siṅgabhūpāla]. Ed. T. Venkatacharya. Adyar, Madras: Adyar Library and Research Centre, 1979; ed. Ganapati Sastri. Trivandrum: Government Press, 1916.

Rasasindhu of Pauṇḍarika Rāmeśvara. Rajasthan Oriental Research Institute, Jodhpur, ms. nos. 28529 and 33913.

Rasataraṅgiṇī of Bhānudatta. In *The Bouquet of Rasa and the River of Rasa*, ed. and trans. Sheldon Pollock. New York: New York University Press, 2009.

Ratnāvalī of Harṣavardhana. Ed. Kasinath Pandurang Parab and Visvanath Sastri Joshi. Bombay: Nirnaya Sagar Press, 1888.

Sāhityadarpaṇa of Viśvanātha with the *Lakṣmī* commentary. Ed. Krsnamohan Sastri. Benares: The Chowkhamba Sanskrit Series Office, 1947–1948; with the *Vivṛti* of Rāmacaraṇa Tarkavāgīśa Bhaṭṭācārya, ed. Durgaprasad. Bombay: Nirnaya Sagar Press, 1922; with the *Locana* of Anantadāsa and the *Vijñapriyā* of Maheśvara Tarkālaṅkāra Bhaṭṭācārya, n.e. Lahore: Motilal Banarsidass, 1938.

Sāhityasudhāsindhu of Viśvanāthadeva. Ed. Ram Pratap. Delhi, Varanasi: Bharatiya Vidya Prakashan, 1978.

Śakatatrayam of Bhatṛhari with the commentary of Rāmacandra Budhendra. Ed. D. D. Kosambi. Bombay: Nirnaya Sagar Press, 1957.

Saṃgītaratnākara of Śārṅgadeva, with the commentaries of Kallinātha and Siṃhabhūpāla, v. 4. Ed. S. Subrahmanya Sastri. Adyar: Theosophical Society, 1953.

Sāṃkhyatattvakaumudī of Vācaspatimiśra. Ed. Ramasastri Bhandari. Varanasi: Chowkhamba Sanskrit Series Office, 2001.

Sarasvatīkaṇṭhābharaṇālaṅkāra of Bhoja, with the commentaries of Ratneśvara and Jagaddhara. 1979. Ed. Kedarnath Sarma. Bombay: Nirnaya Sagar Press, 1924; ed. Biswanath Bhattacharya. Varanasi: Banaras Hindu University.

Sarasvatīkaṇṭhābharaṇālaṅkāra commentary of Bhaṭṭa Narasiṃha. Kerala University Manuscripts Library: Paliam 14758 (partial transcript: Government Oriental Manuscripts

Library, Madras: MT. 2499; SKĀ 5.1–3 also edited in Raghavan 1963: 412–14); with the commentary of Ājada. Shri Mahavir Jain Aradhana Kendra, Gyanmandir, Koba (Gujarat): Patasanghvi 102–1.

Śārṅgadharapaddhati: The Paddhati of Śārṅgadhara. Ed. Peter Peterson. Bombay: Government Central Book Depot, 1888.

Sattasaī. See Gāthāsaptaśatī.

Setubandha of Pravārasena. Ed. R. Basak. Calcutta: Asiatic Society of Bengal, 1959.

Ślokatrayaṭīkā (Bhāgavataprathamādhyāyasya) of Madhusūdana Sarasvatī. Pothikhana Jaipur ms. #4186.

Śrīmadalaṅkārakaustabha of Karṇapūra, with the commentary of Viśvanātha [Lokanātha?] Cakravartin. Ed. Haridasa Sastri. Vrindavan: Shrigadadhara Gaurahari Press, 1989.

Śrī-Prītisandarbha of Jīva Gosvāmin. Ed. Chinmayi Chatterjee. Calcutta: Jadavpur University, 1988.

Śṛṅgāraprakāśa of Bhojarāja, 2 v. Ed. Rewaprasada Dwivedi and Sadashivakumara Dwivedi. New Delhi: Indira Gandhi National Centre for the Arts, 2007; (v. 1 only), ed. V. Raghavan. Cambridge, Mass.: Harvard University Press, 1997; ed. G. R. Joyser. 4 v. Mysore: Coronation Press, 1955-[69].

Subhāṣitāvali of Vallabhadeva. Ed. Peter Peterson. Bombay: Education Society's Press, 1886.

Sūktimuktāvalī. Ed. Embar Krishnamacharya. Baroda: Oriental Institute, 1938.

Svāyambhuva Nāṭyaśāstra. Ed. Rewaprasad Dwivedi. Simla: Bharatiya Ucca Adhyayana Samsthan and Aryana Books International, New Delhi, 2005.

Tantrāloka of Abhinavagupta with the commentary of Jayaratha, v. 12. Ed. Madhusudan Kaul Shastri. Bombay: Nirnaya Sagar Press, 1938.

Tāpasavatsarāja of Mātrarāja. Ed. B. Goswami. Calcutta: Sanskrit Pustak Bhandar, 1998.

Tarkasaṃgraha of Aṇṇaṃ Bhaṭṭa. Ed. Mahadevasarma Bakre. Bombay: Nirnaya Sagar Press, 1919.

Tattvaprakāśa of Bhoja. Ed. Kameshwar Nath Mishra. Varanasi: Chaukhambha Orientalia, 1976.

Uddyota of Nāgeśa Bhaṭṭa, in *Kāvyaprakāśa of Mammata*. Ed. B. Bhattacharya and Jaya Shankar Lal Tripathi. Varanasi: Banaras Hindu University, 2003.

Ujjvalanīlamaṇi of Rūpa Gosvāmin. Ed. Durgaprasad and Wasudev Laxman Sastri Pansikar. Bombay: Nirnaya Sagar Press, 1932.

Uttararāmacarita. See Pollock 2007.

Vakroktijīvita of Kuntaka. Ed. K. Krishnamoorthy. Dharwar: Dharwar University Press, 1977; ed. S. K. De. Calcutta: Firma K. L. Mukhopadhyay, 1961.

Vākyapadīya of Bhartṛhari. Ed. Wilhelm Rau. Wiesbaden: Steiner, 1977; Kāṇḍa 1. Ed. K. A. Subramania Iyer. Poona: Deccan College, 1966; Part III, Vol. II with the commentary *Prakāśa* by Helārāja and *Ambākartrī* by Raghunatha Sarma. Varanasi: Sampūrṇānandasaṃskṛtaviśvavidyālaya, 1979.

Veṇīsaṃhāra of Bhaṭṭa Nārāyaṇa, 9th ed. Ed. Kasinath Pandurang Parab. Bombay: Nirnaya Sagar Press, 1940.

Viṣṇudharmottarapurāṇa Third Khaṇḍa. Ed. Priyabala Shah. Baroda: Oriental Institute, 1958.

Vyaktiviveka of Mahima Bhaṭṭa, with the commentary of Ruyyaka. Ed. Rewaprasada Dwivedi. Varanasi: Chaukhambha Sanskrit Sansthan, 1983.

SECONDARY SOURCES

Bansat-Boudon, Lyne. 1989–1990. "The *Sāmānyābhinaya*, or How to Play the Game." *Indologica Taurinensia* (15–16): 67–77.
——. 1992a. *Poétique du théâtre indien: Lectures du Nāṭyaśāstra*. Paris: École Française d'Extrême-Orient.
——. 1992b. "Le cœur-miroir. Remarques sur la théorie indienne de l'expérience esthétique et ses rapports avec le théâtre." *Les Cahiers de Philosophie* 14: 133–54.
——. 2004. *Pourquoi le théâtre? La réponse indienne*. Paris: Mille et Une nuits.
——. 2011. *An Introduction to Tantric Philosophy*. Abingdon: Routledge.
Beardsley, Monroe. 1981 (1959). *Aesthetics: Problems in the Philosophy of Criticism*. 2nd ed. Indianapolis: Hackett.
Behl, Aditya. 2012. *Love's Subtle Magic: An Indian Islamic Literary Tradition, 1379-1545*. New York: Oxford University Press.
Bhaduri, Nrisinha P. 1988. "Bhakti (Devotion) as an Aesthetic Sentiment." *Journal of Indian Philosophy* 16, 4: 377–410.
Bhattacharyya, Sivaprasad. 1963. "Bhoja's Rasa-Ideology and Its Influence on Bengal Rasa-*śāstra*." *Journal of the Oriental Institute* (Baroda) 13, 2: 106–19.
——. 1964. *Studies in Indian Poetics*. Calcutta: Firma KLM.
Böhtlingk, O., ed. and trans. 1890. *Daṇḍin's Poetik*. Leipzig: H. Haessel.
Bourdieu, Pierre. 1984. *Distinction: A Social Critique of the Judgement of Taste*. Cambridge, Mass.: Harvard University Press.
Bronkhorst, Johannes. 2008. "Udbhata, a Grammarian and a Cārvāka." In *Linguistic Traditions of Kashmir*, ed. Mrinal Kaul and Ashok Aklujkar. New Delhi: D. K. Printworld, 281–99.
Bronner, Yigal. 2011. "A Question of Priority: Revisiting the Bhāmaha-Daṇḍin Debate." *Journal of Indian Philosophy* 40, 1: 67–118.
——. Forthcoming. "Understanding Udbhaṭa." In *Around Abhinavagupta*, ed. E. Franco.
Busch, Allison. 2014. "Poetry in Motion." In *Culture and Circulation*, ed. Thomas de Bruijn and Allison Busch. Leiden: Brill.
Chintamani, T. R. 1927. "Fragments of Bhatta Nayaka." *Journal of Oriental Research*, Madras 1: 267–76.
Chitambaran, P. 1998. *Svatmayogapradipaprabodhini*. Trivandrum: Swantham Books.
Clough, Patricia Ticineto and Jean Halley, eds. 2007. *The Affective Turn: Theorizing the Social*. Durham, N.C.: Duke University Press.
Cohen, Ted. 2004. "The Philosophy of Taste: Thoughts on the Idea." In *The Blackwell Guide to Aesthetics*, ed. Peter Kivy. Oxford: Blackwell.
Coulson, Michael. 1981. *Three Sanskrit Plays*. Harmondsworth: Penguin.
Danto, Arthur C. 1981. *The Transfiguration of the Commonplace: A Philosophy of Art*. Cambridge, Mass.: Harvard University Press.
Davies, R. T. 1965. *Samuel Johnson Selected Writings*. Evanston: Northwestern University Press.
De, Sushil Kumar. 1932. "The Bhakti-Rasa-Śāstra of Bengal Vaisnavism." *Indian Historical Quarterly* 8, 4: 643–88.
——. 1988. *History of Sanskrit Poetics*, 2 vols. Calcutta: Firma KLM.
Della Volpe, Galvano. 1991. *Critique of Taste*. London: Verso.
Delmonico, Neil. 1998. "Rasaśāstra of Rūpa Gosvāmi." *Journal of Vaishnava Studies* 6, 1: 75–98.

Dimitrov, Dragomir, ed. and trans. 2002. *Mārgavibhāga: Die Unterscheidung der Stilarten.* Marburg: Indica et Tibetica Verlag.

——. 2014. *The Legacy of the Jewel Mind: On the Sanskrit, Pali, and Sinhalese Works by Ratnamati. A Philological Chronicle.* Marburg: Marburg University Habilitationsschrift.

Dindayal. 2004. *Dev aur unkā bhāvvilās.* Delhi: Navlok Prakashan.

Dufrenne, Mikel. 1973. *The Phenomenology of Aesthetic Experience.* Trans. Edward S. Casey et al. Evanston: Northwestern University Press. Original French edition, 1953.

Dwivedi, Rewaprasad. 2005. *Alaṃ brahma: sāhityaśāstre apūrvā dṛk.* Varanasi: Kalidasasamsthan.

Eagleton, Terry. 1990. *The Ideology of the Aesthetic.* Oxford: Blackwell.

Feagin, Susan and Patrick Maynard, eds. 1997. *Aesthetics.* Oxford and New York: Oxford University Press.

Filliozat, Pierre-Sylvain, trans. 1963. *Le Pratāparudrīya de Vidyānātha.* Pondicherry: Institut Français d'Indologie.

Fisher, Elaine. 2013. "A New Public Theology: Sanskrit and Society in Seventeenth-Century South India." Ph.D diss., Columbia University.

Gadamer, Hans-Georg. 2004. *Truth and Method.* New York: Continuum.

Gengnagel, Jörg. 1996. *Māyā, Puruṣa und Śiva.* Wiesbaden: Harrassowitz.

Gerow, Edwin. 1994. "Abhinavagupta's Aesthetics as a Speculative Paradigm." *Journal of the American Oriental Society* 114, 2: 186–208.

Gerth, H. H. and C. Wright Mills. 1946. *From Max Weber: Essays in Sociology.* New York: Oxford University Press.

Gnoli, Raniero. 1968. *The Aesthetic Experience According to Abhinavagupta*, 2nd ed. Varanasi: Chowkhamba Sanskrit Series Office.

Gode, P. K. 1934. "A Manuscript of the Rasasindhu." *Calcutta Oriental Journal* 2, 1: 30–32.

Gross, Daniel. 2010. "Defending the Humanities with Charles Darwin's *The Expression of the Emotions in Man and Animals* (1872)." *Critical Inquiry* 37: 34–59.

Gupta, P. S. 1963. "Śaṅkuka, a Buddhist Logician." *Vishveshvaranand Indological Journal* 1, 2: 315–19.

Haberman, David L. 2003, ed. and trans. *The Bhaktirasāmṛtasindhu of Rūpa Gosvāmin.* Delhi: Indira Gandhi National Centre for the Arts.

Harpham, Geoffrey Galt. 2005. "Returning to Philology: The Past and Future of Literary Study." In *New Prospects in Literary Research*, ed. Geoffrey Galt Harpham and Ansgar Nünning. Amsterdam: Royal Netherlands Academy of Arts and Sciences.

Ingalls, Daniel H. H. 1965. *An Anthology of Sanskrit Court Poetry.* Cambridge, Mass.: Harvard University Press.

——, J. M. Masson, and M. V. Patwardhan, trans. 1990. *The Dhvanyāloka of Ānandavardhana.* Cambridge, Mass.: Harvard University Press.

Jacobi, Hermann, trans. 1908. "Ruyyaka's *Alaṃkārasarvasva.*" *Zeitschrift der Deutschen Morgenländischen Gesellschaft* 62: 289–336.

Kamimura, Katsuhiko. 1976. "Bhatta Narasiṃha's *Sarasvatīkaṇṭhābharaṇa-vyākhyā* (Pariccheda I)." *Bukkyō kenkyū*: 100–40.

Kane, P. V. 1971. *History of Sanskrit Poetics.* Delhi: Motilal Banarsidass.

Kangle, R. P. 1973. *Rasa-Bhāva-Vicāra.* Bombay: Maharashtra Rajya Sahitya-samskrti Mandal.

Kidd, David Comer and Emanuele Castano. 2013. "Reading Literary Fiction Improves Theory of Mind." *Treatise* 342: 377–80.

Korsmeyer, Carolyn, ed. 1998. *Aesthetics: The Big Questions.* Oxford: Blackwell.

—. 2001. "Taste." In *The Routledge Companion to Aesthetics*, ed. Berys Gaut and Dominic McIver Lopes. London: Routledge.

—. 2008. "Taste, Food, and the Limits of Pleasure." In *Aesthetic Experience*, ed. Richard Shusterman and Adele Tomlin. New York: Routledge.

Krishnamoorthy, K. 1968. "Traditional Indian Aesthetics in Theory and Practice." In *Indian Aesthetics and Art Activity* (no ed.). Simla: Indian Institute of Advanced Study.

—. 1979a. *Studies in Indian Aesthetics and Criticism*. Mysore: D. V. K. Murthy.

—. 1979b. "Udbhaṭa's Original Contribution to Sanskrit Literary Theory." In *Ludvik Sternbach Felicitation Volume*, ed. J. P. Sinha. Lucknow: Akhila Bharatiya Sanskrit Parishad, 303–11.

—, ed. and trans. 1988. *Abhinavagupta's Dhvanyāloka-Locana with an Anonymous Sanskrit Commentary*. New Delhi: Meharchand Lachhmandas Publications.

Kulkarni, V. M. 1989. *Prakrit Verses in Sanskrit Works on Poetics*. Delhi: Bhogilal Leherchand Institute of Indology.

—. 1991. *Bhoja and the Harivijaya of Sarvasena*. Ahmedabad: Saraswati Pustak Bhandar.

—. 2003. *Abhinavabhāratī Text: Restored, and Other Articles*. Ahmedabad: Shresthi Kasturbhai Lalbhai Smarak Nidhi.

Kundu, Mohendra Narayan. 2000. "A Critical Edition of the Devanagari Recension of the *Daśarūpaka* and the *Avaloka*." Ph.D. diss., University of Edinburgh.

Kunjunni Raja, R. 1994. "Ākṣepa, Arthāpatti and Lakṣanā." In *Cultura Indica*, ed. Vishvanatha Devasarma et al. Delhi: Sharada Publishing House, 103.

Levinson, Jerrold. 2003. "Philosophical Aesthetics: An Overview." In *The Oxford Handbook of Aesthetics*, ed. Jerrold Levinson. Oxford: Oxford University Press.

Leys, Ruth. 2011. "The Turn to Affect: A Critique." *Critical Inquiry* 37, 3: 434–72.

Masson, Jeffrey M. and M. V. Patwardhan. 1969. *Śāntarasa and Abhinavagupta's Philosophy of Aesthetics*. Pune: Bhandarkar Oriental Research Institute.

McCrea, Lawrence. 2009. *The Teleology of Poetics in Medieval Kashmir*. Cambridge, Mass.: Harvard University Press.

—. 2011. "Prajñākaragupta on the Pramāṇas and Their Objects." In *Religion and Logic in Buddhist Philosophical Analysis*, ed. Helmut Krasser et al. Vienna: Verlag der Österreichischen Akademie der Wissenschaften, 319–28.

Minkowski, Christopher Z. 2011. "Advaita Vedānta in Early Modern History." *South Asian History and Culture* 2, 2: 205–31.

Nagendra, and Visvesvara Siddhantasiromani, eds. and trans. *Abhinavabhāratī ke tīn adhyāya* [chapters 1, 2, 6]. Delhi: Dilli Visvavidyalaya, Hindi Vibhag, 1960.

Narayana Rao, V., et al. 1992. *Symbols of Substance: Court and State in Nayaka Period Tamil Nadu*. Delhi: Oxford University Press.

Narayana Rao, V., and David Shulman. 2012. *Shrinath: The Poet Who Made Gods and Kings*. New York: Oxford University Press.

Neill, Alex. 2003. "Art and Emotions." In *The Oxford Handbook of Aesthetics*, ed. Jerrold Levinson. New York: Oxford University Press.

Ollett, Andrew. 2012. "Rasa-bhākhā: Some Vernacular Concepts of Rasa." Paper delivered at the 15th World Sanskrit Conference, New Delhi.

—. 2015. "Ritual Texts and Literary Texts in Abhinavagupta's Aesthetics: Notes on the Beginning of the 'Critical Reconstruction.'" *Journal of Indian Philosophy*. DOI 10.1007/s10781-015-9277-4.

Pandey, K. C. 1963. *Abhinavagupta: An Historical and Philosophical Study*. Varanasi: Chowkhamba Sanskrit Series Office.
Plamper, Jan. 2010. "The History of Emotions." *History and Theory* 49: 237–65.
Pollock, Sheldon. 1998a. "Bhoja's *Śṛṅgāraprakāśa* and the Problem of Rasa: A Historical Introduction and Translation." *Asiatische Studien/Études asiatiques* 70, 1: 117–92.
—. 1998b. "The Cosmopolitan Vernacular." *Journal of Asian Studies* 57, 1: 6–37.
—. 2001a. "The Death of Sanskrit." *Comparative Studies in Society and History* 43, 2: 392–426.
—. 2001b. "The New Intellectuals in Seventeenth-Century India." *Indian Economic and Social History Review* 38, 1: 3–31.
—. 2001c. "The Social Aesthetic and Sanskrit Literary Theory." *Journal of Indian Philosophy* 29, 1–2: 197–229.
—. 2003. "Sanskrit Literature from the Inside Out." In *Literary Cultures in History: Reconstructions from South Asia*, ed. Sheldon Pollock. Berkeley: University of California Press.
—. 2005. *The Ends of Man at the End of Premodernity*. Amsterdam: Royal Netherlands Academy of Arts and Sciences, Stichting J. Gonda-Fonds.
—. 2006. *The Language of the Gods in the World of Men: Sanskrit, Culture, and Power in Premodern India*. Berkeley: University of California Press.
—, ed. and trans. 2007. *Rāma's Last Act by Bhavabhūti*. New York: New York University Press.
—. 2010. "What Was Bhaṭṭa Nāyaka Saying? The Hermeneutical Transformation of Indian Aesthetics." In *Epic and Argument in Sanskrit Literary History*, ed. Sheldon Pollock. Delhi: Manohar, 143–84.
—. 2011. "The Languages of Science in Early-Modern India." In *Forms of Knowledge in Early Modern Asia*, ed. Sheldon Pollock. Durham: Duke University Press, 19–48.
—. 2012a. "From Rasa Seen to Rasa Heard." In *Aux abords de la clairière: Études indiennes et comparées en l'honneur de Charles Malamoud*, ed. Caterina Guenzi and Sylvia d'Intino. Paris: Brepols.
—. 2012b. "*Vyakti* and the History of Rasa." *Vimarsha, Journal of the Rasthriya Sanskrit Sansthan* (World Sanskrit Conference Special Issue), 6: 232–53.
—. 2014. "What Was Philology in Sanskrit?" In *World Philology*, ed. Sheldon Pollock et al. Cambridge, Mass: Harvard University Press.
Raghavan, V. 1932. "Writers Quoted in the Abhinavabharati." *Journal of Oriental Research*, Madras 6: 149–70; 199–223.
—. 1975. *The Number of Rasas*. 3rd rev. ed. Adyar: Adyar Library and Research Centre.
—. 1978. *Bhoja's Śṛṅgāraprakāśa*. 3rd ed. Madras: Punarvasu; 2nd ed., 1963.
Rajendran, C. 2003. *Vyaktiviveka: A Critical Study*. Delhi: New Bharatiya Book Corporation.
—. 2004. "Influence of Pūrvamīmāṃsā on Alaṅkāraśāstra." In *Understanding Tradition*. Calicut: Calicut University Press, 111–18.
Ramaraju, B. 2002. *Contribution of Andhra to Samskrit Literature*. Hyderabad: B. Ramaraju.
Robinson, Jenefer. 1983. "Emotion, Judgment, and Desire." *Journal of Philosophy* 80: 731–41.
—. 2005. *Deeper Than Reason: Art, Emotions and Ethics*. New York: Oxford University Press.
Rorty, Richard. 1989. *Contingency, Irony, and Solidarity*. Cambridge: Cambridge University Press.
Rosenwein, Barbara H. 2005. "Worrying About Emotions in History." *American Historical Review* 107: 821–45.
Sanderson, Alexis. 2005. "A Commentary on the Opening Verses of *Tantrasāra*." In *Sāmarasya*, ed. Sadananda Das and Ernst Fürlinger. New Delhi: D. K. Printworld.

——. 2007. "The Śaiva Exegesis of Kashmir." In *Mélanges tantriques à la mémoire d'Hélène Brunner*, ed. Dominic Goodall and André Padoux. Pondicherry: Institut Français d'Indologie/École française d'Extrême-Orient.
Sellars, Wilfrid. 1963. *Science, Perception and Reality.* London: Routledge & Kegan Paul.
Shulman, David. 2012. *More Than Real: A History of the Imagination in South India.* Cambridge, Mass.: Harvard University Press.
Solf, W. 1886. *Die Kaçmîr-Recension der Pañcâçikâ.* Kiel: C. F. Haeseler.
Solomon, Robert C. 2002. "Back to Basics: On the Very Idea of 'Basic Emotions.'" *Journal for the Theory of Social Behaviour* 32, 2: 115–44.
Shrinivasan, Shrinivasa Ayya. 1980. *On the Composition of the Nāṭyaśāstra.* Reinbek: Verlag für Orientalistische Fachpublikationen.
Stainton, Hamsa. 2013. "Poetry and Prayer: Stotras in the Religious and Literary History of Kashmir." Ph.D diss., Columbia University.
Thrailkill, Jane F. 2007. *Affecting Fictions: Mind, Body, and Emotion in American Literary Realism.* Cambridge, Mass: Harvard University Press.
Tubb, Gary and Yigal Bronner. 2008. "*Vastutas tu*: Methodology and the New School of Sanskrit Poetics." *Journal of Indian Philosophy* 36: 619–32.
Varma, K. M. 1958. *Seven Words in Bharata: What Do They Signify?* Bombay: Orient Longmans.
Wellek, René. 1974 (1942). "Literature and the Arts." In *Literary Criticism—Idea and Act,* ed. W. K. Wimsatt. Chicago: University of Chicago Press.
Wimsatt, W. K. and M. Beardsley. 1949. "The Affective Fallacy." *Sewanee Review* 57, 1: 31–55.

Index

ābhāsa. *See* semblance of rasa
Abhinavabhāratī, xviii
Abhinavagupta, 187–93; on aesthetic elements, 196, 200–201, 202–3; and Anandavardhana, 188–89; on animals, 248–49; and Bhatta Nayaka, 19, 144, 150–51, 190–91, 192; on Bhatta Tota, 181, 182, 183, 187; on *camatkāra*, xv; and chronology, 36–37; and commentary, 38–39; on didactic function of rasa, 68, 85; and documentary lacunae, 37–38; on emotions, xvi; on epistemology, 210–18; on imitation, 195, 211, 220–21; importance of, 49; and Jagannatha, 315, 316; and Mahima Bhatta, 106; and Mammata, 189, 224; on *manas*, xvii; on manifestation, 13–14, 188, 189, 192; and methodology, xiii; minimal influence of, 35; on peaceful rasa, 22, 48, 193; and philosophy, 188; on proper terms, 78; and Ramachandra/Gunachandra, 189, 239; on rasa as enhancement of stable emotions, 15, 281; on rasa as instruction, 32, 33, 192–93; on rasa as residing in the character, 15; on rasa typology, 33, 48, 206–7, 216; on *rasikas*, 34; on reception theory, 19–20, 37, 38, 99, 189, 190, 191; and religion, 21, 22, 36, 302; and Ruyyaka, 235; on semblance of rasa, 27–28, 213–14; on stable emotions identified with rasa, 195–96, 201–2; on storyworld, 20–21; on taste, 43, 190, 205–6; text selections, 193–223; on tragic rasa, 27; on typology of stable emotions, 198, 199; and Vedanta, 24; and Vishvanatha, 261; and Vishvanathadeva, 311. *See also* *The New* Dramatic Art
absorption (*viśrānti*), 18–19, 147, 153, 191
acting, 6. *See also* drama; *Treatise on Drama*
The Actor's Sutras, 47
actualization (*bhāvanā*): Abhinavagupta on, 38; Bhatta Nayaka on, 18, 146, 147, 149, 151, 152, 153–54, 190; Dhanamjaya/Dhanika on, 172–73, 175, 177; Jagannatha on, 320, 322; translation of, xv; Vidyanatha on, 255–56, 257
Advaita, 24, 36
aesthetic elements (*vibhāvādi*): Abhinavagupta on, 196, 200–201, 202–3; Anandavardhana on, 97; Bhoja on, 130, 135; as figures of speech, 11; Kuntaka on, 98; Mahima Bhatta on, 106–7, 108, 109; and philosophy/religion, 36; Pratiharenduraja on, 71; and rasa as instruction, 32–33; rasa as residing in the character, 25; and rasa as residing in drama, 7–9; and reception theory, 25–26, 156; Rupa Gosvamin/Jiva Gosvamin on, 304; Singabhupala on, 274; terms for, xv, 27; *Treatise on Drama* on, 7–8, 26–27;

aesthetic elements (*continued*)
Udbhata on, 11; Vidyadhara on, 251, 252; Vishvanatha on, 263. *See also Sutra on Rasa*; *specific elements*
aesthetics, 1–5; beauty in, 3; and creativity, 2; and intellectual history, 35–41; and interpretation, 3; and separate cultural domains, 2; *Sutra on Rasa* as foundational text of, 7; and taste, 41–44. *See also* Western aesthetics
aesthetics revolution. *See* reception theory
affectionate utterances: Bhamaha on, 56, 57, 58; Bhoja on, 114, 129, 134–35; Dandin on, 59, 61–62, 134–35; Kuntaka on, 99, 104; Pratiharenduraja on, 69–70; Udbhata on, 66, 68, 70. *See also* emotion tropes
affective fallacy, 44–45
ahaṃkāra, xvii
alaṅkāraśāstra (poetics), 6–7, 10, 56, 84–86
Amaranandayogin, 256
Amaru, 276
Ambrosial River of the Rasa of Devotion (Rupa Gosvamin), 303–6. *See also* Rupa Gosvamin
American New Criticism, 5, 15
Analysis of Literature (Dhanika), 155
Analysis of "Manifestation" (Mahima Bhatta), 107–9. *See also* Mahima Bhatta
Anandavardhana, 87–89; and Abhinavagupta, 188–89; on aesthetic elements, 97; and Arjunavarmadeva, 276; and Bhatta Lollata, 75; Bhatta Nayaka on, 144, 145, 146–47; and chronology, 37, 77; on conflicting rasas, 29, 94, 95–96; on emotion tropes, 11–12, 89, 91–93; on flaws of rasa, 224–25; identity of, 87; *Light on Implicature* (Anandavardhana), on rasa as instruction, 32; on manifestation, xv, 12–13, 88–89, 90–91, 93, 95, 97, 188; on proper terms, 43, 78, 88, 90; on rasa as residing in the character, 15–16, 19, 20, 88, 89, 188; on rasa as residing in the poet, 5; and rasa theory expansion from drama to poetry, 12; text selections, 90–97; and Vidyadhara, 248
Anantadasa, 263, 265
animals: Abhinavagupta on, 248–49; Bhoja on, 127; Pratiharenduraja on, 68, 70; Singabhupala on, 249, 270–71, 273–74; Vidyadhara on, 248–49, 254–55, 270
antaḥkaraṇa, xvi, xvii
anubhāva. See reactions
anuvyavasāya, 38, 190
aphorism on rasa. *See Sutra on Rasa*
arising of rasa. *See* epistemology
Arjunavarmadeva, 31, 276–77; on emotion tropes, 279–80; text selections, 276–80
Arnold, Matthew, 4
arthavāda. See eventful narrative
audience as site of rasa. *See* reception theory

Bahurupa Mishra, 157–80
Bana, 16
Baumgarten, Alexander, 4
Beardsley, Monroe, 44, 45
The Bearer of the Ganges of Rasa (Jagannatha), 317–26. *See also* Jagannatha
beauty (*saundarya*), 3
Bhāgavatapurāṇa, 22, 23, 285, 302
Bhamaha, 55–57; on emotion tropes, 10–11, 56–58, 85; on rasa as instruction, 31; text selections, 57–58
Bhanudatta, 280–82; and chronology, xiii; poetry by, xiv, 40; on stable emotions, 76, 280–81, 283; text selections, 282–85
Bharata, 7, 47. *See also Treatise on Drama*
Bhasarvajna, xvi–xvii
Bhatta Lollata, 74–76; and chronology, 74; and Kuntaka, 98; on ontology of rasa, 89; on rasa as enhancement of stable emotions, 23, 75–76, 195, 281; on rasa as residing in the character, 15, 23, 89; Shri Shankuka on, 74, 79; on *Sutra on Rasa,* 75–77; text selections, 76–79
Bhatta Narasimha: and Bhatta Nrisimha, 157; and documentary lacunae, 111; on rasa as residing in the character, 113–14, 115–16
Bhatta Narayana, 37
Bhatta Nayaka, 16–19; and Abhinavagupta, 19, 144, 150–51, 190–91, 192; on absorption, 18–19, 147, 153; and chronology, 37, 181–82; on commonization, 18, 33, 67, 145, 146, 149, 153, 154; and Dhanamjaya/Dhanika, 144, 156; and documentary lacunae, 144; on

experientialization, 18, 19, 38, 146, 147, 151, 152, 153; identity of, 144–45; Jagannatha on, 147–48, 316, 319–20; and Mahima Bhatta, 106; on manifestation, 13, 20, 146–48, 149, 150–51, 153; and Mimamsa, 36, 145, 146, 147, 190; and philosophy, 36; on rasa as instruction, 31–32, 33, 192; on rasa as residing in the poet, 6; on reception theory, xv, 16–19, 38, 145, 147–48, 150–51; and religion, 21, 256; text selections (*Commentary on the* Treatise on Drama), 148; text selections (*Mirror of the Heart*), 149–54
Bhatta Nrisimha, 157–80
Bhatta Tota, 181–82; Abhinavagupta on, 181, 182, 183, 187; and chronology, 37, 181–82; on rasa as instruction, 32, 192; on rasa as residing in the poet, 6; on rasa theory expansion from drama to poetry, 14; on reception theory, 182; on religion, 21; on Shri Shankuka, 78, 182, 183–86; text selections, 182–87
Bhavabhuti, 13
bhāvakāvya. *See* emotion poetry
bhāvanā. *See* actualization
bhāvas. *See* emotions
bhāvayan (bringing into being), 6
bhāvukas, 22
Bhoja, 110–14; and chronology, xiii, 154, 155; on didactic function of rasa, 68, 85; and documentary lacunae, 111; elite status of, 39; on emotion tropes, 114, 128–30, 134–35; and Kavikarnapura, 291; Mammata on, 224; and methodology, xiii; minimal influence of, 35; and philosophy, 36; and Ramachandra/Gunachandra, 239; on rasa as love, 111–12, 291; on rasa as residing in the character, 16, 113, 157; on rasa theory expansion from drama to poetry, 14; on rasa typology, 15, 41, 132–33; and reception theory, 113, 114, 156; and Samkhya, 36, 112, 122; on sense of self, 36, 112, 120, 123, 134, 135–36; text selections (*Light on Passion*), 119–43; text selections (*Necklace for the Goddess of Language*), 115–19; and Vishvanatha, 261
Blazing Sapphire (Ujjvalanīlamaṇi), 302
bliss. *See* rasa as pleasure
Bouquet of Rasa (Rasamañjarī) (Bhanudatta), 40, 280
Brief Annotation (Bhatta Nrisimha), 157–80. *See also* Bhatta Nrisimha
Brief Elucidation (Pratiharenduraja), 68–70, 71, 72–73, 74. *See also* Pratiharenduraja
buddhi, translation of, xvi, xvii
Buddhism, 27, 78, 196, 207

camatkāra, xv
cause and effect: Mahima Bhatta on, 107; *Treatise on Drama* on, 51–52
The Central Gem (Mallinatha), 249, 250, 252, 253, 254, 255. *See also* Mallinatha
Chaitanya, 22, 290–91, 293, 300, 301
Chandidasa, 227
character as site of rasa. *See* rasa as residing in the character; rasa as residing in drama
chronology, xii–xiii, 36–37. *See also specific authors*
cittavṛtti (psychological modality), xvi, 19, 89, 106, 189
colonialism, 4, 40
comic rasa, xvii, 131
commentary: and intellectual history, 38–39, 190; and methodology, xiii. *See also specific authors*
Commentary (Lokanatha Chakravartin), xiii, 291, 293, 294, 295, 296, 298
Commentary on Analysis of "Manifestation" (Ruyyaka), 237–38. *See also* Ruyyaka
**Commentary on the* Treatise on Drama (Bhatta Lollata), 76–79. *See also* Bhatta Lollata
**Commentary on the* Treatise on Drama (Bhatta Nayaka), 144, 148
**Commentary on the* Treatise on Drama (Shri Shankuka), 79–84. *See also* Shri Shankuka
commonization (*sādhāraṇīkaraṇa*): Abhinavagupta on, 194, 203–4; Bhatta Nayaka on, 18, 33, 67, 145, 146, 149, 153, 154; Vishvanatha on, 262
compassion, 27

Compendium of Tropes (Ruyyaka), 235
conflicting rasas: Anandavardhana on, 29, 94, 95–96; Arjunavarmadeva on, 276–77; Dhanamjaya/Dhanika on, 29–31, 161, 162–64; Kuntaka on, 103–4; Mammata on, 29, 30, 225. *See also* mixture of rasas
The Connoisseur's Sport (Sahṛdayalīlā), 235
consciousness: Kuntaka on, 98–99; and Vedanta, 24–25
content rasa, 59
Critique of Judgment (Kant), 4

Dandin, 58–60; and Bhamaha, 56, 57; Bhoja on, 114, 128, 129, 134–35; and chronology, 36; on emotion tropes, 10–11, 59–60, 61–65, 85, 134–35; importance of, 59; on rasa as residing in the character, 15; on rasa as residing in the poet, 6; text selections, 60–65
Darwin, Charles, 8–9, 15
Dev, 281
devotional rasa, 41; Jagannatha on, 316–17, 325–26; Kavikarnapura on, 291, 294, 299; Rupa Gosvamin/Jiva Gosvamin on, 300, 301, 302, 303–10; Vopadeva on, 22, 286, 287–89. *See also* religion
Dhanamjaya, 154–57; and Abhinavagupta, 190, 191; and Bhatta Nayaka, 144, 156; and chronology, xiii, 154; and epistemology, 155–56; on rasa as instruction, 32; on rasa typology, 15; on reception theory, 155–56, 174; text selections, 157–80; and Vidyadhara, 248; and Vishvanatha, 261
Dhanika, 24, 154–57; and Abhinavagupta, 190, 191; and Bhatta Nayaka, 144, 156; and chronology, xiii, 154–55; on conflicting rasas, 29–30; and documentary lacunae, 155; and epistemology, 155–56; on manifestation, 13, 20, 167–70, 172, 174–75; on rasa as instruction, 32; on rasa typology, 15; on reception theory, 20, 155–56, 157, 158, 175; text selections, 157–80; and Vedanta, 256; and Vidyanatha, 255; and Vishvanatha, 261
Dharmadatta, 261
Dharmakirti, 78
dhṛti, xvi
dhvani (implicature). *See* manifestation
didactic function of rasa: Abhinavagupta on, 68, 85; Bhoja on, 68, 85; and Rudrata, 85; and Udbhata, 67–68
Divine Jewel of Ornamentation (Kavikarnapura), xiii, 293–99. *See also* Kavikarnapura
documentary lacunae: and intellectual history, 37–38; and methodology, xi, xii, 35, 37; and *Treatise on Drama,* 49. *See also specific works*
drama: Abhinavagupta on, 190, 191, 196–97, 207–10, 218–22; Bhatta Tota on, 182, 183; Ramachandra/Gunachandra on, 246–47; rasa as residing in, 7–9, 48–49, 66, 243. *See also* rasa theory expansion from drama to poetry; *Treatise on Drama*
Druhin, 50
Dufrenne, Mikel, 26, 42

Eagleton, Terry, 39
The Earring of the Many-Colored Lotus (Shri Shankuka), 77
ego. *See* sense of self
elites, 39
Elixir for the Rasika (Arjunavarmadeva), 277–80. *See also* Arjunavarmadeva
emotion poetry (*bhāvakāvya*): Arjunavarmadeva on, 276; Mammata on, 225; Pratiharenduraja on, 68, 69–70; Rupa Gosvamin/Jiva Gosvamin on, 302
emotion tropes: Anandavardhana on, 11–12, 89, 91–93; Bhamaha on, 10–11, 56–58, 85; Bhoja on, 114, 128–30, 134–35; Dandin on, 10–11, 59–60, 61–65, 85, 134–35; Kuntaka on, 12, 99, 102–5; Pratiharenduraja on, 11, 66, 69–71; Ramachandra/Gunachandra on, 245; Rudrata on, 84; Udbhata on, 11, 66, 68, 70
emotions: Bhoja on, 112, 133; Dandin on, 59; definitions of, xvi, 6; delimiting of, 7–9; Dhanamjaya/Dhanika on, 156, 159; *Treatise on Drama* on, 6, 7–8, 49, 53–55; Western aesthetics on, 4–5, 44–45. *See also* stable emotions; transitory emotions
encomia. *See* praise poems

epistemology, 15–16, 155–56; Abhinavagupta on, 210–18; Anandavardhana on, 19–20, 89; Bhatta Nayaka on, 17; Dhanamjaya/Dhanika on, 20; Shri Shankuka on, 89; and Vedanta, 315–16. *See also* actualization; imitation; manifestation
erotic rasa: Anandavardhana on, 97; Arjunavarmadeva on, 276–77, 278–79; Bhamaha on, 57; Bhanudatta on, 280; Bhoja on, 125, 126, 131; and religion, 22; Rudrata on, 85, 86; and semblance of rasa (*ābhāsa*), 28; translation of, xvii; *Treatise on Drama* on, 22, 52–53; Vopadeva on, 286, 289–90. *See also* erotic thwarted rasa
erotic thwarted rasa (*vipralambhaśṛṅgāra*): Kuntaka on, 100, 103–4; Pratiharenduraja on, 71; vs. tragic rasa, 53; translation of, xv–xvi; *Treatise on Drama* on, 22, 52–53; Udbhata on, 71
Essence of Literary Art (Modak), 40
Essential Component of the Ornament of Poetry (Udbhata), 68–74. *See also* Udbhata
eventful narrative (*arthavāda*), 36
Examination of Literature (Shrivatsalanchana), 311
Examination of The Wishing Vine (*Kalpalatāviveka*), 189
Exegesis (Abhinavagupta), 181, 187
Exegesis of Rasa (Bhatta Lollata), 74–75
Exegesis (Tilaka), 68, 69, 70, 71, 74. *See also* Tilaka
experientialization, 18, 19, 38, 146, 147, 151, 152, 153
expression theory, 5–6
The Eye (Anantadasa), 263, 265
Eye for Light on Implicature (Abhinavagupta), 49, 187, 188. *See also* Abhinavagupta

fantasy rasa, 40–41, 132
figures of speech. *See* emotion tropes
flaws of rasa, 29, 224–25, 228–35. *See also* conflicting rasas
foundational factors: Bhanudatta on, 280; Bhatta Nayaka on, 18, 150, 152, 154; *bhāva* as representing, xvi; Bhoja on, 130–31; Dhanamjaya/Dhanika on, 158, 175–77; Kuntaka on, 101; Pratiharenduraja on, 69; Ramachandra/Gunachandra on, 243–44; and rasa as residing in drama, 7; translation of, xiv–xv; *Treatise on Drama* on, 7. *See also* aesthetic elements

Gadamer, Hans-Georg, 4
The Girl Named Digit-of-the-Moon (Vishvanatha), 261
Gracian, Balthasar, 43
Grice, H. P., xv
Guarding the Tradition (Vadijanghala), 59, 60, 61
Gunachandra, 239–40; and Abhinavagupta, 189, 239; text selections, 241–55
guṇas (language qualities), 59

haughty declarations: Bhamaha on, 56, 57, 58; Bhoja on, 114, 128; Dandin on, 59, 64–65; Kuntaka on, 99; Udbhata on, 66
Hegel, G. W. F., 4
Hemachandra: and Abhinavagupta, 189; on Bhatta Lollata, 74–75; and Bhatta Tota, 181; and Ramachandra/Gunachandra, 239; and religion, 22; and Shri Shankuka, 77
Hemadri, 286
hermeneutics, 147. *See also* Bhatta Nayaka; reception theory
heroic rasa, 131–32, 277, 279
Hṛdayadarpaṇa (Mirror of the Heart) (Bhatta Nayaka). *See Mirror of the Heart*
Hume, David, 42, 43
Hundred of Amaru, 28
Hundred Poems to the Goddess (Devīśataka) (Anandavardhana), 87
Hutcheson, Francis, 4

imitation: Abhinavagupta on, 195, 211, 220–21; Bhatta Tota on, 182, 183–86; Ramachandra/Gunachandra on, 240, 246–47; Shri Shankuka on, 2, 36, 78–79, 182, 183–85
Immortal Life of Chaitanya (Caitanyacaritāmṛta), 301
implicature (*dhvani*), xv. *See also* manifestation
Induraja. *See* Pratiharenduraja
An Inquiry Concerning Beauty (Hutcheson), 4

instruction. *See* rasa as instruction
intellectual history, 35–41; Abhinavagupta on, 191; and chronology, 36–37; and commentary, 38–39, 190; and documentary lacunae, 37–38; and Jagannatha, 316; and Kavikarnapura, 293; and philosophy/religion, 35–36, 44, 188; and Vidyanatha, 256
interpretation, 3
intimation of rasa, 22
Introduction to Linguistic Modalities (Śabdavyāpāraparicaya) (Mammata), 224

Jagannatha, 314–17; on Bhatta Nayaka, 147–48, 316, 319–20; and chronology, 37; on rasa typology, 41; and religion, 36; on semblance of rasa, 29, 315, 326; on *Sutra on Rasa,* 48, 323–24; text selections, 317–26; and Vedanta, 24–25, 315; and Vishvanathadeva, 310, 311, 315
Jain tradition, 191, 240
James, William, 8
The Jewel Store (Kumarasvamin), 257–58, 259, 260–61. *See also* Kumarasvamin
Jiva Gosvamin, 36, 300–3; and chronology, xiii; and Jagannatha, 315, 316; and Kavikarnapura, 291, 292, 293; and rasa as residing in the character, 23, 304; text selections (*Passage Through the Impassable*), 303, 304, 305, 306–10; text selections (*Treatise on Divine Love*), 306–10

Kalhana. *See River of Kings*
Kalidasa, 10, 47
Kant, Immanuel, 4, 33
karuṇa rasa. *See* tragic rasa (*karuṇa*)
Kavikarnapura, 23, 290–93; and chronology, xiii, 293; on erotic rasa, xvii; text selections, 293–99
kāvya. *See* literature
Kulapati Mishra, 40
Kumarasvamin, 255, 256; text selections, 257–58, 259, 260–61
Kumarila, 147
Kuntaka, 98–99; on Anandavardhana, 89; and chronology, 37; on emotion tropes, 12, 99, 102–5; on imitation, 79; and manifestation, 13; on rasa as enhancement of stable emotions, 98, 99, 100; Ruyyaka on, 37; text selections, 99–106

The Lamp (on the *Ten Forms*) (Bahurupa Mishra), 157–80
Lamp for Spiritual Discipline of the Inner Self (Amaranandayogin), 256
Latour, Bruno, 4
Light on Fundamental Principles (Bhoja), 112
Light on Implicature (Anandavardhana), 90–97
Light on Passion (Bhoja), 110, 119–43. *See also* Bhoja
Light on Poetry (Mammata), 226–35. *See also* Mammata
Literary Investigations (Bhatta Tota), 182–87. *See also* Bhatta Tota
literature (*kāvya*): Abhinavagupta on, 189–90; Bhatta Tota on, 182; and decline of rasa theory, 40, 41; Mammata on, 224; vs. *nāṭya* (drama), 56; and religion, 21, 23–24, 302–3; translation of, xvii–xviii; and *vakrokti,* 98; Vishvanatha on, 261, 263
locus of rasa (*rasāśraya*): Anandavardhana on, 89; Bhanudatta on, 281; Bhatta Narasimha on, 157; Bhatta Nayaka on, 17; Dhanamjaya/Dhanika on, 20; and epistemology, 155–56; Kavikarnapura on, 291; Kumarasvamin on, 260; Ramachandra/Gunachandra on, 240, 242; Singabhupala on, 270; Vidyadhara on, 249; Vidyanatha on, 256, 257; Vishvanatha on, 262, 264. *See also* rasa as residing in the character; rasa as residing in drama; reception theory
Lokanatha Chakravartin, xiii, 291, 293, 294, 295, 296, 298
Looking Glass of Poetry (Dandin), 60–65. *See also* Dandin

macabre rasa, 292
Mahābhārata, 87, 93, 304, 325
Mahima Bhatta, 106–7; and chronology, 37, 106; commentaries on, xiii; on manifestation, 13, 106–9; and Shri Shankuka, 78, 106; text selections, 107–9

Mallinatha, 111, 153–54, 249; text selections, 250, 252, 253, 254, 255
Mammata, 224–25; and Abhinavagupta, 189, 224; and Arjunavarmadeva, 276; on Bhatta Nayaka, 151; and chronology, 37; on conflicting rasas, 29, 30, 225; and documentary lacunae, 38; on flaws of rasa, 29, 224–25, 228–35; importance of, 224; and Kavikarnapura, 291; on manifestation, 189; Paramananda Chakravartin on, 227–28; on peaceful rasa, 21, 225, 226; on proper terms, 192, 225, 229, 231; and Ramachandra/Gunachandra, 239; on religion, 22; Ruyyaka on, 226, 235; and Shri Shankuka, 77; and Shrivatsalanchana, 311; text selections, 226–35; and Vidyadhara, 248; and Vishvanatha, 227, 261
manas, xvi–xvii
manifestation (*vyakti*, *vyañjanā*): Abhinavagupta on, 13–14, 188, 189, 192; Anandavardhana on, xv, 12–13, 88–89, 90–91, 93, 95, 97, 188; Bhatta Nayaka on, 13, 20, 146–48, 149, 150–51, 153; Bhoja on, 119, 121–22; Dhanamjaya/Dhanika on, 13, 20, 167–70, 172, 174–75; Jagannatha on, 316, 317–18; Mahima Bhatta on, 13, 106–9; and rasa as residing in the character, 89; and rasa theory expansion from drama to poetry, 12–14; and reception theory, 19–20, 38; Ruyyaka on, 189, 235, 236–38; taxonomy of, 12–13; Vidyadhara on, 249; Vidyanatha on, 255; Vishvanatha on, 262–64, 265
Manual of Poetry (Hemachandra), 239
Mayura, 78
methodology, xi–xviii; and access to intellectual history, 35; and chronology, xii–xiii; citations, xviii; and commentary, xiii; and documentary lacunae, xi, xii, 35, 37; exclusions, xii; and poetry examples, xiii–xiv; and terminology, xiv–xviii
Mimamsa: and Bhatta Nayaka, 36, 145, 146, 147, 190; on emotion tropes, 11; and rasa as residing in the character, 17, 18; and Vedanta, 311
mimesis. *See* imitation
Mirror of Drama (Ramachandra and Gunachandra), 241–55. *See also* Gunachandra; Ramachandra
Mirror of the Heart (Hṛdayadarpaṇa) (Bhatta Nayaka), 149–54; and chronology, xiii. *See also* Bhatta Nayaka
Mirror of Literary Art (Vishvanatha), 263–69. *See also* Vishvanatha
Mirror of Poetry (Rajacudamani Diksita), 39–40
mixture of rasas, 138–42, 279–80. *See also* conflicting rasas
Modak, Acyutaray, 40
modernity, 4, 315
The Moon on the Rasa Ocean (Singabhupala), 271–75
Moonlight of Rapture (Vishveshvara), 269
Moonrise of Chaitanya (Caitanyacandrodaya) (Kavikarnapura), 293
The Moon's Crescent (Mṛgākalekhā) (Vishvanathadeva), 310
Mukula Bhatta, 60
mundane vs. supermundane rasas: Abhinavagupta on, 20–21, 201–3, 219, 302; Bhanudatta on, 281–82, 284; Bhatta Nayaka on, 152; Dhanamjaya/Dhanika on, 20; Jagannatha on, 317; Ramachandra on, 252; Rupa Gosvamin/Jiva Gosvamin on, 23, 301, 302, 305, 306, 307–9; Vidyanatha on, 256, 257–58, 259, 260; Vishvanatha on, 266
music (*saṃgīta*), 2

Nagesha Bhatta, 311–12
Namisadhu, 84, 85, 86
Naraharisuri, 256
Narayana, 261
nāṭya (drama), 56
nāṭyaśāstra (theory of drama), 6. *See also* *Treatise on Drama*
Necklace for the Goddess of Language (Bhoja): authorship of, 110; text selections, 115–19. *See also* Bhoja
The Nectar Ocean of Literary Art (Vishvanathadeva), 312–14. *See also* Vishvanathadeva
The New Dramatic Art (Abhinavagupta), 49, 189, 193–223. *See also* Abhinavagupta

New Logic, 314
New Scholars, 316, 320–22
noble rasa, 135
Notes (Namisadhu), 84, 85, 86

Observations (Dhanika), 157–80
ontology of rasa. *See* locus of rasa
Ornament of the Fame of King Prataparudra (Vidyanatha), 257–61. *See also* Vidyanatha
Ornament of Poetry (Bhamaha), 57–58. *See also* Bhamaha
Ornament of Poetry (Rudrata): text selections, 85–86. *See also* Rudrata
ornaments. *See* emotion tropes

painting, 2, 24, 280
Panini, 47
Paramananda Chakravartin, 227–28
Passage Through the Impassable (Jiva Gosvamin), 303, 304, 305, 306–10. *See also* Jiva Gosvamin
passion. *See* sense of self
peaceful rasa: Abhinavagupta on, 22, 48, 193; Bhatta Tota on, 187; Bhoja on, 133; Dhanamjaya/Dhanika on, 165, 179; dispute over, 15; Jagannatha on, 324–25; in *Mahābhārata,* 87; Mammata on, 21, 225, 226; and religion, 21–22; and *Treatise on Drama,* 48
Pearls of the Bhāgavata (Vopadeva), 287–90. *See also* Vopadeva
pedagogy. *See* rasa as instruction
Philosopher's Stone of the Four Ends of Man (Caturvargacintāmaṇi), 286
philosophy: and intellectual history, 35–36, 188; Vedanta, 24–25, 256, 310–14, 315–16; Vishvanatha on, 262
physical reactions. *See* reactions
pleasure. *See* rasa as pleasure
poetics (*alaṅkāraśāstra*), 6–7, 10, 56, 84–86
poetry. *See* literature
postcolonial thought, 44
praise poems, 247–48, 255, 261
Pratiharenduraja: and chronology, 37; on didactic function of rasa, 85; on emotion poetry, 68, 69–70; on emotion tropes, 11, 66, 69–71; on proper terms, 67; on quiescence, 72–73; on rasa as instruction, 31; on rasa as residing in the character, 67; on stable emotions, 31, 32, 67, 70; text selections, 68–70, 71, 72–73, 74; on Udbhata's identity, 65, 66
proper terms: Anandavardhana on, 43, 78, 88, 90; Kuntaka on, 102–3; Mammata on, 192, 225, 229, 231; Shri Shankuka on, 78, 192; Udbhata on, 11, 67, 78, 88, 192
propriety, 43–44; Anandavardhana on, 93–94; Kavikarnapura on, 295–96; Mammata on, 225; and rasa as instruction, 32, 33; Udbhata on, 72. *See also* semblance of rasa; social states
psychophysical responses (*sāttvikabhāvas*), 7, 55, 84, 160. *See also* aesthetic elements
purāṇas, 325

"The Quest for the Golden Flowers" (*Saugandhikāharaṇa*), 261
quiescence: Bhoja on, 140; Dhanamjaya/Dhanika on, 165; Pratiharenduraja on, 72–73; Ratnashrijnana on, 67; Udbhata on, 11, 66, 72, 73

Rajachudamani Dikshita, 37, 39–40
rajaḥ, xv
Ramachandra, 239–40; and Abhinavagupta, 189, 239; text selections, 241–55
Rāmāyaṇa (Valmiki), 5, 28
rapture. *See* rasa as pleasure
rasa, translations of, xvii, 4
rasa as instruction, 31–34; Abhinavagupta on, 32, 33, 192–93
rasa as love: Bhoja on, 111–12, 291; Kavikarnapura on, 299
rasa of phenomenal reality, 285
rasa as pleasure: Abhinavagupta on, 191, 195, 210, 239–40, 292; Dhanamjaya/Dhanika on, 292; Jagannatha on, 321–22; Kavikarnapura on, 292, 295, 297; Mahima Bhatta on, 109; Ramachandra/Gunachandra on, 239–40, 241–42, 292; Vidyadhara on, 252–53; Vishvanatha on, 265–66
rasa as residing in the character, 15–16, 19, 20; and aesthetic elements, 25;

Anandavardhana on, 15–16, 19, 20, 88, 89, 188; Bhatta Lollata on, 15, 23, 89; Bhatta Narasimha on, 113–14, 115–16; Bhoja on, 16, 113, 157; and epistemology, 155–56; and Mimamsa, 17, 18; Pratiharenduraja on, 67; and religion, 23, 301, 304. *See also* emotion tropes; locus of rasa
rasa as residing in the drama, 7–9, 48–49, 66, 243. *See also* locus of rasa
rasa as residing in the poet, 5–6. *See also* locus of rasa
rasa as residing in the reader/viewer. *See* reception theory
rasa theory: decline of, 39–41; origins of, 39; relevance of, 45. *See also* intellectual history; methodology; rasa theory expansion from drama to poetry
rasa theory expansion from drama to poetry, 6–7, 9–16; and emotion tropes, 10–12; and manifestation, 12–14; and *Ornament of Poetry*, 56; and rasa typology, 11, 14–16; and translation, xviii; transparency of, 9–10
rasa typology: Abhinavagupta on, 33, 48, 206–7, 216; Bhoja on, 15, 41, 132–33; and conflicting rasas, 29–31; and decline of rasa theory, 41; Kavikarnapura on, 293–94; Pratiharenduraja on, 70; and rasa theory expansion from drama to poetry, 11, 14–16; Rudrata on, 85, 86; Rupa Gosvamin on, 300; and semblance of rasa, 29; Shri Shankuka on, 80–81; Tilaka on, 70; *Treatise on Drama* on, 48; Udbhata on, 11, 66, 70; Vopadeva on, 287–88. *See also specific rasas*
rasa-laden statements: Anandavardhana on, 89, 91, 92; Arjunavarmadeva on, 279–80; Bhamaha on, 56, 57, 58; Bhoja on, 114, 128–29; Dandin on, 59–60, 62–64; Kuntaka on, 99, 102, 103; Pratiharenduraja on, 70–71; Ramachandra/Gunachandra on, 245; Udbhata on, 66, 70. *See also* emotion tropes
rasāśraya. *See* locus of rasa
rasasūtra. *See Sutra on Rasa*
rasikas: Anantadasa on, 265; Bhoja on, 125; Dhanamjaya/Dhanika on, 171, 174; and rasa as instruction, 34; and religion, 22; Ruyyaka on, 236; translation of, xvii; Vishvanatha on, 34, 264. *See also* reception theory
Ratna's Glory (Ratnashrijnana), 6, 60, 61–62, 63, 64, 65. *See also* Ratnashrijnana
Ratnashrijnana, 6, 59; text selections, 60, 61–62, 63, 64, 65
ratyādi. *See* stable emotions
reactions (*anubhāva*): Bhanudatta on, 281, 283; Bhatta Lollata on, 75; Bhoja on, 118–19, 136–37, 142; Dhanamjaya/Dhanika on, 156, 159; Ramachandra/Gunachandra on, 242; and reception theory, 156, 281; translation of, xv. *See also* aesthetic elements
reader/viewer as site of rasa. *See* reception theory
reception theory, 5; Abhinavagupta on, 19–20, 37, 38, 99, 189, 190, 191; and aesthetic elements, 25–26, 156; Bahurupa Mishra on, 176; Bhanudatta on, 280; Bhatta Narasimha on, 115; Bhatta Nayaka on, xv, 16–19, 38, 145, 147–48, 150–51; Bhatta Tota on, 182; and Bhoja, 113, 114, 156; Dhanamjaya/Dhanika on, 20, 155–56, 157, 158, 174, 175; and epistemology, 155–56; Kavikarnapura on, 292, 294–95, 296–98; Kuntaka on, 98–99; and Mahima Bhatta, 106; and manifestation, 19–20, 38; and Pratiharenduraja, 67; and storyworld, 20–21
religion, 21–26; *Bhāgavatapurāṇa*, 22, 23, 285, 302; and intellectual history, 35–36, 44; and Jagannatha, 316–17; and Kavikarnapura, 290–91, 292; and locus of rasa, 256; and peaceful rasa, 21–22; and poetry, 40; and rasa as residing in the character, 23, 301, 304; religious literature as sole repository of rasa, 23–24, 302–3; and Rupa Gosvamin/Jiva Gosvamin, 293, 300, 301, 302; and Western aesthetics, 3–4. *See also* devotional rasa; philosophy
religious rasa, 291
River of Kings (Kalhana), 65, 77, 87, 145
River of Rasa (Bhanudatta), 282–85. *See also* Bhanudatta

Rorty, Richard, 33
Rousseau, Jean-Jacques, 112
Rudra Bhatta, 56, 239
Rudrata, 10, 11, 84–85, 114; text selections, 85–86
Rupa Gosvamin, 36, 300–3; and chronology, xiii; and Jagannatha, 315, 316; and Kavikarnapura, 291, 292, 293; and rasa as residing in the character, 23, 301, 304; text selections, 303–6
Ruyyaka, xiii, 235–36; and Abhinavagupta, 235; on Bhatta Nayaka, 151–53; and chronology, 37; on Mammata, 226, 235; on manifestation, 189, 235, 236–38; text selections, 236–37

śabdavṛtti (linguistic modality), 19, 89, 106, 189
sāhitya (literary art), 261
sāmājika (audience), 12. *See also* reception theory
saṃgīta (music), 2
Samkhya, xv, 36, 112, 122
samuparañjakatva, xv
sattva, xv, 8. *See also* psychophysical responses
sāttvikabhāvas. See psychophysical responses
saundarya (beauty), 3
Schleiermacher, Friedrich, 4
scientific rationalism, 4
Secret of Rasa (Kulapati Mishra), 40
Sellars, Wilfrid, 191
semblance of rasa (*ābhāsa*), 27–29; Abhinavagupta on, 27–28, 213–14; Bhoja on, 117, 127, 139–40, 142; Jagannatha on, 29, 315, 326; Kavikarnapura on, 291, 295–96; Kuntaka on, 106; Singabhupala on, 28, 269–70, 271–73; Udbhata on, 11, 28, 66; Vidyadhara on, 254
sense of self (passion), 36, 112, 120, 123, 134, 135–36
sensitivity. *See* psychophysical responses
Shaivism, 187
Short Explanation of Light on Poetry (Ruyyaka), 236–37. *See also* Ruyyaka
Shri Shankuka, 77–79; Abhinavagupta on, 211; on Bhatta Lollata, 74, 79; Bhatta Tota on, 78, 182, 183–86; and chronology, 77; and documentary lacunae, 77; on epistemology, 89; on imitation, 2, 36, 78–79, 182, 183–85; and Mahima Bhatta, 78, 106; and manifestation, 13; and Ramachandra/Gunachandra, 239; on rasa typology, 80–81; text selections, 79–84
Shridhara, 226, 227, 228, 307
Shrivatsalanchana, 311
Simhabhupala, on Bhatta Nayaka, 154
Singabhupala, 269–71; on animals, 249, 270–71, 273–74; on consciousness, 98–99; on semblance of rasa, 28, 269–70, 271–73; text selections, 271–75
The Single Strand (Vidyadhara), 249–55. *See also* Vidyadhara
śloka (versified poetry), and rasa as residing in the poet, 5
social status, 27, 43–44, 93, 199, 225, 226
śoka (grief), 5
sound rasa, 59
śṛṅgāra (erotic love), xvii. *See also* erotic rasa
stable emotions (*sthāyibhāva*): as basic emotion, 7, 25; omission from *Sutra on Rasa,* 75, 82; as *sāmānyarūpa,* 67; Sanskrit term for, xv. *See also* aesthetic elements; foundational factors; imitation; manifestation
stable emotions, defined: Bhanudatta on, 283; Bhatta Lollata on, 76; Bhoja on, 118, 125–26; Dhanamjaya/Dhanika on, 29–30, 161; Ramachandra/Gunachandra on, 241; Vishvanatha on, 264
stable emotions identified with rasa: Abhinavagupta on, 195–96, 201–2; Ramachandra/Gunachandra on, 245–46
stable emotions, rasa as enhancement of: Abhinavagupta on, 15, 281; Anandavardhana on, 15–16; Bhanudatta on, 76, 280–81; Bhatta Lollata on, 23, 75–76, 195, 281; Bhatta Nayaka on, 18; Kuntaka on, 98, 99, 100; Pratiharenduraja on, 32, 70; Rudrata on, 85; Rupa Gosvamin on, 300–301; Shri Shankuka on, 79–80
stable emotions, typology of: Abhinavagupta on, 198, 199; Bhoja on, 117; Dhanamjaya/

Dhanika on, 164–65; Kavikarnapura on, 293; *Treatise on Drama* on, 50
sthāyibhāva. *See* stable emotions
stimulant factors, 7, 101, 158. *See also* aesthetic elements
The Story of the Beautiful Woman of Avanti (Dandin), 58
storyworld, 20–21, 156, 244, 286, 292, 301
stotra, 21–22
subjective state. *See* reception theory
Sutra on Rasa (rasasūtra) (*Treatise on Drama*): Abhinavagupta on, 203; Anandavardhana's ignoring of, 87; Bhatta Lollata on, 75–77; Bhoja on, 128, 130; importance of, 7, 48; Jagannatha on, 48, 323–24; omission of stable emotions from, 75, 82; Shri Shankuka on, 81; text of, 50; Tilaka on, 69; *Treatise on Drama* on, 53. *See also* aesthetic elements

tamaḥ, xv
taste, 41–44; Abhinavagupta on, 43, 190, 205–06; Dhanamjaya/Dhanika on, 174; and reception theory, 49, 150; and totality of rasa, 26; *Treatise on Drama* on, 9, 49, 50–51; Western aesthetics on, 4, 43
tātparya (sentence intentionality, purport), 13
The Ten Dramatic Forms (Dhanamjaya), 157–80. *See also* Dhanamjaya
terminology translations, xiv–xviii. *See also specific terms*
Tilaka: and commonization, 67; and methodology, xiii; text selections, 68, 69, 70, 71, 74; and Udbhata, 60, 235
totality of rasa, 26
tragic rasa (*karuṇa*), 27; Anandavardhana on, 89, 91; Arjunavarmadeva on, 276–77, 278–79; vs. erotic thwarted rasa, 53; Kavikarnapura on, 292; Kuntaka on, 100–101, 103–4; and rasa as residing in the poet, 5; Shri Shankuka on, 78, 83; *Treatise on Drama* on, 53
transitory emotions (*vyabhicāribhāva*): Abhinavagupta on, 200, 207; Bhanudatta on, 284–85; Bhoja on, 117, 118, 131, 132, 136–37; Dhanamjaya/Dhanika on, 160; Mammata on, 228; Pratiharenduraja on, 69–70; Ramachandra/Gunachandra on, 244–45; *Treatise on Drama* on, 7–8, 50, 52–53, 55. *See also* aesthetic elements
Treatise on Divine Love (Jiva Gosvamin), 306–10. *See also* Jiva Gosvamin
Treatise on Drama (*Nāṭyaśāstra*), 47–49; on aesthetic elements, 7–8, 26–27; authorship of, 7, 47; Bhatta Nayaka on, 148; Bhoja on, 111, 132, 134; on cause and effect, 51–52; and chronology, xii–xiii; commentaries on, 49; constituent parts of drama in, 7–8; on emotions, 6, 7–8, 49, 53–55; on erotic rasa, 22, 52–53; and peaceful rasa, 48; on rasa as residing in drama, 7–9, 48–49; on rasa as residing in the poet, 6; rasa typology in, 48; on social states, 27; text selections, 50–55; on transitory emotions, 7–8, 50, 52–53, 55; on typology of stable emotions, 50. *See also* Abhinavagupta; Bhatta Lollata; *Sutra on Rasa*; Udbhata
tropes. *See* emotion tropes

Udbhata, 65–68; on aesthetic elements, 11; commentaries on, xiii; and documentary lacunae, 49; on emotion tropes, 11, 66, 68, 70; identity of, 65–66; on intimation of rasa, 22; and manifestation, 13; on proper terms, 11, 67, 78, 88, 192; on rasa typology, 11, 66, 70; on semblance of rasa, 11, 28, 66; as source for *Treatise on Drama* content, 47; text selections, 68–74; and Tilaka, 60, 235
Upanishads, 25, 311, 315
Utpaladeva, 22

Vachaspatimishra, 112
Vadijanghala, 59, 60, 61
Vaishnava tradition: *Bhāgavatapurāṇa*, 22, 23, 285, 302; and Jagannatha, 316–17; and Kavikarnapura, 290–91, 292; and poetry, 40; and religious literature as sole repository of rasa, 23–24, 302–3; and Rupa Gosvamin/Jiva Gosvamin, 293, 300, 301, 302
vakrokti (striking usage), 98
Vatsyayana, on *buddhi*, xvii
Vedanta, 24–25, 256, 310–14, 315–16

Vedas, 17, 18. *See also* Mimamsa
vibhāvadi. *See* aesthetic elements
vibhāvana, xv
Vidyadhara, 247–49; and Anandavardhana, 248; and Mammata, 248; Singabhupala on, 270; text selections, 249–55; and Vishvanatha, 261
Vidyanatha, xiv, 98, 255–56; text selections, 257–61
viewer/reader as site of rasa. *See* reception theory
violent rasa, 57
vipralambhaśṛṅgāra. *See* erotic thwarted rasa
Vishvanatha, 261–63; and chronology, 261; and Mammata, 227, 261; on *rasikas*, 34, 264; and Shrivatsalanchana, 311; text selections, 263–69; and Vedanta, 24, 256
Vishvanathadeva, 310–12; and Jagannatha, 310, 311, 315; and religion, 36; text selections, 312–14; and Vedanta, 24–25, 310–11
Vishveshvara, 270
viśrānti. *See* absorption
The Vital Force of Literary Language (Kuntaka), 99–106. *See also* Kuntaka
Vopadeva, 285–87; and chronology, xiii; and religion, 22; and Rupa Gosvamin, 300; text selections, 287–90
vyabhicāribhāva. *See* transitory emotions
vyakti. *See* manifestation
vyañjanā. *See* manifestation

Ways of a Lovely Woman (Bhāminīvilāsa) (Jagannatha), 315
Weber, Max, 3–4, 44
Wellek, René, 44–45
Western aesthetics: art as unified sphere in, 2; and elites, 39; on emotions, 4–5, 44–45; and philosophy, 36; and rasa as instruction, 33; and religion, 3–4; on taste, 4, 43
Wimsatt, W. K., 44, 45

GPSR Authorized Representative: Easy Access System Europe, Mustamäe tee 50, 10621 Tallinn, Estonia, gpsr.requests@easproject.com

www.ingramcontent.com/pod-product-compliance
Lightning Source LLC
Chambersburg PA
CBHW082057090726
47909CB00011B/3065

* 9 7 8 0 2 3 1 1 7 3 9 1 9 *